POLITICS OF MULTICULTURALISM IN THE POST OBAMA ERA

A Reader

Bassim Hamadeh, CEO and Publisher
John Remington, Senior Field Acquisitions Editor
Gem Rabanera, Project Editor
Alia Bales, Production Editor
Miguel Macias, Senior Graphic Designer
Trey Soto, Licensing Coordinator
Don Kesner, Interior Designer
Natalie Piccotti, Director of Marketing
Kassie Graves, Vice President of Editorial
Jamie Giganti, Director of Academic Publishing

Cover image copyright© 2017 iStockphoto LP/JTSorrell, Copyright © 2016 iStockphoto LP/swedewah.

Printed in the United States of America.

ISBN: 978-1-5165-3057-1 (pbk) / 978-1-5165-3058-8 (br)

POLITICS OF MULTICULTURALISM IN THE POST OBAMA ERA

A Reader

Edited by Christopher Xenakis

SUNY - Cortland

 cognella® | ACADEMIC PUBLISHING

CONTENTS

INTRODUCTION

What is the Future of Multiculturalism and American Diversity Now That Barack Obama Has Left the Oval Office?

On June 16, 2015, Donald J. Trump came down that gilded escalator in Trump Tower and announced his unlikely presidential campaign with the promise to "Make America Great Again." And since then—and more notably, since Trump's surprising 2016 victory and since January 20, 2017, when the new president raised his right hand before Chief Justice John Roberts and grasped the reins of American power—the new administration has not forestalled American demographic and political change; if anything, social transformations have accelerated in the United States; this is a time of tremendous political upheaval and societal change! Indeed, we may not know with a high degree of certainty what Trump meant by making America great again, but he surely *did not* mean that he would prevent demographic change from taking place, or that he would take America back to some past "golden age." Instead of restoring America to something it once was, or halting the social and economic advances of the past two decades, the Trump administration has aroused and revitalized the forces of transformation.

Repealing Obamacare, building a wall along the U.S.-Mexican border, and gutting the Environmental Protection Agency—three of President Trump's signature executive actions—do not in and of themselves make America great again, or halt social change, or restore the 1950s or the 1960s. Make no mistake about it: the Trump era is proving to be—rather ironically—a time of seismic demographic shifts in the United States. It is a time when the traditional cultural dominance of white European heterosexual males is being challenged as never before.

It was evident on Wednesday morning, November 9, 2016—once we cleared the sleep out of our eyes and realized that Trump had really won the election—that the new administration was going to be different from the Barack Obama presidency that had preceded it. It was most evident in two important respects: first, everything would depend on how President Trump acknowledged and honored (or failed to acknowledge

and honor) the multiculturalism that already exists in the United States, and second, much would depend on how (or rather, if) the new Trump Administration would support and protect America's racial, ethnic, religious, and sexual/gender diversity. In these respects, more than one year in, we can say that the new administration seemed to be failing. It has regressed and has been moving backward since taking office. Instead of expanding the freedoms and rights of people in the United States, the Trump Administration has contracted them. I might add that this was not merely the partisan judgment of Democrats and liberal critics of the new administration; Republicans and conservatives have noted pointedly that instead of striving to expand his base, President Trump seemed to be *playing only* to his GOP base—and to the most extreme and reactive elements of his base, at that. The new administration has been running away from, if not denying outright the existence of, the American people.

In the first weeks and months following the 2016 election, it seemed as if the whole country, and especially rural and working-class White people, had abandoned Obama and turned to Trump—who had famously announced during a campaign rally that he and America had no time for political correctness, diversity, and multiculturalism—for solutions to their problems. This early impression was exaggerated, of course, but even if it had not been—even if most Americans really had gone down a conservative/nationalistic road in late 2016 and repudiated Obama—it was obvious, even on Wednesday morning, November 9, 2016, that if the new administration was to succeed, it would have to be responsive to the problems, needs, and aspirations of the American people.

This was no naïve aspiration or hope—it was clear-sighted and calculated political reality. It was what Cold War policymaker and foreign policy expert George F. Kennan had signaled when he articulated his famous "imperial analogue" in a much different discussion 60 years earlier.[1] Even a brutal dictator whose seizure and iron rule of a country is illegitimate, Kennan said then, would have to be concerned about the people's welfare and betterment—about whether or not they had enough food to eat, and if they had adequate housing and were relatively content—if only to deter a revolution or a coup d'etat from deposing that dictator! Of course, Trump is no Soviet-style dictator, but Kennan's Cold War dictum remained oddly relevant: the Trump administration would have to champion the American people's interests—and this meant *all of the American people's interests,* including African American interests, Latino American interests, Muslim American interests, and immigrant interests—or it would lose the support of a broad swath of the electorate. This is still true today.

Studying and embracing America's multiculturalism transcends partisan politics—diversity is not just a Democratic Party value or a Republican Party value. Even so, it may be helpful for us to recall the course of American politics over the past half-century, to remember that it was as far back as the 1960s (long before anyone could imagine Obama or Trump in the Oval Office), when the influence of the Democratic Party began to slowly wane in the American South and Midwest, and the Republican Party began evolving and quietly embracing a new constituency—White, economically challenged, and undereducated voters who once had been the backbone of the Democratic Party. This was the coalition that supported Ronald Reagan's successful candidacy for President in 1980, and it swept Donald Trump into the White House in 2016. (Little wonder that Trump declared, during a particularly self-revelatory moment in a February 2016 rally in Nevada: "I love the poorly educated!")

Not long ago, the Republican Party represented America's professional, business owner, and executive classes. Republicans were the community leaders and members of Chambers of Commerce throughout small-town America. But today, many more Republicans are rural and working-class Americans—who are vulnerable to economic downturns and may themselves seek government assistance when they are out of work. They may not like Obamacare (largely, I suspect, because they do not like Barack Obama), but many don't have health insurance, and are one paycheck away from bankruptcy or financial catastrophe. This group of American voters substantially, if not exclusively, voted for Trump and made up much of his base.

At the beginning of 2018, Trump was president, and both houses of Congress were controlled by Republicans. Even so, our country has continued to transform itself demographically—becoming less White, less heterosexual, less paternalistic, and less Christian in character. And Kennan's imperial analogue has continued to be important: consequently, if a major constituency of the Republican Party continues to be the rural and working-class poor, and if the party wants to continue to win elections and remain nationally relevant, it will have to embrace at least some of the "safety-net" policies and programs—such as Social Security, Medicare and Medicaid (as well as some form of nationalized health insurance), and other forms of assistance to the poor, the disabled, and the elderly—that millions of good Republicans, Democrats, and independent voters throughout rural and working-class America will demand.

This reader is about American multiculturalism at the end of the Obama presidency and at the start of the Trump Administration. It has been compiled and edited as an introductory textbook for college and university students in the firm belief that this is a pivotal moment in American history. I decided to embark on this project a couple years ago, when I was using a perfectly serviceable older reader for my politics and multiculturalism classes, but found myself giving students more and more outside readings on such "newer" but vitally important developments as the 2012 killing of Trayvon Martin, an unarmed African American teenager, by George Zimmerman, a White neighborhood watch coordinator; a series of fatal shootings of unarmed Black men by White police officers in Ferguson, Missouri, Baltimore, Staten Island, and other cities; and the Black Lives Matter movement that emerged from these tragedies. That older reader also did not discuss the grassroots #MeToo and #TimesUp campaigns that sprang up suddenly in 2017 and have confronted sexism, and aimed their spotlight on widespread and ongoing patterns of sexual harassment and violence against women—and, in the process, have brought down a number of prominent and/or powerful male predators in business, politics, journalism, the media, and entertainment. Nor did it cover the increased reliance of central New York dairy farms on undocumented immigrant workers, or the unlikely presidential campaign and election to the Oval Office of Trump—a hotel and casino developer and reality show star who has repeatedly called for a sharp curtailment of immigration, and who has insulted people of color, women, Muslims, and people of disability.

Why Study Multiculturalism? Why Should We Appreciate America's Diversity? For Reasons of Self-Interest

There are two salient reasons for studying multiculturalism and learning to appreciate America's rich sociocultural diversity: *self-interest* and *the general interest*.

By *self-interest*, I mean that America's multiculturalism affects and benefits you directly. It is an undeniable fact that the U.S. population is becoming less White, less European, and more global in appearance and outlook. Our nation has evolved over the past 241 years, from its origins as a Eurocentric, patriarchal, heteronormative, and Christian hegemonic culture to what it is today—a country that more accurately reflects the racial, ethnic, religious, lingual, and cultural diversity that is evident in the rest of the world. And our *perception* of our country—the way we think about America—has evolved in similar ways.

Consider what Robert P. Jones, CEO of the Public Religion Research Institute, had to say about just two aspects of this demographic shift—race and religion—in a recent *Atlantic* article. His words are worth quoting at length:[2]

> The remarkable truth is this: America is no longer a White Christian country. And that's going to have profound implications. In the early 1990s, fewer than one in ten Americans said that they were religiously unaffiliated. That number today is nearly a quarter—23 percent. About two-thirds of seniors identify as White and Christian. But [among] the youngest Americans, those under the age of 30, only 29 percent identify as White and Christian.

For Jones, a "key question is, 'What does it mean to be an American?'"

> What is the image of America that comes to people's minds when they hear the word, "American?" Many White Evangelicals see something that looks like a Norman Rockwell painting—a White Protestant family gathering around the Thanksgiving table—and that evokes th[e] era of the 1950s, [when] White Conservative Christian values held sway. Compare that to the Coca-Cola commercial that aired during the Super Bowl: [It featured] all kinds of families—Black, White, Latino, Asian, Muslim, and Christian—and [it] set off a firestorm of controversy. Many Conservative White Christians [reacted to that commercial by saying, in effect, that a multicultural America] "is not the America we ought to be celebrating; in fact, it's a departure from th[e] image that we have!"
>
> People fight like that when they are losing a sense of place, a sense of belonging, and a sense of the country that they understand and love. So thinking about the descendants of White Christian America [who] are still here with us today—and it's still 45 percent of the country; it's a lot of people—how do they re-engage in public life when they can't be the majority? On the one hand, there are leaders such as Russell Moore, of the Southern Baptist Convention, who [are] trying to take these shifts seriously, and [are trying] to engage in a way where they're taking one seat at the table, and not pretending that they own the whole table. On the other hand, [we've seen] some [hostile] reactions against [multiculturalism, among] Evangelical leaders who are calling for Christians to reclaim their dominant space in public life.

A key sentence from the above statement bears repetition: "People fight like that when they are losing a sense of place, a sense of belonging, and a sense of the country that they understand and love." But importantly, we should note, the 2016 election of Trump did nothing to change these demographics or to lessen their significance for the future of multiculturalism in America. Trump's victory *did not* mark a White Christian resurgence—because, "there just aren't the numbers out there for that to happen. America is no longer a majority White Christian country." If anything, Trump won the 2016 election because many White Democrats, ethnic minorities, and people of color who had voted for Obama were relatively less enthused about Trump's electoral opponent, Hilary Clinton, and stayed home or simply voted for Trump on Election Day.

And although "nonwhites still punch below their weight on Election Day," as Paul Taylor and the *Pew Research Center* admit, that is quickly changing:

Many are still too young to vote, many aren't citizens, and many aren't politically engaged, [and many are] barred from voting due to restrictive I.D. laws, put in place by Republican statehouses. [Even so,] over time, a mix of demographic and behavioral change is likely to shrink all of these deficits. The U.S. Census Bureau projects that nonwhites will become the majority of the U.S. population in 2043, and by that time, it's a good bet that the[y] will have closed the gap with their population count.[3]

Given these long-term demographic and electoral shifts, it is perhaps paradoxical that, in the words of my SUNY-Cortland colleagues, Seth N. Asumah and Peggy Murphy, "the concepts of democratic pluralism and 'melting pot' theory have contributed to the *marginalization* of different groups within the [American] body politic. Institutional democratization *has not* quite resulted in equality under the law, freedom, and social justice—and *has not* enabled us to celebrate our diversity, engage in healthy discourse, and learn from the collective experiences of humankind (Black or White, male or female, rich or poor, old or young, gay or heterosexual, able or disabled, Muslim, Jewish, or Christian)."[4]

Asumah and Murphy are right; indeed, as many a social studies teacher has remarked to her high school students, perhaps we would be better off thinking of America *not* as a "melting pot" that homogenizes Americans as well as immigrants with their diverse cultures, religions, languages, ethnicities, traditions, colors and flavors, into a dull gray sameness—but instead, we should think of America as a kind of "salad bowl" filled with a nearly endless variety of fresh, colorful, and delicious vegetables and food items, which look and taste very different from each other, but combine to create a beautiful and tasty meal.

Whatever President Trump meant by his promise to restore America to some past measure of "greatness," and despite his disdain for political correctness, we do live in a new America. This is no longer your parents' or grandparents' America, and White nostalgia is not going to bring the 1950s back! We live in an America in which people of color and non-Christians make up (or will soon comprise) the majority population. Only those who understand multiculturalism and can celebrate the diversity of this new America will be able to thrive, or for that matter, survive, in it. So discovering and learning to appreciate America's diversity is a matter of self-interest to you. Bottom line: unless you plan on being a hermit for the rest of your life, working and living in complete isolation from others, you will have to learn how to get along with people who are not like you—people who look, talk, worship, and love differently than you. You will likely encounter and rub shoulders with such people every day, for the rest of your life.

This fact alone has serious implications for how multiculturalism and diversity are taught in colleges and universities. Unlike some academic disciplines and courses of study in which education seems to be a matter of rote memorization, and students "learn" a body of material just long enough to regurgitate it verbatim on a quiz or exam, the study of multiculturalism is different. To be sure, there is a certain amount of cognitive learning (and memorization) that students will have to do. But the more important objective of a course on multiculturalism—and of this reader—is to enable students to arrive at a place, personally and emotionally as well as intellectually, where they value and celebrate the diversity that defines America today.

A Second Reason to Study Multiculturalism and Appreciate America's Diversity: Because of the General Interest

Another reason to study multiculturalism and celebrate the sociocultural diversity that defines America has to do with *the general interest*: an appreciation of multiculturalism and the celebration of our country's rich social diversity are good for America, and more broadly, they are good for humanity at large.

If self-interest and America's new demographic realities are not strong enough reasons for us to study multiculturalism, then perhaps we should reflect more deeply on the still-unfulfilled promises of America, voiced by our Founding Fathers (such as, "all men are created equal"); and/or on the yawning socioeconomic disparity between the rich and the poor in America; and/or on the enduring legacy of the Stonewall demonstrations and the civil rights movement of the 1960s; and/or on the power of 2.6 million women marching in Washington, DC, and throughout United States in January 2017, and again in 2018; and/or on the still-electrifying words of Dr. Martin Luther King from the Lincoln Memorial ("I have a dream that my four little children will one day live in a nation where. ..."). Perhaps we can accede to the simple but profound demands of justice in our treatment of others who are different from us.

And then there is the imperative of the good life. In addition to heeding and being attentive to current social realities, it may be useful to root our study of multiculturalism and our appreciation of America's social diversity in the teachings of ancient political, social, and religious thinkers about "the good life," as well as in the natural rights tradition of the seventeenth century, and in more recent expressions of human rights.

Indeed, if the defense of multiculturalism and diversity studies that I have outlined above, on the basis of America's shifting demographics, seems to accord fundamentally with a liberal (and/or a Democratic Party) political orientation or ideology, we can also set forth a classically conservative rationale (which might be more congruent with a Republican Party political ideology) for such studies, based on Plato's and Aristotle's writings about the ideal *polis*, or political regime, and the good life; on the teachings of Christianity and other world religions; and on the writings of John Locke and other seventeenth-century thinkers about natural rights—which in turn influenced the American drafters of the Declaration of Independence, the U.S. Constitution, and many of our other foundational documents. Indeed, we can see a continuity—a long-standing intellectual tradition—stretching from Plato's and Aristotle's arguments about the good life, to Locke's and the American Founding Fathers' discussions about natural rights, to the human rights that were inscribed in the United Nations Universal Declaration of Human Rights in 1948, and finally, to the national conversation we are engaged in today about multiculturalism and American diversity.

Multiculturalism and Diversity Studies Enable Us to Live the Good Life

Plato and Aristotle believed that the purpose of politics is to enable people to live the good life. They admired the Greek city-state of Athens, but they criticized the Athenian rival, Sparta, in large part because Sparta was one-dimensional—it was little more than a militarized national security state. Athens and Sparta were the "rival superpowers" of the ancient Hellenic world in 450 B.C.E., but whereas the citizens of Athens enjoyed and taught their children music, art, gymnastics, literature, politics, and various trades, the Spartans focused only on one thing: soldiering. From an early age, Spartan children joined children's battalions, were subjected to military discipline and training, and learned how to fight and use weapons. Militarism was a dominant way of life in Spartan society and families. Indeed, Plato's and Aristotle's final word about Sparta—and their ultimate condemnation of that Greek city-state—was that despite her fearsome power, her superb military prowess and technology, and the fighting spirit of her soldiers, for all of those things, Sparta had lost the good life.

The good life is the ancient idea that life should be about more than making money, getting ahead, and fighting wars and defeating enemies. It is the idea, so evident in the earliest days of our Republic, of civility and decency, of looking out for one another, and of self-development. It is the idea that any of us may have grown up harboring chauvinistic, exclusive, and bigoted opinions about ourselves, other people, and the world around us, but through an intentional process of education and contemplation, we can better ourselves, overcome our childhood prejudices, and refine our opinions and beliefs.

Although Plato and Aristotle did not place a high value or priority on democracy and social diversity in the same way that we Americans understand these ideals, their observations about Athens, Sparta, and the good life have direct bearing on U.S. culture and politics today. America is—or should be—much more than the world's preeminent military superpower and national security state. She should also be the preeminent *civilized* country in the world—a place where the good life is enjoyed by all people who reside on her soil. Indeed, the very idea of "the good life" brings to mind quality-of-life concerns—enhancing and guaranteeing the welfare, the living standards, the happiness, and the rights of all citizens and resident noncitizens. Fulfilling these concerns is, or should be, the primary goal of the American government.

The "good life"—attaining it, nurturing it, and protecting it—is at the heart of all of the various ways we talk about "the American Dream" today. And if you think about it, the good life—protecting and enhancing the liberties and the welfare of people—is ostensibly why any country, including the United States, would want to be militarily powerful and vigilant about national security in the first place! In fact, our government already does many things to enhance and guarantee the quality of life, living standards, and rights of its people. Some of these things may seem bureaucratic—like raising and collecting taxes, monitoring economic and unemployment statistics, and passing cost-of-living-adjustment legislation that benefits Social Security recipients—but make no mistake: the core purpose of all of these governmental activities—and the core goal of every country including our own—is (or should be) to protect the quality of life of all of its people.

Similarly, virtually all of the world religions have been, since their ancient origins, keenly interested in social welfare: in caring and advocating for people, in feeding and housing the poor; in embracing the marginalized and the dispossessed; in fighting social injustice, oppression, and discrimination; and in welcoming the immigrant and the stranger in their midst.

I realize that some readers will disagree with this assessment of the societal benefit of religion—particularly if they have come to think of religious institutions and leaders as perpetrators of sexism, racism, homophobia,

and cultural xenophobia. Sadly, there is some validity in such a discordant perspective. But many faith communities and many people of faith are centrally concerned about strengthening and affirming human relationships, and emphasize civility, truthfulness, and respectful communication. And all of the world religions emphasize the need for human interactions based on love and toleration of friends and enemies alike.

Importantly, Islam, Judaism, and Christianity share in these social concerns, and they have done so since antiquity. In addition, most of the world religions contain in their sacred writings some version of the "golden rule"—the familiar injunction to "do unto others as we would like them to do unto us." Religious organizations have been a powerful force in promoting social welfare throughout American history. Religious denominations, churches, mosques, synagogues, and houses of worship have contributed to the advancement of humane programs and policies throughout the United States, and have assisted countless orphans, immigrants, and other marginalized and/or impoverished peoples.

At rock bottom, the ancient Greek thinkers as well as the founders and purveyors of most of the world's religions believed that the purpose of politics and of government was to help and affirm people, to enable them to live the good life. Achieving these ends today requires civility and mutual respect; it requires fighting racism, sexism, homophobia, ableism, classism, and Islamophobia. It requires coming to terms with America as it really is, rather than as it once was, or as we'd like it to be. It requires an appreciation for, and a celebration of, our country's multiculturalism and diversity.

An Appreciation of America's Multiculturalism and Diversity Is in Keeping with Modern Natural Rights and Human Rights Traditions

During the seventeenth century, the natural rights tradition of John Locke and of other scholars—and more recently, the Universal Declaration on Human Rights, proclaimed by the United Nations General Assembly in Paris on December 10, 1948—have summarized and reified many of these ideas. Established as "a common standard of achievements for all peoples and all nations," the Universal Declaration "se[t] out fundamental human rights to be universally protected."[5]

Many conservative political scholars today cherish the natural rights pronouncements of Locke, Jefferson, and Madison, but reject the Universal Declaration of Human Rights (as well as other modern formulations of "human rights"), arguing that they are overly expansive in their expression, thereby encouraging governments to provide their citizens with an endless and costly array of entitlement programs. Such modern articulations of human rights are starkly different, these conservative scholars argue, from Locke's conception of natural rights, or from the rights enshrined in the Declaration of Independence—and hence, are illegitimate. Thus, *Heritage Foundation* political scholar Peter C. Myers argues that for natural rights to be valid, they "must be grounded in a defensible account of our morally distinctive nature, and subject to a sound limiting principle." Unlike modern conceptions of human rights, they must be "liberty rights that contain in themselves no guarantee of any specific distributive outcome."[6] Even so, the careful reader will note that many of the human rights that are enumerated in the Universal Declaration *meet Myers's requirement* and possess the character of natural rights! These rights are not "asking for things," or demanding any kind of payment from the state. Indeed, one suspects that America's Founding Fathers (and Mothers) would have approved of them. Examples of these rights in the Universal Declaration, that have the character of natural rights, include the following:

- All human beings are born free and [are] equal in dignity and rights. They are endowed with reason and conscience and should act toward one another in a spirit of brotherhood (Article 1).
- Everyone is entitled to all the rights and freedoms set forth in this Declaration, without distinction as to race, color, sex, language, religion, political or other opinion, national or social origin, property, birth, or other status (Article 2).

- Everyone has the right to life, liberty, and security of person (Article 3).
- No one shall be held in slavery or servitude; slavery and the slave trade shall be prohibited in all their forms (Article 4).
- All are equal before the law and are entitled without any discrimination to equal protection of the law (Article 7).
- No one shall be subjected to arbitrary arrest, detention, or exile (Article 9).
- Men and women of full age, without any limitation due to race, nationality, or religion, have the right to marry and to found a family. The family is the natural and fundamental group unit of society and is entitled to protection by society and the state (Article 16).

We may conclude that there is a much closer congruence between the human rights that are enumerated in the Universal Declaration and the natural rights tradition of Locke and the American Founding Fathers than Myers and other conservatives would like to think. Collectively, these rights make the multiculturalism argument for us. They tell us in no uncertain terms that we must celebrate people—not just the people of our country, or those who look exactly like us and share our culture—but all the people who reside in our land, in all of their magnificent diversity.

ABOUT THIS READER

This reader was compiled as a textbook for college- and university-level introductory courses on American multiculturalism and diversity. It consists of 45 articles, contained in five broad sections.

Most of the articles in Section I are introductory theoretical readings and demographic studies. The first two articles in Section I make formidable cases *against* American multiculturalism and social diversity. Conservative commentator Selwyn Duke's "Multiculturalism," condemns multiculturalism and immigration as socially corrosive, both in Europe and in the United States, and accords in substance and tone with Samuel F. Huntington's celebrated 1993 essay, "The Clash of Civilizations?" It may be fair to say that Duke's

article sets forth, in fairly coherent, nonideological, and nonhistrionic prose, some of the intellectually foundational ideas of the Alt-Right movement. The second of these two articles, written by CUNY sociologist Richard Alba, is critical of demographic analyses that suggest that the White majority in America is collapsing. These two articles are included in the reader in the belief that students will be better off for having familiarized themselves with some of the prevailing arguments *against* multiculturalism.

Section II is on gender, masculinity, homophobia, patriarchy, and sexism. It is, perhaps, too soon to know if the grassroots #MeToo and #TimesUp campaigns of 2017 will lead to lasting change—and perhaps, to the eradication of sexism, sexual harassment, and sexual violence against women—but these campaigns have already evolved into a robust social movement across America. If there's one thing that we have learned from the recent wave of revelations of predatory sexual abuse by rich, powerful, and famous men, it is that sexism and patriarchy are not just bad habits of the past—anachronistic behaviors from the "anything-goes" 1960s and the "boogie-nights" 1970s that men no longer engage in. Rather, sexism and patriarchy continue to harm women immeasurably, and to plague American culture (as well as dehumanizing American masculinity). Analogously, despite recent landmark Supreme Court decisions making marriage equality the law of the land, Americans who are lesbian, gay, bisexual, transgender, and/or queer (LGBTQ) still do not enjoy all the rights that their heterosexual sisters and brothers take for granted. Even today, in this second decade of the twenty-first century, landlords and employers can evict, fire, and discriminate against LGBTQ people. Indeed, there is some indication that LGBTQ rights are quietly being rolled back in the post-Obama era. The readings in this section explore these topics.

Section III addresses race and racism in the United States. If Americans thought that the election and re-election of Barack Obama to the presidency in 2008 and 2012 marked the end of racism and the beginning of a new "color-blind" era in American society and politics, those hopes were dashed in 2016, by Trump's electoral victory and the resurgence of White supremacy movements under a new "Alt-Right" label—but also by a number of disturbing and widely publicized hate crimes and shootings committed by White offenders against people of color. The truth is that, by almost any statistical metric one can think of—education, housing, income and wealth, arrest and incarceration rates, health and morbidity data—Americans of color continue to experience systemic disadvantages and suffer from abject forms of racial discrimination in 2018. The articles in this section explore both the topic of race and these malignant patterns of racism in America—and they consider several ongoing controversies over White privilege and affirmative action.

The articles in Section IV cover the difficult topic of class and economic inequality in America. What seems to be happening is nothing less than the hollowing out of the American middle class: the wealthy are getting wealthier, while the poor are becoming poorer—and the floor of the middle class is collapsing beneath the feet of a great many Americans, causing them to fall into poverty. This is ominous for America's future. One of the most important correlates of democracy—a key requirement for democracy to work in any country, including the United States—is the presence of a robust middle class, in which people are relatively satisfied with their level of affluence and quality of life, and are optimistic about the future. Accordingly, when the middle class disintegrates and millions of Americans become impoverished, what's left is a distorted class system with a very small wealthy upper class, a shriveled middle class, and a bloated—and immense—lower class. This is an inherently dangerous socioeconomic alignment, because it sets the stage for economic and political instability—and perhaps civil war or revolution—as a frustrated and resentful lower class is tempted to turn on the upper class, possibly with murderous rage and violent intent. The readings in this section will focus on these unhappy themes.

Section V deals with "Other Multiculturalisms." These include ableism and disability; the continued marginalization and mistreatment of Native Americans; Islamophobia; and the political hysteria emanating out of Washington, DC, over immigration—and especially over the presence of undocumented immigrants in the United States. The election of President Trump—and many of the things that Trump has said, both before and after becoming president—have brought these populations into sharp focus, and we will discuss their issues and concerns in this section.

Finally, for your convenience, a title and author index is included at the back of this reader.

One of the strengths—but also, sometimes, a chief frustration—of readers and anthologies is that they speak in many voices. Because I teach multiculturalism and this reader is about cultural diversity, it may not be a huge intellectual leap for you to imagine that I view this reader's disparate voices as a strength. It is my hope that you will benefit from the diversity of authors, writing styles, and arguments that you will encounter in these pages.

In this regard, no effort was made to ensure that all of the articles in the reader, or their authors, are in complete agreement when it comes to definitions (for example, of racism), or even the relative importance of multiculturalism and cultural diversity. Thus, as I have already noted, the first two articles in Section I make rigorous cases *against* multiculturalism. Ultimately, I find their arguments to be unpersuasive, but this reader is a better and a more complete resource because of their inclusion.

Many of the articles that you will find in this reader are almost completely unedited, due both to copyright and publisher restrictions and to my desire that you read them in their original form. Some articles are taken from chapters (or are themselves entire chapters) in other academic works; may contain odd wording, such as, "in this chapter . . .," or may call attention to past or future chapters; or may contain passing references to persons or incidents that are neither fully introduced or explained nor germane to the topic at hand. Other articles may be fraught with ungrammatical sentence constructions. I have tried to minimize these occurrences, but at least one article is a chapter from another academic work, in which specific individuals and accounts of discrimination are alluded to but never explained, because they were discussed fully in a previous chapter—which is not included in this reader!

Several words of thanks are in order. I wish to thank several individuals at Cognella Academic Publishing—notably, my acquisitions editor, John Remington, and my project editor, Gem Rabanera—for their guidance, advice, and reassurance throughout all stages of this reader's development and editing. Gem, you made this reader a better and clearer resource for students. In addition, Miguel Macias's cover art is tremendous. Thanks also to Susana Christie, Kate Ready, Jess Wright, Danielle Menard, Alia Bales, and Jon Preimesberger.

Special thanks to Seth Asumah and Peggy Murphy, my colleagues at SUNY-Cortland for several conversations, some of which were brief, but too many of which stretched into the wee hours of the morning, about American multiculturalism and diversity. Their tutelage, advice, and suggestions amounted to a graduate course on the nexus between American politics and multiculturalism. In addition, I owe a debt of gratitude to my students who inspired my choice of articles to include in this reader, and who contributed so much to my own education through their questions and discussion.

Thanks to you, Marsha Williams of the New York Conference of the United Church of Christ, for your passion, your song, your anger, and your urgency—all of which are so important in confronting racism, sexism, homophobia, and complacency.

And thanks, Susan Fast, for reminding me that we must neither rest on the laurels and accomplishments of the past nor become discouraged when progress seems slow. Because, you said, every generation has to be taught anew to fight racism, homophobia, sexism, and religious parochialism and bigotry.

The shortcomings of this reader are my own, but to the extent that it accurately and intelligently reflects on America's current condition, and what we need to do about it, is largely due to the generous assistance of all of these amazing people.

C. I. X.
March 24, 2018
Cortland, New York

ENDNOTES

1. Kennan's imperial analogue was part of a broader State Department discussion that took place during the early days of the Cold War. The American diplomat was discussing Soviet policy—and specifically, he was addressing the question of what, if anything, the United States could do to ameliorate Soviet dictator Joseph Stalin's tyrannical rule; Kennan was *not* responding to any popular concerns about the domestic policies of the Truman or Eisenhower administrations—as we are doing today with respect to the Trump Administration!

2. Robert P. Jones, Daniel Lombroso, and Caitlin Cadieux, "We've Reached the End of White Christian America (video), *The Atlantic*, October 13, 2016, https://www.theatlantic.com/video/index/504065/america-post-christianity/.

3. Paul Taylor and the Pew Research Center, "Introduction," in *The Next America: Boomers, Millennials, and the Looming Generational Showdown* (New York: Public Affairs, 2014), 2.

4. Peggy Murphy and Seth N. Asumah, POL 110/AAS 120, Politics and Multiculturalism Course Syllabus, State University of New York College at Cortland, Cortland, New York. Italics are mine.

5. "Universal Declaration of Human Rights," *United Nations*, http://www.un.org/en/universal-declaration-human-rights/index.html.

6. Peter C. Myers, "From Natural Rights to Human Rights—and Beyond," *Heritage Foundation*, December 20, 2017, http://www.heritage.org/progressivism/report/natural-rights-human-rights-and-beyond.

Introduction and Some Theory

READING 1.1

MULTICULTURALISM

BY **Selwyn Duke**

Multlculturalists believe that dissimilar cultures within a nation strengthen it and that assimilation is condescending to immigrants, but in fact 'diversity' divides countries.

It is 1991, and Yugoslavia, born of the ashes of WWI, is starting to break up. It is a violent affair that will be long, painful, bloody, and complex. Numerous wars in the multi-ethnic region will be fought, with Slovenia, Croatia, and Bosnia declaring independence from Serb-dominated Yugoslavia and, in turn, Serb minorities seeking independence from the last two regions. Slovenes, Croats, Bosnians (virtually all Muslim), and Albanians (largely Muslim) will battle Serbs. Croats and Bosnians will unite to battle them—then fight each other as well—then unite again; and Albanians will take up the sword against Macedonians. Muslims will burn churches, and minority populations will be purged from many of these regions. They are the first conflicts since WWII to be formerly deemed genocidal, and these wars will introduce English-speakers to a new term: ethnic cleansing.

None of this was any surprise. Ethnic and cultural ties ultimately trump citizenship status just as family ties do. This is why East and West Germany were reunited two decades ago: Their peoples were both German and shared the same culture, making their separation artificial and, therefore, temporary. Yet artificial unity tends to be no less temporary; it teaches us that, sometimes, the sum of the parts can be greater than the whole. And while Yugoslavia may be the current poster boy for this phenomenon, many other states are similarly diverse and, to varying degrees, struggle with ethnic/sectarian turmoil. Some, such as Iraq and Rwanda, are still making history; others, such as the Soviet Union and Czechoslovakia, are history. And then there are yet other nations. These are not places conceived in the ashes of war or the minds of colonial masters, but lands, such as the United States, Britain, and France, in which unprecedented immigration is creating a situation described by another term born of that tumultuous part of southeastern Europe: balkanization.

For most of man's history, the norm was to keep foreign elements out of your land. When a people couldn't, it often meant their conquest and subjugation—if not subsumption, as happened to the Ainus on the Japanese islands. Things have changed in modern times, however; the practice of inviting foreigners to your shores, known as immigration, has become a Western norm. But man's nature doesn't change. Thus, invitations cannot prevent the clash of civilizations that will inevitably result when a flood of new arrivals overwhelms a society's ability to acculturate them.

Traditionally, assimilation was thought the solution to this problem. In fact, it was expected. For example, our 26th President, Teddy Roosevelt, did insist in 1919 that an immigrant must be treated just like any other American. But he also issued the following caveat:

> But this is predicated upon the man's becoming in very fact an American and nothing but an American. If he tries to keep segregated with men of his own origin and separated from the rest of America, then he isn't doing his part as an American. There can be no divided allegiance here. ... We have room for but one language here, and that is the English language, for we intend to see that the crucible turns our people out as Americans, of American nationality, and not as dwellers in a polyglot boardinghouse; and we have room for but one soul loyalty, and that is loyalty to the American people.

Yet it turned out that this wasn't to everyone's liking. Just as a Bosnian doesn't wish to assimilate and become Serbian, many of today's immigrants don't want to become American. Their credo seems to be, "The American way need not apply."

REVERSE ASSIMILATION

Unlike in Teddy Roosevelt's America, there today is insufficient will to countervail this desire. The modern West is now like a man whose belief in himself and sense of purpose are so shattered that he has begun to think the world would be better off without him. It is a civilization that has gone from proud to prostrate, transitioning from the proposition that it is wrong to impose your ways on others in their lands to the proposition that it is wrong to impose your ways on others in your land. And this belief has a name: multiculturalism.

Multiculturalists say that the proverbial American melting pot must be replaced by the "salad bowl," the idea that culturally dissimilar ingredients can co-exist and complement each other. According to them, "diversity" isn't a problem to be overcome but a strength to be celebrated—and intensified through programs such as ethnic studies. Oh, it's not that they're unaware of man's tendency toward bigotry and Balkan-like strife. It's just that they think they have the answer: teach tolerance. This, ostensibly, is facilitated by the doctrine that all cultures are morally equal. The thinking is that if I don't consider my culture superior, I'll have no reason to look down on others, impose my ways on them, or persecute them.

> East and West Germany were reunited two decades ago: Their peoples were both German and shared the same culture, making their separation artificial and, therefore, temporary. Yet artificial unity tends to be no less temporary.

While there is a philosophical contradiction in this theory—one that must and will be addressed later—first note that it's only a theory. In practice, multicultural programs don't just intensify ethnic pride; they nurse ethnic grudges. For example, about an ethnic-studies course in Arizona's Tucson Unified School District (TUSD), Ashley Thome writing at the National Association of Scholars website reported:

> We observed that two of the main books for the TUSD program were Paulo Freire's *Pedagogy of the Oppressed* and *Occupied America: A History of Chicanos,* by Rodolpho [sic] Acuña [who is an actual member of the Communist Party]. Freire's book, of course, argues that teachers must train students to acquire "critical consciousness"

Race is irrelevant: Strife arises from cultural differences more so than racial ones. This fact plays out time and again in Africa, where blacks of one tribe—such as the Kikuyu men shown here—abuse and kill rival tribal members—such as this Luo woman—with machetes, clubs, and guns.

Neighbors, Not Friends or Countrymen: While the dictator Josip Broz Tito controlled Yugoslavia, ethnic groups that normally held grudges against each other intermingled, but when the control ended, so did harmony. Here Croat patients flee a hospital. The Yugoslav army killed 261 Croat men from that hospital.

(an understanding that they are oppressed); to give voice to their grievances; and to liberate themselves from the bonds of imposed assimilation. ... This revolutionary fervor is even more pronounced in *Occupied America,* which tells the story of the Southwestern United States from the perspective of Mexican Americans and has been called "the Chicano bible." The book is sympathetic to Mexico in a reference to the battle at the Alamo. In another place. Acuña wrote:

> Gutiérrez [co-founder of the Raza Unida Party Jose Angel Gutiérrez] attacked the gringo establishment angrily at a press conference and called upon Chícanos to "kill the gringo," which meant to end white control over Mexicans.

Clearly, some people think the American "salad" would be better off if the carrots eliminated the lettuce.

Note that the title *Occupied America* refers to the notion—advanced by groups such as the Chicano Student Movement of Aztlán (MEChA)—that the United States is, to quote MEChA's website, "an oppressive society that occupies our [Latinos'] land." These groups encourage the *Reconquista,* or the reconquest; this is an effort to "liberate" the mythical Aztec homeland called Aztlán—which, mind you, would include parts of the United States. And to see how this idea is being mainstreamed, just open the textbook *The Mexican American Heritage*; on page 84 is a map of Aztlán that includes seven U.S. states and parts of one other. Its author, Carlos Jimenez, unapologetically states on page 107, "Latinos are now realizing that the powers to control Aztlán may once again be in their hands."

Not surprisingly, what these textbooks claim Latinos need liberation from isn't your grandfather's oppression. For example, *Occupied America* cites free English classes offered to Mexicans in the 1950s by the Catholic Church as an effort to rob Latinos of their culture. So the message to American (at least in name) students is clear: assimilation equals oppression.

The above two textbooks aren't anomalies, either; rather, they are part of a festering multicultural trend that serves to demonize traditional American culture and alienate citizens—and those who may one day be citizens—from it. And a good example is the guidelines of textbook publisher McGraw-Hill. As author Diane Ravitch writes on page 44 of her book *The Language Police*:

> [The] guidelines express barely conceded rage against people of European ancestry. They deride European Americans for exploiting slaves, migrant workers, and factory labor; they excoriate the land rapacity of the pioneers and mock their so-called courage in fighting Native Americans: "Bigots and Bigotry," say the guidelines, referring to European Americans, "must be identified and discussed." European Americans, the guidelines suggest, were uniquely responsible for bigotry and exploitation in all human history.

Yet it isn't just through textbooks that multiculturalism is spread. Another way is through the unequal application of the now misunderstood First Amendment. That is to say, the "separation of church and state" dictum (a basis for which is no where to be found in the Constitution) has long been used as a pretext for things such as removing crosses and other Christian symbols from public property and city seals, renaming Christmas trees "Holiday trees," and prohibiting mention of our foundational faith in schools; at the same time, however, it is ignored when social engineers want to pave the way for foreign religions and their symbols. For example, the prohibitions against Christian expression get as nauseatingly ridiculous as a Wisconsin elementary school changing the lyrics of the carol "Silent Night" to "Cold in the night, no one in sight" and schools renaming Valentine's Day "Friendship Day." Meanwhile, the Byron, California, Union School District requires its seventh-grade students to attend an Islamic immersion course that critics say is nothing short of indoctrination. Writes WorldNetDaily.com:

> The course mandates that seventh-graders learn the tenets of Islam, study the important figures of the faith, wear a robe, adopt a Muslim name and stage their own jihad. Adding to this apparent hypocrisy, reports ANS [ASSIST News Service], students must memorize many verses in the Koran, are taught to pray "in the name of Allah, the Compassionate, the Merciful" and are instructed to chant, "Praise to Allah, Lord of Creation." ... There are 25 Islamic terms that must be memorized, six Islamic (Arabic) phrases, 20 Islamic proverbs to learn along with the

Five Pillars of Faith and 10 key Islamic prophets and disciples to be studied.

With such courses being disgorged by American education, it's no wonder that some have called multiculturalism "reverse assimilation." Whatever you call it, though, "wise" is not an adjective that leaps to mind. And this is readily acknowledged when the matter is discussed absent the mind-chains of multiculturalist dogma.

BLOOD OVER BORDERS

Just consider, for instance, Edwin M. Yoder, Jr.'s commentary about the Balkan crisis in his book *The Historical Present: Uses and Abuses of the Past*. He writes, "As we saw in the cruel civil war in Bosnia, it involved the displacement of ethnic minorities trapped among majorities. ... In the years when Marshal Tito held Yugoslavia together,

Occupied America cites free English classes offered to Mexicans in the 1950s by the Catholic Church as an effort to rob Latinos of their culture. So the message to American (at least in name) students is clear: assimilation equals oppression.

personal inclination and opportunity led to much internal migration, accompanied by a healthy forgetfulness of ethnicity, as it does in all federal states." Now, note that the area's woes were ultimately exacerbated by this "internal migration," as it was "internal" only to the *artificial construct called Yugoslavia*. As far as the ethnic, blood-thicker-than-citizenship regions destined to become nations went, however, it amounted to something quite different: immigration without assimilation.

And the problem today in the West—be it Muslims in England or France, or Mexicans and a salad-bar-full of others in the United States—is that the rate of immigration long ago exceeded the rate of assimilation. And how many immigrants are necessary for this to happen, anyway, with multiculturalism discrediting acculturation?

Most interesting, however, is what Yoder casually takes for granted as true. A "healthy forgetfulness of ethnicity" *is* a positive thing. It is also the precise opposite of multiculturalism's prescription. Second, there is a reason why Yugoslavia had to be "held" together (which, as with all communist governments, Tito managed through the iron fist of tyranny): As Yoder acknowledged about the wider European multicultural morass a few paragraphs later, "These [ethnic] fissures

Regional Differences: Multiculturalists like to point to countries such as India, which has any languages and religions, to prove that multiculturalism works, but India is hardly strife free, with its "untouchables" and persecution of Christians. And relative calm can be attributed to group separation within the country.

haven't vanished; they have simply been hiding," Ethnic fissures are appearing in the United States, too. And without a Tito to keep them in check, they're not hiding very well.

Of course, some will say that many "multicultural" societies function quite nicely. For example, Switzerland has four official languages: German, French, Italian, and Romansch; many people in Belgium speak French; and India has approximately 250 different languages and dialects and a plethora of different religions. And, in reality, no nation is completely homogeneous. The difference, however, lies in degree and kind.

It is as with the small nation called a family. Since nobody is a carbon copy of another, there will obviously be differences among even the most closely knit family members; the husband may like one color for drapes while the wife likes another, and the children may have varying tastes in food. Yet there is little threat of family disunity and dissolution as long as these differences are relatively minor. But families can and do go their separate ways, and the split isn't always amicable. It isn't unheard of, for instance, for a teenager who has tastes in music and lifestyle that his parents find highly objectionable to strike out on his own. Let us be clear,

> We see people of opposing ideologies get together for a friendly game of golf. It's quite a different matter, however, when you have to devise laws and social codes; then your religion and culture, which shape your worldview, really do matter.

however, on what happens when a teen embraces his different "lifestyle": Just as the 1960s generation was a world apart from their WWII-era parents, he essentially becomes culturally dissimilar enough from his father and mother to create a rift.

The same thing occurs in nations when differences become great enough—and, even more to the point, when they involve not just taste but conceptions of Truth. Sure, some will say, "Let us simply live and let live. Can't we all just be like children, who play with one another happily regardless of race, creed, or color?" Well, first, while we love to exalt the innocence of childhood, children can be cruel, and their taunts can be centered on race just as easily as size or appearance. But insofar as religious and cultural differences really are insignificant in childhood but start to carry weight

We're One: America has historically been viewed as a melting pot, with people of all races and colors becoming Americans, assimilating and striving to take part in the unique opportunities provided by Americans exceptionalism. It worked well, but now assimilation is actively discouraged.

as people emerge from it, we ought to note why. Is it just an inevitable corruption that age brings? Perhaps ... to an extent. But there is also the very obvious fact that children don't have to run society. It's easy to get along when your agenda consists only of arranging a game of basketball or "kick the can"; after all, even in the adult world we see people of opposing ideologies get together for a friendly game of golf. It's quite a different matter, however, when you have to devise laws and social codes; then your religion and culture, which shape your worldview, really do matter. For example, consider a situation in which one group is so pious that it would criminalize any representation of its religious figures while another group believes that any prohibition against free expression is a type of secular sacrilege. Can there be compromise? Will it satisfy both groups if the religious figures in question are made fair game half the time? As anthropologist Dr. Harry V. Herman wrote, "The designers of 'multiculturalism' forgot perhaps that laws and rules of behaviour are a part of culture, and that society may have difficulty accommodating several different laws and rules of behavior, which may contradict each other." Without a doubt.

At this point, some may aver that differences do not an ethnic conflict make, that for it to erupt there must be some secondary factor such as economic distress or competition for resources. But even if true, isn't this the point? What if I said to you, "Yeah, I have a great family. As long as life is easy, we're just like two peas in a pod;

Our Town, Chinatown: Major cities throughout the United States have ethnic communities where American culture can be, and is, ignored. Such areas often spawn gangs, and the community members often take on an "us versus them" mentality.

it's only when times are tough that we're at each other's throats"? Obviously, problems will find you in life. And if opulence and absence of hardship are necessary for tranquility, it doesn't say much for the given group's unity and sense of brotherhood, does it? It is only when a people's mettle is tested that you find out if it is *a* people—or just *people*.

PEDAGOGY WITHOUT A PLAN

Yet the deepest point has not yet been made. Even if the multiculturalists were correct that a new regime of tolerance could negate man's nature and usher in a new age of peace, they haven't the foggiest idea about how to achieve it. For their ideology contains a fatal flaw: that supposedly tolerance-inducing message that "all cultures are morally equal." Oh, why they embrace it is understandable. It is the same thinking that states that since feelings of racial superiority can justify racial oppression, we need to purge those feelings. But what eludes multiculturalists is that race is a physical characteristic and, as such, doesn't involve a set of values. Different cultures, however, *do* espouse different values; therefore, not all cultures can be morally equal unless *all values are so.* But if all values are equal, how can tolerance be better than intolerance? How can loving another be better than persecuting him? Thus, like all relativism-based beliefs, multiculturalism collapses upon itself into a black hole of irrationality. Metaphorically speaking, you could say that if multiculturalism is true, multiculturalism is false.

This is why its adherents cannot live up to—or, I should say, down to—their own creed. That is to say, multiculturalists will often state things such as, "To co-exist, all cultures must be tolerant and operate within a model of secular government." But to say that a person can have his culture *as long as* he does this or that is to set boundaries; it is to demand that he accept an imposition of your values and thus implies their superiority. And, of course, this is no different from what any staunch nationalist does. Thus, in theory, multiculturalists have an abiding respect for all cultural values, but in practice the value-equality card is pulled only when it can be used to tear down Western culture's

traditions. And when foreign values smack of those traditions—the promotion of religion (the promotion of religiosity), patriarchy, emphasis on modesty in dress and chastity, etc.—the multiculturalists will also, sometimes, break from their dogma. We then learn again that indeed some values are more equal than others.

Today, America is no longer a melting pot. It isn't even a nice tossed salad. Because of relativistic multiculturalism, it is turning into a witch's brew. And, at risk of overfilling readers already sated with gastronomic metaphors, I will say that we can view a successful civilization as a culinary delight. Since a certain recipe was used to create it—with each cultural element being an ingredient—we must remember and continually recreate that recipe to perpetuate the civilization. Of course, this doesn't mean that adding an ingredient won't enhance the meal further, but this must be done with an eye toward improvement of the dish. As it stands currently, we just haphazardly throw things into the cauldron, blind to their effects and behaving as if ingredients can exist separate from—and unaffected by—one another.

To state the matter literally, a healthy culture reflects Truth, and our goal should be to continually bring ours closer to that perfection. Thus, if a foreign cultural element is found superior, by all means make it an American one. But insofar as our culture better aligns with Truth, we should make clear that newcomers don't just have a vested interest in embracing it. We will insist they do so.

In recent discussion of the economy, we've heard much about this or that "bubble." This refers to a situation wherein something (i.e., real estate a few years ago) is tremendously overvalued and, therefore, is destined to come crashing down to the level at which market realities dictate it should be; this is when the bubble bursts. Well, there is also an Ethnicity Bubble. This is when the group patriotism of cultures within a nation starts to increase to dangerous proportions. And when it becomes sufficiently overheated, the nation can burst. This was Yugoslavia's fate. If we keep treading the multiculturalist road, it may be ours also.

DISCUSSION QUESTIONS

Selwyn Duke's article, on the dangers of multiculturalism and multicultural expression, both in the United States and globally, is dark, Hobbesian, and similar in spirit to Samuel F. Huntington's influential *Clash of Civilizations?* argument. If you have not read Huntington's *Clash of Civilizations?* essay, you might want to take a look at it.

1. Duke's article reminds us of the argument of Thomas Hobbes, who believed that human nature is essentially dark and violent, and that the life of human beings is "solitary, poor, nasty, brutish, and short." Do you believe, as Duke suggests, that the human "tendency" is "toward bigotry and Balkan-like strife?" Why or why not?

2. Evaluate Duke's argument that the idea that we need to be "teaching tolerance," and the belief that all cultures are "morally equal," is faulty. "Multicultural programs don't just intensify ethnic pride; they nurse ethnic grudges." Do you agree or disagree? Why?

3. Are some cultures morally better, or more virtuous, than others? Are some cultures morally worse, or more evil? Should the United States welcome, exclude, and/or deport entire populations of immigrants, based on their culture—that is, based on where they came from? Explain your answer.

READING 1.2

THE LIKELY PERSISTENCE OF A WHITE MAJORITY

How Census Bureau Statistics Have Misled Thinking about the American Future

BY **Richard Alba**

Has the notion of demography as destiny ever enjoyed so much credence? The disappearance of a white majority in the United States by the middle of this century is now widely accepted as if it were an established fact. Projections by the Census Bureau have encouraged those expectations, and people on both the right and left have seized on them in support of their views. On the right, the anxieties about the end of white majority status have fueled a conservative backlash against the growing diversity of the country. On the left, many progressives anticipate an inexorable change in the ethno-racial power hierarchy. Numerous sites on the web offer advice and counsel on how whites can handle their imminent minority status,

But what if these different reactions are based on a false premise—actually two false premises? The first stems from the Census Bureau's way of classifying people by ethnicity and race, which produces the smallest possible estimate of the size of the non-Hispanic white population. Whenever there is ambiguity about ethno-racial identity, the statistics publicized by the bureau count an individual as minority. This statistical choice is particularly important for population projections because of the growing number of children from mixed families, most of whom have one white parent and one from a minority group. In the Census Bureau's projections, children with one Hispanic, Asian, or black parent are counted as minority (that is, as Hispanic or nonwhite). The United States has historically followed a "one-drop" rule in classifying people with any black ancestry as black. The census projections, in effect, extend the one-drop rule to the descendants of other mixed families. A great deal of evidence shows, however, that many children growing up today in mixed families are integrating into a still largely white mainstream society and likely to think of themselves as part of that mainstream, rather than as minorities excluded from it.

Under alternative ways of counting, the potential range of variation in the size of the white population is quite large. In unpublicized tables, the Census Bureau itself provides a measure of how wide that variation is. If we were to go to the opposite extreme from the bureau's official projections and adopt a white one-drop rule—that is, to classify anyone with some white ancestry as white—the data show that whites would make up three-quarters of the population at mid-century, when the Census publicly claims that whites will be in the minority. To be sure, neither extreme is credible; the white share of the population will lie somewhere in between these poles.

A second reason to be skeptical about the excited talk about the end of a white majority is that it ignores the potential for blurring the boundary between mainstream and minority. The United States has previously seen excluded minorities such as the Irish, Italians, and Jews assimilate into the mainstream. Although the channels of assimilation are narrower today because of heightened inequality, many recent immigrant families seem to be on the same path as their predecessors. The likely result will be to enlarge the mainstream and alter the circumstances under which individuals are seen as belonging to marginalized minorities.

To raise these questions is not to minimize the significance of the growing diversity of American society, stimulated above all by the mass immigration since the late 1960s. Nor is it to deny the loss by whites of majority status in many parts of the United States, such as California. But it is to peer beneath the surface of census data to the little-understood processes behind their construction and to correct distortions of social reality that the official population statistics encourage. And it is to suggest that longstanding processes of assimilation

could produce a white-dominated mainstream at the national level and in many regions for the foreseeable future.

THE CENSUS AND CHILDREN OF MIXED FAMILIES

Population projections, whether by the Census Bureau or anyone else, are not properly understood as forecasts. As any demography textbook can tell you, a projection is a numerical exercise for working out the implications of a set of assumptions about demographic variables such as birth and death rates. Over an extended period, the assumptions are virtually certain to diverge from demographic realities. Nonetheless, the Census Bureau and, more recently, the Pew Research Center have not hesitated to project an exact year when whites will lose majority status—2044 and 2055, respectively—encouraging the popular view that they are making forecasts.

Projected changes in the racial and ethnic composition of a society also depend on the rules for classifying people. The Census Bureau assumes that every individual is either white or minority and resolves the complexities of multiple heritages by assigning people with any mixed background to the minority side of the white/nonwhite divide. Individuals with both Hispanic and non-Hispanic ancestries cannot even be identified as such in census data; according to the bureau's rules, they are only Hispanic. Since 2000, individuals with a mixed racial heritage can claim it on census forms, but they are, without exception, considered minorities in population statistics. The Census Bureau's report on its latest projections declares that a minority group is "any group other than non-Hispanic white alone." Most readers probably cannot decode the full implications of this formulation.

The bias in the Census Bureau's practices has its largest impact in estimating the ethno-racial backgrounds of children, because it is among children that we first see the consequences of the rapidly rising number of mixed families. To estimate how many children are from mixed families, I used data for 2013 on the families of infants from the American Community Survey, which is conducted by the Census Bureau. (I focused on infants because the chance of obtaining data on both parents is greatest when a child has recently been born, and we need to look at parents' own reports to avoid the biases inherent in the census data for the children themselves.) Although the Census Bureau declared in 2012 that nonwhite births for the first time outnumbered white

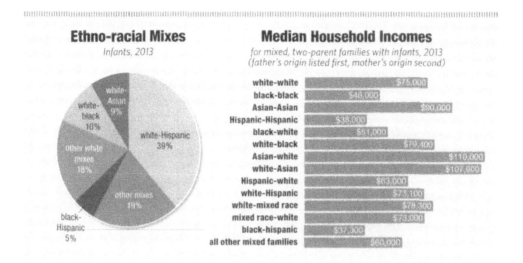

Ethno-racial Mixes
Infants, 2013

Median Household Incomes
for mixed, two-parent families with infants, 2013
(father's origin listed first, mother's origin second)

ones, 60 percent of the 2013 infants have a white parent. About 10 percent, then, have both a white and minority parent. These infants are counted as minorities in census statistics. And they are regarded as permanently so in census projections.

Overall, about one of every seven infants comes now from an ethno-racially mixed family. The largest group by far of these infants, as the pie chart shows, consists of those with one non-Hispanic white and one Hispanic parent They are nearly 40 percent of the total. Other sizable groups are mixed white and Asian, white and black, and white and mixed-race parentage.

Social-science research on children from mixed families is limited. But three kinds of evidence, in concert, indicate persuasively that the Census Bureau data exaggerate the decline of the white population by failing to take into account that many children from mixed backgrounds will likely be integrated into largely white social milieus and identify, at least some of the time, as white. This evidence involves the incomes of mixed families, the social identities of individuals with mixed backgrounds, and their marriage patterns.

Income of mixed families: The household incomes of many mixed families indicate that they are closer socioeconomically to mainstream white families than to disadvantaged minority ones.

As the chart above shows, unmixed Asian families have higher median incomes than unmixed white families, and mixed Asian and white families have the highest incomes of all. The incomes of mixed Hispanic and white families are also very different from those of unmixed Hispanic parents. When the non-Hispanic

white parent is the father (true for about half of the white-Hispanic mixed infants), the median family income is scarcely any different from that of white-only families. When the Hispanic parent is the father, the average income is lower but still much higher than is typical for Hispanic-only families.

Since income is a primary determinant of where families reside, these patterns imply that many of the mixed white and minority children are growing up in neighborhoods where many whites also reside, and outside of areas of minority concentration. These ethno-racially mixed children will have peers from white families and likely learn to get on with them from an early age.

There is one major exception to the pattern in family incomes. Although white-black families have incomes close to those of whites when the father is white, that is not true when the father is black, which is the more common situation in black-white families. The infants with mixed, only-minority parentage also come predominantly from families with incomes between those of black-only and white-only families.

Social identities: Unlike census data, data from a 2015 survey by the Pew Research Center illuminate the feelings and experiences of individuals with mixed backgrounds. According to "Multiracial in America," the Pew report based on the survey, most Americans from mixed backgrounds do not think of themselves as multiracial. For those who are white and Asian, the affinities with the white group are strong. By a two-to-one margin, they say that they have more in common with whites than with Asians. They report, in addition, feeling more accepted by whites and having more white than Asian friends. Those who are white and black exhibit a very different profile. The majority believe that others see them as black. They also have much closer ties to their black relatives and are very likely to report encountering discrimination, including being "unfairly stopped by the police."

The Pew survey found many more multiracial Americans than the census does, which implies that adults with mixed backgrounds often appear in the census in single-group categories (that is, as unmixed white, black, and so on). In fact, an internal Census study, "America's Churning Races," shows that large numbers of people who identify themselves as multiracial in one census identify themselves as white in another.

For instance, of those who reported a mixture of Asian and white parentage in either 2000 or 2010, 36 percent appeared as only white in the other census (and 22 percent as only Asian). Those who report mixed white and Hispanic family backgrounds to the census are counted as Hispanics of white race, a huge group that includes about half of all the nation's Hispanics. Yet, of the individuals who appeared in this group in either 2000 or 2010, 12 percent said they were *non-Hispanic* and white in the other year. In other words, many Americans with mixed Asian or Hispanic family origins identify with the white majority some of the time.

The one exception to this pattern of "leaning" white involves individuals of mixed white and African American heritages, who are much more likely to indicate that they are only black than only white (33 percent versus 16 percent). This exception conforms to the consistent research finding that Americans with visible African ancestry confront more virulent everyday prejudice and discrimination than other minorities do. The one-drop rule appears not to have lost its power in their case.

A Minority Majority? The Census Bureau classifies children of mixed marriages as members of the "minority" population. Under those definitions, three of the four people in this picture—Senator Ted Cruz and the two children he has had with his wife Heidi Nelson Cruz—are part of the minority population that the Census projects to be a majority in 2044. In popular media, this projection is routinely equated with the end of a white majority and an emerging majority of "people of color." Cruz himself is the son of a mother of Irish and Italion extraction and a father born in Cuba.

Intermarriage: Finally, there are the marriage patterns associated with mixed backgrounds, which are indicative of the social milieus into which individuals have been integrated. For individuals who are partly white and partly minority, the likelihood of choosing a white spouse is much higher than it is for those with the same minority ancestry only.

A powerful demonstration of this pattern comes from a unique study of Mexican Americans, which followed families from 1965, when the original survey was conducted, to the late 1990s, when researchers tracked down the original participants who were still alive, as well as their children. In their book, *Generations of Exclusion*, based on these data, the sociologists Edward Telles and Vilma Ortiz report that the odds of intermarriage were five times higher for the children of intermarriages than for those from Mexican-only backgrounds. These intermarriages were overwhelmingly with non-Hispanic whites. Scholars of intermarriage have also found higher rates of marriage with whites among individuals who are mixed white and Asian compared with those who are Asian only. In sum, many partly white adults appear to have been integrated into largely white social worlds.

These data about family income, social identity, and intermarriage raise serious questions about the Census Bureau's practice of counting children of mixed families as members of ethno-racial minorities. In collecting data, the Census relies on what parents say about their children's ethno-racial backgrounds. Parents are very likely in doing so to try to honor both sides of their offspring's family origins. When their children grow up, however, many of them may view themselves as whites. Future white counts are therefore likely to be substantially larger than one would predict from current census data.

ASSIMILATION INTO THE MAINSTREAM

Children from mixed backgrounds are only one aspect of a broader social process under way that is mixing together different groups in American society. Multicultural critics of assimilation have rejected it as a goal, but the concept remains essential for sociological analysis if we are to understand important changes taking place. Some people from minority as well as mixed backgrounds are being attracted into a still heavily white mainstream, changing the mainstream even as it continues to be dominated by whites.

The mainstream, of course, is not the whole of American society. Rather, it is the part that mistakes itself for the whole. In a society where racial and ethnic origins historically have confined Americans to different social strata, the mainstream has been long associated with the social spaces and cultural practices of white Americans. That is now changing as the boundaries of the mainstream expand.

One momentous change involves the rapidly growing presence of Americans from recent waves of immigration at the top of the U.S. workforce, in domains that were previously monopolized by native whites. Guillermo Yrizar Barbosa and I have analyzed this change in an article that appears on the website of the journal *Ethnic and Racial Studies*. We focus especially on the upper quarter of all workers who hold top occupations as defined by annual earnings. Until recently, 85 percent to 90 percent of these workers were whites (and non-Hispanic). But among the young workers who have entered this tier since about 2000, the share represented by whites has dipped below 70 percent. The Great Recession did not reverse this trend. Since the socioeconomic ascent by minorities closely correlates with the declining white share of young adults, it is a safe prediction that it will continue as ethno-racial diversity rises among youth.

*"Whiteness" is a malleable concept, and it is **on its way to changing again**, as it has before.*

The expanding groups in the upper ranks of the workforce are Asians, both immigrant and U.S.-born, and U.S.-born Latinos. Black Americans are also increasing their numbers, but not to the same extent as the others.

The growing diversity at or near the top of the occupational ladder does not mean that whites on these rungs have lost all their advantages, at least not yet. With educational level taken into account, we found that whites generally are better placed occupationally than minorities, and when compared with minorities in the same occupation, they earn more on average. White advantages could decline as the numbers of individuals from minority backgrounds increase in the top tiers, bringing more of them into positions of authority where they can make decisions about hiring and promotions. But it is premature to predict how the struggles of whites to hold onto their diminishing advantages will turn out.

Individuals from minority backgrounds who hold prestigious and visible posts in the workforce, or positions of civic leadership, are part of the mainstream, in any sensible definition of it. Their ascent echoes an earlier transformative moment in our history. In the quarter-century after World War II, the mainstream was joined en masse by the descendants of Irish and southern and eastern European immigrants, Jews, Catholics, and Orthodox Christians. Assimilation today is more selective, not as massive. But as in the earlier period, when hyphenated identities became acceptable, it does not require the obliteration of ethnic and racial identities, just their muting, to allow individuals to function in social worlds that, while increasingly diverse, are still home to many whites. The motive for assimilation is, as before, to gain for oneself and one's children access to the greater opportunities that are available in mainstream settings.

This assimilation should disabuse us of the fantasy of the imminent demise of the white majority and its loss of power. Not all the newcomers to the mainstream will identify as whites, and its visibly growing diversity will be a key development of the early 21st century, as the election of the nation's first black president unmistakably signals. "Whiteness," however, has never been fixed; it is a malleable concept, and it is on its way to changing again, as it has before.

Yet it is critical not to lapse immediately into another fantasy, namely, the belief that assimilation will prove a panacea for still-glaring ethno-racial disparities. Contemporary assimilation is simply not on the same scale as that of the mid-20th century, when, for example, Italians caught up to other whites in education and socioeconomic attainment in just a 25-year period after World War II. Assimilation today is crimped by greatly heightened inequalities and is leaving many outside its reach, including many Hispanics, such as the undocumented and their children, even those who are U.S. citizens because they were born here. In one respect, however, the earlier and current patterns of assimilation are similar: African Americans are participating only to a limited extent. Indeed, one could even say they are being bypassed.

To think clearly about the American future, we need not only the right concepts but also accurate data. The Census Bureau, the public agency we all rely on for neutral representations of social realities, is failing us. Not only do its rigid and illogical classifications distort important new realities, the bureau is also not forthcoming about the errors and uncertainties involved. Instead, it continues to promulgate "firsts"—in June, it declared that for the first time minorities are the majority of children under the age of 5—as if the data were unimpeachable. Given the political resonance of its statistics, which reverberate on the right and left of the spectrum, there is not a moment to lose in demanding that, in its official projections and pronouncements, the Census present a more nuanced view of the nation's demographic future and acknowledge the alternative ways in which Americans may come to think about themselves.

Richard Alba *is a Distinguished Professor of Sociology at the Graduate Center, City University of New York. He is the recent co-author of* Strangers No More: Immigration and the Challenges of Integration in North America and Western Europe.

DISCUSSION QUESTIONS

1. Are you concerned about the persistence of a White majority in the United States? Why or why not?

2. Richard Alba's argument that a White majority will persist in the United States is based on the idea that people of mixed ethnicities and races are fundamentally White--they grow up White, they live White, and they identify as White—even if their skin color happens to be brown. Do you find Alba's argument persuasive? Do you think that White supremacists, and others concerned about the racial and ethnic makeup of the United States will accept Alba's argument? Why or why not?

3. Alba's article calls to mind a notorious court case in 1982–1983 that challenged the State of Louisiana's 1/32nd rule, and the earlier "one-drop" rule. Google these rules. How did they define Blackness? What do they mean? Who was Susie Guillory Phipps? What did she do?

4. If a White person with 1/32nd Black blood, or even a single drop of Black blood, is actually Black—then might a person who looks Black but has 1/32nd White blood—or even a single drop of White blood actually be White? Why or why not? Since many or most Americans today have a mixed heritage, are Blackness and Whiteness meaningful concepts? Explain your answer.

5. Alba says: "Whiteness has never been fixed; it is a malleable concept, and it is on its way to changing again, as it has before." Do you agree? Do you think the definition of Whiteness in America is evolving or expanding in a more inclusive direction?

INTRODUCTION

The Next America Boomers, Millennials, and the Looming Generational Showdown

BY **Paul Taylor; Pew Research Center**

LONGER LIVES, FEWER BABIES, MORE IMMIGRANTS

The fundamentals of our demography are these: in 2014, about 4 million Americans will be born, roughly 1 million will arrive as immigrants, and about 2.5 million will die. "Generational replacement" is the demographer's term of art for the population change produced by this churn. In some eras the process can be relatively uneventful, but not so in the America of the early twenty-first century, when young and old are so different from each other. Of the myriad forces that bear on these numbers, none has been more inexorable or important than the rise in human longevity. Advances in health care, nutrition, and sanitation have increased life expectancy at birth in the US from 47 years in 1900 to 62 years in 1935 (the year Social Security was enacted) to 79 today to a projected 84.5 by 2050. In the first part of the twentieth century, most of the gains came as a result of improvements in the survival rate of newborns; in the second half, most gains came from medical advances that have prolonged the lives of older adults. And there's more to come. While it sounds like the stuff of science fiction, some biomedical researchers believe that by mid-century, bionic bodies embedded with computer chips and fortified by as-yet-uninvented medications will make life spans of 120 or more years attainable, perhaps even commonplace. If so, just imagine the quality-of-life issues—to say nothing of the retirement finances!—that future generations will need to sort out.

Longer life spans beget lower birthrates. As living standards improve and people grow more confident that their children will survive to adulthood, succeeding generations reduce the number of children they have. In the twentieth century, the world's population grew by nearly fourfold. In this century, however, it is expected to grow only by about another 50% before eventually stabilizing at roughly 10 billion.[1] Over the long haul, this is good news for all who worry about the sustainability of the earth's resources. But in the short and medium term, it can create social, economic, and political dislocations, especially in countries like the US that have large cohorts entering old age and smaller cohorts in the workforce. However, all of our biggest economic competitors face even more challenging age pyramids. China's median age will rise from 35 now to 46 by 2050, surpassing the projected median of 41 in the US. Germany's will be 52. And in Japan, where birthrates have been among the lowest in human history for the past generation, the market for adult diapers now exceeds the market for baby diapers. Japan's median age will be 53 by 2050. If present trends continue, there won't be nearly enough Japanese youngsters to care for its oldsters, which helps explain why Japan is the global leader these days in the development and manufacture of caretaker robots.

One way for nations to prevent the economic sclerosis that can occur when their populations age is to replenish their workforce with immigrants. In this realm, the US boasts the world's most enviable demographics. The third great wave of immigration to the US, which began when Congress reopened America's doors in 1965, is now more than 40 million strong. Based on current mortality-fertility-immigration trends, roughly 90% of the growth in the US labor force between now and mid-century will be from new immigrants and their children. Immigration waves always produce political and cultural backlashes; this one has been no exception, especially since more than a quarter of the modern-era immigrants are living here illegally. As columnist Fred Barnes has written, we have a history of hating immigrants before we love them.[2] But no nation has been better served than ours by immigration, and judging by the tens of millions of people from all over the world still clambering to come here, there's every reason to expect our long winning streak to continue.

RACE AND RELIGION

The modern immigration wave has done more than boost our economy. It has given us a racial makeover. Until the middle of the last century, our racial checkerboard was white with a smattering of black. Now it's multicolored, and whites are on a long, steep slide toward losing their majority status. Moreover, in today's America, our old racial labels are having trouble keeping up with our new weddings. More than a quarter of all recent Hispanic and Asian newlyweds married someone of a different race or ethnicity; so did 1 in 6 black and 1 in 11 white newlyweds. Not too long ago these marriages were illegal and taboo; now they barely raise an eyebrow. As these couples procreate, what race will society call their children? What will the children call themselves? For centuries we've used the "one-drop rule" to settle such questions—if you're not all white, you're not white at all. Going forward, we'll need a more nuanced taxonomy. America isn't about to go color-blind; race is too hardwired into the human psyche. But race is becoming more subtle and shaded, and most Americans (especially the young) are at ease with the change.

As noted, the new rainbow America has had a big impact on presidential politics. There's an interesting history here. After he lost the Hispanic vote in 1980, Ronald Reagan described Hispanics as "Republicans who don't know it yet." Three decades later they apparently *still* haven't figured it out. To the contrary, they've grown even more Democratic. In 2012, 71% voted for Obama (up from the 56% who voted for Jimmy Carter over Reagan in 1980), as did a record 73% of Asian Americans. Block voting is nothing new among minority groups in America; blacks have supported Democrats by even more lopsided margins for generations. But these new patterns are ominous for the GOP. Hispanics and Asians today compose 22% of the US population; by 2060 they will make up nearly 40% (while blacks will remain constant at about 13%). They embrace values common to immigrant groups—they're hardworking, family-oriented, entrepreneurial, and freedom loving—all of which, as Reagan rightly observed, could easily make them natural Republicans. Yet they also favor an active government and tend to be social liberals. And

many have been put off by the anti-immigrant rhetoric of the GOP in recent years. "If we want people to like us, we have to like them first," said Bobby Jindal, the Indian-American Republican governor of Louisiana, after the 2012 election. The growing partisan divisions by race and ethnicity coincide with the growing divisions by ideology and age. These deep divisions aren't healthy for the polity; they're especially perilous for the Republicans, who find themselves on the wrong side of the new demography.

Race isn't the only demographic characteristic changing before our eyes. Religion is another. In 2012, for the first time ever, not one of the four major party candidates for president and vice president was a white Anglo-Saxon Protestant (one was black, one Mormon, two Catholic). Nor was the Speaker of the House (Catholic), the majority leader of the Senate (Mormon), or any of the nine justices of the US Supreme Court (six Catholics, three Jews). WASP dominance of our nation's political institutions pretty much peaked at the opening bell in 1776, when 55 of the 56 signers of Declaration of Independence were white Protestants. It has been falling ever since, and the pace of decline has ramped up in the half century since John F. Kennedy became the first non-WASP president in 1960 and Congress was still three-quarters Protestant (as opposed to 56% now). However, it's not just that the American public is becoming less white and less Protestant—it's also becoming less attached to religious denominations in general. A record 1 in 5 American adults today—and fully a third under the age of 30—is religiously unaffiliated. Of these so-called "nones," roughly a quarter describe themselves as atheists or agnostics; the remainder believe in God but have no religious affiliation. The US is still the most religiously observant nation among the world's great powers. But led by today's young, it's growing more pluralistic and less connected to traditional religious institutions.

A HOLLOWING OF THE MIDDLE

For the past decade and a half, America's middle class has suffered its worst economic run since the Great Depression. It has shrunk in size, fallen backward in income and wealth, and shed some—but by no means all—of its characteristic faith in the future.[3] Median household income in this country peaked in 1999 and still hasn't returned to that level, the longest stretch of stagnation in modern American history. As for median household wealth—the sum of all assets minus all debt—it has fallen by more than a third since peaking at the height of the housing bubble in 2006. Not surprisingly, an overwhelming share of Americans—85%—say it has become tougher to live a middle-class lifestyle than it was a decade ago. Yet most middle-class Americans say they have a better standard of living than their parents had at the same stage of life (the economic data bear them out) and a plurality expect their children will do even better than them. The trademark optimism of the American middle class may not be as robust as it was a decade ago, but it hasn't disappeared. It may, however, not be as well founded as it used to be.

This hollowing out of the middle has been accompanied by a sharp rise in income inequality. One standard measure is known as the Gini Index, which ranges from 0 to 1, with 0 representing perfect equality (everyone has equal income) and 1 perfect inequality (one person has all the income). In the US, the index rose to .477 in 2012 (the latest year for which such data are available) from .404 in 1980, an increase of 18%.[4] On the global scale, this means we're not as unequal as many African and South American countries, but we're more unequal than most European and Asian nations. We still think of ourselves as the land of opportunity, but a child born into poverty in Canada and most Western European countries has a statistically better chance of making it to the top these days than does a poor kid in the US.[5] The two decades after World War II were a period of declining inequality in the US—all income groups did well, but in relative terms, those at the bottom did best. Since then, all groups have done less well, and in relative terms, those at the top have done best.

Moreover, when one looks at wealth rather than income, the gaps since the 1980s have ballooned into chasms and are starkly aligned with race and age. As of 2011, the typical white household had 14 times the wealth of the typical black household (up from 7 times in the mid-1990s) and the typical older household had 26 times the wealth of the typical younger household (up from 10 times in the mid-1980s).[6] There's little evidence

Figure 1 Average Annual Change in Mean Family Income, 1950–2010

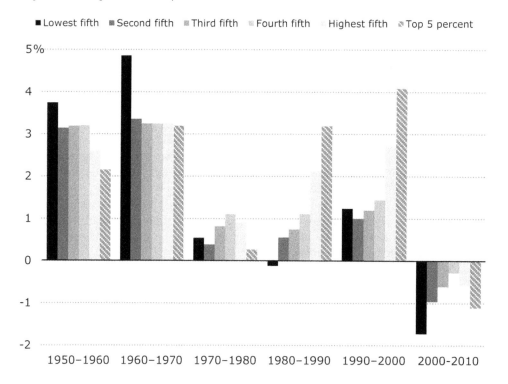

Source: Pew Research Center analysis of US Census Bureau, Historical Family Income Tables, Table F-3 for 1966 to 2010, and derived from Tables F-2 and F-7 for 1950 to 1965

from public opinion surveys that Americans resent the rich. But in growing numbers, they resent the policies and institutions—political as well as economic—that they believe are rigged in favor of the rich.

The rise in inequality is driven in large measure by a workforce that has begun to resemble an hourglass—bulging at the top and bottom; contracting in the middle. The leading culprit is technology. Whole categories of good-paying midlevel white- and blue-collar jobs have been wiped out in recent decades, first by computers and more recently by robots. "The factory of the future will have just two workers," goes the gallows humor in manufacturing towns. "A man and a dog. The man is there to feed the dog. The dog is there to make sure the man keeps his hands off the equipment." This pessimism may prove overwrought. Over time, technological revolutions typically create more jobs than they destroy, and in a 2013 paper, economists Frank Levy and Richard Murnane counted 3.5 million jobs—software engineers, systems analysts, data experts, and so on—created by computer technology. Most, however, demand more advanced skills and training than the middle-level jobs they replace. In America the key to preserving social and civic cohesion among a diverse population is a dynamic economy that offers plenty of work for a sprawling middle class, with lots of on-ramps from below. Today there are fewer such jobs and

on-ramps. At least so far, the digital revolution has left the middle class in worse shape than it found it.

CULTURE, GENDER, MARRIAGE, FAMILY

When the Baby Boomers came of age with a great primal scream of social protest in the 1960s, the electoral backlash was immediate and enduring. In 1968 Richard Nixon won the presidency as the champion of the "silent majority"—by which he meant all the folks who *weren't* protesting. In 1972 he was reelected in a landslide over a Democratic opponent he mocked as the candidate of "acid, amnesty, and abortion." In the ensuing decades the GOP's most effective alliterative attack lines migrated a few notches down the alphabet—to god, guns, and gays—but the basic political calculus never changed. Whenever culture wars flared, Republicans profited—that is, until 2012. In that election year, gay marriage state ballot initiatives, after having gone 0-for-32 during the previous decade, went 4-for-4. Also, voters in Washington and Colorado became the first to legalize the recreational use of marijuana. And in Missouri and Indiana, Republican candidates lost eminently winnable US Senate races because of their tone-deaf remarks about rape and women's reproductive rights. To be sure, the culture wars are far from over. The landmark 2013 Supreme Court rulings that struck down the federal Defense of Marriage Act left the same-sex marriage issue to be fought out state

Figure 2 Views of Legalizing Marijuana: 1969–2013

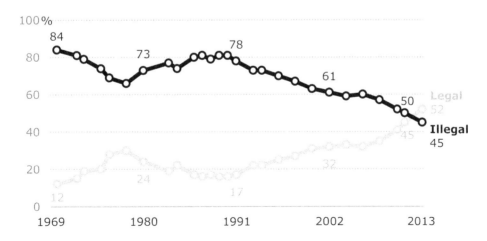

Source: Pew Research Center surveys, 2010–2013; 1973–2008 data from General Social Survey; 1969 and 1972 data from Gallup

by state, likely ensuring it will be contested terrain for a long time to come. That has been the pattern with abortion. Four decades after the court's landmark *Roe v. Wade* decision, abortion is still fiercely contested; in 2013 alone, legislatures in several dozen states tested the limits of that ruling by passing bills to tighten restrictions on abortion. But even as these moral issues continue to play differently in different states and regions, the overall trends in public opinion have put social conservatives on notice. As younger adults age into the electorate and older adults age out, the old wedge issues simply don't work the way they once did. "It's not that our message didn't get out," R. Albert Mohler Jr., president of the Southern Baptist Theological Seminary, told the *New York Times* a few days after the 2012 election. "It did get out. It's that the entire moral landscape has changed. An increasingly secularized America understands our positions, and has rejected them."[7]

One casualty of the new economic and cultural order has been traditional marriage, which has suffered a dramatic loss of market share. In 1960, 72% of all adults ages 18 and older were married; by 2011, just 51% were. In the old days, people in all social classes married at roughly the same rate; today marriage is much less prevalent at the bottom than the top. Pew Research surveys find that adults on the lower rungs are as just likely as others to say they want to marry, but they place a higher premium than others on economic security as a precondition for marriage—a threshold they themselves are unable to cross. These attitudes are self-fulfilling. Marriage brings economies of scale and a heightened commitment to financial responsibility, which means that the growing marriage deficit among poorer adults both reflects and reinforces their growing income deficits. This is worrisome for society. A large body of social science research shows that children born to single parents tend to have a more difficult path in life, even when one holds constant other socioeconomic factors.[8] The same holds for elderly adults who don't have a close relationship with their children.

As marriage has declined, gender roles have converged. Today women are the sole or primary breadwinners in 4 in 10 households with children; a half century ago, this was the case in just 1 in 10 such households. A majority of these "breadwinner moms" are unmarried, but a significant share (37%) are wives who earn more than their husbands. Men are having a tougher time than women adjusting to the demands of the modern knowledge-based economy, and it shows in the way they rank their life priorities. A 2011 Pew Research poll found that 66% of young women say that being successful in a high-paying career or profession is a very important life priority for them. That number may not seem remarkable, except for this: just 59% of young men said the same.

This reversal of traditional gender aspirations comes at a time when nearly 6 in 10 college and graduate students are female; nearly half the labor force is female; and working fathers are just as likely as working mothers to say they find it difficult to balance work and family—and more likely to say they don't spend enough time with the kids. The public overwhelmingly supports the trend toward more women in the workforce and more egalitarian marriages. Nonetheless, Americans are cross-pressured on these topics, and many traditional gender norms endure. For example, a 2013 Pew Research survey found that about half of respondents say that children are better off if the mother stays at home and doesn't hold a job, while just 8% say the same about the father. Also, twice as many Americans say it is very important for a prospective husband to be a good provider than say the same about a prospective wife.[9] In sync with those norms, the decline of marriage has been

Figure 3 Women and Men Approach Parity in Labor Force

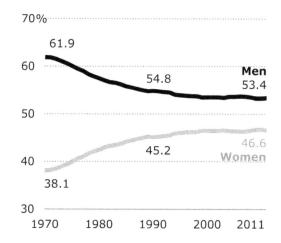

Share of labor force that is men, women, 1970–2011

Note: Annual averages based on civilian noninstitutional population age 16 and older. For changes to the Current Population Survey (CPS) over time, see www.bls.gov/cps/eetch_methods.pdf.

Source: Pew Research Center analysis of US Bureau of Labor Statistics, "Women in the Labor Force: A Databook," Table 2, Feb. 2013.

greatest in the communities where women have the greatest potential to outearn men. For example, fewer than a third of black adults today are married, down from 61% in 1960. As men and women navigate a brave new world of gender convergence, it's not clear how well the institution of marriage will survive.

Families and living arrangements have changed, too. Nearly 3 in 10 households in America today contain just one person, double the share in 1960. Among American women in their early 40s, 1 in 5 have never had children, double the share of 30 years ago. A 2013 memoir by comedian Jen Kirkman, *I Can Barely Take Care of Myself: Tales from a Happy Life Without Kids*, serves up an amusing string of anecdotes from the front lines of childlessness. ("Who'll take care of you when you're old?" "Servants!") Demographer Joel Kotkin has coined the term "post-familialism"; others talk about "the new singleism." It's a global phenomenon, having taken root not just in the US but in Canada, much of Europe, and the wealthy countries of East Asia. It's linked to urbanization, secularism, women's economic empowerment, and higher standards of living. There's a lively debate among cultural arbiters over whether it will deliver more or less happiness over the long haul for the people who make these choices. Clearly, though, it poses a dilemma for humankind as a whole. Societies with fewer young people tend to have less energy, dynamism, and innovation. Societies dominated by the old risk becoming sclerotic. The old require the care of the young. If fewer people form families to play that role, then governments will need to fill more of the gap—but this is a burden they already struggle to bear.

...

All these data points and trends, squeezed between the covers of one book, can create a sense of foreboding about America's future. They portray a society tugged apart by centrifugal forces. And they show that the two institutions we rely on to be repairers of the breach—the government and the family—are themselves being shaken to their core. Yet this isn't a gloom-and-doom book. There are too many findings from the Pew Research Center's surveys that give voice to the optimism, pragmatism, and resilience of the American public, even in the teeth of dysfunctional politics, rising inequality, frayed families, and anemic labor markets. America *isn't* breaking apart at the seams. The American dream isn't dying. Our new racial and ethnic complexion hasn't triggered massive outbreaks of intolerance. Our generations aren't at each other's throats. They're living more interdependently than at any time in recent memory, because that turns out to be a good coping strategy in hard times. Our nation faces huge challenges, no doubt. So do the rest of the world's aging superpowers. If you had to pick a nation with the right stuff to ride out the coming demographic storm, you'd be crazy not to choose America, warts and all.

ENDNOTES

1. All long-term demographic projections in this book should be taken with a grain of salt—and the longer the term, the larger the grain. They're based on the best available data and analysis. But things change.
2. Fred Barnes, "America and Its Immigrants, A Hate-Love Relationship," *Weekly Standard*, July 29, 2013.
3. Pew Research Center, "The Lost Decade of the Middle Class," August 22, 2012. In this report, our analysis of long-term US Census data showed that the share of adults in the middle class declined from 61% in 1971 to 51% in 2011. We defined a "middle class" adult as one living in a household with an annual income between 67% and 200% of the national median—an income range of $39,418 to $118,255 in 2011 dollars (all incomes were scaled to reflect a three person household). We tested other middle income boundaries—some wider, some narrower—but always found the same pattern: the middle-income tier has been shrinking steadily for many decades. Our analysis also found that the share of adults in the upper and lower income tiers have each risen steadily over time—the lower tier to 29% in 2011 from 25% in 1971; the upper tier to 20% in 2011 from 14% in 1971. See http://www.pewsocialtrends.org/2012/08/22/the-lost-decade-of-the-middle-class/.

4. A 2011 cross-national analysis by the Organization for Economic Co-operation and Development (OECD) found that the United States ranked fourth from highest in income inequality among 34 of the world's most advanced economies—behind only Turkey, Mexico, and Chile. That study, which took into account the impact of taxes and public cash transfers, put the US Gini Coefficient at 0.38, lower than the measure of income inequality in the US before taxes and transfers. Both measures have risen more sharply in the US over the past several decades

than in all but a handful of the world's other wealthy countries. See www.oecd.org/els/soc/49499779.pdf.

5. Julia B. Isaacs, "International Comparison of Economic Mobility," in *Economic Mobility in America*, Brookings Institution and the Economic Mobility Project of the Pew Charitable Trusts.

6. Based on a Pew Research Center analysis of wealth data from the Census Bureau's Survey of Income and Program Participation (SIPP).

7. Laurie Goodstein, "Christian Right Failed to Sway Voters on Issues," *New York Times*, November 9, 2012.

8. See, for example, Sara S. McLanahan, "Life without Father: What happens to the children?" Center for Research on Child Wellbeing, Princeton, NJ, 2001.

9. Pew Research Center, "The Decline of Marriage and Rise of New Families," November 2010.

DISCUSSION QUESTIONS

1. In what directions are the two main American political parties evolving? What will the likely effect be of the increased influence within the Republican Party of rural White working-class voters and interests? How is the Democratic Party changing?

2. Paul Taylor writes that "as a people, we're growing older, more unequal, more diverse, more mixed race, more digitally linked, more tolerant, less married, less fertile, less religious, less mobile, and less confident." What are the implications of these changes? What surprises you in this article?

3. Discuss this statement: "There's little evidence from public opinion surveys that Americans resent the rich. But in growing numbers, they resent the policies and institutions—political as well as economic—that they believe are rigged in favor of the rich." Do you agree? Why or why not?

4. What data does Taylor cite to support his claim that

   a. Americans' understanding of and attitudes about gender roles are changing?

   b. Americans' views of race (what is "Whiteness," and what is "Blackness") are changing?

READING 1.4

HAPA NATION

The Next America Boomers, Millennials, and the Looming Generational Showdown

BY **Paul Taylor; Pew Research Center**

When Barack Obama's parents married in 1961, the best estimates are that perhaps 1 marriage in 1,000 in the US that year was, like theirs, between a black person and a white person.

Anti-miscegenation laws were still in force in 16 states, and racial intermarriage was a gasp-inducing taboo virtually everywhere else. That was then. Now 15.5% of all new marriages in the US are between spouses of a different race or ethnicity from each other. This cultural sea change has been driven not just by blacks and whites, but by a wave of Hispanic and Asian newcomers who've produced a new American tapestry more complex than anything our nation has ever known.

Few families embody this transformation better than the one that resides at 1600 Pennsylvania Avenue.[1] President Obama's wife is a descendant of an African-American slave and a white slave owner. His wife's brother is married to a white woman of Scottish/Irish heritage. His half-sister is an Indonesian American married to a Chinese Canadian. The president himself is the product of an African father raised in Kenya and a white mother raised in Kansas. According to genealogy.com, he too is the descendant of a slave—but on his white mother's side, not his black father's. Obama was born in Hawaii, America's most Technicolor state, where the word "hapa" (half or part) is meant to describe someone of mixed Asian heritage, but colloquially has come to mean a mixed-race person of any kind—a "mutt," as Obama sometimes calls himself.

The fact that no racial label neatly fits our sitting president is in its way fitting for a society that is struggling to find a modern vocabulary for race. Our labels, categories, and classification schemes haven't kept up with our behaviors, attitudes, and weddings. This is new. In one form or another, America has been confounded by race—our original sin—for four centuries. But for most of that history, racial identification had been a simple matter of black or white, with the "one-drop rule" the line of demarcation. The rigidity of this either/or formulation obscured the racial intermixing that has always been a part of our national DNA—but that, of course, was exactly the point. Mixing was deemed to be not just illegal but sinful, so it couldn't be acknowledged above a whisper. Now the stigma is receding. And so too is our exclusively black-or-white racial checkerboard, rendered obsolete by the more than 30 million Hispanic and Asian immigrants who have come to the US since 1965. Today's immigrants and their children are in the vanguard of the modern intermarriage trend. What should we call the children of such marriages? As a society, we don't yet know. No one—not the Census Bureau, not those children themselves, not Americans of different races—has come up with a common vocabulary.

Consider again the man who lives in the White House. Racially speaking, who is Barack Obama? Well, it depends on whom you ask. Given a choice between calling the president black or calling him mixed race, most blacks (55%) say Obama is black; just a third (34%) say he is mixed race. Among whites, the pattern is reversed. Most (53%) say he is mixed race, while just a quarter (24%) say he is black. And among Hispanics (who have their own unique set of challenges finding a racial label that fits their group), 6 in 10 say Obama is mixed race.

Nor is Obama the only object of semantic confusion. When a Pew Research survey asked respondents in 2009 to state what race they themselves are (the choices were white, black, Asian, or some other race) and told they could choose as many categories as they wished, just 1% chose to identify with more than one category. However, later in the same survey, when respondents were asked explicitly if they considered themselves to be mixed race, fully 1 in 6 (16%) said they did, including 8% of whites, 20% of blacks, and 37% of Hispanics. In short, responses to racial identity questions vary widely depending on wording and context—another sign that our traditional categories aren't very good at capturing our new racial landscape in all of its complexity.

Some groups are more disoriented by and disapproving of all these changes than others—and here's where a big generation gap emerges. As noted in Chapter 3, just 29% of Silents say that "more people of different races marrying each other" has been a change for the better in America. This share rises to 36% among Boomers, 47% among Xers, and 60% among Millennials. And when a similar question is

---

Figure 4 Do You Think of Obama as Black or Mixed Race?

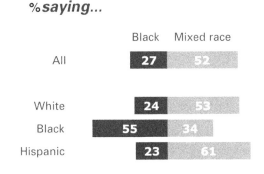

Note: "Both/neither" and "Don't know/Refused" responses not shown. Question wording: Do you mostly think of Obama as a black person or mostly as a person of mixed race?

Source: Pew Research Center survey, Oct.–Nov. 2009, N=2,884 US adults

posed in explicitly personal terms—how comfortable would you be if someone in your family were to marry someone of a different race?—the generational differences grow even sharper. Just 38% of Silents say they would be comfortable, compared with 85% of Millennials.

Whether Americans are ready for them or not, racial and ethnic intermarriages are happening in record numbers.

THE RISE OF INTERMARRIAGE

Some 15.5% of all new marriages in 2011 were either interracial or interethnic, a sixfold increase over the share in 1960. Looking at all current marriages in 2011, irrespective of the year they began, 8.6% were interracial or interethnic, an all-time high.[2]

There are distinctive patterns by race and ethnicity. Among all newlyweds in 2010, 9% of whites, 17% of blacks, 26% of Hispanics, and 28% of Asians married someone whose race or ethnicity was different from their own.

Even though the rate is lowest among whites, they are still by far the nation's most numerous race group. As such, in 70% of all new mixed marriages, one spouse is white. Of the approximately 275,500 new interracial or interethnic marriages in 2010, white/Hispanic couples accounted for more than 4 in 10 (43%), white/Asian couples made up 14%, and white/black couples made up 12%. About 3 in 10 new intermarriages were among a mix of different non-white spouses (Figure 5).

Gender patterns vary widely—and these variances are highly race-specific. Black men are nearly three times more likely than black women to "marry out." By contrast, Asian-American women are more than twice as likely as Asian-American men to marry out. Cultural norms and gender and racial stereotypes help explain these patterns. A 2013 PBS documentary, *Seeking Asian Female,* about a marriage initiated on the Internet between a 60-year-old white American man and his 30-year-old Chinese bride, sparked an animated online debate about the way American pop culture tends to sexualize Asian women and emasculate Asian men. These stereotypes, to some degree, establish the contours of the out-marriage market for Asian Americans of both genders; they also complicate romantic couplings among Asian Americans themselves. The marital dynamics between black men and women are even more fraught. Marriage rates in the African-American community have fallen to their lowest levels in modern history, a trend driven by the disparate impact of the

changing economy on black men and women and exacerbated by gender tensions arising from the fact that among the declining ranks of black men who do marry, a record share (more than 1 in 5) choose a bride who is not black. Among whites and Hispanics, by the way, there is no gender difference in intermarriage rates.

There are also distinctive socioeconomic patterns among intermarried couples, based on the race, ethnicity, and gender of the partners. Some of the differences reflect the overall characteristics of these different groups in society at large, and some appear to be the result of a selection process. For example, among intermarried newlywed couples involving whites, white/Asian couples have the highest combined annual earnings (nearly $71,000), much higher than the earnings of white/Hispanic couples (about $58,000) as well as white/black couples (about $53,000). Also, white/Asian couples have higher combined earnings than either white/white or Asian/Asian couples. Meanwhile, the combined median earnings of white/Hispanic couples are lower than those of white/white couples but higher than those of Hispanic/Hispanic couples. The earnings

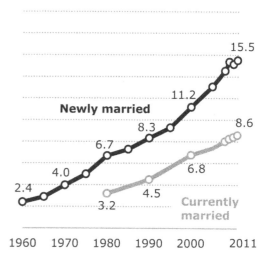

Figure 5 Intermarriage Trend, 1960–2011

% of marriages involving spouses of a different race/ethnicity from each other

Source: Pew Research Center analysis of 1960–2011 American Community Survey and Census data (IPUMS). For 1960–2008, figures are calculated base on 1980 and 2008 data. For more details see Pew Research Center's "Marrying out: One-in-Seven New US Marriages is Interracial or Interethnic," June 4, 2010.

of intermarried white/ black couples fall between those of white/white and black/black couples.

When it comes to education, white newlyweds who married Asians are more educated than whites who married whites, blacks, or Hispanics. More than half of the white men (51%) and white women (57%) who married an Asian spouse are college-educated, compared with only 32% of white men and 37% of white women who married a white spouse. Also, about 6 in 10 Asian newlyweds who married whites are college-educated.

Newlywed Hispanics and blacks who married a white spouse are more likely to be college-educated than those who married within their group. About 23% of Hispanic men who married a white wife have a college degree, compared with just 10% of Hispanic men who married a Hispanic woman. Likewise, 1 in 3 (33%) Hispanic women who married a white husband are college-educated, compared with about 13% of Hispanic women who "married in." The educational differences among blacks who "marry in" and "marry out" are less dramatic but follow a similar pattern.

Marrying out is much more common among the native-born population than among immigrants. Native-born Hispanics were nearly three times as likely as their foreign-born counterparts to marry a non-Hispanic in 2010. The disparity among native- and foreign-born Asians is not as great, but still significant: nearly 4 in 10 native-born Asians (38%) and nearly a quarter (24%) of foreign-born Asians married a non-Asian in 2010.

Among Asian newlyweds, the intermarriage gap between native and the foreign born is much bigger for Asian men than for Asian women. In 2010, native-born Asian male newlyweds were about three times as likely as the foreign born to marry out (32% versus 11%). Among newlywed Asian women, the gap between native and foreign born is much smaller (43% versus 34%). The gender differences are not significant among Hispanic native- and foreign- born newlyweds.

REGIONS AND STATES. Intermarriage in the US tilts west. About 1 in 5 (22%) of all newlyweds in western states married someone of a different race or ethnicity between 2008 and 2010, compared with 14% in the South, 13% in the Northeast, and 11% in the Midwest. At the state level, more than 4 in 10 (42%) newlyweds in Hawaii between 2008 and 2010 were intermarried; the other states with an intermarriage rate of 20% or more are all west of the Mississippi River. For new marriages between whites and Hispanics, states with the highest prevalence rates are New Mexico (19%), Arizona (12%), and Nevada (11%). The highest shares of intermarried white and Asian couples are in Hawaii (9%), District of Columbia (7%), and Nevada (5%). And the top states for white/black intermarried couples are Virginia (3.3%), North Carolina (3.2%), and Kansas (3%).

DIVORCE. Several studies using government data have found that overall divorce rates are higher for couples who married out than for those who married in— but here, too, the patterns vary by the racial and gender characteristics of the couples. An analysis conducted a decade ago found that 10 years after they married, interracial couples had a 41% chance of separation or divorce, compared with a 31% chance among couples who married within their race, according to a study based on the 1995 National Survey of Family Growth (NSFG).[3] A subsequent study that analyzed 2002 NSFG data found that "although interracial marriages overall are more vulnerable to divorce, this reflects the experience of some but not all couples." It found that after 10 years of marriage, interracial marriages that are most vulnerable to divorce involve white females and nonwhite males (with the exception of white females/ Hispanic males). Conversely, there is little or no difference in divorce rates among white men/nonwhite women couples, and white men/black women couples are actually substantially less likely than white/white couples to divorce by the 10th year of marriage.[4]

Figure 6 Intermarriage Rates, by Race and Ethnicity, 2010

% of newlyweds married to someone of a different race/ethnicity

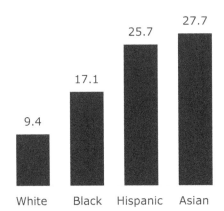

Note: Asians include Pacific Islanders.

Source: Pew Research Center analysis of 2010 American Community Survey, IPUMS.

Figure 7 Intermarriage Rates of Newlyweds, by Gender, 2010

% of newlyweds married to someone of a different race/ethnicity

No gender difference for these groups ...

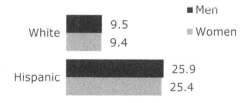

Big gender difference for these groups ...

Note: Asians include Pacific Islanders.

Source: Pew Research Center analysis of 2010 American Community Survey, IPUMS.

Another study using 1990 to 2001 data from the Census Bureau's Survey of Income and Program Participation (SIPP) found that on the whole, interracial marriages are less stable than same-race same-ethnicity marriages, but marital dissolution was found to be strongly associated with the race or ethnicity of the individuals in the union. The authors found that "the results failed to provide evidence that interracial marriage per se is associated with an elevated risk of marital dissolution."[5] Mixed marriages involving blacks and whites were the least stable followed by Hispanic/white couples, whereas mixed marriages involving Asians and whites were more stable than same-race white marriages.

RACIAL IDENTITY AND LABELS

The US is on a demographic track to become a majority nonwhite (or, in the evocative oxymoron, "majority minority") nation sometime between 2040 and 2050. But by then, with an ever rising share of the population likely to be the product of mixed marriages, how much sense will these categories make? History offers some limited lessons. Until a few generations ago, "marrying

out" mainly referred to crossing entrenched boundaries of religion or ancestry (race was still beyond the pale). Families would object to—and might sometimes block—marriages between a Protestant and Catholic, an Italian American and an Irish American, or a Jew and a gentile. Today such unions are so commonplace that they rarely set off family crises and barely attract notice of any kind in the wider society. (A 2013 survey of Jews by the Pew Research Center found that among Jews who have married since 2000, nearly 6 in 10 have a non-Jewish spouse.[6]) Yes, these "mixed" couples and their children have to figure out where to worship and which relatives to visit on which religious holidays, but they don't typically have to confront existential questions about who they are, where they fit, and how society labels them. So one lesson of our history is that identity markers that once seemed impenetrable have a way of becoming porous. And people have a way of adapting.

Race, however, poses a more profound identity challenge than does religion or ancestry. In America, it comes freighted with centuries of slavery and other forms of state-sanctioned discrimination; no other group cleavage in our national life is as deep or painful—or visible. Few people in this country wear their religion in public, but there's no hiding one's race. And nowadays, few seem to want to. Our culture has traded the melting pot for the mosaic. We glory in our distinctive hues. In this new milieu, being mixed race—a stigma not just in our society but in most societies for most of human history—now carries cultural cachet. Pick your favorite mixed-race celebrity, it's quite an A-list: Halle Berry, Beyoncé, Keanu Reeves, Salma Hayek, Derek Jeter, Mariah Carey, Norah Jones, Tiger Woods, Barack Obama.

To be sure, there are still plenty of holdouts from this new racial kumbaya. When General Mills ran a television commercial in 2013 that featured a little girl with a white mom and black dad (the cute plot line had the girl, upon hearing that Cheerios are good for the heart, dumping a bunch of them on the chest of her napping father), two interesting things happened. The first was that the interracial marriage and biracial child were presented without gawking or editorial comment—just your basic TV ad family. The second was that the reaction to the ad got so ugly on the comment section on YouTube that it had to be taken down. There was a similar outbreak of online bigotry when a young woman who is the daughter of Indian immigrants was crowned Miss America in the fall of 2013. Obviously we haven't become a "postracial" society; human beings don't seem to be wired that way. But there are fewer out-and-out bigots than there once were. And increasingly, our new racial landscape is bursting with nuance, shadings, subtleties, possibilities, ironies. A few years ago California-based artist Kip Fulbeck put together the Hapa Project, a photographic exhibition that consisted of a series of portraits of multiracial children and adults. Below each portrait was a short personal statement. "My last boyfriend told me he liked me because of my race," wrote one attractive young woman of middle hue and indeterminate race. "So I dumped him."

There's always been a political dimension to identity labels. In 1997, two of the nation's most powerful civil rights groups, the NAACP and the National Council of La Raza, testified in Congress in opposition to the Census Bureau's proposal to allow people to identify with more than one race on the 2000 decennial census. They feared it would reduce the size of traditionally disadvantaged race groups, thereby "diluting benefits to which they are entitled as a protected class under civil rights law," as the NAACP said in its written testimony. A small group called the Association of Multiethnic Americans countered that the census should concern itself first and foremost with accurate racial identification: "We want a choice in the matter of who we are, just like any other community. [We find it] ironic that our people are being asked to correct by virtue of how we define ourselves all of the past injustices of other groups of people." Another small multiracial advocacy group, Project Race, said in its testimony: "Multiracial children who wish to embrace all of their heritage should be allowed to do so. They should not be put in the position of denying one of their parents to satisfy arbitrary government requirements."

THE HISPANIC IDENTITY CONUNDRUM

Those multiracial groups carried the day back in the late 1990s, but even so, racial and ethnic labeling on the census remains today what it has always been: a confusing maze. No group struggles more with this nation's official race categories than the nation's 53 million Hispanics. They are classified by the federal government as an ethnic group, not a racial group. This is a nod to the genetic reality that Hispanics are a mix of races—with bloodlines flowing from Europe, Africa, and the indigenous Native American tribes of North, Central, and South America. But they all have a connection to Spanish language, culture, and heritage—which are standard markers of ethnicity. The designation of Hispanics as an ethnic group was mandated by Congress in 1976 in response to pressure from

Hispanic political and civil rights leaders who wanted official data about their community so they could press claims for equal treatment and benefits under the law. This was the first (and so far only) time in US history that an ethnic (as opposed to racial) group had been singled out this way. And it has led to a census form that, for many Hispanics, reads like a riddle.

Race and ethnicity are covered by questions 8 and 9 on the 10-question 2010 census form. Respondents are explicitly instructed to answer BOTH (all caps on the form) questions. Question 8 asks all Americans whether they are Hispanic, and if so, to mark their Hispanic country of origin (Mexico, Cuba, etc.). The question notes that "for this census, Hispanic origins are not races." This is the question that produces the government's official count of Hispanics and—as has been the custom in census-taking since the middle of last century—it is based entirely on self-identification.[7] Question 9 then asks people to state their race, and provides a total of 15 different boxes (including white, black, American Indian, 11 Asian race boxes, and "some other race"—but not including Hispanic). On the 2010 census, about half (53%) of all those who self-identified as Hispanic in question 8 checked the "white" box in question 9, while 3% checked black and 8% checked mixed race or other—and fully 37% checked "some other race."

Those responses stand as a rebuke to the classification system that produced them. If more than a third of our nation's largest minority group finds itself without a race box to check on the census form, it may be time to come up with a different taxonomy.

For Hispanics, the identity riddle doesn't stop there, however. Four decades after the terms "Hispanic" and "Latino" were affixed to them by the federal government, Hispanics themselves haven't fully embraced those labels. Only about one-quarter (24%) of Hispanic adults say they most often identify themselves by either of those pan-ethnic terms, according to a 2011 Pew Research Center survey. About half (51%) say they identify themselves most often by their family's country or place of origin (using such terms as Mexican, Cuban, Puerto Rican, Salvadoran, or Dominican), and 21% say they use the term "American" most often (a share that rises to 40% among those who were born in the US). The terms "Hispanic" and "Latino" are American confections—they get little use in the 20-plus countries where Spanish is the official language. Plus, many Hispanics in this country are frankly doubtful about just how much they have in common with other Hispanics.

Figure 8

→ NOTE: Please answer BOTH Question 8 about Hispanic origin and
Question 9 about race. For this census, Hispanic origins are not races.

8. Is Person 1 of Hispanic, Latino, or Spanish origin?

☐ **No,** not of Hispanic, Latino, or Spanish origin
☐ Yes, Mexican, Mexican Am., Chicano
☐ Yes, Puerto Rican
☐ Yes, Cuban
☐ Yes, another Hispanic, Latino, or Spanish origin — *Print origin, for example,
Argentinean, Colombian, Dominican, Nicaraguan, Salvadoran, Spaniard, and so on.* 7

9. What is Person 1's race? *Mark ☒ one or more boxes.*

☐ White
☐ Black, African Am., or Negro
☐ American Indian or Alaska Native — *Print name of enrolled or principal tribe.* 7

☐ Asian Indian ☐ Japanese ☐ Native Hawaiian
☐ Chinese ☐ Korean ☐ Guamanian or Chamorro
☐ Filipino ☐ Vietnamese ☐ Samoan
☐ Other Asian — *Print race, for* ☐ Other Pacific Islander — *Print*
example, Hmong, Laotian, Thai, *race, for example, Fijian, Tongan,*
Pakistani, Cambodian, and so on. 7 *and so on.* 7

☐ Some other race — *Print race.* 7

In response to another 2011 Pew survey question, about 7 in 10 (69%) Hispanics say that Hispanics in the US have many different cultures; just 29% say they share a common culture. That doesn't mean the labels serve no purpose. They make sense to Hispanic leaders and institutions that want to preserve their power base and to a majority white host culture that, despite its growing ease with racial diversity, still isn't ready to stop putting labels on people it deems to be different.

One of the most interesting demographic, sociological, and political dramas of the coming century will be whether the Hispanic identity marker recedes over time, as it did for the European immigrants. The answer isn't yet clear. Proximity, modern communication technology, and the relative ease of international travel make it much easier for today's Hispanic immigrants and their children to keep their ties to their ancestral countries and language. Plus, the mainstream culture's new embrace of ethnic diversity reduces the incentives for minorities to shed their ethnic identity. On the other hand, if a quarter of Hispanics continue to marry non-Hispanics, these ethnic identity markers are bound to blur over time.

What boxes will the children of these marriages discover on the 2050 census? If history is a guide, they'll be different from the ones in use now. In fact, several

changes are already in the works. In 2012, the Census Bureau announced it was contemplating whether to drop the separate Hispanic origin question from its 2020 form and combine it with the race question. If it were to do so, it could then ask a single follow-up question about the national origin of the respondent's family. The net result, according to Kenneth Prewitt, a former director of the US Census Bureau and leading proponent of the change, would be to hold all major racial and ethnic groups harmless in terms of their population counts while at the same time eliminating the confusing conflation of race, ethnicity, and national origin.

BLACKS IN OBAMA'S AMERICA

The Census Bureau has already decided to drop the word "Negro" from the 2020 form because its surveys have determined that a dwindling share of blacks—mostly older adults living in the South—still use the term. (Going forward, blacks will still be able to check the box "black" or "African American.") No population group has been subject to more classification changes than this one. The first census, in 1790, distinguished between free white persons and slaves. The term "color" (not "race") first appeared in the 1850 census, with three options: white, black, or mulatto. By 1890, census takers had the option of describing nonwhites as "quadroons" or "octoroons." In 1910, census takers were instructed to write "B" for "black only" and "Mu" for mulatto, a category meant to include "persons who have some proportion or perceptible trace of Negro blood." By 1930, these terms had been dropped, replaced by instructions that said that persons who were a mix of "white and Negro blood" were to be counted by census takers as "Negro" no matter how small the share of Negro blood—an explicit affirmation of the long-standing but unofficial "one-drop rule." By 1970, the race box was no longer to be filled out by the census enumerators based on observations from in-person visits; instead, it was to be done by Americans themselves, checking boxes on forms sent to them in the mail. That remains the practice to this day.

Over the years, as different labels have come into and out of vogue, the real problem for blacks comes not from the words themselves, but from the enduring power of the one-drop formula. When President Obama filled out his census form in 2010, he could have checked black, he could have checked white, or he could have checked *both* black and white. He checked black—a decision that disappointed many mixed-race Americans who'd hoped he would use this official declaration of racial identity to signal that it was time to move beyond the old formula. The president's defenders countered that anyone who looks like him has lived the life of a black person, and that it would be a denial of reality to pretend otherwise. Obama's ambiguous racial identity in a one-drop world is one reason he is such a compelling historical figure. Over the years he has been well served by political instincts that have taught him to be wary of the topic of race, but when it comes up—as with the Reverend Jeremiah Wright controversy in 2008; or the arrest of a prominent black Harvard professor at his home in Cambridge in 2009; or the killing of a black teenager in Florida in 2012 by a white/Hispanic neighborhood watch volunteer—Obama is frequently eloquent. He knows that in post–civil rights America, the only way for a black politician to be a national figure is to talk about race in the language of inclusion, not grievance. Here's what he said in 2008 when his candidacy was briefly threatened by a videotape that surfaced of an anti-white, anti-American tirade delivered by Wright—his pastor, mentor, and friend—from the pulpit of his Chicago church:

> I am the son of a black man from Kenya and a white woman from Kansas. I was raised with the help of a white grandfather who survived a depression to serve in Patton's army during World War II and a white grandmother who worked on a bomber assembly line at Fort Leavenworth while he was overseas .... I am married to a black American who carries within her the blood of slaves and slaveowners—an inheritance we pass on to our two precious daughters. I have brothers, sisters, nieces, nephews, uncles, and cousins, of every race and every hue, scattered across three continents, and for as long as I live, I will never forget that in no other country on Earth is my story even possible. It's a story that hasn't made me the most conventional candidate. But it is a story that has seared into my genetic makeup the idea that this nation is more than the sum of its parts—that out of many, we are truly one.

Obama has a complicated relationship with his black constituents. A *Washington Post* article captured a telling moment in 2007 when then-candidate Obama was meeting with a group of black advisers and scholars as he rehearsed for a forthcoming Democratic candidates' debate at predominantly black Howard University.[8] In the article's opening scene, Obama struggles to find the right tone and cadence. "I can't sound like Martin," he finally tells the group. "I can't sound like Jesse." Sometimes his challenge of finding a voice that can straddle the gap between our black and white cultures has produced moments of sweet irony. A few days before his 2009 inauguration, the president-elect stopped by Ben's Chili Bowl, a landmark eatery in Washington, DC's black community, with the usual press gaggle in tow. After paying for his chili dog, Obama was asked by the cashier if he wanted change back from his twenty. "Nah, we straight," he replied.[9] The pool reporter chose to clean up the president-elect's dialect and wrote that he said, "No, we're straight." But a video of the exchange became an Internet hit, especially among blacks who got a kick out of their Harvard-educated president sounding, as one hip-hop commentator put it, "mad cool" with his black street slang.

As president, Obama has faced a quiet but persistent undercurrent of criticism from black leaders who feel he's been too timid about addressing ongoing racial imbalances in the economy and in society at large. Television host and political activist Tavis Smiley complained during the 2012 campaign that "tragically ... the president feels boxed in by his blackness." Smiley went on: "It has ... been painful to watch this particular president's calibrated, cautious and sometimes callous treatment of his most loyal constituency. African Americans will have lost ground in the Obama era."[10] Others say the problem isn't that Obama's boxed in by being black—it's that he's not black enough. Typical of the genre: a headline on a column by black *New York Daily News* columnist Stanley Crouch: "What Obama Isn't: Black Like Me." And for others, Obama's mixed-race heritage is fodder for satire. "The first black president!" black comedian Wanda Sykes marveled at a White House Correspondents' Association dinner in 2009, as the president sat a few feet away on the dais. "I'm proud to be able to say that. That's unless you screw up. And then it's going to be, 'What's up with the half-white guy?'"

There's no group in America for whom the election of the nation's first black president has had a more positive impact than African Americans. A nationwide Pew Research survey of blacks conducted in November 2009, a year after Obama's election victory, found that across a wide range of measures—satisfaction with the direction of the country, the state of race relations, the pace of black progress, their personal economic circumstances—black attitudes were significantly more positive than in 2007. On many of these measures, blacks were more upbeat than whites, a reversal of patterns that had prevailed for decades.

Figure 9 Blacks' Sense of Progress, 1981–2013

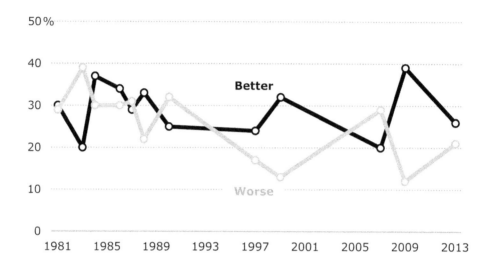

% of blacks who say blacks are better/worse off now than five years ago

Note: In surveys in 2005 and earlier, blacks include Hispanic blacks. In surveys in 2007 and later, blacks include only non-Hispanic blacks. "Same" response not showed.

Source: Pew Research Center surveys, 1981–2013.

This spike in attitudes came in the teeth of an economy that had been in a deep recession for those two years, a downturn that hit blacks especially hard. Nevertheless, twice as many blacks in 2009 (39%) as in 2007 (20%) said that the "situation of black people in this country" was better than it had been five years earlier; this more positive view had taken hold among blacks of all ages and income levels. Asked to look ahead, blacks were also more upbeat. More than half (53%) said that life for blacks in the future will be better than it is now, while just 10% said it will be worse. In 2007, 44% said things would be better for blacks in the future, while 21% said they would be worse.

Much of this post-election glow would eventually dim. By 2013, when Pew Research asked blacks those same questions in a new survey, the share who said things had gotten better for blacks over the past five years—26%—had fallen most of the way back to its 2007 level, even though this new five-year assessment period encompassed all of Obama's tenure in the White House.

That 2013 survey was taken around the time of the commemoration of the 50th anniversary of Dr. King's famous "I Have a Dream" speech on the steps of the Lincoln Memorial in Washington, DC. It found that just a third of blacks feel there has been a lot of progress toward reaching racial equality over the past half century, while 8 in 10 say much more needs to be done. Whites were more mixed in their assessments. Half said a lot of progress has been made, and 44% said a lot more needs to be done.

Those mixed views on progress toward racial equality were echoed in a Pew Research Center analysis of long-term US government trend data on indicators of well-being and civic engagement, including personal finance, life expectancy, educational attainment, and voter participation. The data looked at equality of outcomes rather than equality of opportunity.

Our analysis found that the economic gulf between blacks and whites that was present half a century ago largely remains. When it comes to household income and household wealth, the gaps between blacks and whites have widened. On measures such as high school completion and life expectancy, they have narrowed. On other measures, including poverty and homeownership rates, the gaps are roughly the same as they were 40 years ago (see appendix Figure 7A.5).

FINANCES. Between 1967 and 2011 the median income of a black household of three rose from about $24,000 to nearly $40,000.[11] Expressed as a share of white income, black households earn about 59% of what white households earn, a small increase from 55% in 1967. But when expressed as dollars, the black-white income gap widened, from about $19,000 in the late 1960s to roughly $27,000 today. The race gap on household wealth has increased from $75,224 in 1984 to $84,960 in 2011.

Other indicators of financial well-being have changed little in recent decades, including homeownership rates and the share of each race that live above the poverty line. The black unemployment rate also has consistently been about double that of whites since the 1950s.

EDUCATION. High school completion rates have converged since the 1960s, and now about 9 in 10 blacks and whites have a high school diploma. The trend in college completion rates tells a more nuanced story. Today white adults 25 and older are significantly more likely than blacks to have completed at least a bachelor's degree (34% versus 21%, a 13 percentage point difference). Fifty years ago, the completion gap between whites and blacks was about 6 percentage points (10% versus 4%). But expressed a different way, the black completion rate as a percentage of the white rate has improved from 42% then to 62% now.

FAMILY FORMATION. The analysis finds growing disparities in key measures of family formation. Marriage rates among whites and blacks have declined in the past 50 years, and the black-white difference has nearly doubled. Today about 55% of whites and 31% of blacks ages 18 and older are married. In 1960, 74% of whites and roughly 6 in 10 blacks (61%) were married. The share of births to unmarried women has risen sharply for both groups; in 2011, more than 7 in 10 births to black women were to unmarried mothers, compared with about 3 in 10 births to white women (72% versus 29%).

INCARCERATION. Black men were more than six times as likely as white men to be incarcerated in federal and state prisons and local jails in 2010, the last year complete data are available. That is an increase from 1960, when black men were five times as likely as whites to be incarcerated.

VOTER TURNOUT. Participation rates for blacks in presidential elections has lagged those of whites for

Figure 10 Blacks' View of Why Many Blacks Don't Get Ahead

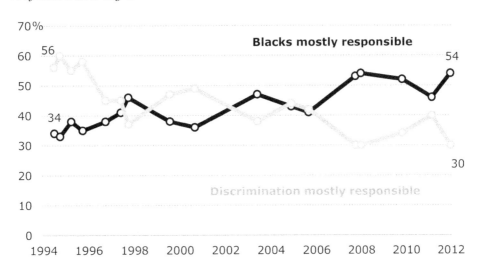

% of blacks who say ...

Note: In surveys in 2005 and earlier, blacks include Hispanic blacks. In surveys in 2007 and later, blacks include only non-Hispanic blacks. Question wording: Which of these statements comes closer to your own view—even if neither is exactly right. Racial discrimination is the main reason why many black people can't get ahead these days, OR, Blacks who can't get ahead in this country are mostly responsible for their own condition.

Source: Pew Research Center surveys, 1994–2012.

most of the past half century but has been rising since 1996. Buoyed by the historic candidacies of Barack Obama, blacks nearly caught up with whites in 2008 and surpassed them in 2012, when 67% of eligible blacks cast ballots, compared with 64% of eligible whites.

LIFE EXPECTANCY. The gap in life expectancy rates among blacks and whites has narrowed in the past five decades from about seven years to four.

In 2012, when a Pew Research survey asked why many blacks have not advanced in this country, a majority of black respondents (54%) said those who cannot get ahead are mainly responsible for their own situation, whereas 3 in 10 (30%) said that racial discrimination is the main reason. Fifteen years before, most blacks held the opposite view. Multiple surveys taken since 1994 show that this shift in blacks' perceptions has occurred in fits and starts over time, and that the change predates Obama's election.

In one of the most intriguing findings of the 2009 survey, most blacks joined with most whites in saying that the two racial groups have grown more alike in the past decade, both in their standards of living and their core values. Seven in 10 whites (70%) and 6 in 10 blacks (60%) said that the values held by blacks and whites have become more similar in the past 10 years. Similarly, a majority of blacks (56%) and nearly two-thirds of whites (65%) said the standard-of-living gap between whites and blacks has narrowed in the past decade.

In fact, most of the racial gaps in key personal finance indicators widened during the 2007–2009 recession and have remained at elevated levels since. But when it comes to race and economics during the Age of Obama, reality is one thing, perception another. In 2013 blacks were still only about half as likely as whites to rate the national economy as poor, and twice as likely to say things will be better in the coming year. They were also more upbeat than whites in their perceptions of the housing market and the job market.

All of these attitudes suggest that Obama's presidency has had a salutary impact on African Americans that's hard to measure but impossible to ignore. Not on their economic circumstances, obviously, but on their

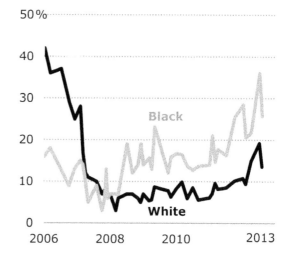

Figure 11 Whites, Blacks Assess the National Economy

% saying national economy is excellent/good

Source: Pew Research Center surveys, 2006–2013.

sense of belonging. I was a reporter in South Africa for three years in the mid-1990s during the transition from apartheid to democracy. Despite surface similarities, that country's racial dynamics are completely different from ours. No matter what the white settlers had done over the centuries in South Africa, blacks there have always known it was their country, their place—the land of their ancestors. The same can't be said of blacks in America; their ancestors arrived in chains. For them the color line has been more than an instrument of discrimination, it has been a badge of unbelonging. But when 130 million of their fellow Americans take part in two successive elections that choose Barack Obama as the nation's leader, that badge loses some of its oppressive power. The black-white divide is still America's deepest cleavage, and Obama's presidency hasn't made it go away. But it has made it smaller. To paraphrase Dr. King, the arc of our history is bending toward inclusion.

ENDNOTES

1. The de Blasios can give the Obamas a pretty good run for their money on the diversity front. I happened to be in Munich, Germany, last fall, two days after Bill de Blasio was elected mayor of New York City. Both Munich newspapers featured giant front page, above-the-fold photos of the winning candidate and his striking interracial

family—his black wife, Chirlane McCray; their son Dante, sporting his massive Afro; and their daughter Chiara, who adorned her loose, kinky locks with flowers. Interest in the family was even more intense in Italy, the ancestral home of de Blasio's mother, where one restaurant near Naples named a dessert in their honor—a sponge cake filled with hazelnut and white chocolate. See http://www.nytimes.com/2013/11/15/nyregion/his-roots-in-italy-de-blasio-now-has-fans-there.html?hp&_r=0. Bill De Blasio had started out as a longshot in the mayor's race and wound up winning by a landslide. Some analysts credit the family itself (especially a TV ad featuring Dante and his huge Afro) for the turnaround. It's hard to imagine the New York City of 1950—or, for that matter, of 2000—embracing that family. But in America, norms change. And the rest of the world watches with fascination.

2.   For background information on intermarriage, see Pew Research Center Social & Demographic Trends project; and see Wendy Wang, "The Rise of Intermarriage," February 16, 2012.

3.   M. D. Bramlett and W. D. Mosher, "Cohabitation, Marriage, Divorce, and Remarriage in the United States," *Vital and Health Statistics* 23, no. 22 (2002).

4.   J. L. Bratter and R. B. King, "'But Will It Last?' Marital Instability among Interracial and Same-Race Couples," *Family Relations* 57, no. 2 (2008): 160–171.

5.   Y. Zhang and J. Van Hook, "Marital Dissolution among Interracial Couples," *Journal of Marriage and Family* 71, no. 1 (2009).

6.   Pew Research Center's Religion & Public Life Project, "A Portrait of Jewish Americans," October 1, 2013.

7.   Prior to 1970, the US Census Bureau would have its enumerators make racial judgments about the identities of the people they counted, based on their in-person observations. Since then, Americans have been allowed to label themselves on their census form, and the bureau has adopted a you-are-whoever-you-say-you-are approach to racial labeling. So if an immigrant from Ghana, or a second-generation Chinese American, or a descendant of an Anglo-Saxon family that arrived on the *Mayflower* were, for whatever reason, to choose to identify as Hispanic, that's how he or she would be counted. And if a recent arrival from Mexico City decided to say she wasn't Hispanic, that's how she would be counted.

8.   Peter Wallsten, "Obama Struggles to Balance African Americans' Hopes with Country's as a Whole," *Washington Post*, October 28, 2012.

9.   Nia-Malika Henderson, "Blacks, Whites Hear Obama Differently," *Politico*, March 3, 2009.

10. Jodi Kantor, "For President, a Complex Calculus of Race and Politics," *New York Times*, October 21, 2012, p. A1.

11. For more information, see Pew Research Center Social & Demographic Trends project, "King's Dream Remains an Elusive Goal; Many Americans See Racial Disparities," August 22, 2013, http://www.pewsocialtrends.org/2013/08/22/kings-dream-remains-an-elusive-goal-many-americans-see-racial-disparities/#fn-17618-1.

DISCUSSION QUESTIONS

1.   What are the implications for multiculturalism of the trends that Paul Taylor discusses in this chapter?

2.   What does Taylor mean when he says that our society "is struggling to find a modern vocabulary for race. Our labels, categories, and classification schemes haven't kept up with our behaviors, attitudes, and weddings"?

3.   Taylor cites the criticism of talk show host Tavis Smiley about Barack Obama: "Tragically," Smiley noted, "the president feels boxed in by his blackness. It has ... been painful to watch [his] calibrated, cautious, and sometimes callous treatment of his most loyal constituency. African Americans will have lost ground in the Obama era." What did Smiley mean by this comment? Do you agree or disagree with him? Were Obama's election victories in 2008, and again in 2012—and his entire presidency—proof that we now live in a postracial society?

4.   Taylor writes: "All of these attitudes suggest that Obama's presidency has had a salutary impact on African Americans that's hard to measure but impossible to ignore. Not on their economic circumstances, obviously, but on their sense of belonging. ... The Black-White divide is still America's deepest cleavage. And Obama's presidency hasn't made it go away. But it has made it smaller." What does Taylor mean by these words? Do you agree or disagree with him?

READING 1.5

BREAKING THE CYCLE

Implicit Bias, Racial Anxiety, and Stereotype Threat

BY **Rachel D. Godsil**

Our country is in the midst of a racial cataclysm. Deaths of black men and boys at the hands of police, combined with grand juries' failure to indict, have spurred grief, rage and protest across the country. The reactions to the events are not uniform, however. A deep polarization along racial lines has emerged that contributes to the feeling among many people of color that black lives don't matter.

Neither these tragedies nor the racial disconnect that followed occur in isolation. People of color experience obstacles rooted in racial or ethnic difference with alarming frequency. And yet most Americans espouse values of racial fairness. How can we make sense of these seeming contradictions? And how can we work to change the conditions that set the stage for daily challenges and tragic endings that are linked to race?

In November 2014, the Perception Institute, along with the Haas Institute for a Fair and Inclusive Society, and the Center for Police Equity, issued the first in a series of reports entitled, *The Science of Equality: Addressing Implicit Bias, Racial Anxiety, and Stereotype Threat in Education and Health Care*, co-authored by Rachel Godsil, Linda Tropp, Phillip Atiba Goff and john powell. The goal of this series of reports is to synthesize and make accessible the advances in neuroscience, social psychology and other "mind sciences" that have provided insight into otherwise confounding contradictions between our country's stated commitment to fairness and the behaviors that lead both to tragic outcomes and day-to-day indignities linked to race.

Our report includes a lengthy discussion of social psychological research focusing on "implicit bias"—the automatic association of stereotypes or attitudes with particular social groups. We place particular emphasis on new research on reducing bias or, as Patricia Devine and colleagues describe, "Breaking the Prejudice Habit" (Devine 2014) and research identifying best practices

to prevent implicit bias from affecting decision-making and behavior.

Understanding implicit bias can help explain why a black criminal defendant charged with the same crime as a white defendant may receive a more draconian sentence, or why a resume from someone named Emily will receive more callbacks than an otherwise identical resume from someone named Lakeisha. This work confirms that people of color whose experiences of the world make abundantly clear that "race matters" are not simply oversensitive, while also explaining how whites who consider themselves non-racist may be sincere, even if their behavior sometimes suggests otherwise.

This is not meant to suggest that racialized outcomes are only a result of individual actions; cumulative racial advantages for whites as a group have been embedded into society's structures and institutions. However, as john powell and I argued in these pages in 2011 ("Implicit Bias Insights as Preconditions to Structural Change," *P&R*, Sept./Oct. 2011), there are two key reasons why structural racism cannot be successfully challenged without an understanding of how race operates psychologically. First, public policy choices are often affected by implicit bias or other racialized phenomena that operate implicitly. As a result, the changes in policy necessary to address institutional structures are dependent upon successfully addressing implicit biases that can affect political choices. Second, institutional operations invariably involve human behavior and interaction: Any policies to address racial inequities in schools, workplaces, police departments, courthouses, government offices and the like will only be successful if the people implementing the policy changes comply with them (Crosby & Monin, 2007).

Although implicit phenomena have the potential to impede successful institutional change, implicit racial bias is not the only psychological phenomenon that blocks society from achieving racial equality. We risk being myopic if we focus only on people's cognitive how we navigate racial interactions. These can translate into racial anxiety and stereotype threat which, independent of bias, can create obstacles for institutions and individuals seeking to adhere to antiracist practices. Indeed, research suggests that some forms of anti-bias education may have detrimental effects, if they increase *bias awareness* without also providing skills for managing anxiety.

Skills are needed for managing racial anxiety.

Racial anxiety refers to discomfort about the experience and potential consequences of inter-racial interactions. It is important to distinguish this definition of racial anxiety from what social scientists refer to as "racial threat," which includes the anger, frustration, uncertainty, feelings of deprivation and other emotions associated with concern over loss of resources or dominance. People of color may experience racial anxiety that they will be the target of discrimination and hostile treatment. White people tend to experience anxiety that they will be assumed to be racist and will be met with distrust or hostility. Whites experiencing racial anxiety can seem awkward and maintain less eye contact with people of color, and ultimately these interactions tend to be shorter than those without anxiety. If two people are both anxious that an interaction will be negative, it often is. So racial anxiety can result in a negative feedback loop in which both parties' fears seem to be confirmed by the behavior of the other.

Stereotype threat refers to the pressure people feel when they fear that their performance may confirm a negative stereotype about their group (Steele, 2010). This pressure is experienced as a distraction that interferes with intellectual functioning. Although stereotype threat can affect anyone, it has been most discussed in the context of academic achievement among students of color, and among girls in science, technology, engineering and math (STEM) fields. Less commonly explored is the idea that whites can suffer stereotype threat when concerned that they may be perceived as racist. In the former context, the threat prevents students from performing as well as they ought, and so they themselves suffer the consequences of this phenomenon. Stereotype threat among whites, by contrast, often causes behavior that harms others—usually the very people they are worried about. Concern about being perceived as racist explains, for example, why

some white teachers, professors and supervisors give less critical feedback to black students and employees than to white ones (Harber et al., 2012) and why white peer advisors may fail to warn a black student but will warn a white or Asian student that a certain course load is unmanageable (Crosby & Monin, 2007).

In other words, cognitive depletion or interference caused by stereotype threat can affect how one's own *capacity,* such as the ability to achieve academically, will be judged; this causes first-party harm to the individual whose performance suffers. However, as is explored in more detail below, stereotype threat about how one's *character* will be judged (i.e., being labeled a racist) can cause third-party harms when suffered by an individual in a position of power.

Implicit bias, racial anxiety and stereotype threat have effects in virtually every important area of our lives. In the first report, we illustrate the interrelated implications of the three phenomena in the domains of education and healthcare. Education and healthcare are of critical importance for obvious reasons, and an abundance of research has highlighted the role race plays in unequal outcomes in both domains.

The report also emphasizes the interventions that are emerging in the research that institutions can begin to use to prevent continuing racialized obstacles. Ideally, this work will happen at the structural and institutional level—but many of us don't want to wait, and the social science research shows that we are not wholly without agency or tools. The interventions described below can, even in absence of wide-scale institutional change, help individual teachers or medical providers begin at least to ameliorate implicit bias, racial anxiety and stereotype threat.

"DEBIASING" AND PREVENTING EFFECTS OF IMPLICIT BIAS

While the research on debiasing is fairly new, recent studies by Patricia Devine and colleagues have found success in reducing implicit racial bias, increasing concern about discrimination and awareness of personal bias by combining multiple interventions to "break the prejudice habit." The strategies quoted below (thoughtfully utilizing findings from research by Nilanjana Dasgupta and others) included:

- *Stereotype replacement:* Recognizing that a response is based on stereotypes, labeling the response as stereotypical and reflecting on why the response occurred creates a process to consider how the biased response could be avoided in the future and replaces it with an unbiased response.

- *Counter-stereotypic imaging:* Imagining counter-stereotypic others in detail makes positive exemplars salient and accessible when challenging a stereotype's validity.
- *Individuation:* Obtaining specific information about group members prevents stereotypic inferences.
- *Perspective-taking:* Imagining oneself to be a member of a stereotyped group increases psychological closeness to the stereotyped group, which ameliorates automatic group-based evaluations.
- *Increasing opportunities for contact:* Increased contact between groups can ameliorate implicit bias through a wide variety of mechanisms, including altering their images of the group or by directly improving evaluations of the group.

The data showing reduced bias from Devine and colleagues "provide the first evidence that a controlled, randomized intervention can produce enduring reductions in implicit bias" (Devine et al. 2012). The findings have been replicated by Devine and colleagues, and further studies will be in print in 2015.

Whites can also suffer stereotype threat.

PREVENTING IMPLICIT BIAS FROM AFFECTING BEHAVIOR

To the extent that debiasing is an uphill challenge in light of the tenacity of negative stereotypes and attitudes about race, institutions can also establish practices to prevent these biases from seeping into decision-making. Jerry Kang and a group of researchers (Kang et al. 2012) developed the following list of interventions that have been found to be constructive:

Doubt Objectivity: Presuming oneself to be objective actually tends to increase the role of implicit bias; teaching people about non-conscious thought processes will lead people to be skeptical of their own objectivity and better able to guard against biased evaluations.

Increase Motivation to be Fair: Internal motivations to be fair rather than fear of external judgments tend to decrease biased actions.

Improve Conditions of Decisionmaking: Implicit biases are a function of automaticity (Daniel Kahneman's "thinking fast"—Kahneman, 2013). Thinking slow by engaging in mindful, deliberate processing and not in the throes of emotions prevents our implicit biases from kicking in and determining our behaviors.

Count: Implicitly biased behavior is best detected by using data to determine whether patterns of behavior are leading to racially disparate outcomes. Once one is aware that decisions or behavior are having disparate outcomes, it is then possible to consider whether the outcomes are linked to bias.

INTERVENTIONS TO REDUCE RACIAL ANXIETY

The mechanisms to reduce racial anxiety are related to the reduction of implicit bias—but are not identical. In our view, combining interventions that target both implicit bias and racial anxiety will be vastly more successful than either in isolation.

Direct Inter-group Contact: Direct interaction between members of different racial and ethnic groups can alleviate inter-group anxiety, reduce bias, and promote more positive inter-group attitudes and expectations for future contact.

Indirect Forms of Inter-group Contact: When people observe positive interactions between members of their own group and another group (vicarious contact) or become aware that members of their group have friends in another group (extended contact), they report lower bias and anxiety, and more positive inter-group attitudes.

STEREOTYPE THREAT INTERVENTIONS

Most of these interventions were developed in the context of the threat experienced by people of color and women linked to stereotypes of academic capacity and performance, but may also be translatable to whites (Erman & Walton, in press) who fear confirming the stereotype that they are racist.

Social Belonging Intervention: Providing students with survey results showing that upper-year students of all races felt out of place when they began but that the feeling abated over time has the effect of protecting students of color from assuming that they do not belong on campus due to their race and helped them develop resilience in the face of adversity.

Wise Criticism: Giving feedback that communicates both high expectations and a confidence that an individual can meet those expectations minimizes uncertainty about whether criticism is a result of racial bias or favor (attributional ambiguity). If the feedback is merely critical, it may be the product of bias; if feedback is merely positive, it may be the product of racial condescension.

Behavioral Scripts: Setting set forth clear norms of behavior and terms of discussion can reduce racial anxiety and prevent stereotype threat from being triggered.

Growth Mindset: Teaching people that abilities, including the ability to be racially sensitive, are learnable/incremental rather than fixed has been useful in the stereotype threat context because it can prevent any particular performance from serving as "stereotype confirming evidence."

Value-Affirmation: Encouraging students to recall their values and reasons for engaging in a task helps students maintain or increase their resilience in the face of threat.

Remove Triggers of Stereotype Threat on Standardized Tests: Removing questions about race or gender before a test, and moving them to after a test, has been shown to decrease threat and increase test scores for members of stereotyped groups.

INTERVENTIONS IN CONTEXT

The fundamental premise of this report is that institutions seeking to alter racially disparate outcomes must be aware of the array of psychological phenomena that may be contributing to those outcomes. We seek to contribute to that work by summarizing important research on implicit bias that employs strategies of debiasing and preventing bias from affecting behavior. We also seek to encourage institutions to look beyond *implicit bias* alone, and recognize that *racial anxiety* and *stereotype threat* are also often obstacles to racially equal outcomes. We recommend that institutions work with social scientists to evaluate and determine where in the institution's operations race may be coming into play.

The empirically documented effects of implicit bias and race as an emotional trigger allow us to talk about race without accusing people of "being racist," when they genuinely believe they are egalitarian. The social science described in this report helps people understand why inter-racial dynamics can be so complicated and challenging for people despite their best intentions. The interventions suggested by the research can be of value to institutions and individuals seeking to align their behavior with their ideals. Yet for lasting change to occur, the broader culture and ultimately our opportunity structures also need to change for our society to meet its aspirations of fairness and equal opportunity regardless of race and ethnicity.

WORKS CITED

Crosby, J. R. & Monin, B. (2007). Failure to warn: How student race affects warnings of potential academic difficulty. *Journal of Experimental Social Psychology, 43,* 663–670.

Dasgupta, Nilanjana, 2013 "Implicit Attitudes and Beliefs Adapt to Situations: A Decade of Research on the Malleability of Implicit Prejudice, Stereotypes, and the Self-Concept," in P.G. Devine & E.A. Plant (eds.), *Advances in Experimental Social Psychology* (Vol. 47, pp. 233–79).

Devine, P. G., Forscher, P. S., Austin, A. J., & Cox, W. T. L. (2012). Long-term reduction in implicit race bias: A prejudice habit-breaking intervention. *Journal of Experimental Social Psychology, 48,* 1267–1278.

Devine, Patricia, et al. *Breaking the Prejudice Habit* (Guilford Publications, 2014).

Erman, S. & Walton, G. M. (in press). Stereotype threat and anti-discrimination law: Affirmative steps to promote meritocracy and racial equality. *Southern California Law Review.*

Harber, K. D., Gorman, J. L., Gengaro, F. P., Butisingh, S., William, T., & Ouellette, R. (2012). Students' race and teachers' social support affect the positive feedback bias in public schools. *Journal of Educational Psychology, 104(4),* 1149–1161.

Kahneman, Daniel, *Thinking Fast and Slow* (Farrar, Straus and Giroux, 2013).

Kang, J., Bennett, M., Carbado, D., Casey, P., Dasgupta, N., Faigman, D., Godsil, R. D., Greenwald, A. G., Levinson, J. D. & Mnookin, J. (2012). Implicit bias in the courtroom. *UCLA Law Review, 59(5),* 1124–1186.

Steele, C. M. (2010). *Whistling Vivaldi: And other clues to how stereotypes affect us.* New York, NY: Norton.

DISCUSSION QUESTIONS

1. Rachel Godsil writes: "People of color experience obstacles rooted in racial or ethnic difference with alarming frequency. And yet most Americans espouse values of racial fairness. How can we make sense of these seeming contradictions?" How would you answer her question?

2. How does Godsil define "implicit bias," "racial anxiety," and "stereotype threat?" How do these concepts explain specific acts of racial injustice in America?

3. What strategies does Godsil suggest for preventing implicit bias, racial anxiety, and stereotype threat from poisoning our attitudes and behavior toward others—and particularly toward those people who look, love, worship, and live differently from us?

Gender, Masculinity, Homophobia, and Sexism

READING 2.1

GENDER

Inequality in America Race, Poverty, and
Fulfilling Democracy's Promise

BY **Stephen Caliendo**

SEX AND GENDER

Many researchers hold that the term "sex" refers to anatomical and physiological differences, whereas "gender" refers to the social construct that differentiates men from women. For instance, the fact that only women can become pregnant is a function of sex; the fact that women are disproportionately expected to be child care providers is a function of gender. Beyond breastfeeding, there is nothing inherent about a man's biology that makes him less capable of caring for infants or children than a woman, but there are significant social constraints about parental responsibilities that center on gender.[1]

SEXISM AND MISOGYNY

As with racism, the important element that is often neglected in discussions of sexism is power. False equivalency claims are common: real or perceived disadvantages of men are presented as evidence that sexism "goes both ways." As with racism, the word "sexism" is most accurately reserved for the idea that men are superior to women. This systemic hierarchy is known as *patriarchy*, and it involves largely unspoken and powerful assumptions and expectations that privilege men in our society.

This dynamic is reflected in the language that we have available for communication. For instance, we have no gender-neutral singular pronoun—we only have "he or she," and "him or her." We are forced to consider gender, even when it should not matter. This is important with respect to occupations too (e.g., fireman, policeman, mailman, and, pertinent to the topic at hand, congressman). Even though political scientists and most journalists use the more acceptable term "member of Congress" or the clumsier "congressperson," most Americans continue to refer to members of

Congress as congressmen. This matters for more than symbolic reasons (though they are also important). First, it does not accurately reflect the idea that it is designed to capture (i.e., there are women who are members of Congress) and, second, it perpetuates gender inequality by setting up an abstract ideal against with which women must compete (in addition to competing with their opponents in the race) when they run for election. Men are advantaged by having the vague term presented as a gendered construct because they can more easily present themselves as closer to the ideal.

This is an example of *sexism*. It is systemic and often subconscious. *Misogyny*, on the other hand, while it can also be subconscious, most accurately refers to individual-level resentment or even outright hatred for women. There is no question that misogyny is rooted in sexism, but it is important, as with racism, to separate the systemic from the individual so that we can adequately address both without conflating the concepts.[2] At the individual level, women can harbor resentment toward men. We might refer to that as *prejudice* or *bigotry*, but calling it sexist undermines the historic reality of male privilege in the same way that using the term "racist" to refer to animosity toward whites by persons of color does.[3]

SOCIALIZATION

The process by which we acquire beliefs, attitudes, and behaviors from previous generations is referred to as *socialization*. It is certainly clear by now that we absorb racist ideas throughout our lives; sexist beliefs are acquired in much the same way. There is ample anecdotal evidence to support the notion that we are socialized into accepting gender roles even earlier and more deliberately than we are with respect to racial categorizations. For gender, the work begins in utero. With ultrasound

Stephen Caliendo, "Gender," Inequality in America: Race, Poverty, and Fulfilling Democracy's Promise, pp. 142-153, 155-156, 158-159, 161, 243-251. Copyright © 2014 by Taylor & Francis Group. Reprinted with permission.

technology, it is common for parents to learn the sex of their unborn as early as the twentieth week of pregnancy, at least partially driven by a desire to buy clothes and decorate a nursery in colors that are considered appropriate. As soon as a baby is delivered, the first question most folks ask is, What is it? Advertisements, catalogs, and websites for toy companies are clearly delineated in blue and pink tones, and stories (both in print and on film) that are directed to toddlers contain powerful messages relating to gender norms and expectations.

Fairy tales and Disney princess movies are prime carriers of sexist messages about the proper roles for men and women in society. Cinderella sings as she cleans and dreams of attending a grand ball to be chosen by the prince, and Ariel from *The Little Mermaid* literally gives up her voice so that she can be with a man, for that is how women are taught that they will find happiness.[4] Messages about standards of beauty are also prevalent in these stories, as are stereotypes about appropriate appearance, attitudes, and behavior for men and boys.[5]

FEMINISM

Sometimes referred to as the "f-word" by feminists,[6] the word *feminism* has been attacked for decades and saddled with much pejorative baggage. Most Americans assume that feminists are women, though many men criticize patriarchy and advocate for increasing equality between men and women.[7] Many Americans believe that feminists hate men and wish to see a world where women are superior. Feminists, however, come from many perspectives,[8] and the zero-sum mentality mirrors concerns that whites harbor with respect to increasing racial equality.

It is mostly agreed that feminism can be conceptualized historically into three waves.[9] The first wave dealt primarily with women's suffrage (late nineteenth and early twentieth centuries); the second wave (1960s through 1980s) centered on consciousness raising, equal rights more broadly, and (at least toward the end), expanding consideration of nonwhite women's voices; the third wave began in the 1990s and is concerned with a sophisticated critique of the conceptualization and construction of gender.[10]

One particularly compelling perspective emerged from the second wave and persisted into the third: the notion of the male gaze. In the 1970s, Laura Mulvey[11] put forward a critique of film that invoked the notion that there is a tendency for the world to be seen (and filmed) from the perspective of men. This notion has come to serve as a theoretical lens through which all aspects of culture can be viewed. Central to this perspective is the notion of women as objects (rather than subjects). Some third wave theorizing and activism has involved women reclaiming their sexuality in ways that make some second wave feminists uncomfortable.[12] Beyond content, however, third wave feminists are using modern technology and cultural trends to engage with one another and with the world in ways that would have been impossible for their predecessors. Blogs and social networking have afforded these writers the opportunity to express themselves without filters or editors, but they face pressures that are inherent in this type of communication, as well (see Box 1).

Third wavers have been more intentional about recognizing their own social, sexual orientation and racial

---

BOX 1.
Representing: JESSICA VALENTI

Jessica Valenti is cofounder and former managing editor of Feministing.com, "an online community for feminists and their allies." She was named one of the top 100 inspiring women in the world by *The Guardian* in 2011,[1] and she is the author of three books: *Full Frontal Feminism: A Young Woman's Guide to Why Feminism Matters; He's a Stud, She's a Slut, and 49 Other Double Standards Every Woman Should Know;* and *The Purity Myth: How America's Obsession with Virginity Is Hurting Young Women.*[2] She currently writes for *The Nation.*

Valenti started Feministing because she felt that young women's voices were not being heard. While feminists are often considered to be politically liberal, Valenti notes that reaching conservatives is an important goal. She wants to make feminism accessible and says that "more people are feminists than they realize … they hear the word, and they don't want to identify as feminists, but they believe in feminist values [such as] equal pay for equal work, [eliminating violence against women, and] reproductive justice." Feministing is characterized by humor and insight that are consciously designed to be accessible.[3]

---

1   Homa Khaleeli, "Jessica Valenti: Pioneering Blogger Whose Online Activism Dragged Feminism into the 21st Century," *Guardian*, March 7, 2011, http://www.guardian.co.uk/books/2011/mar/08/jessica-valenti-100-women.

2   JessicaValenti.com.

3   "A Big Think Interview with Jessica Valenti," Big Think, December 21, 2009, http://bigthink.com/ideas/17880.

BOX 1.
Representing: JESSICA VALENTI
(*Continued*)

Feministing, like other online efforts, has struggled with economic viability. Foministing has advertising, but some users prefer not to see ads. Valenti notes, however, that revenue is important to sustain the site, that profits are distributed equitably among staffers, and that contributors are compensated.[4]

Valenti recognizes that white, middle-class women are still disproportionately at the helm of feminist institutions, but she is consistently reflective about her own organization and about advocating for more voices to be heard.[5]

---

4   "Interview with Jessica Valenti: Feminist Writer and Founder of Feministing.com," The Daily Femme! June 16, 2010.

5   Ibid.

BOX 2. *What Can I Do?*:
BLOGGING

Reading feminist blogs is a useful (and enjoyable) way to stay apprised of the way contemporary culture can be viewed through feminist lenses. Below is a list of some prominent feminist blogs, but it is important to stay alert because new outlets are being created all the time. Since blogging avoids gatekeepers, writing one's own analysis of current events, popular culture, or other interesting aspects of life can be a meaningful form of expression with a potential to reach a very wide audience. Make sure that your blog is integrated with your other social networking sites like Twitter and Facebook, and do not be shy about tagging more established bloggers and columnists to try to get them to read what you are writing. A well-placed re-tweet or share from someone with many followers can garner attention and give you a chance to interact in a meaningful and fulfilling way with others.

The Angry Black Woman: http://theangryblackwoman.com/

Blogs by Latinas (portal): http://blogsbylatinas.com/

Feministe: http://www.feministe.us/blog/

Feministing: http://feministing.com/

Jezebel: http://jezebel.com/

TransGriot: http://transgriot.blogspot.com/

Yes Means Yes!: http://yesmeansyesblog.wordpress.com/

privilege (when and where it exists) and being inclusive of voices that previous generations of feminists have been accused of neglecting.[13] One might speculate that the more democratic nature of our communication has converged with theoretical and empirical work by scholars to create an ideology that is better positioned to consider the ways that various hegemonic forces intersect to provide advantages and disadvantages, privileges and challenges.

INTERSECTIONALITY

As noted in the Introduction, we cannot simply assume that privilege (or disadvantage) is additive, as if being white has privilege and being male has privilege, then being white and male carries twice as much privilege. Sometimes that is the case,[14] but interactions among demographic elements are complex and sometimes counterintuitive. As we consider the degree to which gender intersects with economic inequality in the United States, we must also consider how race forms an interaction that will complicate our work.

GENDER INEQUALITY AND POVERTY

Much has been written about how patriarchy operates in the United States and globally, but here we will focus on ways that these systemic and attitudinal factors relate to economic inequality. Like each topic we have explored, this one is complicated, though it is rarely presented that way in public discourse.

Income and Wealth

The most visible element of gender inequality in the United States is the wage gap. It is well documented that women earn between seventy-two and seventy-nine cents for every dollar men earn.[15] This gap has been relatively consistent for decades—at least since women began to enter the paid workforce in high numbers.[16] One reason for such inequity could be interpersonal—women are not valued as much as men, so they are paid less. However disturbing this may be, it is also too simple and far too convenient. If the problem of pay equity were limited to men in power not valuing women they hire, then the solution would be to punish those who are making inequitable decisions or wait until they retire and then replace them with younger Americans who tend to have more explicitly egalitarian views. Unfortunately, the reality is not so straightforward.

The share of women in the labor market has increased steadily since the 1980s,[17] but women have not yet achieved pay equity in most occupations. Women are disadvantaged for a number of reasons relating to deeply held beliefs about their proper place (in the home versus in the workplace), their abilities and intelligence, and their biology. With respect to the latter, it is important to understand the notion of the mommy track,[18] which is a result of women taking time away from workplace participation as a result of childbirth and sometimes child rearing. While biology necessitates rest and healing after childbirth, cultural pressures dictate that women function as the primary caretaker of children,[19] which results in longer periods of time away from careers. When a woman returns to the office or worksite, a man who was hired at the same time and performed comparably will have advanced, while she returns to the position that she had before her leave. A heterosexual couple with both adults working outside the home may choose to have multiple children, and with each child the woman's career may be suspended, leading to disparities in pay and rank.[20]

Further, there are deeply held beliefs in our culture about what types of jobs are appropriate for men and for women. Figure 1 reveals the ratio of women's pay to men's pay in a number of occupations. While women make more than men in a few positions, the vast majority of jobs feature a substantial pay gap. But this only tells part of the story. Women are hired disproportionately into occupations that have lower pay (see Figure 2). These so-called pink collar occupations (most often service-oriented positions such as cashiers, food servers, and caretakers for the sick, elderly, and children)[21] are disproportionately populated by women and pay much less than those that are populated primarily by men. In this way, women face systemic challenges to equality that are much more complicated than our colloquial understanding of sexism as individual-level preferences for men over women with respect to workforce participation.

All of this contributes to what has been termed the feminization of poverty.[22] Using the federal poverty level guidelines:

> more than 17 million women lived in poverty in 2010, and nearly 44 percent of these women (7.5 million) lived in extreme poverty, with incomes less than half of the federal poverty level.... black and Hispanic women experienced even greater increases in poverty between 2009 and 2010 than women overall, as did single mothers. Poverty rates for all groups of women in 2010 were substantially higher than poverty rates for their male counterparts.[23]

Approximately 1 million women in the United States earn minimum wage (and constitute about one-third of all minimum wage workers). This is less a result of direct gender discrimination as it is workforce gender segregation. In 2012, "the three largest occupational groups, making up 67 percent of minimum-wage jobs, are 65 percent female."[24] Food service is the largest sector for minimum wage workers; nearly 60 percent of food service workers are women.[25]

As noted in Chapter 2, however, poverty has at least as much to do with wealth as it does with income. While it is often difficult to measure wealth from the perspective of gender because wealth is measured as a function of household rather than individuals, we can gain an appreciation for the relationship between gender and poverty if we consider the case of single women. Households led by women that do not have other adult earners in the home constitute the highest levels of poverty. In 2010, the poverty rate for households headed by women that included children was 40.7 percent as compared to households headed by men with children (24.2 percent) or households with children headed by a married couple (8.8 percent).[26] It will be no surprise to readers at this point that race factors into these numbers in predictable ways: the poverty rate for households with children headed by black women (47.5 percent) and Latinas (50.3 percent) was higher than that for white women (32.7 percent).[27] Further, Native American women and Latinas are more than twice as likely to head households with family members as white women; black women are three times as likely (see Figure 3).

Women who are divorced are likely to have custody of children, and if they were not working outside the home while they were married, they find themselves at a competitive disadvantage for gainful employment (not to mention struggles with finding affordable child care if the children are not in school) after separation.[28] Senior women face similar challenges. Though women account for more than half of all Social Security beneficiaries, their benefits are smaller because their earnings, on average, were lower. In 2010, the average retired woman earned $1,023 per month in Social Security benefits compared to $1,323 for men.[29] Widows are more likely to be impoverished than widowers. Because women tend to live longer than men, widows have a longer period of time to live without their partners than widowers do. Two-fifths of women experience poverty within five years of the death of their husband.[30]

...

Figure 1 Ratio of Women's to Men's Earnings, Selected Occupations, 2010

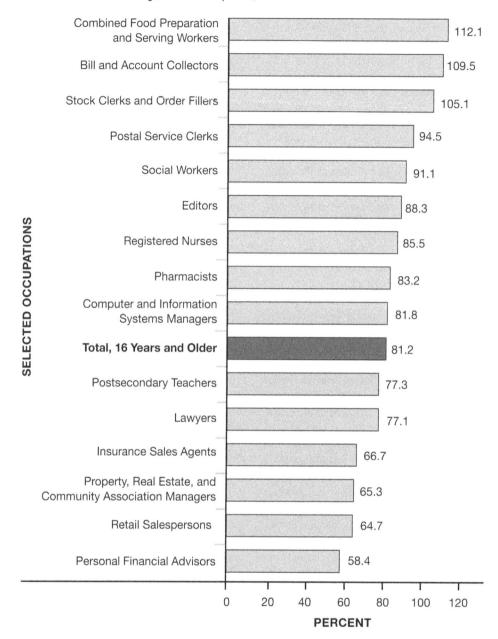

Source: US Bureau of Labor Statistics, "Women at Work," 2011, http://www.bls.gov/spotlight/2011/women.

Figure 2 Usual Median Weekly Earnings and Employment of Full-Time Wage and Salary Women Workers, Selected Occupations, 2009

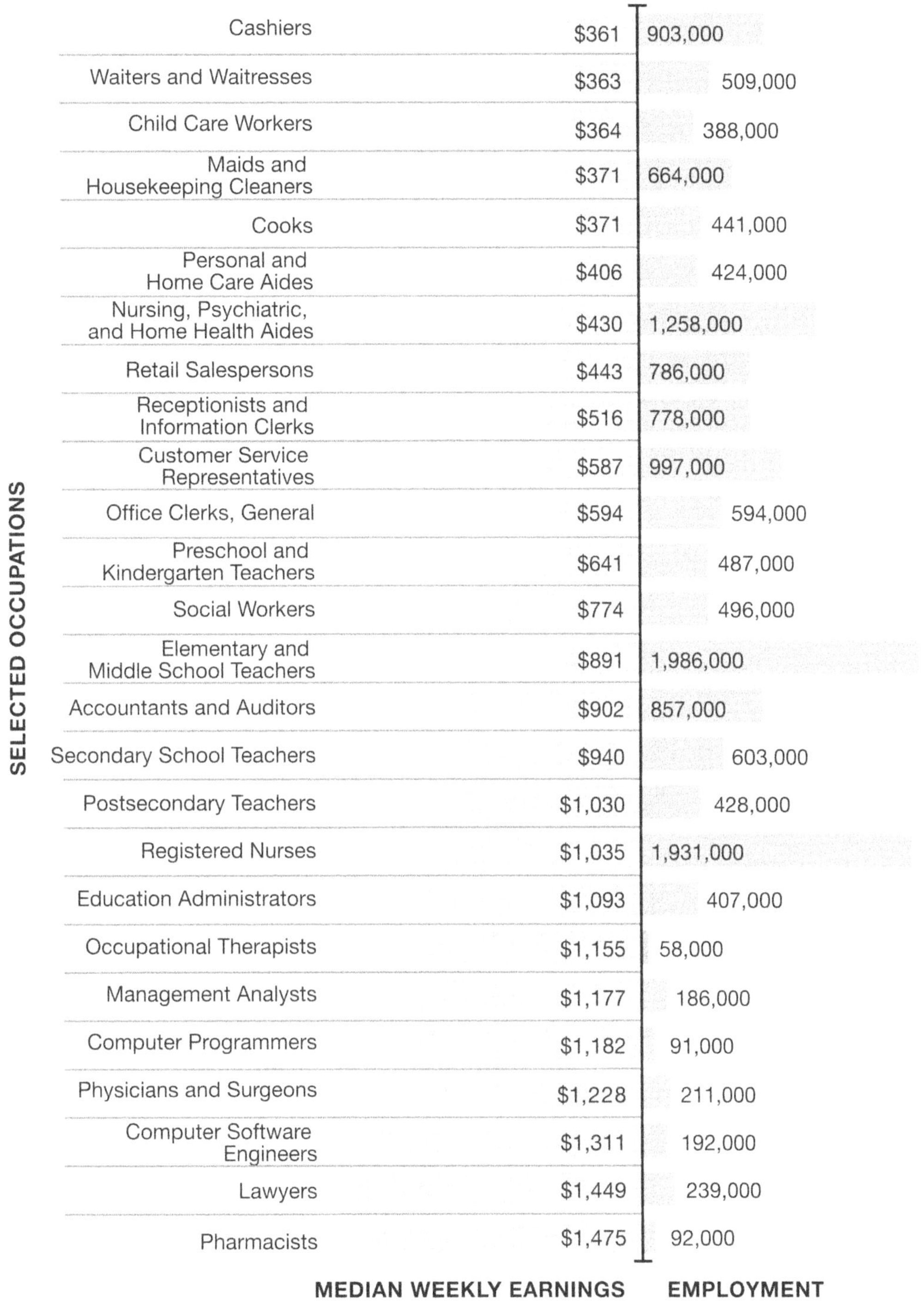

SELECTED OCCUPATIONS	MEDIAN WEEKLY EARNINGS	EMPLOYMENT
Cashiers	$361	903,000
Waiters and Waitresses	$363	509,000
Child Care Workers	$364	388,000
Maids and Housekeeping Cleaners	$371	664,000
Cooks	$371	441,000
Personal and Home Care Aides	$406	424,000
Nursing, Psychiatric, and Home Health Aides	$430	1,258,000
Retail Salespersons	$443	786,000
Receptionists and Information Clerks	$516	778,000
Customer Service Representatives	$587	997,000
Office Clerks, General	$594	594,000
Preschool and Kindergarten Teachers	$641	487,000
Social Workers	$774	496,000
Elementary and Middle School Teachers	$891	1,986,000
Accountants and Auditors	$902	857,000
Secondary School Teachers	$940	603,000
Postsecondary Teachers	$1,030	428,000
Registered Nurses	$1,035	1,931,000
Education Administrators	$1,093	407,000
Occupational Therapists	$1,155	58,000
Management Analysts	$1,177	186,000
Computer Programmers	$1,182	91,000
Physicians and Surgeons	$1,228	211,000
Computer Software Engineers	$1,311	192,000
Lawyers	$1,449	239,000
Pharmacists	$1,475	92,000

Source: US Bureau of Labor Statistics, "Women at Work," 2011, http://www.bls.gov/spotlight/2011/women/.

Figure 3 Female Heads of Households by Race

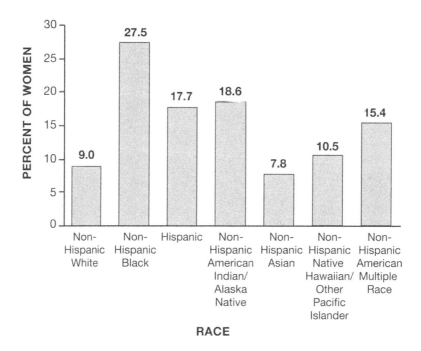

Note: Includes the civilian, non-institutionalized population; includes those who are heads of hourseholds and have children or other family members, but not spouse, living in a house that they own or rent.

Source: Maternal and Child Health Bureau, Women's Health USA, 2011 (Rockville, MD: US Department of Health and Human Services, 2011), http://www.mchb.hrsa.gov/whusa11/popchar/pages/104hc.html.

GENDER AND HOUSING ACCESS

As is the case with wealth, it is difficult to discuss housing inequality with respect to gender because men and women cohabitate at far greater rates than do members of different racial and ethnic groups. As was the case with wealth, statistical analysis is largely limited to women who are heads of household, whether or not they are raising children.

In a broader sense, the notion of home has been intricately linked with women throughout the nation's history. In the nineteenth century a haven model of domestic life emerged that "emphasized the importance of sequestering women in private homes, and focused on making the home a relaxing respite from the competition of capitalist society for the husband/father and a nurturing environment for the children, maintained by the wife/mother."[31] This separate spheres approach maintained public space as the dominion of men and reserved the private sphere for women. Government policies designed to encourage

home ownership in the early part of the twentieth century often included explicit policies that disadvantaged women.[32] As divorce rates climbed or children were born out of wedlock, women were in a position to find safe, affordable housing for their families. Many of the resulting issues in this area converge with our broader discussion of housing in Chapter 3 (public housing, Section 8, etc.), but we should keep in mind that women and men often experienced these challenges differently.

GENDER INEQUALITY AND EDUCATION

The existence of gender inequality in education is well documented. Data collected over the past few decades do not present a clear picture of inequity (e.g., some of the differences in achievement shift when considered at different ages, and socioeconomic status is a relevant consideration), but girls tend to have lower achievement in science and mathematics and higher scores in reading, particularly at younger ages.[33] Research demonstrates that the gender gap with respect to quantitative reasoning tends to widen during K–12 schooling and that biology interacts with environmental factors to produce such divergence.[34]

In the United States girls tend to finish high school at higher rates than boys, a trend that persists across racial and ethnic groups.[35] In the past two decades, men have been less likely than women to enroll in college directly after high school, which correlates positively with college enrollment (delaying enrollment tends to result in lower eventual attendance rates).[36] Boys have consistently outperformed girls on the Scholastic Aptitude Test (SAT),[37] particularly on the mathematics section, with the 2012 results revealing a thirty-three-point gap (532 to 499).[38] The science and mathematics gap persists into college[39] and is reflected in the workforce: the pay gap for women in their first year out of college is only slightly less (82 percent of men's salaries) than the overall gender wage gap.[40]

However, women are attending college and graduating at higher rates than their male counterparts, and the pattern holds across racial groups:

> Women earn 66% of all bachelor's degrees awarded to blacks; the figures are 61% for Hispanics, 60% for Native Americans, 55% for Asians, and 57% for whites.... Note that the especially large gender gap for blacks does not constitute a reversal but, rather, a continuation of a long female-favorable trend.[41]

Women drop out of college at lower rates, finish their degrees more quickly, and are now more likely than men to attend graduate school. They earn 59 percent of master's degrees, 49 percent of doctoral degrees, 49 percent of law degrees, 47 percent of medical degrees, and 44 percent of dentistry degrees.[42] Even so, the wage gap persists. These statistics reveal the complexity of how advantage and disadvantage work in the United States.

...

GENDER, REPRODUCTIVE RIGHTS, AND HEALTH

While space does not permit a thorough discussion of gender disparities related to health,[43] we will look at the most politicized of women's health issues: reproductive rights. Strong moral and ethical issues are intertwined with the question of whether terminating a fetus is appropriate (including the philosophical question of whether life begins at conception, at some stage during gestation, or at birth), but few women have been part of the decision-making process. Most elected officials at all levels of government, as I will explain in greater detail below, are and have been men, as are most judges, including US Supreme Court justices, who have the last word on many aspects of this debate. In 1973 an all-male Court declared that terminating a pregnancy in the first two trimesters was a constitutionally protected right,[44] lending support for the substantive representation model of governance.

In recent years, a number of states have attempted to pass so-called personhood amendments to state constitutions, as well as the US Constitution. Such provisions would designate a fertilized human egg as a legal person, thus protecting it from termination.[45] Pro-choice advocates view such positioning as pitting the rights of a fetus against the rights of a woman.[46] In 2012 five Republican presidential hopefuls signed pledges to support the notion of fetal personhood,[47] and a flurry of other legislative and judicial activity has swirled about in the past few years.[48]

These issues are connected to broader elements of women's reproductive health and sexual violence. Georgetown University law student Sandra Fluke achieved a tremendous amount of attention[49] in 2012 when she was called a "slut" and a "prostitute" by a conservative talk radio host for demanding that her birth control pills be covered by the Catholic institution's health care policy. The attacks on Fluke went beyond reasonable disagreement about religious freedom or reproductive rights; she became a symbol of the collective view of women held by many Americans. Later that year, a number of Republican candidates found themselves heavily criticized for their comments about rape (as it relates to exceptions for abortion), with Missouri's Todd Akin opining that pregnancy as a result of rape is rare because if a woman is the victim of a "legitimate rape, the female body has ways to try to shut that whole thing down"[50] and Indiana's Richard Mourdock noting that if a woman does become pregnant as a result of a rape, the pregnancy (though presumably not the assault) is a "gift from God."[51] Both candidates lost their races.

The symbolic importance of men making statements that are factually inaccurate (Akin) and woefully insensitive (both candidates) cannot be ignored. If we revisit our consideration of symbolic and substantive representation from Chapter 1, we will be in a stronger position to examine the degree to which having more women in office might affect decisions relating not only to reproductive rights and women's health but also to core policy issues discussed throughout this chapter and book including housing, education, and crime.

Beyond reproductive rights, there are related issues that highlight health disparities with respect to child bearing. For example, a recent study found that depression caused by discrimination leads to low birth weight in babies. Babies born to white women and Latinas are at half the risk of low birth weight as babies born to black women. The study showed, however, that even holding race constant (as well as age and type of discrimination), women who reported discrimination had higher levels of depression and babies who weighed less than those who did not report facing discrimination.[52]

Intersectional explanations for mortality and morbidity (being unhealthy) disparities over the past three decades are available as well, and this trend is not completely driven by level of education or socioeconomics; African American women with college degrees report worse health conditions than African American men with a high school education.[53] As highlighted in the previous chapter, women of color face a variety of health disparities compared to white women. These challenges can result from disproportionate poverty and contribute to economic challenges.

...

SUMMARY

All of this calls into question Americans' commitment to women's rights broadly. If we limit our discussion to narrow issues such as closing the pay gap, reducing health disparities, or being attentive to the achievement gap in education, we miss an opportunity to critique patriarchy as a powerful systemic force that undergirds these public policy issues. The Nineteenth Amendment became law in 1920, solidifying the status of women as full participants in the formal democratic process. But the bulk of the work of dismantling the systemic roots of gender inequality has taken place in the past century, with much more work to be done.

Three years after adoption of the Nineteenth Amendment, women's rights activist Alice Paul wrote another amendment espousing equality between men and women. The Equal Rights Amendment (ERA) states that "equality of rights under the law shall not be denied or abridged by the United States or by any state on account of sex," and it gives Congress the ability to enforce the amendment through legislation.[54] A bill was introduced in every Congress until 1972, when it was finally passed and sent to the states for ratification. To date, thirty-five states have ratified it, which is three short of the number needed for it to become an amendment.[55]

As complicated as our treatment of these issues has been to this point, the thorniest part is still ahead. Acknowledging the history and persistence of inequality is challenging enough, but finding consensus about how to rectify the situation to reduce (and eventually eliminate) disparities in these areas is far more controversial. The most comprehensive attempt to do so is referred to collectively as affirmative action, which is where we turn our attention next.

ENDNOTES

1. While this conceptualization is still prevalent, there is notable criticism of its limitations. Some writers have argued that the binary distinction relating to sex is also socially constructed, and consequently the convenient sex-gender binary is not an adequate tool for understanding that construction. Diane Richardson, "Conceptualizing Gender," in *Introducing Gender and Women's Studies*, ed. Diane Richardson and Victoria Robinson, 3rd ed. (New York: Palgrave Macmillan, 2007), 3–19.

2. Similarly, the term "heterosexism" refers to the hegemonic norm that leads individuals to assume that people are heterosexual unless they know otherwise. For instance, sex-segregated rest rooms are grounded in the premise that everyone is heterosexual; otherwise, there is little point in ensuring that men and women do not see one another in states of undress. There is nothing particularly malicious or individualistic about this tendency, or the fact that most laws centering on couples are rooted in similar assumptions. The more common term "homophobia" refers to resentment, animosity, or hatred of folks who are not heterosexual. Such individual-level attitudes are rooted in heterosexism to the extent that the belief that heterosexuals are normal and those who are not are deviant, but the constructs should be considered separately.

3. For an interesting discussion about the difference between sexism and misogyny in the context of an

Australian dictionary's decision to shift the definition of the latter to include "entrenched prejudice against women" (rather than only hatred of them), see Naomi Wolf et al., "Sexism and Misogyny: What's the Difference?" *Guardian*, October 17, 2012, http://www.guardian.co.uk/commentisfree/2012/oct/17/difference-between-sexism-and-misogyny. *New York Times* columnist Nicholas Kristof has struggled with the difference between these concepts and how each contributes to violence against women in a global context. Nicholas D. Kristof, "Misogyny vs. Sexism," *New York Times*, April 7, 2008, http://kristof.blogs.nytimes.com/2008/04/07/misogyny-vs-sexism/.

4. The effects of such messages can be observed in (and are then reinforced by) much of reality television programming. For a thorough treatment, see Jennifer L. Pozner, *Reality Bites Back: The Troubling Truth About Guilty Pleasure TV* (Berkeley, CA: Seal Press, 2010).

5. The literature—both scholarly and popular—is extensive in this area. See, for example, Lori Baker-Sperry and Liz Grauerholz, "The Pervasiveness of the Feminine Beauty Ideal in Children's Fairy Tales," *Gender & Society* 17, no. 5 (2003): 711–726; Elizabeth Bell, Lynda Haas, and Laura Sells, eds., *From Mouse to Mermaid: The Politics of Film, Gender and Culture* (Bloomington: Indiana University Press, 2008); Donald Haase, ed., *Fairy Tales and Feminism: New Approaches* (Detroit: Wayne State University Press, 2004); U. C. Knoepflmacher, *Ventures into Childland: Victorians, Fairy Tales, and Femininity* (Chicago: University of Chicago Press, 1998); Karen E. Rowe, "Feminism and Fairy Tales," *Women's Studies: An Interdisciplinary Journal* 6, no. 3 (1979): 237–257; Ella Westland, "Cinderella in the Classroom: Children's Responses to Gender Roles in Fairy-tales," *Gender and Education* 5, no. 3 (1993): 237–249.

6. Amy Siskind, "How Feminism Became the F-Word," The Daily Beast, January 11, 2009, http://www.thedailybeast.com/articles/2009/01/11/how-feminism-became-the-f-word.html.

7. For a study about how men and women come to embrace feminism, see Rebecca L. Warner, "Does the Sex of Your Child Matter? Support for Feminism Among Women and Men in the United States and Canada," *Journal of Marriage and Family* 5, no. 4 (1991): 1051–1056.

8. For a thoughtful, concise overview of different aspects of feminism, see Jarrah Hodge, "Femisisms 101," Gender Focus, November 13, 2010, http://www.gender-focus.com/tag/types-of-feminism/.

9. Martha Rampton, "The Three Waves of Feminism," *Pacific* 41, no. 2 (2008), http://www.pacificu.edu/magazine_archives/2008/fall/echoes/feminism.cfm.

10. Ibid.

11. Laura Mulvey, "Visual Pleasure and Narrative Cinema," *Screen* 16, no. 3 (1975): 6–18, http://imlportfolio.usc.edu/ctcs505/mulveyVisualPleasureNarrativeCinema.pdf.

12. For a thoughtful, accessible elaboration on this dynamic, see Susan J. Douglas, "Girls 'n' Spice: All Things Nice?" in *Mass Politics: The Politics of Popular Culture*, ed. Daniel M. Shea (New York: St. Martin's/Worth, 1999), 45–48.

13. For examples of work that highlights the gaps in second wave feminist thought, see, for instance, Patricia Hill Collins, "The Social Construction of Black Feminist Thought," *Signs* 14, no. 4 (1989): 745–773; Patricia Hill Collins, *Black Feminist Thought: Knowledge, Consciousness, and the Politics of Empowerment* (New York: Routledge, 1999); Alma M. Garcia, ed., *Chicana Feminist Thought: The Basic Historical Writings* (New York: Routledge, 1997).

14. For example, black women are disproportionately underrepresented in corporate America. A recent study found that black women in that context face more criticism than white women or black men: what the authors refer to as "double jeopardy." Ashleigh Shelby Rosette and Robert W. Livingston, "Failure Is Not an Option for Black Women: Effects of Organizational Performance on Leaders with Single Versus Dual-Subordinate Identities," *Journal of Experimental Social Psychology* 48, no. 5 (2012): 1162–1167.

15. Frank Bass and Jennifer Oldham, "Wage Gap for U.S. Women Endures Even as Jobs Increase," Bloomberg Businessweek, October 25, 2012, http://www.businessweek.com/news/2012-10-25/wage-gap-for-u-dot-s-dot-women-endures-even-as-jobs-increase; Maloney and Schumer, "Women and the Economy 2010."

16. Susan Thistle, *From Marriage to the Market: The Transformation of Women's Lives and Work* (Berkeley: University of California Press, 2006).

17. Sylvia Allegretto and Devon Lynch, "The Composition of the Unemployed and Long-Term Unemployed in Tough Labor Markets," *Monthly Labor Review*, October 2010, http://www.bls.gov/opub/mlr/2010/10/art1full.pdf.

18. Elizabeth Ty Wilde, Lily Batchelder, and David T. Ellwood, "The Mommy Track Divides: The Impact of Childbearing on Wages of Women of Differing Skill Levels," National Bureau of Economic Research Working Paper no. 16582, December 2010, http://www.nber.org/papers/w16582; Rebecca Korzec, "Working on the 'Mommy-Track': Motherhood and Women Lawyers," *Hastings Women's Law Journal* 8 (1997): 117–126; Mary C. Noonan and Mary E. Corcoran, "The Mommy Track and Partnership: Temporary Delay or Dead End?" *Annals of the American Academy of Political and Social Science* 596, no. 1 (2004): 130–150; E. Jeffrey Hill et al., "Beyond the Mommy Track: The Influence of New-Concept Part-Time Work for Professional Women on Work and Family," *Journal of Family and Economic Issues* 25, no. 1 (2004): 121–136; Paula England, "Gender Inequality in Labor Markets: The Role of Motherhood and Segregation," *Social Politics* 12, no. 2 (2005): 264–288.

19. Paternity leave is common in many European democracies, but not in the United States. Lisa Belkin,

"Should Fathers Get Paid Paternity Leave?" *New York Times*, January 28, 2010, http://parenting.blogs.nytimes.com/2010/01/28/paid-paternity-leave-in-britain/; Jens Hansegard, "For Paternity Leave, Sweden Asks If Two Months Is Enough," *Wall Street Journal*, July 31, 2012, http://online.wsj.com/article/SB10000872396390444226904577561100020336384.html. While the Family and Medical Leave Act of 1993 allows fathers to take up to twelve weeks away from work without being fired, that time is unpaid, and few families can afford to take advantage of it. "Leave Benefits: Family & Medical Leave Act," US Department of Labor, http://www.dol.gov/dol/topic/benefits-leave/fmla.htm#.ULjwauOe8f8.

20. In 2013, Facebook chief operating officer Sheryl Sandberg wrote a best-selling book designed to encourage women and men to think differently about the oft repeated rallying cry of the second wave feminist movement that women can "have it all" (at the office and at home). In *Lean In*, Sandberg describes the current state of women in corporate America and encourages both women and men to work together in both settings for greater gender equity.

21. See Kim V. L. England, "Suburban Pink Collar Ghettos: The Spatial Entrapment of Women?" *Annals of the Association of American Geographers* 83, no. 2 (2005): 225–242; Joseph H. Michalski, "Resource Structuralism and Gender Economic Inequality," *Michigan Sociological Review* 18 (2004): 23–63; England, "Gender Inequality in Labor Markets"; Tony Tam, "Sex Segregation and Occupational Gender Inequality in the United States: Devaluation or Specialized Training?" *American Journal of Sociology* 102, no. 6 (1997): 1652–1692.

22. Johanna Brenner, "Feminist Political Discourses: Radical Versus Liberal Approaches to the Feminization of Poverty and Comparable Worth," *Gender & Society* 1, no. 4 (1987): 447–465; Martha E. Gimenez, "The Feminization of Poverty: Myth or Reality?" *Critical Sociology* 25, no. 2–3 (1999): 336–351.

23. "Poverty Rates Among Women and Families, 2000–2010: Extreme Poverty Reaches Record Levels as Congress Faces Critical Choices," National Women's Law Center, September 2011, http://www.nwlc.org/sites/default/files/povertyamongwomenandfamilies2010final.pdf.

24. Bryce Stucki, "Life at the Bottom," *American Prospect*, March 8, 2013, http://prospect.org/article/life-bottom.

25. Ibid.

26. "Poverty Rates Among Women and Families, 2000–2010."

27. Ibid. See also Anastasia R. Snyder, Diane K. McLaughlin, and Jill Findeis, "Household Composition and Poverty Among Female-Headed Households with Children: Differences by Race and Residence," *Rural Sociology* 71, no. 4 (2006): 597–624.

28. Richard R. Peterson, *Women, Work, and Divorce* (Albany: State University of New York Press, 1989); Teresa A. Mauldin, "Economic Consequences of Divorce or Separation Among Women in Poverty," *Journal of Divorce and Remarriage* 14, no. 3–4 (1991): 163–178; James B. McLindon, "Separate but Unequal: The Economic Disaster of Divorce for Women and Children," *Family Law Quarterly* 21 (1987–1988): 351–409; Terry J. Arendell, "Women and the Economics of Divorce in the Contemporary United States," *Signs* 13, no. 1 (1987): 121–135.

29. "Fact of the Day #80: Gender Inequality in Social Security Benefits," Huffington Post, October 17, 2012, http://www.huffingtonpost.com/2012/10/17/social-security-benefits-men-women_n_1973828.html.

30. Cathleen D. Zick and Ken Smith, "Patterns of Economic Change Surrounding the Death of a Spouse," *Journal of Gerontology: Social Sciences* 46, no. 6 (1991): 310–320. For a concise review of the literature on this topic, see Youngae Lee and Jinkook Lee, "The Poverty of Widows: How Do They Become the Poor?" Ohio State University, http://paa2006.princeton.edu/papers/61592.

31. Megan Kelly Reid, "A Disaster on Top of a Disaster: How Gender, Race, and Class Shaped the Housing Experiences of Displaced Hurricane Katrina Survivors" (PhD diss., University of Texas, 2011), 58–59, http://repositories.lib.utexas.edu/bitstream/handle/2152/ETD-UT-2011-05-2926/REID-DISSERTATION.pdf.

32. Ibid., 51.

33. For a comprehensive overview of the statistics in this area, see Christianne Corbett, Catherine Hill, and Andresse St. Rose, *Where the Girls Are: The Facts About Gender Equity in Education* (Washington DC: American Association of University Women, 2008), http://www.aauw.org/research/where-the-girls-are. For a thorough review of the scholarly literature, see Claudia Buchmann, Thomas A. DiPrete, and Anne McDaniel, "Gender Inequalities in Education," *Annual Review of Sociology* 34 (2008): 319–337. For a discussion of differentials with respect to science, technology, and mathematics, see Roland G. Fryer Jr. and Steven D. Levitt, "An Empirical Analysis of the Gender Gap in Mathematics," National Bureau of Economic Research Working Paper no. 15430, October 2009, http://www.nber.org/papers/w15430; Glenn Ellison and Ashley Swanson, "The Gender Gap in Secondary School Mathematics at High Achievement Levels: Evidence from the American Mathematics Competitions," National Bureau of Economic Research Working Paper no. 15238, http://www.nber.org/papers/w15238; August 2009; Ismael Ramos and Julia Lambating, "Risk Taking: Gender Differences and Educational Opportunity," *School Science and Mathematics* 96 no. 2 (1996): 94–98; Gijsbert Stoet and David C. Geary, "Can Stereotype Threat Explain the Gender Gap in Mathematics Performance and Achievement?" *Review of General Psychology* 16, no. 1 (2012): 93–102.

34. The biological element of this is not straightforward. The suggestion that biology is at work is not necessarily sexist. Such evidence of intrinsic skills does not suggest that one sex is "smarter" than the other but rather that

there may be developmental differences that manifest in abilities being formed at different rates, particularly at very young ages. The way that we react to those tendencies can create environmental effects that will be important as children grow and develop cognitively. See Buchmann, DiPrete, and McDaniel, "Gender Inequalities in Education," 323–324, for a review.

35. However, as noted in Chapter 4, there are significant racial gaps in high school graduation rates.

36. Buchmann, DiPrete, and McDaniel, "Gender Inequalities in Education."

37. Martha Groves, "SAT's Gender Gap Widening," *Los Angeles Times*, August 29, 2001, http://articles.latimes.com/2001/aug/29/news/mn-39684; American Physical Society, "Fighting the Gender Gap: Standardized Tests Are Poor Indicators of Ability in Physics," *APS News* 5, no. 5 (1996), http://www.aps.org/publications/apsnews/199607/gender.cfm.

38. Keith Ashley, "Personhood Republican Presidential Candidate Page," Personhood USA, December 15, 2011, http://www.personhoodusa.com/blog/personhood-republican-presidential-candidate-pledge.

39. Laura Bassett, "On International Women's Day, Congress Debates Measure to Limit Reproductive Rights," Huffington Post, March 8, 2012, http://www.huffingtonpost.com/2012/03/08/international-womens-day-congress-abortion_n_1332143.html; "Three Rulings Against Women's Rights," *New York Times*, July 31, 2012, http://www.nytimes.com/2012/08/01/opinion/three-rulings-against-womens-rights.html.

40. Fluke was nominated for *Time* magazine's Person of the Year Award in 2012. Kate Pickert, "Who Should Be TIME's Person of the Year 2012? The Candidates: Sandra Fluke, *Time*, November 26, 2012, http://www.time.com/time/specials/packages/article/0,28804,2128881_2128882_2129176,00.html. See also Leslie Marshall, "No Fluke that Sandra's on *Time's* List," *U.S. News & World Report*, November 28, 2012, http://www.usnews.com/opinion/blogs/leslie-marshall/2012/11/28/sandra-fluke-belongs-on-times-person-of-the-year-list.

41. Aaron Blake, "Todd Akin, GOP Senate Candidate: 'Legitimate Rape' Rarely Causes Pregnancy," *Washington Post*, August 19, 2012, http://www.washingtonpost.com/blogs/the-fix/wp/2012/08/19/todd-akin-gop-senate-candidate-legitimate-rape-rarely-causes-pregnancy/.

42. Michael R. Crittenden, "Mourdock's Rape Remark Sets Off Firestorm," *Wall Street Journal*, Washington Wire, October 24, 2012, http://blogs.wsj.com/washwire/2012/10/24/mourdocks-rape-remark-touches-off-firestorm/.

43. Valerie A. Earnshaw et al., "Maternal Experiences with Everyday Discrimination and Infant Birth Weight: A Test of Mediators and Moderators Among Young, Urban Women of Color," *Annals of Behavioral Medicine*, August 28, 2012, as reported by Christine Kearney, "Discrimination Can Lead to Low Birth Weight in Babies," Medical News Today, August 27, 2012, http://www.medicalnewstoday.com/articles/249507.php.

44. Jason L. Cummings and Pamela Braboy Jackson, "Race, Gender, and SES Disparities in Self-Assessed Health, 1974–2004," *Research on Aging* 30, no. 2 (2008): 137–168.

45. "ERA: A Brief Overview," EqualRightsAmendment.org, http://www.equalrightsamendment.org/overview.htm.

46. Ibid.

DISCUSSION QUESTIONS

1. Stephen Caliendo notes that most Americans think that "sexism is simply and solely about [employment and remuneration—about] equal pay for equal work." Accordingly, they often think that the cure for sexism is the common "'add women and stir' approach that treats sexism with quota-like solutions." What is wrong with such understandings of sexism? Are there better ways of thinking about sexism and how to overcome it? Explain.

2. How are power and patriarchy related to sexism?

3. Comment on Caliendo's statement that, "the share of women in the labor market has increased steadily since the 1980s, but women have not yet achieved pay equity in most occupations. Women are disadvantaged for a number of reasons relating to deeply held beliefs about their proper place (in the home versus in the workplace), their abilities and intelligence, and their biology." Do you agree with Caliendo? Why or why not?

4. According to Caliendo, "there is a stigma attached to receiving some forms of public assistance in the United States. Although few harbor animosities toward those who receive veterans' benefits, social security, Medicare, or even unemployment compensation, many resent Americans who participate in assistance programs such as

Temporary Assistance for Needy Families, the Women, Infants, and Children (WIC) program, and the Supplemental Nutrition Assistance Program (SNAP; formerly food stamps)." What is Caliendo saying here? What is the nature of this stigma, and what is the difference between noncontroversial programs such as social security and more controversial programs such as WIC and SNAP? Why are the former programs noncontroversial, and the latter programs controversial?

5. Caliendo concludes his article with these words: "All of this calls into question Americans' commitment to women's rights broadly. If we limit our discussion to narrow issues such as closing the pay gap, reducing health disparities, or being attentive to the achievement gap in education, we miss an opportunity to critique patriarchy as a powerful systemic force that undergirds these public policy issues." What do these words mean? Is Caliendo right or wrong? Explain.

READING 2.2

REQUIEM FOR THE CHAMP[1]

Some of Us Did Not Die New and Selected Essays

BY June Jordan

Mike Tyson comes from Brooklyn. And so do I. Where he grew up was about a twenty-minute bus ride from my house. I always thought his neighborhood looked like a war zone. It reminded me of Berlin—immediately after World War II. I had never seen Berlin except for black-and-white photos in *Life* magazine, but that was bad enough: Rubble. Barren. Blasted. Everywhere you turned your eyes recoiled from the jagged edges of an office building or a cathedral, shattered, or the tops of apartment houses torn off, and nothing alive even intimated, anywhere. I used to think, "This is what it means to fight and really win or really lose. War means you hurt somebody, or something, until there's nothing soft or sensible left."

For sure I never had a boyfriend who came out of Mike Tyson's territory. Yes, I enjoyed my share of tough guys and/or gang members who walked and talked and fought and loved in quintessential Brooklyn ways: cool, tough, and deadly serious. But there was a code as rigid and as romantic as anything that ever made the pages of traditional English literature. A guy would beat up another guy or, if appropriate, he'd kill him. But a guy talked different to a girl. A guy made other guys clean up their language around "his girl." A guy brought ribbons and candies and earrings and tulips to a girl. He took care of her. He walked her home. And if he got serious about that girl, and even if she was only twelve years old, then she became his "lady." And woe betide any other guy stupid enough to disrespect that particular young black female.

But none of the boys—none of the young men—none of the young Black male inhabitants of my universe and my heart ever came from Mike Tyson's streets or avenues. We didn't live someplace fancy or middle-class, but at least there were ten-cent gardens, front and back, and coin Laundromats, and grocery stores, and soda parlors, and barber shops, and Holy Roller churchfronts, and chicken shacks, and dry cleaners, and bars-and-grills, and a takeout Chinese restaurant, and all of that usable detail that does not survive a war. That kind of seasonal green turf and daily-life supporting pattern of establishments to meet your needs did not exist inside the gelid urban cemetery where Mike Tyson learned what he thought he needed to know.

---

1   *The Progressive*, February 1992

I remember when the City of New York decided to construct a senior housing project there, in the childhood world of former heavyweight boxing champion Mike Tyson. I remember wondering, "Where in the hell will those old people have to go in order to find food? And how will they get there?"

I'm talking godforsaken. And much of living in Brooklyn was like that. But then it might rain or it might snow and, for example, I could look at the rain forcing forsythia into bloom or watch how snowflakes can tease bare tree limbs into temporary blossoms of snow dissolving into diadems of sunlight. And what did Mike Tyson ever see besides brick walls and garbage in the gutter and disintegrating concrete steps and boarded-up windows and broken car parts blocking the sidewalk and men, bitter, with their hands in their pockets, and women, bitter, with their heads down and their eyes almost closed?

In his neighborhood, where could you buy ribbons for a girl, or tulips?

Mike Tyson comes from Brooklyn. And so do I. In the big picture of America, I never had much going for me. And he had less. I only learned, last year, that I can stop whatever violence starts with me. I only learned, last year, that love is infinitely more interesting, and more exciting, and more powerful, than really winning or really losing a fight. I only learned, last year, that all war leads to death and that all love leads you away from death. I am more than twice Mike Tyson's age. And I'm not stupid. Or slow. But I'm Black. And I come from Brooklyn. And I grew up fighting. And I grew up and I got out of Brooklyn because I got pretty good at fighting. And winning. Or else, intimidating my would-be adversaries with my fists, my feet, and my mouth. And I never wanted to fight. I never wanted anybody to hit me. And I never wanted to hit anybody. But the bell would ring at the end of another dumb day in school and I'd head out with dread and a nervous sweat because I knew some jackass more or less my age and more or less my height would be waiting for me because she or he had nothing better to do than to wait for me and hope to kick my butt or tear up my books or break my pencils or pull hair out of my head.

This is the meaning of poverty: when you have nothing better to do than to hate somebody who, just exactly like yourself, has nothing better to do than to pick on you instead of trying to figure out how come there's nothing better to do. How come there's no gym/no swimming pool/no dirt track/no soccer field/no ice-skating rink/no bike/no bike path/no tennis courts/no language arts workshop/no computer science center/no band practice/no choir rehearsal/no music lessons/no basketball or baseball team? How come neither one of you has his or her own room in a house where you can hang out and dance and make out or get on the telephone or eat and drink up everything in the kitchen that can move? How come nobody on your block and nobody in your class has any of these things?

I'm Black. Mike Tyson is Black. And neither one of us was ever supposed to win anything more than a fight between the two of us. And if you check out the mass-media material on "us," and if you check out the emergency-room reports on "us," you might well believe we're losing the fight to be more than our enemies have decreed. Our enemies would deprive us of everything except each other: hungry and furious and drug-addicted and rejected and ever convinced we can never be beautiful or right or true or different from the beggarly monsters our enemies envision and insist upon, and how should we then stand, Black man and Black woman, face to face?

Way back when I was born, Richard Wright had just published *Native Son* and, thereby, introduced white America to the monstrous product of its racist hatred.

Poverty does not beautify. Poverty does not teach generosity or allow for sucker attributes of tenderness and restraint. In white America, hatred of Blackfolks has imposed horrible poverty upon us.

And so, back in the thirties, Richard Wright's Native Son, Bigger Thomas, did what he thought he had to do: he hideously murdered a white woman and he viciously murdered his Black girlfriend in what he conceived as self-defense. He did not perceive any options to these psychopathic, horrifying deeds. I do not believe he, Bigger Thomas, had any other choices open to him. Not to him, he who was meant to die like the rat he, Bigger Thomas, cornered and smashed to death in his mother's beggarly clean space.

I never thought Bigger Thomas was okay. I never thought he should skate back into my, or anyone's community. But I did and I do think he is my brother. The choices available to us dehumanize. And any single one of us, Black in this white country, we may be defeated, we may become dehumanized, by the monstrous hatred arrayed against us and our needy dreams.

And so I write this requiem for Mike Tyson: international celebrity, millionaire, former heavyweight boxing champion of the world, a big-time winner, a big-time loser, and African-American male in his twenties, and, now, a convicted rapist.

Do I believe he is guilty of rape?

Yes I do.

And what would I propose as appropriate punishment?

Whatever will force him to fear the justice of exact retribution, and whatever will force him, for the rest of his damned life, to regret and to detest the fact that he defiled, he subjugated, and he wounded somebody helpless to his power.

And do I therefore rejoice in the jury's finding?

I do not.

Well, would I like to see Mike Tyson a free man again?

He was never free!

And I do not excuse or condone or forget or minimize or forgive the crime of his violation of the young Black woman he raped!

But did anybody ever tell Mike Tyson that you talk different to a girl? Where would he learn that? Would he learn that from U.S. Senator Ted Kennedy? Or from hotshot/scot-free movie director Roman Polanski? Or from rap recording star Ice Cube? Or from Ronald Reagan and the Grenada escapade? Or from George Bush in Panama? Or from George Bush and Colin Powell in the Persian Gulf? Or from the military hero flyboys who returned from bombing the shit out of civilian cities in Iran and then said, laughing and proud, on international TV: "All I need, now, is a woman"? Or from the hundreds of thousands of American football fans? Or from the millions of Americans who would, if they could, pay surrealistic amounts of money just to witness, up close, somebody like Mike Tyson beat the brains out of somebody?

And what could which university teach Mike Tyson about the difference between violence and love? Is there any citadel of higher education in the country that does not pay its football coach at least three times as much as the chancellor and six times as much as its professors and ten times as much as its social and psychological counselors?

In this America where Mike Tyson and I live together and bitterly, bitterly, apart, I say he became what he felt. He felt the stigma of a prior hatred and intentional poverty. He was given the choice of violence or violence: the violence of defeat or the violence of victory. Who would pay him to rehabilitate inner-city housing or to refurbish a bridge? Who would pay him what to study the facts of our collective history? Who would pay him what to plant and nurture the trees of a forest? And who will write and who will play the songs that tell a guy like Mike Tyson how to talk to a girl?

What was America willing to love about Mike Tyson? Or any Black man? Or any man's man?

Tyson's neighborhood and my own have become the same no-win battleground. And he has fallen there. And I do not rejoice. I do not.

DISCUSSION QUESTIONS

1. What, according to June Jordan, is Mike Tyson's understanding of what it means to be a man? What is Tyson's view of women?

2. What "causes" or "influences" an individual to adopt sociopathic and misogynistic attitudes and behaviors? Jordan implies that Tyson's Brooklyn neighborhood—the ugliness and hopelessness that he saw every day while growing there—put him on the path toward violence. Do you agree or disagree that early-childhood environmental factors, such as where one grows up, and/or perhaps watching violent television programs, and playing violent video games causes or influences a person to exhibit violent and/or sociopathic attitudes and behaviors? Why or why not?

3. Evaluate Jordan's argument that kids in rough and broken neighborhoods learn to fight because of the boredom and futility of their environment and because "some jackass" decides to pick a fight with them. "This is the meaning of poverty," she says—"When you have nothing better to do than to hate somebody." Do you agree or disagree? Why?

OUR WOODY ALLEN PROBLEM

BY **James Rosen**

" As the director turns 80 and releases his 45th film,
long-time fans must decide if they can still admire
the artist while being put off by the man

"The heart wants what it wants," Woody Allen famously said in August 1992, at the zenith of the scandal frenzy that erupted when the public learned that the celebrated comedian and director—acclaimed for iconic, Oscar-winning movies like *Annie Hall* (1977) and *Hannah and Her Sisters* (1986)—had ended his 12-year relationship with actress Mia Farrow in the ugliest possible way: a secret affair with Farrow's 18-year-old adopted daughter, Soon-Yi Previn, apparently exposed when Farrow discovered nude pictures of the girl in Allen's apartment. "There's no logic to those things," Allen told *TIME'S* Walter Isaacson. "You meet someone and you fall in love and that's that."

That's that. Allen, who turns 80 in December, has been married to Previn for 17 years, making it the longest of his three marriages. Their two adopted daughters are teenagers. And this summer, 50 years after the release of his first feature film as a director, *What's New Pussycat?*, he premiered his 45th, *Irrational Man.* These landmarks have sparked fresh interest in this exceedingly complex figure.

Allen's cinematic career survived the tumult of a quarter-century ago. The consistently high caliber of his work has allowed him to maintain his stature as one of the country's great filmmakers. But the moral taint has never fully dissipated, in large part because Allen has never conceded how dramatically the origin of his relationship with Previn differed from that of most romantic couplings, even by the generous standards of celebrity matches. His transgressions—against his ex-lover, her children, and the social fabric—were broader and more acute.

THE ARTIST AND THE MAN

There is a grand lineage of great artists, from Benvenuto Cellini to Richard Wagner, who have forced us to confront the paradox of *l'homme* vs. *l'ouevre*—that uncomfortable situation when life and work stand locked in moral conflict.

Among contemporary artists, Allen may trigger even greater cognitive dissonance, due to his indelible onscreen persona as a lovable *schlemiel* and the moral themes and psychological acuity that pervade his work. Allen's early material was never far removed from the cruelty and horrors of World War II, and his later films brim with keen observations on human relations; all the more disturbing, then, to see the man appear to treat the people around him so callously, as an ensemble of characters easily recast or written out of his script altogether.

Yet Allen has remained defiant in interviews and in testimony during his epic child-custody battle with Farrow. Broken-hearted fans who had long cherished the Allen *weltanschauung* simply couldn't believe that this genius could not readily understand that when the heart wants something it *shouldn't*, especially if it will inflict pain on those closest to us, we tell the heart "no." The most nagging and troubling notion is that his cognitive dissonance—his gift for creating fully realized human characters coupled with his own seeming lack of human character—has somehow fueled his achievement.

For his part, this stylized sculptor of words and pictures has demanded that his audience accept his version of messy facts, in which his relationship with Soon-Yi is no problem at all. From that same *TIME* interview with Isaacson:

ISAACSON: How could you get involved with someone who was almost a daughter?
ALLEN: I am not Soon-Yi's father or stepfather. I've never even lived with Mia. I've never in my

entire life slept at Mia's apartment, and I never even used to go over there until my children came along seven years ago. I never had any family dinners over there. I was not a father to her adopted kids in any sense of the word.

ISAACSON: But wasn't it breaking many bonds of trust to become involved with your lover's daughter?

ALLEN: There's no downside to it. The only thing unusual is that she's Mia's daughter. But she's an adopted daughter and a grown woman. I could have met her at a party or something.

No downside. We should perhaps remember that Allen was, as a child, a practitioner of magic and card tricks, and, later, a creator of similarly entrancing cinematic visions. Only then can we understand how readily project *himself* into a reality in which he "could have" met Soon-Yi in a context unrelated to Mia Farrow and her other children.

SLINGS AND ALLEGATIONS

On the spectrum of transgressions by great artists, where do Allen's fall, and should the longevity and apparent success of his marriage be mitigating factors in our judgment? Others have faced allegations which, if true, would represent transgressions far more serious—the acts of child molestation imputed to, and denied by, the late Michael Jackson; the drugging and raping of multiple women imputed to, and contested by, Bill Cosby; and the statutory rape of a 13-year-old girl that Roman Polanski still maintains was "consensual." Allen's *genuinely* consensual relationship, albeit with the adopted daughter of his longtime lover, may be deeply troubling, but it is not criminal.

SHIFTING TIES Woody Allen and Mia Farrow, above, in 1986, with Dylan Farrow [in Farrow's arms] and Soon-Yi Previn, right.

the *auteur* behind *The Purple Rose of Cairo* (1985)—in which a Depression-era waitress, menaced by her loutish husband, is comforted by a lover who literally leaps off a matinee screen and into her arms—could, amid the self-inflicted complexities of his personal life,

Yet the business of being a late-career Woody Allen fan is made even more complicated by the claims of child molestation Mia Farrow and her family have leveled against him since 1992. These allegations got a fresh public hearing in 2014, when, shortly after Allen was presented a lifetime achievement award at the Golden Globes, the *New York Times* published a scathing open letter on its op-ed page from the alleged victim, Dylan Farrow, about her childhood with Allen—her first public comment on the case. While partisans on both sides remain steadfast in their version of events, here the untidy evidence appears to be on Allen's side. In a sworn statement issued in April 1993, John M. Leventhal, head of a Yale-New Haven Hospital team that spent six months investigating the charges, discounted them in full, saying medical examinations found no evidence and that young Dylan's account—a choppy statement made with Farrow's assistance and video-tape editing—"had a rehearsed quality." "We had two hypotheses," Leventhal testified. "One, that these were statements made by an emotionally disturbed child and then became fixed in her mind. And the other ... that she was coached or influenced by her mother."

With this complicated record in mind, we cognitively subdivide Allen into more categories than the careers of most great artists typically demand: There is the towering neurotic genius who evolved from gag writer to stand-up comic, author, and, most prominently, creator of complex films that chronicle our times. There is the extraordinarily selfish and unrepentant man, giver to his heart of whatever it wants, and whenever it wants it, consequences be damned. And there is the apparently wronged public figure, target of the worst kind of reputational smear.

> Allen has long demanded that we **accept his version of reality.**

I still love the artist. Less-of-the-moment than his past works and less likely to include himself as a lead player, Allen's recent movies do not command the attention they once did; but the varied work of his prime, staged across a variety of platforms over three decades starting in 1965, still delights and tugs at my heart. Growing up Jewish with glasses in 1970s New York, I venerated Allen. Here was a hilarious comedian, intellectual in bent but also given to arresting non sequiturs and calamitous slapstick; a gifted and innovative filmmaker and pioneer of new technologies like the morphing effect in *Zelig* (1982); and, most important, a resilient, irrepressibly Jewish voice just a generation after the Holocaust.

THE NEUROTIC AND HIS LEGACY

This skinny, bespectacled, and somehow cute Brooklyn Jew, an urban-neurotic koala bear, improbably made the cover of *TIME* in 1972, at a time when casual anti- Semitism was only beginning to recede from American public life. He did not shrink from his Jewishness nor from the global ugliness of his childhood years; rather, he incorporated both. In his movies, Allen allowed himself to be physically menaced in ways that recalled the Nazis and their victims—in *Take the Money and Run* (1969), for example, nearly everyone his character encounters, beginning in childhood and including even a presiding judge, smashes Allen's eyeglasses beneath their feet. And his *shtick* often made explicit reference to the Final Solution, as when he cited in his stand-up act his wife's preparation of "Nazi recipes" like "Chicken Himmler."

Allen's early and always winning appearances on *The Dick Cavett Show* and *The Tonight Show* with Johnny Carson, redoubts of mainstream American WASP cool, likewise represented a triumph for postwar American Jews. In the resurrection of Jewish culture and thought after the Shoah, Allen's voice was at least as important to my generation as Primo Levi's or Elie Wiesel's, his permeation into American, and even world, consciousness arguably wider and deeper. Just 12 years after Alvy Singer courted Diane Keaton's Annie Hall in spite of his Otherness, Jerry Seinfeld plausibly embodied The Everyman in a top-rated sitcom. This was a measure of Allen's success in changing American perceptions of leading men.

The achievements that made Allen such a revolutionary figure make it correspondingly difficult to remain a fan post-Soon-Yi. One recalls the joke Alvy Singer relates to the camera at the end of *Annie Hall*: "This guy goes to a psychiatrist and says, 'Doc, uh, my brother's crazy. He thinks he's a chicken.' And, uh, the doctor says, 'Well, why don't you turn him in?' And the guy says, 'I would, but I need the eggs.'"

Like that patient considering his lycanthropic brother, we recognize in Allen both the need for radical intervention and the undeniable fruits of radical self-invention. And we can also imagine that long after their deeply flawed deliverer is gone, his treasured eggs will endure.

JAMES ROSEN is chief Washington correspondent for Fox News and author of *The Cheney Tapes* (Regnery, November 2015).

DISCUSSION QUESTIONS

1. What is the "Woody Allen problem" to which James Rosen refers?

2. Film director Woody Allen said, concerning his marriage to his former lover's 18-year-old adopted daughter, Soon-Yi Previn, that "the heart wants what it wants. There's no logic to those things. You meet someone and you fall in love and that's that." Do Allen's comments make sense? Why or why not? Do men who marry their former lovers' adopted daughters, or who sexually harass or assault women, do so out of love? If their actions are not motivated by love, what are they motivated by? Explain your answer.

3. The author writes that "broken-hearted [Woody Allen] fans simply couldn't believe that this genius could not readily understand that when the heart wants something it shouldn't, especially if it will inflict pain on those closest to us, we tell the heart no." What does this statement mean? Do you agree with it?

4. Rosen praises Allen for his comic genius and film-making artistry. But he concludes that "the achievements that made Allen such a revolutionary figure make it correspondingly difficult to remain a fan post-Soon-Yi." Discuss Rosen's ambivalent feelings. Do you feel similar ambivalence about Michael Jackson, Bill Cosby, Michael Weinstein, Charlie Rose, Kevin Spacey, Al Franken, and other famous and/or talented men who have been accused of predatory sexual harassment or assault? Why or why not?

5. What corrective actions or "punishments" are just or appropriate for rich, powerful, famous, and/or extremely talented people who are outted for their past and/or present-day sexual abuse, violence, and harassment? Should they go to jail? Should they be exiled from their profession, and/or ordered into therapy? Should Allen have gone to jail for marrying Soon-Yi Previn?

6. Is there a legitimate case to be made for maintaining a double standard in the case of extremely talented people who sexually abuse? As Rosen admits, "there is a great lineage of great artists from Benvenuto Cellini to Richard Wagner who have forced us to confront the paradox of *l'homme* vs. *l'ouevre*—that uncomfortable situation when life and work stand locked in moral conflict." Should sexual abusers who are extremely talented and acclaimed, as actors, directors, journalists, businessmen, teachers, political leaders, and heart surgeons, be allowed to continue to serve the public and benefit humankind in their chosen profession?

WHEN THE STORY is ABOUT YOU

BY **Julia Park Tracey**

Thirty years later, with the backdrop of rape being discussed—and botched—in news reporting, one journalist tells the story she couldn't tell while in school.

In the first week of my first journalism class at community college, I was told, as so many students are, never use first person. Never say "I." The story is not about you.

Using "this reporter" is not a work-around. Stay out of the story, no matter what. And also: Spell everyone's name right, don't use passive voice, and don't screw up the reporting.

Everything I needed to know about journalism, I learned in that first week.

Shortly after starting school, I went out on assignment to interview a guy running a local access TV show in a rural area of California. The tiny studio was housed in a barn with electricity. I didn't know what exactly running a cable TV show entailed, and it seemed like a fun story (more fun than, say, my incomprehensible visit to the mainframe in the computer studies wing of the science building, and not understanding what bits and bytes were).

I drove out to the boonies and soon was scrawling in my new Reporter's Notebook. I was on the staff of the college tabloid, getting my first bylines, learning to ask better questions than "Who's your favorite teacher?" But I was confused by technology like the computer lab or the TV station in those analog days. I didn't have a larger frame of reference—no iPhone, no laptop—like today's new journalists do. (Realize that the student newspaper was still using typewriters for stories, a darkroom for photos and light tables for paste-up. We manually counted points for heds. There was no Google, only the Yellow Pages.)

The TV guy showed me around, pointed out the equipment, nattered on about how great it was to run a cable station, and then invited me to the comfy couch to finish the interview. I sat down to ask a few more not-so-probing questions, and then he put his arm along the back of the sofa toward me and said, "How about a neck rub?"

What would you have said? I was 18 and in my first semester of college. I was a good girl who did what she was asked, including going out to a remote barn alone with a man I had never met before—without a cell phone.

I said, "Uh, ok." He laid his head in my lap and I massaged his neck. Was I weirded out? Completely. Did I want to get out of there? Absolutely. But I didn't know how to say no to a command from an adult yet, and I was trying to learn the ropes in this new world of journalism. Maybe this was part of the job.

Things hadn't changed a few months later when a fellow journalism student, who'd come over to do homework, sexually assaulted me from behind in my own apartment. I didn't pursue any police action, and I certainly didn't tell the school or the student newspaper; I'd already seen what could happen to people who tell.

Lucky for me, he had enough neck rub after a few minutes and wanted to go somewhere for a drink, but I said the equivalent of, "I think I hear my mom calling." I wasn't 21 and couldn't drink, and I had to get the car home or I'd get in trouble. That adherence to the rules is probably what saved me from more than a neck rub.

I didn't tell anyone at home or at the student newspaper about the incident because it didn't occur to me in 1981 that there was anything that wrong with him asking. I had already been exposed to bad behavior from a couple of creeps on the local transit going to and from college—you'd put your backpack on the seat next to you and pray that Andy wouldn't get on the bus. And that he wouldn't sit next to you. And if he did, that he wouldn't pin you in the corner and try to grab your boobs or your ass—which he did every single time. It was just a hazard of riding the No. 70 bus to Santa Rosa, any day of the week.

Two years later, I transferred to San Francisco State, where in my news-writing class, the professor asked if there was anything we had learned from our reporting so far that we wanted to share with other students. I raised my hand and boldly said that female students should be careful going alone to interviews because of the neck rub incident, explaining what had happened to me. And for the rest of that semester, the professor insisted on asking me for a neck rub as often as he could. It was a joke the whole class enjoyed.

Things hadn't changed a few months later when a fellow journalism student, who'd come over to do homework, sexually assaulted me from behind in my own apartment. I didn't pursue any police action, and I certainly didn't tell the school or the student newspaper; I'd already seen what could happen to people who tell.

In the 30 years since then, how much have things changed? Is it safe for female reporters to go out into the world in search of stories, and do they come back unscathed? Whether something inappropriate like a neck rub, or worse like blatant sex acts, is she allowed to leave unscathed? And when she tells someone about it, is she greeted with scoffs and bawdy jokes and taunted about the incident for as long as it amuses the crew? Does talking about it affect her career?

I've pondered the questions endlessly over the years, as a freelancer, a reporter, an editor and an author—that "What should I have done, what would I do next time?" conundrum. And I always come back to: I wouldn't tell. I might fight, scream, swear or drink heavily afterward—or refuse to cover their story. But would I tell? Would I write about it? I haven't yet—until now.

Flashbacks of the neck-rub incident and the assault at my apartment came up for me as I read of the Bill Cosby rape accusations and the victims' hounding in the media. The Rolling Stone article about rape at the University of Virginia, and the fallout after Rolling Stone had to retract parts of its story because of its incomplete reporting, has a similar result: excoriating the victim's choices, intelligence and intentions.

Coincidentally, shortly after my own assault, another student said she was raped on campus, and one of our staffers reported on the incident. But the campus police couldn't corroborate her story. There were no witnesses, and she dropped out of sight. After reporting her assault in the paper one week, the next week we had to recant.

The experience led the entire journalism program into discussions about how not to be duped by subjects of a story, and how to pursue due diligence in reporting from every source. Truth—and trust—is everything in reporting the news.

Of course, that only underscored my fear of telling my story. Not only would I be exposed, but I would be cross-examined—By a reporter! By an editor! By the copy desk! By whoever sought to poke holes in my narrative in case I was lying. And could I blame them? Who wants to be the reporter caught not doing his or her job? Even if doing that job (or my homework) got me raped?

Have things changed since I started journalism classes? When I see the #yesallwomen hashtag and the #nomeansno campaign, I hope that the tide is turning. My four daughters—feminists, all of them—have so far escaped the statistics; their stories are still unfurling.

It took me a while to say what happened, even in therapy. As a journalist, it was OK to tell stories, just not your own. I got the interviews, wrote the stories, got my assignments in by deadline. And I kept quiet, which is what the perpetrators wanted, and what society still seems to want: strong women who focus on the work, who get the job done and don't talk about what might have happened.

I understand completely how the Cosby women did not have the guts or the stamina to tell their stories back when it happened. I do believe something bad happened to Jackie, the University of Virginia student; but, traumatized, she couldn't tell it or told it badly. And with Rolling Stone's ham-fisted reporting, her shot at justice is as good as gone. It doesn't take much to assault the victim again in the press.

Telling your secret may seem like the path to a book or a movie deal, but that doesn't usually happen to average people. Rape, though, happens to average folks—to about 20 percent of all women, according to the Rape, Abuse & Incest National Network. Statistically speaking, you're sitting in an office or a subway car with a handful of assault victims. You just can't tell by looking at them.

It's taken a long time for me to start talking about it, to put pen to paper, fingers to keyboard, because it isn't an easy story to tell. My story, if not on the front page, is written into my body—in my refusal to walk the neighborhood alone after dark, in the way I startle violently when surprised, in my loathing of elevators and stairwells where people stand behind me. My story is written under my skin as permanently as the quill pen tattooed on my sacrum.

Have things changed since I started journalism classes? When I see the **#yesallwomen** hashtag and the **#nomeansno** campaign, I hope that the tide is turning. My four daughters—feminists, all of them—have so far escaped the statistics; their stories are still unfurling.

Only now—three decades later—this reporter is beginning to tell what happened, reopening old wounds. Because it turns out my first professors were wrong. Sometimes you have to become part of the story to change it. And you have to face down the fear of telling to step toward true healing. And I consider that a good ending.

What would you have done if you were in my shoes, back before cell phones or Twitter-shaming or hashtags to share your feels? Whom would you have told? How would your story have been different—or would it? And—be honest—how many of you journalists, male or female, haven't told your stories yet?

JULIA PARK TRACEY is a reporter, blogger and author from Northern California. She is the founding editor of the Alameda Sun newspaper and has written for the San Francisco Chroni-cle, East Bay Express and Thrillist. On Twitter: @juliaparktraceyHave

DISCUSSION QUESTIONS

1. Why do you think Julia Park Tracey refrained from reporting the TV station guy who had asked her for a neck rub? And why didn't she "pursue any police action" a few years later after she was sexually assaulted in her own apartment? Is remaining silent a common experience for women who are assaulted? If so, why?

2. Tracey explained her silence with these words: "I'd already seen what could happen to people who tell." Explain what Tracey means: what *could* happen to people who tell? What needs to be done for women to feel safe reporting incidents of sexual harassment or sexual attack?

3. Tracey wonders if things have changed for women—and to what extent—in the 30 years since the mid-1980s. "Is it safe for female reporters to go out into the world in search of stories, and do they come back unscathed? Whether something inappropriate like a neck rub, or worse like [a] blatant sex ac[t happens], when she tells someone about it, is she greeted with scoffs and bawdy jokes and taunted about the incident? Does talking about it affect her career?" How would you answer Tracey's questions? How much have things changed over the past 30 years?

4. Tracey says: "It took me a while to say what happened, even in therapy. As a journalist, It was OK to tell stories, just not your own. I got the interviews, wrote the stories, got my assignments in by deadline. And I kept quiet, which is what the perpetrators wanted and what society still seems to want." What does this statement mean? Is Tracey right? Explain your answer

5. Tracey concludes her article with this question: "What would you have done if you were in my shoes? Whom would you have told? How would your story have been different—or would it? And—be honest—how many of you journalists, male or female, haven't told your stories yet?" How would you respond to Tracey's questions?

READING 2.5

PATRIARCHY, THE SYSTEM: AN IT, NOT A HE, A THEM, OR AN US

The Gender Knot: Unraveling Our Patriarchal Legacy

BY **Allan Johnson**

PATRIARCHY

The key to understanding any system is to identify its various aspects and how they are arranged to form a whole. To understand a language, for example, we have to learn its alphabet, vocabulary, and rules for combining words into meaningful phrases and sentences. A system like patriarchy is more complicated because there are many different aspects, and it can be difficult to see how they are connected.

Patriarchy's defining elements are its male-dominated, male-identified, male-centered, and control-obsessed character, but this is just the beginning. At its core, patriarchy is based on a set of symbols and ideas that make up a culture embodied by everything from the content of everyday conversation to the practice of war. Patriarchal culture includes ideas about the nature of things, including women, men, and humanity, with manhood and masculinity most closely associated with being human and womanhood and femininity relegated to the marginal position of other. It is about how social life is and what it is supposed to be, about what is expected of people and about how they feel. It is about standards of feminine beauty and masculine toughness, images of feminine vulnerability and masculine protectiveness, of older men coupled with younger women, of elderly women alone. It is about defining women and men as opposites, about the 'naturalness' of male aggression, competition, and dominance on the one hand and of female caring, cooperation, and subordination on the other. It is about the valuing of masculinity and manhood and the devaluing of femininity and womanhood. It is about the primary importance of a husband's career and the secondary status of a wife's, about child care as a priority in women's lives and its secondary importance in men's. It is about the social acceptability of anger, rage, and toughness in men but not in women, and of caring, tenderness, and vulnerability in women but not in men.

Above all, patriarchal culture is about the core value of control and domination in almost every area of human existence. From the expression of emotion to economics to the natural environment, gaining and exercising control is a continuing goal. Because of this, the concept of power takes on a narrow definition in terms of 'power over'—the ability to control others, events, resources, or oneself in spite of resistance—rather than alternatives such as the ability to cooperate, to give freely of oneself, or to feel and act in harmony with nature.[1] To have power over and to be prepared to use it are culturally defined as good and desirable (and characteristically masculine), and to lack such power or to be reluctant to use it is seen as weak if not contemptible (and characteristically feminine).

This is a major reason that patriarchies with the means to do so are often so quick to go to war. Studies of the men who formulate U.S. military strategy, for example, show that it's almost impossible to lose standing by advocating an excessive use of force in international relations (such as the U.S. response to terrorism and the 2003 invasion of Iraq). But those who advocate restraint in the use of force risk being perceived as less than manly and, therefore, lacking credibility.[2]

The main use of any culture is to provide symbols and ideas out of which to construct a sense of what is real. Thus, language mirrors social reality in sometimes startling ways. In contemporary usage, for example, the words 'crone,' 'bitch,' and 'virgin' describe women as threatening or heterosexually inexperienced and thus incomplete. In their original meanings, however, these words evoked far different images.[3] The crone was the old woman whose life experience gave her insight, wisdom, respect, and the power to enrich people's lives. The bitch was Artemis-Diana, goddess of the hunt, most often associated with the dogs who accompanied her. And the virgin was merely a woman who was unattached, unclaimed, and unowned by any man and therefore independent and autonomous. Notice how each word has been transformed from a positive cultural image of female power, independence, and dignity to an insult or a shadow of its former self, leaving few words to identify women in ways both positive and powerful.

Going deeper into patriarchal culture, we find a complex web of ideas that define reality and what is considered good and desirable. To see the world through patriarchal eyes is to believe that women and men are profoundly different in their basic natures, that hierarchy is the only alternative to chaos, and that men were made in the image of a masculine God with whom they enjoy a special relationship. It is to take as obvious the ideas that there are two and only two distinct sexes and genders; that patriarchal heterosexuality is natural and same-sex attraction is not; that because men neither bear nor breastfeed children, they cannot feel a compelling bodily connection to them; that on some level every woman, whether heterosexual, lesbian, or bisexual, wants a 'real man' who knows how to take charge of things, including her; and that females cannot be trusted, especially when they're menstruating or accusing men of abuse.

In spite of all the media hype to the contrary, to embrace patriarchy still is to believe that mothers should stay home and that fathers should work outside the home, regardless of men's and women's actual abilities or needs.[4] It is to buy into the notion that women are weak and men are strong and that women and children need men to support and protect them, despite the fact that in many ways men are not the physically stronger sex, that women perform a huge share of hard physical labor in many societies (often larger than men's), that women's physical endurance tends to be greater than men's over the long haul, and that women tend to be more capable of enduring pain and emotional stress.[5]

And yet, as Elizabeth Janeway notes, such evidence means little in the face of a patriarchal culture that dictates how things *ought* to be and, like all cultural mythology, "will not be argued down by facts. It may seem to be making straightforward statements, but actually these conceal another mood, the imperative. Myth exists in a state of tension. It is not really describing a situation, but trying by means of this description *to bring about* what it declares to exist."[6]

To live in a patriarchal culture is to learn what is expected of men and women—to learn the rules that regulate punishment and reward based on how individuals behave and appear. These rules range from laws that require men to fight in wars not of their own choosing to the expectation that mothers will provide child care. Or that when a woman shows sexual interest in a man or merely smiles or acts friendly, she gives up her right to say no and to control her own body from that point on. And to live under patriarchy is to take into ourselves ways of feeling—the hostile contempt for women that forms the core of misogyny and presumptions of male superiority, the ridicule that men direct at other men who show signs of vulnerability or weakness, or the fear and insecurity that every woman must deal with when she exercises the right to move freely in the world, especially at night and by herself in public places.

Such ideas make up the symbolic sea we swim in and the air we breathe. They are the primary well from which springs how we think about ourselves, other people, and the world. As such, they provide a taken-for-granted everyday reality, the setting for our interactions with other people that continually fashion and refashion a sense of what the world is about and who we are in relation to it. This does not mean that the ideas underlying patriarchy determine what we think, feel, and do. But it does mean they define what we have to deal with as we participate in it.

The prominent place of misogyny in patriarchal culture, for example, doesn't mean that every man and woman consciously hates all things that are culturally associated with being female. But it does mean that to the extent that we do not feel such hatred, it is *in spite of* prevailing paths of least resistance. Complete freedom from such feelings and judgments is all but impossible. It is certainly possible for heterosexual men to love women without mentally fragmenting them into breasts, buttocks, genitals, and other variously desirable parts. It is possible for women to feel good about their bodies, to not judge themselves as being too big, to not abuse themselves to one degree or another in pursuit of impossible male-identified standards of beauty and sexual attractiveness.

All of this is possible, but to live in patriarchy is to breathe in misogynist images of women as objectified sexual property valued primarily for their usefulness to men. This finds its way into everyone who grows up breathing and swimming in it, and once inside us it remains, however unaware of it we may be. When we hear or express sexist jokes and other forms of misogyny, we may not recognize it, and even if we do, we may say nothing rather than risk other people thinking we're too sensitive or, especially in the case of men, not one of the guys. In either case, we are involved, if only by our silence.

The symbols and ideas that make up patriarchal culture are important to understand because they have such powerful effects on the structure of social life. By 'structure,' I mean the ways privilege and oppression are organized through social relationships and unequal distributions of power, rewards, opportunities, and resources. This appears in countless patterns of everyday life in family and work, religion and politics, community and education. It is found in family divisions of labor that exempt fathers from most domestic work even when both parents work outside the home, and in the concentration of women in lower-level pink-collar jobs and male predominance almost everywhere else. It is in the unequal distribution of income and all that goes with it, from access to health care to the availability of leisure time. It is in patterns of male violence and harassment that can turn a simple walk in the park or a typical day at work or a lovers' quarrel into a life-threatening nightmare. More than anything, the structure of patriarchy is found in the unequal distribution of power that makes male privilege possible, in patterns of male dominance in every facet of human life, from everyday conversation to global politics. By its nature, patriarchy puts issues of power, dominance, and control at the center of human existence, not only in relationships between men and women but among men as they compete and struggle to gain status, maintain control, and protect themselves from what other men might do to them.

To understand patriarchy, we have to identify its cultural elements and how they are related to the structure of social life. We must see, for example, how cultural ideas that identify women primarily as mothers and men primarily as breadwinners support patterns in which women do most domestic work at home and are discriminated against in hiring, pay, and promotions at work. But to do anything with such an understanding, we must also see what patriarchy has to do with us as individuals—how it shapes us and we shape *it*.

ENDNOTES

1. For a thorough discussion of this distinction, see Marilyn French, *Beyond Power: On Men, Women, and Morals* (New York: Summit Books, 1985).

2. See Carol Cohn, "Sex and Death in the Rational World of Defense Intellectuals," *Signs* 12, no. 4 (1987): 687–728; Brian Easlea, "Patriarchy, Scientists, and Nuclear Warriors," in *Beyond Patriarchy: Essays by Men on Pleasure, Power, and Change*, edited by Michael Kaufman (New York: Oxford University Press, 1987); and Myriam Miedzian, "'Real Men,' 'Wimps,' and Our National Security," in *Boys Will Be Boys: Breaking the Link between Masculinity and Violence* (New York: Doubleday, 1991), 18–38.

3. For discussions of language and gender, see Jane Caputi, *Gossips, Gorgons, and Crones* (Santa Fe, NM: Bear, 1993); Mary Daly, *Gyn/Ecology: The Metaethics of Radical Feminism* (Boston: Beacon Press, 1978); Margaret Gibbon, *Feminist Perspectives on Language* (New York: Longman, 1999); Dale Spender, *Man Made Language* (London: Pandora, 1980); Robin Lakoff, *Language and Woman's Place*, rev. ed. (New York: Harper and Row, 2004); Barbara G. Walker, *The Women's Encyclopedia of Myths and Secrets* (San Francisco: Harper and Row, 1983); and Barbara G. Walker, *The Woman's Dictionary of Symbols and Sacred Objects* (San Francisco: Harper and Row, 1988). For a very different slant on gender and language, see Mary Daly (in cahoots with Jane Caputi), *Webster's First New Intergalactic Wickedary of the English Language* (Boston: Beacon Press, 1987).

4. See Arlie Hochschild, *The Second Shift: Working Parents and the Revolution at Home*, rev. ed. (New York: Viking/Penguin, 2012).

5. See, for example, Rosalyn Baxandall, Linda Gordon, and Susan Reverby, eds., *America's Working Women: A Documentary History—1600 to the Present*, rev. ed. (New York: Norton, 1995); Ashley Montagu, *The Natural Superiority of Women* (New York: Collier, 1974); Robin Morgan, ed., *Sisterhood Is Global* (New York: Feminist Press, 1996); and Marilyn Waring, *If Women Counted: A New Feminist Economics* (San Francisco: HarperCollins, 1990).

6. Elizabeth Janeway, *Man's World, Woman's Place: A Study in Social Mythology* (New York: Dell, 1971), 37.

DISCUSSION QUESTIONS

1. Discuss the causes and origins of sexism, racism, and classism. Are they caused by men, Whites, and the wealthy? Or are they instigated by the failures of women, people of color, and the poor? Are they, perhaps, collective problems that are endemic to American society? Or do you think they are systemic problems, present everywhere in the United States and the world, as common as the air we breathe? Explain your answer. Relatedly, is there any one "best" way to study and think about sexism, racism, and classism? Explain your answer.

2. Allan Johnson says that "patriarchy is a kind of society organized around certain kinds of social relations and ideas that shape paths of least resistance." What does he mean by this, and is he right?

    If he is, what are the implications of men and women following "the paths of least resistance" as they live, work, and interact in American society?

3. Do you agree with Johnson that we live in a patriarchal culture? Why or why not?

4. Johnson writes that "because patriarchy is, by definition, a system of inequality organized around culturally created gender categories, we cannot avoid being involved in it. All men and all women are therefore involved in this oppressive system, and none of us can control whether we participate." What does he mean by this? Do you agree with him? Why or why not?

READING 2.6

WHY PATRIARCHY?

The Gender Knot: Unraveling Our Patriarchal Legacy

BY **Allan Johnson**

MISSING LINKS: CONTROL, FEAR, AND MEN

Perhaps more than anything else, what drives patriarchy as a system—what fuels competition, aggression, oppression, and violence—is a dynamic relationship between control and fear.[1] Patriarchy encourages men to seek security, status, and other rewards through control, to fear other men's ability to control and harm them, and to identify being in control as both their best defense against loss and humiliation and the surest route to what they need and desire. In this sense, although we usually think of patriarchy in terms of women and men, it is more about what goes on *among men*. The oppression of women is certainly an important part of patriarchy, but, paradoxically, it may not be the *point* of patriarchy.

Why does control have such cosmic importance under patriarchy? One possibility is that control may be inherently so terrific that men just can't resist organizing their lives around it. In other words, men control because they *can*. But this puts us back in the arms of dead-end essentialism and up against the fact that the more people try to control other people and themselves, the more miserable they seem to be. And the idea that what men might get through control, such as wealth or prestige, is inherently so appealing that they would participate routinely in the oppression of their mothers, sisters, daughters, and wives isn't much better. For that to be true, we would first have to explain how control and its rewards could possibly outweigh the horrendous consequences of oppression, especially involving groups as intimately involved as are women and men. A common explanation is, "That's the way people (men) are. They'll always compete for wealth, power, and prestige." But this is the kind of circular reasoning that essentialism so often gets us into: men are that way because that's the way men are.

An essentialist approach also ignores the prominent role that fear plays in most men's lives. Unlike control, fear may be one of the most powerful and primal of all human motivations, more deeply rooted than greed, desire, lust, or even love. Nothing matches fear's potential to twist us out of shape, to drive us to abandon everything we otherwise hold dear, to oppress and do violence to one another—fear of death, of loss, of pain, of shame or rejection. And the most powerfully oppressive systems are organized in ways that promote fear.

What patriarchy accomplishes is to make men fear what other men might do to them—how control might be turned on them to do them harm and deprive them of what matters most to them. This encourages men to feel afraid of being ridiculed and deprived of recognition as real men.[2] They're afraid other men will use economic power to take away jobs or hold them back or make their work lives miserable. They're afraid men will beat them up or kill them if they're unlucky enough to provoke the wrong one. They're afraid men will wage war against them, destroy their communities and homes, beat, torture, rape, and kill those they love. In short, patriarchy encourages men to fear all the things that other men might do to exert control and thereby protect and enhance their standing as real men in relation to other men.

Women, of course, have many reasons to fear men, but this is not what shapes and defines patriarchy as a way of life. Men's fear of other men is crucial because *patriarchy is driven by how men both cause and respond to that fear.* Because patriarchy is organized around male-identified control, men's path of least resistance is to protect themselves by increasing their own sense of control, and patriarchy provides many ways of doing that. For some, it may be holding their own in aggressive male banter, whatever their particular group's version of 'doing the dozens'[3] happens to be. Or keeping their

feelings to themselves rather than appearing vulnerable at the wrong moment to someone looking for an advantage. Or learning to win an argument, always having an answer, and never admitting they're wrong. They learn early on not to play with girls unless it's in the backseats of cars, and they may go out of their way to avoid the appearance that women can control them. They may pump iron, talk and follow sports, study boxing and martial arts, learn to use guns, or play football or hockey or rugby. In all these ways they may try to cope with their own fear and at the same time inspire it in others, all the while maintaining an underlying commitment to men and what men do and the system of privilege that binds them together.

Men's participation in patriarchy tends to lock them in an endless pursuit of and defense against control, *for under patriarchy, control is both the source of fear and the only solution offered for it.* The more invested a man is in the control-fear spiral, the worse he feels when he doesn't feel in control. And so on some level he is always on the lookout for opportunities to renew his sense of control while protecting himself from providing that same kind of opportunity for others, especially men. As each man pursues control as a way to defend and advance himself, he fuels the very same response in *other* men. This dynamic has provided patriarchy with its driving force for thousands of years.

Men pay an enormous price for participating in this. The more in control men try to be, the less secure they feel. They may not know it because they're so busy trying to be in control, but the more they organize their lives around that effort, the more tied they are to the fear of *not* being in control.

As Marilyn French puts it, "A religion of power is a religion of fear, and ... those who worship power are the most terrified creatures on the earth."[4] Dig beneath the surface appearance of 'great men' and you will often find deep insecurity, fear, and a chronic need to prove themselves to other men. As president of the United States, for example, one of the most powerful positions on Earth, George H. W. Bush was obsessed that people might think he was a 'wimp.' Before him, President Lyndon Johnson continued the Vietnam War in part because he was afraid of being considered less than manly if he didn't.[5] Rather than making men feel safe, great power makes them need still greater control to protect themselves from still more powerful men locked into the same cycle. To make matters worse, control itself is a fleeting, momentary experience, not a natural, stable state. And so, as Marilyn French and

Simone Weil argue, control is always on the edge of slipping away or falling apart:

> Power is not what we think it is. Power is not substantial; not even when it takes substantive form. The money you hold in your hand can be devalued overnight .... A title can be removed at the next board meeting .... A huge military establishment can disintegrate in a few days ... a huge economic structure can collapse in a few weeks....
>
> "All power is unstable .... There is never power, but only a race for power .... Power is, by definition, only a means ... but power seeking, owing to its essential incapacity to seize hold of its object, rules out all consideration of an end, and finally comes ... to take the place of all ends."[6]

The religion of fear and control also blocks men's need for human connection by redefining intimacy. Men are encouraged to see everything and everyone as other, and to look on every situation in terms of how it might enhance or threaten their sense of control. Every opportunity for control, however, can also be an occasion for a failure of control, a fact that can inject issues of control and power into the most unlikely situations. Intimacy is lost as a chance to be open and vulnerable on the way to a deeper connection. Sexual intimacy in particular can go from pleasure in a safe place to a male performance laced with worry about whether the penis—that notorious and willful 'other' that so often balks at men's efforts at control—will 'perform' as it's supposed to. Dictionaries typically define impotence as the *inability to achieve or sustain* an erection, as if an erection is something a man *does* and not something he experiences, like sweating or having his heart beat rapidly or feeling happy. The more preoccupied with control men are, the more lovers recede as full people with feelings, thoughts, will, and soul and become vehicles for bolstering manhood and relieving anxiety. And even though a woman's opinion of a man's sexual 'performance' may seem to be what matters, her words of reassurance are rarely enough, for it is always a patriarchal male gaze that's looking at him over her shoulder and judging him.

Patriarchy is grounded in a Great Lie that the answer to life's needs is disconnection, competition, and control rather than connection, sharing, and cooperation. The Great Lie separates men from what they need most by encouraging them to be autonomous and disconnected when in fact human existence is fundamentally relational.[7] What is a 'me' without a 'you,' a 'mother' without a 'child,' a 'teacher' without a 'student'? Who are we if not our ties to other people—"I *am* ... a father, husband, worker, friend, son, brother"?[8]

But patriarchal culture turns that truth inside out, and 'self-made man' goes from oxymoron to cultural ideal. And somewhere between the need for human connection and the imperative to control, the two merge, and a sense of control becomes the closest many men ever come to feeling connected with anything, including themselves.

PATRIARCHY AS A MEN'S PROBLEM

Patriarchy is usually portrayed as something that is primarily between women and men. At first blush this makes a lot of sense given that 'male' and 'female' define each other and that women occupy an oppressed position in relation to male privilege. Paradoxically, however, the cycle of control and fear that drives patriarchy has more to do with relations among men than with women, for it is men who control men's standing *as men*. With few exceptions, men look to other men—not women—to affirm their manhood, whether as coaches, friends, teammates, coworkers, sports figures, fathers, or mentors.

This contradicts the conventional wisdom that women hold the key to heterosexual men's sense of manhood. It is true that men often use women to show that they measure up—especially by controlling women sexually—but the standards that are used are men's and not women's. Men also may try to impress women as 'real men' in order to start and keep relationships with them, to control them, or to get sexual access and personal care. This is not enough to secure manhood, however. For affirmation of that, they must go to a larger male-identified world—from the local bar to sports to work—which is also where they are most vulnerable to other men. Whether in locker rooms or the heat of political campaigns, when a man is accused of being a wimp or of otherwise failing to measure up, it almost always comes from another man. And when a man suspects *himself* of being less than a man, he judges himself through a patriarchal male gaze, not from a woman's perspective.

Although men often use women as scapegoats for their bad feelings about themselves, women's role in this is indirect at most. If other men reject a man's claim to manhood, how his wife or mother sees him usually makes little difference, and if women's opinions *do* matter to him, his manhood becomes all the more suspect to other men.[9] Women's marginal importance in the manhood question is plain to see in the risks men take to prove themselves in spite of objections from wives, mothers, and other women who find them just fine the way they are. The record books are full of men who seize on *anything*—from video games to extreme sports to being the first to get somewhere or discover something—as a way to create competitive arenas in which they can jockey for position and prove themselves among men.[10] If a man must choose between men's and women's views of what makes for true manhood, he will choose men's views most of the time. "A man's gotta do what a man's gotta do," is typically spoken by a man to a woman as he goes off to do something with other men, and just what it is he's got to do is determined by men and patriarchy, not by women. It isn't up to women to decide what a real man is. Her role is to reassure men that they meet the standards of a male-identified patriarchal culture.

When a woman does question or attack a man's masculinity, the terms of the attack and the power behind it are based on men's standards of patriarchal manhood. She is not going to attack his manhood, for example, by telling him he isn't caring enough. When she uses what are culturally defined as *women's* terms—"You're not sensitive, nurturing, open, or vulnerable, and you're *too* controlling"—the attack has much less weight and produces far less effect. But when women do not play along—when they criticize or question or merely lose enthusiasm for affirming patriarchal manhood—they

risk the wrath of men who may feel undermined, abandoned, and even betrayed. Men may not like being criticized for failing to measure up to women's ideas of what men should be, but it's nothing compared to how angry and violent men can be toward women who dare to use men's weapons against them by questioning their manhood.

In the patriarchal cycle of control and fear, no man is safe from challenges to his manhood, which is why even the rich and powerful can be so quick to defend themselves. In his analysis of John F. Kennedy's presidency, for example, David Halberstam argues that Kennedy initiated U.S. involvement in the Vietnamese civil war in part because he failed to appear sufficiently tough and manly at his Vienna summit meeting with Soviet premier Nikita Khrushchev. Khrushchev challenged Kennedy from the start, and Kennedy, surprised, responded in kind only toward the end. Upon returning home, he felt the need for an opportunity to right the impression he had made and remove any doubts about his manhood. "If he [Khrushchev] thinks I'm inexperienced and have no guts," Kennedy told *New York Times* reporter James Reston, "... we won't get anywhere with him. So we have to act ... and Vietnam looks like the place."[11]

And so the horror of U.S. involvement in Vietnam turned on a political system organized in part around men's ability to impress one another with claims to manhood. And this no doubt played a prominent role in the tortured progress of that war and the stubborn refusal of all sides to compromise or admit defeat.

ENDNOTES

1. The following discussion draws on many sources, especially R. W. Connell, *Gender and Power: Society, the Person, and Sexual Politics* (Stanford, CA: Stanford University Press, 1987); Eisler, *The Chalice and the Blade*; Fisher, *Woman's Creation*; French, *Beyond Power*; David D. Gilmore, *Manhood in the Making: Cultural Concepts of Masculinity* (New Haven, CT: Yale University Press, 1990); Miriam M. Johnson, *Strong Mothers, Weak Wives: The Search for Gender Equality* (Berkeley: University of California Press, 1988); Lee and Daly, "Man's Domination"; Lerner, *The Creation of Patriarchy*; and Michael Schwalbe, *Manhood Acts: Gender and the Practices of Domination* (Boulder, CO: Paradigm, 2014).

2. For more on this, see, for example, Michael Kaufman, "The Construction of Masculinity and the Triad of Men's Violence," in Kaufman, *Beyond Patriarchy*, 1–29.

3. A form of ritual aggression most often associated with African American males in which the contest is to trade progressively harsher insults until one or the other contestant either gives up or cannot better the previous insult.

4. French, *Beyond Power*, 337.

5. See Doris Kearns Goodwin, *Lyndon Johnson and the American Dream* (New York: St. Martin's Press, 1991); and Jackson Katz, *Leading Men: Presidential Campaigns and the Politics of Manhood* (Northampton, MA: Interlink, 2012).

6. French, *Beyond Power*, 508, quoting Simone Weil, "Analysis of Oppression," in *Oppression and Liberty*, translated by Arthur Wills and John Petrie (Amherst: University of Massachusetts Press, 1973).

7. For pioneering work on a relational model of human development, see Jean Baker Miller, *Toward a New Psychology of Women*, 2nd ed. (Boston: Beacon Press, 1986).

8. This was the subject of a now-classic experiment in social psychology. See Manford Kuhn and Thomas McPartland, "An Empirical Investigation of Self Attitudes," *American Sociological Review* 19 (1954): 68–76.

9. Anyone who doubts this needs look no further than the nearest school playground and the persecution endured by boys who show any interest in playing with girls. Among adults, woe betide the man who openly prefers the company of women. See Barrie Thorne, *Gender Play: Girls and Boys in School* (New Brunswick, NJ: Rutgers University Press, 1993).

10. I haven't done the research, but I'd guess that men comprise the overwhelming majority of entries in the *Guinness World Records* book.

11. David Halberstam, *The Best and the Brightest* (New York: Random House, 1972), 76.

DISCUSSION QUESTIONS

1. Why does patriarchy occur? Why is it found in undeveloped societies in Africa, Asia, and the Middle East, but also in highly developed countries in Europe and the United States?

2. Is patriarchy the natural order of things? What arguments does Allan Johnson provide against "essentialism?"

3. Johnson says that patriarchy is "a men's problem," that it's a way men measure themselves against other men: "Modern patriarchy is driven by the dynamic between control and fear, of men seeking status and security through control, fearing other men's control over them, and seeking still more control as the only solution." Do you agree or disagree? Why? What role do women play in maintaining patriarchy?

4. What is misogyny? How is it expressed in our society today? How is it related to patriarchy?

5. Explain and evaluate the following statement: "Patriarchy's roots are also the roots of most human misery and injustice, including race, class, and ethnic oppression, and the ongoing destruction of the natural environment. The spiral of control and fear underlies a global reliance on militarism and toughness to solve problems and resolve disputes ... . In modern patriarchal societies, the default condition is to be running scared most of the time."

HOMOPHOBIA IN SPORT

Ice 'n' Go: Score in Sports and Life

BY **Jenny Moshak and Debby Schriver**

German psychologist Karolyn Maria Benkert first coined the term "homosexuality" in the late nineteenth century. While the word is relatively modern, lesbians, gays, bisexuals, and transgendered (LGBT) people have always existed. Historically, the ancient Greeks accepted and celebrated same-sex relationships through the teachings of Plato and the writings of Aristophanes. Voices of the fifth century BCE speak of gender attraction as a personal matter rather than a moral issue. In the present day, sexual orientation and gender expression are serious points of contention, sparking emotional, political, religious, and civil debate. In the sports world, homophobia, which is a generalized fear or intolerance of lesbians, gay men, bisexuals, and transgendered people, is rampant.

Because people fear difference, the fear of LGBT people is not so surprising. Homophobia rages in almost every segment of American society: young, middle-aged, and elderly; poor, middle-class, and rich; male and female. It can be found in every religion and in every city and town. It impacts workers in arts and culture, professional, and laboring positions. And of course, in sport.

What does this fear have to do with sport? Everything and nothing. Everything, because sport is not immune to social ills. Historically, people in all areas of sport were actively discriminated against based on race, gender, ethnicity, and religion. Racism played a key role in denying access to professional sports. Women once were perceived to be too weak for marathon running, weight lifting, and cycling. Following Hitler's rise to power in 1933, Nazi officials expelled top German athletes who were Jewish. Today, sexual orientation is the target of overt and silent discrimination at every level of sports—professional, Olympic, college, high school, and youth. And fear should have nothing to do with sports, because—just as with an athlete's race, gender, ethnicity, or religion—sexual orientation or identity has no bearing on athletic ability, leadership skills, or capacity for sportsmanship and heart.

Dr. Pat Griffin, Professor Emerita at the University of Massachusetts, Amherst, and author of *Strong Women, Deep Closets: Lesbians and Homophobia in Sport*, is working with the Gay, Lesbian and Straight Education Network (GLSEN) to address bias and behavior in sports at the K-12 levels. With a history of more than thirty years in higher education, Dr. Griffin has witnessed a changing climate regarding attitudes and acceptance. "When I started doing this work, I was a lone voice in the wilderness. It is good to see change and so many more people doing the work."

While LGBT people have gained some visibility and acceptance in the general culture through the media, athletic culture lags behind. Dr. Griffin feels that we need to consider the role sport has played historically in the larger culture. "Sport has defined masculinity. Sport is where boys learn to be men," Dr. Griffin explains. "I think that whether it is women in general or gay men and lesbians in particular who want to participate, they are a threat to that historical function."

Homophobia is so menacing and powerful that it stops people from coming out, from being who they are, from reaching their full potential, and it discourages them from playing sports or participating fully in society. In athletics, males and females can experience this differently. Athletics has historically been defined by masculinity and perpetuates a culture that is binary—male or female—with only two ways to fit. In general women can stretch the binary rules of male and female and be accepted as tomboys. Males are not allowed to stretch these rules with the effeminate stereotypes of gay men. The macho locker room is an inner sanctum populated by all the strong masculine stereotypes and follows the scripted military policy (at least until recently) of "Don't ask; don't tell."

Consider a quarterback of a top-ten college team or an All-America point guard. Their images have been cast in a mold that does not allow for differences. Universities have rich though sometimes narrow traditions. The phenomenon of student-athletes representing these traditions to alumni, fans, and the general public leaves little room for diversity.

Coming out is often a difficult decision. A few athletes choose to do so while at the peak of their career, some after their career has ended, and some are out long before they become involved in sports. It is rarely easy; it is sometimes disastrous; sometimes it is nearly a non-event. The positive side to coming out allows you to be true to self; puts an end to lies; often encourages others to come out; helps biased people realize they already knew and loved a gay person; and helps to normalize LGBT people to others. The negative aspects of coming out may include rejection and ridicule by family, friends, teammates, coaches, fans; ridicule by opponents; hate actions and threats; loss of endorsements; and loss of popularity. In spite of the possible negative ramifications, the widespread consensus is that life is better after coming out.

The number of professional athletes who have come out is miniscule. Most have done so after their playing careers have ended. Some of these sport greats include tennis icon Billie Jean King; football stars Esera Tauolo and David Kopay; baseball's Billy Bean and Glen Burke; and basketball center John Amaechi. A fine example of an athlete who came out during her playing career is tennis superstar Martina Navratilova. One bold sport administrator has come out while on the job. Rick Welts, then president and chief executive officer of the NBA Phoenix Suns, came out as gay on May 15, 2011, in an interview with the *New York Times*. The following fall he took a similar job with the Golden State Warriors in northern California to be closer to his partner. By comparison, the number of college athletes who have come out is astronomical, though in the grand scheme of things it is still quite small.

Andrew Langenfeld grew up playing sports. He also grew up knowing that he was different. As early as age six he vividly remembers asking his parents questions about sex and roles in male/female relationships, and by age seven he realized he was gay. He confided in his mother, but she convinced him that he would outgrow this phase. Growing up in a small mid-western town, Andrew says that he worried most about how close friends and family members would respond when he came out. He feared abandonment. When he was eighteen years old, he again told his mom that he was gay, and then in college, where he experienced his first relationship, he came out publicly. A standout swimmer, he earned a scholarship at the University of West Virginia and then transferred to Purdue University. He not only came out to his teammates, but he also took on the responsibility to educate them and carry the message to others.

Knowing the challenges that gay athletes can face, I asked Andrew how he found the strength to step forward. "Being a student-athlete is one of the most incredible experiences of your life, and you really want to have no regrets," he said. "I know a lot of people give up sport because they know they are gay, when really all they want is to be able to integrate all the parts that make up who they are."

Andrew has encountered positive and negative reactions. "At West Virginia, a friend and fellow athlete had preconceived ideas, but when he learned that I am gay, he realized that people are people. We started to hang out together. Then when some of his friends began asking him if we were dating, that really scared him. Eventually he told me that he could not continue to be friends with me because other people would think he was gay, too. That hurt."

At Purdue University, Andrew continued to be an advocate for gay athletes. When he became aware of derogatory language in the locker room, he suggested that he and his teammates write an email calling for change. "We were not just competitors in the pool. We were a family. There are athletes everywhere who don't have a gay teammate or who don't know another gay athlete. We realized there needed to be leadership and role models. This really sparked us to create an organization to help other student-athletes and form a national support network."

Andrew advises gay athletes to take it one step at a time. "Coming out is a process. I made sure that before I came out, I met a few other gay people so I had someone to talk to. I told a straight friend, and then I told my mom, taking my time, on my own terms. This pace made it so much easier for me. Word spreads quickly through a team. Make sure that you have a support group that's going to be there for you."

Dr. Sue Rankin, research associate in the Center for the Study of Higher Education at Pennsylvania State University, finds that individuals come out selectively to people they trust. "Out is on a continuum: out to your friends is one part; out to your nuclear family is another; out to your extended family; out to professional colleagues, if you are a coach, for example. There are very secretive pockets in athletics. Coming out is a daily process and is incredibly stressful."

Mother of a gay son, Meg McDaniel urges youth to love themselves first and find the courage to be who they are. Then, she says, they will find those who will love and embrace them. Meg says, "I have grown and learned so much from both of my sons. My message to parents of children who are LGBT is to let them know that your love is unconditional. My favorite quote is from author Anne Wilson Schaef, 'Children are the best teachers for helping us unlearn what we have learned.'" Meg says that she now knows that her son kept a lot of his thoughts and feelings from her because he was so conflicted about being gay. "I wish with all my heart I would have known what he was going through, because I would have been his chief ally."

Gay people are coming out much younger because of social networking, media exposure to role models, and greater public acceptance. Athletics, however, continues to perpetuate the binary culture that makes it impossible to be different in this system, according to Dr. Rankin. "If you don't fit what it means to be masculine or feminine, then you don't fit on that athletic team, and so you are weeded out; and in youth sports I think athletes experience that early."

Lee Turner played basketball as a child, and his experiences bear witness to Dr. Rankin's observations. Lee knew that he was different from other boys, and when he was in second grade, he began to understand that he is gay. He protected his secret until graduating from college. Lee remembers the alienation and isolation he experienced in the midst of homophobic comments and attitudes, particularly in sports. The male macho culture was frightening to him. "I never felt comfortable in the locker room and really would have preferred tennis to the team sports that were most popular for boys to play. Even though my brother was very good at baseball, I never played. The macho environment of that sport scared me."

One of the areas where homophobia is prevalent is in athletic recruiting. In "The Positive Approach: Recognizing, Challenging And Eliminating Negative Recruiting Based On Sexual Orientation," a paper Dr. Pat Griffin co-authored, she defined negative recruiting as when "coaches or other school representatives make negative comments or inferences about other schools and athletic programs rather than focusing on the positive qualities of their own school."[1] Negative recruiting is alive and well in women's athletics. One of our student-athletes told me that she experienced it. "On recruiting visits to another school the coaches reassured me and my family that we didn't have to worry about lesbianism—'We don't do that,' they boasted, and they were saying this to the parents of a girl who is gay." The actual or perceived sexual orientation of any coach, player, or staff member has no place in the recruiting process.

The documentary *Training Rules* tells the story of the destructive tragedy of homophobic practices by Rene Portland, the former women's head basketball coach at Penn State, and investigates why the university, which established policies to protect gay students, had done nothing to end this common form of victimization of their student-athletes. Coach Portland enforced three rules during her 26-year career: "(1) No drinking, (2) No drugs, and (3) No lesbians." The film's synopsis offers a chilling description of this real-life story: "Training Rules examines how a wealthy athletic department, enabled by the silence of a complacent university [blinded by winning records], allowed talented athletes, thought to be gay, to be dismissed from their college team. In 2006, student-athlete Jennifer Harris, in conjunction with the National Center for Lesbian Rights, filed charges against Penn State and Coach Portland for discrimination based on sexual orientation. This lawsuit inspired others whose lives were shattered during [her] reign to come forward."[2]

I saw Coach Portland's homophobic creed in action when I was an athletic trainer at Penn State from 1988–1989. One day I was covering a women's basketball practice as the softball team walked through the gym. Coach Portland said to me, "They are all a bunch of lesbians, and my goal is to get that team off this campus." As a lesbian, I knew I could not work with an actively homophobic coach in that targeted, unhealthy environment. That summer I accepted a position at the University of Tennessee.

Dr. Rankin finds that while progress in the battle against homophobia has been made on an institutional level, its impact has not been significantly felt for athletics. One student-athlete confided to her, "My coach and I kind of had a bumpy road in my career. He didn't communicate with me; he kind of cut me off. He was trying to get me to leave, and I never really understood why—all the older players warned me about him. Sometimes the coaches would say 'you need to be careful about who you hang out with' or they'd warn younger players not to hang out with certain teams, 'they will get you.'" Lauren P. shared her experience about being a lesbian collegiate volleyball player. "Being in the closet absolutely had an effect on me as a player. I find that a lot of energy goes into hiding a part of yourself from everybody around you. This is all driven by anxiety worrying about what everybody is going to think if they find out. It's sad when you can't be honest with the people you are closest to. This process is exhausting and depressing. It absolutely affected how I played. By the time you reach Division I college athletics, I truly believe it's about 20 percent physical and 80 percent mental. Generally, everybody at this level is physically similar, so the more successful athletes are the mentally tough ones. To carry on a charade like this affected my focus. I didn't feel that I could let down my guard and just relax because I was afraid. I always had to be 'on.' I don't feel that my teammates got to know the real me. It's not that being gay is such a huge part of who I am, but when you work so hard to hide it from other people, you end up hiding other parts of yourself."

Lauren P. went on to say, "My junior year I started to come out to a select few. When my roommate found out, she did not speak to me for three months and ended up transferring. That was a very difficult time. I heard gay slurs in the athletic department and all over campus. I eventually found a support network that made all the difference. I began to feel comfortable with myself and came out to family and friends. I remember when I came out to my sister, and she encouraged me to come out to my parents as well. I was terrified. She told me 'you need to give Mom and Dad more credit.' And she was right. My dad, who used the term 'faggot' more than I care to admit, now writes letters to the editor of our Ohio small town newspaper about his daughter having the right to marry just like anyone else. It was a pretty amazing transformation."

Endorsements, playing time, scholarships, coaching positions, and teaching and working with youth may be compromised when a female athlete discloses her sexual orientation. Sociologist Dr. Jay Coakley warns that "homophobia affects all women, lesbian and straight alike; it creates fears, it pressures women to conform to traditional gender roles, and it silences and makes invisible the lesbians who manage, coach, and play sports."[3]

One woman who preferred to remain completely anonymous told me, "When I was in high school and getting ready for college, I was deep in the closet and really feminine. Nobody ever suspected I was gay. I had a personal trainer who was an All-American, and one of the first things she talked to me about was that her first roommate was gay and to be careful. Little did she know, she was warning the wrong person." All through college she remained closeted to everyone except the select few she could trust.

With a desire to go into coaching, she feared her silence needed to continue, and this fear was confirmed. As a young club team coach, she was approached by some of the team's parents with an offer to help her select an interview outfit for a college coaching job. "They said, 'We will help you out—we can get something that looks professional, and still look feminine enough because you don't want to be labeled one of those dykey coaches.'" She said, "I know that there's a lot of homophobia in my sport, and it's a big concern for me. I know that I can't be out and be coaching."

Gay and lesbian coaches experience discrimination, as well. Lisa Howe, former soccer coach at Belmont University in Nashville, Tennessee, told me her story. She had been a head soccer coach for seventeen years in collegiate athletics. During her six years at Belmont, she won the 2008 Atlantic Sun Conference tournament and participated in the NCAA tournament for the first time in school history. Coach Howe found herself thrown into the national spotlight in December 2010 when, at the height of her career, this celebrated coach was forced to sign a "mutual agreement" with the university ending her coaching position. This agreement was made after she came out to her team as a lesbian and informed them that she was having a baby with her partner, Wendy. The team was very supportive; the administration was not. Her players and others close to the program told reporters she was fired for revealing the fact she was having a baby with her partner. Lisa grieved, saying, "I felt sad, angry, and, as my family's financial provider, fearful." The support poured in from faculty, students, and boosters, and from the local community and people across the country. The media took notice, creating a frenzy of debate with the majority speaking out against the injustice of the university's actions. Although Lisa is no longer coaching, her courage resulted in progress at Belmont. In January 2011, the board of trustees added sexual orientation to the school's non-discrimination policy. Lisa and Wendy named their little daughter Hope.

Lisa is currently executive director of the Nashville GLBT Chamber of Commerce. She knows that sport success is tied to diversity, and her goal is to show businesses that diversity and equality increase capacity and are positively tied to performance. Her advice to other lesbian and gay coaches is, "You are not alone. There is nothing more important to me than to live my life honestly and authentically. I know that people have to feel safe. Everyone has their own timing, and it's a very personal journey. You are not alone; there are lots of us out there."

The most recent LGBT issue in athletics today is the transgendered athlete. This issue is the only sexual orientation/gender identity topic addressed by NCAA legislation. The NCAA Inclusion of Transgender Student-Athletes policy "ensures transgendered student-athletes fair, respectful and legal access to college sports teams based on current medical and legal knowledge." The policy guides institutions to safeguard the privacy, safety, and dignity of transgendered student-athletes. Kye Allums is the first Division I transgendered student-athlete—female to male—basketball player on the George Washington University women's basketball team. He was allowed to continue playing on the team as long as he did not take the male hormone testosterone. In all other aspects he was treated as a male.

He had access to male locker rooms and restroom facilities in accordance with the Washington, D.C., law that ensures individuals the right to use gender-specific facilities that are consistent with their gender identity or expression. Male pronouns were used in the media guide, marketing, and coaching. Kye felt a great relief and satisfaction with his decision to be who he really is. He told the NCAA, "With the love and respect of the people around me, I no longer feel like I have to choose between being true to myself and staying in school playing the sport I love."[4]

Dr. Rankin makes a strong case for the prevention of prejudicial behavior through education. "Educate—get rid of the ignorance. Parents and institutional policy makers need to be educated. The discussion needs to be about power—who has it; what is it; how is it used; what privilege comes along with that power?"

Society dictates power and privilege according to how people are identified. White privilege is defined as a "right, advantage, or immunity granted to or enjoyed by white persons beyond the common advantage of all others."[5] White privilege is prevalent in our society, and most whites have no idea that they are privileged, which in and of itself proves that they are. Not long ago, a Caucasian friend of mine was at a convention with several colleagues. Due to a check-out time misunderstanding, the key to her hotel room did not work. She went to the front desk and asked for a new key. The clerk readily gave her one. Shortly thereafter, an African American colleague also asked for a new key. The clerk asked to see her ID.

Privilege extends to gender as well. Recently, my sister went to buy a car. The salesperson directed all eye contact and conversation to her husband, even saying, "Will the little lady be driving it as well?" They immediately walked out of the dealership. Ironically, at this time in their professional careers, she was the breadwinner of the household.

Occurrences of privilege exist even when the power characteristic is not overtly visible but assumed. Two qualified female candidates were the finalists for an assistant strength and conditioning position. One had more experience and stronger references; however, a key member of the search committee dismissed her, saying she was "not a good fit." While the actual words were not spoken, the rest of the committee assumed it was because she appeared to be a lesbian. The other candidate was hired.

In virtually every group, even those whose members have been discriminated against historically in this country, privilege and power exist. My brother overheard his African American neighbors talking about a Hispanic landscaping crew working next door. One said, "Bet those guys are illegals—ten bucks says they don't have papers."

Dr. Rankin is so right when she goes on to say, "We need people to be free to talk about what they think and how they feel about these issues," because a way to eliminate fear is to engage in open, inter-group dialogue. Putting names, faces, personal experiences, and emotions front and center will help us realize that we can accept people for who they are and celebrate our differences. I participated on campus with other administrators in a workshop designed to educate, stimulate conversation, resolve issues of conflict, and evaluate our current status as a just and diverse university. After getting to know me through group dialogue activities, one white, heterosexual, middle-aged male administrator came away with understanding, a greater awareness, compassion, and respect for gay people and is now actively working to improve our campus climate.

Struggles for acceptance in the sports world are not limited to athletes. Lindsy McLean, the highly respected head athletic trainer for the San Francisco 49ers, spent twenty-four years living in two worlds before his retirement. As McLean talked with me about his experiences, I felt anger for what he went through and admiration for the courage he brought to his athletic training room every day. McLean says he was aware of his sexual orientation as early as grammar school, when he had a crush on a classmate. Societal messages clearly denounced same sex dating, and McLean held onto the possibility that he might outgrow it. After dating a few women, he accepted that he is gay.

From 1968 to 1979, McLean was head athletic trainer at the University of Michigan, and during this time he came out to friend and colleague Dr. Robert Anderson, Michigan's team physician, whom he trusted. Although McLean found support within athletics, he did not experience that security across the board. One assistant football coach told McLean that he thought he had been "come on to" in the locker room at another school, saying, "I beat the pulp out of that guy." Despite the intolerance and even hostility he encountered, McLean said, "I still got up and did my job every day."

In 1979, he became the head athletic trainer for the San Francisco 49ers. McLean had a partner and didn't hide his sexual orientation, but he didn't go out of his way to mention it either. "I was working in a profession that wasn't accepting of gays, especially the players. I heard talk in the locker room that made me aware that they knew, and they didn't know quite how to deal with it, and that made me uncomfortable about coming out." At times he did feel supported by assistant athletic trainers, head coaches, and general managers.

During his career, he did suffer some physical and emotional attacks by players. Through it all, he remained professional and valued by the organization. Reflecting on those times, he theorizes why people are so homophobic. "It is something people don't understand, and they are fearful of the unknown." When McLean announced his retirement from the 49ers, a reporter from the *Santa Rosa Press Democrat* wrote a story about him that included his sexual orientation. "Before I agreed to do the article, I thought about it, talked to my partner, and I read a book, *Setting Them Straight: You CAN Do Something about Bigotry and Homophobia in Your Life*, by Betty Berzon. She motivated me when she wrote, 'The single most effective thing you can do to eliminate homophobia and bigotry is to come out.' So that convinced me to do the article."

He said that he feels almost universal support from peers across the profession. When I asked him how he would advise others who are gay, McLean said, "I don't suggest that they stay in the closet. Live your life without compromises but don't flaunt the fact that you are gay. If you let little comments get to you, you just can't survive. Earn respect by doing your job." A member of the National Athletic Trainers' Association Hall of Fame, Lindsy McLean's exemplary career illustrates that one's sexual orientation should not be an issue.

However, today, a person can be fired for their sexuality in twenty-nine states. Homophobia is pervasive. I feel gut-wrenching outrage at the unwillingness of educational institutions, governing sports organizations, and administrators to step up and say, "No more." During my twenty-five years, I have seen athletes leave their treasured sports because of their coach's prejudicial behavior toward them. To blend in, athletes change how they dress, how they act, how they talk—all attempts to hide who they really are. I have seen them create a phantom date or guy back home to disguise their lesbianism. I have seen academic troubles, falling grades, affected performance, and depression. I have seen an athlete be open to one person or group and closeted to another. I have seen conflict with parents and family as they apply pressure to conform to beliefs taught in their religious faith. I have heard the general athletic training room talk, the thoughtless use of slang such as the phrase, "that's so gay," and seen its powerful impact on the faces of athletes in the room. I have seen an athlete kicked off a team for vague reasons listed under the heading of attitude, when the true reason is that she is a lesbian or thought to be. I have seen athletes turn to alcohol for comfort in order to cope with their fear, because they feel they have no place to turn and no real protection. I have seen their spirits slip away bit by bit.

We must work to educate people who express homophobic and other discriminatory behaviors that threaten individuals. I am a leader on my campus, working with colleagues, faculty, and students to ensure that equality, acceptance, and respect are championed at the very top level and throughout the organization. I continue to educate my staff and athletes and create a culture where every individual can be their best regardless of sexual orientation or gender identity. One of the focal points in the athletic training room is my office's Diversity Window with its collage of stickers with slogans, symbols, and pictures of various cultures, religions, ethnicities, sexual orientations, and disabilities. It gets a lot of attention and encourages dialogue.

I have seen young women simply eager to grow, make lasting friends, develop their talents, become contributing citizens and find personal meaning just like everybody else. Athletes ask me advice about coming out. I tell them, "Be great at what you do. Be respectful, positive, and pleasant to everyone. If you are someone who people want to be around, how can they hate you? When you do come out, be comfortable with people who accept you and patient with those who don't."

Diversity window.

The slow change in culture, politics, and sport is frustrating. Equality will be attained through policy and governance to bring about social justice nationally and culturally by changing one person at a time. It requires commitment, courage to confront obstacles, patience, daily vigilance, and an open door. These are some of the very qualities that define a high-performing athlete. Despite how behind the culture of sport is regarding homophobia, I choose to believe that one day it will be a non-issue.

ENDNOTES

1. *Training Rules*, Woman Vision Production, 2009.
2. Coakley, *Sport in Society*, 212.
3. "Transgender Man Kye Allums Playing NCAA Women's Basketball," *San Diego Voice & Viewpoint*, http://sdvoice.info/index1.htm.
4. Kendall Clark, "Defining White Privilege," http//academic.udayton,edu/race/whiteness05.htm.

DISCUSSION QUESTIONS

1. Jenny Moshak and Debby Schriver consider the question of why there is so much homophobia in sports. They write: "While LGBT people have gained some visibility and acceptance in the general culture through the media, athletic culture lags behind." They seem to have a point; it is notable, for example, how few current MLB, NFL, and NBA players are out. What reason(s) do they give for this? What do you think of their explanation(s)?

2. What are some of the horror stories that Moshak and Schriver tell regarding homophobia in sports and discrimination against LGBT athletes?

3. What suggestions do Moshak and Schriver offer for combating homophobia in sport?

READING 2.8

SAFE SCHOOLS FOR TRANSGENDER AND GENDER DIVERSE STUDENTS

BY **National Association of School Psychologists**

The National Association of School Psychologists (NASP) supports efforts to ensure that schools are safe and inclusive learning environments for all students, family members, and school staff, including those who are transgender or gender diverse. NASP respects a person's right to express gender identity, and the right to modify gender expression when necessary for individual well-being. In addition, NASP supports all students' right to explore and question their gender identity. NASP is committed to a policy of nondiscrimination and the promotion of equal opportunity, fairness, justice, and respect for all persons (NASP, 2012).

NASP acknowledges that neither having a transgender identity nor being perceived as gender diverse is a disorder, and that efforts to change a person's gender identity are ineffective, harmful, and discriminatory. NASP works to ensure that settings in which school psychologists work are safe and welcoming and provide equal opportunity to all persons regardless of actual or perceived characteristics, including gender, gender identity, gender expression, sexual orientation, and any other personal identity or distinguishing characteristics (NASP, 2010). A glossary of terms may be found at the end of the statement.

NEEDS OF TRANSGENDER STUDENTS

In many communities, it is dangerous to be gender nonconforming or to be known as transgender. Many children, youth, and adults blend with their chosen gender, and are safe to the extent that their transgender status is hidden. Data concerning school-age transgender youth are limited, but what data are available suggest that more action by school officials is needed to ensure schools are settings in which students can thrive.

Because transgender youth are so hidden, it would be easy to believe that these students are extremely rare. It is extremely difficult to estimate the prevalence of transgender students in school (Meier & Labuski,

2013). One of the few large districts to gather data is San Francisco. In 2011, 0.5% of San Francisco high school students self-identified as transgender on the annual Youth Risk Behavioral Survey (Timothy Kordic, personal communication, December 20, 2013). The prevalence of self-identified transgender adults has been estimated as 0.3% of the U.S. general population (Gates, 2011).

The experiences that transgender students have at school appear to have effects on their well-being as adults. Toomey, Ryan, Diaz, Card, and Russell (2010) showed that while gender nonconformity alone had no direct effect on these outcomes, the victimization experienced at school associated with gender nonconformity had a lasting impact and put these children at risk for negative mental health outcomes in adulthood. Harassment and assault lead to anxiety about school, leading to missing days of school. Nearly half (46%) of transgender students reported missing at least one school day in the previous month because they felt unsafe (Greytak, Kosciw, & Diaz, 2009).

Research suggests that gender diverse children are at higher risk of physical, emotional, and sexual abuse and are at higher risk of posttraumatic stress disorder (PTSD) in adulthood, with about a third of the higher risk of PTSD accounted for by being abused as a child (Roberts, Rosario, Corliss, Koenen, & Austin, 2012). Coming out to family members often results in physical assault and expulsion from the family home (Ray, 2006). In one study, more than half of transgender youth reported initial parental reaction to coming out as negative or very negative (Grossman, D'Augelli, & Frank, 2011). Young adults who experience low family acceptance of identity are more likely to be at risk for depressive symptoms, substance use, and suicidal ideation and attempts (Ryan, Russell, Huebner, Diaz, & Sanchez, 2010). In addition to longitudinal outcome risks, transgender youth face immediate challenges during their school-age years. Transgender youth are often desperate to transition. However, even if they have medical insurance, the healthcare procedures necessary to transition are explicitly excluded from most health insurance plans. Psychotherapy for gender dysphoria is often excluded. Transgender youth may take hormones obtained on the street or through the Internet without medical supervision, and take excessive doses. They may seek silicone injections at "pumping parties," resulting in severe disfigurement or death.

Despite these challenges, many transgender youth are resilient and there are a number of factors that may help them guard against the worst outcomes. Resilience

in children and youth appears to depend on personal characteristics like being outgoing, resourceful, and having a positive self-concept. In addition, social relationships, such as having an emotional bond with at least one adult over a period of time, and having a supportive community are associated with resilience (Werner, 1995). Specifically for transgender and gender diverse children, attention has been focused on *family acceptance* and *school acceptance*. LGBT youth from families rated high in acceptance (e.g., they discuss their child's gender identity or sexual orientation openly, integrate their child's LGBT friends into family activities, express appreciation for their child's clothing choices even if the clothing was gender nonconforming) reported better self-esteem, better health, lower levels of depression, lower rates of substance abuse, lower rates of suicide attempts, and lower rates of risky sexual behavior (Ryan, Russell, Huebner, Diaz, & Sanchez, 2010). These findings suggest that similar acceptance in school environments is recommended.

CONSIDERATIONS FOR PARENTS, PHYSICIANS, AND SCHOOLS

To adequately support their child's growth, parents must allow their child's personality to unfold while simultaneously protecting them from harm (Ehrensaft, 2011). Families go through a developmental process in accepting a transgender or gender diverse child. Much depends on a parent's beliefs and understanding of child development and of gender. Some children have unexpected gender behavior at an early age, which persists in spite of parent attempts to divert the child to gender conforming behavior. Parents may be embarrassed or ashamed of their child's behavior, depending on conformity pressures coming from extended family members, neighbors, clergy, daycare providers, and others. Parents may fear the future for their child, as well as their own future as they are judged by other adults. The parent who is the same sex as the child may question his or her own effectiveness as a role model. Children and youth are more likely to have successful outcomes if parents work to create safe and supportive spaces for their child within the home, require others to respect their child, and express love for their child (Brill & Pepper, 2008).

The World Professional Association for Transgender Health (WPATH) *Standards of Care* for the psychiatric, psychological, medical, and surgical management of gender transition notes that "Treatment aimed at trying to change a person's gender identity and expression to become more congruent with sex assigned at birth has been attempted in the past without success. Such treatment is no longer considered ethical" (Coleman et al., 2011, p. 175).

Some students arrive at kindergarten already living in their asserted gender, while others express a desire to make a gender transition later in elementary or in secondary school. The majority of gender diverse children under age 9 who assert that they are a different gender than assigned at birth do not persist in asserting that gender in adolescence and early adulthood. By comparison, the majority of youth age 11 and older asserting a gender different than assigned at birth persist in that identity throughout adolescence and adulthood (Steensma, Biemond, de Boer, & Cohen-Kettenis, 2011). For children under age 9, only reversible social transitions are recommended (e.g., clothing, hair styles, activity preferences). For children age 11 or older, other treatments may be appropriate. A reversible medical treatment involving the administration of a gonadotropin-releasing hormone agonist (GnRH) in early puberty can put puberty on hold for several years, allowing the child time to mature and be ready for permanent changes. After puberty, youth can make more informed decisions regarding long-term treatment (Delemarre-van de Waal & Cohen-Kettenis, 2006; Spack, et al., 2012).

Educational persistence of transgender and gender diverse students may depend on their sense of safety and belonging in the school environment. Title IX of the Education Amendment Act of 1972 prohibits harassment of students on the basis of gender expression. Schools have a duty to ensure that gender diverse and transgender students are included in all school infrastructure. For example, providing gender-neutral bathroom options and avoiding the use of gender segregation in practices such as school uniforms, school dances, and extracurricular activities are structural ways to provide safer school environments (Toomey et al., 2010). The presence of a Gay–Straight Alliance (GSA) in school can lead to greater feelings of safety and belonging, better attendance, and lower rates of harassment (Toomey, Ryan, Diaz, & Russell, 2011). Comprehensive antiharassment policies that include protections for transgender and gender diverse students are helpful for all students. Adult intervention is helpful when homophobic or transphobic statements are heard (Case & Meier, 2014). Written policies and procedures addressing the needs of transgender and gender diverse students are helpful for staff and administrators and all students and families (e.g., Gay, Lesbian and Straight Education Network/National Center for Transgender Equality, 2011; Massachusetts DOESE, 2012).

ROLE OF THE SCHOOL PSYCHOLOGIST

The school psychologist should be in tune with the needs of students and staff, and can provide evidence-based information about transgender issues. The school psychologist should be welcoming and supportive of transgender and gender diverse staff and parents, and be able to foster a climate of acceptance and security for all (Case & Meier, 2014). A student's transgender status or history must be kept confidential and within the student's control. In all cases, school psychologists must be sensitive to the needs and welfare of all individuals at their school sites, including transgender and gender diverse students and staff. School psychologists must advocate for the civil rights of all students, including those who are transgender or gender diverse. This can be accomplished by:

- Advocating for gender-neutral spaces and helping establish safe zones for transgender students
- Seeking additional training or supervision as needed regarding issues affecting transgender and gender diverse people
- Modeling acceptance and respect
- Providing staff training to increase awareness regarding transgender issues in the schools
- Responding to bullying, intimidation, and other forms of harassment whether perpetrated by students or staff
- Minimizing bias by using phrasing and pronouns that are not gender specific and by avoiding gender stereotypes
- Providing counseling and attending to the social–emotional needs of transgender and gender diverse students in school
- Acquiring and providing information on community agencies that provide services and supports to the transgender community
- Supporting or contributing to research regarding best practices for integrating transgender and gender diverse students in school

Gender diverse and transgender students might be referred to a school psychologist due to school victimization or bullying, suicidal ideation or attempts, nonsuicidal self-injury, sexual orientation instead of gender issues, social anxiety, and/or autism spectrum symptoms. School psychologists should be aware of resources for these children and their families. Transgender and gender-diverse students may benefit from learning healthy coping skills and building resilience, but interventions for associated social–emotional problems should not attempt to enforce gender stereotypical behavior.

NASP's *Principles for Professional Ethics* (NASP, 2010) include provisions that pertain to gender diverse and transgender individuals, including the following:

- *Standard I.2.6*: School psychologists respect the right of privacy of students, parents, and colleagues with regard to sexual orientation, gender identity, or transgender status. They do not share information about the sexual orientation, gender identity, or transgender status of a student (including minors), parent, or school employee with anyone without that individual's permission.

- *Standard II.1.2*: Practitioners are obligated to pursue knowledge and understanding of the diverse cultural, linguistic, and experiential backgrounds of students, families, and other clients. When knowledge and understanding of diversity characteristics are essential to ensure competent assessment, intervention, or consultation, school psychologists have or obtain the training or supervision necessary to provide effective services, or they make appropriate referrals.

- *Principle I.3*: In their words and actions, school psychologists promote fairness and justice. They use their expertise to cultivate school climates that are safe and welcoming to all persons regardless of actual or perceived characteristics, including race, ethnicity, color, religion, ancestry, national origin, immigration status, socioeconomic status, primary language, gender, sexual orientation, gender identity, gender expression, disability, or any other distinguishing characteristic.

School psychologists should encourage schools to develop and implement policies and procedures to prevent harassment of gender diverse and transgender students in order to promote safe schools for all students. School psychologists can provide education about gender expression and LGBT issues to teachers, administrators, students, and staff (Toomey et al., 2010). School psychologists should encourage the formation of support or social groups for gender diverse and transgender students (Goodenow, Szalacha, & Westheimer, 2006; Toomey et al., 2010). School psychologists can work with teachers and administrators to serve as mentors for these students. Being accepted by even just one coach, teacher, or administrator can serve as a protective factor against negative psychosocial outcomes for these youth.

GLOSSARY

Language is evolving rapidly. Some terms that were considered acceptable in the past may be offensive in the present. Some previously offensive terms have been reclaimed by newer generations. We have attempted to use currently acceptable terms in this glossary. A glossary that is frequently updated is the *Media Reference Guide* available online from the Gay and Lesbian Alliance Against Defamation (GLAAD, 2010).

Asserted Gender. The gender a person declares to be, verbally, nonverbally, covertly, or overtly. A transgender person's gender is usually affirmed insistently, consistently, and persistently over years. In transgender people, there is a difference between birth-assigned gender and affirmed gender. In *cisgender* people, affirmed gender aligns with birth-assigned gender. Depending on ecological safety, gender affirmation may be nonverbal and covert, or it may be a verbal declaration ("coming out") in a safe place.

Cisgender. A person whose sex assigned at birth matches current gender identity. The opposite of *transgender*. "Nontransgender" is sometimes used, but implies that being transgender is not a normal variant of human difference.

Gender. *Gender* implies the psychological, behavioral, social, and cultural aspects of being male or female (VandenBos, 2007). Gender refers to the socially constructed roles, behaviors, activities, and attributes that a given society considers appropriate for boys and men or for girls and women (APA, 2011). While sex is a biological construct, gender is a social construct. As most people's sex and gender align, the two terms are sometimes used interchangeably.

Gender Assignment. *Gender assignment* is the classification of an infant at birth as either male or female (VandenBos, 2007); this assignment of a legal gender (sex) to a child triggers a variety of social events and developmental tasks related to gender role.

Gender Constancy. *Gender constancy* is a child's emerging sense of the permanence of being a boy or a girl (VandenBos, 2007), an understanding that occurs in stages but is mostly complete by age 7. School entry presents greater pressure to conform to gender expectations. At this age, some children with a gender identity incongruent with their birth-assigned sex may experience distress if they are not permitted to express and be witnessed as their gender. At clinically significant levels, this is called *gender dysphoria* (VandenBos, 2007).

Gender Dysphoria. Discontent with the physical or social aspects of one's own sex (VandenBos, 2007). The degree of distress can vary from mild to severe, and can be life long, although not all transgender people experience gender dysphoria. The child with gender dysphoria may demonstrate symptoms of depression, anxiety, self-harm, or oppositionality (APA, 2013).

Gender Diverse. Someone is *gender diverse* if his or her *gender expression* does not match what is culturally expected for the sex assigned at birth (Gender Equity Resource Center, n.d.). Individuals may dress or act in ways that others believe are not feminine enough or not masculine enough. Gender expression has become one aspect of diversity in human resource practice and in civil rights law, including nondiscrimination laws. Gender diverse implies that all humans express gender, and that no gender expression is inherently better than another. Gender diverse is an alternative term for *gender nonconformity*, which implies that gender diverse people are violating rules for gender expression; it is also an alternative for *gender variant*, which implies difference from a norm. Other respectful terms for gender diversity include *gender creative* and *gender expansive*.

Gender Expression. *Gender expression* refers to how a person represents or expresses gender identity to others, often through behavior, clothing, hairstyles, voice, or body characteristics (NCTE, May 2009). Gender expression is visible, while gender identity is not. Being gender diverse means having an unexpected gender expression; being transgender means having an unexpected gender identity. Some transgender people do not appear gender diverse. Some people with diverse gender expression are happy with their sex assigned at birth and have no desire or intention to transition genders.

Gender Identity. *Gender identity* is a person's internal sense of being male, female, both, or neither (APA

2011). This sense of maleness or femaleness typically develops from a combination of biological and psychic influences (VandenBos, 2007). Shortly after children begin to speak, most are able to state whether they are a boy or a girl, and this identity is stable and resistant to change. Gender identity typically forms between 2 and 5 years of age. For most people, gender identity is consistent with sex assigned at birth.

Genderqueer. A person who defies or does not accept stereotypical gender roles and may choose to live outside expected gender norms may self-identify as genderqueer. (Center for Excellence in Transgender Health, April, 2011). Genderqueer people may or may not avail themselves of hormonal or surgical treatments.

Sex. The term sex refers to a person's biological characteristics, including chromosomes, hormones, and anatomy (VandenBos, 2007).

Sexual Orientation. A person's gender identity is distinct from sexual orientation. *Sexual orientation* refers to an enduring pattern of emotional, romantic, and/or sexual attractions to men, women, both sexes, transgender people, no one, or all genders (APA, 2008; VandenBos, 2007). A transgender adult may be attracted to women, to men, to both women and men (bisexual), to no one (asexual), and/or to other transgender people. One's sexual orientation identity label is typically derived from gender identity, and not birth assigned sex. For example, a female-to-male transgender man who is primarily attracted to other men is likely to self-identify as gay. A male-to-female transgender woman who is primarily attracted to men is likely to identify as straight. Transgender people are more likely to also identify as LGBQ than cisgender people.

Trans. Shorthand term for a variety of transgender identities. Also, trans people or transpeople (Center for Excellence in Transgender Health, April 2011). Because there are a variety of disputes about the terms *transgender* and *transsexual*, trans is seen as a more widely accepted and respectful term than transgender. There are other terms which are more universally perceived as offensive, such as "tranny." See the GLAAD *Media Reference Guide* (2010) for terms that are universally offensive.

Transgender. *Transgender* refers to having a gender identity that differs from culturally determined gender roles and biological sex (VandenBos, 2007). It is an umbrella term that includes diverse identities and includes persons identifying as female-to-male, male-to-female, two-spirit, genderqueer, and other terms (APA, 2011). The transgender umbrella includes those assigned female at birth who are or who wish to be living as men (*transgender men*), and those assigned male at birth who are or who wish to be living as women (*transgender women*). Many transgender people appear indistinguishable from *cisgender* people. They may or may not desire body modifications to express their asserted gender. Body modifications may be temporary (e.g., shaving, changing hair style, binding, using hormone blockers) or permanent (e.g., hormones, electrolysis, surgeries; APA, 2011). Medical assistance can help transgender people live more comfortable lives as they may be better able to blend in as their affirmed gender. Transgender women typically identify as *women*, and transgender men typically identify as *men*.

Transition. The process of changing gender expression from that of one gender to another is called *transition* (APA, 2011). *Social transition* may include changes in clothing, grooming, pronouns, names, and identity documents. Children, adolescents, and adults may undergo social transition at any time. Medical transition may include hormones and surgeries. Surgeries are only available after age 18, after at least one year of living persistently and consistently as the desired gender. Youth who have lived persistently in their preferred gender and who have reached Tanner Stage 2 for their birth sex (around age 12 for female-born youth and about 14 for male-born youth) may be eligible for medication that can suppress puberty until they reach age 16 or older when they may be eligible to be treated with hormones appropriate to their desired gender, saving much of the expense, pain, and cost of medical transition for adults.

Acknowledgment of position statement writing group members: Jill Davidson (chair), Karla Anhalt, Lindsey Garzajohanson, Jim Hanson, Mary Beth Klotz, and Colt Meier. Acknowledgment is also extended to the Welcoming Schools Project of the Human Rights Campaign Foundation for their input.

Please cite this document as: National Association of School Psychologists. (2014). Safe schools for transgender and gender diverse students [Position statement]. Bethesda, MD: Author.

REFERENCES

American Psychiatric Association. (2013). *Diagnostic and statistical manual of mental disorders.* (5th Edition). Arlington, VA: American Psychiatric Publishing.

American Psychological Association. (2008). *Answers to your questions: For a better understanding of sexual orientation and homosexuality.* Washington, DC: Author. Retrieved from www.apa.org/topics/sorientation.pdf

American Psychological Association. (2011). *Answers to your questions about transgender people, gender identity, and gender expression.* Washington, DC: Author. Retrieved from http://www.apa.org/topics/sexuality/transgender.pdf

Brill, S., & Pepper, R. (2008). *The transgender child: A handbook for families and professionals.* San Francisco, CA: Cleis Press.

Case, K., & Meier, C. (2014). Developing allies to transgender and gender-nonconforming youth: Training for counselors and educators. *Journal of LGBT Youth, 11:1*, 62–82. doi:10.1080/193653.2014.840764

Center for Excellence in Transgender Health. (2011, April). *Primary care protocol for transgender patient care.* San Francisco, CA: University of California at San Francisco, Department of Family and Community Medicine. Retrieved from http://www.transhealth.ucsf.edu/trans?page=protocol-terminology

Coleman, E., Bockting, W., Botzer, M., Cohen-Kettenis, P., DeCuypere, G., Feldman, J., & Zucker, K. (2011). Standards of care for the health of transsexual, transgender, and gender-nonconforming people, Version 7. *International Journal of Transgenderism, 13*, 165–232. doi:10.1080/1553 2739.2011.700873

Delemarre-van de Waal, H. A., & Cohen-Kettenis, P. T. (2006). Clinical management of gender identity disorder in adolescents: A protocolon psychological and paediatric endocrinology aspects. *European Journal of Endocrinology, 155*, S131–S137. doi:10.1530/eje.1.02231

Ehrensaft, D. (2011). *Gender born, gender made.* New York, NY: The Experiment.

Gates, G. (2011, April). *How many people are lesbian, gay, bisexual, and transgender?* Los Angeles, CA: The Williams Institute, UCLA. Retrieved from http://williamsinstitute.law.ucla.edu/wp-content/uploads/Gates-How-Many-People-LGBT-Apr-2011.pdf

Gender Equity Resource Center. (n.d.). Gender diverse. *Definition of terms.* Berkeley, CA: University of California at Berkeley. Retrieved from http://geneq.berkeley.edu/lgbt_resources_definiton_of_terms#genderdiverse

GLAAD. (2001). *Media Reference Guide, 8th Edition.* Gay and Lesbian Alliance Against Defamation. Retrieved from http://www.glaad.org/files/MediaReferenceGuide2010.pdf

GLSEN/NCTE. (2011). *Model district policy for transgender and gender nonconforming students.* New York, NY: Gay, Lesbian and Straight Educators Network/National Center for Transgender Equality. Retrieved from http://www.glsen.org/binary-data/GLSEN_ATTACHMENTS/file/000/001/1977-1.pdf

Goodenow, C., Szalacha, L. A., & Westheimer, K. (2006). School support groups, other school factors, and the safety of sexual minority adolescents. *Psychology in the Schools, 43,* 573–589. doi:10.1002/pits.20173

Grant, J. M., Mottet, L. A., Tanis, J., Harrison, J., Herman, J. I., & Keisling, M. (2011). *Injustice at every turn: A report of the national transgender discrimination survey.* Washington, DC: National Center for Transgender Equality and National Gay and Lesbian Task Force. Retrieved from http://www.thetaskforce.org/reports_and_research/ntds

Greytak, E. A., Kosciw, J. G., & Diaz, E. M. (2009). *Harsh realities: The experiences of transgender youth in our nation's schools.* New York, NY: Gay, Lesbian and Straight Education Network. Retrieved from http://www.glsen.org

Grossman, A. H., D'Augelli, A. R., & Frank, J. A. (2011). Aspects of psychological resilience among transgender youth. *Journal of LGBT Youth, 8,* 103–115.

Massachusetts Department of Elementary and Secondary Education. (2012). *Guidance for Massachusetts public schools creating a safe and supportive school environment: Nondiscrimination on the basis of gender identity.* Malden, MA: Author. Retrieved from http://www.doe.mass.edu/ssce/GenderIdentity.pdf

Meier, C., Pardo, S., Olson, J., & Sharp, C. (2014). *Demographics of gender non-conforming children in the United States.* Submitted for presentation at the biennial symposium of the World Professional Association for Transgender Health in Bangkok, Thailand, February 2014.

Meier, S. C., & Labuski, C. M. (2013). The demographics of the transgender population. In A. K. Baumle (Ed.), *International handbook on the demography of sexuality* (pp. 289–327). New York, NY: Springer.

National Association of School Psychologists. (2010). *Principles for professional ethics.* Retrieved from http://www.nasponline.org/standards

National Association of School Psychologists. (2012). *Nondiscrimination and equal opportunity policy.* Retrieved from http://www.nasponline.org/leadership/nondiscrimination_equal_opportunity.pdf

NCTE. (2009, May). *Transgender terminology.* Washington, DC: National Center for Transgender Equality. Retrieved from http://transequality.org/Resources/NCTE_Trans Terminology.pdf

Ray, N. (2006). *Lesbian, gay, bisexual and transgender youth: An epidemic of homelessness.* New York, NY: National Gay and Lesbian Task Force Policy Institute and National Coalition for the Homeless. Retrieved from http://www.thetaskforce.org

Roberts, A. L., Rosario, M., Corliss, H. L., Koenen, K. C., & Austin, S. B. (2012). Childhood gender nonconformity: A risk indicator for childhood abuse and posttraumatic stress in youth. *Pediatrics, 129,* 410–417. doi:10.1542/peds.2011-180

Ryan, C., Russell, S. T., Huebner, D., Diaz, R., & Sanchez, J. (2011). Family acceptance in adolescence and the health of LGBT young adults. *Journal of Child and Adolescent Psychiatric Nursing, 23,* 205–213. doi:10.1111/j.1744-6171.2010.00246.x

Spack, N. P., Edwards-Leeper, L., Feldman, H. A., Leibowitz, S., Mandel, F., Diamond, D., & Vance, S. R. (2012). Children and adolescents with gender identity disorder referred to a pediatric medical center. *Pediatrics, 129,* 418–425. doi:10.1542/peds.2011-0907

Steensma, T. D., Biemond, R., de Boer, F., & Cohen-Kettenis, P. T. (2011). Desisting and persisting gender dysphoria after childhood: A qualitative follow-up study. *Clinical Child Psychology and Psychiatry, 16,* 498–516. doi:10.1177/1359104510378303

Toomey, R. B., Ryan, C., Diaz, R. M., Card, N. A., & Russell, S. T. (2010). Gender-nonconforming lesbian, gay, bisexual, and transgender youth: School victimization and young adult psychosocial adjustment. *Developmental Psychology, 46,* 1580-1589. doi:10.1037/a0020705

Toomey, R. B., Ryan, C., Diaz, R. M., & Russell, S. T. (2011). High school Gay–Straight Alliances (GSAs) and young adult well-being: An examination of GSA presence, participation, and perceived effectiveness. *Applied Developmental Science, 15,* 175–185. doi:10.1080/10888691.2011.607378

Travers, R. (2012). Mental Health. In *Improving the health of trans communities: Findings from the Trans PULSE project.* Ottawa, Canada: Rainbow Health Ontario Conference.

VandenBos, G. R. (Ed.). (2007). *APA dictionary of psychology.* Washington, DC: American Psychological Association.

Werner, E. E. (1995). Resilience in development. *Current Directions in Psychological Science, 4,* 81–85.

DISCUSSION QUESTIONS

1. Given the fact that transgender students make up only 0.3% of students, is the National Association of School Psychologists (NASP) statement, "Safe Schools for Transgender and Gender Diverse Students" necessary? Explain your answer.

2. Discuss the following statement: "To adequately support their child's growth, parents must allow their child's personality to unfold while simultaneously protecting them from harm. Families go through a developmental process in accepting a transgender or gender diverse child." Do you agree or disagree? Why? What sort of developmental process do parents of transgender or gender diverse children go through?

3. The NASP statement says that "some students arrive at kindergarten already living in their asserted gender, while others express a desire to make a gender transition later in elementary or secondary school." Evaluate this statement. Can children that young know that they need to make a gender transition? If so, what does this reality imply about how elementary and secondary schools interact with and teach their students?

READING 2.9

WHO PUT THE 'HETERO' IN SEXUALITY?

Transgender Identities: Towards a Social
Analysis of Gender Diversity

BY **Angie Fee**

PSYCHOLOGICAL CONSTRUCTION OF HETEROSEXUALITY

The identity categories of sex, gender, and sexual orientation are central to people's descriptions of their identity. Sexologists (Hirschfield 1868–1935; Kraft-Ebbing 1840–1902) of the late nineteenth and early twentieth centuries, studied sexual and gendered diversity and this laid the groundwork in establishing normative opposing gender and sexed distinctions based on a dualistically opposed sex/gender system. These historical and cultural conditions had a profound and long lasting impact on the emergence of heterosexuality as a dominant discourse for how people organised their sexual and gendered identities.

Katz's (1995) exploration of the concept of heterosexuality as a twentieth-century creation explores how Freud's (1962 [1905]) theory of the Oedipal complex both relies on, and creates, the institution of heterosexuality. It is this particular matrix—with its arrangement of gender, sex and desire—that influences the way people experience and think about their sexual and gendered identities. The Oedipal complex resides in different-sex desire, subsequently leading to a heteronormative theory of dichotomous gender development, and it is

a cornerstone of twentieth-century psychological theories. The Oedipal complex structures the direction of
identification and desire, in that identification is what
one would *like to be*, and desire is what one would *like
to have* but one cannot identify and desire the same
object. In this way, the concepts of identification and
desire are gendered and heterosexualised. Homosexual
desires are seen as heterosexual desires stemming from
the wrong identifications. The Oedipus complex is the
story that Freud creates about growing up and taming
these initial multiple desires.

It is worth questioning whether Freud's 'normal'
negotiation of the Oedipus complex is ever achieved.
My own psychotherapeutic work with people is testimony to how fluid desire is and how it flows in many
directions breaking up all kinds of imposed moral
codes (Moon 2008; Sanger 2008). In Freudian terms,
we can—at any point in life—still be at the mercy of
the pre-Oedipal state of 'polymorphous perversities'—a
time when neither we, nor the objects of our desire,
were defined through sexual difference, a time before
our gendered fate was sealed by strongly embedded
cultural messages. If Freud's theory that all children are
polymorphously perverse is to be believed, it is difficult
to understand how these multitudinous, undifferen-
tiated desires get so narrowly channelled into adult
procreative heterosexuality. His theory of identity does
not allow for diverse identifications and contradictions,
and the free play of polymorphous perversities are
constrained within the dominant cultural heterosexual
matrix. The Oedipal system entrenches, and continues
the reproduction of heterosexuality within the family,
repressing anything that is different. In these ways, the
Freudian view brought about increasingly rigid social
classifications of drives, desires and sexual relationships.

The Oedipal trajectory manifests itself in the construction of dualistic and hierarchical gender categories
whereby, traditionally, sexual orientation is dictated
by gender identity. The Oedipus myth, by relying on
a heterosexual psychic structure, accepts the social,
political and religious forms of domination in modern
Western society which effectively control and define
desire. Western heterosexuality defines what is male
and female, and gender is thus derived from it. This heterosexual matrix is unconsciously lived out to the extent
that it is marked as natural and given (Warner 2002).

Katz (1995) describes Freud's theory of psychosexual
development as an ethical journey, with the individual
working through the various stages from immature to
mature sexuality. Failure to achieve this progression

results in the homosexual who is fixated at an early
psychosexual stage; thus they are immature and polymorphously perverse—unsocialised and wild. Freud's
linear psychosexual development implies that the ideal
is an exclusive heterosexual who has learned to socially
restrict his or her roving sexual instinct. This position is
full of ethical meaning and, subversively, suggests that
heterosexuals are made, not born (de Beauvoir 1987
[1949]).

As the preceding discussion has demonstrated, the
Oedipal complex has been hugely influential in developing an associated heteronormative theory of sexed and
gender development where difference or otherness is a
condition of sexual desire. Richardson underlines how
the privileging of heterosexual relations as the bedrock
of social relations has reinforced the idea that 'heterosexuality is the original blueprint for interpersonal
relations' (1996: 3). As such, heterosexual identities
remain unremarkable, escaping critical scrutiny (Yep
2003: 29). Society uncritically incorporates and maintains 'heterosexuality' as an unchanging, unquestioned,
ahistorical idea, instead of seeing it as it actually is: one
particular arrangement of the sexes and their pleasure.
The next section examines how this alternative view
was advanced by Foucault (1978), who challenged the
heteronormative underpinnings of the institutions of
western society.

HISTORICAL CONSTRUCTION OF HETEROSEXUALITY

Foucault (1978) emphasises sexuality as having complex
roots in western culture and history. The first volume of
his *History of Sexuality* is a powerful account of different
views of sex and sexuality across various cultures and
periods of time. His 'archaeology of sex' illustrates how
our sexual beliefs and values are influenced by the social
institutions and discourses of the time in which we live.
He challenges the idea that sexuality is a natural 'truth',
arguing that it is a constructed category of experience
which has historical and cultural origins. Foucault
(1985) examines discourses from the ancient Greeks
to the Enlightenment with a view to examining how
discourses on sex and sexuality produce categories of
sexual practices and sexual identities which marked
people out as particular types. For instance, the
Greeks did not have the same social organisation of
sexed difference and eroticism as that which prevails
in contemporary Western society, and they did not
have a heterosexual/homosexual dualism. Foucault
(1978) notes how the Greeks saw sex as one of many

social activities compared to the dominant attitude in the Enlightenment where sexual activity reflected our 'true' identity. Individuals, and not just their acts, were labelled as normal and abnormal. This continues in modern discourses where there is a desire to classify and categorise particular sexualities and new ways of viewing people are produced. A key point in the history of sexuality occurred when people's sexuality was no longer used simply to classify them, but also to ascribe values and rights/privileges to these categories. This interest in sex in western societies is an example of what Foucault (1984) calls 'power-knowledge' which limits the possibilities of subjectivity—both of who we can be and the kinds of relationships that are possible. Thus we can begin to understand why he views sex and sexuality as phenomena that have much to do with social discourse and laws, and less to do with bodies and desires.

Foucault (1984) describes the defining event of the eighteenth century as the heterosexualisation of modern society where forms of knowledge established norms that were linked to the social order of the time. Garlick's (2003) paper, *What is a Man?*, explores Tim Hitchcock's (1996) account of heterosexualisation at work in eighteenth-century England, which involved a redefinition of what constituted 'sexual intercourse'. At the beginning of the century it was characterised by kissing, caressing, touching, and masturbation (what we now call foreplay by heterosexual definition). This changed at the end of century when it became more phallocentric; thus sexual intercourse referred explicitly to putting a penis in a vagina. Certainly, reproductive activity increased in the eighteenth century and Garlick (2003) cites Abelove's (1992) suggestion that this may be linked to the emphasis on production in the Industrial Revolution where the focus was on sex for reproduction rather than for pleasure. In this way, heterosexuality emphasises reproduction as an acceptable normative practice, but again this was responding to a broader need in society. It is within this context that homosexuals came to be seen as a 'species', one that did not fit with the nineteenth-century medical science framework.

Foucault (1978) highlights the regulating of sexuality, asserting that the category of modern homosexuality grew out of a specific historical context. At this point, the binary opposition between homosexuality and heterosexuality began to be formulated. Foucault (1978) argues that the normalisation of these ideas came about by repeating cultural practices and techniques, which continue to infiltrate minds and bodies and which,

in turn, cultivate beliefs and behaviours as seemingly natural qualities embedded in the individual psyche. Foucault's (1984) answer to this tendency is to demand an analysis of the historical, cultural and social politics of the time. He is less concerned with the essence of sexuality than with how it functions as a structure of power in society. Foucault's ideas paved the way for feminist theorists Butler (1990), Rich (1980), and Wittig (1992) who continued to critique the unquestioned assumptions of heterosexuality and its capacity to shape identity and desire by creating a 'compulsory heterosexuality' (Rich 1980: 23).

COMPULSORY HETEROSEXUALITY

Heterosexuality offers normative sexual positions that are intrinsically impossible to embody, and the persistent failure to identify fully and without coherence with these positions reveals heterosexuality itself not only as a compulsory law, but as an inevitable intrinsic comedy ... a constant parody of itself.

(Butler 1990: 122)

Much feminist writing has sought to argue that gender roles are not biologically given and natural, but socially and culturally constructed (Rich 1980; Butler 1990; Wittig 1992). In a highly influential book, Rich (1980) questions the assumption that women are naturally heterosexual and explores the links between heterosexuality and procreational economics. Rich's (1980) essay on compulsory heterosexuality was pioneering in her depiction of heterosexuality as yet another socially produced fiction that constructed and maintained a binary heterosexual order on which the foundation of gender was built. She emphasises how heterosexuality, as an institution, maintains the oppression of women. French feminist theorist Wittig (1992) continues this debate, arguing that the categories of men and women, indeed all sexual categories, are the products of a gender hierarchy which is institutionalised as heterosexuality. Rich (1980) and Wittig (1992) challenge the idea of heterosexuality as 'natural', and view it as a social construct. Whether sexuality is seen as a something that is psychologically achieved or socially constructed, Freud, albeit perhaps unwittingly, and the feminist theorists, draw attention to the notion that heterosexuality is not a 'natural' state.

Wittig (1992) and Rich (1980) paved the way for Butler's (1990) postmodern critique of heterosexuality as an unexamined discourse. Butler's (1990: 151) translation of the unrelenting tyranny of heterosexuality is described as the 'heterosexual matrix', which designates that grid of cultural intelligibility through which bodies, genders and desires are naturalised. Butler (1990: 15) argues that this results in the heterosexualisation of desire which requires and institutes the production of discrete and asymmetrical oppositions between feminine and masculine. The normalisation of heterosexuality is a social phenomenon and promotes a sexuality that is based on the principle that opposites attract which, in turn, perpetuates the reproduction of a binary gender system. In this way, heterosexual identity is affirmed and stabilised through sexual and gendered categories that become norms. Butler (1990) argues that this exclusive binary framework of sexual duality has key consequences in how desire is constructed and in how homosexuality is interpreted as a failed development. Sex, gender, and sexuality are thought of as distinct variables described as having binary characteristics: bodies are either female or male; gender presentation, behavioural dispositions, and social roles are either masculine or feminine; and sexuality is either heterosexual or homosexual (Lorber 2000: 144). The gendered idea of biological sex produces the binary notion of 'opposite sexes' that maintain the workings of the heterosexual matrix. These then become the basis of social identities that often remain unquestioned.

Butler's (1990) critique of the heterosexual matrix exposes the unquestioned intelligibility of individuals who conform and define within a binary oppositional relation. The heterosexual matrix describes the boundaries of expression and social acceptance by defining what is natural and unnatural within the governing law, and this matrix is reinforced by those that fall outside it. Butler (Butler, Osborne and Segal 1994: 4) is alert to the possible reification of the heterosexual matrix, as explored in *Gender Trouble* (1990), whereby it becomes a 'kind of totalizing symbolic'. Butler (1993) uses the term 'heterosexual hegemony' in her subsequent publication *Bodies that Matter* as a way of suggesting that this matrix is open for rearticulation. In this way, Butler draws attention to how any discourse can become hegemonic and produce identities that then become normative by repeating and producing specific modes of expression and behaviour. From this point, the following section examines the ways that heterosexuality

has become hegemonically embedded as a deep social norm and considers how it influences the ways in which people identify their sexual and gendered identities, and impacts upon the kind of relationships they have.

Heterosexuality is not simply a form of sexual expression or practice; it is institutionalised through the law and the state and is embedded in social interaction and practice. Normative heterosexuality describes a particular traditional gender arrangement and is based on the western sex/gender model—one based on difference, particularly the physical difference between sexes; and then gender is mapped onto this. In the 1990s, the theoretical concept of heteronormativity became established in gender/feminist/queer studies (Rosenberg 2008), and was used to describe the social norm of heterosexuality which has become embodied and is lived without question.

One of the most common heteronormative assumptions is that woman and men are 'made for each other', with vaginal penetration by a penis seen as '*the* sex act' (Hitchcock 1996: 79). This assumption remains entrenched, along with the belief that male and female sexuality are naturally different. These assumptions are continually produced and reproduced in social practice. One example of how this happens comes from Celia Kitzinger's (2005) work on displays of heterosexual identity through talk. She found that many people have a normative understanding of families as related by law and blood. Studying everyday social interactions make visible the mundane ways in which people, not on purpose, reproduce a world that marginalises non-heterosexuals. She illustrates how the role of biological parents in families is prioritised over non-biological parents. An example of this is the mother of a lesbian whose partner gave birth to a daughter. When this mother was asked to treat the child as her 'granddaughter' she could not do so and called her 'my daughter's friend's daughter' instead (Epstein 1994: 83). The heterosexual family produces familial terminology that takes for granted non-recognitional person references such as wife, husband, and son—membership categories that do not require you to use the person's name. There is no name for an intimate caring social unit that does not rely on a normative understanding of family as something which comprises of one father and one mother.

Heterosexuality is a particular historical arrangement of human relationships, of the sexes, their pleasures and desires, and it can limit our vision of any other sexed community. Dominant western heteronormative discourse dictates how the categories of sex, gender, and sexuality should interact with each other and this has had significant limitations for the development of categories outwith a binary system. Can we create a space outside the assumptions of heterosexuality? Would this change the way we understand ourselves, and open new possibilities for sexual expression, awareness and acceptance? There is an important developing body of work that poses challenges to the heterosexualisation of identities and desires (Califia 1997; Hines 2007; Monro 2007; Moon 2008; Sanger 2008). My own research and psychotherapeutic work makes it clear that there are multiple ways of being identified, embodied and having sexual relationships, and yet, the dominance of the hegemonic heterosexual discourse is still evident as a constraint on self-identification. In order to begin to imagine a space without sexed and gendered binary identities we need to become more aware of how they are woven into everyday social life and practices that take for granted such presumptions. These include the idea that there are only two sexes; that it is natural for people of opposite sexes to be attracted to each other; that these attractions may be publicly displayed and celebrated; and that the social institution of marriage and the notion of family are all organised around opposite sex coupling. Thus 'same sex' couples are, if not 'deviant', at least seen as 'alternative'. In these ways, heterosexuality is continually reproduced as natural and unproblematic, and in consequence, anything else is seen as unnatural, problematic and less valuable.

So far, this chapter has illustrated the significance and influence of cultural and collective processes on how people understand and experience sexed and gendered identities, and how heterosexuality has become a naturalised status. I will now turn to an examination of the emergence of transgender as a category within the dominant culture of heterosexuality.

...

DECONSTRUCTING HETEROSEXUAL IDEOLOGY

In the last 30 years, gender and cultural studies, feminist theory and queer theory have all made significant contributions to the destabilisation and demystification of heteronormative ideology. One of the first feminist critiques of the social structuring of heterosexuality emerged from the development of sexual politics with the feminist movement linking 'the sexual' with power and politics. Feminist theory (Crawford 1993; Jackson

1995, 1996, 1999, 2006; Richardson 1996) examines how 'normative' heterosexuality affects the lives of heterosexuals. Jackson is keen to remind us of a neglected legacy that 'institutionalised, normative heterosexuality regulates those kept *within* its boundaries as well as marginalising and sanctioning those *outside* them' (2006: 105). This illustrates a key point; that heteronormativity is concerned with not only normative sexuality but also with normative ways of life.

The processes of normalisation that sustain the current heteronormative paradigm have been taken up by queer theorists such as Butler (1990, 1993, 1997a, 1997b, 1999, 2004), Stone (1991), Sedgwick (1985, 1990), Warner (1993, 1999), Halperin (1990, 1995), Seidman (1996), Halberstam (1998, 2005), and Garber (1992). They all significantly build on Foucault's (1978) argument that sexuality is discursively produced, and extend it to include gender. Queer theorists argue that it is possible to have a society that is not organised by a heterosexual norm and that sexuality and gender need not be reducible to each other. In other words 'queer' is concerned with challenging basic hegemonic assumptions about the social and political world by subverting the normative rules of the heterosexual matrix and opening up spaces between the sexual and gender binaries. As Warner (1993) emphasises, 'queer' does not define itself against the heterosexual but against the very notion of the normal.

Feminist psychoanalysts (Benjamin 1988, 1996, 1998; Dimen 2002, 2003; Goldner 2002) are contesting the normalising knowledge of heterosexuality. Benjamin (1998) and Dimen (2002) have been questioning whether a single unified gender identity is necessary to be considered healthy. Maybe, they suggest, it is actually the attempt to create a single gender identity which creates pathology (Goldner 2002), These analysts have begun to question the taken for granted assumptions of everyday thinking on gender, advocating new ways of bringing this thinking into the consulting room. This means being able to stay with multiple meanings, shifting identifications, as well as bearing contradictions and ambiguities that cannot be understood within the gendered, binary language of psychotherapy. At the same time, it is necessary to resist the temptation of assuming a gender free space, a liberal post-modern stance of flexibility and ambiguity, which denies the inevitable gender ideology that society has internalised. Even though I advocate challenging the gender binary, the reality that gender is a central organising principle cannot be ignored. The thought of not having a stable gender identity is a frightening one for many—what would our point of reference be if we were not categorised as a man or a woman?

Being part of an established and recognised group in society is an important aspect of developing self-esteem and an identity. The formation of an individual's identity requires recognition that the individual exists, and in this way, people are dependent on what is outside of them to reflect back a sense of being. In my work as a psychotherapist and trainer, I am witness to how it is a struggle for many people to become an intelligible and recognisable human within the current theoretical and political discourse of heteronormativity and the

laws of desire that operate within this. Heterosexuality is a potent sign and it influences how we live our lives, how we learn and how we see desire and this is why it is so difficult to destabilise. We rarely study the norm or social process of normalisation—it is easier to probe and study the abnormal and the deviant, hence the many studies and research projects on transvestites, transsexuals, gays and lesbians. Although society has become more affirming of diversity and difference, heterosexuality is still treated as a monolithic and unitary concept (Crawford 1993; Eliason 1995; Jackson 1996, 1999; Smart, 1996; Yep 2003)

REFERENCES

Abelove, H. (1992) 'Some speculations on the history of "sexual intercourse" during the "long eighteenth-century" in England', in A. Parker, M. Russo and P. Yaeger (eds) *Nationalisms & Sexualities*, New York: Routledge.

Beasley, C. (2005) *Gender and Sexuality: Critical Theories, Critical Thinkers*, London: Sage.

Benjamin, J. (1988) *The Bonds of Love: Psychoanalysis, Feminism, and the Problems of Domination*, New York: Pantheon Books Inc.

_____. (1996) *Like Subjects, Love Objects: Essays on Recognition, Identification, and Difference*, New Haven: Yale University Press.

_____. (1998) *Shadow of the Other: Intersubjectivity and Gender in Psychoanalysis*, London: Routledge.

Bornstein, K. (1994) *Gender Outlaw: On Men, Women, and the Rest of Us*, New York: Routledge.

_____. (1998) *My Gender Workbook: How to Become the Kind of Man or Women You Always Thought You Could Be ... or Something Else Entirely*, New York: Routledge.

Butler, J. (1990) *Gender Trouble: Feminism and the Subversion of Identity*, New York: Routledge.

_____. (1993) *Bodies That Matter: On the Discursive Limits of 'Sex'*, New York: Routledge.

_____. (1997a) *The Psychic Life of Power: Theories in Subjection*, Stanford, California: Stanford University Press.

_____. (1997b) 'Performative acts and gender constitutions: an essay in phenomenology and feminist theory', in K. Conboy, N. Medina and S. Stanbury (eds) *Writing on the Body: Female Embodiment and Feminist Theory*, New York: Columbia University Press.

_____. (2004) *Undoing Gender*, New York: Routledge.

Butler, J., Osborne, P. and Segal, L. (1994) 'Gender as performance: an interview with Judith Butler', *Radical Philosophy*, 67: 32–39.

Califia, P. (1997) *Sex Changes: The Politics of Transgenderism*, San Francisco: Cleis Press.

Crawford, M. (1993) 'Identity, "passing" and subversion', in S. Wilkinson and C. Kitzinger (eds) *A Feminism and Psychology Reader*, London: Sage.

Cromwell, J. (1999) *Transmen and FTMs: Identities, Bodies, Genders and Sexualities*, San Fransisco: Cleiss Press.

De Beauvoir, S. (1987 [1949]) *The Second Sex*, trans. H. M. Parsley, London: Penguin Books.

Devor, H. (1989) *Gender Blending: Confronting the Limits of Duality*, Bloomington: Indiana University Press.

Devor, A H. and Matte, N. (2004) 'ONE Inc. and Reed Erickson: the uneasy collaboration of gay and trans activism, 1964–2003', *GLQ: A Journal of Lesbian and Gay Studies*, 10(4): 179–209.

Dimen, M. (2002) 'Deconstructing difference: gender, splitting, and transitional space', in M. Dimen and V. Goldner (eds) *Gender in Psychoanalytic Space*, New York: Other Press LLC.

_____. (2003) *Sexuality, Intimacy, Power (Relational Perspectives Book Series)*, New York: Routledge.

Eliason, M. J. (1995) 'Accounts of identity formation in heterosexual students', *Sex Role*, 32: 821–834.

Epstein, R. (1994) 'Lesbian parenting: cracking the shell of the nuclear family', in M. Oikawa, D. Falconer, and A. Decter (eds) *Resist: Essays Against a Homophobic Culture*, Toronto: Women's Press.

Feinberg, L. (1993) *Stone Butch Blues: A Novel*, New York: World View.

_____. (1996) *Transgender Warriors: Making History from Joan of Arc to Rupaul*, Boston: Beacon Press.

Foucault, M. (1978) *The History of Sexuality: An Introduction (Vol. 1)*, New York: Pantheon Books.

_____. (1984) 'Nietzsche, genealogy, history', in P. Rainbow (ed.) *The Foucault Reader*, New York: Pantheon Books.

_____. (1985) *The History of Sexuality: The Use of Pleasure (Vol. 2)*, New York: Vintage Books.

Freud, S. (1962 [1905]) *Three Essays on the Theory of Sexuality*, trans. and ed. J. Strachey, New York: Basic Books.

Fuss, D. (1989) *Essentially Speaking: Feminism, Nature and Difference*, Routledge: London.

Garber, M. (1992) *Vested Interests: Cross Dressing and Cultural Anxiety*, New York: Routledge.

Garlick, S. (2003) 'What is a man? Heterosexuality and the technology of masculinity', *Men and Masculinities*, 6(2): 156–172.

Gilbert, M. A. (2000) 'The transgendered philosopher', *International Journal of Transgenderism*, 14(3). http://www.haworthpress.com/store/product.asp?sku=J485 (accessed 12 May 2009).

Goldner, V. (2002) 'Toward a critical relational theory of gender', in M. Dimen and V. Goldner (eds) *Gender in Psychoanalytic Space*, New York: Other Press.

Halberstam, J. (1998) *Female Masculinity*, Durham, NC: Duke University Press

_____. (2005) *In a Queer Time and Place: Transgender Bodies, Subcultural Lives*, New York: New York University Press.

Halperin, D. (1990) *One Hundred Years of Homosexuality and Other Essays on Greek Love*, New York: Routledge.

_____. (1995) *Saint Foucault: Towards a Gay Hagiography*, New York: Oxford University Press.

Hines, S. (2007) '(Trans)forming gender: social change and transgender citizenship', *Sociological Research Online*, 12(1). http://www.socresonline.org.uk/12/1/hines.html (accessed 26 May 2009).

Hird, M. J. (2002) 'For a sociology of transsexualism', *Feminist Theory*, 36(3): 577–95.

Hitchcock, T. (1996) 'Redefining sex in eighteenth-century England', *History Workshop Journal*, 41: 73–90.

Jackson, S. (1995) 'Heterosexuality, power and pleasure', *Feminism and Psychology*, 5(1): 131–135.

_____. (1996) 'Heterosexuality as a problem for feminist theory', in L. Adkins and V. Merchant (eds) *Sexualising the Social: Power and the Organisation of Sexuality*, New York: St Martin's Press.

_____. (1999) *Heterosexuality in Question*, London: Sage.

_____. (2006) 'Gender, sexuality and heterosexuality', *Feminist Theory*, 7(1): 105–121.

Katz, J. (1995) *The Invention of Heterosexuality*, London: Penguin Books.

Kitzinger, C. (2005) 'Heteronormativity in action: reproducing the heterosexual nuclear family in after-hours medical calls', *Social Problems*, 52(4): 477–498.

Kuhling, C. and Kinsman, G. (2002–3) 'Addressing the politics of social erasure: making transsexual lives visible—an interview with Vivian K. Namaste', *New Socialist Magazine*, 39: http://www.newsocilaist.org/magazine/39/article04.html (accessed 12 April 2009).

Lazenby, J. M. (2007) *The Early Wittgenstein on Religion (Continuum Studies in British Philosophy)*, London: Continuum International Publishing Group.

Lorber, J. (2000) 'Using gender to undo gender: a feminist degendering movement', *Feminist Theory*, 1(1): 79–95.

Monro, S. (2007) 'Transmuting gender binaries', *Sociological Research Online*, 12(1). http://www.socresonline.org.uk/12/1/hines.html (accessed 16 March 2009).

Moon, L. (2008) 'Queer(y)ing the heterosexualisation of emotion', in L. Moon (ed.) *Feeling Queer or Queer Feelings? Radical Approaches to Counselling Sex, Sexualities and Genders*, East Sussex: Routledge.

Namaste, V. K. (2000) *Invisible Lives: The Erasure of Transsexual and Transgendered People*, Chicago: University of Chicago Press.

_____. (2005) *Sex Change, Social Change: Reflections on Identity, Institutions, and Imperialism*, Toronto: Women's Press.

Prosser, J. (1995) 'No place like home: the transgendered narrative of Leslie Feinberg's *Stone Butch Blues*', *Modern Fiction Studies*, 41(3/4): 483–514.

_____. (1998) *Second Skins: The Body Narratives of Transsexuality*, New York: Columbia University Press.

Rich, A. (1980) *Compulsory Heterosexuality and Lesbian Existence*, London: Onlywomen Ltd. Press.

Richardson, D. (1996) 'Heterosexuality and social theory', in D. Richardson (ed.) *Theorising Heterosexuality: Telling it Straight*, Buckingham: Open University Press.

Rosenberg, T. (2008) 'Locally queer: a note on the feminist genealogy of queer theory', *Graduate Journal of Social Science*, 5(2). http://www.gjss.org (accessed 3 May 2009).

Sanger, T. (2008) 'Queer(y)ing gender and sexuality: transpeople's lived experiences and intimate relationships', in L. Moon (ed.) *Feeling Queer or Queer Feelings? Radical Approaches to Counselling Sex, Sexualities and Genders*, East Sussex: Routledge.

Sedgwick, E. (1985) *Between Men: English Literature and Male Homosexual Desire*, Columbia: Columbia University Press.

_____. (1990) *Epistemology of the Closet*, Berkeley: University of California Press.

Seidman, S. (1996) 'Introduction', in S.Seidman (ed.) *Queer Theory/Sociology*, Cambridge, MA: Blackwell.

Smart, C. (1996) 'Collusion, collaboration and confession: on moving beyond the heterosexuality debate', in D. Richardson (ed.) *Theorising Heterosexuality: Telling it Straight*, Buckingham: Open University Press.

Stone, S. (1991) 'The empire strikes back: A post-transsexual manifesto', in: D. Epstein and K. Straub (eds) *Body Guards: The Cultural Politics of Gender and Ambiguity'*, London: Routledge Publications.

Stryker, S. (1994) 'My words to Victor Frankenstein above the village of Chamounix: performing transgender rage', *GLQ: A Journal of Lesbian and Gay Studies*, 13: 237–254.

Stryker, S. (2006) '(De)subjugated knowledges: an introduction to transgender studies', in S. Stryker and S. Whittle (eds) *The Transgender Studies Reader*, New York: Routledge.

Warner, M. (1993) 'Introduction', in M. Warner (ed.) *Fear of a Queer Planet: Queer Politics and Social Theory*, Minneapolis: University of Minnesota Press.

_____. (1999) *The Trouble with Normal: Sex, Politics, and the Ethics of Queer Life*, New York: The Free Press.

_____. (2002) *Publics and Counterpublics*, New York: Zone Books.

Whittle, S. (1996a) *The Transvestite, the Transsexual and the Law*, 3rd Edition, London: Beaumont Trust.

_____. (1996b) 'Gender fucking or fucking gender?' in R. Ekins and D. King (eds) *Blending Genders: Social Aspects of Cross-Dressing and Sex Changing*, London: Routledge.

_____. (1999) 'Transgender rights: the European Court of Human Rights and new identity politics for the new age', in A. Hegarty and S. Leonard (eds) *Human Rights: An Agenda for the 21st Century*, London: Cavendish Publishing.

_____. (2006a) 'Foreword', in S. Whittle and S. Stryker (eds) *The Transgender Studies Reader*, New York: Routledge.

_____. (2006b) 'Where did we go wrong? Feminism and trans theory–two teams on the same side?' in S. Stryker and S. Whittle (eds) *The Transgender Studies Reader*, New York: Routledge.

Whittle, S. and Turner, L. (2007) '"Sex changes"? Paradigm shifts in "sex and gender" following the Gender Recognition Act', *Sociological Research Online*, 12(1). http://www.socresonline.org.uk/12/1/whittle.html (accessed 12 February 2009).

Wilchins, R. A. (1997) *Read My Lips: Sexual Subversion and the End of Gender*, Ithica: Firebrand.

Wittig, M. (1998 [1992]) 'The straight mind', in S. Jackson and S. Scott (eds) *Feminism and Sexuality*, New York: Harvester Wheatsheaf.

Yep, G. (2003) 'The violence of heteronormativity in communication studies: notes on injury, healing, and queer world-making', in G. A. Yep, K. Lovaas and J. P. Elia (eds) *Queer Theory and Communication: From Disciplining Queers to Queering the Discipline(s)*, New York: Harrington Park Press.

DISCUSSION QUESTIONS

1. How has heterosexuality become an organizing principle in understanding and experiencing sexual and gendered identities?

2. What are the cultural conditions that shape and regulate our understanding of sex, gender, and desire?

3. How does the term "transgender" fit into our discussions of sex and gender? What does the word "transgender" mean? What does it not mean? How is transgender identity constructed and produced in Western societies today?

4. Evaluate the following statements. What does each statement mean? Do you agree or disagree with the statement? Why or why not?

5. "Society uncritically incorporates and maintains 'heterosexuality' as an unchanging, unquestioned, ahistorical idea instead of seeing it as it actually is: one particular arrangement of the sexes and their pleasure."

6. "Heterosexuality needs to be deconstructed and the discourse reformulated, if the lived experiences and aspirations of most people, not only transgendered people, are to be heard and accommodated."

READING 2.10

TRANS: A PERSONAL STORY

BY **Jill Davidson**

I am a school psychologist, a member of NASP, and a woman of transgender history. If you meet me, you've met only one trans person; we all have different stories and different places we have located ourselves in the gender universe.

Assigned male at birth, I knew by age 4 (1959) that I was more like the girls in my neighborhood. I transitioned to female in 2010, by which time it had become safe to do so.

Much has changed in my lifetime. The flared slacks, blouse, and blazer I might confidently wear to work today would have gotten me arrested in 1970 in most U.S. cities, if I was perceived by the arresting officer to be biologically male. The crime might be called vagrancy, impersonation, fraud, or moral turpitude, but the real crime would be gender nonconformity. If I had been arrested, I might have been offered "treatment" in lieu of jail, which might include hospitalization, electroconvulsive therapy, extra testosterone, or other treatments without evidentiary support. Today, many trans people still believe their safety depends on "passing"; that is, their safety depends on being invisible.

My early childhood seemed gender free. We all climbed trees, built forts, had chicken fights, learned to cartwheel, and played with Barbies. But I knew I wasn't like the boys. Gender policing became intense when I entered elementary school. Boys were not supposed to cry. Boys were supposed to fight to defend themselves. I was praised for fighting. My parents put me in Little League. Uncorrected myopia made it difficult to see the ball. I believed that I was bad at baseball, not because I couldn't see, but because I should have been a girl. I didn't see girls playing, and I assumed girls couldn't play ball. I didn't correct that error until I met several champion female ball players.

The 1960s were isolating for young transgender people. I believed I was the only person who thought they were the other gender and was sure that no one would understand me. At age 11, I heard a news story about

Christine Jorgensen, an American soldier who had medically transitioned in 1952, and realized that there were people like me. She was not the first person to medically transition, but she was one of the first to talk about her transition, and she became a media celebrity. I wanted my parents to help in the transition process, but knew they would not. My dad was critical of "queers" and anyone who didn't measure up to his idea of masculinity. I knew people could be involuntarily hospitalized, and was sure that would happen if my parents knew about my true identity. I had a bout of major depression at age 11, as male puberty started early, complete with acne and whiskers.

I survived by going "undercover." I could live my life as if I were spiritually female. It helped that I was popular, smart, and had many adults watching out for me. I spent time in libraries, scouting books and articles about transgender people. My disappointment in psychology was in how little information there was in the scholarly literature about transgender people or gender nonconformity. This was just not discussed in the 1970s.

At age 19, I was in college and living in a house off campus. I had answered an ad seeking a housemate. The five other housemates were gay, lesbian, and bisexual. I was happy to be in a "queer" house, with people who seemed like me. One housemate had a large collection of literature about gay men, another had an extensive lesbian library, and I explored my own identity reading extensively and having many conversations. Christine Jorgensen gave a lecture on campus, advocating acceptance for transgender youth. I was still in denial about my own need to transition.

I had panic attacks since high school. These intensified and became more frequent during the first few weeks at the "queer" house. One night I became suicidal when I could not stop a panic attack that was lasting for hours. My girlfriend Linda took me to an emergency room where I was given Valium and told I must get counseling. My counselor believed I was dealing with "identity issues." I never told him about the gender issues, fearing I would be hospitalized. By senior year of college, I was interested in children's mental health. Because nearly all children go to school, I was interested in school psychology. I was accepted at the University of Texas at Austin. Linda and I were married. We thrived in Austin, my panic attacks and all, and I entered the school psychology work force.

> I knew that transition was something I needed to do for my own well-being. How could I transition without harming students, their families, or the district? There were no role models. I knew of no other school psychologists who had successfully transitioned gender on the job.

As I began my professional life, most trans people were still in hiding. Films and TV talk shows depicted trans people as deceitful, immoral, or crazy. Those who were "out" commonly lost jobs, houses, and families. As the Internet became accessible, transgender people had a tremendous resource for information, friendship, and organizing. By 1995, I had a dozen trans friends and many practical resources for transitioning. My gender identity was still a secret known only to me. I did not want to lose my family. In 2003, our only child began college, and I came out to Linda. My panic attacks stopped. Linda stood by me. Our relationship would transition from a straight to a gay relationship and that took some

adjusting. In 2006, my state passed a nondiscrimination law that included protections for gender identity, gender expression, and sexual orientation. I began gender psychotherapy that year, and hormone therapy in 2008. I then began negotiating my transition with my school district. Still presenting male, I had to bind my breasts during the 2009–2010 school year.

I knew that transition was something I needed to do for my own well-being. How could I transition without harming students, their families, or the district? There were no role models. I knew of no other school psychologists who had successfully transitioned gender on the job. One option was "going stealth"—giving up my career and starting over elsewhere, with no one the wiser. That was the traditional thing to do. But why should I deprive my schools of the skills and relationships I had developed? Always worrying about my past being discovered was no way to live either.

School psychology training was ideal preparation for transitioning gender in a large organization. My training in consultation, organizational development, and advocacy were most relevant. I may not have needed to do my job backwards and in heels, but I had to be a very good school psychologist. The district could not fire me for being transgender, but they could fire me over late evaluations, or for other transgressions having nothing to do with gender. I had accrued 10 years of satisfactory personnel evaluations and I had a large group of supporters among families I served.

I understood a successful transition plan would depend on my consultation and advocacy skills. I had many audiences. I had to frame the transition conversation in ways that made sense to them, while at the same time countering myths about transgender people. I carried pictures of myself as Jill, because I knew they expected a man in a dress who would alienate families, and I wanted them to see the real me (who isn't very fond of dresses). I knew that while I had many allies and they would understand, we'd have to communicate with district leaders who had no idea who I was. I had to become knowledgeable about the various cultures in my buildings, and how those cultures viewed women and men and transgender people.

I approached our district's employee assistance program (EAP) director. We met over many months, my proposing how I might proceed, and the EAP director countering with what might go wrong. Eventually, we worked out a way to proceed. She first informed the superintendent and school board members. I wanted to inform my principals, but their supervisors, the school directors, would have to be informed first. We waited more than 6 months before finding the right time politically to tell the school directors. Seattle had had some financial scandals, rapid turnover in leadership, and understandably risk-averse managers. My transition was perceived as a potential public relations disaster. We put together a transition team, including my supervisor; and the district directors for public information, safety and security, and special education; an LGBT family liaison; a Somali community liaison; and others. The EAP director then informed my principals. Each principal supported me. I was then able to inform the teams I worked with in my buildings, and then my psychology colleagues. Messages emphasized my friendship and respect for my colleagues that I was the same person I'd always been, and that when we returned for the 2010–2011 school year, I would be female and known as Jill Davidson. If they had concerns or questions, they were given the EAP number to call.

My team expected the worst when I began the year as Jill. However, nearly everyone was accepting. Word spread fast among families. I think it helped that they saw this as personal, and not an abstract event. I was a person they knew. "Did you hear the news about John?" not "Did you here there is a transsexual in our school?"

The most common student question was, "Are you a boy or a girl?" "I'm a woman" satisfied most of them, who seemed to be asking what pronoun to use. Some said, "But your voice is funny," and I would say, "Women come in all shapes and sizes and have different voices." Students and adults often gave me compliments (e.g., "I like your necklace," or "I love your hair"). I realized that girls and women greet each other with a compliment.

This has made social interaction more delightful than I imagined. Parents seemed more interested in what I was going to do for their child than what my gender was. Sometimes parents seemed confused by my name, asking me to spell it more than once, especially on the phone. I would explain that I was transgender, and that I was still working on my voice. I was prepared to follow this with, "I know you may have many questions about me being transgender, but I really am here to help your child." Most parents just said, "Oh," and quickly moved on to talking about their child. In the first year, I had parents tell me that they were very happy I was in their child's building, and that they found my transition inspiring. I've had parents and colleagues compliment me on outfits, and have received bags of castoff clothes that they thought I would make good use of ("hand-me-rounds"). My schools serve two Orthodox Jewish communities and immigrant communities from East Africa, Central America, and Southeast Asia. Only two families took exception to me during the first year. One was an Orthodox Jewish family who did not like that they had to answer questions from their 11-year-old before they were ready. The second was a Sunni Muslim single mother who requested that a cisgender woman do direct testing with her daughter. We accommodated that family in a way I felt comfortable with. I am respected and loved by many families from these communities who know me and understand my history. They know my being transgender is not the most important fact about me. In the four years since transitioning, my transness has faded into the background, as I act, sound, and feel more natural. I am a better employee, bringing my full authentic self to work.

DISCUSSION QUESTIONS

1. How did Jill Davidson know that she was not like all the other boys at a very young age? Why didn't gender role stereotyping by her parents reinforce the idea that she was a boy?

2. Davidson writes: "I knew that [the] transition was something I needed to do for my own well-being. How can I transition [as an adult school psychologist] without harming students, their families, or the district? There were no role models. I know of

no other school psychologists who had successfully transitioned gender on the job." Comment on this statement. How did Jill negotiate the transition from a male self- (and public) identity to a female self- (and public) identity?

3. Do you know someone who is transgendered, or is considering becoming transgendered? Is her or his story similar to Jill's?

A DRAFT FOR WOMEN?
A SURPRISING SPLIT
AMONG REPUBLICANS

BY **John McCormack**

*Female Marines finish a 10-kilometer hike carrying 55-pound packs
at Camp Lejeune, North Carolina, February 22, 2013.*

Should women be required to register for the Selective Service in case there's ever a draft again? It's an obvious question now that the Obama administration has ruled—over the objections of the Marine Corps—that all combat roles must be open to women.

In testimony to Congress February 2, the commandant of the Marine Corps and the chief of staff of the Army both said women should sign up for the Selective Service just as young men are required to do: "Now that the restrictions that exempted women from [combat jobs] don't exist, then you're a citizen of a United States," Gen. Robert B. Neller, the Marine Corps commandant, told a Senate panel. "It doesn't mean you're going to serve, but you go register."

The issue was injected into the Republican presidential race during the February 6 GOP presidential debate,

when three candidates—Marco Rubio, Jeb Bush, and Chris Christie—were asked if women should register for the Selective Service. All three said yes.

"I have no problem whatsoever with people of either gender serving in combat so long as the minimum requirements necessary to do the job are not compromised," Rubio said. "I do believe that Selective Service should be opened up for both men and women in case a draft is ever instituted."

The next day, Ted Cruz came out as a voice of dissent among GOP contenders: "I didn't have an opportunity to respond to that particular question," Cruz said. "But I have to admit as I was sitting there listening to that conversation, my reaction was, 'Are you guys nuts?'"

Cruz denounced the idea as dangerous political correctness and said "the idea that we would draft our daughters to forcibly bring them into the military and put them in close combat I think is wrong. It is immoral, and if I'm president, we ain't doing it."

Heading into the South Carolina primary, the issue could help Cruz peel away support from Bush and Rubio. A national poll conducted by Rasmussen found that 53 percent of Republicans oppose requiring women to register for the Selective Service. The issue may have even more resonance in conservative South Carolina.

But it's unclear just how much of an advantage Cruz really has. Questions about a draft are highly theoretical, and lawmakers will likely act to ensure that no changes are made without congressional approval.

Senator Mike Lee of Utah is drafting a bill that will prevent the executive branch or the courts from changing current law. "We simply can't trust this president or the courts to honor the law and protect our daughters," Lee said in a statement. "We need new legislation making clear that if the United States is going to change this policy, Congress must be the one to do it." Congress would then have the authority to prevent women from being drafted into combat units, should a draft ever be instituted. Rubio and Cruz will cosponsor the Lee bill, according to their spokesmen.

On the real and immediate issue of opening up combat infantry roles to women, Cruz and Rubio essentially have had the same position. When I asked Rubio last October about a Marine Corps study showing that integrating women into combat units harmed unit cohesion and performance, he replied that the Armed Forces "should be able to perform at peak efficiency" and "if there's evidence that any sort of change would undermine that, it's something we should be deeply concerned about. I don't believe that the military should be used to make social impact statements."

But then Rubio hedged, saying, "as you've seen through the Ranger program and others, it is clear that women already serve a role in combat. They do in the Air Force, increasingly in the Army. We interacted with them during my visit to Afghanistan. They're playing a critical role in combat operations that are occurring."

The Obama administration ruled in December that all combat roles must be open to women, and in January Ted Cruz told the Center for Military Readiness that the Marine Corps request for exceptions "must be reconsidered." He added that as "long as the requirements are fair and universally applied, the military must always place the best person for the job at hand, whether male or female, but we cannot let political correctness compel the military to lower its standards."

Yes, physical standards—such as whether female members of the infantry would be at a disadvantage in hand-to-hand combat or would struggle to carry a wounded 230-pound infantryman to safety—matter. But it also matters a great deal that gender integration harms social bonding and unit cohesion.

In other words, Rubio and Cruz both believe that as long as physical standards aren't lowered, they have no problem with the full gender integration of the infantry.

But critics have two main objections. The first is that political pressure will inevitably lead to the lowering of physical standards, despite current promises to the contrary from the Obama administration and Republican presidential candidates.

The second objection is equally significant. Yes, physical standards—such as whether female members of the infantry would be at a disadvantage in hand-to-hand combat or would struggle to carry a wounded 230-pound infantryman to safety—matter. But it also matters a great deal that gender integration harms social bonding and unit cohesion.

Lance Cpl. Chris Augello was one of the Marines who participated in the Marine Corps study that found that exclusively male units outperformed gender-integrated units on 93 of 134 battlefield tasks. Augello "arrived at the integrated task force believing that women should get a shot at service in the infantry as long as they could meet existing standards," the *Marine Corps Times* reported. But by the time the study was done, he had changed his mind: "The female variable in this social experiment has wrought a fundamental change in the way male NCOs think, act and lead," Augello wrote in a 13-page paper he presented to Marine leaders and shared with the *Marine Corps Times*. Those changes, he wrote, are "sadly for the worse, not the better."

Put young men and women together day and night for months in close quarters: No amount of social conditioning will prevent some from becoming romantically involved with each other. No amount of social conditioning will teach men to ignore their natural instinct to protect women. And the problems that necessarily arise from gender differences in this context—favoritism, jealousy, resentment—will lead to much worse consequences in infantry units that face more stress and danger than support units do.

If Ted Cruz wants to have a debate about the far-off possibility of women being drafted, he's free to do that. But if he, or any other candidate, really wants to stand up for the military, he'll speak out against the Obama administration's decision, which, for the sake of gender equality, is weakening the infantry and needlessly endangering the lives of American troops.

DISCUSSION QUESTIONS

1. What is the place of women in the U.S. Armed Forces, and particularly, in combat? Should women be required to register for the Selective Service in case there's a draft again? If drafted, should women serve in combat roles? Or is the idea of sending women into combat just plain "nuts," as Sen. Ted Cruz says? Explain your answer.

2. Does gender integration in the armed forces harm social bonding and unit cohesion? Evaluate John McCormack's argument that "put[ting] young men and women together night and day for months in close quarters" will inevitably lead to "romantic involvement[s]" that "no amount of social conditioning will teach men to ignore their natural instinct to protect women and to "favoritism, jealous[ies], and resentment[s]." Is he right? If some of these incidents were to occur, would they justify barring all women from all military combat roles?

3. Do you know any women or men who are currently serving, or who have served, in the military? What is their opinion regarding this debate?

READING 2.12

MEDIA, GIRLS, AND BODY IMAGE: HOW IMPOSSIBLE IMAGES OF PHYSICAL PERFECTION ARE MAKING OUR GIRLS SICK

Taking Back Our Lives in the Age of Corporate Dominance

BY **Ellen Schwartz**

The tyranny of the ideal image makes almost all of us feel inferior ... We are taught to hate our bodies, and thus learn to hate ourselves. This obsession with thinness is not a trivial issue; it cuts to the very heart of women's energy, power, and self-esteem. This is a major health problem.

—Jean Kilbourne, in *Feminist Perspectives on Eating Disorders*

The anorexic is weak, voiceless, and can only with difficulty focus on a world beyond her plate.

—Naomi Wolf, *The Beauty Myth*

Many of our girls have "the look of sickness, the look of poverty, and the look of nervous exhaustion."

—Ann Hollander, *Seeing Through Clothes*

A plague is abroad in the land. It has not been caused by rats or mosquitoes, but by profit-driven industries relentlessly marketing an ideal body image impossible to attain. The victims of this epidemic? Our young women and girls.

Initiate an action with a young girl on an issue of mutual interest that goes beyond your own lives, such as attending a rally against land mines, speaking up at a school board meeting about the use of pesticides on school grounds, starting an organic garden, writing a letter together to an elected official, or … ?

Watch MTV or a sitcom with a girl you love. During the program, or at the commercial breaks with the sound off, talk with her about how women and their bodies are treated (through clothes, words, and camera angles). Ask her how she feels about peer pressures and expectations regarding her body. Ask her what she wants in a relationship with a boy.

Compliment girls you know on their achievements to emphasize that these are more important than how they look. Encourage non-stereotypical goals, roles, and dreams.

What gesture could you make to a girl within your sphere to help her bring more balance, health, and wholeness into her life?

BOMBARDED WITH BARBIES

The onslaught starts with a seemingly innocuous toy. While Barbie is presented as fun and wholesome, her image sets the tone for what girls come to expect of themselves in real life. Her unnaturally thin body makes even little girls with normal bodies unhappy with their appearance.

Although my own daughter is supple and athletic, at age nine she declared she was fat because her tummy showed. Many first-grade teachers tell me about the lunches thrown in the trash because these girls are "on a diet." The Barbie message is amplified by advertisers: models who, twenty years ago, were 9% thinner than the average girl are now 23% thinner. Only 5% of the population naturally falls into this body type. For the majority of girls, this is a cruel impossibility.

The pressure of the body image is inherent in the doll; another part of the package is what children learn from playing with Barbie. Through play, children make sense of the world. The primary way girls play with Barbie is changing her outfits. Most of Barbie's clothes are not just stylish, but skimpy and suggestive. This emphasis on clothes leads to enormous pressures in pre-teen and teenage years to own sexy Calvin Klein jeans and trendy Nike shoes instead of generic brands at half the cost.

Barbie makeup kits lead girls to feel they're not really pretty without makeup, and set them up as eager consumers of the multi-billion dollar cosmetics industry. And if that's not enough, the doll itself is made of polyvinyl chloride (PVC), and its manufacture and disposal creates deadly toxins.[1]

GIRLS AS DISEMBODIED SEX OBJECTS

The early childhood playtime emphasis on the external (perfect body, alluring clothes) is the beginning of a continuum which for girls in our society flows seamlessly into the pre-teen years. In middle school, Barbie is supplanted by MTV. MTV not only showcases music videos but powerfully projects highly crafted images of relationships between the sexes. Ninety percent of the videos are directed by men, and the roles girls play are male fantasies. The girls are not presented as real people with hopes and dreams of their own. Camera angles focus on breasts and buttocks; often the faces of the young women are not even shown. Women are presented as having limitless appetites for sex with any available man.

I can hear some of you saying: "Oh, but that's just TV. Everybody knows that's not real life." Are you sure? In a survey of 1,700 seventh-, eighth-, and ninth-grade boys, the question was asked: "When is it okay to force sex on a girl against her will?"[2] Twenty-four percent said it was okay if they had spent "a lot" of money on her ($10 to $15); 31% agreed it was all right if she had "done it" with other boys; 65% thought it was okay if they had been dating a long time (6 to 12 months). This survey seems to be borne out in real life: *32% of our young people have had sex by ninth grade!*[3]

MTV images are not the only ones fueling this behavior. Think about the familiar motif of television and movie stories (written mostly by men): Boy meets girl. Boy makes advances to girl. Girl is intrigued by boy, enjoys the kissing but rebuffs further sexual advances. Girl runs away. Pursuit ensues. Upon capture, boy forces a passionate embrace upon girl. Girl struggles momentarily, then sinks into sexual desire. Seeing this again and again, is it any wonder that boys get the idea that no means yes?

Most young girls want someone to have fun with, someone who treats them sweetly and with respect. They want companionship. Older girls like hugs and kisses, but don't want to have to worry about getting pregnant. This reality is very different from the male fantasy we see reiterated on TV.

FANTASY IMAGES ARE MAKING OUR GIRLS SICK

A homogeneous culture is sweeping our country, created by the mass media. Prettily packaged but with harsh undertones, it endangers our girls both in urban areas and in the heartland of America. Mary Pipher, author of *Reviving Ophelia*, is a psychologist in Lincoln, Nebraska. For twenty years, her focus has been on girls and their families. At first, girls came to her because they felt fat or ugly, or hated their parents. The four principal reasons why girls now seek her help are anorexia, bulimia, gang rape, and self-mutilation. Why are there such enormous pressures on our girls? How is it they find themselves so besieged that they feel nothing except when they're scarring their bodies?

What has happened to childhood? What has happened to adolescence as a time when girls are testing their wings, delighting in the vistas of the world opening up to them? Courage and exhilarating adventure should be the hallmark of their days as they explore budding talents and hone their skills.

We have stood by as the commercial media, with technological glitter and glitz, reduced the acceptable female body size by one-quarter. The misery deliberately engendered by the pervasive marketing of this impossible body ideal is incalculable. The diet business has tripled in the last ten years, from a $10 billion to a $33 billion industry. Yet of those who drop twenty-five pounds or more on a weight loss diet, 90% regain the weight within two years, 98% within five years.

The natural physiological increase of body fat during adolescence is now viewed by many girls as nasty. Their attempts to force their bodies into the unrealistic ideal can lead to severe dieting and semi-starvation, often with diet pills. The negative consequences are many. Psychological effects include irritability, poor concentration, chronic anxiety, depression, apathy, mood swings, insecurity, fatigue, and feelings of social isolation. Physical risks include heart and kidney damage, hypertension, stroke, rotting of teeth (from vomiting), disruption of the menstrual cycle, loss of skin tone, lack of mental clarity, and decreased energy.

BRINGING BALANCE WITH BETTER ROLE MODELING

The mass media will not tell the whole truth about this story. It would cut into sponsor profits and corporations would pull their advertising dollars. It is up to us to make this a prime topic of conversation with all of our girls—daughters, granddaughters, nieces, neighbors, friends' children. We must help them gain perspective on the tyranny that puts such crushing pressure on them.

To help our girls find their natural weight, we must focus on balance and wellness, not a number on a scale. We must emphasize eating nutritious food—centered around fruits, vegetables, and grains—in a relaxed and satisfying manner. We must support them in keeping movement in their lives, such as gymnastics, ballet, hiking, swimming, or gardening.

Naomi Wolf (author of *The Beauty Myth*), points out that the paring down of female body size intensified in the 1960s. When women's houses no longer confined them, their bodies became the new prisons.[4] Many of our young girls' attitudes are absorbed from their mothers' experiences. How much are we still buying into this hype? In addition to working full-time, getting the laundry done, helping with homework, schlepping the kids around, and holding the family together emotionally, must we women also struggle for a great figure? *Do we put even one-tenth the time into bringing about societal change as we do into diet strategies?* Perhaps if our daughters saw us working to stop the rollback of wages and healthcare benefits, or attempting to halt the destruction of the ozone, they would realize that having a perfect body is a trivial pursuit.

QUESTIONS FOR REFLECTION

- Do you have memories of being made to feel "less than" as you grew up seeing advertising and movie images? Are you comfortable with your body now?

- How do you think the messages sent by the fashion and diet industry affect our girls? Think about girls you know or have known.

- What was something wonderful about your childhood and adolescence that girls rarely get to experience today?

ENDNOTES

1. *New Age Journal*, July/August 1996, 21.
2. Sut Jhally. *Dreamworlds* (documentary video).
3. "Youth Risk Behavior Survey." The National Center for Health Statistics and the Alan Guttmacher Institute, 1995.

4. Naomi Wolf. "Hunger." Essay in *Feminist Perspectives on Eating Disorders*, 94.

DISCUSSION QUESTIONS

1. On the first page of this article, Ellen Schwartz quotes Jean Kilbourne: "The tyranny of the ideal [body] image makes almost all of us feel inferior. ... We are taught to hate our bodies, and thus [we] learn to hate ourselves. This obsession is not a trivial issue: It cuts to the very heart of women's energy, power and self-esteem." Evaluate this statement.

2. Who is responsible for this "tyranny"—advertisers, MTV, movies, and the media? Plastic surgeons and the manufacturers of diet foods and cosmetics? Men, who tell their wives and girlfriends that they need to stay thin and beautiful to be loved? Someone else? Evaluate each of these answers.

3. What solution(s) does Schwartz propose to counteract the ideal of physical perfection that is so ubiquitous in the media?

THE RISE OF HIPSTER SEXISM

BY Meghan Murphy

Describing the hipster is something you aren't supposed to do. The mere mention of the fact that there are hipsters outs you as not being one. The point of being a hipster, after all, is to be over everything already—including yourself.

Luckily, having already outed myself as someone who cares about things beyond the rescue of sufficiently derelict but repopularized bars, I am free to discuss the hipster and hipster culture with wild abandon.

Notoriously apathetic, one of the issues hipster culture doesn't concern itself with is sexism. In a comedic video, "You're Probably a Hipster," PBS *Idea* host Mike Rugnetta describes the hipster as a person who enjoys things "ironically" instead of with genuine enthusiasm and has an air of "smugness or arrogance."

But the cultural backlash against hipsters, evidenced by a number of blogs and sites that started popping up around the mid-2000s, like Look at This Fucking Hipster (later a book), grew out of much more than smugness. The backlash against hipster culture also developed as accusations of cultural appropriation arose.

Hipsters have been criticized for appropriating working-class culture from a place of privilege. Douglas Haddow talked about this in an article in *Adbusters* back in 2008 and described how symbols and icons of working-class culture "have become shameless clichés of a class of individuals that seek to escape their own wealth and privilege by immersing themselves in the aesthetic of the working class."

Co-opting culture isn't limited to class. A website called Native Appropriations called out the trend of young white people donning native headdresses and war paint as fashion. The native-culture-as-fashion trend was first documented at music festivals like Coachella in California in 2010. Adrienne Keene, the face behind Native Appropriations, described how the trend reinforces stereotypes about native culture,

co-opts culturally and spiritually significant symbols, and ignores the deeply oppressive and exploitative colonial history of Aboriginal people in North America. She concludes that the trend, while not limited to hipsters, is no different than wearing blackface

When you critique this behaviour, expect to be told that you just don't get it. Irony functions as a disguise that protects hipsters from critique. It's the "Don't you get the joke?" defence against offensiveness.

Hip-hop music critic and radio deejay Jay Smooth argued in his video blog that cultural appropriation is a weak form of humour, writing that "irony is now the last refuge of a coward. A singularly dishonest and deluded sort of coward who imagines his behaviour a mark of courage, as he fearlessly refuses to take anything seriously. Cowardice is the root of all hipster irony. And this is never more obvious or more ugly than when issues of race are involved."

When it comes to race, class and gender oppression, Andrea Plaid, a contributor to the website Racialicious, questions whether racism and sexism need to be funny.

"The reality is that the many, many people who have to deal with racist and/or sexist oppression daily don't find it funny at all.... That person who needs to use racism and/or sexism to be so funny may be the same person who will, say, be making hiring decisions, which can affect a person's survival."

Anita Sarkeesian takes on "retro sexism" or "ironic sexism" in her video series Feminist Frequency. She defines retro sexism as "modern attitudes and behaviours that mimic or glorify sexist aspects of the past, often in an ironic way."

It's the idea that, because we all know that what we are seeing is sexism, we are in on the joke—which supposedly negates the sexism. Sarkeesian sees this as "the normalization of sexism through irony."

The neo-burlesque trend is an example of a "sexism is fun for everyone" ethos that pushes us to get in on the joke. I am just as uncomfortable watching a woman strip on a stage under the burlesque banner for a mixed audience as I am watching straight male audiences ogle exotic dancers at strip clubs. To me, burlesque often replicates those same images, and the women on a burlesque stage are still performing for a male gaze.

When I wrote a blog post recently about the normalization of pornographic imagery in hipster culture, some people were livid. As an example, I pointed to some party photos taken at a local bar in which women posed with their legs spread and breasts jutting out. Among the responses that came back were, "We're just having fun and being sexy" and "We love sex, and this is how we party." The refusal to engage in a critique of why these women would mimic porn poses for a camera shouldn't have surprised me. In hipster culture, there is a stubborn refusal to look at the larger context of a society that values women based on their desirability and over-sexualized bodies.

The kind of soft-core pornographic imagery depicted in the party photos was strikingly similar to the style of photography popularized by *Vice,* a magazine that helped fashion hipster culture. It's the same overly sexualized style used by fashion photographer Terry Richardson and in advertisements for clothing company American Apparel. In fact, a number of American Apparel's ads have been banned by the U.K. Advertising Standards Authority after being deemed "gratuitous ... pornographic and exploitative."

Part of the phenomenon stems from the idea that pornography has become retro and is therefore chic, or hip. What's old is new again, and feminists who are critical of this behaviour or imagery are behind the times. We are humourless curmudgeons. We are expected to be unfazed by strip shows and porn. We are supposed to be having fun—like the boys. The hippest way to fake empowerment is not only to be okay with sexism, but to make it our own.

The hippest way to fake empowerment is not only to be okay with sexism, but to make it our own.

Connected to the idea of hipster sexism is hipster racism. In fact, the two often play together. This happened recently during the Oscars, when someone tweeting for *The Onion* "jokingly" called nine-year-old actor Quevenzhané Wallis *(Beasts of the Southern*

Wild) a cunt. *The Onion* has since apologized and deleted the tweet. In response, Falguni A. Sheth wrote on *Salon* that this kind of racist misogyny "gain[s] an easy acceptability, precisely because it plays into the ironic hipster self-aware racism of 'being so cool that we know it's racist that it's okay to participate in it. We're above it.'"

The term "hipster racism" was coined in 2005 by Carmen Van Kerckhove, founder of the site Racialiscious, who, in an article called "Dude Where's my White Privilege," critiqued "Kill Whitey" parties being held in Brooklyn, New York. The parties provided an opportunity for white hipsters to dance to raunchy hip-hop and, according to Kill Whitey creator Tha Pumpsta, to "kill the whiteness inside."

At the time, Van Kerckhove wrote, "Essentially, these parties are creating a safe space where white people who are scared of black people can get together and enjoy/mock black culture without worrying about retribution from black people."

Michelle Garcia, who covered the emergence of these parties for the *Washington Post*, wrote that they had "something to do with young, white hipsters believing they can shed white privilege by parodying the black hip-hop life."

Andrea Plaid defines hipster racism as "ideas, speech, and action meant to denigrate another person's race or ethnicity under the guise of being urbane, witty (meaning 'ironic' nowadays), educated, liberal, and/or trendy." Similarly, she says, hipster sexism is "ideas, speech and action meant to denigrate female-bodied people under the guise of being urbane, witty (meaning 'ironic' nowadays), educated, liberal, and/or trendy."

An example Plaid points to is a drag performance by Texas-based comedian Chuck Knipp called *Welfare Queen*, an act that employs race, class and gender stereotyping under the guise of humour. Knipp performs character Shirley Q. Liquor in blackface, and has described her as an "inarticulate black welfare mother with 19 children." After complaints flooded a Portland, Oregon gay men's bar following performances of *Welfare Queen* last year, the remainder of Knipp's Portland shows were cancelled.

With hipster racism and hipster sexism, humour side steps critical points about inequity or oppression, serving as a kind of get-out-jail-free card. This brand of humour suggests that we live in a post-sexist and post-racist society now and that these issues are safe to joke about.

Comedy can, in fact, be an effective way to critique racism and sexism. Eddie Murphy once performed a skit on *Saturday Night Live* in which he dressed up to go undercover as a white man. The skit served, says Plaid, to "expose the everyday privileges of simply existing as a white person, specifically a white man."

In a similar vein, feminist writer and rape survivor Kate Harding compiled an online list of "Rape Jokes that Work" (mainly comedy skits). They work because, rather than making the victim the butt of the joke, they include some form of social commentary or make it clear that rape is something women are made to fear daily.

Using humour isn't the problem, in other words.

The problem comes when sexism and racism are billed as "ironic" by those whose very privilege makes them largely immune from racism or sexism themselves. When this happens humour is used to silence dissent and dodge accountability, and it starts to look like the same old problems wrapped up in hipster clothing.

DISCUSSION QUESTIONS

1. What is hipster sexism or retro sexism?

2. Meghan Murphy writes that "retro sexism" or "ironic sexism" has to do with "modern attitudes and behaviors that mimic or glorify sexist aspects of the past, often in ironic ways. Because we all know that what we are seeing is sexism, we are in on the joke, which supposedly negates the sexism." But the problem is that "many people who have to deal with sexist oppression daily don't find it funny at all." Is she right? Why or why not? Are we seeing the rise of a too-cool-for-school cultural appropriation of the sexism and misogyny of the past? How do you know?

3. What do you think—are "neo-burlesque" shows, attended by mixed affluent audiences any less sexist than "exotic dancers at strip clubs, being ogled by straight male audiences?" Are photos of seminude models that mimic porn in fashion and sports magazines any less sexist than real porn?

READING 2.14

HOW TO HACK SEXISM

Meet the 27-year-old Engineer who Forced Silicon Valley's Gender Problem Into the Open

BY **Hannah Levintova**

Back in October 2013, Tracy Chou, a top engineer for the social scrapbooking site Pinterest, was flying home to San Francisco with fellow attendees of the annual Grace Hopper Celebration, the nation's biggest conference for women in computing. "If this flight out of Minneapolis goes down," she tweeted, "Silicon Valley is going to be down a substantial % of female engineers."

She was only half joking. At the conference, Facebook COO Sheryl Sandberg had posited that the Valley's gender gap was actually getting worse, and the comment set Chou's geek gears whirling. "Not that I disagree with the premise," she says. "I just had this thought that nobody actually knows what the numbers are."

For years, Silicon Valley has tried to hide those numbers. Starting in 2008, news outlets filed Freedom of Information Act requests with the Department of Labor, hoping to obtain the workforce diversity data the tech giants refused to release. The companies lawyered up—as of March 2013, most of the top firms (Apple, Google, Microsoft, et al.) had convinced the feds their stats were trade secrets that should remain private.

Their real reason for withholding the data may well have been embarrassment. Although tech employment has grown by 37 percent since 2003, the presence of women on engineering teams has remained flat (at around 13 percent) for more than two decades, and women's share of what the US Census Bureau calls "computer workers" has actually declined since the early 1990s.

In this male-dominated landscape, Chou, 27, is a rising star, with two degrees from Stanford, including a master's in computer science with a focus on artificial intelligence. On her way up, she interned at Google, Facebook, and a rocket science company. Her coding prowess recently landed her on *Forbes'* "30 under 30" and *Fast Company*'s 2015 list of the "most creative people in business." Despite her success, she's more than passingly familiar with the obstacles the Valley's sausage fest creates for women—from brogrammer pickup lines to biased hiring and promotion. (Not to mention pay: As of 2011, census data shows, women in technical fields were making about $16,000 less, on average, than men.)

Fed up with the data void, Chou came home from her conference and wrote a Medium post calling for more transparency: "The actual numbers I've seen and experienced in industry are far lower than anybody is willing to admit," she wrote. "So where are the

Hannah Levintova, "How to Hack Sexism," Mother Jones, vol. 40, no. 4, pp. 29, 58. Copyright © 2015 by Foundation for National Progress. Reprinted with permission. Provided by ProQuest LLC. All rights reserved.

numbers?" With her bosses' permission, she started the ball rolling: Just 11 of Pinterest's 89 engineers (12 percent) were women, she revealed. (Today, it's around 17 percent.)

Her post quickly made its way around programmer circles, and employees of two dozen companies shared gender stats with Chou via Twitter. To keep track of the numbers, she set up a repository on the code-sharing site Github and invited all to participate. As word spread, more techies stepped up. Within a week, her repository had stats on more than 50 firms. (It now has more than 200—including Github, whose 104 coders include just 14 women—making it the most comprehensive available source of coders' gender data.) The numbers were as bad as you might expect: Just 17 of Yelp's 206 engineers (8 percent) were women, for example. Dropbox was barely better, with 26 out of 275 (9 percent). Nextdoor, a social-media tool for neighborhoods, had 29 engineers—all male. Change.org, which bills itself as "the world's platform for change," had less than 13 percent women engineers; it has since changed for the better, with 20 percent.

Chou's project helped fuel the wave of public criticism that has shamed big companies into coming clean. Seven months after the launch, Google disclosed that 17 percent of its tech staff is female. (Chou heard that her Medium post had made it all the way to cofounder Larry Page.) Twitter, Facebook, Yahoo, and dozens of other companies coughed up their stats not long after: Most reported between 10 and 20 percent women in "tech" positions—which can be pretty loosely defined. Some household names, like IBM, Netflix, Oracle, and Zynga, still have yet to produce meaningful diversity data. "The crowdsourced stuff is way better and more reliable than the official party line," notes Silicon Valley diversity consultant Nicole Sanchez, whom Github recently hired as a VP. (The racial diversity numbers are equally cringeworthy; see "How White Is My Valley?" on page 24.)

I sat down with Chou at Pinterest's San Francisco headquarters a few days before an infusion of capital made it one of the world's most valuable startups—$11 billion on paper. In a glass-wrapped conference room, she perched on the edge of her seat, speaking softly, but at a spitfire pace. Chou first learned of the industry's gender problem from her parents, engineers who earned their Ph.D.s together back in the 1980s. "Their names are gender-ambiguous transliterations of their Chinese names," she recalled. "One of the stories my mom told was that she went to pick up

finals for both her and my dad. The professor was really surprised at who was who, because my mom was doing better in the class."

When she started out studying computer science as a Stanford undergrad, "I felt really out of place," she told me. "There weren't many other women." The coursework was tough, and the guys in her classes talked a big game. "My self-calibration was off," she explained. "There's research on how guys are generally inclined to give themselves more credit. So their calibration was 'I'm awesome; this is super easy,' when I felt like I was doing poorly."

Concerned she wasn't qualified for CS, Chou switched to electrical engineering. But the more she excelled, the more pushback she got. Male classmates would interrupt her or tune out when she spoke. During group projects, guys would reject her proposals and debate alternatives for hours before returning to her idea. "It's okay to have a girl in the class if she's not very good," she said. "But it felt like once I became better than they were, it was not okay anymore."

This insidious sexism followed her into the real world. At one diversity event, Chou got into a debate with a male developer over a product built by Quora, where she'd been an early engineer. "Finally, I had to say, 'No, I worked there. Stop shitting on me!'" Another time, at a meet-up, a guy joked about Chou's job at another company: "What do you do there, photocopy shit?" Men tried picking her up with lines like, "You're too pretty to code." Such cluelessness presented a conundrum: "There's always that question of, 'Do I want to be the engineer that always talks about gender? Or do I want to be an engineer that talks about engineering?'"

The Valley's sexism came under renewed scrutiny this year when Ellen Pao, a former partner at Kleiner, Perkins, Caufield, and Byers, sued the VC firm for discrimination. She lost, but the case "raised awareness of the sort of thing that a lot of women face: unconscious bias, messy situations, discrimination that's not clear-cut," Chou said. In her view, getting the numbers out there is merely a first step: "There's an analogy in product development," she said. You can try to grok your users by looking at what people are clicking and how many are creating accounts, but "understanding the *why* in the numbers is pretty important," she added. "We're not quite there yet."

DISCUSSION QUESTIONS

1. Why has Silicon Valley's gender gap in hiring and pay been so bad over the past decade? Why has racial diversity in the computer and information technology industry been almost nonexistent? What should be done to correct these deficiencies?

2. Why don't more women enroll and do well in science, technology, engineering, and math (STEM) courses and majors in high school and college? What can be done to change this trend?

3. Chou says that when she studied computer science and electrical engineering, most of her male classmates "talked a big game," but were inferior to her academically and intellectually—and they were threatened by their own inferiority! Have you ever faced that kind of sexism, in school or the workplace? If so, how did you react? What did you do? Have you ever been surprised that a woman excelled academically, or in her career in a STEM-related field? If so, why were you surprised?

READING 2.15

GENDER INEQUALITY

A Portrait of America: The Demographic Perspective

BY **John Iceland**

Much of what we do is gendered. Boys and girls in school typically have same-sex friends and often role-play games following social norms. Toy stores reinforce this; they are full of toys that are distinctly for boys (action figures) and others that are clearly targeted at girls (dolls and accessories). Gender stereotypes are also perpetuated in the media, as male characters are more likely to act aggressively and be leaders, and females are more likely to be cast in the role of caregivers.[1] Parenting is gendered, with mothers usually playing the leading role in child raising. Housework is gendered, such as with "outdoor" work assigned to men (lawn mowing) and indoor work to women (cooking). Jobs and careers are gendered—construction jobs are still overwhelmingly filled by men, and receptionists are still much more likely to be women. Caregiving for sick family members is gendered, with women more typically caring for aged parents.

However, gender norms, at least in Western countries, are generally more fluid these days than they used to be. A generation ago, a husband taking care of the children while his wife worked would have been a striking oddity and perhaps an object of derision. Today, women can be soldiers, and men can be nurses. Many would argue that women can be smart and tough, and men can be expressive and emotional and still fall within the socially acceptable bounds of femininity and masculinity. The increasing emphasis on individualism and self-actualization discussed in chapter 2 has released people from the tyranny of very tightly bound gender norms. This has led to a withering of gender inequality in the United States and other wealthy, modern countries around the world.

Or has it? How much have gender norms and gender inequality in American society really changed? Are men and women now just about on equal footing? These are the central questions guiding the rest of this chapter. What follows is a review of the evidence on gender inequality in education, labor force attachment and occupations, and earnings. I explore patterns and trends in gender inequality in other countries as well. I evaluate arguments about the rise of women and the decline of men and discuss emerging patterns of gender inequality in American society today.

TRADITIONAL DIVISION OF LABOR IN THE HOUSEHOLD

Conventional wisdom used to hold that differences between men and women, including the division of labor between the two, were rooted in biological differences. For example, researchers writing in the 1960s documented how among some primates the male is dominant and aggressive, extrapolating that humans are much the same. However, others have shown that significant variation occurs in primate social systems, in which females of many species are "fiercely competitive, resourceful and independent, sexually assertive and promiscuous and, in some cases, more prone than males to wanderlust at puberty."[2]

While it would be wrong to say that there are no meaningful biological differences between men and women that can affect their behavior, biological predispositions are strongly affected by social influences and the culture in which individuals are embedded. The goal here is not to definitively determine to what extent biology affects the behavior of boys and girls and men and women, but rather to discuss the role of social constructions of

gender in shaping normative behavior and in particular how such norms have changed over time.

Societies today vary considerably in their level of *patriarchy,* or the systematic dominance of males over females. In several countries in the Middle East and South Asia, women who have committed adultery or have had premarital sex are in some cases killed by their father, brothers, or husbands as a way to protect the family's honor.[3] The practice of purdah in many such societies, or the concealing of women from men, is viewed by many as an institutional method of subordinating women and signals their subjugation (though individual women sometimes choose to wear some kind of covering, such as a *hijab,* for varying personal, cultural, or political reasons).[4] Gender inequality is not confined to developing countries. In the United States into the 1960s and Japan into the 1970s (just to provide two examples), a woman could be legally fired from a job if she married or had children.[5] Thus, there is considerable variation in gender norms across countries that is not necessarily contingent on their level of development or wealth. The overall status of women in Thailand is fairly high; in most professions, in universities, and in the corporate sector, the occupational attainment of Thai women is higher than in most Western industrial nations, including the United States.[6]

Historically, patterns of gender inequality have been linked to changes in the family. As we've seen, in preindustrial America, men and women worked alongside

Figure 1 Percentage of 25- to 29-year-olds who completed four years of college or more, by gender, 1940–2011.

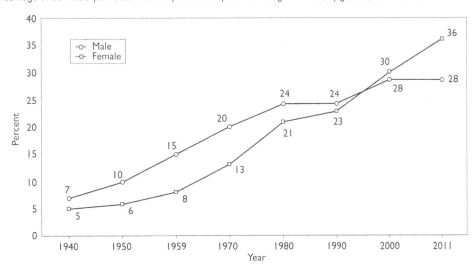

Source: U.S. Census Bureau 2012f.

each other in the home and around it, often specializing in particular activities. The husband was generally seen as the ultimate arbiter and decision maker. With industrialization and urbanization, men increasingly worked away from the home, and the home itself became the province of women, which created different economic spheres for the two. Many advocated for men to be paid a "family wage" that could support not only the husband but the wife and children as well. Henry Ford, for example, promoted paying a family wage to workers in his factories in the early 1900s in part as a way of keeping more women in the home with children.[7] Men's authority as head of the household was reinforced by the money they were responsible for earning to support the family. A significant amount of productive work in which women were engaged (e.g., taking care of the home, childrearing, caring for the sick and elderly, volunteer work) was at least implicitly not valued as highly as men's paid work.

It should be noted, however, that while this traditional family arrangement—the husband earning a family wage and the wife taking care of the home and children—was the cultural ideal, in lower-income families women still continued to work to help make ends meet. Single-parent families were not entirely anomalous either. For example, 9 percent of children lived in such families (mainly with a widowed mother) in 1900.[8] In the 1950s, before the women's rights movement, only about half of all families with children were in the traditional breadwinner/homemaker family model.[9]

Women's labor force participation increased through the twentieth century for several reasons. For one, as family sizes generally declined, less time and energy were needed to care for children and maintain a household. Technological changes, including the invention of time-saving household appliances such as vacuum cleaners, washing machines, refrigerators, dishwashers, and microwaves, all reduced the time needed for housekeeping and the need for a full-time homemaker. The availability of new consumer products and rising living standards may have also made earning money through paid labor more attractive to families.[10]

Changes in the economy, such as the increase in the number of white-collar versus blue-collar jobs, especially with the service sector generating more of the former, provided greater opportunity for women in the paid labor market. Similarly, the rise of women's earnings and the stagnation of men's earnings, especially in the second half of the twentieth century, provided greater impetus for women to work. Increasing divorce

rates likewise led many women to gain job experience to prepare for the possibility of marital dissolution. In the social and cultural realm, changing ideas about gender norms made work for women more socially acceptable, including for mothers of young children. The feminist movement emphasized the importance of women having the ability to pursue independence and self-actualization on an equal footing with men, both in and outside the home.[11] The Civil Rights Act of 1964, along with other anti-discriminatory measures and affirmative action, expanded the opportunities open to women.[12] As a result, women today are better educated and are more likely to work, have higher-status jobs, and receive more in terms of wages than before.

EDUCATIONAL ATTAINMENT

An increasing number of Americans pursue a college degree. However, there are important differences in educational trends by gender. Figure 1 shows the percentage of 25- to 29-year-old men and women who have completed four or more years of college over the 1940 to 2011 period. Men were consistently more likely to be college graduates than women from 1940 to about 1990, when the two lines intersect. For example, in 1940, about 7 percent of young men had completed four or more years of college, compared with 5 percent of women. If anything, the male educational advantage grew larger, such that in 1959 the percentage of men (15 percent) who had completed four or more years of college was nearly double that of women (8 percent). By 1990, however, 24 percent of men and 23 percent of women had four or more years of college, after which women consistently achieved higher levels of educational attainment. In 2011, 36 percent of young women, compared with just 28 percent of men, had finished four or more years of college.[13]

While more women are completing college than men, there are striking differences in the major fields of study chosen by gender (see figure 2). Among 25- to 39-year-olds surveyed in 2009, about 80 percent of engineering majors and 69 percent of majors in computers, mathematics, and statistics were men. In contrast, women were overwhelming concentrated in education (79 percent of education majors were women), psychology (75 percent), and literature and languages (69 percent). Although these differences are notable, the imbalances were even greater among respondents who were 65 years old and over (most of whom presumably finished their bachelor's degrees decades ago). Among this group, 97 percent of engineering majors were men,

Figure 2 Gender distribution by field of study among 25- to 39-year-olds holding bachelor's degrees, 2009.

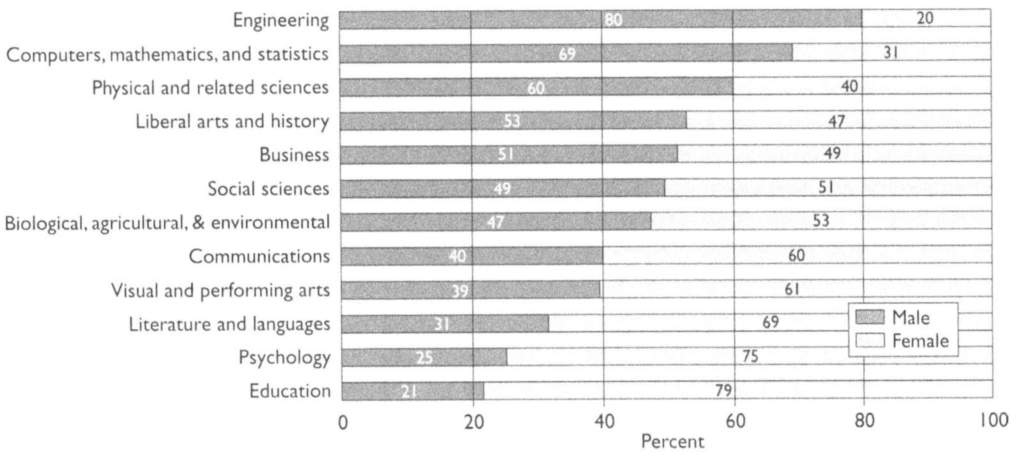

Source: Siebens and Ryan 2012, table 2.

as were 83 percent of those majoring in physical and related sciences.[14] The choice of majors has implications for the types of jobs men and women have and hence gender differentials in earnings. For example, median annual earnings in 2011 for those with degrees in computers, mathematics, and statistics was $80,180, and for those in the physical sciences it was $80,037; in contrast, median earnings among those in education and psychology, both majors in which women are more highly represented, were $50,902 and $55,509, respectively.[15] Many argue that the "choice" of majors should not necessarily be viewed simply as an act of free will; choices are strongly influenced by others' expectations of what is socially acceptable for women and men and also by popular perceptions of their capabilities.[16]

Nevertheless, the increase in women's education has also translated into greater labor market participation. Whereas only 41 percent of women age 16 years and older were employed in 1970, by 2000 that figure had risen to 58 percent, before dipping somewhat to 54 percent in 2010 (see figure 3). Among women with children at home (which includes mainly women who are working age), the proportion who were in the labor force increased from just 47 percent in 1975 to 71 percent in 2007.[17] In contrast to the general upward trend in employment among women, the overall percentage of men age 16 and older who were employed declined slightly, from 76 percent in 1970 to 72 percent in 2000, before falling precipitously to 64 percent in 2010 in the wake of the 2007–9 Great Recession.[18] Thus, the gender employment gap has narrowed significantly in recent decades.

OCCUPATIONAL SEGREGATION

The gender employment gap has narrowed, but to what extent do men and women still have different kinds of jobs? Through most of the twentieth century men and women were concentrated in very different occupations. At times, men actively resisted the entry of women into highly paid "male" jobs, and informal job networks reinforced the gender divide in the workplace. Differences in educational majors also contributed to occupational segregation, many of which persist today. Figure 4 shows that women constitute an overwhelming percentage (over 80 percent) of schoolteachers, social workers, and speech-language pathologists. They are also very highly represented among meeting and event planners and psychologists. At the other extreme, only 4 to 5 percent of firefighters and aircraft pilots and flight engineers are women, as are just 14 percent of architects and engineers. About three-quarters of chief executives are men. Thus, many of the jobs women occupy require a relatively high level of education (a BA or more) but are not known for paying all that well (such as social workers and teachers) for that level of education.

The extent to which men and women are clustered in different occupations has declined over time, though the pace of this decline has slowed in recent years. Figure 5 illustrates the slow of the downward trend using a summary indicator called the segregation (or dissimilarity) index.

Figure 3 Percentage of the population age 16 years and older who are employed, by gender, 1970–2010.

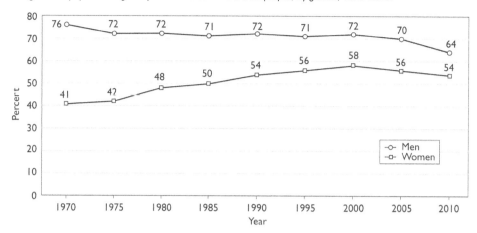

Source: U.S. Bureau of Labor Statistics 2011c, table 2.

This measures the proportion of women or men who would have to change occupations for the occupational distribution of the genders to be the same. The index stood at 64 in 1970, before declining to 54 in 1990. By 2009 it had inched down to 51. The decline was driven much more by women entering what had been male-dominated occupations—mainly white-collar and service jobs—than by men moving into predominantly female ones. More specifically, women have been increasingly likely over time to be employed as management, business, financial, and other professionals, including as lawyers, physicians, and veterinarians.[19] As a result, professional occupations have become less segregated over time, whereas working-class jobs have retained their higher levels of occupational segregation. White middle-class women have benefited most from these changes.[20]

It is not clear if, in the future, men will move into predominantly female occupations, particularly since such jobs continue to pay less than jobs in male-dominated occupations with similar educational requirements (though men in women's occupations typically are paid better than women).[21] Future changes in the labor market may help determine whether men will enter traditionally female occupations. For example, the extent to which manufacturing and other blue-collar jobs continue to disappear may determine if men will increasingly look for jobs in other sectors. Also of critical importance is the extent to which different choices become culturally less gendered, thus permitting both women and men to consider a broader range

of opportunities with little social penalty and greater family and spousal support.[22]

EARNINGS INEQUALITY

As we've seen, gender inequality extends to differences in earnings. Figure 6 shows the change in the female-to-male ratio of earnings since 1960. It relies upon a common indicator of the gender wage gap—women's median annual earnings as a percentage of men's among full-time, year-round workers. While the ratio of earnings did not budge (remaining at close to 60 percent) over the 1960 to 1980 period, it finally began to increase thereafter. By 2011 women earned 77 percent of what men earned.[23] It is important to note that some of the narrowing of the wage gap was a function of the decline or stagnation in men's wages rather than just the increase in women's earnings.[24] Some of the earnings gap is explained by occupational segregation and the tendency for women's work, such as care work, to be devalued.[25] However, women tend to earn less than men even within the same occupational categories. For example, among elementary and middle school teachers, waiters, and chief executives, women earn, respectively, 91 percent, 77 percent, and 69 percent of what men earn, even when only full-time workers are considered.[26]

So why does the gap persist? In contrast to the gap caused by the blatant and broad-based gender discrimination that occurred in the past, the gap today is probably best explained by gender socialization and women's resulting weaker attachment to the labor market, as well

Figure 4 Women as a percentage of the total number employed in selected occupations, 2011.

Occupation	Percent
Aircraft pilots and flight engineers	4
Fire fighters	5
Architects and engineers	14
Chefs and head cooks	19
Security guards and gaming surveillance officers	19
Chief executives	24
Lawyers	32
Physicians and surgeons	34
Computer systems analysts	34
News analysts, reporters and correspondents	34
Postal service mail carriers	36
Total, 16 years and over	47
Retail salespersons	51
Accountants and auditors	61
Hotel, motel, and resort desk clerks	64
Psychologists	71
Tailors, dressmakers, and sewers	75
Meeting, convention, and event planners	76
Social workers	82
Elementary and middle school teachers	82
Speech-language pathologists	96

Source: U.S. Bureau of Labor Statistics 2012c.

as continued discrimination faced by mothers in particular. A greater percentage of women than men still tend to leave the labor force for childbirth, child care, and elder care. As of 2009, about a quarter of married-couple households with children still had a stay-at-home mother (down from 44 percent in 1969), though fewer than 10 percent of mothers stay at home until their oldest child hits the age of twelve.[27] Stay-at-home dads have until recently been viewed as oddities, and this arrangement is still relatively rare. Exiting the labor force or even working part-time, especially if it is for an extended period of time, leads to a lower accumulation of human capital (job-related skills) and hence lower pay, which affects women disproportionately. Similarly, working mothers tend to value workplaces that have "family-friendly" policies; many of these offer less pay, if perhaps better fringe benefits. One study estimated that once many of these factors (such as accumulated human capital and differences in occupations) are taken into account, the gender wage gap is reduced to between 4.8 and 7.1 percent, rather than about 20 percent.[28]

The wage penalty among low-income mothers in particular is not attributable to lost human capital alone; it is also strongly suggestive of continued discrimination and other barriers to work.[29] Some argue that women still

have to strike a delicate balance between femininity and assertiveness in male-dominated environments. Women, for example, have had a notoriously difficult time making inroads into high-paying jobs on Wall Street.[30] Informal job networks and mentoring opportunities may still favor men, and women may be stereotyped as having a low commitment to work and be put on a "mommy track" that keeps them from moving into higher management positions as quickly as men.[31]

Sheryl Sandberg, who has served as the chief operating officer of Facebook, has attributed the gender gap in part to chauvinism and corporate obstacles and in part to socialization early in life that results in women not pursuing economic opportunities as aggressively as men. "We internalize the negative messages we get throughout our lives, the messages that say it's wrong to be outspoken, aggressive, more powerful than men. We lower our own expectations of what we can achieve. We continue to do the majority of the housework and child care. We compromise our career goals to make room for partners and children who may not even exist yet."[32] Others stress that in addition to women choosing to leave the workplace, they also feel pushed out by inflexible workplace environments that are inhospitable to working moms that seek some balance between work and home.[33]

Figure 5 Occupational segregation, by gender, 1970–2009.

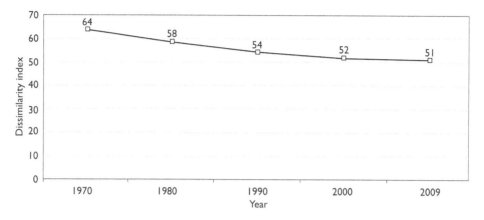

Source: Blau, Brummund, and Yung-Hsu Liu 2012, table 3.

It is important to note that the gender wage gap is smaller among younger workers. For example, one study found that women 16 to 34 years old make somewhere between 91 and 95 percent of what men make, even without taking into account the wide array of factors (e.g., differences in occupations) described above. In contrast, women above 35 years old earn between 75 and 80 percent of similarly aged men.[34] A growing number of women are remaining employed steadily throughout their young adulthood, and this contributes to wage parity. Some of the movement toward gender equality has thus been the result of a gradual process of "cohort replacement," in which younger women are taking on new roles and earning more in the labor market than their mothers. In recent years women have been more likely than in the past to find good jobs, with opportunities for advancement, and to experience social support from their spouses and significant others for their continued employment.[35]

Figure 6 Women's median annual earnings as a percentage of men's earnings for full-time, year-round workers, 1960–2011.

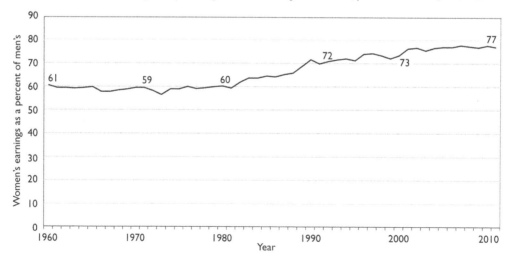

Source: U.S. Census Bureau 2012m.

Figure 7 Trends in average weekly housework hours, by gender, among married women and men of ages 25 to 64, 1965–2010.

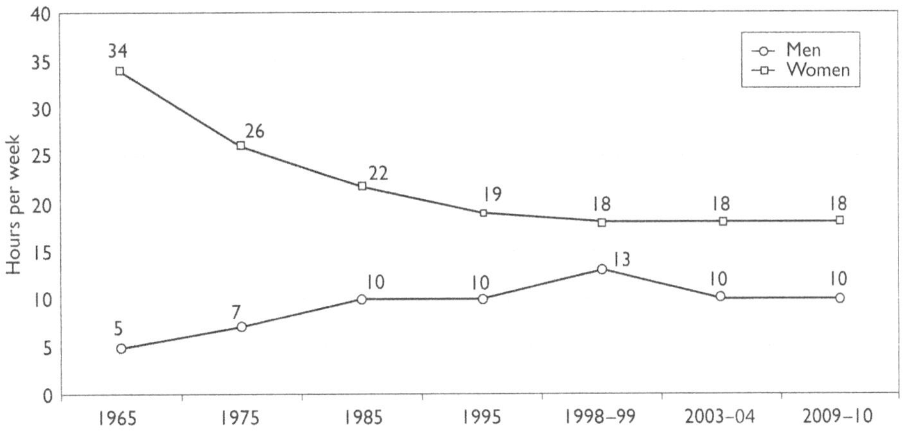

Source: Bianchi et al. 2012, table 1.

The role of socialization and gendered behavior is also reflected in the differing amounts of housework men and women do. In 2009–10, married women ages 25 to 64 reported doing on average 18 hours of housework per week. This is considerably higher than the 10 hours reported by married men in the same age range (see figure 7). Notably, the gap in housework has narrowed over time, though it has changed little since the 1990s. In 1965, married women reported doing 34 hours of housework, compared with only 5 hours among men. The narrowing of the gap is partly accounted for by an increase in housework reported by men and, more important, a sharp decline in housework being done by women. This decline reflects mainly the increase in the number of hours women have come to spend in the paid labor force. Interestingly, both men and women spent more time caring for their children in 2009–10 than in 1975, indicating that childrearing has become more time intensive than it was a generation ago, especially among middle-class families who have adopted the "concerted cultivation" model of raising children.[36] More specifically, the time spent caring for children rose from 7 hours to 14 hours among women and from 2 to 7 hours among men over the 1975–2010 period. Because men are more likely to be in the paid labor force than women, overall work hours (those spent both inside and outside the home) of men and women are quite similar.[37]

* * *

CONCLUSION

American society has traditionally been patriarchal. In the past this has manifested in a number of ways, such as unequal educational opportunities for women, lower rates of female participation in the paid labor force, and lower earnings for women than men. Men have historically excluded women from many kinds of jobs and limited women's social roles more generally. Labor market discrimination is a manifestation of unequal power. First, discrimination occurs when men are paid more than women for the same work. Second, discrimination contributes to occupational gender segregation, when men and women are highly concentrated in different types of jobs. The result is that women's work is typically accorded both lower status and lower earnings than occupations with high concentrations of men.[38] Inequality in the labor market may also result from common social practices or discrimination prior to a person's entrance into the labor market, such as in the education system or in the family. For example, girls have traditionally been socialized into family-oriented roles, while boys and young men have been expected to build careers that pay enough to support a family.[39]

Gender norms have changed, however. The women's rights movement, which took flight in the 1960s, pressed for more equal treatment in the workplace, such as in the form of equal pay for equal work, and for the easing of gender norms that limited women's opportunities in society at large. Until that time, women were rarely in positions of power—be it in private business or in politics—nor were they represented among a wide range of professionals, such as lawyers, judges, doctors, professors, and scientists. For a while, progress in reducing inequalities seemed slow. However, by the 1970s and 1980s there were clear indications that women's educational attainment was rising, women were entering new occupations, and the gender earning gap was beginning to narrow.

By some measures, progress has slowed in recent years. There have been relatively small changes in occupational segregation by gender, and there is a persistent earnings gap, even among full-time workers. By other measures, however, women continue to do very well,

as they now handily surpass men in educational attainment. Job growth is greatest in jobs in which women are currently concentrated. However, women are still much more likely to be caregivers to both children and sick family members and aged parents. This has resulted in women's weaker attachment to the labor force, which in turn has translated into lower lifetime earnings. The extent to which gender norms continue to become more egalitarian in the coming years will likely determine the future level of gender inequality in the labor market.

ENDNOTES

1. Newman 2007, 90.
2. Blau, Ferber, and Winkler 1998, 16.
3. Marger 2011, 336.
4. Blau, Ferber, and Winkler 1998, 19; Nodi 2008, 268–69.
5. Kerbo 2009, 307.
6. Kerbo 2009, 308.
7. May 1982.
8. Blau, Ferber, and Winkler 1998, 20–25.
9. Coontz 1992.
10. Gill, Glazer, and Thernstrom 1992, 184–86.
11. Blau, Ferber, and Winkler 1998, 25; Reskin and Roos 1990.
12. Gill, Glazer, and Thernstrom 1992, 186–88.
13. U.S. Census Bureau 2012f.
14. Siebens and Ryan 2012, table 2.
15. Ryan 2012, 2.
16. Correll 2001; Jacobs 1989.
17. U.S. Bureau of Labor Statistics 2010a.
18. U.S. Bureau of Labor Statistics 2011c, table 2.
19. Blau, Brummund, and Yung-Hsu Liu 2012, 19–22.
20. England 2010; Reskin and Maroto 2011.
21. England 2010, 150; C. L. Williams 1995.
22. An extended discussion of these issues can be found in Damaske 2011; Gerson 2009; Stone 2007; and J. C. Williams 2000.
23. U.S. Census Bureau 2012m, table P-40.
24. Kerbo 2009, 313.
25. England 2005.
26. Institute for Women's Policy Research 2012, table 2.
27. Kreider and Elliott 2010; Frech and Damaske, 2012.
28. CONSAD Research Corp. 2009.
29. Budig and Hodges 2010.
30. Roth 2006.
31. Kerbo 2009, 317.
32. Sandberg quoted in Kristoff 2013.
33. P. Stone 2007.
34. U.S. Bureau of Labor Statistics 2011a, 62–76.
35. See Bianchi 1995, 107–54; Damaske 2011.
36. Lareau 2003.
37. Bianchi et al. 2012, 56–58.
38. England 2010.
39. Polachek and Siebert 1994, 83–89.

DISCUSSION QUESTIONS

1. John Iceland suggests that American women are increasingly marrying down. Why does he say this, and do you agree with him? Why or why not? Is male power declining relative to women's advances in education and earning power? Or do men (who still outearn women, and occupy more CEO and congressional chairs) have more power than women? Explain your answer.

2. What does Iceland mean when he says that "much of what we do is gendered?"

3. How does Iceland explain gender inequality in the labor market?

Race and Racism

WHITE PRIVILEGE

BY **Michael R. Wenger**

On average, African Americans begin life's journey several miles behind their white counterparts as a result of the legacy of our history of racial oppression. This disadvantage is compounded by institutional hurdles they encounter at every stage of the journey: the socioeconomic conditions into which they're born, the system of public education through which they pass, the type of employment they are able to secure, the legacy they are able to leave behind. These hurdles, arduous, relentless, and often withering to the soul, do not confront many white people as they pursue their hopes and dreams. It is at the core of the privilege of being white in our society and it is a reality I have witnessed from a unique perspective—as a white man in an interracial marriage raising three African-American children and now being married to a white woman as we help to guide our four African-American grandchildren and one great grandchild on their life journey.

Whether attending school, leaving home for college, seeking a job, purchasing a house, buying a new car, traveling on vacation, or simply walking down the street, my skin color is never a factor. In most circumstances, it is a huge plus. In school, I experienced only the normal growing-up anxiety about fitting in. My father's connections, which would have been nonexistent had his skin color not been white, were an advantage to me for obtaining summer jobs during high school. When I bought my first car, I had the security of having my father with me, confident that, because of his skin color, he would not be taken advantage of. In seeking my first job out of college, the factor of skin color never entered my mind. After moving to West Virginia, I felt only the anxiety of culture shock in moving from an urban environment to a rural one.

Nevertheless, the concept of white privilege is an understandably difficult concept for white Americans to grasp. Most do not feel privileged in their daily lives. Their income may barely be enough to make ends meet. Economically, they may be only one or two paychecks away from disaster. They fear that if one of the working parents in a two-earner household were to become seriously ill, the deductible for the care they might need, even if they have health insurance, and the loss of time on the job could rip their budget to shreds. Life is a continuing struggle, and the light at the end of the tunnel is dim. To talk about white privilege under these conditions yields an ironic laugh at best and an angry diatribe at worst.

And yet, even with these burdens, I can drive any car that I can afford and not worry about being stopped by the police. I can stop to ask directions of a police officer without concern about the officer's possible reaction. I can read about racial incidents in the newspaper almost every day and not wonder whether it will happen to me. I can make a fool of myself or simply be silent at a meeting without worrying that others will think my performance is reflective of all white people. Within the limits of my budget, I can travel and eat wherever I want without attracting attention. Sociologist Joe Feagin speaks of the innate confidence of being white in a white world. My wife Jackie and I see it every day in the predominantly black community in which we live. We're a distinct minority in our neighborhood, as well as a minority in our county. I'm in the minority in the office where I work. Yet we know innately and instinctively that the world is ours. We see it in newspapers every day. We see it on television. We know it in the way we're greeted when we step out of our community. We know it in terms of our access to economic resources and to political power. And we know it from our government, both historically and contemporarily.

When I begin the discussion of white privilege in my classes, students often ask why I talk about privilege. Isn't it simply another way to describe racial discrimination? In answering the question, I refer to a speech given by then Rep. Henry Hyde (R-IL) from the floor of the House of Representatives. He asserted that the idea of collective guilt for slavery "is an idea whose time has gone. I never owned a slave. I never oppressed anybody. I don't know that I should have to pay for someone who did generations before I was born." In a narrow sense, Rep. Hyde was correct. But what he failed to acknowledge, or probably even to understand, are the benefits that were afforded him simply because he was white. His argument turns on whether or not he engaged in racist behavior. In that context, it's too easy to become defensive and let yourself off the hook by proclaiming that you don't discriminate, or that you don't have a racist bone in your body. But when you come at the issue from the perspective of white privilege, you change the context of the argument from whether someone engages in racist behavior to whether people have benefited from the racist behavior of others in the past. Such an argument eliminates the need for people to be defensive about their own behavior. It gives them the freedom to acknowledge that whether or not racist behavior still exists, the legacy of past racist behavior continues to privilege white people today, and it helps to make them feel more accountable for correcting the inequities that persist.

My skin color is a huge plus.

Thus, while one may not be consciously guilty of racist behavior, understanding the privilege conferred simply because of skin color raises the question, "What will I do to lessen or end racist behavior?"

THE SELF-PERPETUATING CYCLE OF NEGATIVE RACIAL STEREOTYPING

A key aspect of white privilege is not being plagued by negative racial stereotyping. When I was in school, the books we used to learn to read contained nary a black face. Reading these books, one would have thought that the entire population of the United States looked just like me. Compounding the problem was the virtual exclusion of African Americans, except as slaves, from our history of nation-building. The American history I was taught barely touched on the harsh treatment of enslaved people (finally brought alive by Alex Haley in *Roots*) and their countless efforts to escape. It included no contributions by black people to the building of our country other than a line or two about George Washington Carver inventing three hundred uses for the peanut. As a child, I took great pride in reading about white inventors like Thomas Edison and Alexander Graham Bell, and white pioneers like Daniel Boone and Lewis and Clark. My dark-skinned brothers and sisters had no such sources of pride. I was never taught that black people invented the refrigerator and the traffic light, discovered blood plasma, designed Washington, DC, and built the Capitol. Neither was I taught that the concept of mandatory public education emerged from the policies of black-led governments in the South during Reconstruction. Names like Frederick Douglass, W. E. B. DuBois and Ralph Bunche were mentioned only in passing, if at all. But emphasis was placed on the philosophy of Booker T. Washington, who was willing to accept the concept of white social superiority as the price of black job-training.

Our schools, the media and often public officials too often bombard us with negative images of people who are not white, and simply ignore positive images of nonwhite people, making stereotyping virtually impossible to avoid. Unless we can understand and confront this concept, it is unlikely that we will ever be able to overcome the persistent racist behavior that plagues our nation. And make no mistake: Virtually all white people are guilty of such stereotyping, to various degrees. It often occurs subconsciously, despite our best intentions.

We see it clearly whenever a major incident occurs. For example, when a tragic event like the killing of students at Columbine High School or the bombing of the Oklahoma City Federal Building occurs and the perpetrators are white, we spend an interminable amount of time agonizing over why they did it. Did their parents abuse them? Were they taunted by peers for their nonconforming behavior? Did they play too many violent video games? We don't, however, extrapolate from their behavior negative feelings toward the general population of young white men. And yet, when we hear of violence perpetrated by a young black man, we all too often associate such conduct with the majority of young black men. We do not inquire into their individual backgrounds. We simply shake our heads in disgust, even sadness, at the perceived bad behavior of others who look like them.

The reality hit harder more recently, when 17-year-old Trayvon Martin was murdered. There is little doubt that if Trayvon had been white, with his iced tea and his bag of Skittles, he would still be alive, and if George Zimmerman were black, he would have been arrested on the spot. I thought about my grandson, Michael Ian, now 11 and tall and husky for his age. Because of his skin color, he will undoubtedly face challenges that are foreign to young males with my skin color.

I will leave the authoritative explanations to experts in psychology and sociology. What I do know is that this stereotyping—dehumanizing black people—has its roots in efforts to justify slavery in the context of our founding principle that "all men are created equal." And based on my own experiences and observations, it is self perpetuating. Most children grow up in homogeneous racial environments, and people from different racial backgrounds are relatively unknown to them. When they are bombarded by negative racial stereotypes from family and friends, from the inaccurate and incomplete version of American history taught in school, and from inaccurate portrayals by a media more interested in profit than in fairness, they do not have the knowledge or understanding to counteract the bombardment. So, they fall prey to the stereotyping. Even as adults, we have precious little meaningful interaction with people from different racial backgrounds. These negative messages fuel fear and prejudice, which lead to discriminatory or dysfunctional behavior that is often unconscious. This makes meaningful interactions with the stereotyped group even less likely, and in turn, the separation widens and the stereotype intensifies each time we observe behavior that supports it. For example, if we harbor a stereotype that most young black males are dangerous, we will avoid them at all costs. By avoiding them, we give ourselves no opportunity to counteract the stereotype, and the next time we see a violent act by a young black male, our stereotype will be reinforced and our fear and desire for separation will grow. When we do encounter a young black male, we will likely act in ways that reflect the stereotype, which further reinforces and perpetuates it.

We know innately that the world is ours.

WHO PAYS THE PRICE?

But it's not only black people who pay a price for this negative stereotyping. Our nation also pays a heavy price, economically and politically. Negative stereotyping often causes us to avoid hiring people who could make valuable contributions to our businesses and our economic productivity. Such stereotyping contributes to the high level of unemployment for black people and to the cost of that unemployment to society: government assistance we must provide, productivity that is lost, increased crime rates that are often a consequence of unemployment, family dysfunction that arises due to a husband or father's inability to find a good job, and the skyrocketing costs of incarceration that limit government funding for such needs as better schools. In a labor force that is becoming increasingly diverse, this situation weakens our society and our ability to compete in the global economy. It contributes to budget deficits, lowers the standard of living for all of us, and increases racial divisions.

Politically, we pay a price because we are frequently scared into electing public officials whose motivation is victory rather than good public policy. Therefore, we often end up with bad public policies that further exacerbate racial and ethnic divisions and perpetuate societal problems. Perhaps the greatest cost of stereotyping concerns the moral hypocrisy and self-deception we practice. We think of ourselves as a people committed to the principles of justice, fairness and freedom. But each time we unjustifiably discriminate against someone, we puncture our ideals and call our values into question.

Unfortunately, policies that could narrow the gap and strengthen our nation, such as affirmative action, individual development accounts, or even some form of collective reparations, are rejected out of hand by most white Americans. They believe that the playing field of opportunity is essentially level, that any failure to succeed is a matter of personal responsibility and therefore government action to move us closer to racial equity is unnecessary and undesirable. Given the whitewashed (pun intended) version of American history we learn in school, the media's penchant for sensationalism without regard to fairness, and unscrupulous politicians whose win-at-any-cost attitudes border on the unpatriotic, our collective ignorance and our internalized sense of white superiority are not surprising.

If you are not white, the hurdles continue as one emerges from public education to either attend college or enter the workforce. Getting ready for college is an exciting time for young people. After 12 years of regimented schooling, freedom beckons. They'll decide what they want to study, choose their own classes, make their own schedules, decide whether to attend or skip class, and whether and when to do their homework. And they'll be held accountable for whatever consequences their behavior yields. Black children, if they've been able to surmount the hurdles and make it this far, have the added challenge of being marginalized in a predominantly white environment, unless they choose to attend a predominantly black university.

These hurdles continue in the world of work. When white people enter a company, they rarely worry about whether or not they will fit in. Most employees look like they do, grew up in similar environments, and share similar experiences. Rarely does a white person have the experience of going to work in a company with predominantly black employees; rarely does a white person have to adjust to being the odd person out. Affirmative action has been effectively demonized as giving African Americans, women, and Hispanic Americans an unfair advantage. From my perspective, when one is evaluating people with similar qualifications, it is a valuable weapon for confronting the everpresent good-old-white-boy network and moving us closer to a level playing field.

Stereotyping is virtually impossible to avoid.

Even African Americans who have successfully navigated the journey often pay an emotional and physical price that most white people do not pay. The effect of racism is insidious. It's like a worm coursing through your body. Gradually, it creeps through every cell and pore of your body, eating away at your sense of control over your life. Each incident can make you more wary, more suspicious, more agitated. The cumulative effect can make you seethe with resentment. You can't believe that white people are so oblivious to the indignities you endure, and it becomes difficult to view white people as friends or allies. The pressures affect both your emotional and your physical health. According to a recent study, 33% of African Americans suffer from hypertension (high blood pressure), which puts them at greater risk of heart attacks and strokes. Some people attribute this statistic to genetic differences. However, the same study found that only 16% of West Africans and 26% of people from the Caribbean suffer from hypertension. This strongly suggests that the stress is related to racism, as well as to the subtle yet significant consequence of white privilege.

Over 20 years ago, I took a creative writing class and became friendly with a white woman in the class. Over coffee one day, we talked about our respective ambitions. I said I wanted to write a book, but I despaired I'd ever get around to it or that anyone would ever publish it. I must have sounded whiny, because after a minute or two, she snapped at me. "Michael, you're a white male. You're the most privileged person in this society. You can do anything you want. So, don't complain to me." She was, of course, correct.

RESOURCES

Alexander, Michelle. *The New Jim Crow: Incarceration in the Age of Colorblindness*, The New Press, 2012.

Anderson, Elizabeth. *The Imperative of Integration*, Princeton University Press, 2010.

Blackmon, Douglas A. *Slavery By Another Name: Enslavement of Black Americans from the Civil War to World War II*, Anchor, 2009.

Corcoran, Rob. *Trustbuilding: An Honest Conversation on Race, Reconciliation, and Responsibility*, University of Virginia Press, 2010.

Cose, Ellis. *The Rage of a Privileged Class: Why Are Middle-Class Blacks Angry? Why Should America Care?*, Harper Perennial, 1994.

Loewen, James W. *Lies My Teacher Told Me*, The New Press, 2008.

Loewen, James W. *Sundown Towns*, Touchstone, 2006.

Shapiro, Thomas. *The Hidden Cost of Being African American*, Oxford University Press, 2005.

Tatum, Beverly and Perry, Theresa. *Can We Talk About Race? and Other Conversations in an Era of School Resegregation*, Beacon Press, 2008.

DISCUSSION QUESTIONS

1. Why is "the concept of White privilege [so] difficult for White Americans to grasp?"

2. What examples does Michael Wenger cite in this reading of how White privilege works to his advantage every day, socially and at work?

3. Explain "the self-perpetuating cycle of negative racial stereotyping." Wenger notes that "unless we can understand and confront this concept, it is unlikely that we will ever be able to overcome the persistent racist behavior that plagues our nation. And make no mistake: virtually all White people are guilty of such stereotyping to various degrees. It often occurs subconsciously, despite our best intentions." What does Wenger mean by this? Do you agree with him? Why or why not?

READING 3.2

WHITE PRIVILEGE: THE OTHER SIDE OF RACISM

Recognizing Race and Ethnicity: Power, Privilege, and Inequality

BY **Kathleen Fitzgerald**

Part of white privilege involves the treatment of white people as individuals, without all of their actions' being attributed to their membership in a racial group or reflecting on other members of a racial group. An example of white privilege involves media treatment of terrorists or mass murderers. When a white Norwegian man, Anders Behring Breivik, murdered seventy-seven people on July 22, 2011, the media immediately declared him a "lone wolf." The lone-wolf theory implies that this heinous act was committed by a deranged or evil individual, but was not the result of the radical ideologies of some larger group he may be connected to. While we may never fully understand why Breivik committed this horrendous act, the important point for our discussion is that all white people were not implicated by his actions. On the contrary, terrorist acts committed by Muslims result in the extension of collective guilt to the entire Muslim community (Chen 2011). Muslim community leaders are forced to denounce such radical actions and to defend their community and their religion. Similarly, African Americans experience a collective shaming when a mass murderer is found to be black, such as the case of the DC sniper in October 2002. When the news reported the arrest of the DC sniper and it turned out he was a black man, all black people were shamed by his individual actions (Harris Perry 2011). His actions were at least partially interpreted as if they were connected to his blackness.

How are these examples of white privilege? White people have the privilege of being treated as individuals, whose actions are not a reflection of their whiteness. Most mass murderers, for instance, have been white. Yet white Americans do not feel a collective guilt or shaming when the racial identity of a white serial killer is discovered. Even in the case of lynching, which we will explore in greater detail in Chapter 5, which is, at its core, a race-related phenomenon, there is no evidence that whites felt a sense of collective guilt when a person of color was lynched by a white mob. In the late 1990s, there were a number of disturbing mass shootings at US high schools and the FBI insisted there was no profile for the perpetrators. Frustrated by this denial, antiracist activist Tim Wise writes, "White boy after white boy after white boy, with very few exceptions to that rule ... decide to use their classmates for target practice, and yet there is no profile?" (Wise 2001). More recently, the Boston Marathon bombing in April 2013 elicited similar conversations about white privilege and terrorism. As Tim Wise (2013) stated the day after the incident, "White privilege is knowing that even if the bomber turns out to be white, no one calls for whites to be profiled as terrorists as a result, subjected to special screening, or threatened with deportation." The ethnicity of the Boston Marathon bombers and some of their friends were scrutinized, leading to them being "othered" along ethnic lines rather than racial lines. However, their whiteness did not result in the labeling of other whites as terrorists.

In this chapter, the focus is on race privilege, the idea that if some racial/ethnic groups experience disadvantages, there is a group that is advantaged by this very same system. Studying whiteness forces us to acknowledge that all of us have a place in the relations of race. As obvious as this may seem, this is a concept many people are unfamiliar with and it is also a relatively new focus in the social sciences. Prior to the late twentieth century, sociologists were guilty of either ignoring race or focusing on racial/ethnic "others" in their analysis of the "race problem." Scientists avoided analyzing and interrogating the role of whites in American race relations as did the average white American. For people of color, the advantages whites receive due to their racial group membership are more than obvious. As mentioned in Chapter 1, such differences in perspective are at least partially the result of people's standpoint; where one exists in the social structure influences how one views the world. Examples of whiteness as a social construction and white privilege follow:

- Hispanics are being described as the "new Italians," emphasizing their assimilation into whiteness (Leonhardt 2013).

- A Delavan-Darien, Wisconsin, high school "American Diversity" class came under fire for teaching white privilege. A parent's complaint that the subject matter was indoctrinating students into white guilt received national attention ("'White Privilege' lesson ..." 2013).

- White privilege plays out in the restaurant industry, as front-of-the-house, tipped employees are overwhelmingly white, while back-of-the-house, hourly wage employees are overwhelmingly black or Latino.

- White privilege provides its recipients with protection from suspicion; thus, whites are unlikely to face the kind of situation Trayvon Martin faced in February 2012, when a neighborhood watchman decided he looked suspicious and eventually shot the unarmed seventeen-year-old to death.

- European soccer is seen by some fans as the privileged domain of whites, as black players are taunted with racist chants from fans, causing at least one of the black players and his teammates on AC Milan to walk off the field during a match ("AC Milan Players ... " 2013).

THE SOCIAL CONSTRUCTION OF WHITENESS

We introduced the idea of the social construction of race in the previous chapter; to say race is socially constructed is to recognize that racial groups are socially designated categories rather than biological ones; thus, racial categories change across time and place. Whiteness is also a social construction, although recognizing this requires that we first acknowledge that "white" is a race rather than simply the norm. Thus, to say that whiteness is socially constructed is to emphasize which groups have been defined as white has changed across time and place (see Box 2.1 Global Perspectives),

Instead of white being about skin color or one's genetic makeup as we have been socialized to understand it, being designated as white is a social and political process. Many racial/ethnic groups that are considered white today have not always been defined as white. Irish Americans, Italian Americans, Greek Americans, and Jewish Americans have, instead, become white over time. "Becoming white" is a process whereby a formerly racially subordinate group is granted access to whiteness and white privilege, with all the benefits this entails. **White privilege** refers to the rights, benefits, and advantages enjoyed by white persons or the immunity granted to whites that is not granted to nonwhites; white privilege exempts white people from certain liabilities others are burdened with.

RACIAL CATEGORIZATION AND POWER

The privileges associated with being designated white may make it seem like the option of becoming white is in the best interest of racial/ethnic minority groups. However, while racial categorization is fluid and does change over time, racial/ethnic minority groups do not have complete agency in determining whether they become white. During some eras in US history, Mexican Americans demanded they be recognized as white, while at other times they have actively worked to maintain their Mexican heritage (Foley 2008; Rodriguez 2005). This has resulted in Latinos' having a somewhat ambiguous racial status even to this day. Another reason for a group's ambiguous racial status is the power given to official documentation, such as who has been defined as white in legal decisions (Lopez 1996). The US Census, for instance, uses such racial and ethnic categories as "non-Hispanic white" and "Hispanic," which are intended to emphasize the ethnic status of Latinos, but are also about race. Thus, there are **structural** constraints, such as government racial categorizations and legal decisions, to defining a group's racial/ethnic status.

However, there is also **agency**, the extent to which a group of people have the ability to define their own status. People are not simply pawns existing within larger social structures. Individuals and groups act within these structures and, through such actions, can change them.

Since the 1960s, many Mexican Americans have embraced pluralism rather than assimilation. **Pluralism** is when a group embraces and adapts to the mainstream society without giving up their native culture. For instance, Mexican Americans' choosing to keep their language alive by speaking Spanish in their homes while learning English so as to participate in the dominant culture, is an example of pluralism. **Assimilation**, long the preferred model for race relations among the dominant group in American society, is the push toward acceptance of the dominant, Anglo culture, at the expense of one's native culture (see Chapter 5). Groups are expected to become American

by dropping any connection to their native culture, such as language, customs, or even a particular spelling of their name.

Historically, immigrants were encouraged to assimilate into "American" society. What this really meant was that they were expected to assimilate to the white norm, known as Anglo-conformity. Thus, "American" culture was synonymous with "white culture." Previous generations of immigrants were pressured to become American by dropping their accents or native language and cultural practices associated with their native country. Today, the assimilationist thrust remains, as the English-Only movement emphasizes. This is a movement that attempts to make English the national language, to get states to pass laws eliminating bilingual education in schools, and to make government materials, such as signs in Social Security offices or Medicaid brochures, for instance, available only in English.

There are both push and pull factors at work, when it comes to whitening: the dominant group may embrace the assimilation of the subordinate group for political reasons and the subordinate group may seek assimilation, and thus embrace whitening, for access to the privileges it accords. This is accomplished by embracing, or at least acquiescing to, the racial hierarchy. As mentioned previously, racial/ethnic groups do have agency, yet they are not always operating under conditions that allow them to exercise their agency. While some groups challenge the assimilationist push, as did many Chicanos (a term Mexican activists embraced during the 1960s), most succumb. They succumb because access to white privilege makes life easier; such as by offering certain children advantages that every parent hopes for. White privilege is a difficult offer to resist—acceptance versus exclusion; benefits versus obstacles.

BECOMING WHITE

Many groups of people that are today unquestionably seen as white have not always been so. Irish, Greek, Jewish, and Italian Americans have all experienced a "whitening process" in different historical eras, when their group shifted from being perceived as nonwhite to being seen as white. The process of becoming white varied for each group, but each group becomes white in response to larger social and cultural changes. There are three specific eras in the history of whiteness in the United States (Jacobson 1998). The first is the passage of the first naturalization law in 1790 that declared "free white persons" to be eligible for citizenship. The second era (from the 1840s to 1924) emerged as significant numbers of less desirable European immigrants, such as the Irish, challenged this notion of citizenship and required a redefinition of whiteness and, ultimately, the implementation of a white racial hierarchy. Whiteness was redefined again in 1920 at least partially in response to the rural to urban migration of African Americans, which solidified the previously fractured white racial grouping. Groups such as the Irish and Jews, who had held a "probationary" white statuses in previous generations, were now "granted the scientific stamp of authenticity as the unitary Caucasian race" (Jacobson 1998:8).

Irish Americans

Historian Noel Ignatiev (1995) explored how an oppressed group in their home country, the Catholic Irish, became part of the oppressing racial group in the United States. The whitening process for Irish Americans involved the denigration of blacks. This transformation was even more shocking because Irish Americans were not considered white during the early periods of Irish immigration. In fact, early Irish immigrants lived in the

Figure 1 Native American students at the Carlisle Indian School, a government-run boarding school. The primary objective of Native American boarding schools was the forced assimilation of Native American children, as this photo exemplifies by the children's appearance, specifically, their short haircuts and mainstream clothing.

black community, worked with black people, and even intermarried with blacks.

The Irish becoming white, thus increasing their status in the racial hierarchy, has essentially been attributed to a larger political agenda. In this case, the Democratic Party sought the support of the Irish during the antebellum and immediate postbellum eras and was able to attract them primarily due to the party's proimmigrant position at the time. This was a very successful strategy, as Irish voters became the most solid voting bloc in the country by 1844, throwing their support overwhelmingly behind the Democratic Party (Ignatiev 1995).

Although the Democratic Party is recognized today as the party that passed civil rights legislation and generally is supported by the black community, at the time, racial politics looked very different. By the end of the Civil War, southern whites ruled the Democratic Party, and President Lincoln, a Republican, was held responsible for the emancipation of slaves. African American men that could vote during Reconstruction and in the North during Jim Crow tended to support the Republican Party. Most southern whites, on the other hand, overwhelmingly supported the Democratic Party, including their explicitly racist ideologies. Thus, in the mid-nineteenth century, Irish Americans were assimilated into American society through a politics of race: their acceptance as whites hinged on their acceptance and perpetuation of a racist system, particularly, antiblack sentiment (Ignatiev 1995).

Irish Americans intentionally distanced themselves from blacks and even supported Jim Crow and other racist policies that were designed to oppress blacks. An essential truth emerged: in the United States, to be considered white, a person must not be associated with blackness and subordination. Black and white are relational concepts, meaning they only have meaning in relation to each other. We learn to understand who we are partially through an understanding of who we are not. For many groups that are now considered white, distancing themselves from blacks involved accepting the American racial hierarchy and participating in the racism directed at people of color.

Mexican Americans

Racial categorization is not a straightforward process. Some racial/ethnic groups maintain a more fluid racial status. As mentioned previously, Hispanics represent this kind of ambiguity. The term "Hispanic" refers to US residents whose ancestry is Latin American or Spanish, including Mexican Americans, Cuban Americans, Central Americans, and so on. The term "Hispanic" was first used by the US government in the 1970s and first appeared on the US Census in 1980. Thus, all Mexican Americans are considered to be Hispanic, but not all Hispanics are Mexican Americans.

The racial status of Mexican Americans has shifted throughout the nineteenth and twentieth centuries. Mexicans in the newly conquered Southwest at the close of the Mexican-American War in 1848, for instance, were accorded an intermediate racial status: they were not considered to be completely uncivilized, as the indigenous Indians of the region were, due to their European (Spanish) ancestry (Almaguer 1994). They were treated as an ethnic group, similar to European white ethnic immigrants. However, by the 1890s, as whites began to outnumber Mexicans throughout the Southwest, Mexicans became racialized subjects (Rodriguez 2005).

Mexican Americans have been legally defined as white, despite the fact that their social, political, and economic status has been equivalent to that of non-whites (Foley 2008). According to the 2010 US Census, "Hispanic" is an ethnic group, not a racial group. This was not always how the census categorized Mexicans, however. In 1930, the Census Bureau had created a separate racial category for Mexicans, which for the first time, declared Mexican Americans to be nonwhite. This designation did not end the ambiguity surrounding the racial categorization of Mexicans, however. Census takers at the time were instructed to designate people's racial status as Mexican if they were born in Mexico or if they were "definitely not white," with no real instruction for differentiating how anyone would know which Mexican was "definitely not white." Consequently, due to such ambiguity, the US Census discontinued this designation in subsequent censuses. In 1980, the bureau created two new ethnic categories of whites: "Hispanics" and "non-Hispanic" (Foley 2008).

This resulted in many Latinos' choosing "other" for their race, which motivated the Census Bureau to add a question concerning ethnic group membership after the question concerning racial group membership, to try to determine who is Hispanic. The Census Bureau is considering adding "Hispanic" as a racial category on the 2020 census.

While such official maneuverings provided structural constraints on the racial/ethnic identification choices of Latinos, Latinos also exercised their agency. Many Mexican Americans during the 1930s through 1950s, for instance, demanded to be recognized as white as a way to avoid Jim Crow segregation. Much like the whitening process for Irish Americans, for Mexican Americans, distancing themselves from blacks became the objective rather than challenging the racial hierarchy through an embrace of a nonwhite racial status. Mexican Americans, particularly those in the middle class, often supported the racial segregation of schools and the notion of white supremacy. Today, while some Latinos enjoy a status as white ethnics, many others, primarily Mexicans and recent Latino immigrants, remain excluded from the privileges of whiteness. Often this exclusion has been linked to their social class or skin color, as "a dark-skinned non-English-speaking Mexican immigrant doing lawn and garden work does not share the same class and ethnoracial status as acculturated, educated Hispanics ... Hispanicized Mexican Americans themselves often construct a 'racial' gulf between themselves and 'illegal aliens' and 'wetbacks'" (Foley 2008:62–3).

SOCIAL CLASS, MOBILITY, AND "WHITENING"

The process of becoming white has often been directly linked to **collective social mobility**, a group's changing class status over time in the United States. For instance, whitening often occurs simultaneously with a group's entrance into the American middle class, making becoming white and becoming middle class an interconnected phenomenon (Brodkin 2008). Whiteness has also been closely connected to the formation of the American working class (Roediger 1991). Finally, class has been used to divide whites, as in the case of the derogatory notion of "white trash."

Because race is socially constructed, it is always changing, always open to challenge, which means there is always potential for destabilization. Yet, despite this potential, the societal racial hierarchy endures. One of the reasons is that some groups have been provided

---

REFLECT AND CONNECT

Do you belong to a racial/ethnic group that has experienced a changing racial status, such as those discussed here, that became white? If so, were you aware of this? If not, why do you think you were unaware of this? Reflect on the significance of this for your life today.

with membership into the dominant group and have obtained access to white privilege. Thus, the hierarchy remains, with whites at the top and nonwhites at the bottom. For instance, when Irish immigrants were relatively limited in number, their association with the black community and marginalization from the white community was tolerated and even encouraged by many whites. Yet, as their numbers grew and they became a potentially powerful political force, their assimilation into the white mainstream was encouraged and embraced.

Jewish Americans

The process through which Jewish Americans became white involved their simultaneous entrance into the middle class. Today, much like the situation for Irish Americans, most US citizens see Jewish Americans as white ethnics. However, Jewish Americans have not always been considered white in the United States. Prior to World War II, there was considerable anti-Semitism in the United States that manifested in immigration restrictions for Jews and limiting Jewish admission to elite universities, among other forms of discrimination (Karabel 2005; Tichenor 2002). Their whitening process involved access to the GI Bill, which was overwhelmingly denied to black soldiers in the post-World War II era (see Chapter 8). Access to this basic government program enabled Jewish Americans, along with thousands of white Americans, to obtain college educations and enter middle-class professions. In this example, class and race are intertwined, as entering the middle class is part of the whitening process for this previously defined nonwhite group. It is unclear whether becoming white paved the way to their middle-class status or whether their middle-class status contributed to their whitening (Brodkin 2008).

Psychological Wage

One of the most significant ways white privilege has manifested itself has been in the economic sphere, so it is not surprising that there is also a significant link between the emergence of the American working class and whiteness. In 1935, African American sociologist W. E. B. Du Bois argued that white workers, despite their extremely low wages, received an intangible benefit, which he called a **psychological wage**, because they were white. What he meant was that, while all workers were exploited, a racially divided labor force meant that white workers received a psychological boost from simply not being black. This psychological wage manifested

in public deference, titles of courtesy, such as being referred to as "Mr." or "Mrs.," and inclusion at public functions, parks, and countless places that excluded blacks. Later, labor unions continued this practice of offering white workers access to good jobs through the exclusion of black workers from many unionized occupations.

Historian David Roediger (1991) argues that the formation of the US working class is intimately linked to the development of a sense of whiteness because the United States is the only nation where the working class emerged within a slaveholding republic. Thus, the working class defined itself in opposition to slavery, with race attached to each concept; whiteness was connected to the working class, while blackness was linked to slavery. As Roediger argues, "In a society in which Blackness and servility were so thoroughly intertwined—North and South—assertions of white freedom could not be raceless" (1991:49). Part of the whitening process for Irish Americans involved avoiding the stigma of blackness, and one way they did this was through their access to what was known as "white man's work," which simply referred to employment that excluded African Americans (Ignatiev 1995). Irish Americans, for instance, were unwilling to work in the same occupations as free blacks in the North, thus solidifying their whiteness through an insistence on racially differentiated employment.

Race is a fluid category, rather than fixed; the boundaries of whiteness are continually in flux. Inequality exists even within the white racial/ethnic group. We can see this through an exploration of the ways whiteness is related to social class in the notion of "poor white trash" or "white trash." This clearly derogatory notion emerged in the mid-1800s and was created by higher status whites to not just describe poor whites, but to imply their moral inferiority (Wray 2006). The term *cracker*, emerging in the late 1700s, has similar origins. While today *cracker* is a term often used as a generalized racial slur against whites by people of color, it originated as a term higher-status whites used to describe poor whites who were viewed as dangerous, lawless, shiftless, lazy, and people who often associated with other stigmatized groups (Wray 2006). This intersection of class and race is evidence of the power of higher status whites to define who is included in the category of white. Such derogatory terms are used to describe poor whites not just to emphasize their poverty, but to make their racial status questionable as well.

Race Matters

While sociologists speak of race as socially constructed rather than biologically based, it is not meant to imply that race is insignificant and can thus be disregarded. Race still matters. We live in a society that attaches meaning to race and individuals attach meaning to their race. It informs who we are, is an aspect of one's identity if, for no other reason, than it has been externally ascribed to us our entire lives. We learn to see ourselves as white, black, Asian, or Latino, through our interactions with others. Thus, the fact that people racially identify does not negate the idea of the social construction of race. Instead it emphasizes the power of socially defined ideals.

WHITE PRIVILEGE

While the privileges associated with whiteness are not new, the academic exploration and understanding of white privilege is relatively new. Sociologists that study race have shifted the analysis from a focus solely on people of color to one that includes whites and their role in race relations. This necessary shift focuses on what Paula Rothenberg (2008) refers to as "the other side of racism," white privilege. In the United States, individuals identified and defined as white make up the group with the unearned advantages known as white privilege. Whiteness refers to the multiple ways white people benefit from institutional arrangements that appear to have nothing to do with race (Bush 2011). This analytical shift to an analysis of and an understanding of white privilege requires that we recognize "white" as not only a race but as a social construction.

Racial hierarchies, status hierarchies based upon physical appearance and the assumption of membership in particular categories based upon these physical features, exist in the United States and throughout the world, albeit with much variation. Hierarchies imply that a group exists at the top while others exist somewhere in the middle, and still others on the bottom rungs of the hierarchy. The group at the top is the group that benefits from the racial hierarchy in the form of race privilege. The seminal work on white privilege is the self-reflexive essay by Peggy McIntosh (2008), "White Privilege: Unpacking the Invisible Knapsack." McIntosh defines *white privilege* as "an invisible package of unearned assets which I can count on cashing in each day, but about which I was 'meant' to remain oblivious. White privilege is like an invisible weightless knapsack of special provisions,

maps, passports, codebooks, visas, clothes, tools, and blank checks" (2008:123). There are several aspects to this definition that warrant attention: the claims that white privilege is invisible, it is unearned, and that white people are socialized to count on this, while simultaneously not recognizing it as privilege.

Race affects every aspect of our lives: it informs how all of us view the world, our daily experiences, and whether or not opportunities are available due to our membership in particular racial/ethnic groups. While the importance of race has long been recognized for racial/ethnic minorities, until recently, even social scientists have overlooked the significance of race in the daily lives of whites. Part of this problem emerges from a lack of recognition that "white" is a race, rather than merely the norm, the human standard against which all other groups are measured (a perspective which is itself part of white privilege). Some have called for the development of a **new white consciousness**, "an awareness of our whiteness and its role in race problems" (Terry 1970:17). Social scientists have finally heeded this call and white people are now being asked to recognize how race and privilege operate in their world.

WHITE PRIVILEGE AS TABOO

The discussion of white privilege will undoubtedly make many students uncomfortable. Recently, a high school in Wisconsin has come under fire for teaching white privilege in an "American Diversity" class. Some parents complained that the subject matter was akin to indoctrination and meant to divide the students and provoke white guilt (*The Huffington Post* 2013).

This is the invisible side of racism—the advantages offered to the dominant group by an unjust system. Why has it taken so long for social scientists to focus on something as seemingly obvious as the "other side of racism"? A racial bias embedded not only in the discipline of sociology but in our culture is part of the explanation. Additionally, whiteness has been normalized to the point of invisibility in both our culture and in science. In addition, privilege is meant to remain invisible. Those benefiting from such societal arrangements, even if these are people that actively oppose racism, have difficulty seeing the advantages they reap from these arrangements.

Interrogating white privilege is not meant to alienate white people or exclude people of color from conversations concerning race. Instead, it is meant to bring everyone to the table to discuss race, racism, racial inequality, and race privilege. Professor Helen Fox provides a strong argument for why it is so essential to engage white people in discussions of race and privilege:

> I am convinced that learning how to reach resistant white students is central to our teaching about race. These are the future power brokers of America, the ones who by virtue of their class, their contacts, and their perceived "race" will have a disproportionate share of political and economic clout (2001:83).

For people of color, conversations surrounding race are not new; such conversations have likely been quite common for them. People of color experience explicit **racial socialization**, meaning they are taught in their families, in schools, and through the media that their race matters. White people, on the other hand, may have difficulties with the topic of race and privilege for the simple fact that such conversations have likely been uncommon in their lives.

White people experience racial socialization as well, it is just more subtle. White racial socialization comes in the form of an unspoken entitlement. Whites are socialized to protect their privilege, partially through denial of such privilege. White privilege allows whites the privilege of not having to think about race—not having to think about how race might affect them that day.

Whiteness is understood by whites as a culture void, as lacking culture, as an unmarked category in direct opposition to the view that minorities have rich and distinct cultures (Frankenberg 1993). People of color are seen to have a recognizable culture (for instance, the presence of BET (Black Entertainment Television), Latin music, Asian food, etc.) that whites are perceived to lack. For example, Frankenberg (1993) found that white women in interracial relationships often viewed themselves as having no culture, often citing envy of racial/ethnic minorities because of their obvious culture and accompanying identity.

There are some problems with viewing white culture as actually cultureless. The first is that it reinforces whiteness as the cultural norm. Whites are everywhere in cultural representations—advertising, film, television, books, museums, public history monuments—yet the claim is made that this is just culture, not white culture. Additionally, by claiming to be cultureless, whites can ignore white history. Thus, the political, economic, and

REFLECT AND CONNECT

Take a moment and think about your childhood, specifically reflecting on when you discovered your race. When did you discover you were white, African American, or Latino, or whatever? For people of color, this is generally not a difficult task. For whites, this might be more difficult.

WITNESS

"And here I am, just another alienated middle-class white girl with no culture to inform my daily life, no people to call my own" (interviewee quoted in Frankenberg 1993).

social advantages whites have accumulated historically are easier to overlook when claiming there is no such thing as white culture (Frankenberg 1993).

SEEING PRIVILEGE

White privilege—"an elusive and fugitive subject" as Peggy McIntosh described it in 1998—has gone unexamined primarily because it is the societal norm. For sociologists, social norms are a significant aspect of culture and they refer to the shared expectations about behavior in a society, whether implicit or explicit. There are several reasons why white privilege is hard for white people to see. The first problem is the intentional invisibility of white privilege. Privilege is maintained through ignoring whiteness. According to McIntosh, "in facing [white privilege], I must give up the myth of meritocracy … [M]y moral condition is not what I had been led to believe. The appearance of being a good citizen rather than a troublemaker comes in large part from having all sorts of doors open automatically because of my color" (McIntosh 1988). Part of privilege is the assumption that your experience is normal; it does not feel like a privileged existence.

While inequality is easy to see, privilege is more obscure. White people can easily see how racism "makes people of color angry, tired, and upset, but they have little insight into the ways that not having to worry about racism affects their own lives" (Parker and Chambers 2007:17). For people of color, white privilege is not a difficult concept to grasp—it is clear from their standpoint that racial disadvantage has a flip side that amounts to advantages for the dominant group. Despite this, for white people, seeing race is difficult and is the "natural consequence of being in the driver's seat" (Dalton 2008:17).

It is difficult for most white people to discuss ways they benefit from white privilege, and many get offended when asked to think about some advantage they have accrued due to being white. Many students can recognize whether they attended a well-funded public school that adequately prepared them for college. Recognition of privilege does not negate hard work, but it is an acknowledgment that not everyone had the same educational opportunities, particularly individuals that attended poor schools predominantly populated with racial/ethnic minority students.

White privilege is problematic for many white people because it can feel insulting. Americans are taught that we live in a **meritocracy**, where individuals get what they work for, where rewards are based upon effort and talent. This ideology helps us understand poverty along individualized "blame the victim" lines rather than thinking of it as a social problem. In other words, if people are poor, it is presumed to be due to some inadequacy on their part. The opposite of the "blame the victim" ideology is also true. When people succeed in American society their success is often attributed to hard work, motivation, intelligence, or other individualized characteristics that are meant to set the person apart from less successful individuals. The idea of white privilege challenges this. It forces us to recognize that some people, due to their membership in particular racial/ethnic groups, are systematically disadvantaged and face more obstacles in their lives while members of other racial/ethnic groups are systematically advantaged, with more doors opened and more opportunities available to them. It may take their individual talents, motivation and intelligence to take advantage of the open door, but it must be acknowledged that not everyone had the door opened for them in the first place. This is often how privilege manifests itself.

White privilege is uncomfortable for many white students to grasp because the word *privilege* does not appear to describe their life. Poor and working-class white people are often offended by such a notion because they do not see themselves as beneficiaries of the system in any way. They work hard and have very little, relatively speaking. Indeed, many white people are members of the **working poor**, people who work full-time and still fall below the poverty line in the United States. How can

they be considered privileged? To be able to understand this, we have to recognize the complexities involved in the multiple status hierarchies that exist in American society. One can lack class privilege, but still have race privilege, for instance.

The idea of white privilege is that all people identified and treated as white benefit from that status, even if they face disadvantages in other arenas, such as social class. To truly understand how race operates in the United States, it is essential that we recognize this. White privilege offers poor whites something: the satisfaction that at least they do not exist on the bottom rungs of the societal hierarchy—that, despite their poverty, they are at least not black. Additionally, despite any other disadvantages a white person may have, when they walk into a job interview, or restaurant, or any situation, the primary characteristic noted is that they are white, which is their passport for entry, as Peggy McIntosh (2008) describes. Race and gender are what sociologists call **master statuses** in our society, statuses that are considered so significant they overshadow all others and influence our lives more than our other statuses.

The combination of the invisibility of white privilege and the fact that all white people are implicated in the racial hierarchy through their privilege also makes it a disturbing concept for many white people. Interrogating white privilege is a particularly difficult task because it is both structural and personal. It forces those who are white to ask questions that concern not only structural advantage (such as, how are schools structured in ways that benefit white people?) but individual privilege as well (in what ways was my educational attainment at least partially a result of racial privilege?). Again, while it is uncomfortable to acknowledge being unfairly advantaged, this is exactly what white privilege is.

Additionally, it is important to recognize in what arenas we may be advantaged (oppressors) and in what arenas we may be disadvantaged (oppressed). As a white person, I have race privilege (see Box 2.2 Race in the Workplace). As a woman, I have disadvantages within a **patriarchy**, a male-dominated society. On a global scale, there are certain advantages, from my odds of survival to the educational and economic opportunities I have had access to, to having been born in a wealthy, First World country versus in an impoverished nation.

WHITE PRIVILEGE VERSUS WHITE RACISM

Discussing white privilege makes many whites feel uncomfortable because it implicates them in a racist social structure. Thus, doesn't that make them racist? Is there a difference between white privilege and **white racism**? Feagin and Vera (1995) define white racism as "the socially organized set of attitudes, ideas, and practices that deny African Americans and other people of color the dignity, opportunities, freedoms and rewards that this nation offers white Americans" (p. 7). That is clearly a broad definition of white racism—it certainly goes above and beyond the idea that many whites take comfort in, which is that a racist is someone that is actively involved in a white supremacist organization, participates in hate crimes, or believes in the innate inferiority of nonwhites. However, it is not that clear-cut. As the definition implies, as long as people of color are denied opportunities, it is white racism, and what goes unspoken is that the flip side of this racism is that those become opportunities for white people. In other words, these are two sides of the same coin—without white racism, there is no white privilege. To work actively against racism, whites also have to work against privilege. For instance, if a white employee of a restaurant recognizes racialized patterns, such as people of color working in the kitchen and white staff working the dining room, they can point these out to management. Additionally, there are those who argue that simply living in American society makes one racist—it is the norm in our society, found in the subtle messages we all receive every day. Thus, neutrality is not equated with being nonracist. The only way to be nonracist in American society is to actively work against racism, such as by joining a racial justice organization. Many racial justice organizations are affiliated with religious institutions, for instance, or can be found on university campuses. They can also easily be found online by searching "antiracist activism" or "racial justice activism." Beyond actually joining a racial justice organization, one can simply work to be an ally to people of color in the struggle to end racism. Being an ally involves speaking up when you see racial injustice occurring, assuming racism is everywhere, everyday, and understanding the history of whiteness and racism (Kivel 2011).

IDEOLOGIES, IDENTITIES, AND INSTITUTIONS

In the previous chapter, we explored the ways race operates in the form of racial ideologies, racial identities, and institutional racism. We expand on that discussion to show the ways race privilege informs racial ideologies and racial identities, as well as fostering institutional privileges.

Racial Ideologies of Color-blindness

Ideologies are not just powerful; they operate in the "service of power" through providing a frame for interpreting the world (Bonilla-Silva 2010; Thompson 1984). It is through cultural belief systems that so many nonwhite groups embrace the racial hierarchy, embrace racism, as a way to obtain white privilege. The current reigning racial ideology is that of color-blindness.

Color-blindness supports white privilege because it encourages a mentality that allows us to say we don't see race, that essentially we are color-blind. Paradoxically, this ideology persists within a society literally obsessed with race. The elections of President Barack Obama and the ongoing racial discourse surrounding both elections are good examples. In 2007, discussions of race surrounded Super Bowl XLI because it was the first time an African American head coach had led their team to the Super Bowl, much less the fact that both teams, the Chicago Bears and the Indianapolis Colts, had black head coaches. People of mixed-race ancestry continually report being asked, "What are you?," which is evidence of the ongoing significance of race rather than a commitment to color-blindness.

Clearly, Americans see color, we see race, and we attach significance to it. The power of the color-blind ideology is threefold:

1. **We ignore racism.** We have a racist society without acknowledging any actual racists (Bonilla-Silva 2006). Racism is alive and well, yet individuals cling to color-blindness, thus, eliminating their personal responsibility for it. Sociologist Eduardo Bonilla-Silva (2010) argues that the color-blind ideology "barricades whites from the United States' racial reality" (p. 47).

2. **We ignore white privilege.** Haney-Lopez (2006) refers to this as "color-blind white dominance." By claiming color-blindness white people can ignore the ways white privilege benefits them and can ignore ongoing racism.

3. **We perceive whiteness as the norm.** Color-blindness fuels perceptions of whiteness as the norm and as synonymous with racial neutrality.

A glaring example of the preceding third item, perceiving whiteness as the norm, was found in media coverage of Hurricane Katrina in 2005. For days, media coverage showed thousands of displaced and desperate people, overwhelmingly black, seeking shelter from the rising flood waters, yet race was never mentioned. When it finally was mentioned, many white people were angered by what they saw as the media "racializing" what they perceived as a race-neutral tragedy; clinging to color-blind ideologies, they insisted that those left behind to face the devastation were simply people, not black people. The fact that they were black was somehow deemed irrelevant or mere coincidence. Yet, this tragedy was clearly "raced" and "classed" as well. It was not simply coincidence that it was predominantly poor black people that were left behind to drown as the levees broke and the city of New Orleans experienced devastating flooding.

New Orleans is an overwhelmingly black city and a very poor city. When the mayor announced a mandatory evacuation due to the impending hurricane, transportation should have been provided because so many poor, black New Orleanians did not own an automobile. As a matter of public policy, when considering a mandatory evacuation, one has to consider not just transportation but where people are going to go. Poor people are not able to simply get a hotel room in another city to wait out the storm as a middle-class person could.

Racial ideologies change over time as culture changes. What is essential is that we recognize how the racial ideologies manifest themselves in different eras, that we gauge the influence of such ideologies, and perhaps most important, recognize how the dominant group benefits from such ideologies.

WHITE RACIAL IDENTITY

Social scientists have only recently begun studying white racial identity development (Helms 1990; McDermott and Samson 2005). Much effort has been put into the study of white ethnic identity development (Alba 1990; Rubin 1994; Stein and Hill 1977; Waters 1990), black racial identity development (Burlew and Smith 1991; Helms 1990; Resnicow and Ross-Gaddy 1997), and shifting racial identities (Fitzgerald 2007; Korgen 1998; Rockquemore and Brunsma 2002), while white racial identities went unexamined. When sociologists have focused on white racial identity development, it has generally been in conjunction with white supremacist movements, but of course, all whites have a racial identity not just those belonging to such organizations (Dees and Corcoran 1996; Gallagher 2003). Some research finds that white racial identity development is surprisingly similar for white supremacists as well as for white racial justice activists (Hughey 2010, 2012).

Figure 2 A home damaged by the flooding of New Orleans due to the levee breaches after Hurricane Katrina in 2005. These homes are in New Orleans' Ninth Ward, an overwhelmingly poor and African American community that suffered some of the worst flooding. (Photo by Harold Baquet.)

For the most part, people of color have been forced to think about race, not just in the abstract, but as something fundamental to who they are, how they are perceived, and thus, how they see themselves. Whites, however, develop a white racial identity without much conscious thought or discussion. As James Baldwin has said, being white means never having to think about it. Janet Helms (1990) identifies stages of white racial identity development beginning with whites who have had no contact with other races, moving to those who learn about race and privilege, to those who see inequalities as the fault of the other races. For white people progressing through these first three of six stages of racial identity development, the question becomes, how do they get to see themselves as white in a raced world rather than as neutral, nonraced, or the norm?

In the first stage of white racial identity development, whites have had little contact with people of color and thus, have developed a sense of superiority over them based upon social stereotypes and media representations. Whites in stage one have difficulty seeing white privilege and may even resist the idea. Some of these folks are outright racists, while others are not blatant racists but may perceive people of color in stereotypical ways, such as lazy or dangerous. There is nothing inevitable about identity development—most whites are in stage one and many never move beyond the first stage (Helms 1990).

For those whites who progress in their identity development, according to Helms (1990), stage two is characterized by fear and guilt that stems from seeing themselves, perhaps for the first time, as holding racial prejudices. As they learn more about race in American society, it challenges what they thought they knew about the world. They are seeing racism and privilege for the first time. Often, whites respond to this guilt and fear through retrenchment, which is the third stage.

In the retrenchment stage, whites deal with their guilt by blaming the victim, declaring that racial inequality is the fault of minorities. Not all white people move backward at this stage. Instead, some progress through the next stages, eventually developing a healthy white identity that is not based on guilt or a sense of superiority.

Many whites struggle with seeing themselves as white. As mentioned previously, whiteness is viewed by many whites as bland, cultureless, thus, white people are more likely to lack an overt racial identity. In fact, this lack of a sense of white identity is due to the fact that whiteness is generally seen as the norm. By bemoaning their lack of a racial identity, whites help maintain the separate status of racial/ethnic minorities, who are perceived as different, as "other" in American society. What is in operation is white privilege: the privilege to *not* think about race, the privilege to *not* recognize the dominant culture as white culture rather

Figure 3 Antiracist activist, author, and speaker Tim Wise.

than as racially neutral, and the privilege to overlook the fact that whiteness, rather than being absent, is ever present as the unnamed norm.

Identities are more than personal. They are products of particular sociohistorical eras. Thus white identities, like all racial identities, are social, historical, and political constructions. The fact that white as a racial identity is rarely visible is evidence of the operation of white privilege in our lives today. Identities are political and they are a response to changing social and political contexts. Native American activism during the 1970s resulted in more individuals officially identifying as Native American (Nagel 1996). The racial identity of white Americans often goes unacknowledged, with the exception of historical eras that challenge the taken-for-grantedness of whiteness and white privilege. For instance, during the civil rights movement, white Americans began to explicitly claim their whiteness if for no other reason than they viewed the privileges associated with their whiteness as being challenged. The racial socialization of whites, their sense of entitlement, was being challenged every day. As black civil rights activists demanded equal rights, whites counterattacked with rhetoric concerning the perceived loss of their own rights (Sokol 2006). Today, in a less racially charged atmosphere, most whites are unlikely to see themselves in racial terms. However, white people working toward racial justice do view white as a race and their life experiences as racialized (see Box 2.3 Racial Justice Activism).

INSTITUTIONAL PRIVILEGE

Just as sociologists have identified racial discrimination within all of our major social institutions, white privilege can be found in these arenas as well: in banks/lending institutions, educational systems, media, religious institutions, and government, just to name a few. This is the most difficult arena to make race privilege visible. Institutional racism was introduced in the first chapter and refers to everyday business practices and policies that result in disadvantage for some racial groups, intentionally or not. **Institutional privilege** is even more difficult to identify since privilege is designed to remain invisible, in its institutionalized form it becomes even more obscure. In addition to the advantages individuals accumulate through white privilege; it also takes the form of customs, norms, traditions, laws, and public policies that benefit whites (Williams 2003). Throughout this text, various societal institutions will be explored exposing not only the racial inequality embedded in them but also the ways white privilege is built

into the specific business practices and policies within each institution. In exploring institutional privilege, it is useful to ask, what group benefits from a particular arrangement, policy, or practice?

To help understand what is meant by institutional privilege, we explore several policies and practices that have allowed whites to accumulate wealth and inhibited people of color from wealth accumulation. This includes the policies and practices of banking and lending institutions as well as government policies and practices.

Racial minorities have been systematically excluded from wealth creation with very real, concrete consequences. Slavery is the most obvious example. In addition to the cruelty and inhumanity of this institution, it was also a system that deterred wealth accumulation by the great majority of blacks and supported the massive accumulation of wealth by some whites. For over 240 years, blacks labored in America without being compensated. Clearly that places them in a disadvantaged position in terms of wealth accumulation. While only a small portion of the population owned slaves, it is estimated that about 15 million white Americans today have slave-owning ancestors (Millman 2008). Of our first eighteen presidents, thirteen owned slaves. Two recent presidents, father and son George H. W. and George W. Bush, are descendants of slave owners, contributing, of course, to their great wealth and political power to this day.

Upon emancipation, reparations for former slaves were promised, most in the form of land. The promised "forty acres and a mule," however, never materialized. During the Reconstruction era, the federal government established the Freedmen's Bureau to provide food, education, medical care, and in some cases, land, to newly freed slaves as well as to needy whites (see Chapter 5). Although this agency only lasted one year and was unable to meet the needs of the great majority of newly freed slaves, it is significant that more whites benefited from this government agency than blacks.

Native American Land Loss

The exploitation of Native Americans often involved the taking of land; an estimated 2 billion acres of land was transferred to the United States government from American Indian Tribes through treaties in exchange for tribal sovereignty (Newton 1999). European Americans confiscated land that Native peoples populated, forced their removal, and sometimes engaged in acts of genocide so as to acquire land. This theme of Native land loss at the hands of whites is hardly new; most of us learned of this in grade school. However, we need to reflect more on the significance. Native land loss is always presented as a collective problem, which it was, as tribes lost their lands and livelihoods as they were repeatedly relocated to less valuable lands. What we tend not to realize is that this is a significant loss at the individual level as well. Land is equivalent to wealth in the white mainstream culture (Native peoples, however, generally did not believe people could own the land and they instead saw themselves as stewards of the land). Who benefited when all those Native people were forced off of the lands on which they lived? White people took the land as their own, thus acquiring wealth. Native land loss at the hands of whites goes beyond giant land swindles involving treaties between the federal government and tribal governments. Throughout the country there were smaller, everyday, localized swindles. Additionally, many states established laws that did not allow Native people to own land, thus, limiting their ability to accumulate wealth and simultaneously contributing to the ability of white people to accumulate wealth.

Issues of Wealth Accumulation

These historical examples of the exploitation of racial minorities in terms of wealth accumulation have a flip side: white advantage. Whites historically and currently benefit from the exclusion of other racial/ethnic groups. For instance, laws supported the rights of white Americans to own homes and businesses while banks and lending institutions provided them the necessary capital to do so. This was not a given for people of color. Until the 1960s, laws explicitly excluded people of color from obtaining business loans in many places. White people were subsidized in acquiring their own homes, and thus establishing equity, which eventually became wealth that was passed on to the next generation (Oliver and Shapiro 1995). This is significant if for no other reason than wealth accumulates. Federal Reserve studies confirm that even today, minorities get fewer home loans, even when their economic situations are comparable to whites. "The poorest white applicant, according to this [the Federal Reserve] report, was more likely to get a mortgage loan approved than a black in the highest income bracket" (Oliver and Shapiro 1995:20). The consequences of this are profound since for most Americans home ownership represents their primary and often only source of wealth (see Chapter 8).

Ideologies of white supremacy fuel white identities of entitlement and, thus, the creation of institutions that deny access to anyone but whites are deemed acceptable. Ideologies of color-blindness in our current era fuel a

---

REFLECT AND CONNECT

Think about how much white privilege you may have. If you are white, did your ancestors own slaves? Ask your parents the following questions: Did your parents or grandparents have access to home and/or business loans? Did they own their own homes or land? Did your parents or grandparents own a business? Did your parents or grandparents attend college? Have you received or do you expect to receive an inheritance? Are your parents paying for your college, thus making significant student loan borrowing unnecessary? If you can answer yes to any of these, you have more than likely benefited from white privilege in a very material, concrete way.

"raceless" identity in whites that allows them to deny ongoing racism, while still enjoying race privilege.

CHALLENGING WHITE PRIVILEGE

What can or should be done about white privilege? Is it necessary to challenge white privilege? Is it possible? It is easier to condemn racism than to challenge one's own privilege. Understanding white privilege is essential, yet incomplete, because, as McIntosh notes, "describing white privilege makes one newly accountable" (2008:109). In other words, if we see privilege, do we not have an obligation to work to eradicate it? While white privilege allows whites to ignore their race and avoid confronting the advantages associated with it, many white Americans actively challenge white privilege as part of their commitment to racial justice and as a way to challenge their own sense of entitlement (e.g., Warren 2010; Wise 2005). White civil rights activists were rejecting their own race privilege through their activism on behalf of full civil rights for people of color, for instance (e.g., Murray 2004; Zellner 2008).

Racial justice activists argue that white privilege is the proverbial "elephant in the room" that white people agree to ignore (Parker and Chambers 2007). White theologians have called for an end to the silence surrounding white privilege within religious institutions (Cassidy and Mikulich 2007). Stories of racial justice activism are featured in "Racial Justice Activism" boxes in each chapter. Now, we are going to explore why challenging white privilege is not only necessary, but is actually in the interests of white people.

For many white people, being introduced to the concept of white privilege invokes intense feelings of guilt. They often respond by saying they should not be made to feel guilty for being white, as it was hardly their choice. Or they feel that by focusing on privilege, it takes away from their achievements or the achievements of their parents. This is not the intent. White guilt is a normal reaction to learning about historical and current atrocities inflicted upon racial minorities by whites. When it comes to race, our country has an ugly history that cannot be ignored. Guilt is uncomfortable psychologically, so people tend to work to alleviate the feeling. Thus, such guilt has the potential to motivate change, to get white people to understand how they are racist, how they contribute to racial oppression, and what they can do to end it. It is important to recognize white privilege. It is necessary for a complete understanding of the role race plays in all of our lives, both at the individual and societal levels. Additionally, opposing the racial inequities associated with whiteness is not the same thing as opposing white people (Williams 2003).

It is important to critically investigate white privilege because while privilege offers advantages, whites are also losers under this system of structural inequality. There are many unrecognized ways whites lose under this system: it is expensive, financially and morally, to ignore white privilege in the workplace because it remains an uncomfortable environment for people of color and thus, their retention is less likely. The only way white people can remain part of this racial hierarchy is to compartmentalize—separate their head from

their heart. There are long-term consequences of such compartmentalization, primarily in terms of failing to recognize our common humanity (Kendall 2006). Helms's stages of racial identity development are helpful in understanding our common humanity. Through this model, we can see that racial identity is not fixed. We can change; we can progress in terms of understanding ourselves along racial lines as well as understanding the operation of our societal racial hierarchy.

Tim Wise (2008) argues that white people pay a tremendous price for maintaining white privilege and that it is actually in the interest of whites to dismantle the racial hierarchy. Wise offers the following bit of advice to whites interested in working for racial justice: "The first thing a white person must do to effectively fight racism is to learn to listen, and more than that, to believe what people of color say about their lives ... One of the biggest problems with white America is its collective unwillingness to believe that racism is still a real problem for nonwhite peoples, despite their repeated protestations that it is" (2005:67).

One of the reasons offered by whites fighting for racial justice is the moral one: that this is an unjust system and, thus, it should be dismantled. Ignoring both inequality and privilege dehumanizes all of us. Racial justice activists find that they engage in this work because it is personally fulfilling and because they believe that working for racial justice will produce a better society for all. For racial justice activists, having healthier communities, more empowered citizens, and more humane culture that focuses on compassion and community will provide a better society for all (Warren 2010).

Another reason it is in the interest of whites to dismantle white privilege is economic. It is costly to maintain inequality. Whiteness privileges some whites more than others. It is estimated that an affluent 20 percent of whites reap the benefits of whiteness (Hobgood 2007). Having a labor force that is divided along racial lines (see Chapter 8) deflates all workers' wages. The prison industrial complex (see Chapter 9) disproportionately incarcerates racial minority males. The mass incarceration of minority males becomes self-perpetuating in that they become the face of crime, leaving white criminals privileged in that they are not immediately suspect. However, whites are disadvantaged by the mass incarceration of minorities simply because more and more tax dollars go toward incarcerating citizens rather than toward supporting schools, for instance.

WITNESS

"I think it's the price of the soul. You're internally diminished when you dominate other people or when you're trying to convince yourself you're not dominating others" (Warren 2010:88).

WITNESS

One of the racial justice activists interviewed by Warren (2010) explains why she believes this work is part of her civil and political responsibility: "We have got to do something about that for the good of democracy. It's just not healthy for a democracy to have that kind of racism at its core" (Warren 2010:85).

REFERENCES

"AC Milan Players Respond to Racist Chants by Walking off Field, Match against Pro Patria Ends." 2013. *Huffington Post*, January 3. Retrieved May 2, 2013 (http://www.huffingtonpost.com/2013/01/03/ac-milan-players-racist-chants-walk-off-pro-patria_n_2403497.html).

Alba, Richard. 1990. *Ethnic Identity: The Transformation of White Americans*. New Haven and London: Yale University Press.

Bonilla-Silva, Eduardo. 2006. *Racism Without Racists: Color-Blind Racism and the Persistence of Racial Inequality in the United States*, 2nd ed. Lanham, MD: Rowman and Littlefield.

———. 2010. *Racism Without Racists: Color-Blind Racism and Racial Inequality in Contemporary America*, 3rd ed. Lanham, MD: Rowman and Littlefield.

Brodkin, Karen. 2008. "How Jews Became White Folks." Pp. 41–53 in *White Privilege: Essential Readings from the Other Side of Racism*, 3rd ed., edited by P. Rothenberg. New York: Worth Publishers.

Burlew, A. K. and L. R. Smith. 1991. "Measures of Racial Identity: An Overview and a Proposed Framework." *Journal of Black Psychology* 17(2):53–71.

Bush, Melanie. 2011. *Everyday Forms of Whiteness: Understanding Race in a Post-Racial World*, 2nd ed. Lanham, MD: Rowman and Littlefield.

Cassidy, Laurie M. and Alex Mikulich, eds. 2007. *Interrupting White Privilege: Catholic Theologians Break the Silence*. Maryknoll, NY: Orbis Books.

Chen, Michelle. 2011. "Muslim 'Terrorists,' White 'Lone Wolves,' and the Lessons of Oslo." *Colorlines*, July 27. Retrieved July 11, 2013 (http://colorlines.com/cgi-sys/cgiwrap/colorlne/managed-mt/mt-search.cgi?search=Violence%20Against%20Women%20Act&IncludeBlogs=3%2C1%2C3%2C2&limit=10&page=9).

Dalton, Harlon. 2008. "Failing to See." Pp. 15–18 in *White Privilege: Essential Readings on the Other Side of Racism*, 3rd ed., edited by P. Rothenberg. New York: Worth Publishers.

Dees, M. and J. Corcoran. 1996. *Gathering Storm: America's Militia Threat*. New York: HarperCollins.

Feagin, Joe R., Hernan Vera, and Pinar Batur. 1995. *White Racism: The Basics*. New York and London: Routledge.

Fitzgerald, Kathleen J. 2007. *Beyond White Ethnicity: Developing a Sociological Understanding of Native American Identity Reclamation*. Lanham, MD: Lexington Books.

Foley, Neil. 2008. "Becoming Hispanic: Mexican Americans and Whiteness." Pp. 49–60 in *White Privilege: Essential Readings on the Other Side of Racism*, 3rd ed., edited by P. Rothenberg. New York: Worth Publishers.

Fox, Helen. 2001. *When Race Breaks Out: Conversations About Race and Racism in College Classrooms*. New York, Washington, DC: Peter Lang Publishers.

Frankenberg, Ruth. 1993. *White Women, Race Matters: The Social Construction of Whiteness*. Minneapolis: University of Minnesota Press.

Gallaher, Carolyn. 2003. *On the Fault Line: Race, Class, and the American Patriot Movement*. Lanham, MD: Rowman and Littlefield.

Haney Lopez, Ian F. 2006. "Colorblind to the Reality of Race in America." *Chronicle of Higher Education*, November 3. Retrieved July 24, 2013 (http://chronicle.com/article/Colorblind-to-the-Reality-of/12577).

Harris-Perry, Melissa V. 2011. *Sister Citizen: Shame, Stereotypes, and Black Women in America*. New Haven, CT: Yale University Press.

Helms, Janet. 1990. "Toward a Model of White Racial Identity Development." Pp. 49–66 in *Black and White Racial Identity: Theory, Research and Practice*, edited by J. Helms. Westport, CT: Praeger.

Hobgood, Mary Elizabeth. 2007. "White Economic and Erotic Disempowerment: A Theological Exploration in the Struggle against Racism." Pp. 40–55 in *Interrupting White Privilege: Catholic Theologians Break the Silence*, edited by L. M. Cassidy and A. Mikulich. Maryknoll, NY: Orbis Books.

Hughey, Matthew. 2010. "The (Dis)Similarities of White Racial Identities: The Conceptual Framework of 'Hegemonic Whiteness.'" *Ethnic and Racial Studies* 33(8):1289–1309.

Ignatiev, Noel. 1995. *How the Irish Became White*. New York, London: Routledge.

Jacobson, Matthew Frye. 1998. *Whiteness of a Different Color: European Immigrants and the Alchemy of Race*. Cambridge, MA: Harvard University Press.

Karabel, Jerome. 2005. *The Chosen: The Hidden History of Admission and Exclusion at Harvard, Yale, and Princeton*. Boston, New York: Houghton Mifflin Company.

Kendall, Francis. 2006. *Understanding White Privilege: Creating Pathways to Authentic Relationships Across Race*. New York: Routledge.

Kivel, Paul. 2008. "How White People Can Serve as Allies to People of Color in the Struggle to End Racism." Pp. 127–136 in *White Privilege: Essential Readings on the Other Side of Racism*, 3rd ed., edited by P. Rothenberg. New York: Worth Publishers.

Korgen, Kathleen Odell. 1998. *From Black to Biracial: Transforming Racial Identity Among Americans*. Westport, CT: Praeger.

Leonhardt, David. 2013. "Hispanics, the New Italians." *New York Times*, April 20. Retrieved May 20, 2013 (http://

www.nytimes.com/2013/04/21/sunday-review/hispanics-the-new-italians.html?pagewanted=all&_r=0).

Lopez, Ian Haney. 1996. *White By Law: The Legal Construction of Race*. New York: New York University Press.

McDermott, Monica and Frank L. Samson. 2005. "White Racial and Ethnic Identity in the United States." *Annual Review of Sociology* 31:245–261.

McIntosh, Peggy. 2008. "White Privilege: Unpacking the Invisible Knapsack." Pp. 97–102 in *White Privilege: Essential Readings on the Other Side of Racism*, 3rd ed., edited by P. Rothenberg. New York: Worth Publishers.

Millman, Jennifer. 2008. "Slavery Ties: Bush's Long-Held 'Family Secret.'" *DiversityInc.com*, February 20. Retrieved July 11, 2013 (http://www.juneteenth.us/news7.html).

Murray, Gail S. 2004. *Throwing Off the Cloak of Privilege: White Southern Women Activists in the Civil Rights Era*. Gainesville: University Press of Florida.

Nagel, Joane. 1996. *American Indian Ethnic Renewal: Red Power and the Resurgence of Identity and Culture*. New York and Oxford: Oxford University Press.

Newton, Nell Jessup. 1999. "Indian Claims for Reparations, Compensation, and Restitution in the United States Legal System" P. 41 in *When Sorry isn't Enough: The Controversy over Apologies and Reparations for Human Injustice*, edited by R. L. Brooks. New York: New York University Press.

Oliver, Melvin L. and Thomas M. Shapiro. 1995. *Black Wealth/White Wealth: A New Perspective on Racial Inequality*. New York, London: Routledge.

Parker, Robin and Pamela Smith Chambers. 2007. *The Great White Elephant: A Workbook on Racial Privilege for White Anti-Racists*. Mount Laurel, NJ: Beyond Diversity Resource Center.

Resnicow, K. and D. Ross-Gaddy. 1997. "Development of a Racial Identity Scale for Low-Income African Americans." *Journal of Black Studies* 28(2):239–254.

Rockquemore, Kerry Ann and David Brunsma. 2002. *Beyond Black: Biracial Identity in America*. Thousand Oaks, CA: Sage Publications.

Rodriguez, Victor M. 2005. "The Racialization of Mexican Americans and Puerto Ricans: 1890s–1930s." *CENTRO Journal* 17(1):71–105.

Roediger, David R. 1991. *The Wages of Whiteness: Race and the Making of the American Working Class*. London, New York: Verso.

Rothenberg, Paula S. 2008. *White Privilege: Essential Readings on the Other Side of Racism*, 3rd ed. New York: Worth Publishers.

Rubin, Lillian. 1994. *Families on the Fault Line*. New York: Harper Perennial.

Sokol, Jason. 2006. *There Goes My Everything: White Southerners in the Age of Civil Rights, 1945–1975*. New York: Vintage Books.

Stein, Howard and Robert F. Hill. 1977. *The Ethnic Imperative: Examining the New White Ethnic Movement*. University Park: Pennsylvania State University Press.

Terry, Robert W. 1970. *For Whites Only*. Grand Rapids, MI: William B. Eerdmans Publishing.

Thompson, John. 1984. *Studies in the Theory of Ideology*. Cambridge, UK: Polity.

Tichenor, Daniel J. 2002. *Dividing Lines: The Politics of Immigration Control in America*. Princeton, NJ: Princeton University Press.

Warren, Mark R. 2010. *Fire in the Heart: How White Activists Embrace Racial Justice*. Oxford, New York: Oxford University Press.

Waters, Mary. 1990. *Ethnic Options: Choosing Identities in America*. Berkeley, CA: University of California Press.

"'White Privilege' Lesson in Delavan-Darien High School Class in Wisconsin Draws Ire." 2013. *Huffington Post*, January 16. Retrieved May 2, 2013 (http://www.huffingtonpost.com/2013/01/16/white-privilege-class-at-_n_2489997.html?view=print&comm_ref=false).

Williams, Linda Faye. 2003. *The Constraint of Race: The Legacies of White Skin Privilege in America*. University Park: The Pennsylvania State University Press.

Wise, Tim. 2001. "School Shootings and White Denial." *Alternet*, March 5. Retrieved August 20, 2009 (http://www.alternet.org/story/10560/school_shootings_and_white_denial).

———. 2005. *White Like Me: Reflections on Race from a Privileged Son*. Brooklyn, NY: Soft Skull Press.

———. 2005. "Oh, Give Me A Home." *Alternet*, March 10. Retrieved July 25, 2013 (http://www.alternet.org/story/21469/oh,_give_me_a_home).

———. 2008. "Membership Has Its Privileges: Thoughts on Acknowledging and Challenging Whiteness." Pp. 107–110 in *White Privilege: Essential Readings on the Other Side of Racism*, 3rd ed. New York: Worth Publishers.

———. 2013. "Terrorism and Privilege: Understanding the Power of Whiteness." April 16. Retrieved May 21, 2013 (http://www.timwise.org/2013/04/terrorism-and-privilege-understanding-the-power-of-whiteness/).

Wray, Matt. 2006. *Not Quite White: White Trash and the Boundaries of Whiteness*. London and Durham, NC: Duke University Press.

Zellner, Bob and Constance Curry. 2008. *The Wrong Side of Murder Creek: A White Southerner in the Freedom Movement*. Montgomery, AL: New South Books.

DISCUSSION QUESTIONS

1. Explain the social construction of Whiteness and the process of "becoming" White.

2. Explain White privilege: what is it, and how does it work? If you are White, describe at least five ways you have benefited from White privilege. Discuss whether it was difficult to think of five examples, and if it was, speculate on why it was. If you are not White, list five ways you have been discriminated against because of your race. Discuss whether it was difficult to think of five examples, and speculate on why it was or wasn't.

3. Explain how social class, social mobility, and Whiteness are interconnected.

4. Do you belong to a racial or ethnic group that has experienced a changing racial status, such as those discussed in this article, that eventually "became White?" If so, were you aware of this history? If not, why do you think you were unaware of it?

TAKING ACCOUNT OF RACE AND PRIVILEGE

Recognizing Race and Ethnicity: Power, Privilege, and Inequality

BY **Kathleen Fitzgerald**

W. E. B. Du Bois begins his seminal work, The Souls of Black Folk (1989:1), with the prophetic statement, "The problem of the Twentieth century is the problem of the color- line." His comment remains true today, but we would instead say the problem of the twenty- first century remains a problem associated with the **racial order**,1 the collection of beliefs, suppositions, rules, and practices that shape the way groups are arranged in a society; generally, it is a hierarchical categorization of people along the lines of certain physical characteristics, such as skin color,

hair texture, and facial features (Hochschild, Weaver, and Burch 2012). The United States has not resolved the "race problem," as it has historically been referred to by social scientists, and part of the reason is because white people have never considered it to be their problem to solve. The term *race problem* implies a problem of racial minorities. Du Bois expresses this implication in his first chapter: "Between me and the other world there is ever an unasked question ... How does it feel to be a problem?" (1989:3). Race relations in a society, whether problematic or not, involve all racial groups, including the dominant racial group.

The election of President Barack Obama led to im- mediate claims in the media that the United States is a

---

1   Key terms and concepts are indicated in boldface on first definition in the book.

postracial society, a society that has moved beyond race, because Obama could not have won the presidency without a significant number of white votes. However, as sociologists point out, Obama may have won the presidential elections in 2008 and 2012, but most whites did not vote for him (Wingfield and Feagin 2010). While Obama won significant majorities of racial minority votes, from 62 percent of the Asian American vote and 66 percent of the Latino vote to 95 percent of the black vote, he won only 43 percent of the white vote in 2008 (Wingfield and Feagin 2010). The kind of opposition he has faced while governing is virulent and unlike anything past presidents have experienced. For instance, he is the only president to have his birthright questioned. Perhaps even more disturbingly, the US Secret Service has reported approximately thirty death threats against Obama daily,

Figure 1 The election of President Barack Obama, the fi rst African American US president, is evidence of racial progress but not evidence we are a postracial society. Obama could not have won the presidency without a signifi cant number of white votes. However, most whites did not vote for him, while signifi cant majorities of racial minority voters did. (Library of Congress, LC- DIGppbd-00358)

which is four times the number made against the previous president (Feagin 2012).

While much has changed over the last century in terms of race, race remains a central organizing principle of our society, a key arena of inequality, and the subject of ongoing conflict and debate. Race also influences our identities, how we see ourselves. Ongoing evidence of the continuing significance of race manifests in both significant and obscure ways, as the following exemplify:

- The July 2013 acquittal of volunteer neighborhood watchman George Zimmerman for the killing of unarmed teenager Trayvon Martin in Sanford, Florida, has resulted in racially divided opinions on the verdict: 86 percent of African Americans are dissatisfied with the verdict compared to 30 percent of whites, while 60 percent of white Americans think the racial dynamics of the case are being overemphasized compared with only 13 percent of blacks who feel the same way (PEW Research Center 2013).

- A mere ten days before the 2012 presidential election, polls showed that racial attitudes in the United States had not improved since the election of the country's first black president, with 51 percent of Americans expressing explicit antiblack attitudes, up from 48 percent in 2008 (Ross and Agiesta 2012).

- The average white student attends a school where 77 percent of their classmates are also white (Swalwell 2012).

- Several black nurses have sued the Michigan hospital where they work for acquiescing to the demands of a white supremacist who, after exposing his swastika tattoo, demanded that no nurses of color be allowed to care for his baby (Karoub 2013).

- The Pew Research Center released data showing that Asian Americans now outpace Latinos as the fastest-growing immigrant group in the United States (Garafoli 2012).

- Over the past decade, research finds white criminals seeking presidential pardons have been almost four times as likely as racial minorities to receive them (Linzer and LaFleur 2011).

- In 2012, a student at Towson University proposed a campus White Student Union while anonymous students at Mercer University posted fliers on campus declaring November and December to be "White History Month," in response to what they feel is a bias against white students on their campuses.

- The election of the nation's first nonwhite president has contributed to an alarming increase in hate groups and antigovernment groups in the United States (Ohlheiser 2012).

- Even with a black man sitting behind the desk in the Oval Office, a disproportionate number of black men—over one million—are incarcerated in the United States (Ogletree 2012).

- Most Native American mascots, such as the University of North Dakota's Fighting Sioux, remain significant sources of conflict between Native Americans and non-Natives (Borzi 2012). (This text uses the terms "Native American" and "Indian" interchangeably.)

THE SIGNIFICANCE OF RACE

Despite the undeniable racial progress that has been made during the twentieth century, ongoing racism harkens back to earlier eras through racial imagery, for instance. As the opening vignette describes, nooses, visible reminders of an era when whites lynched African Americans, as well as Mexican Americans, Native Americans, Jewish Americans, and many other racial minorities, for real or imagined offenses, are still hung today to intimidate people of color. Lynching imagery was pervasive on the Internet during President Obama's candidacy and eventual presidency (Feagin 2012). In 2007, a noose was hung on the office door of an African American professor who taught courses on race and diversity at Columbia University. That same year on the same campus, a Jewish professor found a swastika on her office door. Both are professors of psychology and education and involved in teaching multicultural education.

What is the message being sent by this kind of racial imagery? The black high school student in Jena, Louisiana, President Obama, and the professors targeted in these examples violate what Feagin et al. (1996) refer to as **racialized space**, space generally regarded as reserved for one race and not another. Both that particular area of the high school campus in Jena and Columbia University were being defined by some students as "white space," a racialized space where nonwhites are

perceived as intruders and unwelcome. Additionally, research on the experiences of Latino college students finds they often refer to institutions of higher education as a "white space," thus, an environment where they feel less than welcome (Barajas and Ronnkvist 2007).

Are these isolated incidents? According to the Southern Poverty Law Center, a nonprofit group that tracks hate crimes and hate group activity, the prevalence of nooses and other symbols of hate, such as swastikas, are not unusual. Often such incidents are explained as a practical joke, which begs the question, what exactly is funny about a noose? A noose is the ultimate symbol of terror directed primarily, but not exclusively, toward African Americans. This symbol is hard to joke about. The parents of some of the white students in Jena explained away their high school children's behavior as a combination of ignorance and humor. We have to challenge such assumptions in the face of the history of this gruesome ritual.

Lynching is generally regarded as a southern type of mob justice perpetrated by whites against blacks. Indeed, the great majority of lynching's fit this profile and thus became the focus of a major antilynching movement during the first half of the twentieth century (which will be discussed in more detail in Chapter 4). However, many more racial/ethnic minorities were targeted for this type of violence. Part of the perceived "taming of the West" involved the lynching of hundreds of Chinese, Native Americans, and Latinos, particularly Mexicans, by Anglo-Americans (Gonzales-Day 2006). In Atlanta, Leo Franck, a Jewish factory manager from Brooklyn, was lynched for the murder of a young female factory worker, despite the fact that the evidence overwhelmingly pointed at someone else as the perpetrator of this crime. After the conviction of this man, a mob broke into the jail and dragged him off to be lynched, rather than allowing his conviction and life sentence to stand. The defendant was described as someone worthy of paying for this horrendous crime, "not just some black factory sweeper, but a rich Jew from Brooklyn" (Guggenheim 1995).

Lynching was a public act—often occurring at night, nevertheless, drawing large crowds of supporters. Photographers routinely captured such moments and often these photographs were made into postcards for popular consumption (Gonzales-Day 2006). Sociologically speaking, the use of public execution is meant to send a message to all members of the community. These are acts of terror, not just actions meant to punish one particular individual; terror is designed to instill fear in more people than the individual or individuals targeted. Thus, anyone currently teaching courses that challenge white supremacy could well interpret the hanging of a noose or a swastika on a professor's door as being directed at them as well. The presence of souvenirs and postcards complicates the picture; beyond terrorizing minority communities, it becomes a morbid celebration of dominant group privilege.

Not long after the hanging of nooses at the school in Jena and at Columbia University, an African American man has been elected president for the first time in US history. The success of Barack Obama's presidential campaign clearly indicates progressive social change. So, what can we make of an era when nooses are still being hung yet a black man finds tremendous support for his presidential candidacy? Such contradictions are actually part of a long history of societal contradictions surrounding the issue of race and are quite common; these may even become obvious to us if we take the time to reflect on some of the lessons we have been taught about race. According to white author and professor Helen Fox, "Everything I learned about race while growing up has been profoundly contradictory. Strong, unspoken messages about how to be racist shamefully contradict the ways I have been taught to be a good person" (2001:15). Students often note that they have been taught to love everyone because "we are all children of God," while simultaneously warned against interracial dating. Clearly, there is a fundamental, though often unrecognized, contradiction embedded in such messages.

Defining Concepts in the Sociology of Race and Ethnicity

This book approaches the study of race/ethnicity through a **sociological** lens. Sociology refers to the academic discipline that studies group life: society, social interactions, and human social behavior. Sociologists that study race and ethnicity focus on such things as historical and current conflict between racial/ethnic groups, the emergence of racial/ethnic identities, racial/ethnic inequality and privilege, and cultural beliefs

about race/ethnicity, otherwise referred to as racial ideologies.

We live in a culture where the meaning of race appears to be clear, yet scientists challenge what we think we know about race. **Race** specifically refers to a group of people that share some socially defined physical characteristics, for instance, skin color, hair texture, or facial features. That definition more than likely reinforces our common understanding of race. Most of us believe we can walk into a room and identify the number of different racial groups present based upon physical appearances. But is that really true? Many people are racially ambiguous in appearance, for any number of reasons, including the fact that they may be multiracial.

A term that is distinct from race, yet often erroneously used interchangeably with it is **ethnicity**. *Ethnicity* refers to a group of people that share a culture, nationality, ancestry, and/or language; physical appearance is not associated with ethnicity. Both of these terms are socially defined and carry significant meaning in our culture; they are not simply neutral and descriptive categories. A challenge social scientists offer is to understand race and ethnicity as **social constructions** rather than biological realities, despite the fact that the definition of race refers to physical appearance. The details concerning this very important distinction will be introduced later in this chapter.

While social scientists distinguish between the two categories of race and ethnicity, they are not mutually exclusive. In other words, people can identify along the lines of their race and their ethnicity. For instance, a Nigerian American immigrant, an African American whose ancestors have been in the United States for hundreds of years, and a black Puerto Rican all have very different ethnicities, yet they are still classified as "black" in our culture. This text uses the term **racial/ethnic** to acknowledge that race and ethnicity overlap. In addition to using the term *racial/ethnic*, the terminology of **people of color** will be used to collectively refer to racial/ethnic minority groups that have been the object of racism and discrimination in the United States, rather than using the term *nonwhite*. To use the term *nonwhite* reinforces white as the norm against which all other groups are defined, which is a perspective this text argues against.

Sociologists often use the terms **minority group** or **subordinate group** to express patterned inequality along group lines. From a sociological perspective, a minority group does not refer to a statistical minority (a group smaller in size). Instead, sociologists are referring

---

REFLECT AND CONNECT

Can you identify any contradictory messages surrounding race that you have been exposed to through the media, at home, in school, or in church?

to a group that is cumulatively disadvantaged in proportion to their population size. For instance, Native Americans are a minority group because they are disproportionately impoverished. Women are a minority group according to the sociological understanding of the term; however, while they qualify as a sociological minority, women are a statistical majority as they represent 51 percent of the US population. The opposite of this is also true: if there are disadvantaged groups, there are advantaged groups that sociologists refer to as a **majority group** or **dominant group**. Again, we are not referring to statistics but instead to a group's disproportionate share of society's power and resources. In terms of race, whites are the dominant, majority group in the United States.

This text emphasizes one status hierarchy: race. However, multiple status hierarchies are significant: there is a gender hierarchy, in which men are the dominant group and women are the minority group. Another status hierarchy of significance relates to sexuality: heterosexuals are the dominant group, while nonheterosexuals comprise what we refer to as sexual minorities.

Racism: Past and Present

Despite undeniable racial progress, our society remains divided along racial lines and racial inequality persists. However, one can look at the previously discussed noose incidents as a sign of that progress: while they are disturbing, racist acts, with the intent of terrorizing minorities, they are only symbolic. Three or more generations ago, they would more than likely have been the "strange fruit" that 1940s-era African American jazz singer Billie Holiday sang of; "strange fruit" referred to lynching and symbolized the bodies hanging from trees.

However, in the face of such a history, we must not underestimate the power of symbols. We live in a symbolic world, which means that we develop a shared understanding of our world through a variety of symbols; meanings are culturally conveyed and understood through symbols. Yet, we all do not have equal power in defining symbols as meaningful. Part of the symbolism of a noose is recognition that, in the United States, the world is still interpreted through a racist lens, even if some people fail to recognize it as such.

The act of hanging nooses, the cultural meaning of this symbol, and any denials of the significance of such symbolism, all amount to **racism**. *Racism* refers to any actions, attitudes, beliefs, or behaviors, whether intentional or unintentional, which threaten, harm, or disadvantage members of one racial/ethnic group, or the group itself, over another. Thus, racism can take many forms. It can manifest as **prejudice**, a belief that is not based upon evidence but instead upon preconceived notions and stereotypes that are not subject to change even when confronted with contrary evidence. Prejudice relegates racism to the realm of ideas and attitudes rather than actions.

The type of racism that most people envision when they hear the word *racism* is actually referring to **individual discrimination**, which refers to discriminatory actions taken by individuals against members of a subordinate group. Not hiring people because they are black is an example of individual discrimination. The minority applicants are not given a chance to even compete for the job, their candidacy dismissed due to the racial/ethnic group to which they belong. This type of racism has declined since the civil rights era simply because it is illegal and thus many employers do not discriminate out of fear of legal retribution.

The most prominent type of racism today is the hardest to see and that is **institutional racism**. It is hard to see because it is found not in individual actions but in everyday business practices and policies that disadvantage minorities and offer advantages to dominant group members; it is often written off as "just the way things are." For instance, schools disproportionately rely on personal property taxes for the majority of their funding, something we will explore in great detail in Chapter 7. This type of a system disadvantages schools that serve predominantly poor communities (because the residents have less personal property and what they do have is valued less, thus fewer tax dollars are collected). As we will discover in the coming chapters, race and class overlap significantly, thus, this type of funding system, while possibly not intentionally racist, manifests as racism because schools that have predominantly minority populations tend to get the least funding.

While the previous examples show that racism has changed over the generations, it remains a significant facet of our society; "Malcolm X used to say that racism was like a Cadillac: they make a new model every year. There is always racism, but it is not the same racism" (Lipsitz 2001:120). Today's racism is certainly different from the racism of the post-Civil War and post-Reconstruction era of segregation known as Jim Crow; however, that does not negate the fact that racism is alive and well and is something people of color experience in their daily lives and to which white Americans are too often oblivious. Race and racism are constantly changing, responding to changing social contexts, societal demands, social movements, and varying political climates, to name a few significant influences.

The Continuing Significance of Race

One of the primary arguments in this text is that all of us are required to take account of race, to recognize the operation of race in our lives. Many of you are taking this course because it is a requirement. That is no accident. In our rapidly changing world, employers need a workforce that is familiar with and comfortable with all kinds of diversity including, but not limited to, racial/ethnic diversity (see Box 1.1 Race in the Workplace). Too often Americans have fooled themselves into thinking we understand one another when we clearly do not. During slavery, for instance, southern slaveholders were astonished at the demands of abolitionists, insisting that they treated "their" slaves well and that it was a mutually beneficial system. Later, during the civil rights movement, many southern whites again misunderstood race relations in their own communities, repeatedly claiming that "their" Negroes were happy and that only outside agitators, primarily those that were communist influenced, were the ones fighting for civil rights. During the early to mid-1970s, as busing became the solution to segregated schools in the north, intense rioting and violent opposition occurred in many cities throughout the north, most notoriously Boston. However, individuals in northern states did not consider themselves racially prejudiced, certainly not in the way southerners were stigmatized as racist. Their reactions to busing revealed a very different picture, however.

More current examples of the continuing significance of race include the efforts during the 2012 presidential election and afterward in numerous states to implement new voter ID laws. The effects of these kinds of laws will likely disenfranchise thousands of mostly poor, black voters simply because significant numbers of poor adults do not have the photo identification that this new legislation requires of voters. Because African Americans overwhelmingly support President Obama and the Democratic Party, such laws are viewed as benefiting the Republican Party. In fact, Pennsylvania House majority leader Mike Turzai said as much, claiming, "voter ID [would] allow Governor Romney to win the state of Pennsylvania" (Johnson 2012).

The Anti-Defamation League provides evidence of ongoing anti-Semitism in the United States and the Southern Poverty Law Center's data on hate crimes and hate group activity highlights the work we still need to do when it comes to understanding one another, particularly those that differ from us on racial/ethnic lines, let alone achieving a postracial society.

To take account of race is to bring it out into the open—to recognize how membership in particular racial/ethnic groups advantages some while hindering others. It exposes how race remains a significant social divide in our culture and, further, how it is embedded in our identities, ideologies, and institutions. Supreme Court justice Harry Blackmun used similar language in his opinion in the affirmative action case *Regents of the University of California v. Bakke* (1978):

> A race-conscious remedy is necessary to achieve a fully integrated society, one in which the color of a person's skin will not determine the opportunities available to him or her ... In order to get beyond racism, we must first take account of race. There is no other way ... In order to treat persons equally, we must treat them differently.

In this opinion, Blackmun emphasizes that we must recognize race to get beyond it, that color consciousness is preferable to color-blindness. Many Americans, particularly white Americans, would rather avoid recognizing the issue of race. Not being victimized by racism can lead many whites to believe that racism is fading away and that any emphasis on race only revives it. Even many progressive white people believe that acknowledging race is a form of racism and that denying race means not discriminating against or holding stereotypical views about racial minorities. This **color-blind ideology** dominates US culture; the idea that we don't see race, that racism is a thing of the past and that if racial inequality still exists, it must be due to other factors, such as culture or personal ineptitude. Claiming we live in a color-blind society isn't polite; it is problematic because it fails to challenge white privilege or acknowledge ongoing racism (Bonilla-Silva 2006; Haney-Lopez 2006; Omi and Winant 1994). Instead, **color consciousness**, recognizing race and difference rather than pretending we don't, allows us to celebrate difference without implying difference is equivalent to inferiority.

UNDERSTANDING RACE AS A SOCIAL CONSTRUCTION

Have you ever questioned this concept called race? For many of us, race has simply been an unquestioned part of our lives. Most white people have not because they view the world from a position of **race privilege**, the advantages associated with being a member of a society's dominant race. Having race privilege allows people to rarely even think about race, much less question its validity. Chapter 2 will explore in more detail this idea of white (race) privilege and the ways it manifests itself. However, it is not only white people that fail to question the notion of race. For people of color, their experiences with racial prejudice and discrimination emphasize the significance of race, and such experiences cause them not to question the concept of race, either. If you experience racial discrimination, race feels very real.

People who question the validity of race tend to be those who live in the racial margins—biracial and multiracial individuals, for instance. Racial categories in our society are treated as absolute, as either/or, and as biologically real. Yet biracial individuals live in a world of both/and—they are members of more than one racial group, so discrete racial categories don't apply to them. For example, monoracial people can fill out their demographic information on standardized test or census forms without question, while biracial and multiracial people find themselves in a predicament. They are forced to think of themselves as *either* black, white, Hispanic, or Native American, when they may be all or some combination of the above categories. Their very existence challenges our societal racial categorization system. Thus, their standpoint on the world and their lived experience allows them to see what for many of us is difficult not only to see but to understand: that race is not real in a biological sense.

Race is a **socially constructed** phenomenon. In other words, race is not biological or genetically determined; racial categories, groups of people differentiated by their physical characteristics, are given particular meanings by particular societies. Beyond the existence of biracial and multiracial people, there is plenty of other evidence to support the idea that race is a social construct rather than a biological reality.

Dislodging the notion that race is "real" in a biological sense is often difficult, particularly if this is your first encounter with this idea (after all, our genes determine what we look like, right?). Next time you walk into a room, see whether you can identify how many racial groups are present. While this may make you uncomfortable, as some people are racially ambiguous and you might hate to be wrong, most people assume that this task is possible. However, scientists know otherwise. Despite the lack of biological validity, race and ethnicity are important socially, which is why a

Figure 2 Despite the fact that Kian (left) looks black and Remee (right) looks white, these little girls are twins, born just a minute apart. This image exemplifies the idea that race is a social construction. (Bancroft Media/Landov)

critical investigation of race, racism, and race privilege are so important. While it may be difficult to dislodge our misconceptions surrounding the biological validity of race, it is important to recognize that there is power in the notion of race as a social construction (see Box 1.3 Global Perspectives). Anything that is constructed can, of course, be deconstructed. In other words, there is nothing inevitable about race, racism, and racial inequality. We could have a society without these problematic divisions, a society without a racial hierarchy.

Race changes across time and place. If race were biologically real, this would not be true. But despite the lack of biological validity, race is a significant delineator in American society because we attach particularly salient meanings to specific physical characteristics and these meanings result in some very real consequences.

The racial category "white" has always been in flux. Groups today that were once considered nonwhite include Irish Americans, Greek Americans, Italian Americans, and Jewish Americans. Their physical appearance never changed, but their social status did, which offers more evidence that race is a socially constructed category. Prior to "becoming white," members of these groups were discriminated against, assumed to be of inferior intelligence, and faced some of the same obstacles that black Americans, for instance, have faced. For example, when Irish Americans were considered to be nonwhite, they were not considered qualified for certain jobs and their housing choices were limited (Ignatiev 1995). Over time, all of these groups came to be considered white, and with that changing racial/ethnic status came advantages that they could use every day (the social construction of whiteness is discussed in detail in Chapter 2).

From a biological science standpoint, it is not hard to recognize that racial categories are social constructions. Quite simply, their argument was that if an animal can breed, and humans are animals, it is of the same species. Any further breakdown in the species "human being," then, is socially generated rather than biologically determined. Additionally, after mapping the human genome, geneticists have not identified a gene that is found strictly in one racial group and not in another.

There is also more genetic variation within a so-called racial group than between groups. Think about this last statement for a moment and challenge how you have been taught to think about race and the world. We all encounter very light-skinned African Americans who are identified and classified as black (in personal interactions or on official documents, for instance) and very dark-skinned individuals who are similarly identified and classified as white. We see these physical variations every day; however, we tend not to let them challenge our assumptions about race. The idea of the social construction of race forces us to recognize that if such

Figure 3 The social construction of race is also exemplified by the changing racial categories on the census. This image is of the racial category question on the 2010 census. Currently, "Hispanic" is not a racial category, according to the US census; however, the Census Bureau is considering adding it as a racial category on the 2020 census. (U.S. Census Bureau, 2010 Census questionnaire)

→ **NOTE: Please answer BOTH Question 5 about Hispanic origin and Question 6 about race. For this census, Hispanic origins are not races.**
5. Is this person of Hispanic, Latino, or Spanish origin?
☐ **No,** not of Hispanic, Latino, or Spanish origin
☐ Yes, Mexican, Mexican Am., Chicano
☐ Yes, Puerto Rican
☐ Yes, Cuban
☐ Yes, another Hispanic, Latino, or Spanish origin — *Print origin, for example, Argentinean, Colombian, Dominican, Nicaraguan, Salvadoran, Spaniard, and so on.* ⤵

6. What is this person's race? *Mark* X *one or more boxes.*
☐ White
☐ Black, African Am., or Negro
☐ American Indian or Alaska Native — *Print name of enrolled or principal tribe.* ⤵

☐ Asian Indian   ☐ Japanese   ☐ Native Hawaiian
☐ Chinese   ☐ Korean   ☐ Guamanian or Chamorro
☐ Filipino   ☐ Vietnamese   ☐ Samoan
☐ Other Asian — *Print race, for example, Hmong, Laotian, Thai, Pakistani, Cambodian, and so on.* ⤵   ☐ Other Pacific Islander — *Print race, for example, Fijian, Tongan, and so on.* ⤵

☐ Some other race — *Print race.* ⤵

glaring contradictions exist, we must challenge our racial categorization system.

Consider a seemingly objective document: the census. Census data has been collected every ten years by the federal government through the Office of Management and Budget since the first census of 1790 under the guidance of Thomas Jefferson. The census is supposed to provide us with a demographic snapshot of the United States: data on the educational levels, age, race, gender, socioeconomic status, and much more about the US population at a particular time (see Image 1.3). The census is assumed to contain objective and nonbiased information. Social scientists use census data regularly in scientific research, thus, affirming the validity of the document and the data collected.

However, racial categories on the census are always changing, which confirms the social construction of race as a reflection of sociohistorical eras. For instance, the first census documented "whites" and "nonwhites," with instructions to not count Native Americans at all. Prior to and following the Civil War, the census had multiple categories for blacks. For instance in 1840, 1850,

REFLECT AND CONNECT

Why were such differentiations and subgroupings of blacks considered necessary during the decades leading up to and immediately after the Civil War, yet have been considered unnecessary since 1890? Can you explain why such racial categorizations of African Americans were politically advantageous in some eras but not others?

and 1860, census takers were provided with a racial category called mulatto, a person of mixed African and white ancestry, although this category was not explicitly defined at the time. In the 1870 and 1880 censuses, the category "mulatto" was defined and differentiated into two subgroups, **quadroons** (the child of a white person and a mulatto) and **octoroons** (which referred to the child of a white person and a quadroon, thus, someone having one black great-grandparent), as well as a category referring to "people having any perceptible trace of African blood." By 1890, census takers were asked to record the exact proportion of African blood, based upon physical appearance and the opinion of the census taker (the census did not begin using racial self-definitions until 1960).

Over the years, such groups as Japanese Americans have been classified on the census as "nonwhite," "Orientals," "other," and currently, "Asian or Asian Pacific Islander." A relatively new census category is that of "Hispanic." Many Latinos do not see themselves as "Hispanic," as it is not a term they have used to define themselves. It is instead a term originated by the United States federal government. The term "Latino" references the Latin American origins of such people, thus, tends to be more commonly used. Currently, "Hispanic" is not classified as a race on the US census despite the fact that whites are referred to as "non-Hispanic whites." As previous eras exposed great interest in African Americans, as emphasized by their census categorizations in the eras surrounding the Civil War, political interest in Hispanics has been emerging since the 1970s.

Why keep track of the racial demographics of society at all? Aren't we all just human beings? The American Civil Liberties Union urged the race category be removed from the census in 1960, but once various civil rights acts were passed, census data on race became useful for gauging compliance with laws barring various forms of discrimination. Thus, we come back to Justice Blackmun's point—to get beyond racism, we must first take account of race.

DEMOGRAPHIC SHIFTS IN THE UNITED STATES

Courses on race and ethnicity are required in many colleges and universities because the face of America is changing demographically. Figure 1.1, based upon Pew Research Center data, shows the demographic breakdown of racial/ethnic groups in the United States for 2005 and predictions for 2050.

REFLECT AND CONNECT

Take a minute to look over the demographic data in Figure 1.1 and analyze the following statement that was reported as part of this national news story: "Pew Center report says nearly 1 in 5 residents will be immigrants, non-Hispanic whites will lose majority status" by 2050 (Olivo 2008). Based upon your understanding of race as a social construction, can you identify potential flaws in this prediction/interpretation of the data?

As the previous discussion makes clear, we cannot be sure that in thirty-something years these will be the census racial categories. Census racial categories have changed over time and it is reasonable to assume this will continue. If so, what changes do you predict in terms of census racial categories? The Pew Research Center warned of the problem of prediction based upon current census categories, but the warnings failed to make it into the news stories.

A second flaw in the statement is the assertion that non-Hispanic whites will "lose majority status." First, that statement is true only if we lump all the other racial groups together (and why would we suddenly do that, when they have been intentionally reported separately?). Second, sociologically speaking, to say that non-Hispanic whites will lose majority status speaks only to numerical status, but says nothing about power and societal dominance. There is no evidence that whites will lose power, resources, and status and certainly no evidence that whites will become a minority group. Such an interpretation presented by the media can be viewed not only as inaccurate but as incendiary in the current climate. It is the kind of statement that strikes fear in whites, increases antagonism toward immigrants, increases racial tensions, and creates a climate of hostility overall.

At the same time, these are significant demographic changes confronting American society; essentially, the face of America is changing dramatically. In two short generations, American society will look very different. Thus, such changes require that we learn to understand one another, particularly cultural differences and across racial/ethnic lines. Future teachers, a population that is still disproportionately white, middle class, and female, will be facing students with much more racial/ethnic diversity than were in the classrooms they grew up in. The hope underlying courses in racial/ethnic diversity or a multiculturalism requirement is that today's college students will come to embrace, not just tolerate, racial/ethnic differences.

Racial Ideologies

Racial ideologies, or cultural belief systems surrounding race, are also significant and have changed over time, generally as a way to meet the needs of a particular era or in response to changing social conditions. Societies establish racial hierarchies to benefit some groups, while disadvantaging others and ideologies serve to justify such arrangements. The current reigning racial ideology in the United States is that of **color-blindness**, or the color-blind ideology. Color-blindness is the idea that race no longer matters, particularly since the civil rights movement, and that if there is evidence of ongoing inequality along racial lines, it must be due to some nonracial factor, such as culture. This is a significant racial ideology because it allows white people, even those that consider themselves liberal and/or progressive, to deny the significance of race in our current society (Bonilla-Silva 2006; Omi and Winant 1994).

This is a justifying ideology because it allows us to think that the social activism of the 1960s resolved racial inequalities and thus we are a society that is beyond race. Color-blindness, for instance, suggests that race no longer matters, and in turn implies that policies with a racial component should also no longer matter. This ultimately allows people to dismiss the necessity of social policies such as affirmative action. And yet, such policies are designed to address not only current racial (and gender) inequality, but also the ongoing effects of historical inequalities; as long as the inequality remains, a need for social policies to address it remains. In previous eras, ideologies based on white supremacy predominated to justify slavery long after slavery had been introduced. Such ideologies served to deflect questions about the morality of slavery because they allowed white people to believe in the complete inferiority and inhumanity of blacks. White supremacist ideologies allowed Anglo-Americans to justify taking land away from Native peoples and engage in genocidal policies against them, due to the perceived inferiority of the Native peoples and the fact that they were viewed as uncivilized heathens.

Institutional Racism

Finally, institutional racism is found in the ways societal institutions, such as educational, economic, political, and legal spheres, are "raced." Institutional racism is the most pervasive form of racism today and also the most subtle because it is found in everyday business practices, laws, and norms that create or maintain racial inequality, whether intentional or not. Institutional racism is often considered to be the most difficult kind of racial discrimination to see because it tends not to be an action taken by a particular person that others can point to and recognize as racism. It is much more subtle than that, despite the fact that the racial manifestations are very real. Because this is the most prominent type of racism in the United States, it may explain why white people and people of color have such divergent views on the extent of racism that still exists in our society.

Racial identities, ideologies, and institutions are intricately interconnected. For instance, when the ideology of white superiority reigned and the one-drop rule was established, biracial individuals saw themselves as black. They did not consider their white heritage as informing their identity in any way, nor were they encouraged to do so. Claiming a biracial or a multiracial identity is a post-1960s phenomenon. Additionally, ideologies inform institutional practices such as public policy making or vice versa. For instance, the emergence of a biracial or multiracial identity came as interracial relationships increased in the post-1960s era, after the last laws forbidding interracial marriage were overturned by the Supreme Court in 1967.

Another example of the interconnections between identities, ideologies, and institutions occurred during the 1990s with the battle for a multiracial category on the census, a clear institutional reflection of this growing movement of people who claim a multiracial identity. The Office of Management and Budget did not opt for a specific biracial or multiracial category, but allowed individuals for the first time to check more than one racial category.

REFERENCES

Barajas, H. L. and Amy Ronnkvist. 2007. "Racialized Space: Framing Latino and Latina Experience in Public Schools." *Teachers College Record* 109(6):1517–1538.

"Big Racial Divide Over Zimmerman Verdict." 2013. PEW Research Center, July 22. Retrieved July 25, 2013 (http://www.people-press.org/2013/07/22/big-racial-divide-over-zimmerman-verdict/).

Bonilla-Silva, Eduardo. 2006. *Racism Without Racists: Color-Blind Racism and the Persistence of Racial Inequality in the United States*, 2nd ed. Lanham, MD: Rowman and Littlefield.

Borzi, P. 2012. "Push to Save Fighting Sioux Name Leaves North Dakota in Costly Limbo." *New York Times*. February 18. Retrieved April 20, 2012 (http://www.nytimes.com/2012/02/19/sports/push-to-save-fightingsioux-name-puts-north-dakota-in-costly-limbo.html?pagewanted=all).

Feagin, Joe. 2012. *White Party, White Government: Race, Class and U.S. Politics*. New York and London: Routledge.

Feagin, Joe R., Hernan Vera, and Nikitah Imani. 1996. *The Agony of Education: Black Students at White Colleges and Universities*. New York and London: Routledge.

Fox, Helen. 2001. *When Race Breaks Out: Conversations About Race and Racism in College Classrooms*. New York, Washington, DC: Peter Lang Publishers.

Garafoli, Joe. 2012. "Asian American Immigrants Outpace Latinos." *San Francisco Chronicle*, June 19. Retrieved June 20, 2013 (http://www.sfgate.com/politics/joegarofoli/article/Asian-American-immigrants-outpace-Latinos-3643191.php).

Gonzales-Day, Ken. 2006. *Lynching in the West, 1850–1935*. Durham, NC: Duke University Press.

Guggenheim, Charles. 1995. *The Shadow of Hate*. Montgomery, AL: Teaching Tolerance/Southern Poverty Law Center.

Haney Lopez, Ian F. 2006. "Colorblind to the Reality of Race in America." *Chronicle of Higher Education*, November 3. Retrieved July 24, 2013 (http://chronicle.com/article/Colorblind-to-the-Reality-of/12577).

Ignatiev, Noel. 1995. *How the Irish Became White*. New York, London: Routledge.

Johnson, Luke. 2012. "Mike Turzai, Pennsylvania GOP House Majority Leader: Voter ID Will Allow Mitt Romney to Win State." *Huffington Post*, June 25. Retrieved May 21, 2013 (http://www.huffingtonpost.com/2012/06/25/mike-turzai-voter-id_n_1625646.html).

Karoub, Jeff. 2013. "Some Patients Won't See Health Care Workers of a Different Race." *Times Picayune*, February 24, p. A17.

Linzer, Dafna and Jennifer Lafleur. 2001. "Presidents More Likely to Pardon White Felons." *Times Picayune*, December 5, p. A3.

Lipsitz, George. 2001. *American Studies in a Moment of Danger*. Minneapolis: University of Minnesota Press.

Ogletree, Charles. 2012. *The Presumption of Guilt: The Arrest of Henry Louis Gates, Jr. and Race, Class and Crime in America*. New York: Palgrave Macmillan.

Ohlheiser, Abby. 2012. "Report Shows 'Stunning' Increase in Anti-Government Groups." *Slatest at Slate.com*, March 8. Retrieved May 20, 2012 (http://slatest.slate.com/posts/2012/03/08/southern_poverty_law_center_hate_group_report_obama_election_triggers_patriot_organization.html).

Olivo, Antonio. 2008. "By 2050, nearly 1 in 5 U.S. residents to be immigrants: Pew Center report says nearly 1 in 5 residents will be immigrants, non-Hispanic whites will lose majority status." *Chicago Tribune*, February 12. Retrieved Feb. 24, 2008 (http://www.chicagotribune.com/20080212-TB-Study-By-2050-nearly-1-in-5-residents-to-be-immigrants-0212)

Omi, Michael and Howard Winant. 1994. *Racial Formation in the United States from the 1960s to the 1990s*, 2nd ed. New York, London: Routledge.

Ross, Sonya and Jennifer Agiesta. 2012. "Poll Shows Racial Attitudes Deteriorate." *Times-Picayune*, October 28, p. A-12.

Swalwell, Katy. 2012. "Confronting White Privilege." *Teaching Tolerance*, 42. Montgomery, AL: Southern Poverty Law Center. Retrieved July 25, 2013 (http://www.tolerance.org/magazine/number-42-fall-2012/feature/confronting-white-privilege).

Wingfield, Adia Harvey and Joe R. Feagin. 2010. *Yes We Can? White Racial Framing and the 2008 Presidential Campaign*. New York and London: Routledge.

DISCUSSION QUESTIONS

1. What is race? What is racism? What do we mean when we say that race and racism are social constructions (or social constructs)?

2. What is "institutional racism?" What are some examples of institutional racism?

3. Did the 2008 election and the 2012 reelection of President Barack Obama prove that America is finally a "postracial" society? Discuss why you think it did or did not.

4. Describe the life experiences that have informed your racial attitudes and beliefs, and reflect on your level of interaction with other racial/ethnic groups. What events in your life have helped you or hindered you?

5. Look around your campus (for example, in your cafeteria, classes, or dormitories). Is there evidence of racial segregation? If so, is it imposed by individuals of one racial group against another racial group, or is it "self-segregation?" Why do you think segregation occurs? Is it harmful? What, if anything, does it tell us about our society? Should we work to eradicate self-segregation?

RACIAL FORMATION: UNDERSTANDING RACE AND RACISM IN THE POST-CIVIL RIGHTS ERA

Racial Formation in the United States: From the 1960s to the 1990s

BY Michael Omi and Howard Winant

In 1982–83, Susie Guillory Phipps unsuccessfully sued the Louisiana Bureau of Vital Records to change her racial classification from black to white. The descendent of an 18th century white planter and a black slave, Phipps was designated "black" in her birth certificate in accordance with a 1970 state law which declared anyone with at least 1/32nd "Negro blood" to be black.

The Phipps case raised intriguing questions about the concept of race, its meaning in contemporary society, and its use (and abuse) in public policy. Assistant Attorney General Ron Davis defended the law by pointing out that some type of racial classification was necessary to comply with federal record-keeping requirements and to facilitate programs for the prevention of genetic diseases. Phipps's attorney, Brian Begue, argued that the assignment of racial categories on birth certificates was unconstitutional and that the 1/32nd designation was inaccurate. He called on a retired Tulane University professor who cited research indicating that most Louisiana whites have at least 1/20th "Negro" ancestry.

In the end, Phipps lost. The court upheld the state's right to classify and quantify racial identity.[1]

Phipps's problematic racial identity, and her effort to resolve it through state action, is in many ways a parable of America's unsolved racial dilemma. It illustrates the difficulties of defining race and assigning individuals or groups to racial categories. It shows how the racial legacies of the past—slavery and bigotry—continue to shape the present. It reveals both the deep involvement of the state in the organization and interpretation of race, and the inadequacy of state institutions to carry out these functions. It demonstrates how deeply Americans both as individuals and as a civilization are shaped, and indeed haunted, by race.

Having lived her whole life thinking that she was white, Phipps suddenly discovers that by legal definition she is not. In U.S. society, such an event is indeed catastrophic.[2] But if she is not white, of what race is she? The state claims that she is black, based on its rules of classification,[3] and another state agency, the court, upholds this judgment. Despite the classificatory standards that have imposed an either-or logic on racial identity, Phipps will not in fact "change color." Unlike what would have happened during slavery times if one's claim to whiteness was successfully challenged, we can assume that despite the outcome of her legal challenge, Phipps will remain in most of the social relationships she had occupied before the trial. Her socialization, her familial and friendship networks, her cultural orientation, will not change. She will simply have to wrestle with her newly acquired "hybridized" condition. She will have to confront the "other" within.

The designation of racial categories and the assignment of race is no simple task. For centuries, this question has precipitated intense debates and conflicts, particularly in the U.S.—disputes over natural and legal rights, over the distribution of resources, and indeed, over who shall live and who shall die.

A crucial dimension of the Phipps case is that it illustrates the inadequacy of claims that race is a mere matter of variations in human physiognomy, that it is simply a matter of skin "color." But if race cannot be understood in this manner, how can it be understood? We cannot fully hope to address this topic—no less than the meaning of race, its role in society, and the forces that shape it—in one chapter, nor indeed in one book. Our goal in this chapter, however, is far from modest: we wish to offer at least the outlines of a theory of race and racism.

WHAT IS RACE?

There is a continuous temptation to think of race as an essence, as something fixed, concrete and objective. And there is also an opposite temptation: to imagine race as a mere illusion, a purely ideological construct that some ideal non-racist social order would eliminate. It is necessary to challenge both these positions, to disrupt and reframe the rigid and bipolar manner in which they are posed and debated, and to transcend the presumably irreconcilable relationship between them.

The effort must be made to understand race as an unstable and "decentered" complex of social meanings constantly being transformed by political struggle. With this in mind, let us propose a definition: _race is a concept that signifies and symbolizes social conflicts and interests by referring to different types of human bodies_. Although the concept of race invokes biologically-based human characteristics (so-called "phenotypes"), selection of these particular human features for purposes of racial signification is always and necessarily a social and historical process. In contrast to the other major distinction of this type, that of gender, there is no biological basis for distinguishing among human groups along the lines of race.[4] Indeed, the categories employed to differentiate among human groups along racial lines reveal themselves, upon serious examination, to be at best imprecise, and at worst completely arbitrary.

If the concept of race is so nebulous, can we not dispense with it? Can we not "do without" race, at least in the "enlightened" present? This question has been posed often, and with greater frequency in recent years.[5] An affirmative answer would of course present obvious practical difficulties: it is rather difficult to jettison widely held beliefs, beliefs which moreover are central to everyone's identity and understanding of the social world. So the attempt to banish the concept as an archaism is at best counterintuitive. But a deeper difficulty, we believe, is inherent in the very formulation of this schema, in its way of posing race as a problem, a misconception left over from the past, and suitable now only for the dustbin of history.

A more effective starting point is the recognition that despite its uncertainties and contradictions, the concept of race continues to play a fundamental role in structuring and representing the social world. The task for theory is to explain this situation. It is to avoid both the utopian framework that sees race as an illusion we can somehow "get beyond," and also the essentialist formulation that sees race as something objective and fixed, a biological datum.[6] Thus we should think of race as an element of social structure rather than as an irregularity within it; we should see race as a dimension of human representation rather than an illusion. These perspectives inform the theoretical approach we call racial formation.

RACIAL FORMATION

We define racial formation as the sociohistorical process by which racial categories are created, lived out, transformed, and destroyed. Our attempt to elaborate a theory of racial formation will proceed in two steps. First, we argue that racial formation is a process of historically situated projects in which human bodies and social structures are represented and organized. Next we link racial formation to the evolution of hegemony, the way in which society is organized and ruled. Such an approach, we believe, can facilitate understanding of a whole range of contemporary controversies and dilemmas involving race, including the nature of racism, the relationship of race to other forms of differences, inequalities, and oppression such as sexism and nationalism, and the dilemmas of racial identity today.

From a racial formation perspective, race is a matter of both social structure and cultural representation. Too often, the attempt is made to understand race simply or primarily in terms of only one of these two analytical dimensions.[7] For example, efforts to explain racial inequality as a purely social structural phenomenon are unable to account for the origins, patterning, and transformation of racial difference. Conversely, many examinations of racial difference—understood as a matter of cultural attributes a la ethnicity theory, or as a society-wide signification system, a la some poststructuralist accounts—cannot comprehend such structural phenomena as racial stratification in the labor market or patterns of residential segregation.

An alternative approach is to think of racial formation processes as occurring through a linkage between structure and representation. Racial projects do the ideological "work" of making these links. A racial project is simultaneously an interpretation, representation, or explanation of racial dynamics, and an effort to reorganize and redistribute resources along particular racial lines. Racial projects connect what race means in a particular discursive practice and the ways in which both social structures and everyday experiences are racially organized, based upon that meaning. Let us

consider this proposition, first in terms of large-scale or macro-level social processes, and then in terms of other dimensions of the racial formation process.

RACIAL FORMATION AS A MACRO-LEVEL SOCIAL PROCESS

To interpret the meaning of race is to frame it social structurally. Consider for example, this statement by Charles Murray on welfare reform:

> My proposal for dealing with the racial issue in social welfare is to repeal every bit of legislation and reverse every court decision that in any way requires, recommends, or awards differential treatment according to race, and thereby put us back onto the track that we left in 1965. We may argue about the appropriate limits of government intervention in trying to enforce the ideal, but at least it should be possible to identify the ideal: Race is not a morally admissible reason for treating one person differently from another. Period.[8]

Here there is a partial but significant analysis of the meaning of race: it is not a morally valid basis upon which to treat people "differently from one another." We may notice someone's race, but we cannot act upon that awareness. We must act in a "color-blind" fashion. This analysis of the meaning of race is immediately linked to a specific conception of the role of race in the social structure: it can play no part in government action, save in "the enforcement of the ideal." No state policy can legitimately require, recommend, or award different status according to race. This example can be classified as a particular type of racial project in the present-day U.S.—a "neoconservative" one.

Conversely, to recognize the racial dimension in social structure is to interpret the meaning of race. Consider the following statement by the late Supreme Court Justice Thurgood Marshall on minority "set-aside" programs:

> A profound difference separates governmental actions that themselves are racist, and governmental actions that seek to remedy the effects of prior racism or to prevent neutral government activity from perpetuating the effects of such racism.[9]

Here the focus is on the racial dimensions of social structure—in this case of state activity and policy. The argument is that state actions in the past and present have treated people in very different ways according to their race, and thus the government cannot retreat from its policy responsibilities in this area. It cannot suddenly declare itself "color-blind" without in fact perpetuating the same type of differential, racist treatment.[10] Thus, race continues to signify difference and structure inequality. Here, racialized social structure is immediately linked to an interpretation of the meaning of race. This example too can be classified as a particular type of racial project in the present-day U.S.—a "liberal" one.

These two examples of contemporary racial projects are drawn from mainstream political debate; they may be characterized as center-right and center-left expressions of contemporary racial politics.[11] We can, however, expand the discussion of racial formation processes far beyond these familiar examples. In fact, we can identify racial projects in at least three other analytical dimensions: first, the political spectrum can be broadened to include radical projects, on both the left and right, as well as along other political axes. Second, analysis of racial projects can take place not only at the macro-level of racial policy-making, state activity, and collective action, but also at the level of everyday experience. Third, the concept of racial projects can be applied across historical time, to identify racial formation dynamics in the past. We shall now offer examples of each of these types of racial projects.

THE POLITICAL SPECTRUM OF RACIAL FORMATION

We have encountered examples of a neoconservative racial project, in which the significance of race is denied, leading to a "color-blind" racial politics and "hands off" policy orientation; and of a "liberal" racial project, in which the significance of race is affirmed, leading to an egalitarian and "activist" state policy. But these by no means exhaust the political possibilities. Other racial projects can be readily identified on the contemporary U.S. scene. For example, "far right" projects, which uphold biologistic and racist views of difference, explicitly argue for white supremacist policies. "New right" projects overtly claim to hold "color-blind" views, but covertly manipulate racial fears in order to achieve political gains.[12] On the left, "radical democratic" projects invoke notions of racial "difference" in combination with egalitarian politics and policy.

Further variations can also be noted. For example, "nationalist" projects, both conservative and radical, stress the incompatibility of racially-defined group identity with the legacy of white supremacy, and therefore advocate a social structural solution of separation, either complete or partial.[13] As we saw in Chapter 3, nationalist currents represent a profound legacy of the centuries of racial absolutism that initially defined the meaning of race in the U.S. Nationalist concerns continue to influence racial debate in the form of Afrocentrism and other expressions of identity politics.

Taking the range of politically organized racial projects as a whole, we can "map" the current pattern of racial formation at the level of the public sphere, the "macro-level" in which public debate and mobilization takes place.[14] But important as this is, the terrain on which racial formation occurs is broader yet.

RACIAL FORMATION AS EVERYDAY EXPERIENCE

Here too racial projects link signification and structure, not so much as efforts to shape policy or define large-scale meaning, but as the applications of "common sense." To see racial projects operating at the level of everyday life, we have only to examine the many ways in which, often unconsciously, we "notice" race.

One of the first things we notice about people when we meet them (along with their sex) is their race. We utilize race to provide clues about who a person is. This fact is made painfully obvious when we encounter someone whom we cannot conveniently racially categorize—someone who is, for example, racially "mixed" or of an ethnic/racial group we are not familiar with. Such an encounter becomes a source of discomfort and momentarily a crisis of racial meaning.

Our ability to interpret racial meanings depends on preconceived notions of a racialized social structure. Comments such as, "Funny, you don't look black," betray an underlying image of what black should be. We expect people to act out their apparent racial identities; indeed we become disoriented when they do not. The black banker harassed by police while walking in casual clothes through his own well-off neighborhood, the Latino or white kid rapping in perfect Afro patois, the unending faux pas committed by whites who assume that the nonwhites they encounter are servants or tradespeople, the belief that nonwhite colleagues are less qualified persons hired to fulfill affirmative action guidelines, indeed the whole gamut of racial stereotypes—that "white men can't jump," that Asians can't dance, etc. etc.—all testify to the way a racialized social structure shapes racial experience and conditions meaning. Analysis of such stereotypes reveals the always present, already active link between our view of the social structure—its demography, its laws, its customs, its threats—and our conception of what race means.

Conversely, our ongoing interpretation of our experience in racial terms shapes our relations to the institutions and organizations through which we are imbedded in social structure. Thus we expect differences in skin color, or other racially coded characteristics, to explain social differences. Temperament, sexuality, intelligence, athletic ability, aesthetic preferences, and so on are presumed to be fixed and discernible from the palpable mark of race. Such diverse questions as our confidence and trust in others (for example, clerks or salespeople, media figures, neighbors), our sexual preferences and romantic images, our tastes in music, films, dance, or sports, and our very ways of talking, walking, eating, and dreaming become racially coded simply because we live in a society where racial awareness is so pervasive. Thus in ways too comprehensive even to monitor consciously, and despite periodic calls—neoconservative and otherwise—for us to ignore race and adopt "color-blind" racial attitudes, skin color "differences" continue to rationalize distinct treatment of racially-identified individuals and groups.

To summarize the argument so far: the theory of racial formation suggests that society is suffused with racial projects, large and small, to which all are subjected. This racial "subjection" is quintessentially ideological. Everybody learns some combination, some version, of the rules of racial classification, and of her own racial identity, often without obvious teaching or conscious inculcation. Thus are we inserted in a comprehensively racialized social structure. Race becomes "common sense"—a way of comprehending, explaining, and acting in the world. A vast web of racial projects mediates between the discursive or representational means in which race is identified and signified on the one hand, and the institutional and organizational forms in which it is routinized and standardized on the other. These projects are the heart of the racial formation process.

Under such circumstances, it is not possible to represent race discursively without simultaneously locating it, explicitly or implicitly, in a social structural (and historical) context. Nor is it possible to organize, maintain, or transform social structures without simultaneously engaging, once more either explicitly or implicitly, in racial signification. Racial formation, therefore, is a kind of synthesis, an outcome, of the interaction of racial projects on a society-wide level. These projects

are, of course, vastly different in scope and effect. They include large-scale public action, state activities, and interpretations of racial conditions in artistic, journalistic, or academic fora,[15] as well as the seemingly infinite number of racial judgments and practices we carry out at the level of individual experience.

Since racial formation is always historically situated, our understanding of the significance of race, and of the way race structures society, has changed enormously over time. The processes of racial formation we encounter today, the racial projects large and small which structure U.S. society in so many ways, are merely the present-day outcomes of a complex historical evolution. The contemporary racial order remains transient. By knowing something of how it evolved, we can perhaps better discern where it is heading. We therefore turn next to a historical survey of the racial formation process, and the conflicts and debates it has engendered.

THE EVOLUTION OF MODERN RACIAL AWARENESS

The identification of distinctive human groups, and their association with differences in physical appearance, goes back to prehistory, and can be found in the earliest documents—in the Bible, for example, or in Herodotus. But the emergence of a modern conception of race does not occur until the rise of Europe and the arrival of Europeans in the Americas. Even the hostility and suspicion with which Christian Europe viewed its two significant non-Christian "others"—the Muslims and the Jews—cannot be viewed as more than a rehearsal for racial formation, since these antagonisms, for all their bloodletting and chauvinism, were always and everywhere religiously interpreted.[16]

It was only when European explorers reached the Western Hemisphere, when the oceanic seal separating the "old" and the "new" worlds was breached, that the distinctions and categorizations fundamental to a racialized social structure, and to a discourse of race, began to appear. The European explorers were the advance guard of merchant capitalism, which sought new openings for trade. What they found exceeded their wildest dreams, for never before and never again in human history has an opportunity for the appropriation of wealth remotely approached that presented by the "discovery."[17]

But the Europeans also "discovered" people, people who looked and acted differently. These "natives" challenged their "discoverers'" preexisting conceptions of the origins and possibilities of the human species.[18] The representation and interpretation of the meaning of the indigenous peoples' existence became a crucial matter, one which would affect the outcome of the enterprise of conquest. For the "discovery" raised disturbing questions as to whether all could be considered part of the same "family of man," and more practically, the extent to which native peoples could be exploited and enslaved. Thus religious debates flared over the attempt to reconcile the various Christian metaphysics with the existence of peoples who were more "different" than any whom Europe had previously known.[19]

In practice, of course, the seizure of territories and goods, the introduction of slavery through the encomienda and other forms of coerced native labor, and then through the organization of the African slave trade—not to mention the practice of outright extermination—all presupposed a worldview which distinguished Europeans, as children of God, full-fledged human beings, etc., from "others." Given the dimensions and the ineluctability of the European onslaught, given the conquerors' determination to appropriate both labor and goods, and given the presence of an axiomatic and unquestioned Christianity among them, the ferocious division of society into Europeans and "others" soon coalesced. This was true despite the famous 16th-century theological and philosophical debates about the identity of indigenous peoples.[20]

Indeed debates about the nature of the "others" reached their practical limits with a certain dispatch. Plainly they would never touch the essential: nothing, after all, would induce the Europeans to pack up and go home. We cannot examine here the early controversies over the status of American souls. We simply wish to emphasize that the "discovery" signaled a break from the previous proto-racial awareness by which Europe contemplated its "others" in a relatively disorganized fashion. In other words, we argue that the "conquest of America" was not simply an epochal historical event— however unparalleled in its importance. It was also the advent of a consolidated social structure of exploitation, appropriation, domination. Its representation, first in religious terms, but soon enough in scientific and political ones, initiated modern racial awareness.

The conquest, therefore, was the first—and given the dramatic nature of the case, perhaps the greatest—racial formation project. Its significance was by no means limited to the Western Hemisphere, for it began the work of constituting Europe as the metropole, the center, of a series of empires which could take, as Marx would later write, "the globe for a theater."[21] It represented this new imperial structure as a struggle between civilization and barbarism, and implicated in this representation all the great European philosophies, literary traditions, and social theories of the modern age.[22] In short, just as the noise of the "big bang" still resonates through the universe, so the overdetermined construction of world "civilization" as a product of the rise of Europe and the subjugation of the rest of us, still defines the race concept.

FROM RELIGION TO SCIENCE

After the initial depredations of conquest, religious justifications for racial difference gradually gave way to scientific ones. By the time of the Enlightenment, a general awareness of race was pervasive, and most of the great philosophers of Europe, such as Hegel, Kant, Hume, and Locke, had issued virulently racist opinions.

The problem posed by race during the late 18th century was markedly different than it had been in the age of conquest, expropriation, and slaughter. The social structures in which race operated were no longer primarily those of military conquest and plunder, nor of the establishment of thin beachheads of colonization on the edge of what had once seemed a limitless wilderness. Now the issues were much more complicated: nation-building, establishment of national economies in the world trading system, resistance to the arbitrary authority of monarchs, and the assertion of the "natural rights" of "man," including the right of revolution.[23] In such a situation, racially organized exploitation, in the form of slavery, the expansion of colonies, and the continuing expulsion of native peoples, was both necessary and newly difficult to justify.

The invocation of scientific criteria to demonstrate the "natural" basis of racial hierarchy was both a logical consequence of the rise of this form of knowledge, and an attempt to provide a more subtle and nuanced account of human complexity in the new, "enlightened" age. Spurred on by the classificatory scheme of living organisms devised by Linnaeus in Systema Naturae (1735), many scholars in the eighteenth and nineteenth centuries dedicated themselves to the identification and ranking of variations in humankind. Race was conceived as a biological concept, a matter of species. Voltaire wrote that "The negro race is a species of men (sic) as different from ours ... as the breed of spaniels is from that of greyhounds," and in a formulation echoing down from his century to our own, declared that "If their understanding is not of a different nature from ours ..., it is at least greatly inferior. They are not capable of any great application or association of ideas, and seem formed neither for the advantages nor the abuses of philosophy".[24]

Jefferson, the preeminent exponent of the Enlightenment doctrine of "the rights of man" on North American shores, echoed these sentiments:

> In general their existence appears to partic-ipate more of sensation than reflection. ... [I]n memory they are equal to whites, in reason much inferior ... [and] in imagination they are dull, tasteless, and anomalous. ... I advance it therefore ... that the blacks, whether originally a different race, or made distinct by time and circumstances, are inferior to the whites. ... Will not a lover of natural history, then, one who views the gradations in all the animals with the eye of philosophy, excuse an effort to keep those in the department of Man (sic) as distinct as nature has formed them?[25]

Such claims of species distinctiveness among hu-mans justified the inequitable allocation of political and social rights, while still upholding the doctrine of "the rights of man." The quest to obtain a precise scientific definition of race sustained debates that continue to rage today. Yet despite efforts ranging from Dr. Samuel Morton's studies of cranial capacity[26] to contemporary attempts to base racial classification on shared gene pools,[27] the concept of race has defied biological definition.

In the 19th century, Count Joseph Arthur de Gobineau drew upon the most respected scientific studies of his day to compose his four-volume Essay on the Inequality of Races (1853–1855).[28] He not only great-ly influenced the racial thinking of the period, but his themes would be echoed in the racist ideologies of the next one hundred years: beliefs that superior races pro-duced superior cultures and that racial intermixtures resulted in the degradation of the superior racial stock. These ideas found expression, for instance, in the eu-genics movement launched by Darwin's cousin, Francis Galton, which had an immense impact on scientific and sociopolitical thought in Europe and the United States.[29] In the wake of civil war and emancipation, and with immigration from southern and Eastern Europe as well as East Asia running high, the U.S. was particularly fertile ground for notions such as social darwinism and eugenics.

Attempts to discern the scientific meaning of race continue to the present day. For instance, an essay by Arthur Jensen that argued that hereditary factors shape intelligence not only revived the "nature or nurture" controversy, but also raised highly volatile questions about racial equality itself.[30] All such attempts seek to remove the concept of race from the historical context in which it arose and developed. They employ an essen-tialist approach that suggests instead that the truth of race is a matter of innate characteristics, of which skin color and other physical attributes provide only the most obvious, and in some respects most superficial, indicators.

FROM SCIENCE TO POLITICS

It has taken scholars more than a century to reject biologistic notions of race in favor of an approach that regards race as a social concept. This trend has been slow and uneven, and even today remains somewhat embattled, but its overall direction seems clear. At the turn of the century Max Weber discounted biological explanations for racial conflict and instead highlighted the social and political factors that engendered such conflict.[31] W. E. B. DuBois argued for a sociopolitical definition of race by identifying "the color line" as "the problem of the 20th century."[32] Pioneering cultural anthropologist Franz Boas rejected attempts to link racial identifications and cultural traits, labeling as pseudoscientific any assumption of a continuum of "higher" and "lower" cultural groups.[33] Other early exponents of social, as opposed to biological, views of race included Robert E. Park, founder of the "Chicago school" of sociology, and Alain Leroy Locke, philosopher and theorist of the Harlem renaissance.[34]

Perhaps more important than these and subsequent intellectual efforts, however, were the political struggles of racially defined groups themselves. Waged all around the globe under a variety of banners such as anti-co-lonialism and civil rights, these battles to challenge vari-ous structural and cultural racisms have been a major feature of 20th century politics. The racial horrors of the 20th century—colonial slaughter and apartheid, the genocide of the holocaust, and the massive bloodlettings required to end these evils—have also indelibly marked the theme of race as a political issue par excellence.

As a result of prior efforts and struggles, we have now reached the point of fairly general agreement that race is not a biologically given but rather a socially constructed way of differentiating human beings. While a tremendous achievement, the transcendence of biologistic conceptions of race does not provide any re- prieve from the dilemmas of racial injustice and conflict, nor from controversies over the significance of race in the present. Views of race as socially constructed simply recognize the fact that these conflicts and controversies are now more properly framed on the terrain of politics. By privileging politics in the analysis that follows we do not mean to suggest that race has been displaced as a concern of scientific inquiry, or that struggles over cultural representation are no longer important. We do argue, however, that race is now a preeminently political phenomenon. Such an assertion invites examination of the evolving role of racial politics in the U.S. This is the subject to which we now turn.

DICTATORSHIP, DEMOCRACY, HEGEMONY

For most of its existence both as a European colony and as an independent nation, the U.S. was a racial dictatorship. From 1607 to 1865—258 years—most nonwhites were firmly eliminated from the sphere of politics.[35] After the civil war there was the brief egali- tarian experiment of Reconstruction which terminated ignominiously in 1877. In its wake followed almost a century of legally sanctioned segregation and denial of the vote, nearly absolute in the South and much of the Southwest, less effective in the North and far West, but formidable in any case.[36] These barriers fell only in the mid-1960s, a mere quarter-century ago. Nor did the successes of the black movement and its allies mean that all obstacles to their political participation had now been abolished. Patterns of racial inequality have proven, unfortunately, to be quite stubborn and persistent.

It is important, therefore, to recognize that in many respects, racial dictatorship is the norm against which all U.S. politics must be measured. The centuries of racial dictatorship have had three very large conse- quences: first, they defined "American" identity as white, as the negation of racialized "otherness"—at first largely African and indigenous, later Latin American and Asian as well.[37] This negation took shape in both law and custom, in public institutions and in forms of cultural representation. It became the archetype of hegemonic rule in the U.S. It was the successor to the conquest as the "master" racial project.

Second, racial dictatorship organized (albeit some- times in an incoherent and contradictory fashion) the "color line," rendering it the fundamental division in U.S. society. The dictatorship elaborated, articulated, and drove racial divisions not only through institutions, but also through psyches, extending up to our own time the racial obsessions of the conquest and slavery periods.

Third, racial dictatorship consolidated the opposi- tional racial consciousness and organization originally framed by marronage[38] and slave revolts, by indigenous resistance, and by nationalisms of various sorts. Just as the conquest created the "native" where once there had been Pequot, Iroquois, or Tutelo, so too it created the "black" where once there had been Asante or Ovimbundu, Yoruba or Bakongo.

The transition from a racial dictatorship to a racial democracy has been a slow, painful, and contentious one; it remains far from complete. A recognition of the abiding presence of racial dictatorship, we contend, is crucial for the development of a theory of racial forma- tion in the U.S. It is also crucial to the task of relating racial formation to the broader context of political practice, organization, and change.

In this context, a key question arises: In what way is racial formation related to politics as a whole? How, for example, does race articulate with other axes of oppression and difference—most importantly class and gender—along which politics is organized today?

The answer, we believe, lies in the concept of hegemony. Antonio Gramsci—the Italian communist who placed this concept at the center of his life's work—understood it as the conditions necessary, in a given society, for the achievement and consolidation of rule. He argued that hegemony was always constituted by a combination of coercion and consent. Although rule can be obtained by force, it cannot be secured and maintained, especially in modern society, without the element of consent. Gramsci conceived of consent as far more than merely the legitimation of authority. In his view, consent extended to the incorporation by the ruling group of many of the key interests of sub- ordinated groups, often to the explicit disadvantage of the rulers themselves.[39] Gramsci's treatment of hegemony went even farther: he argued that in order to consolidate their hegemony, ruling groups must elaborate and maintain a popular system of ideas and practices—through education, the media, religion, folk wisdom, etc.—which he called "common sense." It is through its production and its adherence to this "common sense," this ideology (in the broadest sense of the term), that a society gives its consent to the way in which it is ruled.[40]

These provocative concepts can be extended and applied to an understanding of racial rule. In the Americas, the conquest represented the violent introduction of a new form of rule whose relationship with those it subjugated was almost entirely coercive. In the U.S., the origins of racial division, and of racial signification and identity formation, lie in a system of rule that was extremely dictatorial. The mass murders and expulsions of indigenous people, and the enslavement of Africans, surely evoked and inspired little consent in their founding moments.

Over time, however, the balance of coercion and consent began to change. It is possible to locate the origins of hegemony right within the heart of racial dictatorship, for the effort to possess the oppressor's tools—religion and philosophy in this case—was crucial to emancipation (the effort to possess oneself). As Ralph Ellison reminds us, "The slaves often took the essence of the aristocratic ideal (as they took Christianity) with far more seriousness than their masters."[41] In their language, in their religion with its focus on the Exodus theme and on Jesus's tribulations, in their music with its figuring of suffering, resistance, perseverance, and transcendence, in their interrogation of a political philosophy that sought perpetually to rationalize their bondage in a supposedly "free" society, the slaves incorporated elements of racial rule into their thought and practice, turning them against their original bearers.

Racial rule can be understood as a slow and uneven historical process that has moved from dictatorship to democracy, from domination to hegemony. In this transition, hegemonic forms of racial rule—those based on consent—eventually came to supplant those based on coercion. Of course, before this assertion can be accepted, it must be qualified in important ways. By no means has the U.S. established racial democracy at the end of the century, and by no means is coercion a thing of the past. But the sheer complexity of the racial questions U.S. society confronts today, the welter of competing racial projects and contradictory racial experiences that Americans undergo, suggests that hegemony is a useful and appropriate term with which to characterize contemporary racial rule.

RACE, RACISM, AND HEGEMONY

Parallel to the debates on the concept of race, recent academic and political controversies about the nature of racism have centered on whether it is primarily an ideological or structural phenomenon. Proponents of the former position argue that racism is first and foremost a matter of beliefs and attitudes, doctrines and discourse, which only then give rise to unequal and unjust practices and structures.[42] Advocates of the latter view see racism as primarily a matter of economic stratification, residential segregation, and other institutionalized forms of inequality that then give rise to ideologies of privilege.[43]

From the standpoint of racial formation, these debates are fundamentally misguided. They discuss the problem of racism in a rigid "either-or" manner. We believe it is crucial to disrupt the fixity of these positions by simultaneously arguing that ideological beliefs have structural consequences, and that social structures give rise to beliefs. Racial ideology and social structure, therefore, mutually shape the nature of racism in a complex, dialectical, and overdetermined manner.

Even those racist projects that at first glance appear chiefly ideological turn out upon closer examination to have significant institutional and social structural dimensions. For example, what we have called "far right" projects appear at first glance to be centrally ideological. They are rooted in biologistic doctrine, after all. The same seems to hold for certain conservative black nationalist projects that have deep commitments to biologism.[44] But the unending stream of racist assaults initiated by the far right, the apparently increasing presence of skinheads in high schools, the proliferation of neo-Nazi websites on the Internet, and the appearance of racist talk shows on cable access channels, all suggest that the organizational manifestations of the far right racial projects exist and will endure.[45]

By contrast, even those racisms that at first glance appear to be chiefly structural upon closer examination reveal a deeply ideological component. For example, since the racial right abandoned its explicit advocacy of segregation, it has not seemed to uphold—in the main—an ideologically racist project, but more primarily a structurally racist one. Yet this very transformation required tremendous efforts of ideological production. It demanded the rearticulation of civil rights doctrines of equality in suitably conservative form, and indeed the defense of continuing large-scale racial inequality as an outcome preferable to (what its advocates have seen as) the threat to democracy that affirmative action, busing, and large-scale "race-specific" social spending would entail.[46] Even more tellingly, this project took shape through a deeply manipulative coding of subtextual appeals to white racism, notably in a series of political campaigns for high office that have occurred over recent decades. The retreat of social policy from any practical commitment to racial justice, and the relentless reproduction and divulgation of this theme at the level of everyday life—where whites are now "fed up" with all the "special treatment" received by nonwhites, etc.—constitutes the hegemonic racial project at this time. It therefore exhibits an unabashed structural racism all the more brazen because on the ideological or signification level it adheres to a principle to "treat everyone alike."

In summary, the racism of today is no longer a virtual monolith, as was the racism of yore. Today, racial hegemony is "messy." The complexity of the present situation is the product of a vast historical legacy of structural inequality and invidious racial representation, which has been confronted during the post-World War II period with an opposition more serious and effective than any it had faced before. The result is a deeply ambiguous and contradictory spectrum of racial projects, unremittingly conflictual racial politics, and confused and ambivalent racial identities of all sorts.

ENDNOTES

1. San Francisco Chronicle, September 14, 1982, May 19, 1983. Ironically, the 1970 Louisiana law was enacted to supersede an old Jim Crow statute which relied on the idea of "common report" in determining an infant's race. Following Phipps' unsuccessful attempt to change her classification and have the law declared unconstitutional, a legislative effort arose which culminated in the repeal of the law. See San Francisco Chronicle, June 23, 1983.

2. Compare the Phipps case to Andrew Hacker's well-known "parable" in which a white person is informed by a mysterious official that "the organization he represents has made a mistake" and that "... [a]ccording to their records ..., you were to have been born black: to another set of parents, far from where you were raised." How much compensation, Hacker's official asks, would "you" require to undo the damage of this unfortunate error? See Hacker, Two Nations: Black and White, Separate, Hostile, Unequal (New York: Charles Scribner's Sons, 1992), pp. 31–32.

3. On the evolution of Louisiana's racial classification system, see Virginia Dominguez, White By Definition: Social Classification in Creole Louisiana (New Brunswick: Rutgers University Press, 1986).

4. This is not to suggest that gender is a biological category while race is not. Gender, like race, is a social construct. However, the biological division of humans into sexes—two at least, and possibly intermediate ones as well—is not in dispute. This provides a basis for argument over gender divisions—how natural?" etc.—which does not exist with regard to race. To ground an argument for the "natural" existence of race, one must resort to philosophical anthropology.

5. "The truth is that there are no races; there is nothing in the world that can do all we ask race to do for us. ... The evil that is done is done by the concept, and by easy—yet impossible—assumptions as to its application." (Kwame Anthony Appiah, In My Father's House: Africa in the Philosophy of Culture (New York: Oxford University Press, 1992.) Appiah's eloquent and learned book fails, in our view, to dispense with the race concept, despite its anguished attempt to do so; this indeed is the source of its author's anguish. We agree with him as to the non-objective character of race, but fail to see how this recognition justifies its abandonment. This argument is developed below.

6. We understand essentialism as belief in real, true human essences, existing outside or impervious to social and historical context. We draw this definition, with some small modifications, from Diana Fuss, Essentially Speaking: Feminism, Nature, & Difference (New York: Routledge, 1989), p. xi.

7. Michael Omi and Howard Winant, "On the Theoretical Status of the Concept of Race," in Warren Crichlow and Cameron McCarthy, eds., Race, Identity, and Representation in Education (New York: Routledge, 1993).

8. Charles Murray, Losing Ground: American Social Policy, 1950–1980 (New York: Basic Books, 1984), p. 223.

9. Justice Thurgood Marshall, dissenting in City of Richmond v. J.A. Croson Co., 488 U.S. 469 (1989).

10. See, for example, Derrick Bell, "Remembrances of Racism Past: Getting Past the Civil Rights Decline," in Herbert Hill and James E. Jones, Jr., eds., Race in America: The Struggle for Equality (Madison: The University of Wisconsin Press, 1993), pp. 75–76; Gertrude Ezorsky, Racism and Justice: The Case for Affirmative Action (Ithaca: Cornell University Press, 1991), pp. 109–111; David Kairys, With Liberty and Justice for Some: A Critique of the Conservative Supreme Court (New York: The New Press, 1993), pp. 138–41.

11. Howard Winant has developed a tentative "map" of the system of racial hegemony in the U.S. circa 1990, which focuses on the spectrum of racial projects running from the political right to the political left. See Winant, "Where Culture Meets Structure: Race in the 1990s," in idem, Racial Conditions: Theories, Politics, Comparisons (Minneapolis: University of Minnesota Press, 1994).

12. A familiar example is use of racial "code words." Recall George Bush's manipulations of racial fear in the 1988 "Willie Horton" ads, or Jesse Helms's use of the coded term "quota" in his 1990 campaign against Harvey Gantt.

13. From this perspective, far right racial projects can also be interpreted as "nationalist." See Ronald Walters, "White Racial Nationalism in the United States," Without Prejudice I, 1 (Fall, 1987).

14. Howard Winant has offered such a "map" in "Race: Theory, Culture, and Politics in the United States Today," in Marcy Darnovsky et al., eds., Contemporary Social Movements and Cultural Politics (Philadelphia: Temple University Press, 1994).

15. We are not unaware, for example, that publishing this work is in itself a racial project.

16. Although the Inquisition pioneered racial anti-semitism with its doctrine of "limpieza de sangre" (the claim that Jews could not be accepted as converts because their blood was "unclean"), anti-semitism only began to be seriously racialized in the 18th century, as George L. Mosse shows in Toward the Final Solution: A History of European Racism (New York: Howard Fertig, 1978).

17. As Marx put it:

> The discovery of gold and silver in America, the extirpation, enslavement, and entombment in mines of the aboriginal population, the beginning of the conquest and looting of the East Indies, the turning of Africa into a warren for the commercial hunting of blackskins, signalized the rosy dawn of the era of capitalist production. These idyllic proceedings are the chief momenta of primitive accumulation. (Karl Marx, Capital, Vol. I (New York: International Publishers, 1967), p. 751.)

David E. Stannard argues that the wholesale slaughter perpetrated upon the native peoples of the Western hemisphere is unequalled in history, even in our own bloody century. See his American Holocaust: Columbus and the Conquest of the New World (New York: Oxford University Press, 1992).

18. Winthrop Jordan provides a detailed account of the sources of European attitudes about color and race in White Over Black: American Attitudes Toward the Negro, 1550–1812 (New York: Norton, 1977 [1968]), pp. 3–43.

19. In a famous instance, a 1550 debate in Valladolid pitted the philosopher and translator of Aristotle, Gines de Sepulveda, against the Dominican Bishop of the Mexican state of Chiapas, Bartolome de Las Casas. Discussing the native peoples, Sepulveda argued that

> In wisdom, skill, virtue and humanity, these people are as inferior to the Spaniards as children are to adults and women to men; there is as great a difference between them as there is between savagery and forbearance, between

violence and moderation, almost—I am inclined to say, as between monkeys and men (Sepulveda, "Democrates Alter," quoted in Tsvetan Todorov, The Conquest of America: The Question of the Other (New York: Harper and Row, 1984), p. 153).

In contrast, Las Casas defended the humanity and equality of the native peoples, both in terms of their way of life—which he idealized as one of innocence, gentleness, and generosity—and in terms of their readiness for conversion to Catholicism, which for him as for Sepulveda was the true and universal religion (Las Casas, "Letter to the Council of the Indies," quoted ibid, p. 163). William E. Connolly interrogates the linkages proposed by Todorov between early Spanish colonialism and contemporary conceptions of identity and difference in Identity/Difference: Democratic Negotiations of Political Paradox (Ithaca: Cornell University Press, 1991), pp. 40–48.

20. In Virginia, for example, it took about two decades after the establishment of European colonies to extirpate the indigenous people of the greater vicinity; 50 years after the establishment of the first colonies, the elaboration of slave codes establishing race as prima facie evidence for enslaved status was well under way. See Jordan, White Over Black.

21. Capital, P. 751.

22. Edward W. Said, Culture and Imperialism (New York: Alfred A. Knopf, 1993).

23. David Brion Davis, The Problem of Slavery in The Age of Revolution (Ithaca: Cornell University Press, 1975).

24. Quoted in Thomas F. Gossett, Race: The History of an Idea in America (New York: Schocken Books, 1965), p. 45.

25. Thomas Jefferson, "Notes on Virginia" [1787], in Merrill D. Peterson, Writings of Thomas Jefferson (New York: The Library of America, 1984), pp. 264–66, 270. Thanks to Prof. Kimberly Benston for drawing our attention to this passage.

26. Proslavery physician Samuel George Morton (1799–1851) compiled a collection of 800 crania from all parts of the world which formed the sample for his studies of race. Assuming that the larger the size of the cranium translated into greater intelligence, Morton established a relationship between race and skull capacity. Gossett reports that "In 1849, one of his studies included the following results: the English skulls in his collection proved to be the largest, with an average cranial capacity of 96 cubic inches. The Americans and Germans were rather poor seconds, both with cranial capacities of 90 cubic inches. At the bottom of the list were the Negroes with 83 cubic inches, the Chinese with 82, and the Indians with 79." Gossett, Race: The History of an Idea in America, p. 74. More recently, Steven Jay Gould has reexamined Morton's data, and shown that his research data were deeply, though unconsciously, manipulated to agree with his "a priori conviction about racial ranking." Gould, The

Mismeasure of Man (New York: W. W. Norton, 1981), pp. 50–69.

27. Definitions of race founded upon a common pool of genes have not held up when confronted by scientific research which suggests that the differences _within_ a given human population are every bit as great as those _between_ populations. See L. L. Cavalli-Sforza, "The Genetics of Human Populations," _Scientific American_, (September 1974), pp. 81–89.

28. A fascinating summary critique of Gobineau is provided in Tsvetan Todorov, _On Human Diversity: Nationalism, Racism, and Exoticism in French Thought_, trans. Catherine Porter (Cambridge, MA: Harvard University Press, 1993), esp. pp. 129–40.

29. Two good histories of eugenics are Allen Chase, _The Legacy of Malthus_ (New York: Knopf, 1977); Daniel J. Kelves, _In the Name of Eugenics: Genetics and the Uses of Human Heredity_ (New York: Knopf, 1985).

30. Arthur Jensen, "How Much Can We Boost IQ and Scholastic Achievement?" _Harvard Educational Review_, 39 (1969), pp. 1–123.

31. See Weber, _Economy and Society_, Vol. I (Berkeley: University of California Press, 1978), pp. 385–87; Ernst Moritz Manasse, "Max Weber on Race," _Social Research_, Vol. 14 (1947), pp. 191–221.

32. DuBois, _The The Souls of Black Folk_ (New York: Penguin, 1989 [1903]), p. 13. Du Bois himself wrestled heavily with the conflict between a fully sociohistorical conception of race, and the more essentialized and deterministic vision he encountered as a student in Berlin. In "The Conservation of Races" (1897) we can see his first mature effort to resolve this conflict in a vision which combined racial solidarity and a commitment to social equality. See Du Bois, "The Conservation of Races," in Dan S. Green and Edwin D. Driver, eds., _W. E. B. Du Bois On Sociology and the Black Community_ (Chicago: University of Chicago Press, 1978), pp. 238–49; Manning Marable, _W. E. B. Du Bois: Black Radical Democrat_ (Boston: Twayne, 1986), pp. 35–38. For a contrary, and we believe incorrect reading, see Appiah, _In My Father's House_, pp. 28–46.

33. A good collection of Boas's work is George W. Stocking, ed., _The Shaping of American Anthropology, 1883–1911: A Franz Boas Reader_ (Chicago: University of Chicago Press, 1974).

34. Robert E. Park's _Race and Culture_ (Glencoe, IL: Free Press, 1950) can still provide insight; see also Stanford H. Lyman, _Militarism, Imperialism, and Racial Accommodation: An Analysis and Interpretation of the Early Writings of Robert E. Park_ (Fayetteville: University of Arkansas Press, 1992); Locke's views are concisely expressed in Alain Leroy Locke, _Race Contacts and Interracial Relations_, ed. Jeffrey C. Stewart (Washington, DC: Howard University Press, 1992), originally a series of lectures given at Howard University.

35. Japanese, for example, could not become naturalized citizens until passage of the 1952 McCarran-Walter Act. It took over 160 years, since the passage of the Naturalization Law of 1790, to allow all "races" to be eligible for naturalization.

36. Especially when we recall that until around 1960, the majority of blacks, the largest racially-defined minority group, lived in the South.

37. The construction of whiteness and its tropes of identity is explored in numerous studies, far too many to cite here. Some outstanding examples are Toni Morrison, _Playing In The Dark_: Whiteness and the Literary Imagination (Cambridge, MA: Harvard University Press, 1992); Michael Paul Rogin, _Fathers and Children: Andrew Jackson and the Subjugation of the American Indian_ (New York: Knopf, 1975; Richard Drinnon, _Facing West: The Metaphysics of Indian-hating and Empire-building_ (Minneapolis: University of Minnesota Press, 1980).

38. This term refers to the practice, widespread throughout the Americas, whereby runaway slaves formed communities in remote areas, such as swamps, mountains, or forests, often in alliance with dispossessed indigenous peoples.

39. Antonio Gramsci, _Selections from the Prison Notebooks_, edited and translated by Quintin Hoare and Geoffrey Nowell Smith (New York: International Publishers, 1971), p. 182.

40. Anne Showstack Sassoon, _Gramsci's Politics_, 2nd. ed. (London: Hutchinson, 1987); Sue Golding, _Gramsci's Democratic Theory: Contributions to Post-Liberal Democracy_ (Toronto: University of Toronto Press, 1992).

41. Ralph Ellison, _Shadow and Act_ (New York: New American Library, 1966), p. xiv.

42. See Miles, _Racism_, p. 77. Much of the current debate over the advisability and legality of banning racist hate speech seems to us to adopt the dubious position that racism is primarily an ideological phenomenon. See Mari J. Matsuda et al, _Words That Wound: Critical Race Theory, Assaultive Speech, and the First Amendment_ (Boulder, CO: Westview Press, 1993).

43. Or ideologies which mask privilege by falsely claiming that inequality and injustice have been eliminated. See Wellman, _Portraits of White Racism_.

44. Racial teachings of the Nation of Islam, for example, maintain that whites are the product of a failed experiment by a mad scientist.

45. Elinor Langer, "The American Neo-Nazi Movement Today," _The Nation_, July 16/23, 1990.

46. Such arguments can be found in Nathan Glazer, _Affirmative Discrimination_, Charles Murray, _Losing Ground_, and Arthur M. Schlesinger, Jr., _The Disuniting of America_, among others.

DISCUSSION QUESTIONS

1. In what way is Susie Guillory Phipps's complex racial identity, and her unsuccessful lawsuit against the Louisiana Bureau of Vital Records, a parable of America's unresolved racial dilemma? Discuss.

2. What is the 1/32nd rule? What is the "one-drop" rule? What are the implications of the 1970 Louisiana state law that declared anyone with 1/32nd "Negro blood" to be Black? Do Americans today still believe in the 1/32nd rule or the "one-drop" rule? Does the 1970 law also mean, logically, that anyone with 1/32nd "White blood" (or perhaps, one drop of "White blood") is White?

3. According to Census Bureau statistics, the United States is becoming less White. What are the implications of this and other population trends for racial formation in the United States? How will the United States adapt to these patterns? For example, do you foresee a greater acceptance among Whites of their new minority status? Or do you think there will be greater White hostility toward members of other (non-White) groups?

4. Starting in the 1970s, and continuing more intensively since then, many politicians, academics, and public figures have argued that the United States is becoming a "color-blind" society. Yet survey results continue to show increasing Black-White inequality and persistent beliefs in Black inferiority, laziness, and criminality. Is there a discrepancy here, or can these two trends be reconciled? Discuss how these views on race are conflicting or overlapping racial projects. What does the term "color-blind" mean? Is America today a "color-blind" society?

READING 3.5

COLORBLINDNESS AS A HEGEMONIC RACIAL PROJECT

Racial Formation in the United States: From the 1960s to the 1990s

BY **Michael Omi and Howard Winant**

Today, in the 21st century, the concept of "colorblindness" is hegemonic in the United States. It has become the racial common sense and *desideratum* of our time. This does not mean that it is free of contradictions, however.

Those advocating a colorblind view of race assert that the goals of the civil rights movement have been substantially achieved, that overt forms of racial discrimination are a thing of the past, and that the United States is in the midst of a successful transition to a "post-racial" society. From a colorblind standpoint, any hints of race consciousness are tainted by racism. Thus it is suggested that the most effective anti-racist gesture, policy, or practice is simply to ignore race (Skrentny 1996; Connerly 2007). Critics of colorblindness, in contrast, point to the pervasive presence of race and racism—white supremacy—throughout the U.S. social structure. They emphasize the enduring significance of race and the persistence of racism, arguing that it continues to generate inequality across the entire society, most notably in such areas as education, employment, criminal "justice," health, and housing, but elsewhere as well. In order to address the persistence of racial inequalities, they argue that race-conscious policies and practices are necessary, specifically to target and address the sources and causes of racial disparities (Brown et al. 2003; Feagin 2006; Kennedy 2013).

Both positions lay claim to the legacy of the black movement of the 1950s and 1960s. Indeed, colorblindness itself both reflects and subverts that legacy. Early on, colorblindness provided the general framework for anti-racist movement goals, a moment most familiar from the famous sentence in Dr. King's August 28, 1963, speech: "I have a dream that my four children will one day live in a nation where they will be judged not by the color of their skin but by the content of their character" (King 2002b) [1] But colorblindness represented something very different in the last years of Jim Crow segregation than it did in the early 21st century. In August 1963 as the marchers converged on the Lincoln Memorial and Dr. King's and other civil rights leaders' voices rang out across the capital, overt racism, the U.S. version of *apartheid*, was still the law of the land. Desperate public officials and private citizens, many of them avowed white supremacists, were determined to preserve it at all costs from the growing consensus that sought change.

And things did change. An overtly racist ideology, buttressed by "scientific" claims, was widely disavowed. The Civil Rights Act of 1964 and the Voting Rights Act of 1965 led to the subsequent demise of state and local Jim Crow laws. Anti-miscegenation laws were deemed unconstitutional by the U.S. Supreme Court in 1967. Colorblindness, therefore, cannot simply be seen as a deceptive political hoax or naive matter of wishful thinking. It is a result, however intended or unintended, of the partial dismantlement of the U.S. *apartheid* system in the 1960s. Only by challenging that system, and by creating new, more egalitarian racial dynamics, was it even possible to advance the colorblind position.

"Partial dismantlement." Consider the contrast between the 1960s and today. Half a century later, racism is mostly tacit. Although profiling is ubiquitous and discriminatory practices are often thinly veiled at best, explicitly racial laws are frowned upon. Although race is supposedly a suspect category, courts wink at implicitly discriminatory measures and indeed preoccupy themselves with supposed discrimination against whites. The reforms of the civil rights era seem increasingly ineffective against an ongoing structural racism that sees, hears, and undoes no evil. To ignore ongoing racial inequality, racial violence, racial disenfranchisement, racial profiling, quasiofficial resegregation of schools and neighborhoods, and anti-immigrant racism—it's a long list—under the banner of colorblindness is to indulge in a thought process composed in substantial parts of malice, disingenuousness, and wishful thinking.

Can we really embrace a colorblind approach to race in the face of recurrent nativism with its "show me your papers" laws and extensive network of harassment, imprisonment, and deportation? Can we ignore the existence of a prison system whose highly disproportionate confinement of black and brown people is a national scandal? Mass incarceration has become a racialized system of social control and super-exploitation with blacks and Latinos making up more than 60 percent of the current prison population (Mauer 2006 [1999]; Alexander 2012). Health disparities by race remain clearly evident with regards to access to healthcare, disease prevention, and life expectancy (Smedley, Stith, and Nelson 2003; Ansell 2011). Can we agree with the colorblind approach to race when, as Gary Orfield and Erica Frankenberg (2013), Jonathan Kozol (2012 [1991]), and many others have documented, school segregation has not only persisted but been both exacerbated and normalized in the United States? Can we accept claims that racism is "a thing of the past" when median white net worth is now *twenty times* greater than median black net worth, having *more than doubled* since the onset of the great recession of 2008 (Kochhar et al. 2011; see also Oliver and Shapiro 2006)? Regressive redistribution almost as abysmal has plagued Latin@s over the same period. How can such a rapid shift for the worse, how can a leap in economic inequality of such dramatic scope, be blamed on anything other than the victimization of black and brown people who aspired to middle-class status? How can it be reconciled with the concept of colorblindness? [2] How can we take seriously professions of belief in colorblind attitudes, when they are rife with irrationalities and contradictions (Brown et al. 2003; Carbado and Harris 2008; Bonilla-Silva 2009; Wise 2010)? From the cradle to the grave, race continues to shape and define our prospects, opportunities, life chances, and dreams.

Even more ominous is the realization that even past gains can be rolled back. In June 2013, the U.S. Supreme

Court substantially weakened the Voting Rights Act, thereby allowing nine states to change their election laws without advance federal approval (Liptak 2013). This decision allows states, counties, and municipalities to enact or move forward with voter identification laws that have the effect of disenfranchising groups of color. Was our confidence in Jim Crow's passing premature, as Derrick Bell argued?

The litany of racial inequalities goes on (and on), but the appeal of colorblind ideology cannot be easily dismissed. It promotes a compelling common sense, a general "rule of thumb," to guide and inform both institutional and individual practices. It provides a facile means for individuals to denounce racist beliefs and actions of a certain type—those that are explicit, overt, unconscionable, and morally unacceptable. Colorblindness allows people (mainly whites, but not only whites) to indulge in a kind of anti-racism "lite." While explicit forms of racial animus (such as hate speech) are widely condemned, policies and practices that continue to produce racially disparate outcomes are accepted and even encouraged under the guise of moving us "beyond" race and towards a truly colorblind society.

Not surprisingly, attitudes vary by race regarding the persistence of racial inequality and whether the state needs to proactively do something about racial discrimination. In July 2013, Gallup pollsters asked respondents, "Do you think new civil rights laws are needed to reduce discrimination against blacks?" While only 17 percent of whites replied "yes," 53 percent of blacks and 46 percent of Latinos replied in the affirmative (Gallup 2013). We may all want to get to the post-racial promised land, but group differences abound with respect to how far along the road we are and what are the best means by which to get there.

Despite the withering criticism directed at the concept of colorblindness, we will not succeed in overthrowing colorblindness if we see it as erroneous, deceptive, or merely a hoax. *Colorblindness is also aspirational.* Indeed it is precisely because the old U.S. apartheid system was formally dismantled, and because the new racial dynamic that was substituted for it was more open and fluid, that it became possible to advance the colorblind position. That it has attained hegemonic status as the racial "common sense" of the present has been the outcome of a prolonged period of rearticulation by the political right—a sustained attempt to contain the radical democratic potentialities of what we call the Great Transformation.

As a racial project, indeed as a bid for racial hegemony in the United States today, colorblindness is a rude beast: ineffective, uneven, ungainly, deceptive, contradictory. But since hegemony itself is about the selective and strategic incorporation of opposition, it comes as no surprise that there are contradictions in the very logic of colorblind ideology. In the long run, colorblind racial ideology is only credible and can only "work" to the extent that it reflects the successes of the "post-civil rights" era in ameliorating racial injustice and inequality. A purely fabricated, mythical colorblindness could hardly be sustained intellectually, politically, or even socially in the interactions of everyday life. The effectiveness of colorblind ideology depends on its verisimilitude, on the credibility of its claim that U.S. racial conditions have improved—that we now have less discrimination, less racial violence, less racial repression and, correspondingly, more tolerance, more equality, and more inclusion.

Concepts of race, racial categories, and racial meanings continue to haunt and circulate in all social domains. Both in everyday life and in the political sphere, race organizes U.S. society. In civil society, people continually use race: We rely on perceived racial categories in social interaction, in the presentation of self, and to "navigate" in varied social settings. Consider such matters as getting a job, shopping in a department store, attending university, or dating. In political life too *the state needs race to rule*. Racial profiling and mass (racial) incarceration, for example, have become constitutive of the policies and practices of social control. Patterns of immigration and developing trends in U.S. racial demography have created and revived a whole series of political opportunities. Ongoing nativist appeals exploit white anxieties about the nation's future and fears of the "other" in our midst. Immigrant rights advocates rally an electorate increasingly composed of people of color on behalf of redistributive economic policies and the extension of democratic rights. Overall, however, structural racism still steers the ship of state. Disinvestment in education generates a "school to prison pipeline" (Knefel 2013). Persistent poverty and unemployment, engineered under neoliberalism by the failure to carry out needed social investment, produces increased demand for social control and repression. In the United States, all of this is immediately understood in racial terms.

ENDNOTES

1. Noting the distortions and perversions perpetrated—largely by the right wing—on Dr. King's "I Have a Dream" speech, Michael Eric Dyson once proposed a ten-year moratorium on referring to it (Dyson 2001). That moratorium has now expired. The speech belongs to the tradition that Bercovitch (1978) called the "American Jeremiad."

2. The calamitous 2008 recession impacted groups of color far more than it did whites. From 2005 to 2009, median net worth fell by 66 percent among Latino households, 54 percent among Asian households, and 53 percent among black households compared with a decrease of just 16 percent among white households (Kochhar et al. 2011, 14). The entire subprime mortgage crisis was a racial crisis, with disproportionate numbers of black and Latino borrowers facing foreclosures and losing their homes. Long excluded from equal access to mortgage credit, people of color were first "steered" into unsustainable loans, and then dispossessed of their meager equities through foreclosures, "short sales," and often fraudulent banking practices.

DISCUSSION QUESTIONS

1. Michael Omi and Howard Winant argue that the United States is "a racially organized social and political system," and they regard race as "a master category of oppression and resistance in the United States." What do these claims mean, and what arguments do they make in support of them? Do you agree with their arguments? Why or why not?

2. Omi and Winant argue that the physical "visibility of race"—the fact that a person's skin color is often the first thing about her that we see—"continues to determine popular understandings of race, and thus to shape both White supremacy and color blind hegemony in the United States today." Are they right? Why or why not?

3. What was the Jim Crow era, and how did Jim-Crow-era discrimination end? Did racism end with the passage of civil rights laws in the mid-1960s? Evaluate Daniel Bell's argument that our confidence in Jim Crow's demise may be premature. Was he right? Why or why not?

4. Explain the concept of "colorblindness," which has become hegemonic in the United States during the twenty-first century, and is widely understood as racial "common sense." Is America today a "color-blind" and "postracial" society? Why or why not?

DEFINING RACISM

Why Are All the Black Kids Sitting Together in the Cafeteria? And Other Conversations About Race

BY **Beverly Daniel Tatum**

Early in my teaching career, a White student I knew asked me what I would be teaching the following semester. I mentioned that I would be teaching a course on racism. She replied, with some surprise in her voice, "Oh, is there still racism?" I assured her that indeed there was and suggested that she sign up for my course. Fifteen years later, after exhaustive media coverage of events such as the Rodney King beating, the Charles Stuart and Susan Smith cases, the O. J. Simpson trial, the appeal to racial prejudices in electoral politics, and the bitter debates about affirmative action and welfare reform, it seems hard to imagine that anyone would still be unaware of the reality of racism in our society. But in fact, in almost every audience I address, there is someone who will suggest that racism is a thing of the past. There is always someone who hasn't noticed the stereotypical images of people of color in the media, who hasn't observed the housing discrimination in their community, who hasn't read the newspaper articles about documented racial bias in lending practices among well-known banks, who isn't aware of the racial tracking pattern at the local school, who hasn't seen the reports of rising incidents of racially motivated hate crimes in America—in short, someone who hasn't been paying attention to issues of race. But if you are paying attention, the legacy of racism is not hard to see, and we are all affected by it.

The impact of racism begins early. Even in our pre-school years, we are exposed to misinformation about people different from ourselves. Many of us grew up in neighborhoods where we had limited opportunities to interact with people different from our own families. When I ask my college students, "How many of you grew up in neighborhoods where most of the people were from the same racial group as your own?" almost every hand goes up. There is still a great deal of social segregation in our communities. Consequently, most of the early information we receive about "others"—people racially, religiously, or socioeconomically different from ourselves—does not come as the result of firsthand experience. The secondhand information we do receive has often been distorted, shaped by cultural stereotypes, and left incomplete.

Some examples will highlight this process. Several years ago one of my students conducted a research project investigating preschoolers' conceptions of Native Americans.[1] Using children at a local day care center as her participants, she asked these three- and four-year-olds to draw a picture of a Native American. Most children were stumped by her request. They didn't know what a Native American was. But when she rephrased the question and asked them to draw a picture of an Indian, they readily complied. Almost every picture included one central feature: feathers. In fact, many of them also included a weapon—a knife or tomahawk—and depicted the person in violent or aggressive terms. Though this group of children, almost all of whom were White, did not live near a large Native American population and probably had had little if any personal interaction with American Indians, they all had internalized an image of what Indians were like. How did they know? Cartoon images, in particular the Disney movie *Peter Pan,* were cited by the children as their number-one source of information. At the age of three, these children already had a set of stereotypes in place. Though I would not describe three-year-olds as prejudiced, the stereotypes to which they have been exposed become the foundation for the adult prejudices so many of us have.

Sometimes the assumptions we make about others come not from what we have been told or what we have seen on television or in books, but rather from what we have *not* been told. The distortion of historical information about people of color leads young people (and older people, too) to make assumptions that may go unchallenged for a long time. Consider this conversation between two White students following a discussion about the cultural transmission of racism:

"Yeah, I just found out that Cleopatra was actually a Black woman."

"What?"

The first student went on to explain her newly learned information. The second student exclaimed in disbelief, "That can't be true. Cleopatra was beautiful!"

What had this young woman learned about who in our society is considered beautiful and who is not? Had she conjured up images of Elizabeth Taylor when she thought of Cleopatra? The new information her classmate had shared and her own deeply ingrained assumptions about who is beautiful and who is not were too incongruous to allow her to assimilate the information at that moment.

Omitted information can have similar effects. For example, another young woman, preparing to be a high school English teacher, expressed her dismay that she had never learned about any Black authors in any of her English courses. How was she to teach about them to her future students when she hadn't learned about them herself? A White male student in the class responded to this discussion with frustration in his response journal, writing "It's not my fault that Blacks don't write books." Had one of his elementary, high school, or college teachers ever told him that there were no Black writers? Probably not. Yet because he had never been exposed to Black authors, he had drawn his own conclusion that there were none.

Stereotypes, omissions, and distortions all contribute to the development of prejudice. *Prejudice* is a preconceived judgment or opinion, usually based on limited information. I assume that we all have prejudices, not because we want them, but simply because we are so continually exposed to misinformation about others. Though I have often heard students or workshop participants describe someone as not having "a prejudiced bone in his body," I usually suggest that they look again. Prejudice is one of the inescapable consequences of living in a racist society. Cultural racism—the cultural images and messages that affirm the assumed superiority of Whites and the assumed inferiority of people of color—is like smog in the air. Sometimes it is so thick it is visible, other times it is less apparent, but always, day in and day out, we are breathing it in. None of us would introduce ourselves as "smog-breathers" (and most of us don't want to be described as prejudiced), but if we live

in a smoggy place, how can we avoid breathing the air? If we live in an environment in which we are bombarded with stereotypical images in the media, are frequently exposed to the ethnic jokes of friends and family members, and are rarely informed of the accomplishments of oppressed groups, we will develop the negative categorizations of those groups that form the basis of prejudice.

People of color as well as Whites develop these categorizations. Even a member of the stereotyped group may internalize the stereotypical categories about his or her own group to some degree. In fact, this process happens so frequently that it has a name, *internalized oppression*. Some of the consequences of believing the distorted messages about one's own group will be discussed in subsequent chapters.

Certainly some people are more prejudiced than others, actively embracing and perpetuating negative and hateful images of those who are different from themselves. When we claim to be free of prejudice, perhaps what we are really saying is that we are not hatemongers. But none of us is completely innocent. Prejudice is an integral part of our socialization, and it is not our fault. Just as the preschoolers my student interviewed are not to blame for the negative messages they internalized, we are not at fault for the stereotypes, distortions, and omissions that shaped our thinking as we grew up.

To say that it is not our fault does not relieve us of responsibility, however. We may not have polluted the air, but we need to take responsibility, along with others, for cleaning it up. Each of us needs to look at our own behavior. Am I perpetuating and reinforcing the negative messages so pervasive in our culture, or am I seeking to challenge them? If I have not been exposed to positive images of marginalized groups, am I seeking them out, expanding my own knowledge base for myself and my children? Am I acknowledging and examining my own prejudices, my own rigid categorizations of others, thereby minimizing the adverse impact they might have on my interactions with those I have categorized? Unless we engage in these and other conscious acts of reflection and reeducation, we easily repeat the process with our children. We teach what we were taught. The unexamined prejudices of the parents are passed on to the children. It is not our fault, but it is our responsibility to interrupt this cycle.

RACISM: A SYSTEM OF ADVANTAGE BASED ON RACE

Many people use the terms *prejudice* and *racism* interchangeably. I do not, and I think it is important to make a distinction. In his book *Portraits of White Racism,* David Wellman argues convincingly that limiting our understanding of racism to prejudice does not offer a sufficient explanation for the persistence of racism. He defines racism as a "system of advantage based on race."[2] In illustrating this definition, he provides example after example of how Whites defend their racial advantage—access to better schools, housing, jobs—even when they do not embrace overtly prejudicial thinking. Racism cannot be fully explained as an expression of prejudice alone.

This definition of racism is useful because it allows us to see that racism, like other forms of oppression, is not only a personal ideology based on racial prejudice, but a *system* involving cultural messages and institutional policies and practices as well as the beliefs and actions of individuals. In the context of the United States, this system clearly operates to the advantage of Whites and to the disadvantage of people of color. Another related definition of racism, commonly used by antiracist educators and consultants, is "prejudice plus power." Racial prejudice when combined with social power—access to social, cultural, and economic resources and decision-making—leads to the institutionalization of racist policies and practices. While I think this definition also captures the idea that racism is more than individual beliefs and attitudes, I prefer Wellman's definition because the idea of systematic advantage and disadvantage is critical to an understanding of how racism operates in American society.

In addition, I find that many of my White students and workshop participants do not feel powerful. Defining racism as prejudice plus power has little personal relevance. For some, their response to this definition is the following: "I'm not really prejudiced, and I have no power, so racism has nothing to do with me." However, most White people, if they are really being honest with themselves, can see that there are advantages to being White in the United States. Despite the current rhetoric about affirmative action and "reverse racism," every social indicator, from salary to life expectancy, reveals the advantages of being White.[3]

The systematic advantages of being White are often referred to as White privilege. In a now well-known article, "White Privilege: Unpacking the Invisible Knapsack," Peggy McIntosh, a White feminist scholar, identified a long list of societal privileges that she received simply because she was White.[4] She did not ask for them, and it is important to note that she hadn't always noticed that she was receiving them. They included major and minor advantages. Of course she enjoyed greater access to jobs and housing. But she also was able to shop in department stores without being followed by suspicious salespeople and could always find appropriate hair care products and makeup in any drugstore. She could send her child to school confident that the teacher would not discriminate against him on the basis of race. She could also be late for meetings, and talk with her mouth full, fairly confident that these behaviors would not be attributed to the fact that she was White. She could express an opinion in a meeting or in print and not have it labeled the "White" viewpoint. In other words, she was more often than not viewed as an individual, rather than as a member of a racial group.

This article rings true for most White readers, many of whom may have never considered the benefits of being White. It's one thing to have enough awareness of racism to describe the ways that people of color are disadvantaged by it. But this new understanding of racism is more elusive. In very concrete terms, it means that if a person of color is the victim of housing discrimination, the apartment that would otherwise have been rented to that person of color is still available for a White person. The White tenant is, knowingly or unknowingly, the beneficiary of racism, a system of advantage based on race. The unsuspecting tenant is not to blame for the prior discrimination, but she benefits from it anyway.

For many Whites, this new awareness of the benefits of a racist system elicits considerable pain, often accompanied by feelings of anger and guilt. These uncomfortable emotions can hinder further discussion. We all like to think that we deserve the good things we have received, and that others, too, get what they deserve. Social psychologists call this tendency a "belief in a just world."[5] Racism directly contradicts such notions of justice.

Understanding racism as a system of advantage based on race is antithetical to traditional notions of an American meritocracy. For those who have internalized this myth, this definition generates considerable discomfort. It is more comfortable simply to think of racism as a particular form of prejudice. Notions of power or privilege do not have to be addressed when our understanding of racism is constructed in that way.

The discomfort generated when a systemic definition of racism is introduced is usually quite visible in the workshops I lead. Someone in the group is usually quick to point out that this is not the definition you will find in most dictionaries. I reply, "Who wrote the dictionary?" I am not being facetious with this response. Whose interests are served by a "prejudice only" definition of racism? It is important to understand that the system of advantage is perpetuated when we do not acknowledge its existence.

RACISM: FOR WHITES ONLY?

Frequently someone will say, "You keep talking about White people. People of color can be racist, too." I once asked a White teacher what it would mean to her if a student or parent of color accused her of being racist. She said she would feel as though she had been punched in the stomach or called a "low-life scum." She is not alone in this feeling. The word *racist* holds a lot of emotional power. For many White people, to be called racist is the ultimate insult. The idea that this term might only be applied to Whites becomes highly problematic for after all, can't people of color be "low-life scum" too?

Of course, people of any racial group can hold hateful attitudes and behave in racially discriminatory and bigoted ways. We can all cite examples of horrible hate crimes which have been perpetrated by people of color as well as Whites. Hateful behavior is hateful behavior no matter who does it. But when I am asked, "Can people of color be racist?" I reply, "The answer depends on your definition of racism." If one defines racism as racial prejudice, the answer is yes. People of color can and do have racial prejudices. However, if one defines racism as a system of advantage based on race, the answer is no. People of color are not racist because they do not systematically benefit from racism. And equally important, there is no systematic cultural and institutional support or sanction for the racial bigotry of people of color. In my view, reserving the term *racist* only for behaviors committed by Whites in the context of a White-dominated society is a way of acknowledging the ever-present power differential afforded Whites by the culture and institutions that make up the system of advantage and continue to reinforce notions of White superiority. (Using the same logic, I reserve the word *sexist* for men. Though women can and do have gender-based prejudices, only men systematically benefit from sexism.)

Despite my best efforts to explain my thinking on this point, there are some who will be troubled, perhaps even incensed, by my response. To call the racially motivated acts of a person of color acts of racial bigotry and to describe similar acts committed by Whites as racist will make no sense to some people, including some people of color. To those, I will respectfully say, "We can agree to disagree." At moments like these, it is not agreement that is essential, but clarity. Even if you don't like the definition of racism I am using, hopefully you are now clear about what it is. If I also understand how you are using the term, our conversation can continue—despite our disagreement.

Another provocative question I'm often asked is "Are you saying all Whites are racist?" When asked this question, I again remember that White teacher's response, and I am conscious that perhaps the question I am really being asked is, "Are you saying all Whites are bad people?" The answer to that question is of course not. However, all White people, intentionally or unintentionally, do benefit from racism. A more relevant question is what are White people as individuals doing to interrupt racism? For many White people, the image of a racist is a hood-wearing Klan member or a name-calling Archie Bunker figure. These images represent what might be called *active racism,* blatant, intentional acts of racial bigotry and discrimination. *Passive racism* is more subtle and can be seen in the collusion of laughing when a racist joke is told, of letting exclusionary hiring practices go unchallenged, of accepting as appropriate the omissions of people of color from the curriculum, and of avoiding difficult race-related issues. Because racism is so ingrained in the fabric of American institutions, it is easily self-perpetuating.[6] All that is required to maintain it is business as usual.

I sometimes visualize the ongoing cycle of racism as a moving walkway at the airport. Active racist behavior is equivalent to walking fast on the conveyor belt. The person engaged in active racist behavior has identified with the ideology of White supremacy and is moving with it. Passive racist behavior is equivalent to standing still on the walkway. No overt effort is being made, but the conveyor belt moves the bystanders along to the same destination as those who are actively walking. Some of the bystanders may feel the motion of the conveyor belt, see the active racists ahead of them, and choose to turn around, unwilling to go to the same destination as the White supremacists. But unless they are walking actively in the opposite direction at a speed faster than the conveyor belt—unless they are actively antiracist—they will find themselves carried along with the others.

So, not all Whites are actively racist. Many are passively racist. Some, though not enough, are actively antiracist. The relevant question is not whether all Whites are racist, but how we can move more White people from a position of active or passive racism to one of active antiracism? The task of interrupting racism is obviously not the task of Whites alone. But the fact of White privilege means that Whites have greater access to the societal institutions in need of transformation. To whom much is given, much is required.

It is important to acknowledge that while all Whites benefit from racism, they do not all benefit equally. Other factors, such as socioeconomic status, gender, age, religious affiliation, sexual orientation, mental and physical ability, also play a role in our access to social influence and power. A White woman on welfare is not privileged to the same extent as a wealthy White heterosexual man. In her case, the systematic disadvantages of sexism and classism intersect with her White privilege, but the privilege is still there. This point was brought home to me in a 1994 study conducted by a Mount Holyoke graduate student, Phyllis Wentworth.[7] Wentworth interviewed a group of female college students, who were both older than their peers and were the first members of their families to attend college, about the pathways that lead them to college. All of the women interviewed were White, from working-class backgrounds, from families where women were expected to graduate from high school and get married or get a job. Several had experienced abusive relationships and other personal difficulties prior to coming to college. Yet their experiences were punctuated by "good luck" stories of apartments obtained without a deposit, good jobs offered without experience or extensive reference checks, and encouragement provided by willing mentors. While the women acknowledged their good fortune, none of them discussed their Whiteness. They had not considered the possibility that being White had worked in their favor and helped give them the benefit of the doubt at critical junctures. This study clearly showed that even under difficult circumstances, White privilege was still operating.

It is also true that not all people of color are equally targeted by racism. We all have multiple identities that shape our experience. I can describe myself as a light-skinned, well-educated, heterosexual, able-bodied, Christian African American woman raised in a middle-class suburb. As an African American woman, I am systematically disadvantaged by race and by gender, but I systematically receive benefits in the other categories, which then mediate my experience of racism and sexism. When one is targeted by multiple isms—racism, sexism, classism, heterosexism, ableism, anti-Semitism, ageism—in whatever combination, the effect is intensified. The particular combination of racism and classism in many communities of color is life-threatening.

Nonetheless, when I, the middle-class Black mother of two sons, read another story about a Black man's unlucky encounter with a White police officer's deadly force, I am reminded that racism by itself can kill.

THE COST OF RACISM

Several years ago, a White male student in my psychology of racism course wrote in his journal at the end of the semester that he had learned a lot about racism and now understood in a way he never had before just how advantaged he was. He also commented that he didn't think he would do anything to try to change the situation. After all, the system was working in his favor. Fortunately, his response was not typical. Most of my students leave my course with the desire (and an action plan) to interrupt the cycle of racism. However, this young man's response does raise an important question. Why should Whites who are advantaged by racism *want* to end that system of advantage? What are the *costs* of that system to them?

A *Money* magazine article called "Race and Money" chronicled the many ways the American economy was hindered by institutional racism.[8] Whether one looks at productivity lowered by racial tensions in the workplace, or real estate equity lost through housing discrimination, or the tax revenue lost in underemployed communities of color, or the high cost of warehousing human talent in prison, the economic costs of racism are real and measurable.

As a psychologist, I often hear about the less easily measured costs. When I ask White men and women how racism hurts them, they frequently talk about their fears of people of color, the social incompetence they feel in racially mixed situations, the alienation they have experienced between parents and children when a child marries into a family of color, and the interracial friendships they had as children that were lost in adolescence or young adulthood without their ever understanding why. White people are paying a significant price for the system of advantage. The cost is not as high for Whites as it is for people of color, but a price is being paid.[9] Wendell Berry, a White writer raised in Kentucky, captures this psychic pain in the opening pages of his book, *The Hidden Wound:*

> If white people have suffered less obviously from racism than black people, they have neverthe-less suffered greatly; the cost has been greater perhaps than we can yet know. If the white man has inflicted the wound of racism upon black

men, the cost has been that he would receive the mirror image of that wound into himself. As the master, or as a member of the dominant race, he has felt little compulsion to acknowledge it or speak of it; the more painful it has grown the more deeply he has hidden it within himself. But the wound is there, and it is a profound disorder, as great a damage in his mind as it is in his society.[10]

The dismantling of racism is in the best interests of everyone.

A WORD ABOUT LANGUAGE

Throughout this chapter I have used the term *White* to refer to Americans of European descent. In another era, I might have used the term *Caucasian.* I have used the term *people of color* to refer to those groups in America that are and have been historically targeted by racism. This includes people of African descent, people of Asian descent, people of Latin American descent, and indigenous peoples (sometimes referred to as Native Americans or American Indians).[11] Many people refer to these groups collectively as non-Whites. This term is particularly offensive because it defines groups of people in terms of what they are not. (Do we call women "non-men?") I also avoid using the term *minorities* because it represents another kind of distortion of information which we need to correct. So-called minorities represent the majority of the world's population. While the term *people of color* is inclusive, it is not perfect. As a workshop participant once said, White people have color, too. Perhaps it would be more accurate to say "people of more color," though I am not ready to make that change. Perhaps fellow psychologist Linda James Myers is on the right track. She refers to two groups of people, those of acknowledged African descent and those of unacknowledged African descent, reminding us that we can all trace the roots of our common humanity to Africa.

I refer to people of acknowledged African descent as Black. I know that *African American* is also a commonly used term, and I often refer to myself and other Black people born and raised in America in that way. Perhaps because I am a child of the 1960s "Black and beautiful" era, I still prefer *Black.* The term is more inclusive than *African American,* because there are Black people in the United States who are not African American—Afro-Caribbeans, for example—yet are targeted by racism, and are identified as Black.

When referring to other groups of color, I try to use the terms that the people themselves want to be called. In some cases, there is no clear consensus. For example, some people of Latin American ancestry prefer *Latino,* while others prefer *Hispanic* or, if of Mexican descent, *Chicano.*[12] The terms *Latino* and *Hispanic* are used interchangeably here. Similarly, there are regional variations in the use of the terms *Native American, American Indian,* and *Indian. American Indian* and *Native people* are now more widely used than *Native American,* and the language used here reflects that. People of Asian descent include Pacific Islanders, and that is reflected in the terms *Asian/Pacific Islanders* and *Asian Pacific Americans.* However, when quoting others I use whichever terms they use.

My dilemma about the language to use reflects the fact that race is a social construction.[13] Despite myths to the contrary, biologists tell us that the only meaningful racial categorization is that of human. Van den Berghe defines race as "a group that is socially defined but on the basis of *physical* criteria," including skin color and facial features.[14]

Racial identity development, a central focus of this book, usually refers to the process of defining for oneself the personal significance and social meaning of belonging to a particular racial group. The terms *racial identity* and *ethnic identity* are often used synonymously, though a distinction can be made between the two. An ethnic group is a socially defined group based on *cultural* criteria, such as language, customs, and shared history. An individual might identify as a member of an ethnic group (Irish or Italian, for example) but might not think of himself in racial terms (as White). On the other hand, one may recognize the personal significance of racial group membership (identifying as Black, for instance) but may not consider ethnic identity (such as West Indian) as particularly meaningful.

Both racial and ethnic categories are socially constructed, and social definitions of these categories have changed over time. For example, in his book *Ethnic Identity: The Transformation of White America*, Richard Alba points out that the high rates of intermarriage and the dissolution of other social boundaries among European ethnic groups in the United States have reduced the significance of ethnic identity for these groups. In their place, he argues, a new ethnic identity is emerging, that of European American.[15]

Throughout this book, I refer primarily to racial identity. It is important, however, to acknowledge that ethnic identity and racial identity sometimes intersect.

For example, dark-skinned Puerto Ricans may identify culturally as Puerto Rican and yet be categorized racially by others as Black on the basis of physical appearance. In the case of either racial or ethnic identity, these identities remain most salient to individuals of racial or ethnic groups that have been historically disadvantaged or marginalized.

The language we use to categorize one another racially is imperfect. These categories are still evolving as the current debate over Census classifications indicates.[16] The original creation of racial categories was in the service of oppression. Some may argue that to continue to use them is to continue that oppression. I respect that argument. Yet it is difficult to talk about what is essentially a flawed and problematic social construct without using language that is itself problematic. We have to be able to talk about it in order to change it. So this is the language I choose.

ENDNOTES

1. C. O'Toole, "The effect of the media and multicultural education on children's perceptions of Native Americans" (senior thesis, Department of Psychology and Education, Mount Holyoke College, South Hadley, MA, May 1990).

2. For an extended discussion of this point, see David Wellman, *Portraits of White racism* (Cambridge: Cambridge University Press, 1977), ch. 1.

3. For specific statistical information, see R. Farley, "The common destiny of Blacks and Whites: Observations about the social and economic status of the races," pp. 197–233 in H. Hill and J. E. Jones, Jr. (Eds.), *Race in America: The struggle for equality* (Madison: University of Wisconsin Press, 1993).

4. P. McIntosh, "White privilege: Unpacking the invisible knapsack," *Peace and Freedom* (July/August 1989): 10–12.

5. For further discussion of the concept of "belief in a just world," see M. J. Lerner, "Social psychology of justice and interpersonal attraction," in T. Huston (Ed.), *Foundations of interpersonal attraction* (New York: Academic Press, 1974).

6. For a brief historical overview of the institutionalization of racism and sexism in our legal system, see "Part V: How it happened: Race and gender issues in U.S. law," in P. S. Rothenberg (Ed.), *Race, class, and gender in the United States: An integrated study*, 3d ed. (New York: St. Martin's Press, 1995).

7. P. A. Wentworth, "The identity development of non-traditionally aged first-generation women college students: An exploratory study" (master's thesis, Department of Psychology and Education, Mount Holyoke College, South Hadley, MA, 1994).

8. W. L. Updegrave, "Race and money," *Money* (December 1989): 152–72.

9. For further discussion of the impact of racism on Whites, see B. Bowser and R. G. Hunt (Eds.), *Impacts of racism on White Americans* (Thousand Oaks, CA: Sage, 1981); P. Kivel, *Uprooting racism: How White people can work for racial justice* (Philadelphia: New Society Publishers, 1996); and J. Barndt, *Dismantling racism: The continuing challenge to White America* (Minneapolis: Augsburg Press, 1991).

10. W. Berry, *The hidden wound* (San Francisco: North Point Press, 1989), pp. 3–4.

11. It is important to note here that these groups are not necessarily mutually exclusive. For example, people of Latin American descent may have European, African, and Native American ancestors. The politics of racial categorization has served to create artificial boundaries between groups with shared ancestry.

12. It is difficult to know which is the preferred term to use because different subgroups have different preferences. According to Amado Padilla, younger U.S.-born university-educated individuals of Mexican ancestry prefer *Chicano(a)* to *Mexican American* or *Hispanic*. On the other hand, *Latino* is preferred by others of Mexican ancestry or other Latin American origin. Those of Cuban ancestry may prefer *Cuban American* to *Latino*, whereas recent immigrants from Central America would rather be identified by their nationality (e.g., *Guatematecos* or *Salvadoreños*). A. Padilla (Ed.), *Hispanic psychology* (Thousand Oaks, CA: Sage, 1995).

13. For an expanded discussion of the social construction of race, see M. Omi and H. Winant, *Racial formation in the United States*, 2d ed. (New York: Routledge, 1994).

14. P. L. Van den Berghe, *Race and racism* (New York: Wiley, 1967).

15. See R. Alba, *Ethnic identity: The transformation of White America* (New Haven: Yale University Press, 1990).

16. For a discussion of the census classification debate and the history of racial classification in the United States, see L. Wright, "One drop of blood," *The New Yorker* (July 25, 1994): 46–55.

DISCUSSION QUESTIONS

1. Beverly Daniel Tatum offers two metaphors—breathing smoggy air, and riding on an automated walkway at the airport—to illustrate the ubiquity of active and passive racism in American society. Explain how these metaphors work. In what way does Tatum use them to suggest that all Americans are affected by racism, and that all White people are active or passive participants in the maintenance of racism in America today?

2. Some people define racism as prejudice, or as "prejudice plus power." Tatum prefers to think of racism as a system of advantages based on race. What do you think of these definition? How would you define racism?

3. Can people of color be racists? Or can only White people be racist? Significant arguments can be made for both conclusions, based in part on how one defines racism. Explain both arguments. Which is more persuasive in your view? Why?

4. What is White privilege? How does Tatum defend the reality of White privilege when so many White people don't feel very privileged today?

READING 3.7

RACIST AMERICA: RACIST IDEOLOGY AS A SOCIAL FORCE

Racist America: Roots, Current Realities, and Future Reparations

BY Joe R. Feagin

CREATING A RACIST IDEOLOGY

The dramatic expansion of Europe from the 1400s to the early 1900s eventually brought colonial exploitation to more than 80 percent of the globe. The resulting savagery, exploitation, and resource inequalities were global, and they stemmed, as W. E. B. Du Bois has noted, from letting a "single tradition of culture suddenly have thrust into its hands the power to bleed the world of its brawn and wealth, and the willingness to do this."[1] However, for the colonizing Europeans it was not enough to bleed the world of its labor and resources. The colonizers were not content to exploit indigenous peoples and view that exploitation simply as "might makes right." Instead, they vigorously justified what they had done for themselves and their descendants. Gradually, a broad racist ideology rationalized the oppression and thereby reduced its apparent moral cost for Europeans.

An ideology is a set of principles and views that embodies the basic interests of a particular social group. Typically, a broad ideology encompasses expressed attitudes and is constantly reflected in the talk and actions of everyday life. One need not know or accept the entire ideology for it to have an impact on thought or action. Thus, each person may participate only in certain fragments of an ideology. Ideologies are usually created by oppressors to cover what they do, and counterideologies are often developed by the oppressed in their struggle against domination. Here we examine a critical aspect of the social reproduction of systemic racism from one generation to the next. The perpetuation of systemic racism requires an intertemporal reproducing not only of racist institutions and structures but also of the ideological apparatus that buttresses them.

The early exploitative relationships that whites developed in regard to African Americans and Native Americans were quickly rationalized, and they became enduring racist relations. From the beginning, racial oppression has been webbed into most arenas of American life, including places of work and residence, and activities as diverse as eating, procreating, and child rearing. Racist practices in these life worlds create, and are in turn shaped by, basic racist categories in the language and minds of Americans, especially white Americans. A racist ideology has overarching principles and beliefs that provide an umbrella for more specific racist attitudes, prejudices, and stereotypes.

Major ideological frameworks, including racist frameworks, are typically created, codified, and maintained by those at the top of a society, although this construction takes place in ongoing interaction with the views and practices of ordinary citizens. Those with the greater power have the greater ability to impose their own ideas on others. As Karl Marx and Friedrich Engels long ago pointed out, "the ideas of the ruling class are in every epoch the ruling ideas: i.e. the class, which is the ruling material force of society, is at the same time its ruling intellectual force."[2] Elites have dominated the creation, discussion, and dissemination of system-rationalizing ideas in business, the media, politics, education, churches, and government. While there is indeed much popularly generated racist imagery and discourse, even this is usually codified and embellished by the elites. As with most important ideas, if the elites had been opposed to the development of the racist ideology, they would have actively combated it, and it would likely have declined in importance. Thus, in his detailed analysis of the racist ideas and actions of presidents from George Washington to Bill Clinton, Kenneth O'Reilly has shown that conventional wisdom about presidents following a racist populace is wrongheaded. The historical evidence shows that most of the men who control U.S. political institutions have worked hard "to nurture and support the nation's racism."[3] Racist thought did not come accidentally to the United States. It was, and still is, actively developed and propagated.

THE EMERGING ANTIBLACK IDEOLOGY: EARLY VIEWS

For several centuries white ministers, business people, political leaders, academics, scientists, and media executives have developed and disseminated to all Americans a complex and variegated racist ideology that defends the theft of land and labor from Americans of color. The antiblack version of this ideology is the most developed; it has included a variety of religious, scientific, and psychosexual rationalizations for oppression. Although the ideology has been elaborated and changed somewhat over time, in all its variations it has operated to rationalize white power and privilege.

From the 1600s to the 1800s English and other European Protestants dominated the religious scene on the Atlantic coast of North America, and their religious views incorporated notions of European superiority and non-European inferiority. The early English Protestants regarded themselves as Christian and civilized, but those they conquered as unchristian and savage. Religious and cultural imperialism accompanied economic imperialism.

Most of the new colonists from Europe saw themselves as Christian people of virtue and civilization. From the first century of American colonization these Europeans frequently portrayed themselves as "virtuous republicans." They did not, or should not, have the instinctual qualities of the "creatures of darkness," the black and red Calibans they saw in their stereotyped images. Europeans were rational, ascetic, self-governing, and sexually controlled, while the African and Native American others were irrational, uncivilized, instinctual, and uncontrolled.[4] The first non-Europeans with whom many European colonists came into contact were Native Americans. Rationalizing the often brutal destruction of Native American societies, European colonists developed early on some negative images of Native Americans. Native Americans were "uncivilized savages" to be killed off or pushed beyond the boundaries of European American society. Moreover, much white thinking about indigenous peoples in the first centuries alternated between great hostility, such as can be seen in the Declaration of Independence's complaint about "merciless Indian savages," and the paternalism seen in the image of a "noble savage" who was independent of the vices of Europeans. Novelists such as James Fenimore Cooper heralded what they saw as the diversity in character of the "native warrior of North America. In war, he is daring, boastful, cunning, ruthless ... in peace, just, generous, hospitable, revengeful, superstitious, modest, and commonly chaste."[5]

EARLY COLOR CODING: THE LINK TO SLAVERY

In the first century of North American slavery the antiblack ideology was becoming ever more developed and comprehensive. The emerging ideology increasingly focused not only on the blackness of the others but also on the whiteness of Europeans. Africans and African Americans were viewed as physically, aesthetically, morally, and mentally inferior to whites—differences that were regarded as more or less permanent. "Whiteness" was created in opposition to "blackness," in comparison to which it was not only different but quite superior. Indeed, from the seventeenth century forward black women, men, and children were "constructed as lazy, ignorant, lascivious, and criminal; Whites as industrious, knowledgeable, virtuous, and law-abiding."[6]

Significantly, the antiblack image was not "out there," but rather in the white mind and emotions. In their thinking and imaging, some whites went so far as to view the dark skin of Africans as a "natural infection" or as "pollution." A leading medical educator of the late 1700s, Dr. Benjamin Rush, thought the dark skin color of African Americans resulted from a type of leprosy that could be cured with medical treatment.[7]

The U.S. Constitution recognized the slave economy and implicitly incorporated an ideology of white supremacy in such provisions as the one that counted an African American as only "three-fifths" of a person. After the new nation was created, the unifying of growing numbers of immigrants from various European countries was done in part through the legal and political doctrines buttressing white privilege and superiority. In the first naturalization law in 1790, the new U.S. Congress made the earliest political statement on citizenship. Naturalization was restricted to "white persons." Whiteness thereby became an official government category; only European immigrants could qualify to become citizens of the new United States. The legal doctrines established by Congress and the courts helped to shape and unify the white consciousness, including that of the nation's leadership.[8]

EMOTIONAL UNDERPINNINGS

From the seventeenth century to the present the ideology justifying antiblack oppression, while overtly cognitive and legally enshrined, has had a strong emotional base. Antiblack attitudes and actions among whites have long been linked to or supported by such emotions as hate, fear, guilt, and repulsion. W.E.B. Du Bois suggested that color barriers are created not only out of overt maliciousness but also by "unconscious acts and irrational reactions unpierced by reason."[9]

For instance, many whites have been emotionally obsessed with what they term "racial mixing." Strong and irrational emotions are evident in the taboos and laws against interracial sex and marriage, which have long been considered to be extremely "unnatural" and "abominable" by many whites. In 1662 the colony of Virginia established the first law against interracial sex, and in 1691 a law against interracial marriage was enforced by banishment. White Virginians, scholars have noted, were very "disturbed by the racial intermingling, especially white-Negro mixtures, and introduced laws to prevent what they saw as the 'abominable mixture and spurious issue' by penalizing whites who engaged in interracial sex."[10] Mixed-ancestry Americans were viewed not only as inferior but also as degrading what Benjamin Franklin called a "lovely" whiteness. As Franklin argued, white "amalgamation with the other color produces a degradation to which no lover of his country, no lover of excellence in the human character can innocently consent."[11] Like most whites of the eighteenth century, Franklin seems to have developed a deep fear of black Americans. A slaveholder for several decades, then a leading abolitionist later in life, Franklin openly opposed slavery not because of its inhumanity but because of its negative impact on the whiteness of the American population. Ironically and significantly, for most of American history it was white men who were the most likely to cross the color line and force sex on black women.

Strong emotions are evident in the white violence that has long targeted black Americans. While most of the bloodthirsty lynchings of black Americans took place after the Civil War, they were preceded before that war by barbaric beatings, rape, torture, and mutilation of Africans and African Americans on slave ships, farms, and plantations. The early white notion that African Americans were "dangerous savages" and "degenerate beasts" played a role in rationalizing this violence. To deserve such treatment "the black man presumably had to be as vicious as the racists claimed; otherwise many whites would have had to accept an intolerable burden of guilt for perpetrating or tolerating the most horrendous cruelties and injustices."[12] After slavery, the racist ideology legitimated lynchings, whose sadistic character suggests deep and shared white emotions of guilt, hatred, and fear.

Fear is central to the ideology and attitudes woven through the system of antiblack oppression. Significantly, of the three large-scale systems of social oppression—racism, sexism, and classism—only racism involves the dominant group having a deep and often obsessively emotional fear of the subordinate group. This is not generally true for men, who dominate women in the system of sexism, nor is it true for the capitalists who exploit workers in the class-stratified capitalist system.

DEVELOPING AN EXPLICIT IDEOLOGY OF "RACE"

The ideology rationalizing exploitation did not develop all at once, but was elaborated as colonialism expanded around the globe. First, as we saw above, the "others" were viewed as religiously and culturally inferior. This brought an early accent on a hierarchy of inferior and superior groups. Later on, those oppressed were seen as distinctive "races" that were inferior in physical, biological, and intellectual terms to Europeans. A clearly delineated concept of "race" as a distinctive pseudobiological category was developed by northern Europeans and European Americans about the time of the American Revolution.

By the late 1700s these hierarchical relations were increasingly explained in overtly bioracial terms. This biological determinism read existing European prejudices back into human biology; then it read that biology as rationalizing social hierarchy. Those at the bottom were less than human; they were alleged to have smaller, and thus inferior, brains. Reflecting on European imperialism in the late nineteenth and early twentieth centuries, Frantz Fanon stressed the point that this colonialism was about much more than labor or resource exploitation, for it involved broad social domination constructed in racist terms. European colonialism created the modern idea of "race" across the globe. "In the colonies the economic substructure is also a superstructure. The cause is the consequence; you are rich because you are white, you are white because you are rich."[13] This new racist ideology had three important elements: (1) an accent on physically and biologically distinctive categories called "races"; (2) an emphasis on

"race" as the primary determinant of a group's essential personality and cultural traits; and (3) a hierarchy of superior and inferior racial groups.

America's prominent theorist of liberty, Thomas Jefferson, contended that black Americans were an inferior "race." In *Notes on the State of Virginia*, written in the late eighteenth century, Jefferson articulated what were the first developed arguments by an American intellectual for black inferiority. Blacks are said to be inferior to whites in reasoning, imagination, and beauty. Blacks are alleged to favor white beauty "as uniformly as is the preference of the Oranootan [Orangutan] for the black women over those of his own species." Blacks are alleged to be more adventuresome than whites because they have a "want of forethought," to be unreflective, and—perhaps most amazing—to feel life's pain less than whites. Blacks are alleged to have produced no important thinkers, poets, musicians, or intellectuals. Improvement in black minds comes only when there is a "mixture with whites," which Jefferson argues "proves that their inferiority is not the effect merely of their condition of life."[14]

SCIENTIFIC RACISM

As early as the 1730s the Swedish botanist and taxonomist, Carolus Linneaus, distinguished four categories of human beings—black, white, red, and yellow. Though he did not explicitly use the idea of "race," he associated skin color with cultural traits—with whites being superior and blacks inferior. Between the 1770s and the 1790s the prominent German anatomist and anthropologist, Johann Blumenbach, worked out a racial classification that became influential. At the top of his list of "races" were what Blumenbach called the "Caucasians" (Europeans), a term he coined because in his judgment the people of the Caucasus were the most beautiful of the European peoples. Lower on the list were the Mongolians (Asians), the Ethiopians (Africans), the Americans (Native Americans), and the Malays (Polynesians). "White" was viewed as the oldest color of mankind, and white had degenerated into the darker skin colors.[15]

The new scientific racism firmly encompassed the notion of a specific number of races with different physical characteristics, a belief that these characteristics were hereditary, and the notion of a natural hierarchy of inferior and superior races. In their broad sweep these racist ideas were not supported by careful scientific observations of all human societies but rather were buttressed with slanted reports gleaned by European missionaries, travelers, and sea captains from their experiences with selected non-European societies. Most scientists of the late eighteenth and early nineteenth centuries, while presenting themselves as objective observers, tried to marshal evidence for human differences that the white imperialists' perspective had already decided were important to highlight.[16]

CELEBRATING AND EXPANDING THE RACIST IDEOLOGY

In the United States distinguished lawyers, judges, and political leaders promoted scientific racism and its white-supremacist assumptions. In the first half of the nineteenth century whites with an interest in slavery dominated the political and legal system. This influence was conspicuous in the infamous *Dred Scott v. John F. A. Sandford* (1857) decision. Replying to the petition of an enslaved black American, a substantial majority of the U.S. Supreme Court ruled that Scott was not a citizen under the Constitution and had no rights. Chief Justice Roger Taney, a slaveholder, argued that African Americans "had for more than a century before [the U.S. Constitution] been regarded as beings of an inferior order, and altogether unfit to associate with the white race, either in social or political relations; and so far inferior, that they had no rights which the white man was bound to respect; and that the negro might justly and lawfully be reduced to slavery for his benefit. He was bought and sold, and treated as an ordinary article of merchandise and traffic, whenever a profit could be made by it. This opinion was at that time fixed and universal in the civilized portion of the white race."[17] The Dred Scott decision showed that the racist ideology was both elaborate and well established.

Senators and presidents played their role in articulating and spreading this ideology. President James Buchanan, a northerner, urged the nation to support the racist thinking of the *Dred Scott* decision. Moreover, several years before he became president, in his debate with Senator Stephen A. Douglas, Abraham Lincoln argued that the physical difference between the races was insuperable, saying, "I am not nor ever have been in favor of the social and political equality of the white and black races: that I am not nor ever have been in favor of making voters of the free negroes, or jurors, or qualifying them to hold office or having them to marry with white people. … I as much as any other man am in favor of the superior position being assigned to the white man."[18] Lincoln, soon to be the "Great Emancipator," had made his white supremacist views clear, views later cited by southern officials in the 1960s struggle to protect legal segregation and still quoted by white supremacist groups today.

With the end of Reconstruction in 1877 came comprehensive and coercive racial segregation in the South. Distinguished judges, including those on the Supreme Court, played a key role in solidifying the extensive segregation of black Americans and in unifying white defenses of institutionalized racism. In *Plessy v. Ferguson* (1896) a nearly unanimous Supreme Court legitimated the fiction of "separate but equal" for black and white Americans in a case dealing with racially segregated railroad cars. This separate-but-equal fiction was legal for more than half a century, until the 1954 *Brown v. Board of Education of Topeka* decision and until broken down further by the civil rights laws of the 1960s. There was widespread agreement in the elites and in the general white population about the desirability of thorough and compulsory segregation for black men, women, and children.

SOCIAL DARWINISM

In his influential writings Charles Darwin applied his evolutionary idea of natural selection not only to animal development but also to the development of human "races." He saw natural selection at work in the killing of the indigenous peoples of Australia by the British, wrote of blacks as a category between whites and gorillas, and spoke against social programs for the "weak" because they permitted the least desirable people to survive. The "civilized races" would eventually replace the "savage races throughout the world."[19]

During the late 1800s and early 1900s a perspective called "social Darwinism" developed the ideas of Darwin and argued aggressively that certain "inferior races" were less evolved, less human, and more apelike than the "superior races." Prominent social scientists like Herbert Spencer and William Graham Sumner argued that social life was a life-and-death struggle in which the best individuals would win out over inferior individuals. Sumner argued that wealthy Americans, who were almost entirely white at the time, were products of natural selection and essential to the advance of civilization. Black Americans were seen by many of these openly racist analysts as a "degenerate race" whose alleged "immorality" was a racial trait.[20]

By the late 1800s a eugenics movement was spreading among scientists and other intellectuals in Europe and the United States. Eugenicists accented the importance of breeding the "right" types of human groups. Britain's Sir Francis Galton argued for improving the superior race by human intervention. Like Galton, U.S. eugenicists opposed "racial mixing" (or "miscegenation") because it destroyed racial purity. Allowing "unfit races" to survive would destroy the "superior race" of northern Europeans. Those from the lesser races, it was decided, should be sterilized or excluded from the nation. Such views were not on the fringe, but had the weight of established scientists, leading politicians, and major business leaders. Thus, in 1893 Nathaniel S. Shaler, a prominent scientist and dean at Harvard University, argued that black Americans were inferior, uncivilized, and an "alien folk" with no place in the body politic. In social Darwinist fashion, he spoke of their eventual extinction under the processes of natural law.[21]

Scientific racism was used by white members of Congress to support passage of discriminatory congressional legislation, including the openly racist 1924 immigration law excluding most immigrants other than northern Europeans. In this period overtly racist ideas were advocated by all U.S. presidents. Former president Theodore Roosevelt openly favored scientific racism.[22] President Woodrow Wilson was well-known as an advocate of the superiority of European civilization over all others, including those of Africa. As president, Wilson increased the racial segregation of the federal government. Significantly, no less a racist leader than Adolf Hitler would later report having been influenced by Wilson's writings. (In its contemporary sense, the term *racism* first appeared in a 1933 German book by Magnus Hirschfeld, who sought to counter the Nazi and other European racists' notion of a biologically determined hierarchy of races.)[23]

In 1921 President Warren G. Harding, who had once been linked to the Ku Klux Klan, said he rejected any "suggestion of social equality" between blacks and whites, citing a popular racist book as evidence the "race problem" was a global problem. Not long before he became president, Calvin Coolidge wrote in *Good Housekeeping* magazine, "Biological laws tell us that certain divergent people will not mix or blend. The Nordics propagate themselves successfully. With other races, the outcome shows deterioration on both sides."[24] Ideas of white supremacy and rigid segregation were openly advocated by top political leaders.

PERPETUATING THE RACIST IDEOLOGY: CONTEMPORARY AMERICA

Periodically, the racist ideology framed in the first two centuries of American development has shifted somewhat in its framing or emphases. Those in charge have dressed it up differently for changing social circumstances, though the underlying framework has remained much the same. Some new ideas have been added to deal with pressures for change from those oppressed, particularly ideas about government policy. After World War II, aspects of the dominant racist ideology were altered somewhat to fit the new circumstances of the 1950s and 1960s, during which black Americans increasingly challenged patterns of compulsory racial segregation.

In recent decades white elites have continued to dominate the transmission of new or refurbished ideas and images designed to buttress the system of racial inequality, and they have used ever more powerful means to accomplish their ends. The mass media now include not only the radio, movies, and print media used in the past, but television, music videos, satellite transmissions, and the Internet.

Today, for the most part, the mass media are still controlled by whites. Just under 90 percent of the news reporters, supervisors, and editors at newspapers and magazines across the United States are white. On television whites are overrepresented in managerial jobs, and as on-air reporters; they are greatly overrepresented as "experts" in the mass media. Americans of color have only a token presence in the choice and shaping of news reports and media entertainment. The concentration of media control in a few corporations has increased dramatically in recent decades. In the early twenty-first century, fewer than two dozen corporations control much of the mass media, and that number is likely to decrease further. In addition, the mass media, especially television, are substantially supported by corporate advertisers, and advertisers have significant command over programming. Thus, information about racial matters is usually filtered and whitewashed through a variety of elite-controlled organizations. This filtering is not a coordinated conspiracy, but reflects the choices of many powerful whites socialized to the dominant framing in regard to racial issues.[25]

Looking for data and stories, reporters and journalists typically seek out established government, business, academic, and think-tank reports and experts. The right wing of the U.S. ruling class, a large segment, has historically been the most committed to the racist ideology and has pressed for repression of protests against oppression. The liberal wing of the white elite is much smaller and often more attuned to popular movements; it has been willing to liberalize the society to some degree and to make some concessions to protesters for the sake of preserving the society. (The center of the elite has waffled between the two poles.) In the late 1960s and 1970s many experts consulted by top executives in government and the mass media came from think tanks usually espousing the views of those in the center or on the left of the ruling elite. Becoming very concerned about this, wealthy conservatives began in the 1970s to lavishly fund right-wing think tanks and to press aggressively conservative views of U.S. society on universities, politicians, and media owners. In recent years the right-wing think tanks—including the American Enterprise Institute, the Manhattan Institute, and the Heritage Foundation—have been very successful in getting their experts into mainstream discussions and debates. Working alongside a large group of other conservative intellectuals, media experts, and activists, these right-wing think tanks continue to be successful in an indoctrination campaign aimed at shaping public views on racial and other social issues.[26]

Most Americans now get their news from commercial television and radio programs. The largest single source is local news programming.[27] Using these local and national media, the white elites have the capability to mobilize mass consensus on elite-generated ideas and views; this consensus often provides an illusion of democracy. These elites encourage collective ignorance by allowing little systematic information critical of the existing social and political system to be circulated through the media to the general population.

With the national racial order firmly in place, most white Americans, from childhood on, come to adopt the views, assumptions, and proclivities of previous generations and established white authorities. In this manner the system of racism is reproduced from one generation of whites to the next.

INCREASED EQUALITY RHETORIC

From the 1960s onward the rhetoric of racial equality, or at least of an equality of opportunity, grew in volume among members of the white elite, including presidents and members of Congress. The black protests and rebellions of the 1950s and 1960s had an important effect in eradicating not only the system of the legal segregation but also most public defense of racial discrimination by the nation's white leadership. Since the late 1960s most leaders have proclaimed the rhetoric of racial and ethnic equality.

The structural dismantling of a large-scale system of compulsory segregation did require a new equality emphasis in the prevailing racial ideology. However, while the structural position of whites and blacks had changed somewhat, at least officially, most whites—in the elites and the general public—did not seem interested in giving up significant white power or privilege. Thus, the racist ideology was altered in some ways but continued to incorporate many of its old features, and it continued to rationalize white privilege—now under conditions of official desegregation. There had long been some fairness language in the prevailing ideology—for example, most whites thought blacks were treated fairly—but now notions of fairness and equality of opportunity were moved to the forefront. The acceptance by the white elite and public of the principles of equal opportunity and desegregation in regard to schools, jobs, and public accommodations did *not* mean that most whites desired for the federal government to implement large-scale integration of these institutions.

A MORE CONSERVATIVE ORIENTATION: 1969 TO THE PRESENT

Beginning around 1969, with the arrival of Richard Nixon's presidential administration, the rhetoric of equality was increasingly accompanied by a federal government backing off from its modest commitment to desegregation and enforcement of the new civil rights laws. At the local level, there was increased police repression of aggressive dissent in the black community, such as the illegal attacks on Black Panthers and other militant black groups by local police and FBI agents. The old racist images of dangerous black men and black welfare mothers were dusted off and emphasized by prominent white leaders who often spouted the rhetoric of equality at the same time. Moreover, the liberal wing of the white elite, which had provided some funding for the civil rights movement and other social movements of the 1960s, significantly reduced its support for these movements.[28]

By the mid-1970s the right wing of the ruling elite was accelerating its attack on the liberal thinking associated with the new civil rights laws. Since the 1970s a growing number of conservative organizations have worked aggressively in pressing Congress, the federal courts, and the private sector to eviscerate or eliminate antidiscrimination programs such as affirmative action efforts, as well as an array of other government social programs. This signaled the increasing influence on national policy of a more conservative Republican Party that represented, almost exclusively, the interests of white Americans. Moreover, even at the top of the

Democratic Party there was also some shift to the right, which could be seen in the relatively modest antidiscrimination policies of the Jimmy Carter and Bill Clinton administrations.

The shift away from government action to remedy discrimination was associated with a reinvigoration of notions about inferior black intelligence and culture. In the 1970s, and increasingly in the 1980s and 1990s, numerous white journalists, politicians, and academics were critical of what they saw as too-liberal views in regard to black Americans and remedies for discrimination and defended arguments about black intellectual or cultural inferiority. In public policy discussions, increasingly led by white conservatives, there was a renewed emphasis on the view that only the individual, not the group, is protected from discrimination under U.S. law.

The federal courts provide an important example of this conservative shift. In the decades since the 1970s these courts have often ruled that group-remedy programs against racial discrimination violate the U.S. Constitution, which they assert only recognizes the rights of individuals, not groups. For instance, in 1989 a conservative Supreme Court handed down a major decision, *City of Richmond, Virginia v. J. A. Croson Co.*, which knocked down a local program designed to remedy past discrimination against black and other minority businesses.[29] The high court ruled in favor of a white-run construction company, the plaintiff, which argued that the municipal government had unconstitutionally set aside business for minority companies. The court ruled that the city of Richmond had not made a compelling case for racial discrimination, even though the defendant's statistics showed that in a city whose population was one-half black, *less than 1 percent of the city government's business* went to black-owned firms.

STILL ARGUING FOR BIOLOGICAL "RACES"

In recent years some social and behavioral scientists have joined with certain physical scientists to continue to press for the idea of biological races and to connect that idea to concerns over government social policies. Since the late 1960s several social scientists at leading universities, including Arthur Jensen and Richard Herrnstein, have continued to argue that racial-group differences in average scores on the so-called IQ tests reveal genetic differences in intelligence between black and white Americans. Their views have been influential, especially on white politicians and the white public. In 1969 the *Harvard Educational Review* lent its prestige

to a long article by Jensen, a University of California professor. The arguments presented there and Jensen's later arguments in the next two decades have received much national attention, including major stories in *Time, Newsweek, U.S. News and World Report, Life,* and major newspapers. Jensen has argued that on the average blacks are born with less intelligence than whites, and that the "IQ" test data support this contention. In addition, he has suggested that high birth rates for black Americans could result in a lowering of the nation's overall intelligence level.[30]

Perhaps the most widely read example of biological determinism is a 1990s book, *The Bell Curve*, which sold more than a half million copies. Into the twenty-first century it is still being cited and read. Like Jensen, the authors of *The Bell Curve*—the late Harvard University professor Richard Herrnstein and prominent author Charles Murray—argue that IQ test data show that black (and Latino) Americans are inferior in intelligence to whites. Though the authors have no training in genetics, they suggest that this supposed inferiority in intelligence results substantially from genetic differences. Thus, biological differences account to a substantial degree for racial inequalities. The fact that the book has sold many copies and has been widely debated in the media—in spite of the overwhelming evidence against its arguments—strongly suggests that biologically oriented racist thinking is still espoused by a large number of white Americans, including those who are well-educated. Indeed, Herrnstein and Murray explicitly suggest that their views are *privately shared* by many well-educated whites, including those in the elite, who are unwilling to speak out publicly. This book was launched during a major press conference at the conservative American Enterprise Institute. This publicity insured that the book would get much national attention, while antiracist books have generally gotten far less media play.[31]

Racist arguments about contemporary intelligence levels are grounded in nearly four hundred years of viewing blacks as having an intelligence inferior to that of whites. Today, such views are much more than an academic matter. They have periodically been used by members of Congress and presidential advisors in the White House to argue against antidiscrimination and other government programs that benefit Americans of color. Given this elite activity, it is not surprising to find these views in the white public.

Another aspect of older racist views that can be found in new dress is the idea of what one might call "cultural racism"—the view that blacks have done less well than whites because of their allegedly deficient culture with its weak work ethic and family values. As early as the seventeenth century, black Americans were seen as inferior in civilization and morality to white colonists. These blaming-the-victim views have regularly been resuscitated among the white elites and passed along to ordinary Americans as a way of explaining the difficult socioeconomic conditions faced by black Americans.

Since the 1970s leading magazines have published articles accenting some version of this perspective on what came to be called the black "underclass"; the perspective accents the allegedly deficient morality and lifestyle of many black Americans. Prominent author Ken Auletta wrote an influential set of *New Yorker* articles, later expanded in his book *The Underclass*. He accented the black underclass and its supposed immorality, family disorganization, and substandard work ethic.[32] A later article in the *Chronicle of Higher Education* surveyed the growing research on the underclass, noting that "the lives of the ghetto poor are marked by a dense fabric of what experts call 'social pathologies'—teenage pregnancies, out-of-wedlock births, single-parent families, poor educational achievement, chronic unemployment, welfare dependency, drug abuse, and crime—that, taken separately or together, seem impervious to change."[33] To the present day, similar stories designed to explain black problems in cultural terms regularly appear in the local and national media across the nation.

A WHITEWASHED WORLDVIEW

This antiblack ideology links in so many ways to so much of white thought and behavior that we might speak of it as a broad worldview. Seen comprehensively, all the mental images, prejudiced attitudes, stereotypes, fictions, racist explanations, and rationalizations that link to systemic racism make up a white racist worldview, one deeply imbedded in the dominant culture and institutions. The U.S. system of racism is not just something that affects black Americans and other Americans of color, for it is central to the lives of white Americans as well. It determines how whites think about themselves, about their ideals, and about their nation.

In the early 1900s European immigrants to the United States came to accept this worldview and its implicit assumption that being "American" means being white. This has not changed much in the intervening years. Today the term "American" still means "white"—at least for the majority of white Americans, and probably for most people across the globe. One can pick up most newspapers or news magazines and find "American" or "Americans" used in a way that clearly accents *white* Americans. Take this sentence from a news writer in a Florida newspaper: "The American Public isn't giving government or police officers the blind trust it once did."[34] Clearly, "American" here means "white American," for the majority of blacks have never blindly trusted the police.

One research analysis examined all the articles in sixty-five major English-language newspapers for a six-month period and estimated that there were thousands of references to "black Americans" or "African Americans" in the articles. However, in the same newspapers there were *only forty-six* mentions of "white Americans."[35] In almost every case these mentions by newspaper writers occurred in connection with "black Americans," "blacks," or "African Americans." (The exceptions were three cases in which "white Americans" was used in connection with "Native Americans" or "Korean Americans.") A similar pattern was found for major magazines. Not once was the term "white Americans" used alone in an article; if used, it was always used in relation to another racial category. The same study examined how congressional candidates were described in news articles in the two weeks prior to the November 1998 elections. In every case white congressional candidates were *not* described as "white," but black congressional candidates were always noted as being "black."[36] In the United States blackness is usually salient and noted, while whiteness generally goes unmentioned, except when reference is specifically made to white connections to other racial groups.

Being "American" still means, in the minds of many people, including editors and writers in the media, being white. This need not be a conscious process. For several centuries most whites have probably not seen the routines of their everyday lives as framed in white. "Race" is often not visible when one is at the top of the social hierarchy. Today, major social institutions, those originally created by whites centuries ago, are still dominated by whites. Yet from the white standpoint they are not white, just normal and customary. They are not seen for what they actually are—whitewashed institutions reflecting in many of their aspects the history, privileges, norms, values, and interests of white Americans. When whites live in these customary arrangements, they need not think in overtly racist terms. Nonetheless, when whites move into settings where they must confront people of color in the United States or elsewhere, they usually foreground their whiteness, whether consciously or unconsciously.

FEAR OF A MULTIRACIAL, MULTICULTURAL FUTURE

Today, many white analysts still see Western civilization as under threat from groups that are not white or European. Racist thinking is more than rationalizing oppression, for it also represents a defensive response, a fear of losing power to Americans of color. In recent years many advocates of white superiority have directed their attacks at the values or cultures of new immigrants of color coming to the United States, as well as at black Americans. In one recent interview study elite numerous white men openly expressed some fear of the growth of Americans of color in the United States, seeing Western civilization as under threat.[37]

We observe examples of this fear among U.S. politicians and intellectuals. For example, in several speeches and articles Patrick Buchanan, media pundit and once a candidate for the Republican presidential nomination, has argued that "our Judeo-Christian values are going to be preserved and our Western heritage is going to be handed down to future generations and not dumped on some landfill called multiculturalism."[38] Once again, we see the linkage between religion and a strong sense of European supremacy. We also see a concern for the reproduction of the white-dominated system from current to future generations. In addition, Buchanan told one interviewer that "if we had to take a million immigrants in, say, Zulus next year or Englishmen, and put them in Virginia, what group would be easier to assimilate and would cause less problems for the people of Virginia? There is nothing wrong with us sitting down and arguing that issue that we are a European country, [an] English-speaking country."[39] The Zulus, who are Africans, seem to represent in his mind the specter of strange or savage hordes who would not assimilate well into the nation. Ironically, Africans have been in the nation longer than Buchanan's Irish ancestors, and Virginia has been home to African Americans for nearly four centuries.

CONCLUSION

The systemic racism that is still part of the base of U.S. society is interwoven with a strong racist ideology that has been partially reframed at various points in U.S. history, but which has remained a well-institutionalized set of beliefs, attitudes, and concepts defending white-on-black oppression. Until the late 1940s commitment to a white supremacist view of the world was proud, openly held, and aggressive. Most whites in the United States and Europe, led by elites, took pride in forthrightly professing their racist perspectives on other peoples and their racist rationalizations for Western imperialistic adventures. Brutal discrimination and overt exploitation were routinely advocated. Indeed, white domination of the globe was "seen as proof of white racial superiority."[40]

Beginning in the late 1940s, however, the open expression of a white supremacist ideology was made more difficult by a growing American awareness of actions of the racist regime in Nazi Germany. In addition, by the 1950s and 1960s growing black civil rights protests against U.S. racism—with their counterideology of black liberation—and the U.S. struggle with the Soviet Union made the open expression of a white supremacist ideology less acceptable. The dominant racist ideology changed slowly to reflect these new conditions, with a new accent on equality of opportunity and some support for moderate programs to break down the nation's segregated institutions. Still, as we have seen, many aspects of the old racist ideology were dressed up in a new guise, and they persist, with some barnacle-like additions, to the present day. From the beginning, the age-old idea of the superiority of white (Western) culture and institutions has been the most basic idea in the dominant ideology rationalizing oppression.

For some time now, most whites have viewed the last few centuries of societal development in terms of a broad imagery equating "human progress" with Western civilization. We hear or see phrases like "Western civilization is an engine generating great progress for the world" or "Africans have only seen real advancement because of their contacts with Western civilization." Western imperialism's bringing of "civilization" or "democracy" to other peoples is made to appear as an engine of great progress, with mostly good results. However, this equating of "progress" with European civilization conceals the devastating consequences of imperialism and colonialism. The actual reality was—and often still is—brutal, bloody, oppressive, or genocidal in consequence for those colonized. When whites speak of Western civilization as equivalent to great human progress, they are talking about the creation of social systems that do not take into serious consideration the interests and views of the indigenous or enslaved peoples whose resources were ripped from them, whose societies were destroyed, and whose lives were cut short. Images of Western civilization, like the racist ideologies of which they are often part, are too often used to paper over the sordid realities of Western colonialism and imperialism.

ENDNOTES

1. W.E.B. Du Bois, *Dusk of Dawn: An Essay Toward an Autobiography of a Race Concept* (New Brunswick, NJ: Transaction Books, 1984 [1940]), p. 144.

2. Karl Marx and Friederich Engels, *The German Ideology*, ed. R. Pascal (New York: International Publishers, 1947), p. 39.

3. Kenneth O'Reilly, *Nixon's Piano: Presidents and Racial Politics from Washington to Clinton* (New York: Free Press, 1995), p. 11.

4. Ronald T. Takaki, *Iron Cages: Race and Culture in 19th Century America* (Oxford: Oxford University Press, 1990), pp. 11–14.

5. James Fenimore Cooper, *The Last of the Mohicans* (1826), as quoted in Emily Morison Beck, ed., *John Bartlett's Familiar Quotations*, 15th ed. (Boston: Little Brown, 1980), p. 463.

6. Tomás Almaguer, *Racial Fault Lines* (Berkeley and Los Angeles: University of California Press, 1994), p. 28.

7. Takaki, *Iron Cages*, pp. 30–34.

8. See Frances Lee Ansley, "Stirring the Ashes: Race, Class and the Future of Civil Rights Scholarship," *Cornell Law Review* 74 (September, 1989): 993.

9. W.E.B. Du Bois, *Dusk of Dawn: An Essay Toward an Autobiography of a Race Concept* (New Brunswick, NJ: Transaction Books, 1984 [1940]), p. 6.

10. A. Leon Higginbotham, Jr., and Barbara K. Kopytoff, "Racial Purity and Interracial Sex in the Law of Colonial and Antebellum Virginia," *Georgetown Law Journal* 77 (August 1989): 1671.

11. Benjamin Franklin, quoted in Takaki, *Iron Cages*, p. 50; Claude-Anne Lopez and Eugenia W. Herbert, *The Private Franklin: The Man and His Family* (New York: Norton, 1975), pp. 194–95.

12. George Frederickson, *The Black Image in the White Mind* (Hanover, NH: Wesleyan University Press, 1971), p. 282.

13. Frantz Fanon, *The Wretched of the Earth* (New York: Grove Press, 1963), p. 32.

14. Thomas Jefferson, *Notes on the State of Virginia*, ed. Frank Shuffelton (New York: Penguin, 1999 [1785]), pp. 145, 147–48.

15. William H. Tucker, *The Science and Politics of Racial Research* (Urbana: University of Illinois Press, 1994), pp. 8–9; Ivan Hannaford, *Race: The History of an Idea in the West* (Baltimore: Johns Hopkins University Press, 1996), pp. 205–207.

16. Audrey Smedley, *Race in North America* (Boulder, CO: Westview Press, 1993), p. 26.

17. *Dred Scott v. John F. A. Sandford*, 60 U.S. 393, 407–408 (1857).

18. Abraham Lincoln, "The Sixth Joint Debate at Quincy, October 13, 1858," in *The Lincoln-Douglas Debates: The First Complete, Unexpurgated Text*, ed. Harold Holzer (New York: HarperCollins, 1993), p. 283.

19. Charles Darwin, quoted in Frederickson, *The Black Image in the White Mind*, p. 230.

20. See Joe R. Feagin, *Subordinating the Poor: Welfare and American Beliefs* (Englewood Cliffs, NJ: Prentice-Hall, 1975), pp. 35–36; and Frederick L. Hoffman, "Vital Statistics of the Negro," *Arena* 5 (April 1892): 542, cited in Frederickson, *The Black Image in the White Mind*, pp. 250–51.

21. John Higham, *Strangers in the Land* (New York: Atheneum, 1963), pp. 96–152; Tucker, *The Science and Politics of Racial Research*, p. 35.

22. Tucker, *The Science and Politics of Racial Research*, p. 93.

23. See Theodore Cross, *Black Power Imperative: Racial Inequality and the Politics of Nonviolence* (New York: Faulkner, 1984), p. 157; Magnus Hirschfeld, *Racism*, trans. and ed. by Eden and Cedar Paul (London: V. Gollancz, 1938). The book was published in German in 1933.

24. Warren G. Harding and Calvin Coolidge, each quoted in Tucker, *The Science and Politics of Racial Research*, p. 93.

25. David K. Shipler, "Blacks in the Newsroom," *Columbia Journalism Review*, May/June 1998, pp. 81 26–29; Robert M. Entman et al., *Mass Media and Reconciliation: A Report to the Advisory Board and Staff, The President's Initiative on Race* (Washington, DC, 1998); Edward Herman, "The Propaganda Model Revisited," *Monthly Review* 48 (July 1996): 115.

26. Sidney Blumenthal, *The Rise of the Counter-Establishment* (New York: Times Books, 1986), pp. 4–11, 133–70; Peter Steinfels, *The Neoconservatives: The Men Who Are Changing America's Politics* (New York: Touchstone, 1979), pp. 214–77.

27. Franklin D. Gilliam Jr., and Shanto Iyengar, "Prime Suspects: the Effects of Local News on the Viewing Public," University of California at Los Angeles, unpublished paper, n. d.

28. Thomas Ferguson and Joel Rodgers, *Right Turn: The Decline of the Democrats and the Future of American Politics* (New York: Hill and Wang, 1986), pp. 65–66.

29. *City of Richmond, Virginia v. J.A.Croson Co.*, 488 U.S. 469 (1989).

30. Arthur R. Jensen, "How Much Can We Boost IQ and Scholastic Achievement?" *Harvard 99 Educational Review* 39 (1969): 1–123.

31. Jean Stefancic and Richard Delgado, *No Mercy: How Conservative Think Tanks and 100 Foundations Changed America's Social Agenda* (Philadelphia: Temple University Press, 1996), p. 34.

32. Ken Auletta, *The Underclass* (New York: Random House, 1982).

33. Ellen K. Coughlin, "Worsening Plight of the Underclass Catches Attention," *Chronicle of Higher Education*, March 1988, A5.

34. I draw here on Nick Mrozinske, "Derivational Thinking and Racism," unpublished research paper, University of Florida, fall, 1998.
35. The search algorithm did not allow searches for the word "whites" alone, because this picks up the surnames of individuals in the Lexis/Nexis database.
36. Mrozinske, "Derivational Thinking and Racism."
37. Rhonda Levine, "The Souls of Elite White Men: White Racial Identity and the Logic of Thinking on Race," paper presented at annual meeting, Hawaiian Sociological Association, February 14, 1998.
38. Patrick Buchanan, quoted in Clarence Page, "U.S. Media Should Stop Abetting Intolerance," *Toronto Star,* December 27, 1991, A27.
39. Patrick Buchanan, quoted in John Dillin, "Immigration Joins List of ' 92 Issues," *Christian Science Monitor,* December 17, 1991, 6.
40. Frank Furedi, *The Silent War: Imperialism and the Changing Perception of Race* (New Brunswick, NJ: Rutgers University Press, 1998), p. 1.

SELECTED BIBLIOGRAPHY

Cross, Theodore. *Black Power Imperative: Racial Inequality and the Politics of Nonviolence* (New York: Faulkner, 1984).

Du Bois, W. E. B. *Dusk of Dawn: An Essay Toward an Autobiography of a Race Concept* (New Brunswick, NJ: Transaction Books, 1984 [1940]).

Furedi, Frank. *The Silent War: Imperialism and the Changing Perception of Race* (New Brunswick, NJ: Rutgers University Press, 1998).

O'Reilly, Kenneth. *Nixon's Piano: Presidents and Racial Politics from Washington to Clinton* (New York: Free Press, 1995).

Smedley, Audrey. *Race in North America* (Boulder, CO: Westview Press, 1993).

Takaki, Ronald T. *Iron Cages: Race and Culture in 19th Century America* (Oxford: Oxford University Press, 1990.

Tucker, William H. *The Science and Politics of Racial Research* (Urbana: University of Illinois Press, 1994).

DISCUSSION QUESTIONS

1. Define racist ideology and explain how it developed specifically in North America. What three components (or ideas) made up the new racist ideology? Who is most responsible for the growth and importance of America's racist ideology—White elites, or the general population?

2. In what ways does racist ideology impact America today? Explain.

3. Define scientific racism and explain how it supports racist ideas. Please provide examples of prominent figures that contributed to its development.

4. What is social Darwinism, and how was it important in the development and maintenance of America's racist ideology? Does it continue to play such a role today? How is social Darwinism evident in public policy, and in political leaders' policy proposals?

5. Evaluate the following statement: "Today, many White analysts still see Western civilization as under threat from groups that are not White or European." How widespread are such fears of a multiracial, multicultural American future?

PASSIVITY IN WELL-MEANING WHITE PEOPLE

Silent Racism: How Well-Meaning White People Perpetuate the Racial Divide

BY **Barbara Trepagnier**

PASSIVITY

Passivity regarding racism is not well documented in the race literature. The exception is Joe Feagin (2001), who briefly mentions "bystanders" as a category of white racists that "provide support for others' racism" (p. 140), and who in his work with Hernán Vera and Pinar Batur (2001) suggests that "passivity is a first step in learning to ally oneself with white victimizers against black victims" (p. 49). The latter study deals primarily with passivity in the face of antiblack violence. This follows much of the literature on bystanders, which is based largely on the "anonymous crowd" that colluded with the atrocities of the World War II Holocaust (Barnett 1999: 109). Our interest concerns the passivity of well-meaning white people who collude not with violent acts but with subtle forms of racism.

Ervin Staub (2003), the foremost scholar regarding the bystander role, defines bystanders as people "who are neither perpetrators nor victims" (see Goleman 2003: 29). Bystanders are present in situations where a person or a group is the target of a negative act or statement, whether or not the victim is present at the time. Passivity in bystanders appears to have multiple causes, including alienation from victims, identification with perpetrators, and fear of repercussions. And, although bystanders are neither victims nor perpetrators, their reaction in the situation is important. Passive bystanders differ from "active bystanders" (Staub 2003: 3) in that passive bystanders do nothing in the face of injustice or discrimination; active bystanders interrupt the unjust behavior or discrimination.

Most passive bystanders feel little or no connection to the victim (Barnett 1999). In-group/out-group

differentiation may play a part in the passivity of bystanders because it is easier not to come to the aid of people who are in some way outsiders (Staub 2003). Intergroup theory posits that a primary function of groups, or categories, is to enable their members to distinguish themselves from members of other groups. Categorical differentiation is a means of cognitive sorting that facilitates information processing (Brown 2002). The sorting procedure "sharpen[s] the distinctions between categories and, relatedly, blur[s] the distinctions *within* categories" (Brown 2002: 397, emphasis in original). The resulting emphasis on similarities with in-group members and on differences with members of the out-group cause the in-group to be seen positively in comparison to the out-group. According to intergroup theory, differential categorization accounts for members of out-groups being seen in a less positive light than fellow in-group members and helps explain why people are more likely to be passive bystanders when targets of discrimination are different from themselves. Some have critiqued intergroup theory because it tends to make discrimination appear as though it is a natural occurrence and therefore cannot be avoided (see Fiske 1989).

The just world hypothesis may help explain passivity as well. The *just world hypothesis* refers to the idea that victims of injustice get what they deserve. The premise is that people want a world that is orderly and predictable. And if the world is orderly and predictable, it is also just. In order to sustain this belief, people must either come to the aid of victims of injustice or decide that the victims deserve the treatment they receive. Given that out-group members—people that are different in some way—are more likely to be seen as deserving of discrimination than in-group members, people's level of belief in the just world hypothesis is in inverse relation to the degree of empathy held for the group under attack (Staub 1992). The silent racism in people's minds would tend to support the white belief that blacks in some way deserve discrimination.

Another reason some people are passive bystanders is out of loyalty to the person doing the discriminating. Fear of causing embarrassment or anger may discourage interrupting racism, even if the bystander disapproves of the behavior. Shifting from being a passive bystander to an active one takes moral courage (Staub 2003). This is particularly true in situations where a power differential is in play, such as when one's boss tells a racist joke or makes a racist decision. In this case ambivalence (Smelser 1998) is likely to occur, and the decision of whether to intervene will be weighed against the cost of doing so.

The role of bystanders is important because they have a good deal of influence in how a given situation will proceed (Staub 2003). For example, when people make racist statements and bystanders remain passive, the passivity is perceived as collusion with the exposed racist point of view. This perception, right or wrong, empowers people to persist in their racism. By contrast, when bystanders actively interrupt racist statements, the balance of power shifts away from those making racist statements in support of the target group, blacks or other people of color. This means that despite the connotation of the terms "bystander" and "passivity," neutrality is not an option. Doing nothing creates an alliance with the perpetrator, regardless of the bystander's intention (Barnett 1999). In other words, bystanders, by virtue of being present during a racist incident, align either with the target of discrimination by interrupting the discrimination or with the perpetrator by remaining passive.

A final point about the bystander role is in order. The tendency to remain passive in the face of discrimination tends to continue once the pattern is set (Staub 2003). By the same token, taking an active bystander role by interrupting racism may also become easier with practice.

The data discussed in the next section relate to passivity in the participants. The first form of passivity results from feeling estranged from the target of discrimination because of detachment. Two additional sources of passivity emerged in this study, both of which are latent effects of the "not racist" category: apprehension about being perceived as racist, and confusion about what is racist.

Detachment from Race Issues

The "not racist" category distances well-meaning white people from racism by implication: White people who see themselves as "not racist" are unlikely to see their connection to race or racism. Sharon expressed a sense of detachment from race issues several times during the discussion in her group. The first example was in response to the question, "What do you think needs to happen in order for racism to end?" Sharon said, "Racism has no connection to my life." Later, when asked if she had ever been told by someone else, or realized herself, that she had said or done something racist, Sharon again appears detached. She said, "I can't think of anything. I'm sure there must be, but I can't think of anything. It didn't hit me." Sharon would not regard her indifference as problematic in any way. Rather, as she stated, "Racism has no connection to my life." But Sharon's thinking is faulty: we are all intimately connected with issues of race (Frankenberg 1993).

Sharon's detachment from race issues makes her a passive bystander when confronted with others' racism. For example, when asked, "What do you do when you are around someone who has made a racist remark or tells a racist joke?" Sharon responded, "Nothing, usually." The indifference characterized by Sharon is akin to willful blindness, a term used in reference to the perpetrators of white-collar crime such as Ken Lay, the president of Enron. Lay claims no knowledge of criminal behavior that he and others greatly profited from. Similarly, detachment from race matters serves white people who benefit from the racial status quo. Sharon's detachment from race issues is more striking than any other participant's, although others demonstrated disconnections as well. For example, Karen, in Sharon's focus group, also said that she usually does nothing when confronted with others' racism.

Detachment from racism is not limited to people like Sharon, who came to this study accidentally and who knows very little about racism. Penny is more representative of well-meaning white people who are concerned, yet passive. Penny senses that she should interrupt racism, but she openly admits that often she does not. When Penny answered the question about what she does if someone tells a racist joke or makes a racist comment, her answer illustrates passivity. Penny said, "Ideally, I would say, 'I don't laugh at that.'

Do I say it? [That] depends on how grounded I'm feeling that day or what my relationship, my role in the group, is…. Then you get into the whole thing about, 'Oh, I didn't say it.' And 'I'm complicit.' It can be quite a conundrum." Penny, unlike Sharon, has good intentions about interrupting racism and feels bad about not doing it. Penny mentions that her role in the group could affect her reaction as a bystander. Bystanders who identify with the perpetrator or inhabit a subordinate role in relation to the perpetrator are less likely to take an active role for fear of disapproval or alienation (Staub 2003).

Vanessa said in response to the question about being around someone telling a racist joke, "I probably just don't laugh," an interesting response because the word "probably" casts her answer as a hypothetical statement rather than a statement of fact. A hypothetical answer instead of a factual one about one's behavior is likely to indicate avoidance of the question, perhaps due to being unsure about how the inquiring party might react. Nevertheless, whether Vanessa "just doesn't laugh" or laughs politely, her answer appears to indicate a measure of detachment.

Racist comments and jokes that go uninterrupted implicate the listener as well as the actor. The only way to not comply with racism when it occurs is to interrupt it. It is not correct to think that racism only occurs in interactions between whites and blacks or other people of color. To the contrary, those interactions may demonstrate less racism than comments that occur between or among white people when no blacks are present. Interrupting racism is as important at these times as it is when blacks are present, primarily because not to do so is perceived by perpetrators as encouragement of their racism.

Unintended Consequences

The "not racist" category appears to produce two unintended consequences: apprehension about being perceived as racist, and confusion about what constitutes racism. Both of these consequences result in passive behavior in white people. Differentiating manifest consequences—those that are obvious and intended—from latent consequences—those that are not obvious and not intended—is important in order to avoid confusion between "conscious *motivations* for social behavior and its *objective consequences*" (Merton 1967: 114, emphasis in original). A failure to distinguish between intended and unintended consequences results in flawed theoretical assumptions.

The putative intended function of the oppositional categories is to distinguish between antiblack racists and well-meaning white people who are presumed not to be racist. The unintended consequence is that the "not racist" category produces passivity, which is manifested in two ways: apprehension about being seen as racist, and confusion about what is racist.

Apprehension About Being Seen as Racist. Everyday rules regarding race matters, known as "racial etiquette" (Omi and Winant 1986: 62), are imbued with myriad meanings regarding race and racial difference that produce apprehension in white people. Several participants said that they felt apprehension about being perceived as racist. Elaine articulated her self-consciousness in dealing with black/white difference when she shared a story about meeting Dorothy, the friend of a friend, at a barbecue. Elaine said, "I opened the door and she's *black*. Oh! And I was just so mad at myself, and embarrassed for thinking that. I mean like, 'Oh, did that show?' Really worrying about it; just never getting past that."

Elaine's surprise that Dorothy was black was only exceeded by her embarrassment about being surprised. Based on her past experience, Elaine expected to see only white people at the barbecue. The racial etiquette that Elaine learned in her "all white" upbringing seems to have left her unsure about how to navigate a social setting that included both whites and blacks. The phrase "Did that show?" indicates that Elaine was afraid Dorothy might have noticed her surprise and interpreted it as racist. Apprehension about being perceived as racist troubled Elaine quite a bit, as evidenced by the comment, "Really worrying about it; just never getting past that." Elaine elaborated her discomfort by explaining how she makes sense of her reluctance to initiate friendships with black women. She said, "I do tend to socialize with people that are like me. … It's comfortable, it's easy, the knowns outweigh the unknowns. I think working against racism includes that fear of offending someone or fear of saying/doing the wrong thing and not being conscious of this…. I'm gonna make a mistake and I don't want to have to worry about that."

Elaine's comments do not imply that she thinks it is right to avoid situations in which she might make a misstep, as in her response to Dorothy. Nevertheless, she acknowledges that she often takes the easier path in developing friendships rather than the path that is more likely to provoke her anxiety about race difference. Her apprehension is important because of its own consequences: a tendency to avoid interactions with people of color. Ironically, as we will see in Chapter 5, having close ties with blacks and other people of color is important in developing race awareness—something that would lessen Elaine's apprehension.

Elaine added, "Racism has such a stigma attached to it that yes, we fear it. We don't want to be associated with [it]—we are not supposed to be making any mistakes." The "not racist" category produces fear of losing one's status as not racist and, in the process, lessens the tendency to question ideas about racism.

Karen made a related point in her group when she said, "I sometimes feel a barrier in approaching black women, in that I feel that they don't want to deal with me, and so I feel like I'm being respectful by keeping my distance, or something. I feel more comfortable letting them make the first move instead of me going over and starting conversations." Karen's reluctance to initiate friendships, or even conversations, with black women so they won't have to "deal with her" may relate to the incident described in Chapter 2 when Karen's black friend, Belle, rebuffed Karen's attempt to order her ice cream for her. Belle had not said why she was upset about the incident, and Karen did not ask. Consequently, Karen assumed it was simply because she was white, not realizing that it was because she had expressed a paternalistic assumption.

Apprehension about being perceived as racist keeps well-meaning white people from finding out more about racism. Anita made this point when she said, "[The] fear of saying anything that's going to label you racist ... you're not really dealing with. Well, is it or isn't it [racist], and why do I feel like that?" Lucy makes a similar point when she says, "Something that gets in my way [of dealing with my own racism] is feeling that I've got to be cool, or good, or maybe it's feeling like I try too hard or I care too much. I think it gets in my way because it prevents me from ... acknowledging that I am human." I think what Lucy means by "acknowledging that [she is] human" refers to the inevitability that she will at times be unwittingly racist. Humans make mistakes, and sometimes those mistakes are because of misconceptions or ignorance regarding racism. The need to be seen by oneself and others as "not racist" hinders becoming more aware of race matters. Moreover, people with low race awareness are not likely to be active bystanders who interrupt others' racism; rather, people with low race awareness are likely to be passive bystanders, encouraging racism.

Loretta also indicated apprehension about being perceived as racist. She said, "People silencing themselves out of the fear of not saying the right thing [means] not being able to talk, and therefore not being able to change. Making actual change may mean making a mistake, saying the wrong thing, and having somebody call you on it and having to own that." Loretta's statement shows insight into the paradox of being unable to discuss racism for fear of being perceived as racist. Loretta's comment also shows insight into the danger of seeing racism as deviant. The original definition of *political correctness,* now known as PC, was "internal self-criticism" among liberals (Berube 1994: 94). For example, liberals hoped to raise awareness about biases in language—such as the use of sexist language—because biases in language reinforce biases in society (Hofstadter 1985). Conservatives co-opted the term, mocking liberals by casting political correctness as an attempt to limit the freedom of speech. Today political correctness is widely perceived as destructive, rather than as it was originally intended: an attempt not to be offensive (Feldstein 1997).

Passivity resulting from the apprehension about being perceived as racist is evident in the preceding stories of the well-meaning white women. The fear of being seen as racist paralyzes some well-meaning white people, causing them to avoid meeting and interacting with blacks. This is significant—and ironic—because forming close relationships with blacks and other people of color is the most important step they can take to lessen their apprehension.

Confusion About What Is Racist. Confusion about racism is epitomized by uncertainty and embarrassment and is sometimes related to being apprehensive about being seen as racist. People who see themselves as not being racist often presume that they should know what is racist and what is not, even when they are not sure. Confusion about what is racist is closely related to passivity in that it suppresses action. In the following comments, participants share experiences demonstrating confusion.

Anne spoke of her confusion about whether referring to people as "black" is in itself racist. Anne reported a conversation she had with her mother in reference to a baseball announcer during a New York Yankees game. When her mom asked who announced the game, Anne said that it was Bill White. "My mom asked me, 'Who's Bill White?' I didn't want to say he was black—I thought it would be racist." Anne attempted to avoid using color as a marker for distinguishing among the sports announcers, believing that mentioning his race would have been racist. After describing many details about Bill White—color of hair, size, and so on—Anne could not think of any other way to distinguish him and finally told her mother that he was "the black announcer." This raises an important point of discussion: Was Anne's telling her mother that Bill White was "the black announcer" racist? Was it the same as Ruth, who earlier said she had a bright "black" student in her class? (See Chapter 2.)

I classified Ruth's comment as racist, as did the friend that interrupted it, pointing out that Ruth's reason for mentioning that the student was black was related to the fact that he was bright. However, that is not the case in Anne's situation; saying that Bill White was the black announcer was not related to any negative stereotype but was instrumental in identifying him to her mother.

Some would argue that using "black" as an identifying characteristic is always racist because it reinforces the notion that blacks are racialized and whites are not. This view is called *otherizing* and is thought to marginalize blacks and other minorities. However, sometimes identifying someone as black is pertinent to the context of a situation. To say he was "the black announcer" was not racist in Anne's situation because it was instrumental in that context and in no way reproduced a stereotype about blacks. I agree that white people virtually never use *white* in the same way. Nevertheless, avoiding the word *black* simply because its use is not equivalent to the use of the word *white* seems like faulty logic to me.

While discussing this issue with a black colleague, I was given this response: "Sometimes a person will apologize for saying the word *black* even when it is appropriate to include for clarity. Very often I have had whites apologize for even uttering the word. It's as if, for them, the word *black* is gaining status with *nigger* as a racially sensitive word." Avoiding the use of *black* because it might be racist results from confusion about what is racist. Using *black* as an identifying characteristic is racist when its use is associated with a racist stereotype or if it is tacked on solely because a person is not white. However, rigidly avoiding *black* unnecessarily when its use would serve a purpose is tantamount to pretending that race does not exist or was not noticed, a prime example of racial etiquette (Omi and Winant 1986).[1]

Anne's reluctance to "utter the word" *black* indicates some hesitation about saying the word at all. Anne may have received a message as a child similar to the one Lisa received from her parents. Lisa said that she was told explicitly not to notice race differences. Lisa said that in addition to telling her "colors don't matter," her parents added, "[but] don't ever say the word *black,* don't say the word *Mexican,* and don't ever refer to a person's color. It's offensive to say those words." Lisa said that when she was ten, she and her family moved into a housing project where she would be in close proximity to black children. Since Lisa would undoubtedly play with black children—her new neighbors—Lisa's parents were perhaps trying to prepare her for that experience. By cautioning Lisa to ignore difference—a difference they also denied was there—Lisa's parents wanted to both protect her from any repercussions they thought might occur from pointing out difference *and* teach her about equality. However, parents' double messages about race and racism can cause confusion in their children in terms of what is and what is not racist. In Anne's case, confusion contributed to her apprehension about being racist, which had a paralyzing effect. Avoiding any mention of race or the word *black* rather than acknowledging one's confusion keeps people from understanding what is and what is not racist.

In a related incident, Penny, who grew up in the 1960s, spoke of asking her mother about a house that looked "different" from the ones in their neighborhood—she said that it was pink and had iron grillwork across the front. Penny stated, "My mother said, 'Oh, that's where Egyptians live.' [My mother] didn't think that I'd ever meet Egyptians, and so it was okay for me to think that Egyptians were different." The logic that Penny attributes to her mother's comment—that it was okay to think that Egyptians were different because it was unlikely that Penny would meet any—indicates the lengths to which Penny's mother went in avoiding a discussion about race difference with her children. Although Penny did not recall receiving an explicit message to "not notice" race, it appears that her mother saw the acknowledgment of difference *itself* as problematic and perhaps racist, a confusion of what is racist and what is not.

Although the reluctance to mention race can be referred to as being colorblind, the instances here do not meet the definition of *color-blind racism*: a racial ideology that "explains contemporary [racial] inequality as the outcome of nonracial dynamics" (Bonilla-Silva 2003: 2). Color blindness derives from a racist ideology that is at times racist but that is not necessarily always racist. The individuals described in this section are only color blind in that they did not want to draw attention to race difference for fear it would be racist to do so.

However, I would characterize the reluctance to mention race as confusion about what is racist rather than as racism per se.

Confusion was also evident in Heather's description of an incident that occurred in her high school circle of friends. However, Heather's confusion is not coupled with apprehension. Heather said,

> I just remembered a very good friend of mine in high school who was half black—his dad was black and his mom was white—and he was blond, with blue eyes. There was an incident [in high school] that was really sticky. One of our friends didn't even know that David's father was black, and she made a very bad mistake by telling a joke about a black man and a Jewish man in an airplane—an awful, awful joke that just did not go over [well].... I think part of it was that [David] was such a blond guy. And his father had a Ph.D. in some hard science and has taught at [a major university]; he was on the faculty and then went to work at a laboratory. [David's] mom is a nurse.

Heather characterized the "sticky" incident as "a mistake" and that the friend telling the racist joke "didn't even know that David's father was black." What seems to be problematic for Heather is that David had inadvertently heard the racist joke, not the fact that the joke was racist. This interpretation is substantiated by Heather's comment that the "mistake" resulted from David being "such a blond guy" whose father has a Ph.D. and whose mother is a nurse. Heather's confusion about what is racist concerning the joke incident is likely to result from her not thinking the incident through, and, as a result, excusing her friend's racism by seeing it as harmless rather than as racist.

Confusion was also evident in a statement Alyssa made in her focus group:

> I think that everyone should be noted for their differences and celebrate their differences, instead of just ignoring, and looking through them and saying, "You know, I don't see color." Because you do [see color]. Everyone sees it. You may not think negatively of it, but when you think of the fact that you notice that a person is black, you think it's something bad. But I don't see that as something being bad—you can celebrate a difference.

The confusion in Alyssa's notion of celebrating difference becomes evident when she states inconsistent views centered on the pronoun *you*: "you may not think negatively of it" and "you think it's something bad." Alyssa seems to notice the apparent contradiction between these two thoughts when she quickly distances herself from the second statement by adding, "*I* don't see it as something bad." The confusion in Alyssa's thinking (that noticing race difference is "good" and that being black is seen as "something bad") presumably remains intact in her thinking, perhaps below her awareness. Holding contradictory beliefs without scrutinizing them may explain how many white people harbor racist thoughts about blacks and other people of color without being aware of it.

Loretta talked about the celebration of difference, but without the confusion exhibited by Alyssa. She said, "We can have a kind of 'feel good' cultural diversity yet not be antiracist. We [can] all talk the same talk, isn't this great, and cultural diversity is great. I [can] go to a food fair and taste [different food] and that's great, on one level. But if the reality is that economically only certain people are getting jobs ... and people of color are getting paid less than white people ... then there is still going to be racism." Loretta does not embrace the celebration of difference uncritically, as Alyssa does. Her critical assessment of the concept exposes the danger of celebrating the different cultural traditions of black and white Americans without acknowledging the history of racial oppression in the United States and the current racial inequality that continues today.

Confusion in well-meaning white people does not produce passivity as directly as detachment from race issues does. Neither does confusion produce passivity in the same sense that apprehension about being racist does, through the avoidance of contact. However, confusion is linked to passivity indirectly in that white people who are confused about racism are not likely to take a stand against it; one must be able to conclusively define an act as racist in order to feel justified in contesting it. Only white people who are clear about the historical legacy of racism in the United States, who understand how institutional racism operates, and who sense their own complicity with a system that benefits them to the detriment of people of color are likely to be active in interrupting racism when they encounter it. In this way, confusion along with detachment and apprehension is the antithesis of antiracism. For this reason, I consider it racist and place it just inside the midpoint toward the less racist end of the racism continuum. See Figure 1 for passivity on the racism continuum.

Figure 1 Passivity on the Racism Continuum

The aforementioned data support the claim that the "not racist" category itself produces several latent effects that bring about passivity in well-meaning white people. Just as silent racism produces institutional racism, passivity produces collusion with racism. Said differently, everyday racism could not stand without the participation and cooperation of well-meaning white people. However, before discussing how silent racism and passivity are key ingredients in the production of institutional racism, there is another topic to consider: possible unintended consequences of replacing the oppositional categories with a racism continuum.

ONE MORE UNINTENDED CONSEQUENCE

Would racism increase if people came to believe that all white people are somewhat racist? This concern—that some whites who now suppress their racist thoughts would presume to have permission to express them—is well founded. We saw this effect in Chapter 2 when Vanessa expressed the racist belief that black Americans are essentially different from white Americans. I questioned Vanessa's point that blacks and whites are inherently different, using the analogy of how supposed inherent gender difference between men and women have traditionally been used as a rationale against change for women. Vanessa responded, "Exactly. I just feel safe in saying this; I've never said it anyplace else. ... As a psychologist, I wouldn't dare say what I said [laughter from several group members], but I really do question what people are so quick to say, that all races have to be equally endowed."

Vanessa acknowledged that she has never voiced the opinion before, and that she "felt safe" in saying in the focus group what she "wouldn't dare say" any place else. The idea raised by Vanessa may exemplify what would result if the sanctions against acknowledging racist thoughts were eliminated. In other words, is expressing suppressed racist thoughts a greater harm than the harm caused by their suppression?

Despite her belief in biological race differences, Vanessa expressed pride in her antiracist heritage when she told about her great-grandparents who helped "slaves escape to the North." Vanessa invokes both racist and antiracist sentiments, shifting between the two. The term *drift* can be used to explain juvenile delinquents' movement between two cultures, "convention and crime" (Matza 1964: 28). Similarly, that the focus groups granted permission to talk about race and racism likely explains Vanessa's "drift" into racism. In her journal entry, Vanessa further explained her statement concerning biological determinism:

> I felt a kind of exhilaration in being able to talk openly about a loaded subject. Also, being with others who seemed to totally share my general [antiracist] attitudes on racism was a pleasure. I soon began to view them all with admiration as the stories came forth. Although I told of attitudes and beliefs the others might not agree with offhand, I had the feeling it was a good place to share them—[I thought] they would be fairly considered.

Vanessa appears to offset her statement about biological determinism by stating that she had never said it "anyplace else," that she "wouldn't dare," and that she felt "safe" in saying it in the focus group. *Neutralization* refers to a set of techniques intended to rationalize or justify delinquent behavior (Sykes and Matza 1957). Vanessa's use of a neutralization technique illustrates her awareness that what she said is not acceptable under normal circumstances. Her statement verifies the concern that removing the "not racist" category and its tendency to silence those in it would increase the expression of racist ideas. However, concern about this effect is based on the dubious assumption that suppressed racism is preferable to overt racism. I maintain that even if statements like Vanessa's increased, the benefit of increasing race awareness would outweigh that consequence because the increased race awareness is essential to decreasing the production of institutional racism. The drift into racism demonstrated by Vanessa should not be reason to dismiss rethinking the oppositional categories; on the contrary, Vanessa's statement is evidence that more open discussion about racism is needed. The expression and discussion of racist ideas would be more conducive to understanding racism than the confusion and apprehension that now govern white people who care about racism but feel paralyzed when faced with it.

In the 1950s, whites who stood up against racism were labeled "deviant"; today, the opposite is true: whites who are overtly racist are labeled "deviant." Labeling theory posits that the process of naming people "deviant" pertains to social rules that define deviance (Becker 1963). The deviance literature states that rules concerning who is deviant (and by implication who is not deviant) are imposed from outside, by moral entrepreneurs. In the case of the labels "racist" and "not racist," however, many white people who see themselves as "not racist" impose the rules on themselves. And yet, if the function of the "racist" category is to identify and therefore punish racists, then racism is sustained by the very social regulation intended to curtail it. Furthermore, the label "not racist" produces passivity in well-meaning white people, the supposed allies of blacks and other people of color. Labels imply essences—ways of being rather than merely ways of acting (Katz 1975). This is particularly true in the case of the racism labels; white racists are perceived as qualitatively different from whites presumed to be "not racist." If all whites are somewhat racist, this distinction is false, serving only to protect silent racism, everyday racism, and institutional racism.

CONCLUSION

Passivity is common in well-meaning white people. It is marked by detachment that produces a bystander effect in white people who find themselves in the face of others' racism. In addition, passivity results from apprehension about being seen as racist and from confusion about what is racist—both unintended but direct effects of the "not racist" category. This chapter's central thesis is that *passivity works against racial equality.* Well-meaning white people who are passive bystanders quietly watch America grow more divided over race issues. Yet, these are not innocent bystanders. They profit from the racial divide; they reap the same advantages received by those performing racist acts that they silently witness. The well-meaning whites who are the least aware of this fact feel little or no discomfort about the situation—they do not recognize the benefits that institutional racism affords them. The well-meaning whites who are detached have a measure of race awareness and feel bad about the situation as well as about their own passivity. Other passive bystanders are apprehensive—afraid to make a move for fear that they may be seen as racist. And still others are confused or misinformed, even though most do not recognize their confusion.

Both silent racism and passivity in well-meaning white people, some of which is produced by the category system, are instrumental in the production of institutional racism, described in the next chapter.

ENDNOTE

1. I would like to thank Glynis Christine and Chad Smith for their conversations regarding this topic.

REFERENCES

Barnett, Victoria. 1999. *Bystanders: Conscience and Complicity during the Holocaust.* Westport, CT: Praeger.

Becker, Howard. 1963. *Outsiders: Studies in the Sociology of Deviance.* New York: Free Press.

Berube, Michael. 1994. *Public Access: Literary Theory and American Cultural Politics.* New York: Verso.

Bonilla-Silva, Eduardo. 2003. *Racism Without Racists: Color-Blind Racism and the Persistence of Racial Inequality in the United States.* Lanham, MD: Rowman and Little-field.

Brown, Cynthia. 2002. *Refusing Racism: White Allies and the Struggle for Civil Rights.* New York: Teachers College Press.

Feagin, Joe. 2001. *Racist America: Roots, Current Realities, and Future Reparations.* New York: Routledge.

Feagin, Joe, Hernán Vera, and Pinar Batur. 2001. *White Racism: The Basics,* 2nd ed. New York: Routledge.

Feldstein, Richard. 1997. *Political Correctness: A Response from the Cultural Left.* Minneapolis: University of Minnesota Press.

Fiske, Susan. 1989. "Examining the Role of Intent: Toward Understanding Its Role in Stereotyping and Prejudice." In *Unintended Thought,* edited by Jim Uleman and John Bargh. New York: Guilford.

Frankenberg, Ruth. 1993. *White Women, Race Matters: The Social Construction of Whiteness.* Minneapolis: University of Minnesota Press.

Goleman, Daniel. 2003. "Studying the Pivotal Role of Bystanders." In *The Psychology of Good and Evil: Why Children, Adults, and Groups Help and Harm Others,* edited by E. Staub. New York: Cambridge University Press.

Hofstadter, Douglas. 1985. *Metamagical Themas: Questing for the Essence of Mind and Pattern.* New York: BasicBooks.

Katz, Jack. 1975. "Essence as Moral Identities: Verifiability and Responsibility in Imputations of Deviance and Charisma." *American Journal of Sociology* 80(6): 1369–1390.

Matza, David. 1964. *Delinquency and Drift.* New York: John Wiley.

Merton, Robert. 1967. *On Theoretical Sociology.* New York: Free Press.

Omi, Michael, and Howard Winant. 1986. *Racial Formation in the United States.* New York: Routledge.

Smelser, Neil. 1998. *The Social Edges of Psychoanalysis.* Berkeley: University of California Press.

Staub, Ervin. 1992. *The Roots of Evil: The Origins of Genocide and Other Group Violence.* New York: Cambridge University Press.

———. 2003. *The Psychology of Good and Evil: Why Children, Adults, and Groups Help and Harm Others.* New York: Cambridge University Press.

Sykes, Gresham, and David Matza. 1957. "Techniques of Neutralization: A Theory of Delinquency." *American Sociological Review* 22 (December): 664–670.

DISCUSSION QUESTIONS

1. What is "silent" or "passive" racism? If a White person is silent or passive in the presence of racist acts, or is within earshot of racist comments, can she or he still be racist? Isn't she or he, rather, a kind of "innocent bystander?" Explain your answer.

2. Are some Americans detached from racial issues? Can any American, Black or White, be truly detached from racial issues or from America's racial divide? Explain your answer.

3. Comment on the following statement: "Racist comments and jokes that go uninterrupted implicate the listener as well as the actor. The only way to not comply with racism when it occurs is to [actively] interrupt it."

READING 3.9

AFFIRMATIVE ACTION ENDING?

Certain Legal Cases have Left Experts Speculating where Race-Conscious Admissions are Headed

BY **Kimberly Davis**

As an outgrowth of the civil rights movement, the consideration of race in college admissions became a common way for traditionally White colleges and universities to bolster opportunities and level the playing field for people of color, particularly African-Americans.

Legal actions, such as *Sweatt v. Painter* in 1950, in which a Black applicant, Heman Marion Sweatt, challenged the "separate but equal doctrine" and gained admission to The University of Texas School of Law, paved the way for Blacks to gain equality in higher education. Following *Sweatt, Brown v. Board of Education* outlawed school segregation in 1954 and seemingly opened the gateway to college campuses nationwide.

Even after these cases, however, segregation and de facto segregation (wherein Black applicants were unfairly deemed unqualified) had kept low the percentage of students from marginalized communities who enrolled in traditionally White institutions of higher learning. According to the National Center on Education Statistics (NCES), there have been periods of significant gaps in rates for immediate college enrollment based on race or ethnicity.

But in the early 1960s, following "affirmative action" executive orders by Presidents John F. Kennedy in 1961 and Lyndon B. Johnson in 1965, colleges and universities adopted recruitment strategies designed to deliver on the promise of opportunity to previously barred students.

Prior to these policies, the percentage of minority students had been very low relative to their student-age population and the enrollment gap persisted. In the affirmative action era, according to NCES, those have declined to the point where in 2012—the last year for which data were available—there were no measurable differences.

But along the way, there have and continue to be threats to this type of intervention, with critics arguing that the use of affirmative action has no place in American society because unqualified minority applicants are favored over qualified White applicants. But this argument assumes that non-White applicants are intrinsically unqualified, says Dr. Kecia Thomas, associate dean for faculty leadership development and diversity in the University of Georgia's Franklin College of Arts and Sciences.

"Affirmative action has opened doors of opportunity for women and people of color and their families," says Thomas, who holds a doctorate from Penn State. "Too often, the general public assumes that affirmative action promotes the selection of unqualified workers.... In reality, affirmative action motivates institutions to disrupt often invisible boundaries that have impeded the education and career development of women and people of color."

Affirmative action appears to have paid off for all students, as college enrollment has increased for students across racial and ethnic backgrounds. The most recent NCES report shows that between 1990 and 2012, the immediate college enrollment rate increased for Whites (from 63 to 67 percent), Blacks (from 49 to 62 percent), and Hispanics (from 53 to 69 percent). By that same measure, the enrollment for Asian high school graduates has been higher than any other race or ethnicity each year since that category was separated in 2003. In 2012, 84 percent of Asians enrolled immediately in a two- or four-year college.

Dr. Kecia Thomas is associate dean for faculty leadership development and diversity in the University of Georgia's Franklin College of Arts and Sciences.

William Kidder is assistant executive vice chancellor at the University of California, Riverside.

CHALLENGES PERSIST

Despite these arguments and statistics and following U.S. Supreme Court decisions that upheld some use of race in college admissions in the early 2000s, challenges persist.

Most recently, *Fisher v. University of Texas* has brought to the forefront the accusation that a White student, Abigail Fisher, was discriminated against based on race. For roughly seven years, her case has wound its way through the court system, with her attorneys arguing that she was denied admission to the state's flagship university because she is White. The U.S. Supreme Court remanded the case back to the 5th Circuit Court of Appeals last year, and earlier this summer, a three-judge panel ruled 2-1 that the university had properly applied the concept of "strict scrutiny" to the case.

Edward Blum, the architect of the *Fisher* case, says they will appeal back to the Supreme Court, if it comes to that. In late July, Fisher's attorneys filed a petition asking the full 5th Circuit to review the three-judge panel's ruling.

"The ultimate goal of this case is really simple," says Blum, "and that is that the University of Texas would be found to have violated the constitutional rights of Abby Fisher and all of the other applicants who were denied admission during this period in which they were improperly using race."

Officials of The University of Texas at Austin have consistently stated that they are committed to using race as a "factor of a factor" in their second-tier, holistic admissions process. With students like Fisher, who failed to gain admission under the state's Top 10 Percent Plan, which automatically grants admission to those who graduate in the top 10 percent of their high school class, admissions officers may take into account the applicant's race or ethnicity, socioeconomic background, life experience and desired major, along with other attributes.

In addition to the *Fisher* case, earlier this year, the Supreme Court upheld the state of Michigan's voter-mandated ban on affirmative action. The April ruling in *Schuette v. Coalition to Defend Affirmative Action* essentially means that any challenge to states that have banned affirmative action at the ballot box would also fail.

AFFIRMATIVE ACTION HEADED

According to the Pew Research Center, seven other states—besides Michigan—currently have broad bans on affirmative action, including in college admissions: California, Florida, Washington, Nebraska, Arizona, New Hampshire and Oklahoma. While neither *Fisher* nor *Schuette* reversed earlier rulings about the merits of diversity in college admissions, the way in which that diversity is achieved or not achieved is now in question.

"The reason we thought that the *Schuette* case was so essential for us to win was that it opened the door for every state in this country being able to ban affirmative action through a popular mandate," says Shanta Driver, national chair for the Coalition to Defend Affirmative Action, Integration, and Immigrant Rights and Fight for Equality by Any Means Necessary (BAMN) and the case's lead attorney. "That we lost at the Supreme Court means that we are back, now, in the position where states' rights rules and a racist, White voter majority can take away the basic, fundamental right of Black and

Latino immigrants and other minorities to be able to get an education, get a job [and] be able to defeat the vestiges of racism that still structure every opportunity in this society."

Driver, along with others contacted for this story, say that the writing may be on the wall for the use of race in college admissions, as a conservative Supreme Court appears to favor ending the policy all together. That could clear the way for other states to institute similar bans, although a Pew Research poll shows that Americans favor affirmative action by a roughly 2 to 1 margin.

At the root of the problem is that there are not enough slots for every qualified applicant, says Juan E. Gilbert, a professor of computer and information science and engineering at the University of Florida. As qualified applicants look for reasons they were denied admission, they turn to the differences in each applicant and blame those differences on their failure to gain admission. Gilbert predicts that court challenges to athlete admissions may be on the horizon.

"It's clear where this is headed," says Gilbert, founder of Applications Quest, a college admissions software system designed to help colleges admit diverse classes of students without preferences. "There will continue to be court challenges because these challenges are addressing the wrong problem.... You have more qualified applicants than available positions; therefore, you must turn away qualified applicants."

S.B. Woo, a member of the interim executive committee of the 80-20 Initiative, a political organization that has fought to end affirmative action in college admissions, cites unfairness to Asian Americans and the "mismatch hypothesis" as part of his reasoning for opposing affirmative action policies. The mismatch hypothesis holds that affirmative action is damaging to minority students who are "unprepared" to succeed at the most rigorous colleges and universities and would be better served at other colleges where the curriculum would give them a better opportunity to succeed.

"Those data are undeniable," says Woo, who is of Chinese descent. "I know the believers of affirmative action, from my own experience, deny facts. They don't think that Asian Americans are disadvantaged. ... That is why the court will interfere, because those believers are not facing the facts. They say we have the power; we'll just ignore you. That is not the American ideal; that is not the way to get education to work for the people."

Shanta Driver is national chair for the Coalition to Defend Affirmative Action, Integration and Immigrant Rights and Fight for Equality by Any Means Necessary (BAMN) and the *Schuette* case's lead attorney.

William Kidder, assistant executive vice chancellor at the University of California, Riverside, says that the preponderance of social scientific evidence is against the mismatch hypothesis and that there are certain Asian American student populations that benefit from affirmative action.

According to Kidder, affirmative action is headed in multiple directions, with cases being decided both at the federal level and on a state-by-state basis. Kidder, who has researched diversity in higher education extensively, says one study he authored found that in California, where the percentage of Black and Latino students is "very low" (2 or 3 percent), those students reported feeling less respected based on their race.

"It's a direct measure of students' perception of how welcome they feel and don't feel on campus," says Kidder.

He says that racial and ethnic diversity are essential to ensuring that research institutions contribute to the development of future leaders.

"I think that's important because it really taps into the soul of who we are as Americans," Kidder says. "The diverse fabric of America needs to be reflected in its leaders. If it's not, that could be a basis for questioning the legitimacy of American society."

Editor's Note: Cox, Matthews & Associates, the parent company of Diverse: Issues In Higher Education, *has an ownership stake in Applications Quest.*

DISCUSSION QUESTIONS

1. Is affirmative action (and are affirmative action programs) ending in the United States? Why or why not? What is the future of race-conscious admissions and hiring policies and practices in colleges, universities, government, and the workplace?

2. Comment on the following statement: "Too often, the general public assumes that affirmative action promotes the selection of unqualified [students and] workers. In reality, affirmative-action motivates institutions to disrupt [the] often-invisible boundaries that have impeded the education and career development of women and people of color." Do you agree or disagree? Why?

3. What is the mismatch hypothesis? Do you think the mismatch hypothesis is a valid reason for colleges and universities to end affirmative action programs?

READING 3.10

THE ENDURING RELEVANCE OF AFFIRMATIVE ACTION

BY **Randall Kennedy**

One of the most notable accomplishments of liberalism, over the past 20 years is something that didn't happen: the demise of affirmative action. Contrary to all predictions, affirmative action has survived. This is a triumph not only for race relations but also for the liberal vision of an inclusive society with full opportunity for all.

In the early 1990s, the future of policies aimed at assisting racial minorities seemed bleak indeed. In 1989, the Supreme Court invalidated an affirmative-action plan for government contracts in Richmond, Virginia, holding that such programs at the state and local level must be subject to "strict scrutiny"—the same level of skeptical assessment applied to laws or decisions that had historically disadvantaged racial minorities. That same year, the Court issued decisions that neutered the concept of "disparate impact" as a form of racial discrimination under Title VII of the Civil Rights Act of 1964. Disparate impact required employers not only to desist from intentionally excluding racial-minority applicants because of their race but also to avoid race-neutral screening criteria that had the same effect, unless the criteria could be justified by "business necessity" or shown to be related to job performance. In 1990, when Congress repudiated the Court's regressive interpretation of Title VII, President George H.W. Bush vetoed the legislation, calling it a "quota bill."

The Civil Rights Act of 1991 passed eventually, but not before Bush put a new impediment in the way of affirmative action. He nominated Clarence Thomas, a vehement enemy of affirmative action, to replace Thurgood Marshall on the Supreme Court. This was a momentous shift that would be tantamount to Antonin Scalia being replaced by, say, liberal legal scholar Laurence Tribe. Thomas—a black man who famously overcame racism and impoverishment as a youngster—added extra timbre to the Court's anti-affirmative-action chorus, despite the fact that he was himself a beneficiary of the policy, both at Yale Law School and in the Ronald Reagan and George H. W. Bush administrations.

Conservatives charged that affirmative action amounts to "reverse racism"; discriminates against "innocent whites"; stigmatizes its putative beneficiaries; erodes the incentives that prompt individuals to put forth their best efforts; lowers standards; produces inefficiencies; goes to those racial minorities who need it least; and generates racial resentments. This indictment and the backlash it rationalized resonated not only with Republicans but also with Democrats, some of whom shared the conservatives' philosophical objections to the policy, while others worried simply that supporting it meant electoral suicide.

Writing in these pages in 1990, sociologist William Julius Wilson asserted that "the movement for racial equality needs a new political strategy ... that appeals to a broader coalition." Eschewing affirmative action (though he has subsequently changed his mind), Wilson championed redistributive reforms through "race-neutral policies," contending that they could help the Democratic Party regain lost political support while simultaneously benefiting those further down within minority groups. Similarly, in 1992 *Prospect* founding co-editor Paul Starr lamented that affirmative action "has taken a big political toll," alienating working-class whites, increasing political support for the right, and making it harder to enact "the kind of positive legislation that would especially benefit low- to middle-income Americans of all races."

Politics of Language: "Affirmative action" became "diversity" and survived. That fate wasn't certain back in the summer of 1992.

One key Democrat attracted to this critique is Barack Obama. Writing in *The Audacity of Hope,* he did not expressly condemn affirmative action, but he did consign it to a categoiy of exhausted programs that "dissect[s] Americans into 'us' and 'them'" and that "can't serve as the basis for the kinds of sustained, broad-based political coalitions needed to transform America." As president, Obama has repeatedly eschewed race-targeting (with respect most notably to employment policy) in favor of "universal" reforms that allegedly lift all boats.

Over the years, affirmative action has been truncated by judicial rulings and banned by voters in some states. In one guise or another, however, special efforts to assist marginalized racial minorities remain a major force in many schools and firms, foundations, and governments. Affirmative action survived principally because many rightly believe what President Bill Clinton declared on July 19, 1995, in what is (thus far) the only presidential address wholly devoted to the subject: "Affirmative action has been good for America." Clinton argued that ongoing injuries of past racial wrongs require redress; that affirmative action can usefully serve to prevent new invidious discrimination that is difficult, if not impossible, to reach through litigation; that the adverse consequences of affirmative action on whites are often grossly exaggerated and can easily be minimized; and that better learning and decision-making arise in environments that are racially diverse.

The amorphous and malleable idea of "diversity" provided much needed buoyancy to affirmative action, especially in the 2003 University of Michigan affirmative-action cases when 65 major companies, including American Express, Coca Cola, and Microsoft, asserted that maintaining racial diversity in institutions of higher education is vital to their efforts to hire and maintain a diverse workforce. A group of former high-ranking officers and civilian leaders of the military concurred, declaring that "a highly qualified, racially diverse officer corps ... is essential to the military's ability to fulfill its principal mission to provide national security." Even Theodore Olson, the Bush administration's solicitor general, took pains to defer to "diversity" in a brief on the case.

The rise of the diversity rationale for affirmative action has not been costless, but it has ensured that appreciable numbers of racial minorities are in strategic positions, while dampening certain side effects that attend any regime of racial selectivity. Unlike affirmative action based on grounds of compensatory justice, the diversity rationale is non-accusatory. It doesn't depend on an assumption of culpability for some past or present wrong, and it minimizes the anger ignited when whites are accused of being beneficiaries of racial privilege. Everyone can be a part of diversity.

Many are drawn to the diversity rationale because it frames affirmative action not as special aid for designated groups but as a way of producing better services and products. Businesspeople love to say that "diversity is good for the bottom line." Many of them would be ideologically allergic to a business practice based solely on notions of justice or altruism but comfortable supporting a program that can be seen as reinforcing the principal mission of their enterprises.

The diversity rationale also facilitates the evasion of prickly subjects—for instance, the fact that racial minorities selected for valued positions sometimes have records that, according to certain criteria such as standardized tests, are inferior to those of white competitors. The diversity rationale moves the spotlight from the perceived deficiencies of racial minorities to their perceived strengths. Unlike other justifications for affirmative action that seek to make exceptions to meritocracy, the diversity rationale is consistent with meritocratic premises. This is the most striking and historically significant aspect of affirmative action: It enables racial-minority status for the first time in American history to be seen as a valuable credential. Instead of the presence of blacks and other racial minorities constituting an expiation of past sins, the diversity rationale makes their presence a welcome and positive good.

> Affirmative action in education is vital to American companies' ability to hire and maintain a diverse workforce.

Liberals have been key supporters of the modern struggle for racial equality. Affirmative action is both a major strategy and central accomplishment of that struggle. Its status is paradoxical. The election of the first African American president represents a coming of age of the "affirmative-action babies," but the right has so successfully vilified the policy that Obama is embarrassed by it. He has yet to say forthrightly what Bill Clinton aptly declared: Affirmative action is good for America.

This observation is not necessarily a criticism of Obama. The president should be pragmatic. If quietude about affirmative action serves its purposes or is essential to him retaining office, then by all means he should remain quiet. Fortunately, though, Obama's acts and omissions, justifiable or not, will not prove decisive. The true measure of affirmative action's staying power is that its absence now is virtually inconceivable. Liberalism has made racial homogeneity uncool and unacceptable. Even many conservatives are made uncomfortable by lily-white gatherings—hence the enhanced value to the right of Clarence Thomas, Shelby Steele, Condoleezza Rice, Linda Chavez, and any well-spoken Negro or Latino who consorts with the Tea Party crowd. That conservatives practice affirmative action even as they condemn it is a tribute to liberalism's handiwork.

DISCUSSION QUESTIONS

1. According to Randall Kennedy, "One of the most notable accomplishments of liberalism over the past 20 years is something that didn't happen: The demise of affirmative action." What does this statement mean? Do you agree or disagree with it? Why or why not?

2. Is affirmative action "reverse racism?" Does it "discriminate against 'innocent' Whites; stigmatize its putative beneficiaries; erode the incentives that prompt individuals to put forth their best effort; lower standards; produce inefficiencies; [benefit] those racial minorities who need it least; and generate racial resentments?" Explain your answer.

3. React to, and evaluate the following statement: "The true measure of affirmative-action staying power is that its absence now is virtually inconceivable. Liberalism has made racial homogeneity uncool and unacceptable. Even many conservatives are made uncomfortable by lily-White gatherings. That conservatives practice affirmative action even as they condemn it is a tribute to liberalism's handiwork."

READING 3.11

THE POWER OF BLACK LIVES MATTER

When we Consider Specific Issues of Discrimination, Race Still Trumps Class

BY **Darryl Lorenzo Wellington**

Protesters march against police brutality in Boston.

"Something happening here/What it is ain't exactly clear" sang the Buffalo Springfield, in a song that became definitive of the cultural shifts of the 1960s. The Obama years—meaning the period since 2008—have also sent ripples, even shock waves through the cultural lives of most Americans. Something indeed is happening here and now in America. I don't mean that it is the "hope and change" Obama sloganized in 2008, and yet Obama's election has inadvertently been a catalyst. I don't mean that this awakening is leading us toward the light; indeed, what's happening is that we have been peering more honestly into the abyss. I do mean that, despite so many frustrations, setbacks and strange twists, the past seven years created fertile ground for the reconsideration and excavation of two perpetual themes in American public and intellectual life. They're not new themes. They've always been with us, however obscured, coded or politicized.

Haven't you guessed them yet? The themes that have always brooded beneath the surface, conveniently glossed over until they are roused by public outcry against a new recession, or another incident of police brutality. Class exists. Race matters. Class creates, or diminishes opportunity. Race impacts lives, and minority citizenship at the bottom of the social ladder has destroyed lives. These should be old truisms. These should be stark naked truths. Yet it has taken colorblind idealism, triumphant joy, reactionary racism and widespread shock to seriously begin to unclothe them. It has taken shock after shock throughout the Obama years to begin to make Americans consciously aware of the truths that should be self-evident.

The first shock was that a Black man with a moderately reformist agenda won the hearts of millions of voters. How could America be racist, if a Black Man ascended to the White House? How could the country not be the land of equal opportunity? In a wave of enthusiasm, hypnotized by Obama's eloquence, for a brief post-election moment the questions appeared rhetorical. In fact, they were starkly answerable.

People remembered that in 2008 Obama had delivered "A More Perfect Union," a speech in which he tendered the possibility that America could resolve its problems with class and race together, ignoring the distinctions and refusing to play "a zero sum game." But while he spoke the upper echelons of the White working class were experiencing unprecedented economic disenfranchisement. The housing mortgage crisis made relatively secure middle-class Americans aware of the worsening gap between themselves and the truly insulated wealthy. The financial sector reeled; the troubled banks and corporations were bailed out while, in the words of the Occupy Wall Street movement, "We got sold out!"

The Occupy movement sharpened the American critique of the financial sector by posing a very broad critique of class. From its beginnings in New York City's Zuccotti Park, where the outraged Occupiers camped out and parodied Wall Street bureaucracy, its main meme was "We are the 99 percent!" But the meme that underscored class was itself annoyingly classist.

It referred to the statistic that a privileged one percent of Americans owned 40 percent of the national wealth; in other words all the collected wealth of 99 percent of Americans amounted to substantially less than a privileged one percent.

Occupy camps spread across the country. If the middle class was unhealthy, and lacked chances of upward mobility, so the message went, then they would do whatever they had to do to take back public space and political power. Although Occupiers were usually legitimately struggling, they were playing at being hoboes. The movement's failure to respect the cultural and economic diversity within the 99 percent became a weakness.

Perhaps the initial Occupiers honestly believed, with the characteristic presumptiveness of White privilege, that a great victory in race had been summarily achieved. Such thinking suggested that class obviously trumped race, if a Black president was undercutting the middle class and bailing out the banks. Hence, they reasoned, the time was ripe to sharpen the distinction between opportunities offered the super wealthy and rest of us.

"Black Lives Matter is an ideological and political intervention in a world where Black lives are systematically and intentionally targeted for demise."

For Black Americans considering the Occupy movement, this was problematic. First of all, the Occupy camps suffered from troubles along race lines. Blacks were often in conflict with others in the movement over how to deal with the truly poor and the homeless. Difficulties accumulated as the indigent joined the movement, or in some cases flooded the camps. Many Occupiers were simply embarrassed by them. Efforts were made to expand the objectives of the movement to incorporate issues of gender, sexuality, race and homelessness. But they by and large remained ineffectual.

The Occupy movement asked Blacks to look at the power dynamics emanating from above, and critique a corporatocracy whose influence was rampant, unmerited and had to be reigned in by structural changes. But when Blacks in the movement looked at who really subsisted at the bottom of the 99 percent, was the overwhelming preponderance of people of color only a coincidence?

Tens of thousands marched to protest the grand jury decision after Eric Garner's death.

For all it merits, Occupy failed to appreciate that there could not be an end to racial politics without addressing the structural issues that had afflicted Blacks long before the housing crash. The question that haunted politically conscious Black Americans was not how could race still matter with Obama in the White House. The conundrum was how could a country that elected a Black president still passively let segregated ghettoes and large oases of socio-economic hopelessness remain intact? And turn a blind eye on the rates of Black child poverty and Black incarceration? How could Black people and Native Americans remain the most afflicted of the 99 percent? When we consider specific issues of discrimination, race still trumps class. How could America deny that Black lives mattered?

Black youth in America led the way in encouraging activism that refocused attention away from the clout of the super wealthy and toward systemic racial oppression, particularly in the criminal justice system. Irrational tragedies provoked them. Trayvon Martin's murder. Eric Garner's murder. Mike Brown's murder. A new challenge was born out of the outrage that escalated after each of these killings was legally sanctioned. "Black Lives Matter is an ideological and

political intervention in a world where Black lives are systematically and intentionally targeted for demise. It is an affirmation of Black folks' contributions to this society, our humanity, and our resilience in the face of deadly oppression" writes Alicia Garza, a cultural worker in Oakland, Calif. who founded Black Lives Matter alongside Patrisse Cullors and Opal Tometi. In the same way that Occupy had socially transformative ambitions beyond reforming banking practices, Black Lives Matter, writes Garza, "goes beyond the narrow nationalism that can be prevalent within some Black communities, which merely call on Black people to love Black, live Black and buy Black. Black Lives Matter affirms the lives of Black queer and trans folks, disabled folks, Black-undocumented folks, folks with records, women and all Black lives along the gender spectrum. When we say Black Lives Matter, we are talking about the ways in which Black people are deprived of our basic human rights and dignity."

FACEBOOK ACTIVISM

It's important to distinguish between a hashtag, a movement (singular) and many movements. Black Lives Matter is an organization (singular) founded in 2013 shortly after George Zimmerman was acquitted in the killing of Trayvon Martin. Black Lives Matter soon found that its social media and Twitter hashtag resonated, a banner with broad appeal. Other equally dedicated organizations were founded in the wake of the failures of grand juries to indict the police officers responsible in the deaths of Garner and Brown. The phrase "Black Lives Matter" is often used as a convenient banner encompassing the groups that responded to recent events by disseminating protest—both online and in the streets They include Dream Defenders, The Million Hoodies Movement for Justice, Millennial Activists United and other youth-oriented groups in Ferguson, Mo.

One quality that these youth-led movements share is a heavy investment in social media networking. A few years ago "Facebook activism" was often criticized for being an idle millennial-generation pastime. But by now the evidence has gathered to the point of certainty that social media is a primary 21st century tool. From late last year to MLK Day 2015, "Facebook activism" efficiently organized thousands of marchers in protests against systemic racism and injustice in law enforcement. The leaders of the protests ubiquitously say the swift escalation of a nationwide Black Lives Matter movement would not have been possible without social media. Activist DeRay Mckesson has

Ashley Yates was one of the many Ferguson activists to meet with President Obama.

worked primarily from Ferguson, where police officer Darren Wilson shot Mike Brown to death. He calls social media the next step in the war against silence. "The history of blackness is also a history of erasure." Mckesson says.

Social media has given protesters an amplified voice. Because of "Facebook activism," information about the killing of Mike Brown spread like wildfire, alongside stories and facts about Black life in Ferguson. These authentic accounts of the prevalence of racism and apartheid-level disenfranchisement soon made Ferguson into a symbol of an America in which too little has changed. Mckesson says it happened because "We were able to document that in a way that we never could have without social media. We were able to tell our own stories. What was powerful in the context of Ferguson is that there were many people able to tell their story as the story unfolded."

In November 2014, activists from various groups protesting in Ferguson or marching against police brutality were granted an audience with President Obama. Participants in the meeting say being given 45 minutes with the president confirmed that their work had garnered massive support.

In November 2014, activists from various groups protesting in Ferguson or marching against police brutality were granted an audience with President Obama. Participants in the meeting say being given 45 minutes with the president confirmed that their work had garnered massive support. The activists reported they presented Obama with a list of demands, including: 1) requiring the federal government to use its powers to prosecute police officers that kill or abuse citizens; 2) appointing independent prosecutors to handle cases involving police officers; and 3) establishing independent review boards to handle cases of police misconduct.

They reported that the president encouraged them but reminded them that change is slow. However, there is nothing "slow" about this upsurge of protest activism dominated by youth.

POST-RACIAL FALLACY

In late 2014 I replaced the cover photo on my Facebook page. I put up a stark black image that stated BLACK LIVES MATTER, in contrastingly bright white lettering. Thousands—including people of all races—did the same; in other words people of all races have *acted in solidarity.*

This is Black Lives Matters' primary call to White Americans and other races–that they act in solidarity with the goal of eradicating racism in law enforcement and the school-to-prison pipeline afflicting Black communities. The writings of founding member Alicia Garza have clearly stated that she disapproves of the tendency of some progressive groups to "modify" the rally cry. "When we deploy 'All Lives Matter' as if to correct an intervention specifically created to address anti-Blackness, we lose the ways in which the state apparatus has built a program of genocide and repression mostly on the backs of Black people—beginning with the theft of millions of people for free labor—and then adapted it to control, murder and profit off of other communities of color and immigrant communities," she argues.

Black Lives Matter is a necessary corrective to false notions that we have a post-racial society, or that that successful progressive movements (such as Occupy Wall Street) can only build large coalitions if they are built on the fallacy that class always trumps race. In fact the issues of police brutality and prison industrial complex cannot be addressed without acknowledging a racial stigma. Furthermore, America has resisted acknowledging the plight of impoverished Blacks for so many generations that intentional ignorance has become a habit. Perhaps "All Lives Matter" dilutes the message. The power of the movement is that it is effectively forcing the reality of a racial stigma into the heart of the American consciousness.

DARRYL LORENZO WELLINGTON is a poet and essayist living in Santa Fe, N.M. His work recently appeared in the anthology, MFA vs NYC, edited by Chad Harbach.

DISCUSSION QUESTIONS

1. Comment on Darryl Lorenzo Wellington's assertion that the Obama presidency has brought to the surface two very old themes in American politics that heretofore have been buried or concealed: "Class exists," and "race matters." Do you agree? Why or why not?

2. Answer Wellington's question: "How can America be racist, if a black man ascended to the White House?"

3. What were the objectives of the Occupy movement that began in 2011? In what ways was the movement ineffective in galvanizing, and representing the concerns of, communities of color? How was the Black Lives Matter movement an outgrowth of the Occupy movement?

4. What were the core argument(s) of the Black Lives Matter movement? Was the movement anti-White, or anti-police? Explain.

5. What if anything is wrong with the practice, evident in some White communities, of posting "All Lives Matter" and "Blue Lives Matter" signs, placards, and banners on lawns and billboards in response to the Black Lives Matter movement? How does the "All Lives Matter" message miss the point that the Black Lives Matter movement is making?

Class in America

READING 4.1

INCOME AND WEALTH

Inequality in America: Race, Poverty, and
Fulfilling Democracy's Promise

BY **Stephen Caliendo**

*How can it be that it is not a news item
when an elderly homeless person dies of
exposure, but it is news when the stock
market loses two points?*

—Pope Francis, Evangelii Gaudium,
November 26, 2013[1]

*Today, after four years of economic growth,
corporate profits and stock prices have
rarely been higher, and those at the top have
never done better. But average wages have
barely budged. Inequality has deepened.
Upward mobility has stalled. The cold, hard
fact is that even in the midst of recovery,
too many Americans are working more than
ever just to get by; let alone to get ahead.
And too many still aren't working at all. So
our job is to reverse these trends.*

—President Barack Obama, State of the
Union Address, January 28, 2014[2]

St. John's University education professor Allan
Ornstein argues that "no country has taken
the idea of equality more seriously than the
United States," though he notes that "we are witnessing
the rise of a new aristocratic class, based on wealth
and power, far worse than the European model our
Founding Fathers sought to curtail."[3] Americans
largely accept the notion that capitalism will produce
unequal outcomes with respect to income and wealth,
but we prefer a more equal distribution than currently
exists. Recently, a nationally representative sample of
Americans was asked to (1) estimate the actual level
of wealth inequality in the United States and (2) indicate preferences for ideal distribution of wealth. The
researchers found that:

> Respondents vastly underestimated the actual
> level of wealth inequality in the United States,
> believing that the wealthiest quintile[4] held
> about 59% of the wealth when the actual number
> is closer to 84%. More interesting, respondents
> constructed ideal wealth distributions that were
> far more equitable than even their erroneously
> low estimates of actual distributions, reporting
> a desire for the top quintile to own just 32% of
> the wealth.[5]

The researchers also found that this preference existed across demographic groups (including expressed
presidential vote choice from 2004): "All groups—even
the wealthiest respondents—desired a more equal
distribution of wealth than what they estimated the
current United States level to be, and all groups also desired some inequality—even the poorest respondents."[6]
Finally, and perhaps most interesting, all groups agreed
that the way to move toward this ideal is through
redistributing wealth from the top to the bottom three
quintiles.

The disconnect between what Americans of all ideological backgrounds desire and the reality of inequality
is striking and calls into question the effectiveness of
our representative system. So why is this happening?
One answer could be that our elected officials wish to
make changes to bring the wealth gap more in line with
what Americans want but are constrained by systemic
forces that make such meaningful change possible.

Another answer is that our elected officials, most of whom (at the federal level at least) are wealthier than the average American,[7] are trying to protect themselves and their elite friends and family members. More likely, though, as the researchers suggest, we generally are not aware that the gap is so large; we are optimistic about our chances of getting into higher quintiles; we are not clear about the causes of inequality; and we often do not make a connection between these beliefs and our public policy preferences.[8] In this chapter, we explore the statistical realities of income and wealth inequality, as well as the relationship between that inequality and race. We will focus on the various elements in American society that perpetuate economic inequality in an attempt to understand how the current gap has not only persisted but has been greatly expanded over the past generation or so.

INCOME

Economic inequality is customarily discussed in terms of two distinct but related concepts: income and wealth. Wealth is a person's (or household's) total worth (assets minus debt), while income is simply the amount of money a person (or household) earns in a year. We will explore wealth disparities below, but in this section we consider the differences in annual household income and the ability to provide for oneself or one's family as a result.

Income and Employment

For most Americans, income is tied to employment; we only get paid when we work. Of course, there are exceptions. Disabled and retired individuals can collect Social Security from the federal government. Unemployed workers can receive benefits for a limited period after losing a job. Some wealthy individuals have invested money and earn from dividends and interest. For the most part, though, income is related to work.

Work is related to a number of factors that we will consider in more detail in the chapters that follow (specifically, education opportunities and incarceration rates). Most recently, though, attention has been focused on the sluggish economy and the degree to which it has affected Americans in the workforce. With respect to recessions, it has been said that when America catches a cold, African Americans get the flu. That sentiment was clearly reflected in the recession that began with the housing crisis in 2008. Unemployment rates for October 2012 indicated a nationwide level of 7.9 percent (12.3 million persons), but a closer look reveals that the rate for whites (7.0 percent) was lower than for Hispanics (10.0 percent) or African Americans (14.3 percent, or double the rate for whites).[9] The gap has been even more pronounced among those with a college education. White unemployment among the college educated rose from 1.8 percent in 2007 to 3.9 percent in 2011, while black unemployment among the college educated spiked from 2.7 percent in 2007 to 7.0 percent in 2011.[10]

Unemployment naturally has an effect on earnings. Data from 2011 demonstrate a notable income gap between white, black, and Hispanic families. In that year, the median household income for whites was $52,214, while the median income for African Americans was $32,229, and for Hispanics, $38,624.[11] Those numbers reflect a fairly stable gap over the past two decades.[12]

The income gap is most pronounced among Hispanics and African Americans, but its growth is notable among all segments of the population. In 2009, the highest quintile of earners collected 50 percent of the total income in the United States. In contrast, the bottom three quintiles combined brought in just 26.7 percent of the total income that year (with the second-highest quintile earning 23.3 percent).[13] There has been a steady increase in this trend over the past forty years, such that the top 5 percent of earners in 1970 pulled in 16.6 percent. That number was stable a decade later but rose to 18.5 percent in 1990 and to 22.1 percent in 2000. In 2011, the top 5 percent of households earned 21.5 percent of the total income.[14]

This shift can be analyzed in a variety of ways. One notable trend is that incomes in all ranges rose steadily (and relatively evenly) between the end of World War II and 1979. However, the top 20 percent of earners saw a 49 percent increase (including a 73 percent increase among the top 5 percent and a 224 percent increase among the top 1 percent) since the early 1980s while the bottom, second, middle, and fourth quintiles saw changes of 7 percent, 6 percent, 11 percent, and 23 percent, respectively.[15]

Gender is also related to income disparity. Much attention has been given to the wage gap in recent years, which stands today at about 23 percent. Put another way, women make an average of seventy-seven cents for every dollar a man makes in the United States.[16] The gap is largest for Latinas (39 percent compared to white men) and smallest for Asian American women (88 percent compared to white men). The gap for African American women is 70 percent.[17] About one-third of working women are heads of household in terms of earnings;[18] black women are most likely to be single heads of household (27.5 percent), compared to 9 percent of white women and 17.7 percent of Hispanic women,[19] and this responsibility is related to the decrease in African American women's labor force participation as compared to white women.[20]

On the opposite end of the spectrum, evidence of racial disparity is illustrated by an examination of the board members of America's top corporations. In 2010, white men comprised 72.9 percent of the board members at the largest one hundred companies and 77.6 percent of the largest five hundred companies in the United States. Nonwhite men held 10 percent of those seats, and white women held 13 percent.[21] It was not until 1999 that an African American became CEO of a Fortune 500 company, and there have been only thirteen; in July 2012, there were only six African American CEOs in such positions.[22] Women headed eighteen Fortune 500 companies in 2012,[23] the highest number in history.[24]

Further, there has been a tremendous shift in the ratio of CEO pay to the income of an average worker. Though the ratios found on bumper stickers and pro-union literature vary from 500 to 1 to 431 to 1 to 364 to 1 to 253 to 1,[25] the reality is complicated by the various types of compensation (besides monetary income) that CEOs receive. By one count, however, the ratio grew from 42 to 1 in 1980 to 107 to 1 in 1990 before spiking to its current levels in the last two decades.[26] In 2012, the median overall compensation of the top one hundred CEOs was $15.1 million, which represented a 16 percent rise from the previous year.[27] The monetary portion of these figures relates to gross income (before taxes). Since the United States has a progressive income tax structure (higher annual incomes relate to higher tax brackets), some of this income inequality will ostensibly be resolved once taxes are collected. As we see in the next section, though, it is not that simple.

Minimum Wage and the Poverty Line

In 1938, Congress set a federal minimum wage (at twenty-five cents per hour),[28] but it was not indexed to increase with inflation. As a result, there have been significant lags in the buying power of the dollar for minimum wage workers. The current federal minimum wage, set in 2009, is $7.25 per hour, though the highest level (in real dollars) was in 1968 ($10.04 in 2010 dollars).[29] Eighteen states and the District of Columbia have minimum wages higher than the federal level.[30] Individuals in occupations where tips are expected are not protected by minimum wage laws.

A full-time worker at the federal minimum wage will fall below the poverty line for a family of four. In 1968, a full-time minimum wage worker earned about 90 percent of the poverty level, but from the mid-1980s until Congress raised the minimum wage in 2006, full-time minimum wage workers with a family of four only earned between 50 percent and 60 percent of the federal poverty level.[31]

The poverty line (technically "poverty threshold") is not without its critics (those who think it is too low and those who think it is too high). The poverty threshold was developed in the 1960s and is based on the cost of food, under the assumption that a family of three or more spends about one-third of its income on food.[32] In 2012, the poverty threshold for an individual was $11,170; the threshold for a family of four was $23,050.[33] In 2010, the poverty rate in the United States was the highest since 1993, with 15.1 percent of individuals living in poverty. Twenty-seven percent of African Americans and 26.6 percent of Hispanics lived below the poverty threshold in 2010; less than 10 percent of non-Hispanic whites and 12.1 percent of Asians lived in poverty that year.[34] Once again, gender matters:

> Poverty rates are highest for families headed by single women, particularly if they are black or Hispanic. In 2010, 31.6 percent of households headed by single women were poor, while 15.8 percent of households headed by single men and 6.2 percent of married-couple households lived in poverty.[35]

Poverty rates are even higher for single women of color. In 2010, the rate for Hispanic single mothers was 50.3 percent and the rate for African American single mothers was 47.1 percent, compared with a 32.7 percent rate for white single mothers. Three-fifths of poor single mothers were black or Latino.[36] Because women earn less than men, and because women of color are more likely to be heads of household, a portion of the racial gap in income is related to gender.

Children are also disproportionately affected by poverty. Though they are 24 percent of the population, they represent 36 percent of the poor.[37] Twenty-two percent of all American children live below the poverty threshold: 12.4 percent of white children, 38.2 percent of African American children, 35 percent of Hispanic children, and 13.6 percent of Asian children.[38]

As is always the case with statistics and classifications, there is disagreement about how to appropriately operationalize poverty. Those who argue that the existing formula sets the level too low point to the fact that income from federal programs (often referred to as welfare; see below) is not counted in this calculation.[39] Those who argue that the level is too high note that while the rationale for calculating based on food as one-third of a family budget might have been appropriate a half century ago, housing prices in particular (not to mention transportation and utility costs) have increased at a rate disproportionate to food.[40]

Similarly, there are competing ideas about whether raising the minimum wage would help relieve income inequality. By one calculation, if the minimum wage had risen proportionally with CEO compensation, it would be more than $23 per hour.[41] The wisdom of raising the minimum wage can be considered in terms of our shared American values (*should* the minimum wage rise at the same level as CEO compensation?), as well as in terms of more practical considerations. A *New York Times* editorial in March 2011 argued for a raise, noting that even with the 2009 increase, in real dollars, the minimum wage is still lower than it was thirty years ago.[42] In his 2014 State of the Union Address, President Obama called on Congress to raise the federal minimum wage to $10.10 per hour.[43] Business groups who oppose raising the minimum wage argue that doing so would harm job creation, force layoffs, or lead to hours being cut back for those earning the minimum wage.[44] They note, for instance, that many minimum wage workers are not trying to support families—they have a second earner, have supplemental income (such as Social Security retirement for seniors working part-time), or are students. In combination with other government programs, advocates of this position feel as if there is enough of a safety net in place to protect low-wage workers and that the government should not meddle with the invisible hand of the economy.

Welfare

Many advanced democracies have expansive welfare states that are designed to provide a safety net so that no citizen falls into economic despair. Such societies are generally characterized by high tax rates and active central governments that are involved in many segments of the economy.[45] The United States has sponsored a number of programs over the years that are designed to provide such protections, but the scope and duration of those programs was dramatically reduced in the 1990s.

"Welfare" is a catchall term for government-funded and operated programs that provide different forms of financial assistance to those who need it. While various levels of assistance have been in place since colonial times, New Deal programs established during the Great Depression were more expansive than their predecessors. Many of these programs, such as unemployment compensation, Aid to Families with Dependent Children, and the program that we now know as Social Security are still in place.[46] Though not income per se, health care programs such as Medicare (for senior citizens) and Medicaid (for needy persons who are not seniors) provide additional assistance to offset costs associated with taking care of oneself and one's family.

There has been great debate in the United States about how much assistance should be provided to the needy and under what circumstances. These debates involve conflict of several core values to which Americans subscribe.[47] While Americans have a commitment to equality in a broad sense, we also have a commitment to individualism that has roots deep into our history. Further, the language used to discuss welfare in the 1980s was highly racialized, causing persistent inaccuracies in perceptions about whom these programs benefit and how much money is spent in this area.

Ronald Reagan's reference to a "welfare queen" in Chicago with "80 names, 30 addresses, 12 Social Security cards and is collecting veterans' benefits on four nonexisting deceased husbands" to the tune of $150,000 per year[48] created an enduring image of poverty in America that is characterized by undeserving African Americans who are cheating the system to get rich on the backs of hard-working (white) taxpayers. The story he told on the campaign trail in 1976 about Linda Taylor was likely an exaggeration,[49] but the retelling of the story suggested that she was typical. As a result, the welfare queen script came to dominate the imaginations of white Americans who were asked to consider reforms to the welfare system in the following decade.[50] As political scientist Martin Gilens notes:

> The connection between "poor" and "black" exists simply because African Americans account for a disproportionate number of poor people in the United States. Only one in ten white Americans falls below the official government poverty line, but three out of ten blacks are poor. Still, blacks are a small segment of the American population, and even though they are disproportionately poor, they comprise only a minority (currently about 27 percent) of all poor people.[51]

Gilens's study reveals that white respondents who viewed blacks as hard-working were much less willing to decrease welfare spending than those who viewed blacks as lazy.[52] In this way, it is very difficult to disentangle Americans' views of the poor generally with their perceptions of poor persons of color. Deservedness lies at the heart of welfare policy debates. In a political culture that values individualism and has a history that is deeply rooted in racial animosity toward African Americans in particular (and more recently Latinos), support for benefits to veterans, retired persons, and the physically disabled is more plentiful than support for the working poor, the homeless, or the mentally ill. Further, we must consider that Reagan chose to focus on a welfare queen, not a welfare king. The public disdain for the poor that is reflected in Gilens's study and that led to reforms in the 1990s is rooted in patriarchal views of personhood that marginalize women's voices and delegitimize their lived experiences.[53] In other words, Reagan's simplistic and atypical story resonated with Americans because of preexisting sexist and racist narratives that we hold in our subconscious.

The reality, of course, is much more complicated. Government "handouts" do not only go to the needy. So-called corporate welfare refers to tax incentives and subsidies for businesses.[54] Most Americans may not be aware of these policies, and even if they are, programs such as these are generally not lumped into the category of welfare. Though subsidies and tax breaks to corporations (even if they are profitable) are not income in the individual sense of the word, they help to make businesses successful, which sometimes translates into job creation (and thus income for workers) and often results in increases in wealth for top executives and major stockholders.

WEALTH

While income is the amount of money a person or household earns in a year, wealth is the value of that person or household overall. Wealth is calculated by subtracting debt from assets, and in many ways it is a more accurate window into economic and racial inequality in America. While it is important to understand income gaps as part of the cycle of disadvantage (and advantage) in the United States,

> wealth signifies the command over financial resources that a family has accumulated over its lifetime along with resources that have been inherited across generations. Such resources,

when combined with income, can create the opportunity to secure the "good life" in whatever form is needed—education, business, training, justice, health, comfort, and so on.[55]

Some Americans (both rich and poor) earn no income on an annual basis. In that respect, they are equal in terms of income even though their opportunities may be quite different. Further, wealth and income are not highly correlated, and there is great variation in wealth within income categories.[56] In this section, we will briefly consider some markers of wealth inequality before turning our attention to the systemic factors that reflect and perpetuate the growing gap between the wealthy and the poor in the United States.

Wealth Gap

While the income gap is large (and growing), the wealth gap is even more dramatic.[57] Median household wealth in the United States grew from $79,100 in 1989 to $126,400 in 2007 before falling dramatically to $77,300 in 2010.[58] Rather than accumulating wealth throughout a lifetime, a sizable percentage of Americans struggle through their senior years, living primarily on Social Security. Nearly half of Americans die with less than $10,000 in assets.[59] The Pew Research Center produced a report based on data from the US Census Bureau[60] that found an increasing gap between the rich and poor in America that is more exaggerated when race is factored in. Specifically, the top 10 percent of US households now control 56 percent of the nation's wealth (up from 49 percent in 2005).[61] That increase, however, somewhat masks the reality that is faced by persons of color:

> The median wealth of white U.S. households in 2009 was $113,149, compared with $6,325 for Hispanics and $5,677 for blacks.... Those ratios, roughly 20 to 1 for blacks and 18 to 1 for Hispanics, far exceeded the low mark of 7 to 1 for both groups reached in 1995, when the nation's economic expansion lifted many low-income groups into the middle class. The white-black wealth gap is also the widest since the census began tracking such data in 1984, when the ratio was roughly 12 to 1.[62]

A similar report in 2010 found that nonhousing assets for white families are typically around $100,000 while African American families' assets averaged about

$5,000, with 25 percent of black families having no assets at all.[63] Between 1984 and 2007, white families increased their median value from $22,000 to $100,000 (real dollars) while African American households had nearly imperceptible gains.[64, 65] That has resulted in a near tripling of the black-white wealth gap over the past twenty-five years (from a gap of $85,070 in 1984 to $235,500 in 2009).[66]

At this point, it should come as no surprise that gender is also relevant with respect to wealth, though it is much more difficult to measure since wealth is most often reported at the household, rather than individual, level. The data that are available center on nonmarried households and tend to show that

> women are less likely than men to own almost every type of asset. The median value of assets held by women is almost always lower than that of their male counterparts. A smaller percent of women own stocks, bonds, and other financial assets compared to men. Women are also less likely to hold retirement accounts and a woman's pension is typically smaller than a man's.[67]

When married couples divorce or when a spouse dies, women often face a disproportionate financial burden. If they were not in the labor force during marriage, they are disadvantaged when competing for positions with more experienced candidates. Children most often live with their mother after a separation or divorce, and men are not always willing or able to pay child support.[68] Women are also more likely than men to lose health insurance after a divorce,[69] which, as we will see later, can result in significant, even debilitating, financial strain. A woman whose husband dies tends to own only fifty-nine cents for every dollar of wealth that men have when a wife dies.[70] As we saw with income, because women of color are more likely to be heads of households, there is an interactive effect between race and gender, as well.

The very wealthiest Americans lost a lot during the Great Recession: "The 10 richest Americans lost a combined $39.2 billion" between September 2008 and September 2009 (which represents a 14 percent reduction).[71] One way to look at this, then, is to consider that the wealthiest were hit hardest by the housing crisis and resulting economic troubles. We must ask, though, how the day-to-day lives of those Americans were affected compared to the lives of the poorest Americans. Put another way, if given the choice, would we rather be one of those individuals who lost the most money, or an American living in poverty who either lost a low-wage job or had a harder time finding one as a result of the recession?[72]

SUMMARY

It is tempting to think of income as fluid (relating to securing a job, losing a job, getting a raise or a promotion, etc.) while wealth is more or less stable, growing over time (where possible). This characterization is inappropriate, though, as losses in income or an unexpected rise in expenses (due to an illness, a death in the family, etc.) can lead to a sudden and dramatic drop in wealth. According to sociologist Dalton Conley, "a significant proportion of individuals in the U.S. experience at least one drop in wealth."[73] Whites and African Americans have approximately the same number of drops (on average), but African Americans are more likely to have a greater drop.[74]

Researchers Shapiro, Meschede, and Sullivan argue that while America's racist past is certainly a driving factor behind the existence of the racial wealth gap,

> the four-fold increase in such a short time reflects policies, such as tax cuts on investment income and inheritances which benefit the wealthiest, and redistribute wealth and opportunities. Tax deductions for home mortgages, retirement accounts, and college savings all disproportionately benefit higher income families. At the same time, evidence from multiple sources demonstrates the powerful role of persistent discrimination in housing, credit, and labor markets.[75]

They note that persons of color pay more to access credit and are particularly susceptible to predatory lending in the mortgage industry. In short, while there may be overt, individualized bigotry involved in shaping income and wealth inequality, such incidents cannot come close to explaining these larger trends. First, while income and wealth inequality are pronounced between whites and persons of color, there is a tremendous gap between the highest earning whites and all other whites, as well. Second, the policies that perpetuate and exacerbate these trends are ostensibly colorblind. That is, they are not infused with explicit advantages for whites or disadvantages for persons of color.

Taking a colorblind approach to policy within a racist systemic context cannot lead to increased equality.

As Figure 1 indicates, there is a cycle of advantage and disadvantage that centers on three major elements of American life: jobs, education, and housing. To earn access to the middle class in the twenty-first century, a college degree is increasingly necessary. Gaining admission into and succeeding in college is more difficult if one does not have a rigorous education in high school (which begins in elementary school). Because most areas fund the local public school districts disproportionately through property tax revenues, the neighborhood in which one lives is strongly related to the quality of education that is available. Of course, most people live in the neighborhood they can afford, so having money in the first place is important. This can be thought of as a cycle of disadvantage, but it is also a cycle of advantage. That is, if one is disadvantaged, it is quite difficult to break the cycle and gain access to economic security (let alone prosperity). Conversely, those who are privileged to be in an advantageous position have numerous opportunities to avoid falling into economic despair.

The cycle is not a guarantee of success or failure. There are many Americans who started in poverty and became financially comfortable and even wealthy, and there are wealthy individuals who fall on hard times and are unable to recover. The idea, however, is that the starting line is not the same for everyone, and that far from simply being behind (as the foot race metaphor suggests), there are systemic obstacles that are difficult to overcome. Many ideas and programs have been designed to interrupt this cycle at various points. As will

Figure 1 Cycle of Advantage and Disadvantage

become clear in the following chapters, the reasons for its persistence are complicated and affected by other related elements (such as disparities in health and in the criminal justice system). Solutions are multifaceted and present opportunities and challenges for ordinary Americans to become involved and make a difference.

ENDNOTES

1. Laurie Goodstein and Elisabetta Povoledo, "Pope Sets Down Goals for an Inclusive Church, Reaching Out 'on the Streets,'" *New York Times*, November 26, 2013, http://www.nytimes.com/2013/11/27/world/europe/in-major-document-pope-francis-present-his-vision.html.
2. Federal News Service, "Full Transcript: Obama's 2014 State of the Union Address," *Washington Post*, January 28, 2014, http://www.washingtonpost.com/politics/full-text-of-obamas-2014-state-of-the-union-address/2014/01/28/e0c93358-887f-11e3-a5bd-844629433ba3_story.html.
3. Allan Ornstein, *Class Counts: Education, Inequality, and the Shrinking Middle Class* (Lanham, MD: Rowman & Littlefield, 2007), 117, 150.
4. A quintile represents 20 percent of the population. In this case, if all households in the United States were listed from the wealthiest to the poorest and then divided equally into five groups, the top quintile would be the group that includes the wealthiest 20 percent of households.
5. Michael I. Norton and Dan Ariely, "Building a Better America—One Wealth Quintile at a Time," *Perspectives on Psychological Science*, 6, no. 1 (2011): 9–12.
6. Ibid., 10.
7. In 2009, nearly half of all members of the US Congress (261) were millionaires, with fifty of them having an average wealth of $10 million or more. Eight members were worth over $100 million. Median wealth in the US House of Representatives was $765,010; median wealth in the US Senate was nearly $2.38 million. Both numbers represent increases from the previous year. Center for Responsive Politics, "Congressional Members' Personal Wealth Expands Despite Sour National Economy," OpenSecrets.

org, November 17, 2010, http://www.opensecrets.org/news/2010/11/congressional-members-personal-weal.html. In contrast, the median household income in the United States in 2009 was $49,777, which was virtually unchanged from the previous year. US Census Bureau, "Income, Poverty, and Health Insurance Coverage in the United States: 2009," September 16, 2010, http://www.census.gov/newsroom/releases/archives/income_wealth/cb10-144.html.

8. Ibid., 12.

9. US Bureau of Labor Statistics, "Employment Situation Summary," November 2, 2012, http://www.bls.gov/news.release/pdf/empsit.pdf.

10. Jesse Washington, "The Disappearing Black Middle Class," *Chicago Sun-Times*, July 10, 2011, http://www.suntimes.com/6397110-417/the-disappearing-black-middle-class.html.

11. Carmen DeNavas-Walt, Bernadette D. Proctor, and Jessica C. Smith, "Income, Poverty, and Health Insurance Coverage in the United States: 2011," US Census Bureau, September 2012, http://www.census.gov/prod/2012pubs/p60-243.pdf.

12. In 2008 dollars, the white-black-Hispanic medians were $58,952, $34,212, and $37,419, respectively, in 1990. US Census Bureau, Table 696, Money and Income of Families—Median Income by Race and Hispanic Origin and Constant (2008) Dollars: 1990 to 2008, *Statistical Abstract: Income, Expenditures, Poverty, and Wealth,* 2011, http://www.census.gov/compendia/statab/2011/tables/11s0696.pdf.

13. US Census Bureau, "Income, Poverty and Health Insurance Coverage in the United States: 2009," September 16, 2010, http://www.census.gov/newsroom/releases/archives/income_wealth/cb10-144.html.

14. US Census Bureau, Table 693, Share of Aggregate Income Received by Each Fifth and Top 5 Percent of Households: 1970 to 2008, *Statistical Abstract: Income, Expenditures, Poverty, and Wealth,* 2011, http://www.census.gov/compendia/statab/2011/tables/11s0693.pdf.

15. MoveOn.org, "Something Big Happened to America in 1979," June 7, 2011, http://front.moveon.org/something-big-happened-to-america-in-1979/?rc=fb.fan; Martha Hamilton, "Is It True the Rich Are Getting Richer?" Politifact.com, July 6, 2011, http://www.politifact.com/truth-o-meter/article/2011/jul/06/it-true-rich-are-getting-richer/; William Julius Wilson, "The Great Disparity," *The Nation*, July 10, 2012, http://www.thenation.com/article/168822/great-disparity. Wilson reviews two books on growing economic inequality: Timothy Noah, *The Great Divergence: America's Growing Inequality Crisis and What We Can Do About It* (New York: Bloombury Press, 2013) and Charles Murray, *Coming Apart: The State of White Amerca, 1960–2010* (New York: Crown Forum, 2013).

16. Marina Villeneuve, "Study Shows How Broad Pay Disparities Are Between Sexes," *USA Today*, April 20, 2012, http://www.usatoday.com/money/workplace/story/2012-04-17/gender-pay-gap-study/54368152/1.

17. Ibid.

18. Ibid.

19. Maternal and Child Health Information Resource Center, "Women's Health USA, 2011," http://www.mchb.hrsa.gov/whusa11/popchar/pages/104hc.html.

20. Irene Browne, "Explaining the Black-White Gap in Labor Force Participation Among Women Heading Households," *American Sociological Review* 62, no. 2 (1997): 236–252.

21. Allison Linn, "Minorities Lose Ground in Big Corporate Boardrooms," LifeInc, May 3, 2011, http://thegrio.com/2011/05/04/minorities-lose-ground-in-big-corporate-boardrooms; see also Alliance for Board Diversity, "Missing Pieces: Women and Minorities on Fortune 500 Boards," May 1, 2011, http://the-abd.org/Missing_Pieces_Women_and_Minorities_on_Fortune_500_Boards.pdf.

22. Chris Isidore, "African-American CEOs Still Rare," CNN Money, March 22, 2012, http://money.cnn.com/2012/03/22/news/companies/black-ceo/index.htm.

23. Two of the eighteen women CEOs in 2012 were of color: Ursula Burns (Xerox), who is African American, and Indra Nooyi (PepsiCO), who is Indian.

24. Bianca Bosker, "Fortune 500 List Boasts More Female CEOs Than Ever Before," Huffington Post, May 7, 2012, http://www.huffingtonpost.com/2012/05/07/fortune-500-female-ceos_n_1495734.html.

25. CNN Money, "GDP Growth Not Reaching Paychecks," CNN.com, September 5, 2007, http://money.cnn.com/2007/09/03/news/economy/epi_report/index.htm; Huck Gutman, "Economic Inequality in the US," CommonDreams.org, July 1, 2002, http://www.commondreams.org/views02/0701-05.htm; MoveOn.org, "Something Big Happened to America in 1979."

26. Gutman, "Economic Inequality in the US"; Derrick Z. Jackson, "Income Gap Mentality," *Boston Globe*, April 19, 2006, http://www.boston.com/news/globe/editorial_opinion/oped/articles/2006/04/19/income_gap_mentality.

27. Gretchen Morgenson, "An Unstoppable Climb in C.E.O. Pay," *New York Times*, June 29, 2013, http://mobile.nytimes.com/2013/06/30/business/an-unstoppable-climb-in-ceo-pay.html. An interactive chart is available at http://www.nytimes.com/interactive/2013/06/30/business/executive-compensation-tables.html.

28. Court Smith, "Minimum Wage History," 2011, http://oregonstate.edu/instruct/anth484/minwage.html.

29. Ibid.

30. US Department of Labor, "Wage and Hour Division: Minimum Wage Laws in the States, January 1, 2012," 2012, http://www.dol.gov/whd/minwage/america.htm.

31. Smith, "Minimum Wage History."

32. Jessie Willis, "How We Measure Poverty: A History and Brief Overview," Oregon Center for Public Policy, February 2000, http://www.ocpp.org/poverty/how.htm.

33. US Department of Health and Human Services, *The 2011 HHS Poverty Guidelines*, 2011, http://aspe.hhs.gov/poverty/11poverty.shtml.

34. National Poverty Center, "Poverty in the United States: Frequently Asked Questions," 2012, http.//www.npc.umich.edu/poverty/.

35. Ibid.

36. Legal Momentum, "Single Mother Poverty in the United States in 2010," 2011, http://www.legalmomentum.org/our-work/women-and-poverty/resources–publications/single-mother-poverty-2010.pdf.

37. National Poverty Center, "Poverty in the United States."

38. Ibid.

39. Willis, "How We Measure Poverty."

40. Ibid.

41. Jackson, "Income Gap Mentality."

42. "A Minimum Wage Increase," *New York Times*, March 26, 2011, http://www.nytimes.com/2011/03/27/opinion/27sun2.html.

43. *Washington Post*, January 28, 2014, http://www.washingtonpost.com/politics/full-text-of-obamas-2014-state-of-the-union-address/2014/01/28/e0c93358-887f-11e3-a5bd-844629433ba3_story.html.

44. Marilyn Geewax, "Does a Higher Minimum Wage Kill Jobs?" National Public Radio, April 24, 2011, http://www.npr.org/2011/04/24/135638370/does-a-higher-minimum-wage-kill-jobs.

45. Raymond A. Smith, *The American Anomaly: U.S. Politics and Government in Comparative Perspective* (New York: Routledge, 2011), 165–169.

46. Social Security Administration, "Historical Background and Development of Social Security," 2011, http://www.ssa.gov/history/briefhistory3.html.

47. For example, see Stanley Feldman and John Zaller, "The Political Culture of Ambivalence: Ideological Responses to the Welfare State," *American Journal of Political Science* 36, no. 1 (1992): 268–307.

48. "'Welfare Queen' Becomes Issue in Reagan Campaign," *New York Times*, February 15, 1976, http://picofarad.info/misc/welfarequeen.pdf.

49. Though prosecutors argued that the characterization of her crimes was accurate, she was only indicted for theft of $8,000 from public welfare and for perjury. Dan Miller, "The Chutzpa Queen: Favorite Reagan Target as Welfare Cheat Remains Unflappable at Trial in Chicago, *Washington Post*, March 13, 1977, A3.

50. See Frank Gilliam Jr., "The 'Welfare Queen' Experiment: How Voters React to Images of African-American Mothers on Welfare," UCLA Center for Communications and Community, 1999, http://escholarship.org/uc/item/17m7r1rq; Ange-Marie Hancock, *The Politics of Disgust: The Public Identity of the Welfare Queen* (New York: New York University Press, 2004). Reagan did not mention the woman's race explicitly. Rather, he made references to Chicago or to the South Side of Chicago or to the inner city, which served as code for "African American." Paul Krugman, "Republicans and Race," *New York Times*, November 19, 2007, http://www.nytimes.com/2007/11/19/opinion/19krugman.html. As Gilliam explains, "The implicit racial coding is readily apparent. The woman Reagan was talking about was African-American. Veiled references to African-American women, and African-Americans in general, were equally transparent. In other words, while poor women of all races get blamed for their impoverished condition, African-American women commit the most egregious violations of American values. This story line tips into stereotypes about both women (uncontrolled sexuality) and African-Americans (laziness)."

51. Martin Gilens, *Why Americans Hate Welfare: Race, Media, and the Politics of Antipoverty Policy* (Chicago: University of Chicago Press, 1999), 68.

52. Ibid., 68–69.

53. Hancock, *Politics of Disgust*.

54. Stephen Slivinsky, "The Corporate Welfare State: How the Federal Government Subsidizes U.S. Businesses," *Policy Analysis* 592 (2007): 1–21.

55. Melvin L. Oliver and Thomas M. Shapiro, *Black Wealth/White Wealth: A New Perspective on Racial Inequality*, 10th ed. (New York: Routledge, 2006).

56. Lisa A. Keister, *Wealth in America: Trends in Wealth Inequality* (New York: Cambridge University Press, 2000), 10.

57. Ibid.; Joseph E. Stiglitz, *The Price of Inequality: How Today's Divided Society Endangers Our Future* (New York: Norton, 2012).

58. Figures are expressed in 2010 dollars. Linda Levine, "An Analysis of the Distribution of Wealth Across Households, 1989–2010," Congressional Research Service, July 17, 2012, http://www.fas.org/sgp/crs/misc/RL33433.pdf. Household wealth grew faster than median wealth over that period, suggesting concentration at the upper end of the wealth distribution. As Levine notes, while both declined by 2012, the greater decline in the median reflects that the recession "affected those in the lower half of the wealth distribution more than those higher up in the distribution" (p. 3).

59. Bonnie Kavoussi, "Nearly Half of Americans Die Without Money, Study Finds," Huffington Post, August 6, 2012, http://www.huffingtonpost.com/2012/08/06/americans-die-without-money_n_1746862.html.

60. Paul Taylor et al., "Wealth Gaps Rise to Record Highs Between Whites, Blacks and Hispanics: Twenty-to-One," Pew Research Center, July 26, 2011, http://www.pewsocialtrends.org/2011/07/26/wealth-gaps-rise-to-record-highs-between-whites-blacks-hispanics/.

61. "Census: Wealth Gap Widens Between whites and Minorities," *USA Today*, July 26, 2011, http://www.usatoday.com/news/washington/2011-07-26-census-wealth-data_n.htm.

62. Ibid.

63. Thomas M. Shapiro, Tatjana Meschede, and Laura Sullivan, "The Racial Wealth Gap Increases Fourfold," Brandeis University, May 2010, http://iasp.brandeis.edu/pdfs/Racial-Wealth-Gap-Brief.pdf; Chris McGreal, "A $95,000 Question: Why Are Whites Five Times Richer Than Blacks in the U.S.?" *Guardian*, May 17, 2010, http://www.guardian.co.uk/world/2010/may/17/white-people-95000-richer-black.

64. Shapiro, Meschede, and Sullivan, "Racial Wealth Gap Increases Fourfold."

65. This chapter focuses disproportionately on the black-white income and wealth gaps because most research on the question of race and economic inequality has been focused here. For a broader view, including discussion of Asian Americans and Native Americans, see Jessica Gordon Nembhard and Ngina Chiteji, eds., *Wealth Accumulation and Communities of Color in the United States* (Ann Arbor: University of Michigan Press, 2006).

66. "Study Shows Racial Wealth Gap Continues to Widen," *USA Today*, February 27, 2013, http://www.usatoday.com/story/money/personalfinance/2013/02/27/racial-wealth-gap-growing/1948899/. This report from Brandeis University attributed the widening gap primarily to the housing crisis but also noted the effect of unemployment during the Great Recession, as well as the education gap and the cost of education.

67. Karuna Jaggar, "The Race and Gender Wealth Gap," *Race and Regionalism* 15, no. 1 (2008), http://urbanhabitat.org/node/2815.

68. Megan Thibos, Danielle Lavin-Loucks, and Marcus Martin, "The Feminization of Poverty," YWCA Dallas, 2007, http://www.ywcadallas.org/PDF/womens-health/FeminizationofPoverty.pdf.

69. Bridget Lavelle and Pamela Smock, "Divorce and Women's Risk of Health Insurance Loss in the U.S.," *Population Studies Center Research Report no. 11–734*, Institute for Social Research, University of Michigan, March, 2011, http://www.psc.isr.umich.edu/pubs/pdf/rr11-734.pdf.

70. Jaggar, "Race and Gender Wealth Gap." For more information on gender and race in wealth disparity, especially with respect to homeownership, see Beverlyn Lundy Allen, "Race and Gender Inequality in Homeownership: Does Place Make a Difference?" *Rural Sociology* 67, no. 4 (2002): 603–621.

71. Matthew Miller and Duncan Greenberg, "The Forbes 400: Almost All of America's Wealthiest Citizens Are Poorer This Year," Forbes.com, September 30, 2009, http://www.forbes.com/2009/09/29/forbes-400-buffett-gates-ellison-rich-list-09-intro.html.

72. For a video representation of the US wealth gap, see http://mashable.com/2013/03/02/wealth-inequality/. For a video representation of the racial wealth gap in the United States, see this video from the Urban Institute: http://urban.org/changing-wealth-americans/video/.

73. Dalton Conley, *Being Black, Living in the Red: Race, Wealth, and Social Policy in America*, 10th ed. (Berkeley: University of California Press, 2010), 157.

74. Ibid.

75. Shapiro, Meschede, and Sullivan, "Racial Wealth Gap Increases Fourfold," 2.

DISCUSSION QUESTIONS

1. What explains the hollowing out of the middle class, the near-complete suspension of upward mobility, and the persistence of economic inequality in America? Why are these trends dangerous for the United States? What is the relationship between race and wealth, poverty, and inequality?

2. Stephen Caliendo notes that "women make an average of seventy-seven cents for every dollar [that] men make in the United States. The gap is largest for Latinas and smallest for Asian American women." The gap for African American women is somewhere in between. What do you make of this data? Do you believe it? Why or why not? Why does this gap exist, and what will it take to close it?

3. Caliendo writes that "many advanced democracies have expansive [and generous] welfare programs that provide a 'safety net' so that no citizen falls into economic despair." However, entitlement programs are less expansive and generous, and more controversial in the United States. Is Caliendo right? If he is, why is that? How does Caliendo explain this state of affairs?

CLASS MATTERS

BY **Barbara Ehrenreich***

must admit I am not happy about the continuing relevance of my book, *Nickel and Dimed,* which was published fourteen years ago, in 2001. I didn't expect that book to change the world. That's not how the world changes. But I did expect that the kind of conditions that I described in that book would be improved, reformed, done away with. Conditions like consistent underpayment, humiliating treatment by management. So its depressing to me that all of that is still perfectly relevant, and in fact, some of those conditions are worse, as I'm going to talk about now.

What I learned in the research for *Nickel and Dimed* was basically that a huge number of Americans, probably about 30 percent of working people, are paid less than they can live on, wages that do not allow them to support a family, or maybe even one person, at least if they want to live indoors, as many of us aspire to, of course. Another thing I discovered, and which has loomed much larger as time has gone on, is that the little amounts that people earn in a lot of these jobs are diminished by wage theft, which means the employer makes you work longer hours than you are paid for. It's illegal, but that doesn't matter. It could be in the form of telling you to come in half an hour before the time clock starts running, or to stay an hour after it stops running, and keep working. Most recent estimates are that employers steal at least $100 billion a year from their low-wage employees, in various ways. Think about that; $100 billion is a big number. It's on the order of a major social program, the EITC, Earned Income Tax Credit. So we talk about these things all the time; well, could we give more money to the poor? Why don't we just stop stealing from them?

I also learned that, paradoxically enough, it is expensive to be poor, more expensive in some ways than not being poor. As a journalist, I went out to see what it was like to be poor. I didn't admit I was a journalist, and I would go to different cities, find the cheapest place I could to live in and the best paying job I could get—which meant being a waitress, a cleaner with a housecleaning company, a nursing home aide, and a Walmart associate, among other things. If you can't put enough money together for your first month's rent and security deposit, you cannot rent an apartment. And that's a lot of capital, probably over a thousand dollars. And to many people, that's unthinkable.

So I ended up doing what a lot of people do if they don't have a family they can crash with: I went to a residential motel. They charge outrageous amounts—I was paying $250 a week—but you can get in. You're off the street immediately. Some of these places do not have either a little fridge or microwave oven, nothing. That means that you have to pay more because you're buying food at a convenience store or fast food restaurant.

I'm not complaining about the cuisine, I'm just saying it's expensive. I went into this project thinking, oh, well, how hard can it be? I can make big lentil soups and freeze them and have them one night after another. And yet you have to have a pot to cook them in. It would be nice to have a well-stocked kitchen if you want to live cheaply, and I couldn't do that. If you live in an inner-city area, there may be no grocery stores; you might be in one of our urban food deserts. If you live in a rural area, you will need a working car to go somewhere where you can get your food.

Now, these things are no less true today than they were fourteen years ago. President Obama has just called again for raising the national minimum wage to $10.10 an hour. Which would be nice, right? But it turns out that in this state, New York, a family of two—one adult and one child—needs on average, across the state, to earn $24 an hour to live at a kind of basic minimal

* Barbara Ehrenreich is an award-winning columnist, essayist, and political activist. She is the author of twenty-one books. This essay was delivered on Friday, January 23, 2015 at the Trinity Institute conference, "Creating Common Good."

level. That's what a living wage would be. And the same is true for the state where I now live, Virginia.

This reality helps explain the wrenching news we got recently, that 51 percent of the children in public schools are in poverty and qualify for subsidized meals. It's not because their parents are lazy or incapable of financial planning. They are in poverty because they're not paid enough to live on. That's my theory anyway, which I've been pushing ever since I wrote *Nickel and Dimed:* poverty is not a character failing or a wrongheaded lifestyle. Poverty is a shortage of money. And the chief reason for that shortage of money is lack of adequate pay or lack of any job at all.

The thing that strikes me most all these years after writing that book is that while we talk about what can be done for the poor, the sad truth is, instead of helping the down and out, we have a society that seems to persecute the poor. If you start sliding downhill—even if you started in a white-collar professional life—you stand a good chance of accelerating all the way down to destitution.

So how does this operate? How do people get pushed down further and further? It seems to me that the real question we have to ask is not, What can we do for the poor?, but, What do we need to stop doing to them? Both government and corporations have a tendency to single out people who are in economic difficulty and make things harder for them. For example, there are help-wanted ads out there saying explicitly that no unemployed candidates will be considered. Now, what's that about? You can only hire people who have jobs? That weeds out the financially shaky people. There are only five cities in this country in which that kind of blatant discrimination is against the law; everywhere else, it can be done.

About 60 percent of employers now do a credit check before you can get a job. If you've been unemployed for a while, or if you've been having problems with your finances, you may indeed have a lousy credit rating, which then means you can't get a job, or its much harder to get a job. If you've been relying on a credit card to help you through some hard patches and you fall behind in your monthly payments, or if you are low income and have always been kind of shaky, you can face interest rates of up to 30 percent. And if you think you can get out of those bills by declaring bankruptcy, just leave it behind. I discovered through the bad experience of a member of my own family that the average cost of filing for bankruptcy is $2,000 or even higher. So where are you going to get that?

Now, I particularly want to talk about some of the ways that the government practices its own forms of harassment of the poor. These disproportionately target people of color, like the stop-and-frisk policies that New York was long so notorious for. That racial bias, however, is not what makes harassment so horrendous. Like stop-and-frisk, which now has been reduced or eliminated, no one of whatever color should be subjected to unprovoked searches on the street or any other kinds of abuses. There is racial profiling in what I'm describing, but these are abuses no matter who they're inflicted on.

It is estimated that about ten million people a year in this country are charged with misdemeanors, many of them very minor but still leading to fines and even jail time. And 75 percent of the people charged with misdemeanors are poor or even indigent. They are disproportionately people of color. The average fines for misdemeanors are in the range of $200 to $500, often much more. Even the number of possible misdemeanors has been increasing rapidly just in the last decade.

For example, in New York City it is illegal to put your feet up on the subway car seat, or to put a bag next to you on the seat. Even if the rest of the car is empty and its three in the morning and you're coming back from the late shift, you can't put your feet up. And this is not something where you'll get a warning or a policeperson will say, no, you can't do that. This is grounds for arrest, right there: snatched up, arrested. In Washington, D.C., near where I live, you can be arrested—not just given a warning or citation—for driving with an expired license. All right, it's against the law. But there you are, and you face another cascading number of effects.

In the last few years a growing number of cities and counties have taken to ticketing and sometimes even handcuffing children found on the streets during school hours. In New Mexico, if a child has a second "conviction" for truancy, the parent could face a fine of up to $500, or imprisonment for up to six months. Just think about that. In Illinois, the parents of a child who is absent too often can be fined $1,500 and jailed for up to thirty days. That's going to do a lot for that kid's problem, right? Having the parents go off to jail.

Now, this kind of harassment and heavy-handed law-enforcement has actually increased since the economic crisis of 2008. And the reason everybody cites is that the counties and municipalities have increasingly come to rely on fees and fines to supplement their declining revenues.

Consider the case of Ferguson, Missouri. Naturally, we think of that incident as a huge racial injustice, but here are some facts about Ferguson. The second-largest source of income for the city government there is fees and fines levied on minor offenders. Even if you want to plead guilty for some tiny traffic violation—say, a brake light off—you have to pay $12 for that, and you can even be charged with mileage used by the city officers who had to serve you with a warrant when they drove to do it.

Last spring, an NPR series exposed some shocking facts. Since 2010, forty-eight states have added and/or increased court-related fees. So getting involved in the court system means you're going to be drained of money. At least forty-three states have billed the defendants for the cost of the public defender. This seems like a violation of logic, but that happens. Forty-nine states charge for the electronic monitoring bracelets required for home detention. So you can see all these things building up.

Now, suppose you sink all the way down to homelessness, living on the streets. Then you find a new thing: its virtually illegal to be homeless. At least you're likely to find that most of the biological necessities of life, including sitting, loitering, sleeping, lying down, and relieving yourself, are illegal if you look like you are indigent.

I interviewed a homeless man in Washington, D.C., who had been arrested for an outstanding warrant when he was inside a homeless shelter. He was inside the homeless shelter, and men were sleeping. The police came in, and they did a warrant search to look for anybody who might have an outstanding warrant. They found him, they caught him. And what was his outstanding warrant for? Sleeping outdoors. So there he is, a homeless man, inside a homeless shelter, being arrested for being homeless.

The laws against homelessness vary from state to state. One of my favorites is Sarasota, Florida, where an ordinance makes it illegal to be awakened from sleep and state that you have no other place to live or sleep. So imagine you are a very wealthy person and you decide to go sleep in the park, and a policeman comes along and wakes you up and asks, What are you doing here? You say, well, I got really tired of my penthouse condo and decided to try something else for the night. That's fine, the policeman will say, make yourself uncomfortable. But if you have no other place to go, you are arrested. In other words, it's illegal to be homeless for any reason or live outdoors. It should be noted, though, that there are no laws requiring cities to provide food, shelter, or restrooms for their indigent or any other citizens.

In some cities, and Orlando is one of the biggest, it is even illegal to help the poor. There are laws against sharing food with indigent people in public places. Now, I think that should be seen as a direct attack on Christianity. What are we told to do? Share. Give. How can you make it illegal to share? If you do end up in jail, you face one more nasty surprise. Forty-one states have started charging inmates for their room and board! Why are they in jail? Because they're poor, they couldn't afford a lawyer, they couldn't afford to pay their fees and fines. And if they miss paying those fees and fines, a warrant will go out for them. Then, when they get out of jail, they will get a huge bill in these states. Figure that out.

I really want to do more reporting on this. It is so astounding. Now, what sense does any of this make? You take a hard-working person, say who has a broken tail light that she can't afford to replace, fine her an amount much greater than the cost of a new tail light, persecute her for failing to pay the fine, jail her, and then turn her into a desperately poor person, possibly even a fugitive, since when you have no address, no driver's license, no identification, you enter a land of fugitive status.

Now, I am not building up to a resounding indictment of capitalism, if that's what you're expecting, which would be consistent. Capitalism at least has a logic to it. It makes sense in its own way. What I have been describing does not make sense. If you pay something like 30 percent of the population less than they can live on, they obviously are not going to be able to participate in the economy by buying stuff. And we are certainly well past that point in this country. Even the most conservative economists are now saying, Why are wages so low? Could we do something about that, that doesn't disturb anything else?

Even Walmart is having trouble, and I'll tell you the reason why. Their prices are too high for an awful lot of people. When I worked at a Walmart store, I had co-workers who could not afford even the most deeply reduced items. How could they, when they're making about the equivalent of $9 an hour today? It was out of the question. And the big question is, what is the sense in tormenting and trying to extract more money all the time from people who are already poor? I know that there are people who would make an economic argument in response to that question: it's a capitalist plot in its own way, or it comes from the prison industrial complex, or somebody's making money off this, and that explains it all. I am not totally convinced by that.

What I see is a system of mindless sadism, which is ultimately costly to all of us. Now, we need a lot of changes. We need profound changes in the distribution of wealth and power. But my short-term message is we should just stop the meanness, the relentless persecution of people who are already having a hard time.

Stop the wage theft by employers. Stop treating low-wage workers as criminals, with the drug tests and the constant suspicions that workers are stealing. If they want to organize into unions and associations or whatever, that's their right, but that's not actually possible in most places. Stop penalizing people for having bad credit scores. Stop the banks and credit card people from squeezing more and more money in the form of interest out of people who are poor. Stop harassing the homeless and indigent in public places; that would actually be better for city budgets than going through the trouble of arresting and jailing all these people all the time.

My demand is to stop kicking people who are already down. Of course we could be doing a lot more to help those who are struggling. But I also want us to focus on doing less harm.

DISCUSSION QUESTIONS

1. According to Barbara Ehrenreich, adverse labor conditions, such as the "consistent underpayment" of workers by employers, and the "humiliating treatment [of employees] by management" have increased during the past 10–20 years in the United States. Is she right? Why or why not? What evidence does Ehrenreich cite for her claim?

2. Ehrenreich says that "it's expensive to be poor." What does she mean? What evidence does she cite?

3. Ehrenreich notes that "poverty is not a character failing or a wrongheaded lifestyle. Poverty is a shortage of money." And "while we talk about what can be done for the poor, the sad truth is, instead of helping the down and out, we persecute the poor." So "the real question we have to ask is not, what can we do for the poor?, but what do we need to stop doing to them?" Do you agree? Why or why not? What are some of the things that Ehrenreich thinks we should stop doing to the poor?

READING 4.3

THE AMERICAN DREAM OF MERITOCRACY

The American Dream and the Power of Wealth

BY **Heather Beth Johnson**

The American Dream has been continually re-invented over time, so that for each generation of Americans it has held different meanings. And since the phrase "the American Dream" could mean different things to every one of us, it might be more accurate to call it "the American Dreams." At its core, however, some aspects of the Dream (or Dreams) are consistently fundamental. Simply, the American Dream explains the logic of our country's social system. *It is a way (or perhaps the way) we are to understand how American society operates.* It is how we make sense of our particular social structure. The American Dream rests on the idea that, with hard work and personal determination anyone, regardless of background, has an equal opportunity to achieve his or her aspirations. The American Dream promises that our system functions as a meritocracy. *Within a meritocracy people get ahead or behind based on what they earn and deserve, rather than what circumstances they were born into.* This notion of is central to the American Dream, and is the central logic of how our system is supposed to operate. The American Dream, in many ways, defines us and sets our system apart from others.

Given the importance of the American Dream to our national identity, and the enormity of it in shaping our core ideologies, it is curious how little attention the idea has received in academe, especially in the social sciences. Until relatively recently, no one had traced the history of its origins, meanings, or cultural impacts. In the past decade, however, groundbreaking scholarship on the American Dream has yielded important understandings. We know, for example, that the principles of the American Dream were promoted by even the very first settlers to arrive from Britain. Later, the American Dream was central to the charter of the United States when the Declaration of Independence was created. And although the phrase "the American Dream" does not appear to have been coined until around 1931, it has quickly become recognizable the world over. The American Dream is, for better or for worse, the central creed of our nation.

As a creed, the American Dream represents a basic belief in the power and capacity of the individual. Deeply embedded in this belief is a particular notion of individual agency—the idea that over the course of our own lives we are each accountable for whatever position we find ourselves in. Full collective potential for this agency, though, depends on exactly that which the dream promises: A system of opportunity, so that regardless of background each individual has an equal chance to prosper. The American Dream promises that an egalitarian system will allow individuals to advance based on their own merit. This promise resonates throughout contemporary American society telling us—through multiple variations on a theme, through school assignments and television advertisements, through song lyrics and newspaper stories—that in a meritocratic process we rise or fall self-reliantly. So, despite differences across generations and regardless we each have unique hopes and dreams, we share the American Dream of meritocracy in common: That is, we are each subject—in one way or another—to our nationalist ideology of meritocracy.

Meritocracy explains not only how our society works but how inequality exists. The idea is that what we reap—good or bad—is merited; whatever we have, whatever our status, whatever our place in the social world, we earn. A system of meritocracy does not assert equality *per se*—within any social hierarchy some individuals will inevitably be positioned higher and some lower—rather, it justifies inequality of social positioning by the meritocratic process itself. Inequality of outcomes is justified and legitimized by equality of opportunity. This meritocratic idea has roots dating back to the British colonialists' aspirations for a society founded in a "natural aristocracy." In their vision upward mobility and prominence would be merited and achieved, rather than ascribed. For those first families settling from Europe, this vision was a defiant rebellion from other forms of social structure where social rank was inherited based on such distinctions as family lineage, royalty, and caste. Although they never precisely defined how merit should be measured, it was always clear how it should not be: achievement based on individual merit is not unearned advantage; it is not inherited privilege. A meritocratic system is contingent upon a societal commitment to fair competition so that no individual or group is advantaged or disadvantaged by the positions or predicaments of their ancestors.

The American Dream of meritocracy is at once a simple idea and a complex national ethos. For some people the American Dream may simply represent owning a home, while for others it might represent striking it rich. Although those may be part of what the American Dream means for many people, as a foundational ideology it is about more than material abundance or a place with streets-paved-with-gold. It is about opportunity—not just an opportunity, but equal opportunity. It is about not just a chance, but equal chances. In her landmark book, *Facing Up to the American Dream: Race, Class, and the Soul of a Nation*, political scientist Jennifer Hochschild explicates the American Dream and identifies its main tenets. She distinguishes key premises which interlock to form its philosophical foundation. These premises include meritocracy, the notion that in our social system upward and downward mobility is based on personal achievement so that people get ahead or behind based on merit; equal opportunity, the notion that all members of society are given equal opportunity for social mobility; individualism, the notion that each individual makes it on his or her own; and the open society, the notion that the United States is a free country, the melting pot of the world, the land of opportunity for all people. As Hochschild outlines, the American Dream is a set of deeply held beliefs, a particular mindset. It is a particular way of viewing the world, and it is a particular way in which we want the world to view us. For many Americans, the American Dream is a great source of pride. But even many who question it as an accurate portrayal of social life believe strongly in the egalitarian and inclusive principles for which it stands.

As a dominant ideology the American Dream echoes throughout our nation, it carries on through generations, and can cement in crystal form in our minds. But it can also be easily taken for granted. For as central the American Dream is to our national identity, we don't consciously reflect on it often. As historian Jim Cullen has noted, the American Dream is "an idea that seems to envelop us as unmistakably as the air we breathe." We can be reminded of it, without even being aware, every time we are told that we will achieve if we work hard enough, or that we could have achieved if we had only worked harder. The American Dream can inspire great aspirations and explain great achievements, and it can depress us as we ponder our regrets. It is malleable enough to fit in almost any social situation. We can use it to justify our accomplishments: I earned it on my own. This is the result of my hard work. I deserve this. And we can feel the sting of it as we question ourselves: Should I have worked harder? Could I have gone farther? Why am I not where he is? And, we can use it to question others' social standing: Why doesn't she try harder? Doesn't he want more? Why don't they make better choices? The American Dream is all around us, and, in many ways it is in us.

Ultimately, the American Dream is an explanation for the hierarchical ordering of our class positions in our social world. It explains our relative rank as the result of solely our own doing, not as the result of social forces or the circumstances we find ourselves in. It is not surprising, then, that Americans might genuinely believe that they independently earn and deserve their class positions—the dominant ideology of our culture tells them so. This internalized sense of class positioning has been the subject of scholarly research, especially in regards to working-class and poor families. In Richard Sennett and Jonathan Cobb's pivotal book *The Hidden Injuries of Class*, for example, they discuss the "hidden injury" of the internal class conflict experienced among working-class men. They wrote that "Every question of identity as an image of social place in a hierarchy is also a question of social value. ... This is the context in which all questions of personal and social legitimacy occur."

The American Dream helps to sustain these "hidden injuries" by bombarding people with the message that their social place—and their social value, their self-worth—is directly and exclusively the result of their own actions.

In their interviews for this book, people spoke in depth and at length about the American Dream, despite the fact that in the first 182 interviews the families were not even asked about it. Those parents were told that the project was to study assets and inequality, and during the interviews they were asked to speak about the communities they lived in, their children's schools, and their families' financial histories. Over and over, however, the focus of the interviews turned to beliefs in meritocracy as families repeatedly brought up the subject and wove it into the conversations. I must admit that I myself was surprised with the extent to which the interview findings were so ideological in nature. And I was even more surprised when interviews—including those interviews from the second phase which did directly ask people about their thoughts on the American Dream—revealed the depths of people's commitment to, and belief in, meritocracy as a real and valid explanation for how contemporary American society operates. People from all walks of life spoke forthrightly of their belief in meritocracy, not just as rhetoric, but as an accurate explanation of our social system.

Trying to confirm these findings has been frustrating due to the lack of qualitative studies that have asked people in-depth about their perspectives on the American Dream. Curiously, even in terms of quantitative studies, surprisingly few public opinion polls have been conducted on the subject of the American Dream. However, related social survey data that do exist reflect that Americans overwhelmingly believe that their country operates as a meritocracy. Indeed, after his review of the data political scientist Everett Carl Ladd concluded that survey research "shows Americans holding tenaciously and distinctively to the central elements of their founding ideology." He found Americans' belief in the American Dream to be more intense, pervasive, and firmly entrenched than generally recognized. Very recent qualitative research on post-civil rights views also finds that in in-depth interviews people are remarkably insistent in their beliefs that the playing field is level, that meritocracy is real. While these findings are definitely in line with my own, perhaps the most compelling affirmation for me has been to discover that other sociologists doing in-depth interviewing on subjects not explicitly focused on the American Dream are finding, as I have, that respondents consistently evoke the American Dream—specifically the notion of meritocracy—as their own theme in interviews. In the 200 interviews conducted for this study, what families said, their views, their decisions, and their experiences, were explicitly framed by their belief in meritocracy. These families' perspectives give a vivid account of the place and significance of the American Dream in contemporary life.

The reality of wealth in America though—the way it is acquired, distributed, and the way it is used—is a direct contradiction to these fundamental ideas. In interviews with American families we have seen a way how that plays out. Examining school decision-making (just one arena wherein families potentially experience the ramifications of wealth inequality), those parents from backgrounds of even moderate wealth had a significant advantage over parents with family histories of wealth poverty. Disproportionately white, wealth-holding parents used the financial assistance, intergenerational transfers, and security of their family wealth to help access schools for their own children that were viewed as advantageous by all of the parents. Meanwhile, parents without family wealth to rely upon, who were disproportionately black, were navigating the same arena unaided, with relatively limited resources and constrained capacities. *A central incongruity surfaces when families' school decisions are considered in the context of the American Dream: the assets that the wealth-holding families had owned, relied upon, and utilized in choosing schools had most often originated from non-merit sources.* Inherited wealth and the security of family wealth were critical advantages being passed along to the next generation—advantages often unearned by the parents themselves, and always unearned by their children.

A foundational conflict exists between the meritocratic values of the American Dream and the structure of intergenerational wealth inequality. Simply, advantageous resources inherited and passed along in families are not attained through individual achievement. Although wealth can, of course, be earned by an individual entirely independently, in the case of the families we spoke with it had not. This is the aspect of family wealth that concerns us here. Family wealth generates unearned advantages for those who have it. It is a form of privilege. In light of their beliefs in the American Dream, how do those families who present the most transparent contradiction to the idea of meritocracy—families with wealth privilege—understand their positioning and the unearned advantages they pass along to their children?

We could presume that as with other forms of privilege (such as race privilege or gender privilege) wealth privilege would generally appear invisible and be taken for granted by those who have it. However, one of the most striking aspects of the interviews was the acknowledgement of wealth privilege on the part of wealth-holding families. The parents who had benefited from family wealth acknowledged a structure of wealth inequality that grants privilege to some families and disadvantage to others, and they acknowledged the advantages they were passing along to the next generation through the schools that they chose.

ACKNOWLEDGING ADVANTAGE: A STRUCTURE OF WEALTH INEQUALITY

Given the fact that these families had so vehemently expressed their beliefs in the legitimacy of the American Dream, it was startling to hear them so openly discuss the reality of structured wealth inequality in American society. Not only did parents talk openly about this, they expressed specific views concerning the advantages conferred by wealth. Wealth-holding families thought of wealth as a distinctive resource to be used in particular ways, and even asset-poor families had concrete opinions about how they would use wealth—as opposed to income—if they had it. *Regardless of whether a family had a lot, a little, or none, wealth was thought of as a special form of money, different from income.* Wealth was perceived as a vehicle to provide opportunities, experiences, and material things, as well as a source to provide other less tangible advantages that were harder to articulate but no less important (a sense of security, or confidence about the future, for example). *As a whole, families' perspectives on the advantages of family wealth centered around two notions: wealth as a push and wealth as a safety net.* While families across the board alluded to these ideas, they were especially prevalent among the wealthier families, who emphasized them repeatedly. The first notion—a "push"—or an "edge" as some referred to it, was used by parents to explain how family wealth put some people "ahead" of others right from the start and "paved the way" for them over time.

> Int: Do you believe that you would have achieved the same social and economic situation that you have today if you weren't given the same financial support from your parents?

James: I would say no, because I feel what it has given me is the edge today. But for us today—for what I am, where I work, my abilities as well as my level of education—I feel without that I don't think I would be where I am today. Because the son would not have been successful without his father doing this—

Pamela: Paving the way for him—

James: [Nods] So, his father paved the way for him to start off and climb up the ladder to be what he is right now. Each kid has the potential, aspiration, a dream. And with wealth you can guide them, you can steer them that way. And you can help them, smooth the way for them, open up doors which they had never seen before.

Pamela and James Gordon, just as the other parents from backgrounds of family wealth, had experienced how that wealth had given them a push and believed it had made a positive difference in the trajectory of their life course. And they believed that this same push they were now giving their own children would make a difference for them too down the road.

Some of the wealth-holding families interviewed were more resistant than others to explicitly conceptualize that "push" they referred to, or those "difference down the road," as concrete "advantage." Joel, for example, asserted right away that wealth passed on to children is "not advantage." He did, however, believe that "it helps." While he described the wealth passed along in families as "a pushing factor," he was careful to not suggest that this translated into actual advantage.

Int: Does the financial help in terms of wealth that some people receive from their families give them certain advantages?

Joel: Not advantage, but it helps. It will help.

Int: Do you think it's significant?

Joel: Depends on what kind of financial help you're talking about.

Int: I'm not talking about billionaires. I'm talking, like, giving a kid after he graduates a $45,000 car. Or giving him, like, $30,000 for his wedding gift.

Joel: That helps, yeah, that does help. Yeah, the normal help that the parents give to the children, that is a pushing factor. Just puts you ahead a little bit.

Int: Do you believe those without stable economic situations have a harder time achieving success?

Joel: Yes, I do. That's the rule of life. I mean if you have the money you have peace of mind. So you probably can make better decisions. If you're under pressure for lack of money you could go wrong, you could make wrong decisions, definitely.

Here we see a tension between the ideology of meritocracy and the reality of structured wealth inequality in the nuances of how Joel Conrad talked about, perceived, and made sense of family wealth. While a few other parents expressed similar resistance to acknowledging that the "push" of family wealth was a form of privilege, most families did not. Victoria and Abraham Keenan, for example, conceptualized what they were doing for their own children as "absolutely" giving them advantages. While they were careful to point out that they were not "multi-millionaires" like other people they knew, they did fully believe, and acknowledge, that their family wealth was giving their children "a better chance of becoming successful." Implicit in the way they discussed the passing along of their wealth was their acknowledgement that by doing so they were passing along advantage.

Family wealth was believed to give children a push that, as Abraham said, "gives them a better chance of becoming successful." Some families, of course, can give bigger pushes than others, but even small pushes are clearly advantageous. Children who get the pushes of family wealth benefit from advantages they did nothing to individually earn. The acknowledgement of this on the part of the families who were passing advantages along is an important part of their perspectives on wealth privilege and an important insight to how they think about inequality. The second major way that parents depicted the advantages of family wealth was that it acted as a "safety net" for them in important decisions and throughout their lives. Parents from wealth-holding families repeatedly articulated their sense that family wealth was a "safety net" that gave them tremendous "peace of mind." The Barrys, a white couple whose families on both sides had given them significant financial assets over the years, described their wealth-holdings, and the family wealth they believed they could rely upon in the future, as "a sense of economic security." When asked what that sense of security provides for them, Briggette answered:

Briggette: Sleep at night. It's very non-tangible things. Being able to give my children a sense of peace. Being able to live worry free. It's really non-tangible things. Knowing that I will probably never have the income that my parents had, but still being comfortable with that and being able to provide for my children what they need.

Another parent who explicitly described her family's wealth as a "safety net," went on to explain, "Well, I think just having, um, the assets, just gives us a certain freedom. ... You know? You're more freer and more comfortable." The sense of security parents felt from the safety net of family wealth, their desire to re-establish that safety net for their own children, and their ability to rely on it and expand on it in investing in their children's futures cannot be overemphasized. This was a major way that individuals we interviewed—for example Cynthia and Paul Perkins, a white middle-class couple with three children in Boston—acknowledged the power of wealth and wealth's associated privileges.

When a "safety net" of wealth—or, "a cushion for the future"—could not be relied upon, families without it felt the insecurity of having nothing on which to fall back. This is where the difference between wealth and income is perhaps the clearest. As Lenore Meehan, a young black mother from Boston explained it: "You know, if you look on paper, I make a lot of money, but it doesn't feel like it. ... I mean, I don't feel like I'm economically secure at all." While she was up-front about the fact that she felt she made quite a lot of money working as a dispatcher for the police force, Lenore's income simply could not provide the sense of security that family wealth was granting to other parents who had it. The families interviewed from all race and class backgrounds made a clear distinction between wealth and income and had concrete understandings of the kinds of advantages that family wealth can provide. Their conceptualization of the "push" and the "safety net" that wealth affords for families and children (and that lack-of-wealth prohibits) reveals their intrinsic awareness and understanding of the power of wealth. *Their acknowledgement of the role of wealth in shaping opportunities, life trajectories, and future chances reveals their awareness and understanding of a structure of wealth inequality.*

As Abigail Connor said, "for someone like her" (someone from a wealthy white family with accumulated, historically rooted race and class advantages), intergenerational transfers of wealth along the way had created a real form of contemporary privilege: family wealth advantage that is not earned entirely independently but which make opportunities relatively easier to attain, aspirations relatively more achievable, and life chances relatively more optimistic. When asked to reflect on the way this had played out in their own lives Abigail and others "like her" (others from families of relative wealth privilege) were quite aware of the essential role that their family wealth had played in their lives. Here Emily Mitchel explains:

Int: Do you believe that you would have achieved the same social and economic situation that you have today if you weren't given the same financial support from your parents growing up?
Emily: No.
Int: [silent pause] How essential, if at all, do you believe family wealth is in attaining success?
Emily: I think it certainly helps. I think more people who have money tend to excel than people who have no money. It gives you the education, it gives you the contacts, it gives you the clothes, the way of talking. The things that make life easier. Can you do it without it? Yes. Is it as easy? I don't think so.... I think early in our history hard work was really important. But I think money—you can work really hard and be the best foreman on a construction job, but it's not gonna get you a villa in France or a villa in Tuscany. It's just gonna get you whatever kind of advance you want, and a place to live. So I really think that wealth or family money is one of the essential ingredients.

Parents who had benefited from the advantages of family wealth consistently expressed their beliefs that they would not have achieved their same level of success without the financial support that they had received. Of the families who had benefited from family wealth, in only two cases did a parent insist without any compromise that they would have ended up in exactly the same position without any of the financial support that they had received from their family. And in the two exceptions it is possible, of course, that they are correct. It is also the case that we have no way to really know.

In addition to talking about how it had impacted them, parents with family wealth also discussed how they were using that wealth to shape their own children's lives. They were consciously aware that their own relatively privileged positions were enabling them to pass advantage along to the next generation. From these parents' perspectives, family wealth provided specific advantages such as educational opportunities that without it their children would not have. Elizabeth Cummings, a white mother from a wealthy St. Louis family, explained her perspective:

> Elizabeth: No question about it! I mean, if my parents hadn't had the money to send my kids to *The Hills School*, we couldn't have considered it. We would have had to really do belt tightening, and financial aid, and many more loans, more mortgages. It would have been very difficult and a real strain on us, especially with two. And we probably would have felt like we just couldn't swing it as a family. So, I don't know, I would have had to gone out and gotten a job that would pay enough to justify two kids in private school. With that, it would have meant not being able to mother them as much myself. Or my husband having to change work, and all the soul searching that would have meant for him. It's unimaginable. I can't envision a path that we would have been able to so comfortably just sail on over to *The Hills School*.

The idea that "you have to have wealth to get it" (or, at least, that having wealth makes it relatively easier to get more) and the idea that "wealthier people have better life chances" (or, at least, that wealth confers relatively better chances for success), stood at the heart of the matter in the interviews. And these concepts stand at the heart of the matter here: If family wealth makes the next generation's wealth relatively easier to acquire, and if wealth makes success (however defined) relatively easier to attain, then people born into families with wealth are born with a distinct, unearned advantage. They are born with privilege that others do not have.

CONVICTION IN MERITOCRACY: HARD WORK OR LACK THEREOF

> Carter: The fact of the matter is because you get some assistance from your parents doesn't mean that you haven't primarily achieved anything on your own. The fact of the matter is getting a down payment on a house means you were able to get a house sooner, but you still have to make the payments on the house, you still have to do everything necessary to maintain that house. So yeah, it's a help, but it's not the overriding factor.
>
> Int: You think the overriding factor is your own—
>
> Carter: Your own psyche.... At the end of the day, hard work is the most important ingredient—in anybody's success.
>
> Int: Think so?
>
> Carter: Yes. The determination to be successful is like the tide, you know? You can't stop it.

> Faith & Carter Martin, Homemaker & Attorney, White, Washington, D.C.

Tracei Diamond, a black single mother from St. Louis, spent much of her interview answering "no" to every question regarding any financial assistance she might have received and explaining the lack of any family financial resources available to her. As a full time banquet waitress at a private country club, Tracei's annual income was $24,000, she had zero net financial assets, and held only a high school degree. Tracei talked about how she sees the members of the country club at functions and events and thinks about how they and their children had advantages that she and her three children simply did not have. She spoke at length, for example, about how the schools "out there" (where the country club was located) were "good schools," how the teachers "really work with them" (the students), and how overall "the education is better." In Tracei's view, for as much as she would like to be able to give her kids those same kinds of opportunities, she simply cannot afford the move to such an area. On top of supporting her three children on her own (she was receiving no child support), Tracei also was doing whatever she could to financially support her younger sister and their mother.

Tracei's interview was typical in that she articulated clear recognition of a structured inequality amongst families that blatantly and categorically translates into unequal educational opportunities for children of different family wealth backgrounds. Yet also typical was Tracei's outright rejection of this inequality and of unequal opportunity. Tracei recognized it and rejected it at the same time. After Tracei had talked about how "wealthy families" get the "better schools," she was asked about how a family's wealth plays a factor in their children's access to quality education. She replied: "It really doesn't have an impact on it. I guess pretty much it depends on you, as far as what kind of life you will have for your child." When she was asked if wealth has any impact, she said "I don't really look at it like that. So, like I say, money definitely doesn't have anything to do with it." When asked to explain further, Tracei did:

"It's basically what the parents want or whatever, that's the only thing I really can see. It just depends on how they raise them really." Despite their perspectives that class inequality structures life chances, Tracei and the other families maintained their belief that merit—not money—is what matters; they maintained with conviction their belief in meritocracy.

It was striking to hear disadvantaged parents talk so vehemently about meritocracy, to hear them assert repeatedly that positions in society are earned entirely through hard work and personal achievement, and to hear them deny family wealth inequality as a legitimate explanation. But considering that many of these parents had no direct experience with wealth privilege, that they had no awareness of the extent to which wealthy families are using and extending intergenerational transfers of assets, that they did not know for sure how much others are advantaged by unearned resources, then it makes sense how they clung so resolutely to the dominant ideology. What was most remarkable, however, is that those parents with family wealth who had spoken openly of their unearned advantages, who had so plainly seen and felt and known wealth privilege in motion in their own lives, were, at the same time, insistent that meritocracy is an accurate and realistic explanation for social stratification in America. In an interview in St. Louis, Briggette and Joe Barry spoke in detail of the financial help they had received from their parents. *They openly declared that these resources had allowed for a lifestyle they would not otherwise have had. After listing extensive financial assistance, the security of family wealth, and the many advantages they have had, the Barrys insisted that the way they had earned their assets was through hard work.*

The Barrys were not atypical of the white middle-class families interviewed; on the contrary, they portrayed the sentiments of families like them in the sample. Their socioeconomic positions were due, in large part, to the inheritance and accumulative advantages of family wealth, yet at the same time they were adamant that they single-handedly earned and deserved their places in society. These families' insistence that they had, "worked their butts off" for what they had was astonishing. They listed in detail the help they had received from their families: Financial assistance with major purchases, down payments on houses, school tuition for children, "loans" that were later forgiven, etc. They catalogued the gifts they had received from family members for birthdays, graduations, weddings, and births of children. They discussed the numerous ways

their extended families had been financially generous over the years by providing used cars, old furniture, flight tickets home for holidays, family vacations, dining out, kids' back-to-school clothes, and groceries, to name a few. They described the "push" and the "safety net" that comes with family wealth: Feeling that they have had "a head start" or "an edge" over others, knowing they would have something to fall back on in a financial pinch, and the expectation of future inheritances. While they talked about, listed, and described these things when asked, they repeatedly emphasized how hard they had worked for all that they owned and how much they deserved their stations in life.

Regardless of background, families used the American Dream of meritocracy to explain their assertion that anyone can be anything and do anything and get anywhere with hard work. They stressed that hard work or lack thereof was the determinant of each individual's position in society. But for those with family wealth, what was most notable was how they implied, implicitly and explicitly, that their own advantages as well as the advantages they were passing along to their children were earned and deserved autonomously—through hard work, perseverance, and determination alone.

Another example comes from our interview with Chris and Peter Ackerman, a white couple in their early thirties who lived in a white suburb of St. Louis. They had three kids, ages six, three, and two. They had been married for ten years and both worked in management positions on the staff of a local university. Their combined annual income was $83,000, their net worth $210,000, and their net financial assets totaled $91,500. This couple owned savings accounts, savings bonds, small trust funds for each child, and a boat worth $12,500. They had received significant financial assistance from their families, including help with a down payment on their first home, which they bought when they married. The equity from that house was later used as a down payment for an upgraded home when they had their children. Chris and Peter's parents financed their college educations; they never had to take out student loans; their children regularly received cash gifts and savings bonds from their grandparents on holidays and birthdays; Chris's parents had often paid for the family to vacation with them; Peter's parents had bought many of their major household appliances for them, as well as their car; and so on. They talked about how appreciative they were of all this help, about how they would not be in the position that they are without it. Despite this acknowledgement, Chris and Peter continually insisted that their wealth had been achieved single-handedly:

Int: How did you acquire the assets you own?
Chris: By working.
Peter: Saving, working.
Chris: Working and saving, working and saving. That's basically how we do it.

The Ackermans and many of their peers simultaneously acknowledged the power of their wealth privilege and avowed that it does not really matter. They were resolute in their explanation that hard work and determination had gotten them to where they are. For as much as they were upfront about the structure of wealth, they also depicted social positioning as independently earned and deserved. As one young mother from just outside of New York City put it, "You know—and I'm not bragging, I'm not saying anything—but it just comes from setting your priorities straight, and taking care of business!" In discussing hard work and individual achievement people often spoke louder, quicker, and sometimes at a higher pitch. People leaned forward or moved in toward the tape recorder's microphone as if to want to be sure they were heard clearly on this. They spoke with fervor and conviction when crediting themselves with their own success. For example, in talking with Lily and Jonathan Boothe, a white wealthy family from the New York City area, Jonathan had been quite serene throughout the interview. However, when we began talking about the Boothes' perspectives on success and achievement, Jonathan became noticeably more vivacious.

Just as people with wealth credited themselves for their success, conversely, those who lacked family wealth blamed themselves. Conviction in meritocracy worked both ways, and meritocracy could justify both positions. The themes of "sticking to one's ideals," "being focused," "motivated," and "willing to work hard" were as consistent in interviews with working-class and impoverished families as they were in affluent families. People blamed themselves for their inability to attain what they wished for and wanted for themselves and their children, even when they were starting from the most disadvantaged backgrounds. One parent from Boston explained that, compared to others, she comes up short because "I did a lot of fooling around." A mother from St. Louis said, "I would say that I am a little bit limited. But it's nobody's fault but my own. So I can't complain." And still another

parent lamented, "If I was to make more, better, wiser decisions along the way, I wouldn't have the debt that I have now."

Most people have regrets in life, and maybe if the families who were struggling to make ends meet had made "more, better, wiser decisions along the way," things would have turned out differently for them. Maybe not. But one of the things that stood out the most about this explanation was that many of these families had in fact done extraordinarily well for themselves. More often than not, however, the fruits of unaided self-achievement simply paled in comparison to the results of self-achievement combined with the advantages of family wealth. Still, throughout the interviews, parents from poor and working-class family backgrounds compared themselves to more "well-off" others, blamed themselves, and legitimized their situations by saying they should have worked harder. While to some extent they understood that a structure of wealth inequality existed, and while they recognized the real advantages for those with family wealth, they simultaneously blamed themselves for not having worked harder and done better than they had.

The interviews also show the power of hope. For these families the American Dream was hope. It held out hope that what is wanted will happen, and that what is wanted can be expected. It held out hope that children's life chances were all equally unconstrained. It held out hope that the world is just. To think otherwise (to think that the world is not just) would be heart-breaking to any parent. And, I believe, many parents fear that to think otherwise (to think that the world is not just) could potentially—if conveyed to children—break the spirit of any child. So they hold on to the American Dream, they hold on to their hope. This hope was reflected in the parents' perspectives regarding themselves, the social system they are acting on and within, and—most importantly—their children.

REFERENCES

Hochschild, Jennifer. 1995. *Facing Up to the American Dream: Race, Class, and the Soul of a Nation*. Princeton, NJ: Princeton University Press.

——. 1981. *What's Fair? American Beliefs about Distributive Justice*. Cambridge, MA: Harvard University Press.

Schwartz, John E. 1997. *Illusions of Opportunity: the American Dream in Question*. New York: W. W. Norton.

Sennett, Richard & Cobb, Jonathan. 1972. *The Hidden Injuries of Class*. New York: W. W. Norton.

DISCUSSION QUESTIONS

1. Heather Beth Johnson argues that "the American Dream promises that our system functions as a meritocracy." Explain this assertion; what does Johnson mean by it? What is a meritocracy? And what is the American Dream (or what are the American Dreams)? Is it (are they) still relevant today? How?

2. Johnson notes a significant inconsistency between the mythology of the American Dream as based solely on meritocracy and the reality of wealth inequality in America: Americans "from backgrounds of even moderate wealth have a significant advantage over [other Americans] with family histories of poverty." And inherited wealth is a critical—but often unearned—advantage that is passed on by parents to their children. Which vision of America do you think is more accurate—the idea of America as a meritocracy, or Johnson's revelations about wealth inequality? How do you resolve the inconsistency between the two visions? Is it resolvable?

3. Do Americans achieve wealth (or fall into poverty) solely as the result of hard work and talent (or solely because of the absence of these traits) alone? What makes American believe that "meritocracy is an accurate and realistic explanation for social stratification in America" even when faced with evidence of systematic inequality?

4. How believable is the American Dream in the face of increasing economic inequality and social stratification?

THE AMERICAN GULAG— ENTWINING SCHOOLS IN THE CARCERAL STATE

Prelude to Prison Student Perspectives on School Suspension

BY **Marsha Weissman**

The term "gulag," which originally referred to the Soviet system of penal labor camps (Solzhenitsyn 1973), has come to symbolize prisons generally. Ruth Wilson Gilmore (2007) refers to the "Golden Gulag" in describing the expansion of prisons in California, now the largest state prison system in the United States, which itself maintains the largest prison system in the world. With more than two million people in prison, the US criminal justice system is widely viewed as a system of mass incarceration driven by a confluence of governmental and economic forces now known as the "prison-industrial complex" (Mauer 2001; Simon 2001).

The circumstances and factors that have created the American Gulag have become an increasingly important link in the carceral state. By carceral state, I mean the way that law enforcement techniques, methods, and tools are ubiquitous throughout all facets of American society. A synthesis of ideas from Foucault (1979), Garland (1990, 2001b), Wacquant (2001, 2006), and Simon (2007) suggests that the carceral state consists of spatial ordering of control both within and external to prisons through gated communities, mall security, metal detectors in schools, security cameras, and the physical presence of public and private police, as well as the prisons and detention centers that dot the American landscape. The carceral state also consists of zero tolerance policies that criminalize an increasing range of human behavior including homelessness, mental illness, addiction, and noise on the street, and increasingly, student insubordination and normative adolescent behavior in the schools. Those who transgress are considered different and dangerous and can be incapacitated even outside the prison wall through house arrest and electronic monitoring. They are labeled ex-con and ex-offender, labels that exclude them from participation in most aspects of civil society, for even without incarceration, a criminal conviction of even a minor sort can result in bars to employment, college, housing, licenses, voting, and volunteering.

MASS IMPRISONMENT

In 1971, US prisons captured the attention of the American public with the Attica rebellion that took place in a maximum security prison in Batavia, New York, a small town outside of Buffalo.[1] I was one of those caught up in the unveiling of twentieth-century American punishment. My discovery of these institutions was serendipitous—a product of time and place—as experienced through the eyes of a then young graduate student who in the early 1970s became involved in efforts to defend prisoners charged in the aftermath of the Attica prison uprising of 1971.

In 1971, there were no prisoner's rights projects and only a handful of people were at all concerned about prison conditions. Prisons were a relatively insignificant institution in American life in 1971, with the rate of incarceration (96 per 100,000) relatively constant all through the 1900s to that point in time. In fact, by 1971, there had even been a small decline in the incarceration rate.

There were a few lawyers who did prison work, and they took on the defense of the sixty-one prisoners charged in the uprising and recruited law and graduate students to help with the various aspects of the work. I first became involved in efforts to survey community attitudes toward prisoners as part of the legal strategy to obtain a change of venue to move the trials from the virtually all-white prison town of Batavia to Buffalo, New York, a city with a more diverse population that would be more representative of the largely black and Latino prison population. I also became involved in the community organizing strategy to build support for the "Brothers," as the prisoners charged in the Attica case came to be called. As time passed (the first case went to trial in 1974), more and more of the prisoners were able to post bail and become active in their own legal and community organizing strategies. I came to know many of them, not just as "clients" but as friends. I came to learn firsthand the connections, direct and indirect, between community conditions and pathways into crime, and to think more critically about how the United States constructs its punishment system.

The cumulative experiences stemming from the Attica insurrection—the substantive work, the community organizing, and personal connections—were transformative for me. I spent the last thirty years working in community organizations in an effort to reduce the use of incarceration. Forty years after the rebellion at Attica, the incarceration rate had increased six-fold: in 1980, there were fewer than 140 people per 100,000 in state and federal prisons but by 2011 that rate had risen to just over 716 per 100,000 or more than 1 out of every 130 US residents (Sentencing Project 2011). The incarceration rates for people of color are much higher—black, non-Hispanic males are imprisoned at a rate of 4,749 per 100,000, representing more than 2.3 million people confined in US jails and prisons (West and Sabol 2010). One in nine black men between the ages of twenty and thirty-four is now in prison or jail (Pew Center on the States 2008). America's "gulag" now stretches from coast to coast in institutions that contain men and increasingly women, who are isolated from families and communities.

David Garland (1990) describes mass imprisonment as a form of social control that reflects the social and economic changes of late modernity. In *The Culture of Control*, Garland (2001b) elaborates on the arrival of mass incarceration and its connection to changes in social, economic, and cultural relations ("late modernity") and the ascendance of socially conservative politics. These changes are characterized by the transformation of US capitalism from a manufacturing to a service economy, increasing globalization of capital with the associated insecurity, deterioration of public goods, and increasing income inequality and effects on social reproduction (Katz 2001). The "culture of control" is a reaction to these economic, political, and social changes. Poverty and crime become equated, and both are characterized as the individual choices of unworthy individuals (Hagan 1993). The conflation of poverty and crime has made it easier to replace social welfare programs with punitive crime control policies resulting in a reliance on incarceration (Simon 2007; Garland 2001b).

Through her case study of California, Gilmore (2007) explains the orgy of imprisonment in the United States in the latter part of the twentieth century. She traces the expansion of prisons within the context of changing economic structures and political ideology. Surpluses in capital, land, labor, and state capacity make prisons an increasingly attractive investment. Economic and political changes create a large urban underclass, a surplus humanity that in essence becomes the commodity that stokes the prison-building boom. Prisons were built on surplus land, formerly used for agricultural purposes, in an effort to shore up rural economies that were decimated by climate-induced crises and agribusiness. The prisons were financed by public borrowing that was "off-line," that is, not included in state budgets and therefore immune to right-wing organized taxpayer revolts exemplified by California's famous "Proposition 13," which starved public goods such as education. The dismantling of welfare supports for the poor and near poor was supported by the consolidation of right-wing Republican power through the administrations of Ronald Reagan, George Deukmejian, and Pete Wilson. The politically expedient "get tough on crime" mantra created harsh sentencing laws (e.g., "three strikes") that ensured a steady stream of humanity into the large number of new prisons being built in rural areas throughout the state.

California's "Golden Gulag" is perhaps the most dramatic example of the role of prisons in the political and economic landscape of the late twentieth century, but it is not the only example. New York State mirrors much of the California experience, although the prison expansion in the state occurred under the liberal administration of Mario Cuomo. Sidestepping the state's regular budget process and even its bonding process when the voters of New York rejected a prison bond referendum in 1981, the state government turned to the Urban Development Corporation (UDC) to fund the building of new prisons. UDC was originally established to fund low- and moderate-income housing, but in 1982, during the dramatic increase in homelessness throughout the state, UDC funds were redirected to pay for prison building (Schlosser 1998). There were twenty-eight prisons built in New York between 1981 and 1990, prisons that were readily filled through enforcement of New York's mandatory drug sentencing laws.

Mass incarceration has become a uniquely American institution, one that is intimately tied to structural changes in the larger society, both economic and social (Garland 2001a; Wacquant 2001). Wacquant (2001) specifically considers incarceration to be the most recent iteration of social control of African Americans. He places mass incarceration in the coterie of the American "peculiar" institutions—slavery, Jim Crow, and the ghetto—directed at controlling black people. In keeping with Garland's explanation of prison as the social control mechanism of late modernity, Wacquant asserts that prisons are particularly directed at controlling the no longer employable black population, that is, surplus labor for whom there are no jobs. Under the race-neutral rubric of crime control, "tough on crime" became a code word for containment of the largely African American "castaways" (Wacquant 2006, 5) of the US population. Disciplinary policies and practices, such as those that mandate the suspension of young people out of mainstream schools, play a critical role in rendering young people of color superfluous and unemployable.

RACE AND INCARCERATION

Incarceration rates vary dramatically for whites and minorities. In 2011, the rate of incarceration in state and federal prisons was 478 per 100,000 for white males, 3,023 per 100,000 for black males, and 1,238 per 100,000 for Hispanic males (Sentencing Project 2011). The incarceration rate of black people in the United States exceeds the rate of black incarceration in South Africa at the height of apartheid (Mauer 1994).[2]

The tremendous growth in the numbers of black and Latino males in prison has been the most troubling aspect of the prison-industrial complex, but is not the only demographic characteristic to consider. The number of women incarcerated increased by 757 percent between 1977 and 2004 (Frost, Greene, and Pranis 2006). Racial disparities are even more pronounced among the female prison population: in 2011, black and Hispanic women made up more than half of the population of women incarcerated (Carson and Sabol 2012). The incarceration rate for black women, at 129 per 100,000, was about three times the incarceration rate for white women, which was 71 per 100,000. Hispanic women, with an incarceration rate of 142 per 100,000, were about two times more likely to be incarcerated than white women (Carson and Sabol 2012).

ERECTING THE "PECULIAR INSTITUTION": DRUG LAWS AND MANDATORY SENTENCING

Legislative changes and changes in the implementation of criminal justice procedures and processes have situated the criminal justice system as a critical tool in the management of marginalized populations (Wacquant 2001; Gilmore 2007). The "War on Drugs" is most often pointed to as the cause of the astonishing growth in the US prison population and the specific containment of poor people of color. Indeed, drug laws are considered the single most important legislative factor driving the expansion in imprisonment, first in New York State, and then throughout the United States.

Mandatory prison sentences for drug crimes were first introduced in 1973 in New York State. Under what became known as the Rockefeller Drug Laws, New York's prison population grew from 12,500 in 1973 to a peak of 71,500 in 1999 (Correctional Association of New York 2006a).[3] People convicted of drug offenses were 11 percent of new commitments in 1980, but by 2006, drug offenders represented 36 percent of New York's prison population (Correctional Association of New York 2006b). Drug law reform in New York was enacted beginning in 2004, and by 2012, 14 percent of the state prison population was incarcerated on drug crimes. Despite the reforms, almost 8,000 people are still incarcerated for drug crimes and racial disparities persist with 75 percent of prisoners being people of color (New York State Department of Corrections and Community Supervision 2012).

New York's draconian drug laws were replicated in states across the United States as well as by the federal government. In roughly the two decades between 1980 and 2000 the number of annual drug arrests tripled, reaching 1,579,566 by 2000 (King and Mauer 2002). Between 1980 and 1990 alone, there was a five-fold increase in the rate of imprisonment, from 19 prison commitments per 1,000 arrests to 103 per 1,000 arrests. The rest of the country followed New York's example: prison cells were increasingly taken up by drug offenders. In 1980, people convicted of drug crimes were only 6 percent of the state and federal prison populations, but by 2008, 17 percent of state and federal prison populations were drug offenders (Carson and Sabol 2012).

The enforcement of drug laws—arrest, prosecution, and sentencing—have been most felt in communities of color (Tonry 1995). While drug use is not distinguishable by race or ethnicity among African Americans, Latinos, and whites (Substance Abuse and Mental Health Services Administration (SAMHSA) 2007), drug laws have been far more aggressively enforced in poor communities of color than in white middle class neighborhoods. The result of this disparate application of drug laws is apparent in the US prison population: almost three-quarters of all people in prison for drug offenses are black or Latino (Human Rights Watch 2000; Mauer 2006; Blumstein et al. 1983).

While important, drug laws are not the only laws that have increased incarceration. Mandatory sentencing laws, i.e., laws that require imprisonment for certain crimes (crimes involving the use or possession of a weapon, robbery, and other crimes involving violence, as well as drug crimes) or criminal histories (e.g., the infamous "three strikes" laws) result in the incarceration of people who previously might have received noncustodial (typically probationary) sentences (Wolf and Weissman 1996). By 1996, all states had implemented some form of mandatory sentencing (National Center on Crime and Delinquency 1998). Mandatory sentencing has led to higher incarceration rates (Stemen, Rengifo, and Wilson 2006) and exacerbated racial disparities in the criminal justice system (Mustard 2001; Albonetti 1997). The most egregious examples of these mandatory sentencing laws are federal drug laws that include mandatory minimum sentences for crack and cocaine offenses (US Sentencing Commission 1995; Human Rights Watch 2000; Free 1997).[4] However, state drug laws affect more people, given that law enforcement remains predominantly a state function.

Beyond driving more people into prisons, mandatory sentencing laws also have institutional effects on the administration of justice. The balance of power is shifting in court rooms as mandatory sentencing laws remove judicial discretion and increasingly make prosecutors' charging decisions the key determinants of the sentence outcome (Albonetti 1997; Bureau of Justice Assistance 1996).

Changes in parole and probation supervision have also been a part of the building of the carceral state. First, these community supervision options have been proscribed through mandatory sentencing laws that eliminate the prospect of a noncustodial probation sentence at the front end, and by the elimination of parole at the back end (Wolf and Weissman 1996; Travis and

Lawrence 2002). Federal "truth in sentencing laws," notably The Violent Crime Control and Law Enforcement Act of 1994, as amended in 1996, played a role in eliminating or reducing the use of parole. Under this law, federal funding for prison construction was made contingent upon the state increasing the length of sentences and requiring that certain categories of offenders serve at least 85 percent of the sentence imposed (Sabol et al. 2002). Second, probation and parole supervision approaches moved away from a rehabilitative focus and became increasingly law enforcement oriented (Clear and Byrne 1992) and heavily reliant on sophisticated methods of surveillance and control (e.g., electronic monitoring, urinalysis). These methods in turn resulted in greater numbers of people being returned to prison for "technical" violations[5] of their conditions of release rather than new criminality. Travis and Lawrence (2002) report that the number of parole violators returned to prison increased seven-fold between 1980 and 2000, noting that the number of parole violators re-incarcerated in 2000, 203,000, approaches the total number of people imprisoned in state prisons in 1980. In some states, such as California, parole violators are the largest single segment of the prison population (Travis and Lawrence 2002).

THE COLOR OF JUSTICE: DISPARITIES IN ARREST, PROSECUTION, AND SENTENCING

The socioeconomic characteristics of the US prison population show that the phenomenon of mass incarceration has not affected all segments of the population equally. A body of research and data demonstrates disparities in the criminal justice system by race and ethnicity (Golub, John-son, and Dunlap 2007; Mauer 2006; Tonry 1995; Nelson 1995; Baldus et al. 1998). Discrimination is historical and current, deliberate and inadvertent, and occurs at every stage of the criminal justice system from arrest to sentencing. The stage-based nature of discrimination has a cumulative effect that lends itself to the adage the "the whole is greater than the sum of its parts."

Regardless of the source, the result is the over-representation of minorities at each of the key stages of the criminal justice system. Cumulative disparity plays an insidious role in the criminal justice system. The American Bar Association's (ABA) (2004, 9) Kennedy Commission concluded: "the cumulative effect of discretionary decisions at each step of the process ultimately contributes to the racial disparity in our prisons and jails."

A number of scholars have attributed racially disparate sentencing outcomes, whether or not a person is incarcerated, to legally relevant factors such as longer criminal histories (Hagan 1974; Blumstein et al. 1983). However, legally relevant factors at sentencing cannot be separated from broader criminal justice practices along the continuum of the system, including the harsher treatment of minorities as juveniles (Pope and Feyerherm 1990; Sampson and Lauritsen 1997; Poe-Yamagata and Jones 2000), and at each stage of the [adult] criminal justice system (Nelson 1995). Moreover, the criminalization of student behavior, with its attendant racially disparate effects, positions the school as the new entryway into the criminal justice system continuum.

Studies of each distinct stage of the criminal justice system have found evidence that race influences outcomes. The deployment of police resources in inner cities and certain practices, such as police stops, have been found to result in disparate arrest rates for minorities (Blumstein 1982; Blumstein et al. 1983; Langan 1985; Hawkins and Hardy 1989; Crutchfield, Bridges, and Pitchford 1994). The National Organization of Blacks in Law Enforcement (NOBLE) (2001, 4) asserts that "[b]ias-based policing impacts all aspects of policing and should be considered the most serious problem facing law enforcement today." Blumstein (1982, 1993) found that 75–80 percent of the racial disparity in the prison population is explained by racial differences in arrests. Using different methods and levels of analysis, subsequent research essentially confirmed Blumstein's findings (Langan 1985; Hawkins and Hardy 1989; Crutchfield, Bridges, and Pitchford 1994). Disparity tends to be greater for the less serious and nonviolent crimes where there is typically more discretion in police decision making (Austin and Allen 2000). For example, racial profiling in traffic stops has been a widely acknowledged problem (New Jersey Office of the Attorney General 1999; Ramirez, McDevitt, and Farrell 2000; Harris 2000). While the problem of "driving while black" has been the most visible example of racial profiling, the pattern of police deployment in venues and neighborhoods with higher concentrations of people of color also contributes to the higher arrest rates of minority populations (Cole 1999; Tonry 1995; Sampson and Lauritsen 1997). Between 2002 and 2012, the New York City Police Department made more than four million "stop and frisk" interrogations. The overwhelming majority of people stopped—87 percent—were black and Latino (New York Civil Liberties Union 2012).[6]

Arrest is followed by the decision to detain or to release on recognizance or to set bail: defendants detained pretrial are more likely to be convicted of the charges, and if convicted, are more likely to be incarcerated (Ares, Rankin, and Sturz 1963; Taylor et al. 1972; Hermann, Single, and Boston 1977; Hart and Reaves 1999; Spohn 2000; Williams 2003; Taxman, Byrne, and Pattavina 2005; Phillips 2007). Critical bail and pretrial release decisions are influenced by the defendant's racial and ethnic characteristics, with minority defendants more likely to be detained prior to trial than whites facing similar charges and with similar criminal histories (Goldkamp 1979; Mahoney et al. 2001; Demuth and Steffensmeier 2004; Free 1997). Racial disparities are also present in the next step in the criminal justice system—prosecution and charging decisions. Minorities are less likely to have charges dismissed or reduced. An investigation of about 700,000 criminal cases from California between 1981 and 1990 revealed statistically significant racial disparities in prosecutors' willingness to dismiss charges or reduce charges to crimes that would permit diversion (Schmitt 1991). Albonetti (1997) also found differences by race in federal prosecutors' willingness to grant sentencing reductions based upon "substantial assistance." Whites who provided substantial assistance received an average 23 percent reduction in the likelihood of incarceration, while similarly situated blacks received a 13 percent reduction and Hispanics received a 14 percent reduction. The actions of many different criminal justice system "actors" along a multi-stage continuum impact the basic "in/out" sentencing decision.

ECONOMICS AND SOCIAL CONTROL: THE PRISON-INDUSTRIAL COMPLEX

The tremendous growth in the prison population has made criminal justice big business. The economic interests that now connect industry to prisons go beyond the public sector workforce of police, court personnel, and prison guards. It extends into companies that produce and sell an array of products, both security-related and more basic supplies to these various sectors. It also includes the use of prison labor to produce goods and services at below-market price for private corporations and local government (Nagel 2002). A *New York Times* report (Santos 2008) on a possible prison closing in upstate New York captured the small town dependence on prisons:

The reliance on Camp Gabriels extends well beyond jobs. Small businesses have staked their survival on the prison workers who patronize their stores. Local governments and charities, meanwhile, have come to depend on inmate work crews to clear snow from fire hydrants, maintain parks and hiking trails, mow the lawns at cemeteries and unload trucks at food pantries.

Mike Davis (1995) first introduced the term "prison-industrial complex," likening the burgeoning prison industry to the "military-industrial complex" exposed by President Dwight Eisenhower. Schlosser (1998, 54) defined the term as referring to "a set of bureaucratic, political, and economic interests that encourage increased spending on imprisonment, regardless of the actual need." Like the military-industrial complex, the prison-industrial complex entwines diverse public and private interests. The economic interests include unionized public sector workers, public and private corporations that bond, construct, and supply prisons (architects, construction companies, investment houses, bond counsel firms, and telephone companies), industries devoted to the technology of social control, and the growing role of private corporations in the direct operation of prisons that are contracted out by state and federal government. Private corporations and governments also benefit from the use of prison labor that takes on public sector work (e.g., maintenance of state parks) or joint ventures between states or the federal government and private companies to produce goods and services using prison labor (Sexton 1995).

Prisons are also increasingly privatized and run by large corporations such as the Corrections Corporation of America and Wackenhut, whose profits are dependent upon the continuation of punitive policies. A *Businessweek* article headlined "Private Prisons Have a Lock on Growth" noted that the Corrections Corporation of America stock price rose 26 percent in the first six months of 2006 (Ghosh 2006). The Correctional Corporation of America (the largest private prison company) manages or owns at least sixty prisons in nineteen states and Washington, DC, with these facilities having a "bed" capacity of 80,000 (Correctional Corporation of America 2010). It is a publicly traded corporation and posts a web page for investors with up-to-date share prices. As of 2009, there were 127,688 people held in private prisons under contract to the federal and various state governments. In but one year (July 2005–June 2006), the use of private prisons increased by almost 13 percent (Sabol, Minton,

and Harrison 2007). Moreover, these publicly traded companies, driven by financial profit, have become significant and sophisticated lobbyists on criminal justice legislation[7] that would sustain or increase the prison population (Chang and Thompkins 2002).

Private corporations are not the only group lobbying for tougher sentencing laws and against sentencing reform. Prison guard unions also do so (Doster 2007; Center on Juvenile and Criminal Justice 2007; Chang and Thompkins 2002; Davis 1995). Unions have combined and spawned victims rights groups that together form a formidable lobby for "tough on crime laws." Davis (1995) points to more than one thousand new laws enacted in California between 1984 and 1992 with the strong support of the guards union and victims groups. Rural communities without another source of jobs join in the clamor for prison expansion and prison construction (Gilmore 2007). A *New York Times* article (Confessore 2007), quoting Kent Gardner, president of the Center for Government Research, captures rural support for prisons in New York State: "Up in the north country, you used to just think of hanging out a sign that says 'PrisonsRUs' ... ; pretty much every rural town in the state was angling for these facilities." Prisons have become the largest local employer in many rural communities, which over the last twenty years have become home to about 60 percent of new prisons (Beale 1993, 1997; Wagner 2003).

There are no comprehensive measures of the overall economic power of the prison-industrial complex. However, the Bureau of Justice Statistics tracks employment and spending in various government functions that form the criminal justice system—police, prosecutors, courts, and corrections. Overall, expenditures in the multiple sectors that make up the criminal justice system have increased dramatically between 1980 and 2010. In 1982, criminal justice prison spending was calculated at just under $36 billion dollars. Within ten years, spending grew by 125 percent to $79 billion and by the end of the 1990s, spending exceeded $146 billion, another 85 percent increase in less than ten years and an astounding 300 percent increase between 1980 and 2000 (US Department of Justice 2002).

The increase in spending on corrections has outpaced spending on education. Between 1977 and 2003, corrections spending alone increased by 1,173 percent, while spending on education increased 505 percent. Criminal justice functions became a larger share of state and local spending, while spending on education decreased as a proportion of state and local budgets (US

Department of Justice 2002). Employment in criminal justice functions increased by 77 percent between 1982 and 2003 (US Department of Justice, Bureau of Justice Statistics 2002). By 2006, the federal and state criminal justice systems employed more than 2.4 million people, accounting for 10 percent of federal government employees, 31 percent of state employees, and 58 percent of local government employees (Perry 2008).

MASS INCARCERATION AND THE SOCIAL CONTROL OF SUPERFLUOUS POPULATIONS

While crime control defines the public view of the purpose of prisons, mass incarceration is driven by other agendas, including economics and politics (Garland 2001a; Wacquant 2006; Gilmore 2007). Incarceration rates increase independently of changes in crime rates, growing even when crime rates go down, such as occurred during the 1990s, and outpacing crime rates when these rates are high, such as during the 1980s (King, Mauer, and Young 2005).[8] Moreover, only between 10 and 25 percent of the decrease in crime has been attributed to the increase in incarceration (Levitt 2004; Spelman 2000; Western 2006). Incarceration rates continue to climb even in the face of evidence that it is itself a destabilizing force, particularly when meted out in concentrated forms on specific communities (Rose and Clear 1998).

Mass imprisonment is a tool to address the growing unemployment of young, unskilled men and is most readily imposed upon African Americans. As explained by Western (2006, 53):

> Underlying these political and economic explanations of mass imprisonment is a broader account of political reaction to the upheaval in American race relations through the 1960s and the collapse in urban labor markets for low-skill men. The social turbulence of the 1960s—a volatile mixture of rising crime, social protest, and the erosion of white privilege—sharpened the punitive sentiments of white voters. The economic demoralization of low-skill urban blacks in the 1970s presented a vulnerable target for the punitive turn in criminal justice. These were the basic preconditions for mass imprisonment.

The work of Wacquant (2001, 2006), Gilmore (2007), Garland (2001a), Western and Beckett (1999), Western and Pettit (2005), Western (2006), and Davis (1995) all offer perspectives on the prison as a mechanism for absorbing surplus labor. Western and Beckett (1999, 1031) discuss how prison acts as a regulator of the US labor market, serving the role that social welfare institutions do in European democracies: "Incarceration generated a sizeable, nonmarket reallocation of labor, overshadowing state intervention through social policy."

Incarceration hides joblessness by taking labor out of the market. Western (2006) demonstrates that the economic boom of the 1990s and its ameliorative effect on unemployment and the poverty rate, particularly for African American males, disappears once prisoners are included in calculations of economic well-being.[9]

Wacquant (2001) attributes the rise in incarceration in the late twentieth-century United States to signify the declining ability of the ghetto to contain poor African Americans due to economic restructuring, which included mechanization and globalization that made African American labor even more expendable. Like slavery and Jim Crow laws, prisons are the latest means for keeping (unskilled) African Americans in a subordinate and confined position—physically, socially, and symbolically (Wacquant 2001, 97). Wacquant defines the extreme containment of the prison as the "hyperghetto." The carceral culture has become the dominant culture in poor, urban, African American communities, revealing not only the profound lack of jobs, but also other indices of the abandonment of inner cities: "As the ghetto became more like a prison (what I call the 'hyperghetto') and the prison became more like a ghetto, the two institutions increasingly fused to form the fast-expanding carceral system that constitutes America's fourth 'peculiar institution'" (Wacquant 2001, 103).

Prisons become more like ghettos in their racial divide, increased violence, and chaotic street culture that meshes with convict culture. This should come as no surprise as poor communities of color are populated by people who cycle in and out of prison, doing life on the installment plan. Ghettos take on the culture of prisons, most profoundly, in Wacquant's words, by "official solidification of the centuries-old association of blackness with criminality and devious violence" (2001, 117). The material manifestations of the merging of prison and the street is evident in street gangs in prison and prison gangs in the street, prison slang, such as "homeboy" or "homie," and even fashion trends such as sagging pants, a style with roots in the prohibition against belts in prison. Shabazz Sanders (2008) explored the meshing of the ghetto and prison in the culture and consciousness of black men. He points to the hyper-masculinity of black men, including their body sculpture, tattooing, and physicality as moving from the prison to the community. The ghetto also prepared young black men for prison through the spatial contours of geographical isolation, policing, and surveillance, physical overcrowding, poor nutrition, and compromised health. Shabazz Sanders joins many public health scholars in pointing out the interaction between prison and the ghetto in the spread of HIV (Lane et al. 2004; Freudenberg 2008; Adimora and Schoenbach 2005).

The merging of race and criminality also depoliticizes issues of racism. Under the guise of a race-neutral criminal justice system, social and economic problems of the ghetto that result in alienation and its attendant behavioral manifestations are redefined. For example, the condition of urban schools is transformed from an issue of resource distribution to a problem of violent, delinquent children and their dysfunctional families. Moreover, community level disenfranchisement effects associated with the large number of people barred from voting because of a criminal record undermine the possibility of effecting change in educational practice and policy through the political process (Uggen, Manza, and Thompson 2006).

PRISONIZING SCHOOLS: POLICE, SECURITY, AND SURVEILLANCE

As a core institution, public schools in poor urban communities of color are not immune from the symbiotic relationship between prison and community. "Public schools in the hyperghetto have similarly deteriorated to the point where they operate in the manner of *institutions of confinement* whose primary mission is not to educate but to ensure 'custody and control'—to borrow the motto of many departments of corrections" (Wacquant 2001, 108; emphasis in original).

School as the initiation to mass incarceration is a recent consideration. The ghetto school reflects the carceral culture in many ways, from zero tolerance policies requiring suspension, which can be analogized to mandatory sentencing, to pervasive police presence, pro-arrest policies, and expanded surveillance and security. As Shabazz Sanders (2008) points out, the carceral culture is also seen in the appearance and behaviors of youth. This melding of prison culture and school operation collapses the pipeline: schools become a place that readies some youths for prison.

While there is a rich literature on the role of the school in reproducing cultural and class relationships, until the late 1990s, schools were not thought of as training grounds for prison. The first national level conference to examine the school-to-prison pipeline was held at Harvard University in May 2003. That conference, the research that preceded it, as well as much of the subsequent research has focused on documenting and analyzing the problem, showing how the punitive policies of the criminal justice system have come to permeate the US school system, particularly inner city urban schools. The "school-to-prison pipeline" has become a phrase used to describe the connections among school policies and practices that result in a more punitive approach to student misbehavior.

The links between school disciplinary policies and practices and criminal justice system involvement are both direct and indirect. The direct link is the increased presence of police in schools such that student misconduct and noncompliance that were previously addressed by teachers or school administrators now become the purview of school-based police. Police presence and criminalization of misdeeds have resulted in an increase in the number of in-school arrests (Advancement Project 2005).

Regular police presence in schools is a relatively recent phenomenon. In the late 1970s, there were only 100 school police officers nationwide (Brady, Balmer, and Phenix 2007). Between 1999 and 2003, the number of schools reporting the regular presence of safety and police officers increased by 30 percent, according to the US Department of Education (DeVoe and Kaffenberger 2005). The number of school resource officers peaked at just over 14,300 in 2003 and, due to federal funding cuts, declined to about 13,000 in 2007 (Justice Policy Institute 2012).

By the mid 1990s, the number of police deployed in New York City schools exceeded the size of the entire Boston police force (Beger 2002) and now at 4,600, exceeds the number of officers in most US cities (New York Civil Liberties Union (NYCLU) 2007). As might be expected, police presence results in the treatment of student misbehavior as criminal justice matters. While New York City has refused to disclose the number of arrests made in schools, the NYCLU study shows that increased law enforcement and school security measures are concentrated in schools where the student body is disproportionately students of color: 82 percent of children attending schools with metal detectors were black and Latino, surpassing their representation in the citywide school population by 11 percent.

While national data are not available, information from individual cities show an increasing number of arrests of children while in school. For example, in the 2010–2011 school year, 16,377 students in Florida were sent directly to the juvenile justice system, an average of forty-five students per day. Black students make up only 21 percent of the Florida youth population but made up 46 percent of all 2011 school-related referrals to law enforcement (Florida Department of Juvenile Justice 2011). In 2003 in Chicago, Illinois, 8,539 students were arrested in public schools (Advancement Project 2005). Almost 10 percent were children age twelve or younger. Black students made up 77 percent of the arrests, but were only 50 percent of the school population. Half of the students arrested in Chicago schools are sent to juvenile or criminal court. In Palm Beach County, Florida in 2003, black students make up only 29 percent of the student population but were 64 percent of arrests in school (Advancement Project 2006). The racial disparity in school arrests is not limited to large urban centers: in 2003, according to the *Des Moines Register*, black students constituting 15 percent of Des Moines's high school student population were 33 percent of the 556 arrests in that city's high schools (Deering, Alex, and Blake 2003).

Data on school arrests for school districts with more than fifty thousand were made public by the US Department of Education in 2012. The data showed that over 70 percent of school-based arrests or referrals to law enforcement involved minority students. Males were more likely than females to be arrested in school (US Department of Education 2012).

Especially disturbing is the fact that many of the school arrests are for non-criminal activity and are carried out without regard for the age of the student or the context of the child's misbehavior. Media accounts of these sorts of arrests abound and have been chronicled by the Advancement Project (2006) and the Advancement Project in collaboration with Alliance for Educational Justice, Dignity in Schools Campaign, NAACP, and Legal Defense Fund (2013). Examples include the arrest in St. Petersburg, Florida, in 2005 of a five-year-old African American girl by police for throwing a tantrum and hitting an assistant principal. Also in that year, in New York City, a sixteen-year-old girl was arrested for shouting an obscenity in the hallway. When the school principal attempted to stop the police from detaining the girl, the principal and a school aide were also arrested. In May 2012, an honors student in Houston, Texas spent a night in jail when she missed class to go to work to support her family. In April 2012, a kindergarten student in Milledgeville, Georgia was handcuffed and arrested for throwing a tantrum. In Palm Beach, Florida, 22 percent of the in-school arrests were for miscellaneous non-criminal behaviors such as "disruptive behavior" (Advancement Project 2005, 2006).

The prisonization of schools through ubiquitous presence of the police undermines the authority of principals and other school administrators (Devine 1996). There are formal and informal policies that now require incidents to be turned over to the police for action. Several years back, I attended a meeting of a New York State board with planning responsibility for the state's juvenile justice system. A school administrator was chastised for requesting funding to establish an anti-graffiti program that would retain school authority over such behavior. The administrator was sharply reminded that graffiti was a crime and therefore school police, and not the school principal, were to be the arbiters of whether or not a student could be admitted into the diversion program or arrested and prosecuted under the penal code.

The widespread introduction of police in schools has been accompanied by enhanced security technology. In schools throughout the country, including Syracuse City schools, entryways to schools are often limited to one door. On entering the school, students are subject to metal detectors, wands, electronic identification systems, and biometric technology such as eye-scanning cameras and fingerprinting that allows admission to preapproved students (Atlas 2002; Cohn 2006). Halls are equipped with alarm systems and cameras and some districts have installed panic buttons in classrooms. In addition to hard technology, schools now employ security guards to monitor entry and egress. In some cases of school searches, the police use dogs to sniff out drugs. Data from the US departments of education and justice that track the types of security measures used by schools show that between 1998 and 2000, 75 percent of public schools limited access to schools during school hours, 7 percent used random metal detector checks, 21 percent used dogs for random drug checks, and 19 percent monitored students' whereabouts with security cameras (DeVoe and Kaffenberger 2005). Private security firms have identified schools as a lucrative market, with business magazines sprouting up that focus on the selling of security systems to schools. There are a large number of vendors who set up booths at school-related conferences as well as security industry-organized conferences on the topic of school safety (Casella 2003). The industry magazine *Security Management*, for example, posts a web page[10] listing its collection of articles on school security. There is an overlap between companies that design prisons and jails and sell security equipment to correctional facilities and those that are now involved in designing and equipping K–12 schools.[11]

SCHOOL DISCIPLINARY POLICIES: BRINGING ZERO TOLERANCE TO SCHOOLS

Arresting young people in school is the overt connection between school and the criminal justice system. Increasingly punitive disciplinary policies are less obvious, but play a more significant role in disconnecting youths from education by pushing them out of the school by expulsion or suspension.

Zero tolerance grew out of federal drug enforcement policies of the 1980s and was adapted to aggressive quality-of-life policing in urban centers, notably in New York City during the Giuliani administration (Bowling 1999). The 1994 Gun-Free Schools Act brought the zero tolerance policies of the criminal justice system into the school setting. The act made federal funding to schools contingent upon the local adoption of school disciplinary policies that mandated expulsion for weapons possession.

Much as zero tolerance policing increased the number of people brought into the criminal justice system, zero tolerance disciplinary policies have played a major role in the increase in school suspensions. While the federal law requires a one-year expulsion for possession of a weapon, over time many jurisdictions came to apply mandatory expulsion policies to other behaviors, including drug possession and fighting, and even lesser "offenses" such as swearing (Skiba and Knesting 2001). The interpretation of zero tolerance and expulsion varies by state. In some states, expulsion means virtual exclusion from all educational settings; in others, such as New York, school suspensions can result in assignment to "alternative" educational settings.

By the close of the twentieth century, school suspensions became the indirect link between American education and the US prison system, as suspended students became more likely to drop out of school, and dropouts acquired a high risk of being incarcerated at some point in their lives. Western's (2006) empirical work found education to have the most profound impact on the likelihood of incarceration, with high school dropouts five times more likely to go to prison than high school graduates regardless of race. The combination of race, gender, and education level is devastating. By the late

1990s, one in six black male dropouts annually went to prison. For young black men in particular, dropping out of school foreshadows incarceration. Western, Pettit, and Guetzkow (2002) estimate that one in ten young (age 22–30) white high school dropouts and 52 percent of African American male high school dropouts have been incarcerated by their early thirties.

Educational level demarcates the prison population from the general population. Among whites for example, those with only a high school education get imprisoned at a rate twenty times greater than those with college degrees. Sixty-eight percent of state prisoners in the United States do not have a high school diploma and 41 percent have neither a high school diploma nor a GED[12] compared to 18 percent of the general population (Harlow 2003). While the prison population as a whole is characterized by extraordinary levels of high school dropouts, prisoners of color are more likely to be dropouts than are white prisoners. Forty-four percent of black prisoners and 53 percent of Hispanic prisoners in state prison did not graduate or earn a GED, compared to 27 percent of white inmates (Harlow 2003).

School suspensions, which play a critical role in producing dropouts, have significantly increased over the period of time that also saw the growth in incarceration. US Department of Education, Office of Civil Rights data on school suspensions and expulsions show that between 1974 and 2000, the rate at which America's students were suspended and expelled from schools almost doubled from 3.7 percent of students in 1974 (1.7 million students suspended) to 6.6 percent of students in 2000 (3 million students suspended) (Wald and Losen 2003). By 2012, the number of students suspended at least once reached over three million students, more than seventeen thousand students per day (Orfield and Losen 2012). Much like arrest and incarceration, suspensions fall disproportionately on youths of color. African American students are 3.5 times more likely to be suspended or expelled as white students (US Department of Education 2012). Also, the use of punitive school discipline can be decoupled from school violence in the same way that incarceration rates are not related to crime rates. Out-of-school suspensions increased despite a documented decline in school violence, student victimization, and student fear of violence during the 1990s (Donahue, Schiraldi, and Ziedenberg 1998; Kaufman et al. 2000).

School suspensions are predictors of dropping out of school. The National Center for Educational Statistics shows[13] that 31 percent of students who had been suspended three or more times before the spring of their sophomore year dropped out of school compared to only 6 percent of students who had never been suspended dropping out (Livingston 2006, table 27-2). The dropout rate for suspended high school sophomores is three times greater than for students who were not suspended (Skiba and Peterson 1999). While not all dropouts wind up in prison, dropping out does increase one's prospects for becoming a prisoner and most people in prison are high school dropouts.

We have then a perfect storm: young black men who drop out of school are very likely to wind up in prison; the likelihood of dropping out of school is increased by suspension; and black male students are the most vulnerable to being suspended from school.

ENDNOTES

1. The prison uprising took place at the Attica prison in upstate New York from September 9 through September 13, 1971. Wicker (1975) provides an observer's view of the takeover of the prison by the inmates and the state's retaking of the prison.

2. The incarceration rate for people of color ("blacks" and "coloureds") in South Africa in 1993 was 851 per 100,000.

3. The New York State prison population declined to about 58,000 in 2010 (New York State Department of Correctional Services 2010).

4. There have been recent reforms to federal sentencing guidelines and support for further reforms is gaining momentum. Effective November 1, 2007, the US Sentencing Commission amendment revised the federal guidelines for crack cocaine sentencing and reduced prison time for people convicted of crack offenses. Congressional legislation to eliminate the disparity in crack versus cocaine sentencing is under consideration and, if passed, would equalize federal sentences for offenses involving crack and powder cocaine. Attorney General Eric Holder supported sentencing reform in a June 24, 2009 speech before the Charles Hamilton Houston Institute for Race and Justice and the Congressional Black Caucus Symposium "Rethinking Federal Sentencing Policy: 25th Anniversary of the Sentencing Reform Act." Available at: http://www.usdoj.gov/ag/speeches/2009/ag-speech-0907221.html.

5. A technical violation of parole or probation reflects an alleged failure to abide by conditions of release for reasons other than a new crime. Examples of technical violations include drug use, association with other people on parole, changing residence without parole or probation officer approval, failure to maintain employment, and failure to report.

6. About 90 percent of the stops did not result in any arrest, indicating that stop and frisk practices are less about public safety and more about social control.

7. Seeing detainees as a lucrative market, private prisons are also involved in crafting harsh immigration laws. An investigation by National Public Radio (Sullivan 2010) revealed that the Correctional Corporation for example was involved in the drafting of the 2010 Arizona Immigration Law (S.B. 1070).

8. For example, during the 1990s, the crime rate declined by 17 percent, yet the rate of incarceration increased by 65 percent (King, Mauer, and Young 2005).

9. Western and Pettit (2005) show that by 1999, the exclusion of prisoners in earnings calculations inflated the relative earnings of blacks by between 7 and 20 percent among all working age men, and by as much as 58 percent among young men.

10. See http://www.securitymanagement.com/library/000760.html.

11. Randall Atlas, for example, whose essay is cited above, is vice president of Atlas Safety and Security Design, Inc. His resume describes him as an architect specializing in "criminal justice architecture" and cites his experience as a consultant to the Florida Department of Corrections and the National Institute of Corrections, among others.

12. The majority of prisoners who earned a GED did so while incarcerated (Harlow 2003).

REFERENCES

Adimora, Adaora A., and Victor J. Schoenbach. 2005. "Social Context, Sexual Networks and Racial Disparities in Rates of Sexually Transmitted Infections." *Journal of Infectious Diseases* 191:S115–S122.

Advancement Project. 2005. *Education on Lockdown: The Schoolhouse to the Jailhouse Track*. Washington, DC: Advancement Project.

———. 2006. *Arresting Development: Addressing the School Discipline Crisis in Florida*. Washington, DC: Advancement Project.

Advancement Project, Alliance for Educational Justice, Dignity in Schools Campaign, NAACP, and Legal Defense Fund. 2013. *Police in Schools Are Not the Answer to the Newtown Shooting*. Washington, DC: Advancement Project.

Albonetti, Celesta A. 1997. "Sentencing under the Federal Sentencing Guidelines: Effects of Defendant Characteristics, Guilty Pleas, and Departures on Sentence Outcomes for Drug Offenses 1991–1992." *Law and Society Review* 31:789–813.

American Bar Association. 2004. *Justice Kennedy Commission: 2004 Report to the House of Delegates*. Washington, DC: American Bar Association.

Ares, Charles E., Anne Rankin, and Herbert Sturz. 1963. "The Manhattan Bail Project: An Interim Report on the Use of Pretrial Parole." *New York University Law Review* 38:67–92.

Atlas, Randall. 2002. "Designing Safe Schools." *Campus Security and Safety Journal* (December): 16–42.

Austin, Roy L., and Mark D. Allen. 2000. "Racial Disparity in Arrest Rates as an Explanation of Racial Disparity in Commitment to Pennsylvania's Prisons." *Journal of Research in Crime and Delinquency* 37:200–220.

Baldus, David C., George Woodworth, David Zuckerman, Neil Alan Weiner, and Barbara Broffit. 1998. "Racial Discrimination in the Post-Furman Era: An Empirical and Legal Overview, with Recent Findings from Philadelphia." *Cornell Law Review* 83:1638–1770.

Beale, Calvin L. 1993. "Prisons, Population and Jobs in Nonmetro America." *Rural Development Perspective* 8 (3): 16–19.

———. 1997. "Rural Prisons: An Update." *Rural Development Perspectives* 11 (2): 25–27.

Beger, Randall R. 2002. "Expansion of Police Power in Public Schools and the Vanishing Rights of Students." *Social Justice* 29 (1–2): 119–30.

Blumstein, Alfred. 1982. "On the Racial Disproportionality of United States' Prison Populations." *Journal of Criminology* 73 (3): 1259–81.

Blumstein, Alfred. 1993. "Racial Disproportionality of U.S. Prison Populations Revisited." *University of Colorado Law Review* 64:743–60.

Blumstein, Alfred, Jacqueline Cohen, Susan E. Martin, and Morris H. Tonry, eds. 1983. *Research on Sentencing: The Search for Reform*. Vol. 1. Washing-ton, DC: National Academy Press.

Bowling, Ben. 1999. "The Rise and Fall of New York Murder: Zero Tolerance or Crack's Decline." *British Journal of Criminology* 39 (4): 531–54.

Brady, Kevin P., Sharon Balmer, and Deinya Phenix. 2007. "School–Police Partnership Effectiveness in Urban Schools: An Analysis of New York City's Impact Schools Initiative." *Education and Urban Society* 39 (4): 455–78.

Bureau of Justice Assistance. 1996. *National Assessment of Structured Sentencing*. Washington, DC: US Department of Justice, Bureau of Justice Assistance.

Carson, E. Anne, and William J. Sabol. 2012. *Prisoners in 2011*. Washington, DC: US Department of Justice, Bureau of Justice Statistics.

Casella, Ronnie. 2003. "Security, Schooling, and the Consumer's Right to Segregate." *Urban Review* 35 (2): 129–48.

Center on Juvenile and Criminal Justice. 2007. *Political Power of the CCPOA*. San Francisco: Center on Juvenile and Criminal Justice. http://www.cjcj.org/cpp/political_power.php.

Chang, Tracy F. H., and Douglas E. Thompkins. 2002. "Corporations Go to Prisons: The Expansion of Corporate Power in the Correctional Industry." *Labor Studies Journal* 27 (1): 45–69.

Clear, Todd, and James M. Byrne. 1992. "The Future of Intermediate Sanctions." In *Smart Sentencing: The Emergence of Intermediate Sanctions*, edited by J. M. Byrne, A. J. Lurigio, and J. Petersilia, 319–30. Newbury Park, CA: Sage.

Cohn, Jeffrey P. 2006. "Keeping an Eye on School Security: The Iris Recognition Project in New Jersey Schools." *National Institute of Justice Journal* 254:12–15. http://www.ncjrs.gov/pdffiles1/jr000254.pdf.

Cole, David. 1999. *No Equal Justice*. New York: New Press.

Confessore, Nicholas. 2007. "Spitzer Seeks Panel to Study Prison Closings." *New York Times*, February 5.

Correctional Association of New York. 2006a. *Basic Prison and Jail Fact Sheet*. New York: Correctional Association of New York. http://www.correctionalas-sociation.org/publications/factsheets.htm.

———. 2006b. *Offenders under Custody in NYS Prisons Calendar Years 1970–2005*. New York: Correctional Association of New York. http://www.correctionalassociation.org/publications/factsheets.htm.

Correctional Corporation of America. 2010. "CCA Announces 2010 Fourth Quarter and Full-Year Financial Results." Press release available at http://ir.correctionscorp.com/phoenix.zhtml?c=117983&p=irol-newsArticle&ID=1527174&highlight=.

Crutchfield, Robert D., George S. Bridges, and Susan R. Pitchford. 1994. "Analytical and Aggregation Biases in Analyses of Imprisonment: Reconciling Discrepancies in Studies of Racial Disparity." *Journal of Research in Crime and Delinquency* 31 (2): 166–82.

Davis, Mike. 1995. "Hell Factories in the Field." *Nation*, February 20, 229–34.

Deering, Tara, Tom Alex, and Brianna Blake. 2003. "1 in 3 School Arrests Involved Blacks." *Des Moines Register*, June 17. http://www.uiowa.edu/~nrcfcp/dmcrc/pdf/DM%20Register%206–17-03.pdf.

Demuth, Stephen, and Darrell Steffensmeier. 2004. "The Impact of Gender and Race-Ethnicity on the Pretrial Release Process." *Social Problems* 51 (2): 234 and 237–38.

Devine, John. 1996. *Maximum Security: The Culture of Violence in Inner City Schools*. Chicago: University of Chicago Press.

DeVoe, Jill F., and Sarah Kaffenberger. 2005. *Student Reports of Bullying: Results from the 2001 School Crime Supplement to the National Crime Victimization Survey (NCES 2005–310)*. Washington, DC: US Department of Education, National Center for Education Statistics.

Donahue, Elizabeth, Vincent Schiraldi, and Jason Ziedenberg. 1998. *School House Hype: The School Shootings and the Real Risks Kids Face in America*. Washington, DC: Center for Juvenile and Criminal Justice.

Doster, Adam. 2007. "Correcting the Guards." *American Prospect*, July 2. http://prospect.org/cs/articles?article=correcting_the_guards.

Florida Department of Juvenile Justice. 2011. *Delinquency in Florida's Schools: A Seven Year Study*. Tallahassee, FL: Florida Department of Juvenile Justice. http://www.djj.state.fl.us/docs/research2/2010-11-delinquency-in-schools-analysis.pdf?sfvrsn=0.

Foucault, Michel. 1979. *Discipline and Punish: The Birth of the Prison*. New York: Vintage.

Free, Marvin D. 1997. "The Impact of Federal Sentencing Reforms on African Americans." *Journal of Black Studies* 28:268–86.

Freudenberg, Nick. 2008. "Health Research behind Bars: A Brief Guide to Research in Jails and Prisons." In *Public Health behind Bars: From Prisons to Communities*, edited by Robert Greifinger, 415–33. New York: Springer.

Frost, Natalie A., Judy Greene, and Kay Pranis. 2006. *HARD HIT: The Growth in the Imprisonment of Women, 1977–2004*. New York: Women's Prison Association.

Garland, David. 1990. *Punishment and Modern Society: A Study in Social Theory*. Oxford: Oxford University Press.

———. 2001a. "Introduction." In *Mass Imprisonment: Social Causes and Consequences*, edited by David Garland, 1–3. Thousand Oaks, CA: Sage.

———. 2001b. *The Culture of Control: Crime and Social Order in Contemporary Society*. Chicago: University of Chicago Press.

Ghosh, Palash R. 2006. "Private Prisons Have a Lock on Growth." *Businessweek*, July 5. http://www.business-week.com/print/investor/content/jul2006/pi20060706_849785.htm.

Gilmore, Ruth Wilson. 2007. *Golden Gulag: Prisons, Surplus, Crisis and Opposition in Globalizing California*. Berkeley: University of California Press.

Goldkamp, John S. 1979. *Two Classes of Accused: A Study of Bail and Detention in American Justice*. Cambridge, MA: Ballinger.

Golub, Andrew, Bruce D. Johnson, and Eloise Dunlap. 2007. "The Race/Ethnicity Disparity in Misdemeanor Marijuana Arrests in New York City." *Criminology and Public Policy* 6 (1): 131–64.

Hagan, John. 1974. "Extra-Legal Attributes and Criminal Sentencing: An Assessment of a Sociological Viewpoint." *Law and Society Review* 8:357–83.

———. 1993. "Structural and Cultural Disinvestment and the New Ethnographies of Poverty and Crime." Review of *Streetwise: Race, Class, and Change in an Urban Community*, by Elijah Anderson; *People and Folks: Gangs, Crime and the Underclass in a Rustbelt City*, by John M. Hagedorn; *Going Down to the Barrio: Homeboys and Homegirls in Change*, by Joan W. Moore; and *The Gang as an American Enterprise*, by Felix M. Padilla. *Contemporary Sociology* 22:27–32.

Harlow, Carolyn W. 2003. *Education and Correctional Populations*. Washington, DC: US Department of Justice, Bureau of Justice Statistics.

Harris, David A. 2000. "Driving while Black and Other African-American Crimes: The Continuing Relevance of Race to American Criminal Justice." In *The State of Black America 2000: Blacks in the New Millennium*, edited by Lee A. Daniels. New York: National Urban League.

Hart, Timothy, and Brian A. Reaves. 1999. *Felony Defendants in Large Urban Counties, 1996*. Washington, DC: US Department of Justice, Bureau of Justice Statistics.

Hawkins, David, and Kenneth A. Hardy. 1989. "Black-White Imprisonment Rates: A State-by-State Analysis." *Social Justice* 16:75–95.

Hermann, Robert, E. Single, and J. Boston. 1977. *Counsel for the Poor*. Lexington, MA: Lexington.

Human Rights Watch. 2000. *Punishment and Prejudice: Racial Disparities in the War on Drugs*. New York: Human Rights Watch. http://www.hrw.org/reports/2000/usa/.

Justice Policy Institute. 2012. *Education under Arrest: The Case against Police in Schools*. Washington, DC: Justice Policy Institute.

Katz, Cindi. 2001. "Vagabond Capitalism and the Necessity of Social Reproduction." *Antipode* 33 (4): 708–28.

Kaufman, Philip, Xianglei Chen, Susan P. Choy, Sally A. Ruddy, Amanda K. Miller, Jill K. Fleury, Kathryn A. Chandler, Michael R. Rand, Patsy Klaus, and Michael G. Planty. 2000. *Indicators of School Crime and Safety, 2000*. Washington, DC: US Department of Education and US Department of Justice.

King, Ryan S., and Marc Mauer. 2002. *Distorted Priorities: Drug Offenders in State Prison*. Washington, DC: Sentencing Project.

King, Ryan S., Marc Mauer, and Malcolm Young. 2005. *Incarceration and Crime: A Complex Relationship*. Washington, DC: Sentencing Project.

Lane, Sandra D., Robert A. Rubinstein, Rob Keefe, Noah Webster, Alan Rosenthal, Donald Cibula, and Jesse Dowdell. 2004. "Structural Violence and Racial Disparity in Heterosexual HIV Infection." *Journal of Health Care for the Poor and Underserved* 15 (Aug): 319–35.

Langan, Patrick A. 1985. "Racism on Trial: New Evidence to Explain the Racial Composition of Prisons in the United States." *Journal of Criminal Law and Criminology* 76 (3): 667–83.

Levitt, Steven D. 2004. "Understanding Why Crime Fell in the 1990s: Four Factors That Explain the Decline and Six That Do Not." *Journal of Economic Perspectives* 18 (1): 163–90.

Livingston, Andrea. 2006. *The Condition of Education 2006 in Brief*. Washington, DC: US Department of Education, National Center for Education Statistics.

Mahoney, Barry, Bruce D. Beaudin, John A. Carver III, Daniel B. Ryan, and Richard B. Hoffman. 2001. *Pretrial Services Programs: Responsibilities and Potential*. Washington DC: National Institute of Justice.

Mauer, Marc. 2001. "The Causes and Consequences of Prison Growth in the United States." In *The Culture of Control: Crime and Social Order in Contemporary Society*, edited by David Garland. Chicago: University of Chicago Press.

———. 2006. *The Race to Incarcerate*. New York: New Press.

Mustard, David B. 2001. "Racial, Ethnic, and Gender Disparities in Sentencing: Evidence from the U.S. Federal Courts." *Journal of Law and Economics* 44 (1): 285–314.

Nagel, Mechthild. 2002. "Prisons, Big Business, and Profit: Whither Social Justice?" In *Diversity, Multiculturalism, and Social Justice*, edited by Seth Asumah and Ibipo Johnston-Anumonwo, 361–85. Binghamton, NY: Global.

National Center on Crime and Delinquency. 1998. *1996 National Survey of State Sentencing Structures*. Washington, DC: US Department of Justice, Bureau of Justice Statistics.

National Organization of Blacks in Law Enforcement. 2001. *A NOBLE Perspective: Racial Profiling—A Symptom of Bias-Based Policing*. Alexandria, VA: National Organization of Blacks in Law Enforcement.

Nelson, James F. 1995. *Disparities in Processing Felony Arrests in New York State, 1990–1992*. Albany: New York State Division of Criminal Justice Services, Bureau of Research and Evaluation.

New Jersey Office of the Attorney General. 1999. *Final Report of the State Police Review Team*. Trenton: New Jersey Office of the Attorney General. http://www.state.nj.us/lps/Rpt_ii.pdf.

New York Civil Liberties Union. 2007. *Criminalizing the Classroom: The Over-Policing of New York City Schools*. New York: New York Civil Liberties Union.

New York Civil Liberties Union. 2012. "Stop and Frisk Data" (website). New York: New York Civil Liberties Union. http://www.nyclu.org/issues/racial-justice/stop-and-frisk practices.

New York State Department of Correctional Services. 2010. *Under Custody Report: Profile of the Inmate Population under Custody on January 1, 2010*. Albany: New York State Department of Correctional Services.

New York State Department of Corrections and Community Supervision. 2012. *Under Custody Report: Profile of Incarcerated Offender Population under Custody on January 1, 2012*. Albany: New York State Department of Corrections and Community Supervision.

Orfield, Gary, and Daniel Losen. 2012. "Response to the Release of the 2009–10 Civil Rights Data." *Civil Rights Project* (website). March 8. http://civilrightsproject.ucla.edu/research/k-12-education/civil-rights-data-collection-1/03.08.12-response-to-the-release-of-the-2009-10-civil-rights-data.

Perry, Steve W. 2008. *Justice Expenditure and Employment Extracts, 2006. NCJ 224394*. Washington, DC: US Department of Commerce, Bureau of the Census.

Pew Center on the States. *One in 100: Behind Bars in America 2008*. Washing-ton, DC: The Pew Charitable Trusts.

Phillips, Mary T. 2007. "Bail, Detention and Non-Felony Case Outcomes." In *CJA Research Brief No. 14*. New York: New York Criminal Justice Agency.

Poe-Yamagata, Eileen, and Michael A. Jones. 2000. *And Justice for Some*. Washington, DC: National Center on Crime and Delinquency.

Pope, Carl, and William Feyerherm. 1990. "Minority Status and Juvenile Justice Processing." *Criminal Justice Abstracts* 22:327–36.

Ramirez, Debra, Jack McDevitt, and Amy Farrel. 2000. *A Resource Guide on Racial Profiling Data Collection Systems: Promising Practices and Lessons Learned*. Washington, DC: US Department of Justice.

Rose, Dina R., and Todd R. Clear. 1998. "Incarceration, Social Capital and Crime: Examining the Unintended Consequences of Incarceration." *Criminology* 36 (3): 441–80.

S.B. 1070, 49th Leg., 2nd Reg. Sess. (Ariz. 2010), "Support Our Law Enforcement and Safe Neighborhoods Act," codified at Ariz. Rev. Stat. Ann. §§ 11-1051, 13-1509, 13-3883 (2010).

Sabol, William J., Todd D. Minton, and Paige M. Harrison. 2007. *Prison and Jail Inmates at Midyear 2006*. Washington, DC: US Department of Justice, Bureau of Justice Statistics.

Sabol, William J., Katherine Rosich, Kamala M. Kane, David P. Kirk, and Glenn Dubin. 2002. *The Influences of Truth-in-Sentencing Reforms on Changes in States' Sentencing Practices and Prison Populations*. Washington, DC: Urban Institute.

Sampson, Robert J., and Janet L. Lauritsen. 1997. "Racial and Ethnic Disparities in Crime and Criminal Justice in the United States." *Crime and Justice* 21:311–74.

Santos, Fernanda. 2008. "Plan to Close Prisons Stirs Anxiety in Rural Towns." *New York Times*, January 27.

Schlosser, Eric. 1998. "The Prison-Industrial Complex." *Atlantic Monthly*, December 1, 51–77.

Schmitt, Christopher. 1991. "Plea Bargaining Favors Whites, as Blacks, Hispanics Pay Price." *San Jose Mercury News*, December 8.

Sentencing Project. 2011. *Trends in U.S. Corrections*. Washington, DC: Sentencing Project.

Sexton, George. 1995. *Work in American Prisons: Joint Ventures with the Private Sector*. Washington, DC: US Department of Justice.

Shabazz Sanders, G. Rashad. 2008. "'They Imprison the Whole Population': U.S. and South African Prison Literature and the Emergence of Symbiotic Carcerality, 1900–Present." PhD diss., University of California, Santa Cruz. ProQuest (UMI No. 3317409).

Simon, Jonathan. 2001. "Fear and Loathing in Late Modernity: Reflections on the Cultural Sources of Mass Imprisonment in the United States." In *The Culture of Control: Crime and Social Order in Contemporary Society*, edited by David Garland, 15–27. Chicago: University of Chicago Press.

———. 2007. *Governing through Crime: How the War on Crime Transformed American Democracy and Created a Culture of Fear*. New York: Oxford University Press.

Skiba, Russell J., and Kimberly Knesting. 2002. "Zero Tolerance, Zero Evidence: An Analysis of School Disciplinary Practice." *New Directions for Youth Development: Theory, Practice and Research* 92:17–43.

Skiba, Russell J., and Reece Peterson. 1999. "The Dark Side of Zero Tolerance: Can Punishment Lead to Safe Schools?" *Phi Delta Kappa* 80:372–76.

Solzhenitsyn, Alexander I. 1973. *The Gulag Archipelago, 1918–1956: An Experiment in Literary Investigation*. Vol. 1. New York: Harper and Row.

Spelman, William. 2000. "The Limited Importance of Prison Expansion." In *The Crime Drop in America*, edited by Alfred Blumstein and Joel Wallman, 97–129. Cambridge: Cambridge University Press.

Spohn, Cassia. 2000. "Thirty Years of Sentencing Reform: The Quest for a Racially Neutral Sentencing Process."

In *Criminal Justice 2000*, edited by Julie Horney, 427–50. Rockville, MD: National Institute of Justice.

Stemen Don, Andres Rengifo, and James Wilson. 2006. *Of Fragmentation and Ferment: The Impact of State Sentencing Policies on Incarceration Rates, 1975–2002*. New York: Vera Institute of Justice.

Sullivan, Laura. 2010. "Prison Economics Help Drive Arizona Immigration Law" (radio news story). National Public Radio, October 28. Washing-ton, DC: National Public Radio. http://www.npr.org/2010/10/28/130833741/prison-economics-help-drive-ariz-immigration-law.

Taylor, Jean, Thomas Stanley, Barbara DeFlorio, and Lynn Seekamp. 1972. "An Analysis of Defense Counsel in the Processing of Felony Defendants in San Diego, California." *Denver Law Journal* 49:233–75.

Taxman, Faye S., James Byrne, and April Pattavina. 2005. "Racial Disparity and the Legitimacy of the Criminal Justice System: Exploring Consequences for Deterrence." *Journal of Health Care for the Poor and Underserved* 16 (4): 57–77.

Tonry, Michael H. 1995. *Malign Neglect: Race, Crime and Punishment in America*. New York: Oxford University Press.

Travis, Jeremy, and Sarah Lawrence. 2002. *Beyond the Prison Gates: The State of Parole in America*. Washington, DC: Urban Institute.

Uggen, Christopher, Jeff Manza, and Melissa Thompson. 2006. "Citizenship, Democracy and the Civic Restoration of Criminal Offenders." *Annals of the American Academy* 605:281–310.

US Department of Education. 2000. *Office for Civil Rights Elementary and Secondary School Survey: 2000 National and State Projections*. Washington, DC: US Department of Education, Office for Civil Rights. http://vistademo.beyond2020.com/ocr2000rv30/Table 1 -.

———. 2012. *The Transformed. Civil Rights Data Collection (CRDC): Revealing New Truths about Our Nation's Schools*. Washington, DC: US Department of Education. http://www2.ed.gov/about/offices/list/ocr/. . ./crdc-2012-data-summary.pdf.

US Department of Health and Human Services. 2007. "Results from the 2007 National Survey on Drug Use and Health: National Findings 25." US Department of Health and Human Services, Substance Abuse and Mental Health Services Administration (website). http://www.oas.samhsa.gov/nsduh/2k7nsduh/2k7Results.pdf.

US Department of Justice. 2002. "Trends in Justice Expenditure and Employment, Table 1." Washington, DC: US Department of Justice, Bureau of Justice Statistics. http://www.ojp.usdoj.gov/bjs/data/eetrnd01.wk1.

US Sentencing Commission. 1995. *Special Report to the Congress: Cocaine and Federal Sentencing Policy, 1995.* Washington, DC: US Sentencing Commission.

Wacquant, Loïc. 2001. "Deadly Symbiosis: When Prison and Ghetto Meet and Mesh." *Punishment and Society* 3 (1): 95–134.

———. 2006. *Punishing the Poor: The New Government of Social Insecurity.* Durham, NC: Duke University Press.

Wagner, Peter. 2003. "Rural Areas Have 20% of Population but 60% of New Prisons." *Prison Policy Initiative, Prison Gerrymandering Project* (website). July 28. http://www.prisonersofthecensus.org/news/fact-28-7-2003.html.

Wald, Joanna, and Daniel F. Losen. 2003. *Defining and Redirecting a School-to Prison Pipeline.* San Francisco: Jossey-Bass.

West, Heather C., and William J. Sabol. 2010. *Prisoners in 2009.* Washington, DC: US Department of Justice, Office of Justice Programs, Bureau of Justice Statistics.

Western, Bruce. 2006. *Punishment and Inequality in America.* New York: Russell Sage Foundation.

Western, Bruce, and Katherine Beckett. 1999. "How Unregulated Is the U.S. Labor Market? The Penal System as a Labor Market Institution." *American Journal of Sociology* 104 (4): 1030–60.

Western, Bruce, and Becky Pettit. 2005. "Black-White Wage Inequality, Employment Rates, and Incarceration." *American Journal of Sociology* 111 (2): 553–78.

Western, Bruce, Becky Pettit, and Joshua Guetzkow. 2002. "Black Economic Progress in the Era of Mass Imprisonment." In *Invisible Punishment: The Collateral Consequences of Mass Incarceration,* edited by M. Chesney-Lind and Marc Mauer, 165–90. New York: New Press.

Wicker, Tom. 1975. *Time to Die: The Attica Prison Revolt.* New York: Quadrangle/New York Times Book Company.

Williams, Marian R. 2003. "The Effect of Pretrial Detention on Imprisonment Decisions." *Criminal Justice Review* 28 (2): 299–316.

Wolf, Elaine, and Marsha Weissman. 1996. "Revising Federal Sentencing Policy: Some Consequences of Expanding Eligibility for Alternative Sanctions." *Crime and Delinquency* 42 (2): 192–205.

DISCUSSION QUESTIONS

1. What criticisms does Marsha Weissman level against the American prison system and the "carceral state?" Why does she call the American prison system a "gulag?" What is the "carceral state" to which she refers?

2. According to Weissman, "Mass incarceration has become a uniquely American institution, one that is intimately tied to structural changes in the larger society, both economic and social. Specifically [it is] the most recent iteration of social control of African Americans." Comment on this statement. What does Weissman mean by this assertion? Do you agree or disagree with it?

3. How do arrest, prosecution, sentencing, and incarceration rates vary for Whites and minorities? How have the "war on drugs" and mandatory prison sentencing for drug-related offenses affected these rates?

4. Comment on the following statement: "While crime control defines the public view of the purpose of prisons, mass incarceration is driven by other agendas, including economics and politics." Elaborate on Weissman's argument; what agendas is she talking about? Do you agree or disagree with her? Why or why not?

5. How have public schools become a gateway into the prison system for American youth? Are American school officials, the law enforcement system, and judges incarcerating people who are truly dangerous to society, or are they putting away people who society is angry with, or doesn't know what to do with, people who are identified as nonconformists and/or nuisances?

THE DANGERS OF 'UNDERCLASS' AND OTHER LABELS

The War Against the Poor: The Underclass and Antipoverty Policy

BY **Herbert Gans**

One of America's popular pejorative labels is "slum," which characterizes low-income dwellings and neighborhoods as harmful to their poor occupants and the rest of the community. In the nineteenth century, slums were often faulted for turning the deserving poor into the undeserving poor, but in the twentieth century the causality was sometimes reversed, so that poor people with "slum-dweller hearts" were accused of destroying viable buildings and neighborhoods.

After World War II, "slum" and "slum dweller" as well as "blight" all became more or less official labels when the federal government, egged on by a variety of builder and realty pressure groups, started handing out sizeable sums for the "clearance" of low-income neighborhoods unfortunate enough to fit these terms as they were defined in the 1949 U.S. Housing Act.[2] Although by and large only slums located in areas where private enterprise could build luxury and other profitable housing were torn down, more than a million poor households lost their homes in the next twenty years, with almost nothing done for the people displaced from them.

This chapter is written with that much-told history in mind, in order to suggest that the underclass label—as well as all but the most neutrally formulated behavioral term—can have dangerous effects for the poor and for antipoverty policy. While the emphasis will be on "underclass," the dangers of related labels will be discussed as well.

Labels may be only words, but they are judgmental or normative words, which can stir institutions and individuals to punitive actions. The dangers from such labels are many, but the danger common to all behavioral labels and terms is that they focus on behavior that hides the poverty causing it, and substitutes as its cause moral or cultural or genetic failures.[3]

"THE UNDERCLASS" AS CODE WORD

The term "underclass" has developed an attention-getting power that constitutes its first danger. The word has a technical aura that enables it to serve as a euphemism or code word to be used for labeling.[4] Users of the label can thus hide their disapproval of the poor behind an impressively academic term. "Underclass" has also become morally ambiguous, and as it is often left undefined, people can understand it in any way they choose, including as a label.

Because "underclass" is a code word that places some of the poor *under* society and implies that they are not or should not be *in* society, users of the term can therefore favor excluding them from the rest of society without saying so.[5] Once whites thought of slaves, "primitives," and wartime enemies as the inhuman "other," but placing some people under society may not be altogether different.[6]

A subtler yet in some ways more insidious version of the exclusionary mechanism is the use of "underclass" as a synonym for the poor, deserving and undeserving. While not excluding anyone from society, it increases the social distance of the poor from everyone else. This distance is increased further by the contemporary tendency of elected officials and journalists to rename and upgrade the working class as the lower middle class—or even the middle class.

Because "underclass" is also used as a racial and even ethnic code word, it is a convenient device for hiding antiblack or anti-Latino feelings. As such a code word, "underclass" accommodates contemporary taboos against overt prejudice, not to mention hate speech. Such taboos sometimes paper over—and even repress—racial antagonisms that people do not want to express openly.

Ironically, the racial code word also hides the existence of very poor whites who suffer from many of the same problems as poor blacks. When used as a racial term, "underclass" blurs the extent to which the troubles of whites and blacks alike are generated by the economy and by classism or class discrimination and require class-based as well as race-based solutions.

Like other code words, "underclass" may interfere with public discussion. Disapproval of the actions of others is part of democracy, but code words make covert what needs to be overt in order for the disapproval to be questioned and debated. If openly critical terms such as "bums" and "pauper" were still in use, and if umbrella terms such as "underclass" were replaced with specific ones such as "beggars" or "welfare dependents," upset citizens could indicate clearly the faults of which they want to accuse poor people. In that case, public discussion might be able to deal more openly with the feelings the more fortunate classes hold about the poor, the actual facts about the poor, and the policy issues having to do with poverty and poverty-related behavior.

THE FLEXIBILITY OF THE LABEL

Terms and labels undergo broadening in order to adapt them for use in varying conditions. Broadening also makes labels flexible so that they can be used to stigmatize new populations, or accuse already targeted ones of new failures.

One source of harm to such populations is flexible *meaning*, which stems from the vagueness of a new word, the lack of an agreed-upon definition for it. Since Oscar Lewis once identified nearly sixty-five "traits" for his culture of poverty, there is apt precedent for the flexibility of the underclass label that replaced Lewis's term. Flexibility becomes more harmful when pejorative prefixes can be added to otherwise descriptively used terms; for example, a female welfare recipient can also be described as a member of a permanent underclass, which suggests that she is incapable of ever escaping welfare. An underclass of young people becomes considerably more threatening when it is called "feral," and even worse is the idea of a biological underclass, which implies a genetic and thus permanent inferiority of a group of people whom public policy can render harmless only by sterilizing, imprisoning, or killing them.

Another serious danger follows from the flexibility of *subjects*: the freedom of anyone with labeling power to add further populations to the underclass, and to do so without being accountable to anyone. The poor cannot, after all, afford to bring libel and slander suits. If tenants of public housing are also assigned to the underclass, they are even more stigmatized than when they are coming from "the projects." Illegal immigrants who are refugees from a country not favored by the State Department or the Immigration and Naturalization Service are more likely candidates for public harassment or deportation if their native-born neighbors decide that their behavior marks them as members of the underclass. That they may be doing work that no one else will do or collecting entitlements for which they have paid their share of taxes becomes irrelevant once they have been assigned the label.

THE REIFICATION OF THE LABEL

A further source of danger is the reification of the label, which takes place when a definition is awarded the gift of life and label users believe there to be an actually existing and homogeneous underclass that is composed of whatever poor people are currently defined as underclass. Reification, which turns a definition into an actual set of people, hides the reality that the underclass is an imagined group that has been constructed in the minds of its definers. Once a stigmatized label is reified, however, visible signs to identify it are sure to be demanded sooner or later, and then invented, so that people bearing the signs can be harassed more easily.

Furthermore, once the signs are in place so that imagined groups can be made actual, the labels run the danger of being treated as causal mechanisms. As a result, the better-off classes may decide that being in the underclass is a cause of becoming homeless or turning to street crime. Homelessness then becomes a symptom of underclass membership, with the additional danger of the hidden policy implication: that the elimination of the underclass would end homelessness, thereby avoiding the need for affordable housing or for jobs and income grants for the homeless.

Even purely descriptive terms referring to actual people, such as "welfare recipients," can be reified and turned into causal labels. People may thus persuade themselves to believe that being on welfare is a cause of poverty, or of single-parent families. Once so persuaded, they can propose to eliminate both effects by ending welfare, and without appearing to be inhumane—which is what conservative politicians running for office, and the intellectuals supporting them, have been doing since the early 1990s. They ignore the fact that in the real world the causal arrow goes in the other direction, but they achieve their political aim, even if they also harm poor mothers and their children.

Since popular causal thinking is almost always moral as well as empirical, the reification of a label like "the underclass" usually leads to the assignment of *moral* causality. If the underclass is the cause of behavior that deviates from mainstream norms, the solution is moral condemnation, behavioral modification, or punishment by the elimination of financial aid. Thus people are blamed who are more often than not victims instead of perpetrators, which ignores the empirical causes, say, of street crime, and interferes with the development of effective anticrime policy. Blaming people may allow blamers to feel better by blowing off the steam of righteous (and in the case of crime, perfectly justified) indignation, but even justified blaming does not constitute or lead to policy for ending street crime.[7]

A scholarly form of reification can be carried out with labels that are also scientific terms, so that the former are confused with the latter and thus obtain the legitimacy that accompanies scientific concepts. Conversely, the moral opprobrium placed on the labeled allows social scientists either to incorporate overt biases in their concepts or to relax their detachment and in the process turn scientific concepts into little more than operationalized labels.

A case in point is the operational definition of "the underclass" by Erol Ricketts and Isabel Sawhill, which has been widely used by government, scholars, and in simplified form even by popular writers.[8] The two social scientists argue that the underclass consists of four populations: "high school dropouts," "prime-age males not regularly attached to the labor force," welfare recipients, and "female heads."[9] Ricketts and Sawhill identify these populations as manifesting "underclass behaviors," or "dysfunctional behaviors," which they believe to be "at variance with those of mainstream populations."[10]

The two authors indicate that they can "remain agnostic about the fundamental causes of these behaviors."[11] Nonetheless, they actually adopt an implicit moral causality, because in defining the underclass as "people whose behavior departs from (mainstream) norms" and remaining silent about causality, they imply that the behaviors result from the violations of these values.[12]

Ricketts and Sawhill provide no evidence, however, that the four behaviors in question are actually the result

of norm violation. More important, their operational definition does not consider other causal explanations of the same behavior. No doubt some poor young people drop out of school because they reject mainstream norms for education, but Ricketts and Sawhill omit those who drop out because they have to go to work to support their families, or because they feel that their future in the job market is nil, as well as the youngsters who are forced out by school administrators and who should be called "pushouts."[13]

Likewise, in addition to the "prime-age males" Ricketts and Sawhill believe to be jobless because they do not want to work, some of these men reject being targeted for a career of dead-end jobs, and others, most in fact, are jobless because there are no jobs for them. Indeed, the irony of the Ricketts-Sawhill definition is that when an employer goes out of business, workers who may previously have been praised as working poor but now cannot find other jobs are then banished to the underclass.

Poor mothers go on welfare for a variety of reasons. Some are working mothers who need Medicaid for their children and cannot get health benefits from their employers. Female family heads are often single because jobless men make poor breadwinners, not because they question the desirability of mainstream marriage norms.[14]

If I read the two authors correctly, they are conducting essentially normative analyses of the four types of underclass people they have defined, even if they may not have intended to be normative. Thus, the measures they have chosen to operationalize their definitions bear some resemblance to popular pejorative labels that condemn rather than understand behavior.[15] Conversely, Ricketts and Sawhill do not appear to consider the possibility that the failure of the mainstream economy is what prevents people from achieving the norms they are setting for the poor.

As a result, the two authors make no provision for data that measure the failures of the mainstream economy, and they do not include—or operationalize—a good deal of other information. For example, they could count home, school, and neighborhood conditions that interfere with or discourage learning, and the economic conditions that cause the disappearance of jobs and frustrate the desire for work. In addition, they might obtain information on job availability for jobless prime-age males, as well as for women on welfare—just to mention some of the relevant data that are publicly available. Until they include such data, their definition and operationalization of "underclass" are scientific only because and to the extent that their counting procedures observe the rules of science.[16]

A different approach to the indiscriminate mixing of science and labeling, and to the reification of stereotypes, emerged in some proposals in the late 1980s to measure underclass status by poor people's answers to attitude questions: on their willingness to plan ahead, for example. Such attitude data could be found in the widely used Panel Survey of Income Dynamics. This type of question assumes not only that people should plan ahead, but that their failure to do so reflects their unwillingness, rather than their inability, to plan ahead, which has been documented in many empirical studies. Nonetheless, people whose poverty prevented them from planning ahead and who answered honestly that they did not so plan, would have been assigned a stigmatizing label—merely on the basis of their response to superficial and general questions.[17] Fortunately, this approach to "measuring" the underclass appears not to have been used so far by anyone in an influential position.

A final reification is spatial, an approach in which behavioral labels are applied to census tracts to produce "underclass areas." Such areas derive from statistical artifacts invented by the U.S. Bureau of the Census. The bureau developed the concept of "extreme poverty areas" for those places in which at least 40 percent of the people were poor.[18] While this is inaccurate enough—especially for the 60 percent not poor—Ricketts and Sawhill subsequently identified "underclass areas," in which the proportion of people exhibiting all four of their behavioral indicators for being in the underclass was "one standard deviation above the mean *for the country as a whole*."[19] The two authors did not explain why they chose this measure, even though poverty is not dispersed through the country as a whole but is concentrated in the cities of the northeast, midwest, and south, the latter being also the location of the most severe rural poverty.

Most people lack the methodological skills of social scientists, and do not see the assumptions that underlie the approaches to underclass counting. Once word gets out that social scientists have identified some areas as underclass areas, however, these neighborhoods can easily be stigmatized, the population labeled accordingly and accused of whatever local meanings the term "underclass" may have acquired.[20]

When areas become known as underclass areas, local governments and commercial enterprises obtain legitimation to withdraw or not provide facilities and services that could ameliorate the poverty of the area's inhabitants. Labeling areas as underclass can also encourage governments to choose them as locations for excess numbers of homeless shelters, drug treatment centers, and other facilities that serve the very poor and that are therefore rejected by other neighborhoods.[21]

In fact, "underclass area" is basically a current version of the old label "slum," which also treated indicators of poverty as behavioral failures. In the affluent economy of the post-World War II era, similar defining and subsequent counting activities were used to justify "slum clearance," and the displacement of poor people for subsidized housing for the affluent. And as in all labeling, the poor people who are labeled are left to fend for themselves.

THE DANGERS OF THE UMBRELLA EFFECT

Since "underclass" is an umbrella label that can include in its definition all the various behavioral and moral faults that label-makers and users choose to associate with it, two further dangers accrue to those it labels.

The sheer breadth of the umbrella label seems to attract alarmist writers who magnify the many kinds of moral and behavioral harmfulness attributed to people it names. A correlate of the umbrella effect is amnesia on the part of writers about the extreme and usually persistent poverty of the labeled. Thus, the more widely people believe in the validity of the underclass label, and the broader its umbrella becomes, the more likely it is that political conditions will not allow for reinstituting effective antipoverty policy. If the underclass is dangerous, and dangerous in so many different ways, it follows that the government's responsibility is to beef up the police, increase the punishments courts can demand, and create other punitive agencies that try to protect the rest of society from this dangerous class.

Umbrella labels also do harm when they lump into a single term a variety of diverse people with different problems.[22] This ignores the reality that the people who are assigned the underclass label have in common only that their actual or imagined behaviors upset the mainstream population, or the politicians who claim to speak in its name. Using this single characteristic to classify people under one label can be disastrous, especially if politicians and voters should ever start talking about comprehensive "underclass policies," or what Christopher Jencks has called "meta solutions."[23] For one thing, many of the people who are tagged with the label have not even deviated from mainstream norms, and yet others have done nothing illegal. An underclass policy would thus be a drastic violation of civil rights and civil liberties.

At this writing, electioneering politicians as well as angry voters still remain content with policies that harm the people who bear specific labels, such as welfare recipients, illegal immigrants, and the homeless. In the past, however, the makers of earlier umbrella labels have proposed extremely drastic policies. In 1912, Henry Goddard suggested dealing with the feebleminded by "unsexing ... removing, from the male and female, the necessary organs for procreation." Realizing that there would be strong popular opposition both to castration and ovariectomies, he proposed instead that the next best solution was "segregation and colonization" of the feebleminded.[24] A few decades earlier, Charles Booth had offered the same solution for an equivalent category of poor people, and not long before he was forced to resign as vice president of the United States in 1974, Spiro Agnew suggested that poor people accused of behavioral shortcomings should be rehoused in rural new towns built far away from existing cities and suburbs.

Even a thoughtful underclass policy would be dangerous, because the people forced under the underclass umbrella suffer from different kinds of poverty and, in some cases, poverty-related problems, which may require different solutions. Reducing poverty for able-bodied workers requires labor market policy change; reducing it for people who cannot work calls for a humane income grant program. Enabling and encouraging young people to stay in school requires different policies than the elimination of homelessness, and ending substance abuse or street crime demand yet others. Labelers or experts who claim one policy can do it all are simply wrong.

THE HUMAN DANGERS OF LABELING

Most immediately, the underclass label poses a danger for poor people in that the agencies with which they must deal can hurt clients who are so labeled.[25] For one thing, agencies for the poor sometimes build labels into their operating procedures and apply them to all of their clients. As a result, either evidence about actual clients is not collected, or the label is assumed to fit regardless of evidence to the contrary. Agencies responsible for public safety typically resort to this procedure as a crime prevention or deterrence measure, especially when those labeled have little legal or

political power. For example, in 1993, the Denver police department compiled a roster of suspected gang members based on "clothing choices," "flashing of gang signals," or associating with known gang members. The list included two-thirds of the city's young black men, of whom only a small percentage were actual gang members.[26]

Labeling also creates direct punitive effects of several kinds. Bruce Link's studies of people labeled as mentally ill have found that the labeling act itself can lead to depression and demoralization, which prevent those labeled from being at their best in job interviews and other competitive situations.[27] Likewise, when poor youngsters who hang out on street corners are treated as "loiterers," they may end up with an arrest record that hurts them in later life—which is probably why middle-class teenagers who also hang out are rarely accused of loitering.

Some effects of labels are felt even earlier in children's lives. Teachers treat students differently if they think they come from broken homes.[28] A long-term study of working-class London has found that labeling effects may even be intergenerational. Labeling of parents as delinquent makes it more likely that their children will also be labeled, adding to the numbers in both generations who are accused of delinquent or criminal behavior.[29]

Sometimes the effect of labeling is more indirect: agencies cut off opportunities and the label turns into a self-fulfilling prophecy. When teachers label low-income or very dark-skinned students as unable to learn, they may reduce their efforts to teach them—often unintentionally, but even so students then become less able to learn. If poor youngsters accused of loitering are assumed to have grown up without the self-control thought to be supplied by male supervision, they may be harassed—sometimes to tease and entrap them into an angry response. The arrests and arrest records that inevitably follow may deprive youngsters from fatherless families of legal job opportunities, and help force them into delinquent ones. In all these cases, the self-fulfilling prophecy is used to declare the labeled guilty without evidence of misconduct.

Another variation of the entrapment process takes place in jails. John Irwin's study of San Francisco courts and jails reports that these sometimes punished defendants whether they were guilty or not, and adds that "the experience of harsh and unfairly delivered punishment frequently enrages or embitters defendants and makes it easier for them to reject the values of those who have dealt with them in this way."[30] In this instance, as in many of the other instances when the labels are applied by penal institutions, the labeled are not necessarily "passive innocents," as Hagan and Palloni put it.[31] Instead, labeling sometimes generates reactions, both on the part of the police and of those they arrest, that push both sides over the edge.

The direct and indirect effects of labeling even hurt the poor in seeking help, because when they evoke labels in the minds of service suppliers they may be given inferior service, the wrong service, or none at all. Services for the labeled are normally underfunded to begin with and service suppliers are frequently overworked, so that the agencies from which the poor seek help must operate under more or less permanent triage conditions. One way of deciding who will be sacrificed in triage decisions is to assume that most clients cheat, use every contact with them to determine whether they are cheating, and exclude those who can be suspected of cheating. Since clients are of lower status than service suppliers and lack any power or influence over them, the suppliers can also vent their own status frustrations on clients. An arbitrary denial of services to clients not only relieves such frustrations but also enables suppliers to make the needed triage choices. For that reason alone, poor clients who object to being mistreated are usually the first to be declared ineligible for help.

Labeling clients as cheaters encourages service suppliers to distrust them, and that distrust is increased if the suppliers fear revenge, particularly violent revenge, from these clients. Consequently, suppliers hug the rules more tightly, making no leeway in individual cases, and even punishing colleagues who bend the rules in trying to help clients. When clients, who presumably come with prejudices of their own about agency staffs, develop distrust of the staff, a spiraling effect of mutual distrust and fear is set up. This creates data to justify labeling on both sides. The mutual distrust also encourages the exchange of violence, or the preemptive strikes of staff members who fear violence from angry clients.[32]

Admittedly, labeling of clients is only a small part of staff-client misunderstandings and client mistreatment. The previously noted lack of funds and staff, the stresses of operating in stigmatized agencies and with stigmatized clients, normal bureaucratic rules that always put the demands of the agency and its staff ahead of the needs of clients, as well as differences of class and race between staff and clients, wreak their own cumulative havoc.

The added role of labeling in reducing services is particularly serious for poor people who live at the edge of homelessness or starvation or ill health. Yet another cause for the reduction or ending of already minimal services may push them over the edge, into the streets or an emergency clinic, into chronic illness or permanent disability, or into street crime.

Nevertheless, agencies sometimes actively discourage labeled people from escaping their stigmatized status. Liebow reports a dramatic but typical incident from a women's shelter: two women were trying to escape homelessness by taking second jobs, which they were forced to give up in order to attend obligatory but aimless night meetings so as to retain their beds in the shelter.[33] In unlabeled populations, taking second jobs would have been rewarded as upward mobility; among labeled ones it is identified as evasion of agency rules or flouting of service supplier authority, as well as evidence of the client troublemaking that is often associated with the label.

Consequently, one major ingredient in successful efforts to help the labeled poor is to remove the label. For example, scattered site housing studies suggest that such housing is successful in changing the lives of the rehoused when their origins and backgrounds are kept from their new neighbors, so that these cannot react to pejorative labels about slum dwellers.[34]

The labels that have produced these effects are not created solely from overheated mainstream fears or imaginations. Like all stereotypes, such labels are built around a small core of truth, or apply "to a few bad apples," as lay psychology puts it. Labeling, however, punishes not only the bad apples but everybody in the population to whom the label is applied. By labeling poor young black males as potential street criminals, for example, the white and black populations fearful of being attacked may feel that they protect themselves, but at the cost of hurting and antagonizing the large majority of poor young black males who are innocent. Inevitably, however, a proportion of the innocent will react angrily to the label, and find ways of getting even with those who have labeled them. In the end, then, everyone loses, the label users as well as the labeled.

Nonetheless, labeling is only a by-product of a larger structural process that cannot be ignored. In any population that lacks enough legitimate opportunities, illegitimate ones will be created and someone will take them. When the jobs for which the poor are eligible pay such a low wage that even some of the employed will turn to drug selling or other crime to increase their incomes, the labeling process is set in motion that finally hurts many more people, poor and nonpoor, whether or not they are guilty or innocent. Still, the real guilt has to be laid at the door of the employers that pay insufficient wages and the market conditions that may give some of them little other choice.

ENDNOTES

1. This chapter is a drastically revised version of my "Deconstructing the Underclass: The Term's Dangers as a Planning Concept," *Journal of the American Planning Association* 52 (Summer 1990): 271–77; and chapter 21 of my *People, Plans and Policies* (New York: Columbia University Press, 1991, 1994). I am indebted to Michael B. Katz and Sharon Zukin for comments on these versions, and to the long list of scholars who wrote about the dangers of the term "underclass" before I did, among them Robert B. Hill, Richard McGahey, Jewelle T. Gibbs, and Michael B. Katz.

2. They deserve to be called official labels because the criteria by which federal government described slums and blight had as much to do with the undesirability of their poor inhabitants as with the condition of the housing in which they lived.

3. This is of course one of the virtues of labels for cultural and political conservatives who prefer not to acknowledge the existence of poverty.

4. Irving Lewis Allen distinguishes between euphemisms, which are innocently substituted for labels, and code words, which are intentional substitutes, but empirical researchers will have to discover whether people are willing to discuss the intent involved in Allen's distinction (Irving Lewis Allen, *Unkind Words: Ethnic Languages from Redskin to WASP* [New York: Bergin and Garvey, 1990], chap. 8).

5. European analysts have developed the phrase "social exclusion" to describe both economically excluded native-born people and immigrants who are excluded on ethnic, racial, or citizenship grounds. For a comprehensive analysis, see Hilary Silvery "Social Exclusion and Social Solidarity: Three Paradigms" (Geneva: International Institute for Labour Studies, DP/69,1994).

   While the European phrase is a scholarly concept used for studies concerned with ending exclusion, it is possible to imagine redefinitions, particularly in America, in which the phrase becomes a popular label to condemn the excluded.

6. The prefix "under-" has often been pejorative in America, as in "underhanded," "underworld," and even the untranslated but occasionally used *Untermensch.*

7. Blaming poor people may help lead to their imprisonment, since prisons exist in part to isolate the blamed, but imprisonment does not seem to be an effective policy against street crime either.

8. Erol R. Ricketts and Isabel V. Sawhill, "Defining and Measuring the Underclass," *Journal of Policy Analysis and Management* 7, no. 2 (1988): 316–22.

9. Welfare recipients are a "proxy for women who are not married and not working," while female heads are a proxy for "early child-bearing, risk of dependency, and the possible long-term adverse consequences of children being raised by only one parent." This and all other quotes are from Ricketts and Sawhill, "Defining and Measuring the Underclass," p. 321.

10. Ibid., p. 318. Actually, their quartet of underclass populations consists of people they deem to vary from the mainstream who have also been studied already by the U.S. government. The two authors pointed out that their definition was "heavily influenced by the availability of data," indicating that they would have added street crime and drug use if data had been available (pp. 317, 321).

11. Ibid., p. 318. Isabel Sawhill's "The Underclass: An Overview," *Public Interest* 96 (Summer 1989): 3–15, referred to in chap. 2, suggests that she was not agnostic about causes in a later publication.

12. Ricketts and Sawhill, "Defining and Measuring the Underclass," p. 320. The authors sometimes seem to shift ground from mainstream behavior to mainstream expectations, arguing that "in American society, it is *expected* that children will attend school and delay parenthood until at least age 18 ... work at a regular job ... females will either work or marry ... and that everyone will be law abiding" (p. 319–20, emphasis added). The meaning of this statement depends in part on the definition of "expectations," but if the authors mean aspirations, then the people they call underclass generally share them, as many studies have shown.

13. See, for example, Michelle Fine, *Framing Dropouts: Notes on the Politics of an Urban High School* (Albany: State University of New York Press, 1988), esp. chap. 3.

14. These are all explanations from the current poverty literature, and most can be found in William Julius Wilson's previously mentioned *Truly Disadvantaged* (William Julius Wilson, *The Truly Disadvantaged: The Inner City, the Underclass, and Public Policy* [Chicago: University of Chicago Press, 1987]).

15. The similarity of the authors' analysis to labeling is exemplified by generalizations for which they present no data. They suggest, for example, that an unemployed prime-age male in an underclass area is likely to be engaged in

"hustling." Ricketts and Sawhill, "Defining and Measuring the Underclass," p. 320.

16. For more detailed and somewhat different critiques of the Ricketts-Sawhill definition, see Mark A. Hughes, "Concentrated Deviance and the 'Underclass' Hypothesis," *Journal of Policy Analysis and Management* 8, no. 2 (1989): 274–82; and Robert Aponte, "Definitions of the Underclass: A Critical Analysis," and Walter W. Stafford and Joyce Ladner, "Political Dimensions of the Underclass Concept," in Herbert J. Gans, ed., *Sociology in America* (Newbury Park, Calif.: Sage, 1990), chaps. 8, 9.

17. For the argument on the utility of attitude studies, see Kathleen J. Pottick, "Testing the Underclass Concept by Surveying Attitudes and Behavior," *Journal of Sociology and Social Welfare* 17 (Dec. 1990): 117–25.

18. The census does not, however, identify "extreme wealth areas," since the privacy of the rich is politically and otherwise privileged.

19. Ricketts and Sawhill, "Defining and Measuring the Underclass," p. 321 (emphasis added).

20. William Julius Wilson provides an illustration of this process in writing about the fate of his analysis of the concentration of the poor; pointing out that "arguments in the popular media tended to emphasize a crystallization of a ghetto culture of poverty once black middle-class self-consciously imposed cultural constraints on lower-class culture were removed." Wilson, *The Truly Disadvantaged*, p. 55.

21. Camilo J. Vergara, *The New American Slum* (New Brunswick, N.J.: Rutgers University Press, 1995), forthcoming.

22. William Kornblum, "Lumping the Poor: What *Is* the Underclass?" *Dissent* (Sept. 1984): 295–302.

23. Christopher Jencks, *Rethinking Social Policy: Races Poverty and the Underclass* (Cambridge, Mass.: Harvard University Press, 1992), p. 202.

24. Henry H. Goddard, *The Kallikak Family* (New York: Macmillan, 1912), pp. 105–9, quotes at pp. 105, 107.

25. Such labeling is class-blind; it can hurt rich or poor; and it need not even be pejorative in intent. See, for instance, "A Disabilities Program that Got Out of Hand," *New York Times*, Apr. 8, 1994, pp. Al, B6, which describes the effects of special education experts labeling preschool children at one of New York City's most prestigious private schools.

26. Dirk Johnson, "Two of Three Young Black Men in Denver Listed by Police as Suspected Gangsters," *New York Times*, Dec. 11, 1993, p. B8. This procedure is akin to the one many police department "red squads" once used to list alleged communists.

27. Bruce Link, "Understanding Labeling Effects in the Area of Mental Disorders: An Assessment of the Effects of Expectations of Rejection," *American Sociological Review* 52 (Feb. 1987): 96–112.

28. Nan M. Astone and Sarah McLanahan, "Family Structure and High School Completion" (Madison, Wisconsin: Institute for Research on Poverty, discussion paper 905–9, 1989).

29. John Hagan and Alberto Palloni, "The Social Reproduction of a Criminal Class in Working-Class London," *American Journal of Sociology* 96 (Sept. 1990): 265–99.

30. John Irwin, *The Jail: Managing the Underclass in American Society* (Berkeley: University of California Press, 1985), p. 84. The book, which refers to the underclass only in the title, is full of examples of the role of labeling in creating jail populations and repeaters.

31. Hagan and Palloni, "Social Reproduction," p. 293.

32. For an incisive and data-filled analysis of staff-client interactions, see Elliot Liebow, *Tell Them Who I Am: The Lives of Homeless Women* (New York: Free Press, 1993), chap. 4.

33. Ibid., pp. 139–40.

34. William K. Stevens, "Scattered Low Cost Housing Offers Renewed Hope to Poor and Minorities," *New York Times*, Sept. 18, 1988, p. B6.

35. The demanded goods and services the underclass supplies to the better-off are described in my discussion of the functions of the undeserving poor in chap. 4.

DISCUSSION QUESTIONS

1. What is wrong with using terms such as "slum," "slum-dweller," "blight," and "underclass?" In what way are such labels dangerous? What does Herbert Gans mean when he calls such terms "code words?"

2. Gans writes that it is dangerous "when terms such as "underclass," or even "purely descriptive terms" such as "welfare recipient" are "reified and turned into causal labels." What does he mean by this? Do you agree or disagree with him?

3. In what way is "underclass" an "umbrella label?" What other umbrella labels can you think of? How are such terms dangerous?

Other Multiculturalisms

I'M NOT CRIPPLED; I'M HANDICAPPED

Crises of Identifying: Negotiating and
Mediating Race, Gender, and Disability
within Family and Schools

BY **Dymaneke D. Mitchell**

INTRODUCTION: MEETING KIM

Kim is a divorced African American female with cerebral palsy. She is also a disability activist with a master's degree in political administration.

I met Kim and Starbucks 311 at the same time. When I first met this dynamic twosome, they exuded a level of confidence and independence that I envied. In May of 2006, I noticed them in the audience while I was presenting a paper in Washington, DC. We were all attending the annual conference of the same disability studies organization where I met King, Black Her Story, and José. After the paper session, Starbucks 311 approached me and told me how much she enjoyed the paper I presented, which critiqued the essentialization disability identity and disability culture. During this encounter, she introduced me to Kim.

KIM: CRISES OF IDENTIFYING WITHIN THE FAMILY

Kim was born on January 14, 1970. She was her mother's first and only child. I had also met Kim's mother, who was a disability activist, on several occasions. From Kim's narrative, I got a better sense of the dynamic relationship that existed between Kim and her mom. Unfortunately, her relationship with her father and his family was strained and distant.

> I said before that my mom raised me as a single parent and so I didn't see my dad all too often. But when I did I guess he never—I just never—he was frustrated with me because of my disability.
>
> I had lots of struggles about my dad and what he means in my life. Besides in addition to me having a disability, him not accepting that, I

guess it was combined with him not wanting to be responsible for me or responsible to my mom for me. And so it wasn't only my disability.

> For decades really, I tried to have a relationship with him and with his side of the family. My grandmother on his side is still alive and I have two half-brothers and I have aunts. I have a large family on his side. And I tried to reach out to them until I got married—I tried everything for them to react positively towards me, but it didn't work.

It seemed that Kim's father and his family were experiencing crises of identifying in relation to her disability. Their refusal to negotiate and mediate their crises resulted in Kim never developing a relationship with her paternal family members.

But like José's mother, from the moment she was born, Kim's mother was very diligent about establishing the quality of her life despite the negative reactions from family members around her.

> She accepted it. It was more of other people in our family not accepting me. But she accepted it.
>
> My mom had a major role in how I live my life now. She didn't hold me back. She didn't put ideas in my head like I couldn't do that because I have a disability. If I wanted to do something and I couldn't do it, then she would find a way for me to do it another way or hire someone to help me do it. Yeah.
>
> She was always up front with me. I remember when I was about three or four, I would play in the neighborhood and some kids that I knew

played with they would say, *You're crippled.* And I say, *I'm not crippled; I'm handicapped.* And this was back in the early '70s so the word disability wasn't known yet.

But I guess she always instilled in me, yes, I have a disability. But that's not all you are. Use your mind.

The way Kim's mother identified with her disability influenced the way Kim would develop identification with her disability. By helping her understand from a young age that, although she had a disability, she was not her disability, Kim's mother provided her with the tools to reject negative stereotypes about who or what she was. Kim learned to use her intellect and independence as means for negotiating and mediating her interactions and lived experiences.

I asked Kim to discuss ways her mother's approach to her disability influenced the way she perceived herself.

If I was bad or acting spoiled, you know, some parents would give in because the child has a disability and she can't help that. But my mother didn't ever give in because I had a disability. In fact she was tougher.

I remember coming home from school ... I got off the bus and my mother was walking back to our apartment and she was mad at me. She said, *Why do you let someone put your shoes on the wrong feet? Your shoes are on the wrong feet. Don't you know your left from your right?*

I can't dress myself but she blamed me for having my shoes on the wrong feet. She said you should be able to tell people that it's not on right.

And she tells a story of my first physical therapist when I was—remember I told you I started when I was eight months old, and this therapist took my mom aside because my mom was 22 at the time, and she said whatever you do don't spoil her because she has a disability. And I don't know if I'm thankful for my physical therapist or not. Sometimes I wanted to be spoiled.

I think I had a degree of personal responsibility, just you're responsible; and sometimes I think I'm a Republican because I think hey, it's my fault. Or I'm hard on other people because I think if they didn't get what they want it's their fault because they didn't do such and such. Sometimes I think I'm too hard on people.

This excerpt revealed the impact of a paraprofessional on informing how people with disabilities are constructed. By focusing on Kim as a person, the physical therapist was instrumental in influencing how Kim's mother proceeded in challenging prevalent essentialist discourses concerning her disability. Her mother's persistence in developing a sense of independence in Kim enabled her to develop a strong will that affected her intrapersonal and interpersonal interactions. Although she needed assistance from paraprofessionals, Kim understood that this was just a requirement of her disability.

However, Kim had interactions with other family members were not as supportive and positive.

Well, my great aunt and my cousins. They still—well, all my great aunts are deceased now but they're all treating me like a baby. Even when I got to be a teenager or young adult, I was always a baby.

They just talk to me very juvenile and talk about what boyfriends I had, just kidding, like just joking around. *Who's your boyfriend now?* You know? At some point that should be inappropriate.

I guess I gave into it because I was too afraid to stand up for myself. So I would act—they made me feel like I needed to act that age that they were treating me.

Unfortunately, her family participated in perpetuating and reiterating essentiality discourses regarding Kim's disability. It was interactions and experiences like these within familial contexts that instigated crises of identifying for Kim concerning her race.

I asked Kim if she had any thoughts about why these family members treated her the way they did, especially when she demonstrated that she was just as capable as they were if not more so.

Well, I mean they thought that I had a disability but they said that a person with a disability can't grow up to be an adult, to be an adolescent. They had views of people with a disability, handicapped people as being a perpetual baby who need to be taken care of.

Yeah. I think they're not used to people with disabilities; and we're used to taking care of our own; we're forced to take care of our own even in times of slavery—taking care of whether you had disability or not. And since you couldn't work out in the fields the best thing for you to do is to treat you like a baby so you wouldn't be angry at them.

I could be wrong but that's my theory.

It was interesting that Kim associated her family's attitudes about her with slavery. It provided insight into how perceptions of slaves with disabilities as unproductive and useless by their family and owners may still influence interactions between Black families and family members with disabilities. Treating her like she was infantile could be a result of Kim's family perceiving her needs for services and assistance as pitiful and naïve. Apparently, requiring assistance was misconstrued as a sign of helplessness or weakness.

However, there were several family members that Kim had a positive relationship with. For instance, she had a very close relationship with her grandmother.

My grandmother on my mother's side, my maternal grandmother, I remember stories of her trying to get me to feed myself.

She wanted me to feed myself but I never felt that I wasn't good enough. I never felt that way.

The toys that she gave me, one time she— probably because I asked for it—but she got me a miniature golf set. And you know with my hands, my mother would never buy me that because I would be dangerous with that in my hands. But she got it for me. She gave it to me but my mom goes, *What are you crazy?*

I had two aunts; and the other one, she's great. She is generous. She's like my mother. She always treated me age appropriate. She never treated me like a baby when I was a child.

Kim showed how her grandmother did not allow her interactions with Kim to be defined by social and cultural constructions about what she was capable or incapable of. This motivated Kim to challenge herself by partaking of or participating in things that she would have been discouraged from doing.

Kim's mother was also influential in her identification development as an attractive sexual being. Kim was very open about discussing her sexuality and having boyfriends.

When I was very young [five years old], my mother started teaching me about the birds and bees. She has a book that she read to me about how babies are made; and not only do they go

for humans. I think humans were the last ones; but it went through chickens; it went through dogs; and they got to humans.

Yeah. I guess she wanted to be very honest with me. She encouraged me to explore my sexuality.

But it's funny because when I got to be 11 or 12, even though she told me about the birds and the bees, she forgot. She left out the point that you had to be naked.

These experiences allowed Kim to develop a positive identification with herself as a sexual being. This identification was important, because along with being treated like babies, people with disabilities are often perceived as asexual or irresponsibly promiscuous. It was perceptions like these that often led to the sterilization of people with disabilities.

KIM: CRISES OF IDENTIFYING WITHIN SCHOOLS

Unlike the other participants, Kim attended different types of schools growing up.

Okay. I went—first I went to the boarding school when I was three to five years old. Primarily because I needed intensive therapy and my mother needed to work. So this was a way for us to do what we needed to do.

And then in Philadelphia I went to a school for disabled children from five to eight years old.

And then we came back to New Jersey and I went to another school—a day school, you know, for children with disabilities.

And then I went back to the boarding school; And then I came home again and went to my neighborhood middle school.

Because she left home at such a young age to attend boarding school, I asked Kim about what impact she thought this had on her. She discussed how she felt that it helped her become more independent.

I don't remember—now looking back, I think it began to teach me how to separate from my mom, separate from my family.

The school in Philadelphia played a big role in terms of my independence because it was a large—well everything seems large when you're small. But it was pretty large. One level of the school was done with carpet, wall-to-wall carpeting; and I could walk. So I walked all over that school. I just had a good time. I was a safety patrol. I just had a good time.

Essentialist discourses concerning children with disabilities often influenced perceptions and assumptions about their inability to become independent, capable individuals. However, there were several educational institutions that developed children in ways that challenged these assumptions.

However, because the student population at institutional schools was mostly White, this affected Kim's interactions with Black people, which impacted her identification with Blackness.

And I remember coming home on weekends and me developing a taste for or an ear for country music. I would hear it and I would say, *I like this country song*, or whatever and you know, all I wanted was to listen. Yeah. Because my care providers of the boarding school were mainly White; and they liked it.

I then realize that I wasn't supposed to like it when other people would make comments. When they made comments ... when my family like would make comments ... But I did not know. I liked it. You don't know you're not supposed to like it.

By attending educational institutions for children with disabilities, Kim was able to develop her independence as well as a positive identification with her disability. However, contentions regarding race were exacerbated when she started to transition between mostly White educational contexts and all Black familial contexts.

Kim discussed the effect of being alienated and ostracized by African American people within familial and educational contexts had on her perceptions of being Black.

Again, I mean, I guess in high school I started realizing, *Hey, it's not my fault*. And realizing, hey, that most of my babysitters, most of the people who were in our family and friends, most of my care providers were White; if not all were White. So I'd say of course I can't help it, because look who's assisting me.

That's why maybe it's so easy to adapt their mannerisms because I didn't feel any different.

You know. I didn't get a sense that I was any different.

Obviously, Kim developed a stronger identification with White paraprofessionals in relation to her disability. Because her experiences and interactions with were positive, Kim generally felt more comfortable being around White people than she did Black people.

When she transferred to a school for children with disabilities closer to her home, the repercussions of her having mostly White caregivers became even more problematic for her.

I came home to be with my mom in Philadelphia. She had taken a job in Philly and that was difficult now that I think about it.

The school was great as in it was the best school for children with disabilities. But the kids were hard on me, because these disabled kids they grew up in the city; so I come in and didn't talk *street*. I had a certain way of speaking; so I got it bad. So, it was hard.

Once Kim was transferred to an educational institution for children with disabilities that included more Black children, she started to experience crises of identifying in relation to her race and Black peers. Like King, Kim's mannerisms and speech patterns contributed to her alienation and marginalization by her Black peers. In this educational context, her positive identification with her disability was not enough and her positive identification with White paraprofessionals was too much.

When she went to a public school for the first time, Kim's interactions and experiences in educational contexts became even more contentious. Now she was dealing with essentialist discourses and power and privilege dynamics in a public educational context, general and special education teachers, and students with and without disabilities. Kim's discussion of these experiences ranged from the way teachers and other students interacted with her as a result of her disability to the effect transitioning to a public school had on her positive identification with herself as a female sexual being.

When I was 13 or 14, I went to middle school—the first time I was mainstreamed in general ed classes in a public neighborhood school.

The first example is my sex life went down the tubes once I was in mainstream school. I always had a boyfriend in school for disabled children.

But I just had no problem with boys. And when I got into mainstream school, I still wanted the boys, but they were too afraid of what other people would think of them if they liked me.

Of course I got some teachers who were leery about my ability to compete in public school; and I got some teachers that tried to deny me certain things that they were providing to the other children.

I was the only one who had an assistant at that time in my grade. I think there were people who came behind me who had an assistant. But that was a barrier in terms of making friends. I used to like days when she was off because I would get to be on my own. Sure, it was hard for me trying to do things, but it was a chance for me to be on my own too.

Although she had difficulty in getting a boyfriend in public school, Kim's identification with herself as an attractive sexual being remained positive. Her confidence and previous experiences with having boyfriends kept her from experiencing crises in relation to her attractiveness and sexuality even though it was harder for her to intimately connect with boys in public school. This was also the case with her disability. Negative interactions and experiences with general education teachers because of her disability did interfere with the positive identification she had with her disability.

Nevertheless, there were some things that Kim learned at public school that would be valuable to her identification development.

I had to go to a public school to get history about people with disability.

Actually it was odd because in middle school they showed a movie about people with disability and they showed the movie about the independent living movement. It was how I had to go to a regular public school to get that history.

But when I came home that day, I told my mama I wanted to go to California because that's where the independent living movement began.

Unlike José, Kim's general education teachers did include media and literature concerning people with disabilities in their curricula. Even though Kim had always interacted with people with disabilities in educational institutions as well as maintained a positive identification with her disability, it was at a public school that she learned about people with disabilities as activists and advocates.

NEGOTIATING AND MEDIATING CRISES: CATALYSTS OF LEADERSHIP

Because of her mother's diligence and commitment to her, Kim was provided with support and encouragement that contributed to her developing a positive identification with herself as a female with a disability. Her confidence, independence, and strong will were the source and a reflection of her leadership. However, as a result of interactions in familial and educational contexts, she spent years negotiating and mediating crises regarding her race and Black people. As she became more involved in activism and advocacy with her mother, Kim started to meet and develop positive relationships with African American people with disabilities. These relationships influenced her negotiation and mediation of her crises regarding her race, which led her to a *better* identification with Blackness.

Being around my friends, I have girlfriends who are Black female and they—one has a physical disability and the other's blind and just being around them develop me as a person; And the other person who's blind and she's Black—I don't know; it's like coming home—she reminds me coming home to comfortable Black people because I got to the point that I was uncomfortable around Black people.

By marrying an African American man, Kim experienced more positive interactions with Black people. Her exposure to her husband's family had a significant impact on her identification development with Black people.

I got married almost two years ago; and his family has a reunion every year where they discuss Black values; and I view it as not only coming together as family but coming together as a group of Black folks. And I never had that as a child. And I can feel myself getting stronger in that environment.

Just feeling more comfortable around Black people, and if I can feel comfortable around my own people, that's the only evidence that I'm getting stronger in my own skin.

I guess I'm more tolerant of Black people now. I'm willing to at least give them a try.

Kim's positive interactions with her husband's family and her friendship with several Black people with disabilities started to challenge negative perceptions she had of Black people. This initiated her renegotiation and remediation of her negative interactions and perceptions of Black people.

DISCUSSION QUESTIONS

1. In Dymaneke D. Mitchell's article, we read Kim's story. Why do you think Kim's father had trouble dealing with her disability? Do you think that parental and family alienation (for example, a father blaming the mother, or questioning "whose fault it is" that their child has a congenital disability) is a common experience shared by other people of disability? Why or why not?

2. A children's rhyme has it that "sticks and stones may break my bones, but names will never hurt me." Is that true? Is it innocent, harmless fun when persons of disability are called names such as "crippled," or "spastic," or "retard"? Why or why not?

3. Mitchell writes that Kim's mother "help[ed] her understand from a young age that, although she had a disability, she was not her disability." What did Kim's mother mean by this?

4. Does it surprise you that Kim was able to think of herself as an attractive sexual being, and to express herself sexually? Why or why not? Comment on Mitchell's statement that "people with disabilities are often perceived as asexual or as irresponsibly promiscuous." Do you agree? Why or why not?

5. How did "intersectionality"—the fact that Kim was Black *and* a woman *and* a person of disability—complicate her life and exponentially multiply the many forms of discrimination that she experienced in public school and throughout life?

READING 5.2

NEW ECONOMIES FOR NATIVE NATIONS

BY **Mark Anthony Rolo**

During President Reagan's budget-slashing years in the 1980s, American Indian governments were especially hard hit, facing even greater cutbacks than the rest of the country in federal dollars for health, education, and business development. Tribes were forced into finding economic alternatives to address the deepening poverty brought on by Reaganomics.

There was little to build on in Indian Country. Trailer parks, jewelry and other craft stands for tourists, and humble bingo halls that only appealed to reservation community members could never form the foundation of a strong tribal economy.

Given the federal government's responsibility to tribes, based on treaties, Congress passed the Indian Gaming Regulatory Act of 1988, authorizing tribes to construct casinos. This was seen as the most promising solution to end federal government dependency by promoting economic self-sufficiency.

But nearly three decades later, most of the more than 500 federally recognized tribal nations have not seen the payoff of Vegas style gaming. Today, the unemployment rate among American Indians is still nearly double that of the national average. One in four Indians continue to live in poverty.

The reality is that Indian gaming has not been a panacea. Only those few tribes located next to urban centers like Minneapolis, Los Angeles, Detroit, and San Diego have been able to rake in big revenue.

"What makes for a successful casino? Geography and population," says Joe Kalt, co-founder and co-director of the Harvard Project on American Indian Economic Development. "Since the vast majority of reservations are in much more rural areas, many tribes have small gaming operations. Some year-round truck drivers come through or summer tourists visit, but it really provides only a little cash flow for tribal government services."

Rural reservation life also suffers from other business development barriers. There is the absence of trade routes that carry consumer goods. There is the poor infrastructure (especially telecommunications). Banks are reluctant to lend to individuals or start-up businesses because they have next-to-no collateral. Reservation land is not owned by tribes or private citizens; it is trust land owned by the federal government.

Jacqueline Pata, executive director of the National Congress of American Indians, a legislative advocacy organization made up of more than 250 tribes, says federal policies are another huge hindrance.

"Tribes must wrestle with outdated and unfair laws and policies that put them at a competitive disadvantage and restrict their ability to fully grasp the reins of their economic futures," she says. "Federal law currently does not allow tribal governments the use of critical tools, such as surety bonds and tax exempt bonds that state and local governments have long relied on to seed economic development and job opportunities."

Even seeking to do business with small contractors, such as construction companies, becomes problematic. Because tribes are sovereign nations, they are generally immune to off-reservation lawsuit rulings. If a business,

Indian or non-Native, runs into contractual problems with a tribal government, it can only make an appeal to a tribal court, whose judges are usually hand-picked by the tribal council. Many companies won't even bother doing business with a tribe because, if a dispute arises, seeking recourse through the tribal court system can be futile.

'Tribes must wrestle with outdated and unfair laws and policies that put them at a competitive disadvantage and restrict their ability to fully grasp the reins of their economic futures.'

Finally, when it comes to realizing the dream of tribal economic self-sufficiency, history often stands in the way. When the federal government set up the reservation system a century ago, it imposed oppressive governments on tribes.

"This is really deep historical trauma," Kalt says. "Tribes got saddled with governmental structures that weren't of their own making. They had no legitimacy to the people, and they weren't culturally appropriate. Quite often what you find today is political instability. You want to screw up your economy? Screw up your government."

But there have been some hopeful developments.

According to a February report on the challenges of commercial lending in Indian Country by the U.S. Treasury Department's Office of the Comptroller of the Currency, some tribes have been successful in "asset-based development." This involves building businesses using the tribes' natural resources—including minerals, wildlife, and forests—and their cultural and intellectual property.

The Mississippi Band of Choctaw Indians provides nearly 6,000 jobs for tribal and non-Native community members in areas including manufacturing, retail sales, and tourism. The band's annual payroll tops $100 million. Since 2008, Alaska Native regional corporations have earned just over $5 billion, largely through federal construction and manufacturing contracts provided to minority-owned businesses.

Since the majority of tribes know they will never build huge corporate portfolios, they are looking deeper within their own communities to find economic opportunities. Rather than trying to lure corporate America into coming to them, tribes are investing in their own people through job creation using what limited resources they have at home.

The Red Lake Band of Chippewa in northern Minnesota has built a fishery business that offers decent-paying jobs for tribal members and income to the tribe. It features a sustainable harvesting plan that won't deplete the fish population, and worldwide marketing and distribution.

Samuel Strong, the tribe's director of planning and economic development, says about 500 community members catch and sell walleye and other fish to the Red Lake Nation Fishery, which provides about fifty jobs to members. Fish are among the most important resources on the reservation.

"Fishing is in our blood," Strong says. "We refer to our lake as our storehouse. It provides a means for our livelihood and it allows us to control those means for our people."

The tribe began providing fish for sale to the federal government in order to feed military servicemen during the two World Wars. But decades of illegal angling and selling on the black market nearly wiped out the lake's fish population by the late 1990s. Working with the state's Department of Natural Resources, the tribe banned fishing in order to repopulate the lake. Though this was a severe economic hardship on tribal members who relied on harvesting and selling the fish, most agreed this was needed to save not just the fish, but a traditional way of life.

In 2006, the lake was opened up again to harvesting. "Because we work with the DNR to make sure fishing remains sustainable, the harvest will now be available in perpetuity," Strong says. "This allows us to provide for future generations. Teaching our kids through living this way of life promotes a cycle of reciprocity that is critical to our success."

Merging sustainability with preserving traditional ways has spawned a new economic model in recent years, one built on tribal control.

Since the 1990s, many Plains tribes have had successful intertribal cooperatives in the areas of buffalo restoration and Indian agriculture. The InterTribal Buffalo Council, with fifty-eight member tribes in nineteen states, in 1992 launched a plan to bring the sacred bison back to reservation land for cultural, subsistence, and spiritual purposes. That effort became one of the country's most successful natural resource restoration projects.

"This is all about the tribes," says Dianne Amiotte-Seidel, the council's project director and marketing coordinator. "We are bringing all the tribes together as one, because they have the same belief in one thing, and that's the buffalo."

The council manages a collective herd of more than 15,000 buffalo. Its goal is to engage in education and training programs on herd management and marketing. It works with the National Park Service to relocate surplus bison to tribal land, and provides buffalo meat to reservation people.

"When they took the buffalo away from tribes and gave them food commodities instead, Indian people developed a lot of health problems like diabetes and obesity," Amiotte-Seidel says. "Now, in addition to restoring the buffalo, we are helping to restore Native health by putting buffalo meat in elderly and diabetes programs, and in our school lunchrooms."

Tribal control, Kalt says, is key to creating sustainable economic development. Since the Harvard Project on American Indian Economic Development began conducting research in 1987, all the data on what makes business work in Indian Country points to tribal self-determination.

"In the era before the Indian Self-Determination Act of 1975, overbearing federal control was killing economic development on reservations," Kalt says. "You practically couldn't build a bowling alley without the federal government's approval. But since the passage there has been a rebuilding of governments, an exercising of sovereignty—and economic development is finally taking hold in more and more Indian nations. But self-determination isn't a blank check. It's the tribes that have figured out their own systems for governing themselves well that are developing economically."

While research shows that such economic activities as gaming and manufacturing promote traditional culture and the recovery of indigenous language by providing the financial resources to back these efforts, there is a movement among many Indian communities to go even further in their cultural and economic histories. How did their ancestors devise an economy without disrupting the natural landscape?

INTERTRIBAL BISON COUNCIL

Left: Students from the Blackfeet Nation, Montana, observe the buffalo parts that their ancestors utilized many years ago. Right: A student at Taos Day School, New Mexico.

At the Tyonek Alaskan Native village, located forty-five miles west from Anchorage across Cook Inlet, community members have been "growing local" for the past three years in an effort to bring back traditional gardening practices. It's an attempt to provide their people with sustenance and to revive ancient culture as well.

"We are an off the road' community," says Christy Cincotta, executive director of the Tyonek Tribal Conservation District, one of thirteen such districts in Alaska. "Any food that is not from the community has to get flown in and it is expensive, and often not fresh. Elders remember having vegetable gardens, but that has faded over time. It's lost knowledge."

The district runs a garden project to create raised beds, solar-powered irrigation, and ventilation systems. Native youth interns tend the community garden, which is expanding each year in size. And interest from villagers and surrounding non-Native communities is growing.

"We want to make sure we can provide jobs so that the project can sustain itself," Cincotta says. Elders and youth are the first beneficiaries come harvest season, but Cincotta says a substantial quantity of vegetables are sold outside the community. "People are excited to support this because they know money is staying in their community and not going to a grocery store in Anchorage. And they know where [their food] came from. No harsh chemicals are being used, only renewable energy in a sustainable way."

Paul DeMain, a member of the Oneida Nation of Wisconsin, harvests maple syrup and gathers wild onions. He says making money is not the first priority when it comes to building a sustainable business. "First, there is family helping to harvest maple syrup and wild rice. Next, this food is used for spiritual, ceremonial, and medicinal use."

DeMain believes more can be done to support Native harvesters on the economic level. He would like local food markets to buy Indian-owned sustainable products, and for more public schools to open their cafeterias to Indian vendors. "But in order to do that, our venison and our walleye have to meet USDA health standards," he says. "Right now, the tapping of maple trees and harvesting of wild rice are not considered farming by the federal government. We need to get language in the Farm Bill to support us."

But no one knows how much support American Indian tribes can count on from Congress and the federal government. Some wonder whether Indian nations will have time to pull themselves out of poverty before federal-Indian policy swings back against their economic efforts.

"Sometime in the late 1990s, there was a massive shift in the way Congress deals with tribes," Kalt says. "The Democrats still tend to support spending on tribal issues and tribal sovereignty as forms of social justice. The Republicans, however, have shifted from a party of small government and strong defense for local self-rule—including tribal local self-rule—to a party of social conservatism that tends to see tribal sovereignty as merely special race-based rights for Indians, regardless of the fact that tribal sovereignty is founded on the Constitution and Treaties."

This might mean tribes could find themselves subject to policies that do more than inhibit growth. They could be subject to policies that derail self-sufficient economies for their people.

DISCUSSION QUESTIONS

1. What are the economic challenges confronting Native American reservations? Are these challenges similar to the ones faced by communities of color and immigrants? If not, how are they unique?

2. How has the ceding of control of Native American economies to the federal government hurt those economies? How might the restoration of tribal control rebuild them?

3. What hopeful or positive developments appear on the horizon that promise to bolster Native American economies?

NO HOME IN INDIAN COUNTRY

BY Janeen Comenote

AMERICAN INDIANS AND ALASKA NATIVES: AN OVERVIEW

The United States is an immigrant nation to all but one population, American Indians and Alaska Natives. There are essentially two populations to examine. We have an on-reservation population (governed by tribal governments) and the off-reservation population of Native peoples. However, an added complexity to keep in mind is the notion of citizenship. Native people often hold triplicate citizenship, that of: a) the "home tribe" and "homeland"; b) a citizen of the United States; and c) for off-reservation populations, the city or town in which they reside.

While we can fairly assess that both populations suffer disproportionately from economic stress and lack of access to fair credit and housing, we need to realize that tribal governments operate under a dramatically different set of regulations, rules of law and constituent

---

Janeen Comenote (jcomenote@unitedindians.org), an enrolled member of the Quinault Indian Nation in Washington State, works as a Development Officer at the United Indians of All Tribes Foundation and as Director of the National Urban Indian Family Foundation, both in Seattle. The extensive citations and references in the original version of this article, prepared for the Kirwan Inst, for the Study of Race and Ethnicity, are available from the author.

responsibilities. A simple way of thinking about tribal populations in the United States is to consider that both tribal nations and the U.S. Congress observe a sovereign government-to-goverament relationship between tribes and the United States government formalized in American law in the 1832 case *Worcester* v. *Georgia*. Simply put, when the U.S. was forming, legally binding treaties were made to the tribes who relinquished millions of acres of lands and numerous age-old freedoms. In exchange, the federal government is legally bound to the provision of service, including the provision of housing, to Native people in perpetuity.

THE TRUST RESPONSIBILITIES OF CONGRESS AND THE EXECUTIVE BRANCH

The federal trust responsibility to Indian nations can be divided into three components:

1   The protection of Indian trust lands and Indian rights to use those lands;

2   The protection of tribal sovereignty and rights of self-governance;

3 The provision of basic social, medical and educational services for tribal members.

The U.S. is an immigrant nation to all but American Indians and Alaska Natives.

Often considered an "invisible minority," American Indians and Alaska Natives are often left out or relegated into the category of "other" within the racial equity framework in the United States. The racial equity framework must be adapted and explicitly expanded to include an indigenous lens. American Indian communities often adopt a stance of "measured separatism" that legal writer R.A Williams describes as "much different from the types of minority rights that were and remain at the center of the continuing struggle for racial equality." J.E. Nielsen, citing T. Biolsi, notes: "It may be appropriate for Native communities to adopt a racial equity perspective in some situations/geopolitical spaces—other circumstances/spaces require that we operate from a stance of sovereignty and self-determination—an *indigenous* lens. Opportunity is specialized and may look different in tribal space than in non-tribal space. "

Geography and Demographics: In Census 2000, 4.3 million people, or 1.5% of the total U.S. population, reported that they were American Indian or Alaska Native, representing over 500 individual tribal nations. This number included 2.4 million people, or 1% of the U.S. total, who reported AI/AN as their only race.

The geography of the AI/AN population is widely distributed in the United States, with a majority of Native people residing off-reservation. Slightly over 64% live outside tribal areas; 33.5% live in American Indian Areas (which includes federal reservations and/or off-reservation trust lands, Oklahoma tribal statistical areas, tribal-designated statistical areas, state reservations, and state-designated American Indian statistical areas); and slightly over 2% live in Alaska Native Villages.

Poverty: Regardless of geographic location, poverty remains the singularly most challenging aspect of contemporary AI/AN experience. There is considerable indicative information that Native Americans are disproportionably affected by monetary or economic poverty. The following examples point out some of these disparities:

- 25.3% is the 2007 poverty rate of people who reported they were AI/AN and no other race. However, this does not reflect the poverty rate of those individuals reporting AI/AN alone or in combination with another race.

- Residents of reservations experience deep poverty, meaning they live at less than 75 % of the poverty level, and do so at twice the rate of the total U.S. population (26% for American Indians versus 12% nationally).

- Unemployment in some reservations can be several times the national average.

- Off-reservation and urban AI/AN people also experience disproportionate levels of poverty, three times that of whites.

HOUSING

- 14.7% of homes are overcrowded, compared to 5.7% of homes of the general U.S. population.

- Indian Country has a denial rate for conventional home purchase loans of 23%—twice that of Caucasians.

- The percentage of Indian Country without adequate plumbing facilities is 10 times the general U.S. population.

- 11% of Indian Country lacks kitchen facilities, compared to 1% of the U.S.

- In an 8-state (MN, IA, ND, SD, MT, ID, WA, OR) study of housing needs in 30 Metropolitan Statistical Areas, the 2000 U.S. Census reports that 46% of Indian renters pay more than 30% of their total income for rent. The Census also reveals that 2% of renters are forced to pay at least a half of their monthly income for rent.

In looking at the disparities within the poverty and housing indicators cited above, it becomes clear that there is an interdependence between accessibility to fair credit and housing for AI/AN people regardless of their geographic location on or off the reservation. As such, coordinated national strategies are needed to address these barriers.

Fair Housing: The U.S. Department of Housing and Urban Development (HUD) defines housing affordability by asserting that no more than 30% of a household's income should be dedicated to housing (rent and utilities). The lack of affordable housing is a significant hardship for low-income households, preventing them from meeting their other basic needs such as nutrition and health care, or saving for their future and that of their families. While this holds true for all disadvantaged communities in the United States, it has significant differences when examined from AI/AN perspectives, with a key point being that the federal government has a legal and trust responsibility to provide adequate housing for Native people.

On-Reservation Populations: HUD is charged with housing construction and maintenance on Native American trust lands and reservations. Under the Native American Housing Assistance and Self-Determination Act (NAHASDA) of 1996, the federal government makes block grants to tribes and tribally-designated housing entities. While the block grant program has led to greater local control, its success has been undercut by lack of funding. At its current level, NAHASDA funding will only meet 5% of the total need for housing in Native communities.

Native people often hold triplicate citizenship.

NAHASDA separated Native-American housing from general public housing, both administratively and financially. The Act, recognizing tribal rights to self-governance and self-determination, was designed to permit tribal recipients to manage and monitor housing assistance programs. It is structured to provide flexibility in tribal planning, implementation and administration of housing programs. Given the unique housing challenges Native Americans face—including impoverished economic conditions, restrictions on individual land rights, lack of homeownership, and substandard housing—greater and immediate federal financial support is imperative.

Off-Reservation Populations: In an 8-state community-based research project, over 1,200 urban-dwelling Native people were interviewed in 4 major metropolitan areas regarding a number of poverty indicators, including access to housing. Respondents cited the following barriers to getting into housing: credit checks, low income, lack of affordable housing stock, background checks, and deposits/downpayment requirements. It is likely that these outcomes do not vary significantly nationwide.

Nearly every city represented in the National Urban Indian Family Coalition reports a disproportionate number of Natives in shelter care but very few transitional housing projects serving the Native community. This points to the need for capacity in the Native non-profit sector and for the will and ability of tribal governments to develop collaborative national strategies to impact this on a policy and practice level. It is important to

Airports & Civil Rights

The official name of the Baltimore/Washington International Airport several years ago was changed to the Thurgood Marshall BWI—honoring the Baltimorean who was the nation's first African-American Supreme Court Justice (and providing some political balance to the DC area's 3 airports, the others officially Reagan and Dulles). The Jackson, MS airport is now officially the Medgar Evers Jackson International Airport, and Birmingham's airport now is officially named after Fred Shuttlesworth. It's good to bring this to people's attention (doing so to the Amtrak President got them finally to update the airport station sign and get train and station announcers to call out the airport's full proper name).

note that this remains merely anecdotal information until a research agenda is developed to quantify this experience.

RECOMMENDATIONS

Provide Opportunities and Resources, both on and off the reservation, for Native people to become more financially literate in order to improve both their credit scores and access to homeowner ship:

- Fund and support the continued development of Native community development financial institutions (CDFIs). There are presently 48 U.S. Treasury-certified Native CDFIs, with another 50+ in various stages of emergence, up from just 6 such at the end of 2000. These locally-based, Native institutions have become economic engines for communities, providing homebuyer education, financial education, entrepreneurship, individual development account (IDA) matched savings programs, credit counseling, anti-predatory lending, mortgages and small business loans.

- Explore policies regarding requiring predatory lending institutions and banks to contribute to a general fund designated specifically for financial literacy education. Within this, specify that a percentage of the fund go to tribal governments and Native non-profit organizations to provide financial literacy and relevant economic enhancement services in their communities.

- Fund an Indian community development block grant through HUD or the Administration for Native Americans for tribal governments and Native non-profits to build economic capacity and literacy in their communities. Specific language must be included for off-reservation populations.

A sovereign government-to-government relationship exists between tribes and the U.S. government.

Establish a Research Agenda: AI/AN communities need more research to fully understand the conditions our people are experiencing in tribal and urban settings. We are not interested in merely being the "subjects" of research, however; what we need is the resources that will enable us to build our own capacity to define research questions, gather data, and draw our own conclusions based on those data. Specifically, the National Congress of American Indians Policy Research Center, the Harvard Project on American Indian Economic Development, or other culturally relevant scholars and research institutions should be engaged to conduct the needed research:

- *Access to Fair Housing:* While there exists some research and analysis on housing as it relates to on-reservation housing and access to housing, there exists a clear need to examine this from the standpoint of off-reservation Native populations who now comprise a majority of the AI/AN people in the United States. A comprehensive examination of the current housing crisis for this population needs exploration, with a focus on the equitable distribution of resources compared to the disproportionate local representation in their homeless populations.
- *Access to Fair Credit:* There is very little current information on best practices and strategies for increasing access to credit by AI/AN populations either on- or off-reservation. We need to develop a research agenda to explore this aspect of the AI/AN experience. The 2000 Native American Lending Study was an important first step and led to the creation of the present Expanding Native Opportunity Initiatives of the U.S. Treasury CDFI Fund. More detailed and current information is now required.

Collaborate with the Native Financial Education Coalition (NFEC) to enact policy recommendations: NFEC is a group of local, regional and national organizations and government agencies that have joined together for one purpose: to promote financial education in Native communities.

Each year, the NFEC develops a comprehensive set of policy recommendations relating to Financial Education in Native communities:

Support the development and growth of the newly formed Native CDFI Network: Help to create a policy platform that addresses the broader issues of asset-building and community development in Native communities.

Expand Tribal Housing Authority: Expand the capacity of tribal governments and/or Tribal Designated Housing Entities (TDHE) to develop fair market housing with Indian preference in off-reservation locations. This policy recommendation needs to be crafted in conjunction with appropriate tribal governmental bodies, advocacy and off-reservation organizations.

Explore and enact policy recommendations as laid out in the U.S. Civil Rights Commission report, "A Quiet Crisis in Indian Country": The report focused on the adequacy of federal funding for programs and services targeting American Indians, Federally Recognized Indian Tribal Governments and Native American Organizations. Attention was directed at *unmet needs,* the portion of *basic needs* among Native Americans that the government is supposed to supply but does not. For the purposes of this overview, we are concentrating on the segments of the report focusing on housing.

The report details 11 recommendations with regard to the distribution of federal resources in Indian Country—while each recommendation made by the U.S. Civil Rights Commission deserves and requires additional attention by the federal government, two come to the forefront that might bear fruit when applied towards issues of fair housing and fair credit:

- ***Recommendation 2:*** All agencies that distribute funds for Native American programs should be required to regularly assess unmet needs for both urban and rural Native individuals. Such an assessment would compare community needs with available resources and identify gaps in service delivery. Agencies should establish benchmarks for the elevation of Native American living conditions to those of other

Americans, and in doing so create attainable resource-driven goals.

In addition, each federal agency that administers Native American programs should specifically and accurately document Native American participation in its programs and account for all projects and initiatives. This inventory will provide tribal governments and Native individuals with up-to-date information on the services and programs available and will enable agencies to identify and reduce program redundancies.

- ***Recommendation 8:*** Federal appropriations must account for costs that are unique to Indian tribes, such as those required to build necessary infrastructure, those associated with geographic remoteness, and those required for training and technical assistance. Overall, more money is needed to support independent enterprise, such as through guaranteed loans that facilitate home and business ownership, and to provide incentives for lending institutions, builders, educators and health management companies to conduct business on Indian lands. The federal government should develop widespread incentives to facilitate education and to promote the return of services to Indian communities. In doing so, it will promote economic development in Indian Country, which will eventually reduce reliance on government services.

In addition, the unique needs of non-reservation and urban Native Americans must be assessed, and adequate funding must be provided for programs to serve these individuals. Native Americans are increasingly leaving reservations and their way of life, not always by choice but due to economic hardships. Yet funding for health, education, housing, job training and other critical needs of urban Native Americans is a low priority.

OTHER CONSIDERATIONS

Tribal Sovereignty

The United States government has a unique legal relationship with Native American tribal governments, as set forth in the Constitution of the United States, treaties, statutes and court decisions. As executive departments and agencies undertake activities affecting Native American tribal rights or trust resources, such activities should be implemented in a knowledgeable, sensitive manner respectful of tribal sovereignty. As such, when examining policy and research within the context of Indian Country, this political aspect must be taken into consideration, and any actionable policy recommendations need to be developed in consultation with tribal governments.

Programs that are funded in Indian Country must be enacted under tribal sovereignty and self-determination. Julie Nielsen noted: "There is ample evidence that in Native nations, the best outcomes of federally funded programs emerge when tribal governments are able to exercise their inherent sovereignty and to exercise self-determination. In fact, according to Stephen Cornell and Jonathan Taylor, over 12 years of research and evaluation from both the Harvard Project on American Indian Economic Development and the Udall Center for Public Policy at the University of Arizona indicate that the *only* successful public development strategies in Indian country are those that have been enacted under tribal control. They also suggest that state goals, as well, have been advanced through successful tribal control over publicly funded development."

Consultation

Indian Country has developed infrastructure and experts in the field of housing and credit. The following institutions should be included in future policy development:

Financial Empowerment: First Nations Development Institute, Oweesta, Native Financial Education Coalition

Housing: National American Indian Housing Council, National Congress of American Indians, National Urban Indian Family Coalition

DISCUSSION QUESTIONS

1. Do some independent research: What trust promises and responsibilities were made by the federal government (i.e., by Congress and the executive branch) to Indian nations at the time of the American founding? How well or poorly has the federal government kept those trust promises and responsibilities?

2. Why are Native Americans considered to be an "invisible minority," often left out or relegated to the category of "other" within the racial equity framework of the United States?

3. What recommendations does Janeen Comenote make or cite for improving Native American living and working conditions?

READING 5.4

MUSLIM AMERICAN STUDENTS

An Overview for School Psychologists

BY **Anisa N. Goforth and Ramzi Hasson**

There are an estimated 3.3 million Muslim Americans, and the population will likely double by 2050 (Pew Research Center, 2016). Although a large population in the United States, Muslim Americans are not an official minority and are largely underrepresented in the school psychology research literature. Moreover, the events of September 11, 2001, the subsequent sociopolitical climate, and the recent refugee crisis in Syria and other Middle Eastern countries have led to increased scrutiny of Islam and its followers. Civil rights organizations have noticed an increase in hate crimes and discrimination (Council on American-Islamic Relations, 2008), and the FBI (2013) reported that 13.7% of hate crimes were associated with anti-Islamic bias. This increase in scrutiny, prejudice, and hate crimes warrants our particular attention given that we may be serving Muslim American students in the schools.

School psychologists have an important role in developing a positive school climate for religious minorities. Culturally responsive school psychological practice includes developing knowledge, skills, and awareness about students from diverse backgrounds (Sue, Arredondo, & McDavis, 1992). The purpose of this article is to provide basic foundational knowledge and awareness about Muslim American students. It is the first in a series of articles that will address ways to meet the mental health and academic needs of Muslim American students in schools. We will first provide a general overview of Muslim Americans and an introduction to the Islamic faith and practices. We will then discuss the current research literature that addresses Muslim American students' experiences in the schools and the effects of these experiences on their mental health and academic success.

WHO ARE MUSLIM AMERICAN STUDENTS?

Muslims comprise 1% of the total U.S. population (Pew Research Center, 2016). Unfortunately, statistics on Muslim American students are limited because the U.S. government does not track the religions of new residents. Current estimates, however, suggest that there has been an increase in the number of Muslim immigrants entering the United States as legal permanent residents between 1992 and 2012 (Pew Research Center, 2013). Approximately 64% of immigrants are Muslim, with most Muslim immigrants being from the Middle East/North Africa or Asia and the Pacific.

UNDERSTANDING ISLAM

Islam is a monotheistic religion. In the United States, Islam is one of the fastest growing religions and is the third largest religion behind Christianity and Judaism. Worldwide, there are 1.6 billion Muslims as of 2010, making Islam the second largest of the three major monotheistic religions. Islam is anticipated to be the single biggest religion in the world by 2050 (Pew Research Center, 2011).

Muslims adhere to the five pillars of Islam. The first pillar is *shahada*, or the declaration of one's belief in *Allah*. Allah is the Arabic word for God, and it describes the same entity as in the Judeo-Christian faith. Muslims respect Moses and Jesus as prophets

of God and view the Prophet Mohammed as the last messenger of God. The holy book for Muslims is the Quran, which is believed to be God's word as revealed to the Prophet Mohammed through the angel Gabriel. The Quran contains much of the basic information told in the Hebrew Bible.

The second pillar is *salat* or prayer. Muslims are required to pray five times every day (at dawn, noon, afternoon, sunset, and evening). Most Muslims pray at home, but it is recommended that prayer be conducted collectively in a mosque. Muslims, especially men, are expected to congregate every Friday for afternoon prayer. The third pillar is *zakat*, or charity, for those in need. Depending on interpretation, Muslims are required to give a certain percentage of their accumulated wealth. The giving of charity is considered to be a very important aspect of the Muslim faith. The fourth pillar is *siyam* or fasting from food, water, and other bodily pleasure during the daylight hours in the month of Ramadan. Generally, all Muslims are supposed to fast during this holy month, except if they are young children, elderly, or ill. Finally, the fifth pillar is *hajj* or the pilgrimage to Mecca in Saudi Arabia. Muslims are expected to go to Mecca once in their lifetime if it is physically and economically possible.

There are two major sects within Islam: Sunni and Shi'a. The majority of Muslims (approximately 85%) follow the Sunni sect (Turner, 2011). Although both sects adhere to the five pillars, the primary difference is related to beliefs about the religious leaders following the death of the Prophet Mohammed. This difference between sects has had a significant impact on how the tenets and traditions of Islam are applied culturally (e.g., Shi'a allows for the veneration of saints while the Sunni do not). For many centuries, there has been little emphasis on the difference between the two sects; however, the contemporary sociopolitical climate has intensified the differences (e.g., the civil wars between Sunni and Shi'a in Iraq).

CULTURAL DIFFERENCES WITHIN ISLAM

Muslims reside in many countries around the world and, as a result, there are significant variations in how Islam is applied to daily life. Muslim Americans who have emigrated from Somalia, for example, differ in their cultural practices, clothing, foods, and traditions from Muslim Americans from Indonesia or Egypt. Given the diversity of people who follow Islam, there are also differences in racial and ethnic composition. Although there is often a perception that Muslim Americans are of Arab descent, there are many Americans of different racial and ethnic backgrounds who follow Islam. Arabs make up less than 25% of all Muslims worldwide (Pew Research Center, 2013).

Furthermore, like other religions, there is variation in the degree of religiosity. In the United States, nearly 70% of Muslims consider religion as very important in their lives, and are as religious as Christian Americans (Pew Research Center, 2011). Many Muslim Americans are very concerned about religious extremism and believe that their religious leaders should do more to combat it (Pew Research Center, 2011). Thus, it is important to recognize that Muslim American students and their family may have different cultural practices and levels of religiosity.

One of the most defining aspects of Islam concerns gender roles. Women and men are expected to dress modestly out of reverence for Allah. The application of this expectation is highly variable and often controversial. Muslim women are expected to wear modest clothing and cover their body except for the face and hands. However, in some cultural contexts, women may cover with the *hijab* (head cover), the *niqab* (face and head cover), or the *burka* (full body cover). Of note, not all Muslim women choose to wear these coverings, and there is even variation within countries. For example, Muslim women in Lahore, Pakistan (a large urban city) tend to wear modest, loose clothing with a scarf, while Muslim women in Peshawar, Pakistan (a city located near the border of Afghanistan) are more frequently fully covered with the burka.

Some Westerners may view the conservative religious covering Muslim women wear as repressive. However, there are diverse views on wearing the hijab among Muslim women. Many Muslim women view wearing the hijab and dressing modestly as empowering because it allows them to control their own body image, finding the notions of liberation and being judged by sex appeal to be incompatible (Esposito & Mogahed, 2007). Muslim women also highlight the powerful role women

have played in the formation of Islam and the fact that they were able to vote and be nation rulers since the inception of Islam almost 1,400 years ago (Esposito & Mogahed, 2007). Like many other patriarchal societies, however, there are cultural corruptions within Islam that have sought to strip power away from women. More conservative interpretations of Islamic law, or sharia, have been implemented by some Muslim countries in a manner that is repressive by moderate Muslim standards (Aslan, 2011).

MUSLIM AMERICAN STUDENTS' EXPERIENCES

Like other ethnic and religious minority youth, Muslim American students have varied experiences in schools related to school belongingness and discrimination, depending on their school, neighborhood, or community. School belongingness, or the degree to which a student feels accepted, respected, and included by others (Goodenow & Grady, 1993), has been shown to be a critical aspect of student academic success and social-emotional well-being (e.g., Vaz et al., 2015). To our knowledge, there have been few studies that have examined Muslim American students' sense of school belongingness; however, there has been research to show that Muslim American students have experienced prejudice and discrimination in school.

Muslim American youth experience challenges in the public schools. Results of a qualitative study found that religious minority youth, including Muslim students, report that school institutional policies often do not reflect an understanding or respect for their needs as religious minorities within the school (Dupper, Forrest-Bank, & Lowry-Carusillo, 2015). Religious holidays, for example, were often Christian-based (e.g., spring break is over the weekend of Good Friday and Easter), and the schools did not recognize non-Christian religious holidays. Furthermore, another study found that Muslim high school students experienced challenges in practicing Islam in school, particularly in accessing space to perform their afternoon and late afternoon prayer and in having to explain to teachers and other school staff why these prayers are necessary (Seward & Khan, 2016).

Muslim American students also experience prejudice, discrimination, and microaggressions in the public schools. In a survey of Muslim students in public schools in California, 52% of students reported being verbally abused as a result of their religion (Council of American–Islamic Relations–California [CAIR–CA], 2014). Nearly

Anisa N. Goforth, PhD, NCSP, is the director of the school psychology graduate training programs at the University of Montana. Her research focuses on culturally responsive school psychological practice with children from diverse backgrounds, including Arab Americans. She is Australian American and grew up in seven countries, including Yemen, Indonesia, and Pakistan.

Ramzi Hasson, PhD, is a postdoctoral fellow in pediatric rehabilitation neuropsychology at the University of Michigan department of physical medicine and rehabilitation. He is a first generation Arab American who has conducted research on the clinical utility of intellectual and academic assessment among Arab American adolescents.

30% of students wearing the hijab experienced offensive touching or pulling of their hijab. In a qualitative study using focus groups, Muslim students reported incidents of interpersonal discrimination, most of which occurred in the school setting (Aroian, 2012). In one incident, Muslim students reported that a "new student was easily identified as Muslim because she was wearing a headscarf. When she arrived, a classmate turned around in his seat and whispered to the participant, 'Watch out, she has a bomb'" (Aroian, 2012, p. 209).

Unfortunately, some educators and school staff have also committed discriminatory acts toward Muslim students. One in five Muslim students reported that they experienced discrimination by a school staff member (CAIR–CA, 2014). Some Muslim students in a qualitative study reported that they noticed their teachers perpetuate negative comments about Muslims when discussing American history (Aroian, 2012). Moreover, Seward and Khan (2016) shared one female student's experience:

> Like my English teacher, he was talking about women, and he was like, "And you all know Islam oppresses women or doesn't respect women" … And I was like, "No, it's the culture and not the religion." And he was giving examples of Saudi Arabia and stuff. It's really hard to confront a teacher, and he was like a real respected teacher. (p. 6)

Similarly, in the study by Dupper and colleagues (2015), a Muslim participant reported that she had not been allowed to take a break during her outdoor sports practice "because she was 'choosing to suffer' by fasting during her religious holiday" (p. 42).

These experiences of explicit discrimination may have an effect on Muslim American students' well-being. Research has suggested that perceived discrimination has an effect on overall health among people of ethnic minority backgrounds (Pascoe & Richman, 2009), and perceived discrimination has been found to affect psychological well-being among Muslim adolescents (Goforth, Oka, Leong, & Denis, 2014). Muslim adolescent girls also experienced more perceived ethnic discrimination and problem behaviors than boys (Maes, Stevens, & Verkuyten, 2014). In fact, perceived religious discrimination has been found to be associated with subclinical paranoia among Muslim Americans, perhaps because of more vigilance and suspicion of this ethnic minority group by non-Muslims (Rippy & Newman, 2006).

Although there are risk factors associated with perceived discrimination, religion and religious coping may also be protective factors for Muslim students' well-being. Previous research has found that religion, religious coping, and religious support are associated with less psychological distress for Arab American adolescents (Ahmed, Kia-Keating, & Tsai, 2011) and adult Muslim Arab Americans (Amer & Hovey, 2007). Furthermore, participating in religious organizations, such as attending mosque, has also been associated with less acculturative stress among Muslim adolescents (Goforth, Pham, Chun, & Castro-Olivo, in press). Religious faith and participating in religious organizations may facilitate a sense of community and develop trusting relationships (Ebstyne King & Furrow, 2008).

Fortunately, there have been some positive results related to Muslim students' experience in schools. A majority of the Muslim students in Californian public schools felt safe at school and reported feeling comfortable participating in class discussions about Islam (CAIR–CA, 2014). In fact, 67% of Muslim students reported believing that their teachers and administrators were responsive to their religious needs, such as by providing students time for prayers or excusing absences for Eid (a religious holiday marking the end of Ramadan; CAIR–CA, 2014). Similarly, in a qualitative study, a student reported that her social studies teacher countered the stereotypes students in her seventh grade class had about Muslims and highlighted that few Muslims committed acts of terrorism (Isik-Ercan, 2015). These data suggest that teachers and school staff can provide Muslim students with a safe and comfortable school.

CONCLUSION

As the Muslim American student population increases in the public schools, school psychologists should develop their knowledge, skills, and awareness related to Muslim culture, heritage, and faith. The current rhetoric in the media and sentiments made by politicians may pervade the public school environment, and thus reinforce a view of Muslim Americans as the "other" (Bonet, 2011). School psychologists have an important role to play in countering this negativity and developing a positive school climate for Muslim American students. In the next articles, there will be recommendations and suggestions for ways to facilitate a positive school climate and support Muslim American students' mental health and academic success.

REFERENCES

Ahmed, S. R., Kia-Keating, M., & Tsai, K. H. (2011). A structural model of racial discrimination, acculturative stress, and cultural resources among Arab American adolescents. *American Journal of Community Psychology, 48*, 181–192. doi:10.1007/s10464-011-9424-3

Amer, M. M., & Hovey, J. D. (2007). Socio-demographic differences in acculturation and mental health for a sample of 2nd generation/early immigrant Arab Americans. *Journal of Immigrant Mental Health, 9*, 335–347. doi:10.1007/s10903-007-9045-y

Aroian, K. J. (2012). Discrimination against Muslim American adolescents. *The Journal of School Nursing, 28*, 206–213. doi:10.1177/1059840511432316

Aslan, R. (2011). *No God but God: The origins, evolution, and future of Islam.* New York, NY: Random House.

Bonet, S. W. (2011). Educating Muslim American youth in a post-9/11 era: A critical review of policy and practice. *The High School Journal, 95*, 46–55. doi:10.1353/hsj.2011.0013

Council for American–Islamic Relations–California. (2014). *Mislabeled: The impact of school bullying and discrimination on California Muslim students.* Retrieved from https://ca.cair.com/sfba/wp-content/uploads/2015/10/CAIR-CA-2015-Bullying-Report-Web.pdf

Council on American–Islamic Relations. (2008). *The status of Muslim civil rights in the United States.* Retrieved from https://www.cair.com/images/pdf/CAIR-2008-Civil-Rights-Report.pdf

Dupper, D. R., Forrest-Bank, S., & Lowry-Carusillo, A. (2015). Experiences of religious minorities in public school settings: Findings from focus groups involving Muslim, Jewish, Catholic, and Unitarian Universalist youths. *Children & Schools, 37*, 37–45. doi:10.1093/cs/cdu029

Ebstyne King, P., & Furrow, J. L. (2008). Religion as a resource for positive youth development: Religion, social capital, and moral outcomes. *Psychology of Religion and Spirituality, 40*, 34–49. doi:10.1037/1941-1022.S.1.34

Esposito, J. L., & Mogahed, D. (2007). *Who speaks for Islam? What a billion Muslims really think.* New York, NY: Guilford Press.

Federal Bureau of Investigation. (2013). 2013 Hate Crime Statistics. Retrieved from https://www.fbi.gov/about-us/cjis/ucr/hate-crime/2013

Goforth, A. N., Oka, E. R., Leong, F. T., & Denis, D. (2014). Acculturation, acculturative stress, religiosity, and psychological adjustment among Muslim Arab American adolescents. *Journal of Muslim Mental Health, 8*, 3–19. doi:10.3998/jmmh.10381607.0008.202

Goforth, A. N., Pham, A. V., Chun, H., & Castro-Olivo, S. M. (in press). Association of acculturative stress, Islamic practices, and internalizing symptoms among Arab American adolescents. *School Psychology Quarterly.* doi:10.1037/spq0000135

Goodenow, C., & Grady, K. E. (1993). The relationship of school belonging and friends' values to academic motivation among urban adolescent students. *Journal of Experimental Education, 62*, 60–71. doi:10.1080/00220973.1993.9943831

Isik-Ercan, Z. (2015). Being Muslim and American: Turkish-American children negotiating their religious identities in school settings. *Race Ethnicity and Education, 18*, 225–250. doi:10.1080/13613324.2014.911162

Maes, M., Stevens, G. W. J. M., & Verkuyten, M. (2014). Perceived ethnic discrimination and problem behaviors in Muslim immigrant early adolescents: Moderating effects of ethnic, religious, and national group identification. *The Journal of Early Adolescence, 34*, 940–966. doi:10.1177/0272431613514629 Pascoe, E. A., & Richman, L. S. (2009). Perceived discrimination and health: A meta-analytic review. *Psychologial Bulletin, 135*, 531–554.

Pew Research Center. (2011). Muslim American Survey. Retrieved from http://www.people-press.org/2011/08/30/muslim-americans-no-signs-of-growth-in-alienation-or-support-for-extremism

Pew Research Center. (2013). *The religious affiliation of U.S. immigrants: Majority Christian, rising share of other faiths.* Retrieved from http://www.pewforum.org/2013/05/17/the-religious-affiliation-of-us-immigrants-muslim

Pew Research Center. (2016). *A new estimate of the U.S. Muslim population.* Retrieved from http://www.pewresearch.org/fact-tank/2016/01/06/a-new-estimate-of-the-u-s-muslim-population

Rippy, A., & Newman, E. (2006). Perceived religious discrimination and its relationship to anxiety and paranoia among Muslim Americans. *Journal of Muslim Mental Health, 2*, 5–20. doi:10.1080/15564900600654351

Seward, D. X., & Khan, S. (2016). Towards an understanding of Muslim American adolescent high school experiences. *International Journal for the Advancement of Counselling, 38*, 1–11. doi:10.1007/s10447-015-9252-5

Sue, D. W., Arredondo, P., & McDavis, R. J. (1992). Multicultural counseling competencies and standards: A call to the profession. *Journal of Counseling and Development, 70*, 477–486.

Turner, C. (2011). *Islam: The basics.* New York, NY: Routledge.

Vaz, S., Falkmer, M., Ciccarelli, M., Passmore, A., Parsons, R., Tan, T., & Falkmer, T. (2015). The personal and contextual contributors to school belongingness among primary school students. *PLoS ONE, 10*, 1–21. doi:10.1371/journal.pone.0123353

DISCUSSION QUESTIONS

1. What accounts for the dramatic increase in anti-Muslim scrutiny, prejudice, and hate crimes in America over the past two decades? Is it simply due to the terrorist attacks of 9/11? Or do the causes of American Islamophobia run deeper than 9/11?

2. How many Muslims are there in the United States today? Are they undocumented immigrants? Are they terrorists? Are they productive U.S. citizens? Is Islam a minor religion that can be ignored, or is Islam a major world religion that is rapidly growing in the United States? Should Americans be alarmed by the presence of Muslims, and by the rapid expansion of Islam throughout the United States? Why or why not?

3. Is Islam a radical, and/or a violent, religion? Or conversely, is it a religion of peace, tolerance, and love? How do you know? Discuss the various features and distinguishing characteristics of Islam, and of practicing Muslims, as summarized by Anisa Goforth and Ramzi Hasson.

4. What are the experiences of, and the challenges faced by, American Muslim youth? What role can school psychiatrists and teachers play in resisting Islamophobia and helping Muslim students overcome negative stereotypes and prejudice?

READING 5.5

MUSLIM AND AMERICAN

Living Under the Shadow of 9/11

BY **Beenish Ahmed**

One morning, my uncle arrived at his family medical practice in Toledo, Ohio, to find threats on his answering machine. A muffled voice greeted him with a string of expletives before warning that there would be consequences if he didn't "get the hell out of here." In the 30 years since Uncle Doctor, as I called him, had emigrated from Pakistan to the United States, he had never been singled out for his nationality or religion. It was September 12, 2001, and the dust still hung heavy in Lower Manhattan. A similar message was waiting for him at home.

"The scariest thing about it," my Aunt Kathy says, "was that whoever left those messages knew us. They knew our names. They knew the clinic number and our home number, even though it was unlisted." Today, my aunt and uncle struggle with the details ("It was ten years ago!" my aunt says), but at the time, they felt it was necessary to report the threats to the FBI. A middle-aged agent arrived on their doorstep clad in jeans and a khaki jacket. He spent half an hour listening to the messages and putting a tap on their phone to trace any further calls. None came, and my uncle went to work the next morning.

I was 14 years old and less willing to accept what was happening. My mother and I had our own encounter with what media started calling the "backlash" against Muslims. Like my uncle, my parents had moved to Toledo because it had a decades-old Muslim community. The first to arrive were Syrians and

Lebanese who were attracted to the area's high-paying auto-manufacturing jobs. The 1970s brought a different wave: engineers, doctors, and other professionals from South Asia.

Still shaken by the threats to my uncle, my mother and I stood in the checkout line at our grocery store. She wore a gauzy scarf and a shalwaar kameez—the long tunic and matching pants ensemble that is ubiquitous in South Asia—and I ... in what? Shalwaar kameez as well? My cross-country warmups? Jeans and a T-shirt? I don't remember. In fact, I don't remember any of it, but my mom does.

A woman who was standing behind us asked where we were from. It's a question I still have not learned how to answer. Northwest Ohio or Northwest Pakistan? Perrysburg or Peshawar? Which is the right response? Which me is being asked? A girl who wore flannel shirts and listened to emo bands like Midtown and Brand New in her room or the one who sat down to lentils and rice for dinner and recounted her day to her family in Urdu?

The woman didn't wait for an answer. Instead, she told us in a rush of anger, over the beeps of the register, that we should go back to where we came from. We lived no more than two blocks from the store, but she wasn't telling us to return to our suburban home with white aluminum siding and black shutters. She was telling us to go somewhere that existed in her mind as a place that was foreign and feared.

Maybe my inability to recall this event signals my unwillingness to accept the Islamophobia that rose up after September 11. I wanted to believe I belonged in the United States—the country where I was born. I could chalk up the grocery store incident to the acts of a single, frightened individual, but when my mosque was attacked, it was hard not to feel under siege.

In the middle of sprawling cornfields dotted with red, weathered barns, the Islamic Center of Greater Toledo is an architectural wonder in white. On either side of a vast dome stand two towering minarets that are even taller. Stained-glass windows of turquoise, blue, and vermillion line the inside of the prayer hall. Built in 1983, the center was one of the largest mosques in North America at the time. When I was a kid, my friends asked me in excited playground voices if a princess lived there. I felt ennobled by the place where I had spent nearly every Sunday of my life learning to pray and recite the Quran with melodious precision. Early on the morning of September 12, bullets shattered one of the stained-glass windows.

"People were saying, shall we cancel Friday service? Shall we cancel Sunday school?" says Imam Farooq Abo Elzahab in a lilting Egyptian accent when I recently asked him about the incident. "But we never did that. To the opposite. We unlocked our doors." He didn't waiver despite the profane notes slipped under the center's door and the threats when he answered the phone.

In response to the shooting, a Christian radio station organized a day of prayer, and more than 1,000 people from the community joined hands to encircle the Islamic Center. They made a human shield to protect us from further threats. It was as if they were saying, "You have to go through all of us to get to them." The words "United We Stand" could be found in every corner-shop window and on the bumper of every car in those days, but this interfaith demonstration organized a week after 9/11 was the first time that I felt such unity.

Today, Imam Farooq assures me that the window was easy to replace and that area congregations donated money to cover the costs. Still, I wonder if something irreplaceable wasn't lost that night. Rather than judging Islam by the billions of peaceful practitioners around the world, the shooter had equated all Muslims to the extremists who hijacked my religion along with the planes. I wanted to judge the city that was my home by the mass outpouring of support, not by a single gunman's hatred. Sometimes, though, individual displays of violence speak louder than the peaceful actions of a silent majority.

Four years after 9/11, I bought extra-long twin sheets and took my place in the mass anthropological experiment that is random-room assignment at a public university. The University of Michigan has a large number of Muslim students, though many of them share apartments off campus instead of the dorm life I chose. Like so many other college students, most of what I learned in my first year happened in my residence hall and not in lecture halls. A plate of steamed string beans taught me about vegans, and an offhand reference to a fellow resident who was transitioning from female to male forced me to rethink gender norms.

A woman who was standing behind us asked where we were from. Northwest Ohio or Northwest Pakistan? Which is the right response? Which me is being asked?

When Ramadan began that fall, I came to share something about myself. My hall mates weren't aware of the hunger that came before the Eid, the feast that ends the dawn-to-dusk fasting during Islam's holiest month. Some of my friends even joined me in observing the fasts, and I got used to praying in front of my roommate who had grown up in a town with only one streetlight. I also got used to lifting my feet into a sink in the communal bathroom to complete the pre-prayer ablution known as wadu as other girls rushed in and out in bathrobes, shooting me curious looks. Eventually, I began to feel comfortable enough to leave my door open while I prayed, so my hall mates could observe as I moved through the movements. It made me happy to think of them taking some part in my meditative moments.

One afternoon, as I carried my rented sitar onto an elevator for my weekly lessons in Indian classical music, someone I didn't know stepped in and asked me half-jokingly if I were smuggling a bazooka somewhere. When I recoiled, he said, "I only ask because you seem to be from the part of the world where people like to tote those sorts of things around. Just try to remember, you're in America now." The door opened, and he grinned at me and stepped out.

There was another day when I barreled down the hall, chased by a student who spent his summers volunteering with the Israeli Defense Force. He hollered at me in Arabic until I slipped into my room and slammed the door behind me. It happened time and again, but it wasn't until a Lebanese international student moved onto our floor that I learned what the other student had been saying: "Show me your papers!" and "Stop, or I'll shoot!" I don't speak Arabic, and apparently neither did he, except for those two phrases. He shouted them at me and no one else.

More often, I was asked to explain the basic tenants of my faith, and many times, people responded with their beliefs about Islam. Strangers took it upon themselves to warn me of the dangers of abstaining from food and drink during my fasts, and even longtime friends looked at me woefully for not trading in jeans for cutoffs in the summer. Growing up as a Muslim American, I had often been told to be a good ambassador of Islam, but this notion implies that Muslims will always be emissaries from elsewhere—that we will always be outsiders because of our religion. That it is my fellow Muslims who say this to me makes me wonder if we will ever see ourselves as fully American.

September 11 is part of what divides my parents' generation from mine. Almost half of my life has occurred after the attacks, and I remain profoundly ambivalent about the country where I was born, the country where I am a citizen. There are days I am as hopeful as I was when those hundreds of people joined hands around the Islamic Center of Greater Toledo. Like Catholics and Jews before us, who were also once told to "go back to where they came from," we will prevail, I tell myself. We will become part of this country without losing our identities.

At the same time, public support for Muslims is too often seen as socially suspect and politically imprudent. State legislatures around the country are banning Shariah law—the facet of Islam included in marriage contracts and wills—and city councils around the country have blocked plans to build new mosques. A year ago, plans to expand an Islamic center near Ground Zero sparked a nationwide controversy. Sometimes I wonder whether Muslims will ever be viewed as American without having to defend or explain ourselves. I wonder if 9/11 will come to define my generation.

DISCUSSION QUESTIONS

1. What is your reaction to Beenish Ahmed's very personal story of Islamophobic prejudice directed toward her, her family, and her mosque, in the days following the 9/11 attacks? Why were she and her family attacked?

2. React to Ahmed's reflection, following the attacks on her mosque, that "something irreplaceable" may have been "lost that night.... I wanted to judge the city that was my home by the mass outpouring of support, not by a single gunman's hatred. Sometimes, though, individual displays of violence speak louder than the peaceful actions of a silent majority." Do you agree or disagree? If Ahmed is right, how, if ever, does a person or a community that has been threatened and/or attacked begin to heal and rebuild social trust?

3. In her article, Ahmed recounted several bizarre conversations and experiences—many of them motivated by Islamophobia, not just innocent curiosity about Islam—during her student days at the University of Michigan. In your experience, and from what you know of the experience of others, is it common for students of color and minority ethnicities and religions to experience such bizarre conversations and encounters? Have you, or someone you know, experienced discrimination, and/or had similar strange encounters?

4. Ahmed writes: "I remain profoundly ambivalent about the country where I was born, the country where I am a citizen…. Sometimes I wonder whether Muslims will ever be viewed as American without having to defend or explain ourselves." Can you relate in any way to her statement—have you ever felt that way? Will Ahmed always be a foreigner (even though she was born in the United States), and will she always have to "represent her people?" Can she ever be "fully American?" How? When?

READING 5.6

MELODY

War on Error: Real Stories of American Muslims

BY **Melody Moezzi**

My parents, especially my father, have always cautioned me against religion in general, and for the most part, they have been right in doing so. They never fully endorsed the practice of one religion to the exclusion of any others in raising either my sister or myself. This is perhaps why I was so adamant in my initial refusal to write this chapter. It took a great deal of goading from my agent at the time to do it, and even then, I must admit that I began writing reluctantly. But ultimately, I did write it, not because my agent wanted me to but because I thought it was only fair to subject myself to the same scrutiny to which I had subjected all of the other individuals whose stories I had been entrusted to tell in the pages of this book. I couldn't very well bring myself to tell the stories of others from my own admittedly subjective standpoint if I hadn't first laid out where that subjectivity was coming from.

The last time I remember going to a mosque with my family, I must have been seven or eight years old. We had gone to this mosque in downtown Dayton every couple of weeks since I could remember, and I liked it mostly because they always had doughnuts, which we never had at home, and because the kids were always just playing hide-and-seek when they weren't eating doughnuts. On that last visit, we were greeted by police. The mosque had been vandalized by some neo-Nazi kids who apparently thought it was a synagogue. It was covered in swastikas, and the windows were all broken. We stopped going after that because my dad said it wasn't safe, and eventually, my sister and I started going to piano lessons instead, which I hated because I was always being upstaged at recitals by this Korean prodigy half my age and, to top it off, there were never any doughnuts.

If anything, the religion of our household was education, and focusing on one tradition of any variety—religious, cultural, or otherwise—would only limit our education. My parents had no problem sending us to a Catholic school when it was the best school in our district, and they had no problem sending me to live with nuns in Spain to study alone at the University of Madrid when I was only sixteen because my Spanish teacher assured them that it would be a priceless educational experience. My dad used to make me look up and write down every new word I heard or read in the English language in a steno pad, and he would test me on them weekly. He refused to let me get away with having less than perfect English just because he did.

More than anything else, though, he refused to let me have a chip on my shoulder just because I was the child of immigrants, or looked different from most other kids growing up in Dayton, or spoke a different language, or didn't worship Christ. There was an absolute prohibition on bitching about that kind of thing in the Moezzi household. I remember going to a slumber party in the eighth grade and having a couple of girls corner me as I was trying to go to sleep. They insisted that I accept Jesus Christ as the Son of God before I fell asleep, and they assured me that if I didn't, there was no doubt that I was going to hell. They told me that they wanted to be able to hang out with me in heaven because I was fun and that I had to accept the Savior before I went to sleep that night or we couldn't hang out later. I kept telling them that I thought Jesus was cool and all, and that I thought that he was a Prophet, but that I didn't think God was up for conceiving children. After what seemed like hours, they finally lost hope and left me alone, but not before reminding me that I was definitely going to hell now. When I told my dad about this, he laughed and told me I should have just said, "Yeah, sure, whatever you say," and gone to sleep. When I told him I didn't want them to have the satisfaction, he told me that if I cared so much about God, I wouldn't care what they said or thought.

That same year, when a deathly pale, chubby, red-headed, freckled girl told me that she could no longer be my friend because her mom said that she should have more Christian friends, I was so shocked that I again told my dad, somehow forgetting that whining about such things was strictly forbidden. He told me that he was happy because he could barely stand looking at her, she was so ugly, and that he wished she had said so earlier, before she threw up in our basement at my thirteenth birthday party.

* * *

Both my parents witnessed and lived through Iran's Islamic Revolution—partly in Iran and partly from the United States. I was born in the spring of 1979, at the height of this revolution, not in Iran like my parents but in the middle of America. Having experienced the revolution and its aftermath, my parents have always been understandably averse to anything overtly religious.

They have always strongly advised me never to be the one to bring up the topic of religion, particularly Islam, in conversation or writing—especially with or intended for American audiences: "They'll think you're a fanatic; they'll stop taking you seriously; they don't know any better; it just doesn't look good." They're right. It doesn't look good, in most of the so-called Western world, to say that you are Muslim. But as I age, I am growing less and less concerned with appearances. I am not a terrorist; I do not think women are scum; I do not hate Jews; and I am neither Arab, nor do I speak Arabic.

I don't mean to make presumptions about my reader here. I say all of this as a response to stereotypes with which I have been presented consistently throughout my life. People seem to always want to know what I think about these things when they find out that I am Muslim. Instead of asking about Islam, they ask me what I think of the Israeli-Palestinian debacle or feminist ideals or terrorism. These issues, which are inherently political and/or criminal in nature, have much to do with power and manipulation, but nothing to do with faith. Still, I admit that, even though I don't want it to, at least one such association manages to cross my own mind when a stranger tells me that she or he is Muslim.

This type of disgusting Pavlovian response is, to me, the worst form of cultural oppression, and it is my sincere belief that such oppression can only be combated through education—not necessarily through academia, but through learning, compassion, and understanding. This belief, along with a personal attraction to truth and any journey that might lead to it, most fully explains my motivation in writing this book. Nevertheless, it took a series of unexpected personal experiences, followed by the appalling events of 9–11 and the worldwide response to them, before I could manage to write a single word.

* * *

Several years before 9-11, I was faced with a personal awakening disguised, as many are, in the form of adversity. After nearly twenty years of good health and good fortune, I got sick. The saga began directly after my senior year of high school. My graduation party was shared with several other graduates, all members of our large Dayton Iranian community of friends, who had been my second family since childhood. It was in the ballroom of a Holiday Inn near the Dayton Mall. I remember doing a lot of dancing and consuming an inhuman amount of junk food—brownies, Doritos, cookies, cake—all courtesy of the hotel caterers, who wouldn't allow us to bring our own food. If Iranians know how to do anything, they know how to throw parties, and to our parents' credit, this party (apart from the catering) was no exception.

I wore a bright yellow, knee-length flowing chiffon dress with spaghetti straps. When I look at the pictures now, I cringe. I look like a banana with a little brown head and long flailing limbs to match. Still, all of our friends and family kept telling me how beautiful I looked and how proud they were of my personal and academic accomplishments. My dad, to this day, still says that I was the victim of the evil eye, and that had he burned *esfand* (a heavy, strong-smelling incense that, according to Persian superstition, is supposed to ward off the evil eye) over my head that night, this all probably would have never happened. I don't think he really believes it though.

That night, after opening more gifts than I had ever received in my life, I started having slight stomach pains. They were still there the next day, and by the next night I was in excruciating pain. My parents kept insisting that it was just gas, but I forced them to take me to the emergency room anyway. They were so convinced of the triviality of my condition, though, that they made a pit stop at the Elmis' house en route to the hospital. The Elmis were going to Iran the next day, and my dad insisted that if we didn't drop off the standard shipment of medicines for them to bring along, a bunch of our family members in Iran, short on necessary medications, would be forced to suffer severe mental and physical hardships—all thanks to me and my unrelenting gas.

The Elmis, while not blood relations, have been my second family since I can remember, and while I would generally be excited to see them, I was far from thrilled to be delaying immediate medical attention. Still, being a sucker for guilt trips and genuinely wanting to avoid responsibility for the ill health of anyone in Iran, I grudgingly agreed to the short visit and tried to tolerate the delay by staying in the car, waiting in the backseat with my knees pressed tightly against my chest, and rocking back and forth to distract myself from the pain. I remember that Dr. Elmi—the dad, an orthopedic surgeon, my godfather (who would oversee the ceremony of my marriage some five years later), and Amoo Ali to me (*amoo* meaning "paternal uncle" in Farsi)—came out of the house to offer me some Tylenol. I tried to be polite in refusing it, but I'm sure I came off as a total brat, which at that point in my life was far from an anomaly. I was sure that nothing short of some seriously heavy narcotics could control this pain, and as it turned out, despite my inexperience, I was right.

I was sobbing uncontrollably by the time we got to hospital, and I was rushed into an examination room. After a few lab tests, it became clear that I was having an attack of acute pancreatitis, a sudden inflammation of the pancreas that most commonly affects overweight, middle-aged alcoholic men and people with gallstones—none of which came close to describing me. Everyone was convinced I had been doing some heavy postgraduation celebratory drinking, but after I assured them that I didn't drink at all and that I had not recently been bitten by a snake or a scorpion (apparently another likely cause), the doctors finally ordered a CT scan.

The results suggested the presence of a pseudocyst in the middle of my pancreas, and that night, I nearly died of shock resulting from the pancreatitis. That same night, the doctors arranged to send me via helicopter to a hospital in Indiana for specialized care. I vaguely remember receiving my last rites from a priest before leaving the hospital and being too drugged up to explain to him that I wasn't Christian and too desperate at that point to reject *anyone's* prayers on my behalf.

Not a fan of flying, I asked if we could just drive instead, and while the doctors weren't encouraging, my parents gave in and drove me the one hundred miles to Indianapolis, hanging my IV on the coat hook in the backseat. I made it through the night and was treated for a week in Indianapolis—the treatment consisting mainly of starvation. After that, I started becoming familiar with hospitals around the country. For the next two years, as modern medicine tried to fix me, I was placed on a restrictive diet and underwent several endoscopic procedures in an effort to avoid surgery, all to no avail.

On the morning of April 1, 1999, I was admitted to Chicago's Rush Presbyterian Hospital to undergo a risky invasive operation the name of which I can't pronounce to this day. During the week after the surgery, my family and I were presented with a series of details about my condition: first, I had a tumor, not a cyst; second, this tumor was malignant, and the cancer had spread to outlying tissues; third, I had roughly a year left to live; and finally, two days later, that some dye hadn't been picked up on a few slides, and I had correspondingly been misdiagnosed: the tumor was in fact benign. I was going to live.

* * *

All of this happened while I was an undergraduate at Wesleyan, a freethinking, picturesque liberal arts university in the central Connecticut valley. At the time, I was busy burying my head in the writings of old dead white men, mostly philosophers. I read all of the works assigned assiduously, hoping to reach some great spiritual awakening through reason. Getting sick, however, inspired the collapse of most of my rational faculties for a good while. After being admitted to the ER on several occasions for eating foods that my pathetically deficient pancreatic enzymes were failing to digest—a chocolate chip muffin, overly oiled pasta, anything fried—I made the unilateral decision to stop eating all together.

I had always been thin, and I had never taken any active notice of the food that I put into my mouth or the power that action entailed until I was forced to monitor it, literally to save my life. Out of frustration and despair, I took things to an extreme. As a result, I spent half of my college career with a raging eating disorder and the other half in recovery, undergoing intensive outpatient treatment in the form of psychotherapy, which, by the grace of God, worked.

While I had endured extreme physical pain because of my pancreatic condition, it never came close to matching the pain I inflicted on myself. I have no doubt that I lost my mind for almost two years there, and *that*, not a tumor, was what led me to start contemplating the most selfish of all human acts. I fantasized about suicide incessantly for a period, and by refusing to ingest food, I was well on my way. Every day there was less and less of me, and somehow I found this comforting. My only other comfort was in books, but after a point, all of the philosophers started to sound the same, and I began to question their intentions in writing anything at all.

It was upon reaching this state of desperation that I took an unknowing step toward God, and before I knew it, He had taken a thousand toward me. Having never read the central text underlying the religion to which I had always claimed to subscribe, I decided, out of boredom and frustration with the great rational philosophers, to read the Qur'an. I intended to read it as a break, and began as a literary critic approaching a new genre, but I finished feeling like a naive and misinformed child. To my surprise, I had only three or four points of contention upon completing the text, and those were mostly resolved through a little deeper thought and/or reconciling translations from English to Farsi to Arabic. I had expected, at best, to find the kind of insight I'd found in great novels. My expectations, however, were far surpassed. I had unwittingly found a path that looked as if it could work for me, and the fact that this path accepted the viability of other paths and other pilgrims was what most convinced me of our compatibility.

It was then that I chose to retrieve my mind. After having read less than half of the Qur'an, I began to feel a strength and ease previously unknown to me. It was this strength that finally led me to seek help for my eating disorder on my own terms, for as my family and friends had all made countless well-intentioned attempts to help before, I had not yet been ready to do the work. It was a year after starting this treatment for my eating disorder that I finally underwent surgery to remove the growing mass in my viscera. The final and most pleasant part of my recovery took place less than one month after I was released from the hospital, when, against the advice of my surgeon, my parents, and most everyone who cared, I chose to drive cross-country to spend the summer in the most beautiful territory I had ever, or since, beheld.

I got a job folding T-shirts and making fudge and espresso at a resort at the edge of Glacier National Park, near the Canadian border, and I spent every minute I wasn't working in awe. I learned the words of the Prophet Muhammad's daily prayers in Arabic and, most importantly, their meaning. I began to pray through speaking those delightfully melodic words for the first time in my life. I started carrying an extra set of prayer "materials" in my car: a large soft sheet, or chador, to cover my body (so that I could more easily focus on my soul) and a small prayer rug to keep my feet from getting dirty.

I became increasingly dedicated to performing each of the daily prayers, a practice that has always brought me great solace but that has also, since I learned how to do it, admittedly become a fairly constant source of guilt as well, given my lousiness at it. Today, on a good day, I generally do one or two of the formal prayers, but I am a work in progress. Montana will always maintain a spiritual quality for me, not simply because of its breathtaking scenery but because it was the place where I first fully embraced my faith. Neither before nor since my time there has my practice ever been so disciplined.

Amid the mountains, lakes, and receding glaciers of northwestern Montana, without a mosque, a mullah, or even another Muslim to be found, I came to believe fully, not only in the power, presence, and beauty of God but also in the fact that He had a plan for me and that His grace, patience, and mercy refused to let me forget it. Thus began my genuine attempt to pursue the path of Islam.

I was aware of and experienced a general ignorance about Islam among most Americans, but it was a harmless ignorance, in that I ran across only a few people who actually hated me for having this background or belief. The great majority just didn't know what being Muslim meant, and while they may have had some negative associations with the faith, their ignorance usually prevented them from stating or acting on them.

In Montana, I worked with many other young men and women, mostly college students as well, and to my recollection every single one was Christian—a significant minority of them Mormons, with whom I generally formed a unique bond, given that they were my sole companions in sobriety. While most of them took that sobriety to greater lengths than I (I avoided only alcohol, and they often avoided caffeine as well), there was still clearly a connection based on our mutual distaste for mind-altering substances and the inane behaviors that often result from their consumption. Not a single one of the Mormons I met, moreover, ever held it against me that I worked as a barista at the resort's espresso bar, nor did a single one of them ever actively try to convert me. They knew what it was like to be in the minority, and I think that shared reality helped them steer clear of any missionary work with me as the object.

I remember some of my friends "warning" me about the Mormons, so that I would be prepared for their assumed future attempts to convert me. If anything, however, the Mormons I met in Montana turned out to be my staunchest supporters and defenders. Strange things happen when you're stuck in the middle of nowhere with a bunch of imported college students, there only for the summer. For me, I quite unexpectedly ended up learning a great deal about Mormonism—not by reading the Book of Mormon, which embarrassingly I have yet to pick up, but by meeting and befriending some of its adherents. Likewise, my guess is that my newly befriended Mormon brothers and sisters (none of whom, in all probability, had ever picked up a copy of the Qur'an) got some rather unexpected basic instruction in Islam through our friendships as well.

In a lot of ways, Mormons tend to get a bad rep based on the actions of a few crazy missionaries, just like Muslims tend to get a bad, if not worse, rep based on the actions of a few crazy terrorists. Comparing lunatics aside, the great majority of us are pretty decent people, Muslim and Mormon alike. Turns out that neither is quite that scary after all.

Nevertheless, I was still not only the sole Muslim in residence but the sole non-Christian, brown girl who wasn't a member of the Blackfeet Tribe. There were no Blacks, no Asians, no Arabs, no Hispanics. Just white Americans, Canadians, the Blackfeet, and me.

This brings me to Elizabeth, a girl I worked with at the St. Mary's Lodge and Resort gift shop. Elizabeth was a constant source of amusement for the rest of us, as she was incredibly ignorant in most matters. Nevertheless, she was very sweet and bore no ill will toward anyone. People would come in asking for books on Indian paintbrushes, some of the most popular wildflowers in the park, and she would tell them that we only had normal paintbrushes and that maybe they should drive down to the reservation and ask the Indians about them. She asked me one afternoon, after catching me praying outside, what religion I was. I told her that I was Muslim, and in response, she asked me what denomination of Christianity "Muslim" was. I told her that it was kind of like being Methodist, not being in the mood for long explanations.

* * *

I regret my selfish laziness and arrogance now. Today, the explanations are ten times as long, as the assumptions and perceptions are ten times as misguided. Now, instead of taking a couple of minutes to tell the Elizabeths of the world that Indian paintbrushes are wildflowers and that Islam is a separate religion from Christianity but with similar moral bases, I feel compelled to write an entire book.

Some two years before perhaps the greatest public disservice that has ever been performed for Islam, I began my very private conversion through prayer, study, and thought. Thus, when several murderous, thickheaded zealots crashed civilian airliners into the World Trade Center towers and the Pentagon on September 11, 2001, my first reactions were tears, prayers, and fear. Soon after these subsided, however, I had another familiar response, one that has always accompanied witnessing such mindless, vicious, and surreal acts: "Please, God. Don't let these fools end up claiming Islam." But they did, and I prayed that people would see past the idiocy and sensationalism and realize that they could have claimed anything and it wouldn't matter because they were still murderers of innocent men, women, and children, and I am not aware of any God-loving religion that rewards, encourages, or tolerates such slaughter.

Soon after 9–11, some drunken hick drove his truck into a Hindu temple near my parents' house in Dayton, thinking it was a mosque. A friend's uncle, who is Sikh, was slammed over the head by a two-by-four in a Rochester Home Depot solely because the perpetrator thought his turban alone meant he was Muslim, and therefore deserving. My best friend, Christina, and her family, along with the large Coptic Egyptian community in Dayton, got so much crap from people who thought they were Muslim that they eventually had to schedule an information session to inform everyone that most of the Egyptians in the district were Christian—and on a side note, it's bad to harass Muslims just for being Muslim anyway.

As Sikhs, Hindus, and Christian Arabs were getting mistaken for Muslims, I was waiting tables and living in a tiny apartment with Michael and Wendell, an interracial gay couple, and their five cats, along with their pug, Lilly, whom they had brilliantly trained to use a litter box as well. The apartment, in the middle of a largely Dominican and Puerto Rican neighborhood on the Upper West Side of Manhattan, had one window that overlooked a fallout shelter. As the grief and depression that hovered over New York quickly turned into misdirected rage, slues of Arab-run businesses were being vandalized and harassed all over the city. Muslim women who had previously worn hijab began to refrain from doing so for fear of being attacked, and, overall, hate speech and hate crimes directed toward Muslims and Arabs in particular were seriously on the rise. All the while, I was still being mistaken for a Latina.

Before 9–11, I never felt the need to clarify my origins or faith to those mistaking me for something, anything, else. Everyone in the neighborhood just assumed I was Puerto Rican because I spoke Spanish and because I had brown skin and dark curly hair. I wasn't ashamed of my faith or my heritage. I just didn't see the point in publicizing it unless someone explicitly asked. After 9–11, however, I felt like continuing to "pass" would be wrong.

* * *

I was eating an empanada and waiting for my clothes to dry at a local Laundromat not far from my apartment when María, who worked there, and with whom I'd developed a camaraderie, started talking about how happy she was that the two brothers who owned a nearby convenience store had been forced to shut it down. She told me that she should have known better than to have ever bought even a stick of gum from those disgusting Arabs. Then she told me that we were lucky that we had a glorious, civilized, Catholic culture that helped us stick together and succeed. I told her that I liked the brothers and that I used to watch soccer games in the back of the store with them because they

had satellite. Then she asked me why the hell I did that, given that all they ever watched were Middle Eastern countries' matches. I had told her twice before that I was Iranian, and it now became clear to me that either she had no idea where Iran was or she wasn't listening to me. "María," I told her, "soy iraní. Soy casi árabe, y soy musulmana."* Tears running down my face, I threw the remainder of my empanada at her and ran home, leaving my laundry to fend for itself.

After talking to Michael and crying some more, I went back that night when I knew María would no longer be working. But she was still there, sitting in a lawn chair on the sidewalk in front of the store watching traffic. I walked straight past her without saying a word, and she followed me in. When I asked her why she was still there, she told me that her shift had ended over an hour ago but that she had stayed to wait for me. At this point, I noticed that someone else's clothes were in my drier and mine were nowhere in sight. "Damn it! Where the hell are my clothes?" That was the first time I had ever spoken to her in English.

She took my hand and led me to the back of the store, where she had neatly folded all of my clothes and wrapped them in tissue paper. She apologized and told me that she was embarrassed and ashamed. She then thanked me for being honest and for debunking her prejudices through my example. I have no idea where María is today, or what she is doing, or even her last name. Still, I am grateful for her example as well, for she gave me hope in the persistent power of friendship and human interaction, no matter how brief or minimal, to impact our lives and attitudes. Without this hope, I could have never even begun to write this book. I am the product of my experiences, memories, and relations, and so is each one of the individuals around whom the following chapters revolve. These individuals are not characters, they are not case studies, and they are not literary devices. They are all real, and they are all awake and dynamic. As such, each of them has given me an education for which there is no worthy or appropriate degree, and I thank them.

---

* "I am Iranian. I'm almost Arab, and I'm Muslim."

DISCUSSION QUESTIONS

1. Melody Moezzi is a Muslim—her parents came to the United States from Iran—but she describes her family and her upbringing as secular (nonreligious). Does it surprise you that she is not religious, that she is not a "practicing" Muslim? Does it surprise you that she does not subscribe to radical politics, but rather, is a culturally mainstream American woman? She writes: "I am not a terrorist; I do not think women are scum; I do not hate Jews; and I am neither Arab, nor do I speak Arabic." Are any of these words, or the ways in which she describes herself, unexpected or unusual? Why or why not?

2. Comment on the following statement: "In a lot of ways, Mormons tend to get a bad rep based on the actions of a few crazy missionaries, just like Muslims tend to get a bad, if not worse, rep based on the actions of a few crazy terrorists. Comparing lunatics aside, the great majority of us are pretty decent people, Muslims and Mormons alike. Turns out that neither is quite that scary after all." Do you agree? Do you disagree? Explain why.

3. Are Sikhs Muslims? Do their turbans make them Muslims? Research the Sikh religion. What part of the world do Sikhs come from, and what are the basic tenets of their religion? Are Coptic Egyptians Muslims? If not, what are they? What does it say about American fears (and about American religious ignorance) that Sikhs and Coptic Egyptians in the United States have been mistaken for Muslims and attacked? Can you really tell what religion a person is by the way they look, or even if they seem to be wearing exotic clothing? Why or why not?

4. What is "passing?" Melody writes that before 9/11, she had been happy that her brown skin and curly hair allowed her to "pass" for Puerto Rican; but after 9/11, she no longer wanted to pass as someone other than who she is: a Muslim woman. What was it about 9/11 that prompted Melody's change of heart? Have you ever wanted to pass as someone other than who you are?

5. What was the point of Melody recalling her conversation with Maria at the laundromat? What was important about that conversation? Are there a lot of "Marias" in American society today?

READING 5.7

THE WAR ON IMMIGRANTS

Stories from the Front Lines
Anti-Immigration Policies are Hurting Real People and
Families and Undermining U.s. Ideals of Justice. They
May Also Be Making Us Less Safe from Terrorism.

BY **Cheryl Little**

The U.S. Government's War on Terror has transgressed into a War on Immigrants. Since September 11, 2001, Washington's attempt to secure the nation's borders has not only sent waves of fear through the immigrant community but has undermined the nation's longstanding principles of providing shelter and refuge to those fleeing tyranny, intolerance and hunger.[1]

Federal dragnets with code names like Operation Endgame and Return to Sender target immigrants who have broken no criminal laws, yet are treated like hardened criminals, with no right to a court-appointed lawyer. Fugitive Operations teams from Immigration and Customs Enforcement (ICE) arrested over 30,000 immigrants in fiscal year 2007, nearly doubling the 2006 arrests.[2]

ICE detainees now represent the fastest growing prison population in the U.S., costing taxpayers more than $1.2 billion a year.[3] The new laws, programs and strategies aimed at strengthening our borders and controlling immigration in the aftermath of the 9/11 terror attacks have not only failed to make us safer; they have fueled an anti-immigrant hysteria.

Immigrant neighborhoods around the country have been the targets of massive sweeps by both local and federal law enforcement.[4] Town and state officials have passed laws punishing immigrants and those who offer them shelter. And, as a weakening economy has prodded disgruntled Americans into a search for scapegoats, many hard-working, tax-paying immigrants with significant ties to the U.S., full-time jobs and American spouses and children, have been forced underground.[5]

Even when they have been victims of hate crimes, they avoid contact with law enforcement.

My agency, the Florida Immigrant Advocacy Center (FIAC), has met with thousands of these immigrants since 9/11. A non-profit group dedicated to protecting the basic rights of immigrants, FIAC has documented their stories to put a face on the injustices being committed against them.

Our work has provided ample evidence that the barrage of anti-immigrant laws and regulations, often propelled by right-wing rhetoric, is an assault on the fundamental civil liberties of all. But our research also makes clear that driving immigrants further underground does nothing to fix our broken immigration system.

It only makes matters worse.

BORDER PATROL AGENTS SPEND HOURS LOOKING FOR UNDOCUMENTED IMMIGRANTS DRIVING ON FLORIDA'S TURNPIKE.

OVERZEALOUS LAW ENFORCEMENT

A first step toward changing this situation must be to back away from the exclusive focus on law enforcement as a solution. Florida provides some poignant examples of the current trend. Sheriff deputies from Okaloosa and Santa Rosa counties are arresting immigrants without ICE assistance, claiming they are responding to tips about identity fraud.[6] The sheriff's offices in these counties has a tip line for reporting suspected undocumented workers.[7] Following the narrow defeat of anti-immigrant ordinances in Palm Bay, local police used a trespassing law to bring criminal charges against suspect Hispanics and turn them over to Border Patrol.[8]

In a climate that encourages overzealous policing, elaborate dragnets often employ racial profiling.[9] In Florida, the Bay County sheriff who prosecutes immigrants for using false documents has been accused of such racial profiling by Hispanics.[10] Across the state, immigrants traveling to work or to visit relatives are often targeted. Border Patrol agents spend hours looking for undocumented immigrants driving on Florida's Turnpike.[11]

Law enforcement authorities in Florida and elsewhere are increasingly entering into agreements with the Department of Homeland Security (DHS) to act as ICE agents, a practice which reduces already limited crime-fighting resources of local police.[12] These agreements can be enticing to sheriffs in smaller counties anxious to foster a get-tough reputation and build arrest statistics by detaining suspected "illegals." Although many police chiefs are opposed, such agreements are increasingly attractive to many sheriffs who see this as an easy way to mollify angry constituents.

Last summer, U.S. Congressman Jeff Miller (R-FL) urged ICE Assistant Secretary Julie Myers to open an ICE office in Okaloosa County, Florida.[13] In 2007, the Collier County (Florida) Sheriff's Department signed a Memorandum of Understanding with DHS. More such agreements are sure to follow.[14]

If local sheriffs are overzealous, they are only following a path blazed by federal agents. Earlier this year, congressional witnesses charged that ICE's tactics often resulted in the apprehension of legal residents and citizens without warrants.[15] In April 2005, 114 U.S. citizens and legal residents filed suit against ICE, claiming they were illegally detained and harassed during a workplace raid in Los Angeles.[16] U.S. citizens and legal residents sued ICE last year after being targeted during raids at Swift & Company meat packing plants.[17]

In the absence of comprehensive immigration reform that would offer a more regularized and predictable way of treating immigrants, cities and states nationwide are attempting to take federal responsibilities into their own hands. The result has been a proliferation of local mandates and initiatives that have poisoned the climate even for legal residents.

In 2007 alone, over 1,700 local anti-immigrant ordinances were considered around the U.S.[18] In some locales this has led to a mass exodus of Hispanics, which has devastated local economies, and lawsuits that drain community coffers.[19] State legislatures have become the immigration debate's newest battleground.[20] In Mississippi, for example, undocumented immigrants who have a job can be charged with a felony and are ineligible for bail. Those found guilty are jailed for at least one year, fined at least $1,000, or both.[21]

CHILDREN ARE VICTIMS

The crackdown has traumatized immigrant families. In many cases, families have been forced apart when parents are detained or deported—leaving children to fend for themselves with relatives or strangers. While ICE has the right to arrest those without legal status, the manner in which they carry out their raids is disturbing.

The story of the Sánchez family of Coral Gables, Florida, is typical. On April 17, 2006 at 4 a.m., DHS and local police surrounded the couple's home.[22] "There were so many officers—they even had shotguns," the mother recalled. "They were screaming that we had two minutes to get ready. My young daughters were crying as officers grabbed my husband and handcuffed him. They acted as if we were hardened criminals."[23] The Sánchez family was deported so quickly there was no time to sell their home, gather their belongings or say goodbye to family and friends. An older daughter, married to a U.S. citizen, was also deported even though her application for legal residency was pending.[24]

Children are often among the most deeply affected by ICE roundups. After raids, children have been left with non-family caregivers or placed in state care.[25] Crying infants have been pulled from their mothers by armed officers who deny them any opportunity to make arrangements for their children's care.[26] Even nursing mothers have been detained and forced to leave their babies behind, as have mothers with sick children.[27]

Perhaps the greatest fear parents have is losing their American-born children forever. Blanca Benitez-Banegas knows this firsthand. Blanca and her common-law husband came to the United States in 1999 after Hurricane Mitch. While here, she gave birth to two sons who were age five and seven.

But a traffic stop shortly before Christmas, 2006 brutally divided the family. The two boys were placed in foster care even though Blanca begged ICE to place them with her sister, a legal permanent resident, in Houston, Texas.[28] For two long months, while in ICE detention in a Florida jail and two Texas jails, Blanca had no idea where her sons were, and they had no idea

Welcome Sign: Avon Park, Florida

A Florida resident holds a sign protesting a proposed law targeting immigrants in Avon Park.

where she and their father were.[29] She finally learned that her husband had been sent to Krome and then deported about a month after her arrest. "I saw my children for the first time when I was back at the Broward Transitional Center (BTC)," Blanca remembered. "My eldest son asked why we had abandoned him and then asked if I had killed someone. My youngest son was having nightmares."[30]

When Blanca was transferred back to Florida she had no idea that a court hearing was scheduled to determine who would have custody of her boys. If she did not retain custody, she might not see them again during the 10 years she would be barred from returning to the United States following deportation. Thanks to the Honduran Consulate and pro bono lawyers, Blanca retained custody and her sons returned with her to Honduras.

CAUGHT IN THE BLACK HOLE

Once in custody, detainees often fall into a black hole. Parents held by ICE have limited access to the outside world. It can take weeks to get permission to call an attorney or loved ones to let them know where you are.[31] Without the benefit of legal representation, parents often unknowingly waive their rights and are quickly deported.

The number of children affected is alarming.[32] According to a 2007 study by the non-partisan Urban Institute, for the National Council of La Raza, 5 million children in the U.S. had at least one undocumented parent.[33] Two-thirds of these children were U.S. citizens or legal residents.[34] For every two undocumented workers arrested, one child was left behind.[35]

Older children, many brought to the U.S. as toddlers by their parents, are also being deported. That's what happened to 18-year-old college student Juan Gómez. Juan was 18 months old when his family came to the U.S. from Colombia in 1991 on a tourist visa and applied for asylum. Their case was pending for 11 years. Six years passed before they had a chance to make their case. Meanwhile, Juan's parents started a catering business. Juan excelled in school, scoring 1410 on the SAT, and volunteered at a shelter.[36]

Seventeen years after their lawful arrival, Juan and his family were arrested and taken to jail in handcuffs by ICE. The family was separated and neither Juan nor his brother Alex were allowed to communicate with their parents while in jail. Outraged, Juan's classmates launched a campaign on Facebook to secure their release. The resulting publicity led to the family's temporary release in July 2007. Even then, the parents were deported in October. They have no idea when they'll see their sons again.

When FIAC first met with Juan and Alex in jail, Juan said, "Every experience Alex and I have had, every friend we've made, every pledge of allegiance we've recited, and every pivotal point of development in our lives has been in the U.S." This case is so compelling, that even CNN's Lou Dobbs has said the Gómez brothers should be allowed to remain in this country. Yet, their future looks bleak.[37] Florida Congressman Lincoln Diaz-Balart recently said it's not likely Congress will pass a private bill filed on their behalf because "there are too many similar cases."[38] And passage of the DREAM Act, which would permit students like Juan and Alex to earn legal status if they complete at least two years of college or two years of military service, is an uphill battle.[39] If neither happens, Juan and Alex could be deported next year.[40]

NO SAFE HAVEN

The fear and misery caused by ICE sweeps are widespread, stretching from Hispanic to Haitian communities, and leave few safe havens.[41] The arrest earlier this year of Karina Acosta outside her New Mexico school prompted an outcry from school officials that even schools are no longer safe for undocumented students.[42] The arrest of a Haitian woman in Florida as she was leaving church in late February 2008 stunned pastors and their parishioners,[43] and pastors have complained that congregations are being decimated due to enforcement activities.[44] The Bay County Sheriff even boasted that fewer immigrants attend church or school since they began prosecuting immigrants for using false documents.[45]

As if government crackdowns weren't enough, some vigilante private citizens are attempting to take matters into their own hands. On October 8, 2007, a condominium president in Florida's Deerfield Beach posted a letter informing residents—70 percent of whom were Brazilian—that she was asking ICE to enter their building and "do a door-to-door documentation of everyone's legal status."[46] The warning also noted that if residents did not make themselves available, "I will allow authorities to do whatever they deem necessary, including forcible entry into the unit.[47]

A frantic call to FIAC last year from a U.S. citizen, concerning her Uruguayan-born husband, revealed just how mean-spirited things have become. While filling his gas tank, Miguel was approached by two uniformed men. They flashed badges and claimed they were from "immigration." One pointed to a gun under his uniform. They asked for Miguel's ID, disappeared with his documents and upon return interrogated him at length.

They released him after two hours, but said he had overstayed his visa and would have to appear in court. Yet Miguel is in the U.S. legally. A vendor at the gas station later told him that the so-called ICE officers actually worked for a strip club across the street. The two frequently pose as immigration agents and harass people they suspect are undocumented.[48]

Anti-immigrant groups vow that the war against the current "invasion" is just beginning. At last count Florida had at least a dozen such groups.[49] The website of a Pompano Beach group, www.reportillegals.com, promises visitors that for $10 they'll alert ICE to "illegals" reported to them. Floridians for Immigration Enforcement posts videos of persons suspected of hiring undocumented workers.

Not just fun and games: an anti-immigrant video games

The demonization of immigrants these days is also evident in the media. Billboards across the country have called for Americans to "Stop the Invasion." A computer game, "Border Patrol," encourages players to try to shoot immigrants crossing the border, including a pregnant woman with children.[50] Meanwhile, the media—most prominently FOX News and CNN commentator Lou Dobbs—sensationalize the issue on a daily basis.

THE IMMIGRATON CRACKDOWN IS MAKING US LESS SAFE; OUR GOVERNMENT IS WASTING PRECIOUS RESOURCES TARGETING PEOPLE WHO CAUSE US NO HARM.

Not surprisingly, this harassment has escalated to real violence. Undocumented immigrants in border states are frequently targeted by robbers, armed civilians and rival smugglers.[51] Attacks against Guatemalans are so common in South Florida that perpetrators call their assaults "Guat-bashings." Mexicans are easy prey for armed thugs who break into their homes, take their money and belongings and even shoot them. They call it "Chico-hunting."[52] Most crimes go unreported because the victims fear discovery by ICE. Hate groups like the Ku Klux Klan, Skinheads and neo-Nazis are riding the anti-immigrant wave and recruiting additional support. The Southern Poverty Law Center attributes the 48 percent growth in hate groups in the U.S. since 2000 to growing anti-immigrant sentiment.[53] According to the FBI, anti-Hispanic hate crimes jumped 25 percent since 2004.[54]

THE WRONG TARGET

Is our nation any safer because families like the Gómezes and Benítezes have been deported? It's likely we're actually less safe, because our government is wasting precious resources targeting people who cause us no harm.

DHS Secretary Michael Chertoff conceded last year that his immigration agents were busy chasing maids and landscapers instead of focusing on drug dealers and terrorists. Even former CIA counterterrorism chief Vincent Cannistrano lamented that a system that targets whole classes of people in an effort to prevent terrorism is exactly the wrong way to go about it.

Deportations are not only a drain on federal coffers, they ravage our economy. According to the U.S. Department of Labor, by 2010 America will have 168 million jobs and only 158 million Americans to fill them.

Undocumented workers pay sales taxes, real estate taxes and income taxes. In April 2008, the Congressional Budget Office estimated that a mandatory employment verification system would cut $17.3 billion from federal revenues over nine years by pushing undocumented workers out of jobs where they pay taxes.[55]

Immigrants today feel that the welcome mat has been pulled from under them, driving further underground even those eligible for relief from deportation. Current immigration policy creates an ever-growing undocumented population, permits exploitation and all too often results in human tragedy.

The U.S. can cope with the new groups of immigrants and, at the same time, protect national security, without tarnishing our principles of justice. How? With reality-based immigration reform that permits government officials to track the whereabouts of immigrants, responds to the demands of the U.S. labor market, and preserves the fundamental principle of family unity. Such reform will also undermine the power of smugglers and unscrupulous employers who exploit immigrants. By permitting undocumented immigrants already in the United States to embark on a path to legalization, and controlling future immigration through legal channels, enforcement efforts could focus instead on identifying those with true intent to do us harm.

Clearly, we need to enforce immigration law; but we need laws that can reasonably be enforced. Lawmakers at all levels should abandon measures that squander our funds and misdirect our attention by criminalizing immigrants for civil violations. Legislative reform that treats immigrants humanely will strengthen our economy and will ensure that law enforcement focuses on fighting real threats. Without this, the tragedies represented by the caseloads of agencies like FIAC will continue to grow.

ENDNOTES

1. For a detailed report of government practices and policies post September 11, 2001 see Cheryl Little and Kathie Klarreich, "Securing Our Borders: Post 9/11 Scapegoating of Immigrants," Florida Immigrant Advocacy Center, April 2005.

2. U.S. Immigration and Customs Enforcement, "ICE Fugitive Operations Teams arrests more than 30,000 in FY2007," News Release, December 4, 2007. See also, Ruth Morris, "Crackdown boosts arrests of fugitive immigrants in Florida," *South Florida Sun-Sentinel*, December 5, 2007.

3. Roughly 64% are held in county or city jails and about 84% are without lawyers. The recent surge in immigration detention has greatly benefitted private prison companies, like Corrections Corporations of America and the GEO group, whose stocks increased sharply following President Bush's proposal in February 2006 to increase spending on ICE detention. See e.g., Leslie Berestein, "A once ailing private-prison sector is now a revenue maker," *The Copley News Service*, May 9, 2008.

4. See e.g., Fear and Loathing: Immigration Editions, "Special Report Documents Rhetoric and Hysteria Surrounding Illegal Immigration on Cable News," Press Release, Media Matters, May 21, 2008.

5. Although family unity is the cornerstone of our immigration laws, extra-ordinarily long backlogs for family-based immigration petitions keep families apart for years. At the end of fiscal year 2003, over 1.2 million green card applications were pending. Testimony of Demetrios G. Papademetriou, Senate Hearing on "Evaluating a Temporary Guest Worker Proposal," February 12, 2004.

6. The Santa Rosa County Sheriff is working with Florida's Walton County and Okaloosa County Sheriffs to target undocumented workers in Florida's Panhandle. Press Release, Santa Rosa County Sheriff's Office, March 10, 2008.

7. Louis Cooper, "Santa Rosa going after undocumented workers," *The Pensacola News Journal*, February 24, 2008.

8. Palm Bay immigrant ordinances fail," *Orlando Business Journal*, August 18, 2006; Linda Jump, "Palm Bay Council Nixes Immigration ordinance," *Florida Today*, August 18, 2006; "Central Florida Nixes Immigration Ordinance," *Local 6.com*, August 18, 2006; "Illegal Immigration: Arrest Controversy," *Central Florida News 13*, September 5, 2006.

9. Warrantless raids of Hispanic homes by ICE and a Tennessee county sheriff have been challenged in court. Julia Preston, "No need for a warrant, You're an Immigrant," *The New York Times*, October 14, 2007.

10. S. Brady Calhoun, "Illegals gone from Bay County; Sheriff takes credit," *Florida Freedom Newspaper*, January 29, 2008.

11. Beth Reinhard, "Judge on spot for way he treats illegals." The Miami Herald, March 14, 2006.

12. After 9/11 the Chief of Florida's Department of Law Enforcement asked DHS to grant its 40,000 police officers the power to interrogate, arrest and detain immigrants suspected of violating civil immigration laws. Although this was not done, in the fall of 2002 Florida was the first state to enter into an agreement with Immigration to deputize local law enforcement officers to act as immigration agents.

13. Letter to Julie Myers, Assistant Secretary U.S. ICE, from U.S. Congressman Jeff Miller, August 23, 2007.

14. These include the Florida counties of Duval, Manatee, Santa Rosa, Lee and Bay.

15. Mancha, a U.S. citizen from Mexico, described to the House Judiciary Committee how armed ICE officers knocked down their door without a warrant and demanded to see her mother's immigration paper. She didn't need a green card because she was born in Florida, Mancha told lawmakers. Ben Evans, "Immigration enforcement tactics criticized at House hearing," *The Associated Press*, February 13, 2008.

16. Anna Gorman, "LA civil rights attorney files claims over federal immigration raid," *Los Angeles Times*, April 25, 2008; "114 U.S. Citizens and Lawful Residents File Damage Claims," Center for Human Rights Press Release, April 25, 2008.

17. Julia Preston, "No Need for a Warrant, You're an Immigrant," *The New York Times*, October 14, 2007.

18. "Top 10 Migration Issues of 2007," *Migration Information Source*, Migration Policy Institute, December 2007.

19. See e.g., "What happens when immigrants go away," Editorial, *The Miami Herald*, October 2, 2007; Ken Belson and Jill P. Capuzzo, "Towns Rethink Laws Against Illegal Immigrants," *The New York Times*, September 25, 2007; Julie Preston, "Judge voids ordinance on Illegal Immigrants," *The New York Times*, July 27, 2007.

20. See e.g., Bill Kaczor, "Immigration bills get first heaving, but time running short," The Associated Press, April 8, 2008; "Plans for legislation cover wide spectrum," The Miami Herald, March 31, 2008; Helena Poleo, "Bills Boost Power Over Immigration," The Miami Herald, February 17, 2008; Niala Boodhoo and Beth Reinhard, " State proposals target undocumented workers," The Miami Herald, February 7, 2007; Laura Wides-Munoz, "State Reps. Offer a Slew of Bills to Combat Illegal Immigration," The Associated Press, February 5, 2008.

21. David Bacon, "In Mississippi, Work is Now a Felony for Undocumented Immigrants," http://dbacon.igc.org, April 27, 2008.

22. The family's name has been changed to protect their confidentiality.

23. Declaration of LQ to Florida Immigrant Advocacy Center, May 2, 2006.

24. On March 1, 2003, the Immigration and Naturalization Service (INS), along with 21 other cabinet level agencies, was reorganized under the newly created Department of Homeland Security (DHS). Among the departments formed within DHS to handle enforcement action are the Bureau of Customs and Border Protection and the Bureau of Immigration and Customs Enforcement. They are referred to in this report by their acronyms CBP and ICE, respectively. References to INS predate DHS's creation.

25. See e.g., Ray Henry, "Children Stranded After Immigration Raid, *The Associated Press*, March 7, 2007; David Montgomery, "Poster Child," *The Washington Post*, May 20, 2007; "One Year after the New Bedford raid, has anything changed?," *ACLU Mass Rights Blog*, March 6, 2008.

26. See e.g., Julia Preston, "Immigration Quandary: A Mother Torn from her Baby," *New York Times*, November 17, 2007; Dianna Smith, "Haitians targeted unfairly in immigration sweeps, advocates say," Naples Daily News, February 27, 2005; Dianna Smith, "'Arrest of Illegals' leave behind shattered lives," *Naples Daily News*, February 27, 2005; Waveny Ann Moore, "As Immigration status divides families, 'You can feel the fear'," *St. Petersburg Times*, July 30, 2007; Ana Mendez, "Immigration chaos tears a family apart," *The Miami Herald*, March 7, 2007.

27. See e.g., Julia Preston, "Immigration Quandary: A Mother Torn from her Baby," New York Times, November 17, 2007; Ana Ceron, "Jupiter family tries to survive as mom fights deportation," *Palm Beach Post*, July 21, 2007; Alfonso Chardy, "Detained Haitian mom set free, *The Miami Herald*, October 27, 2007. After much public criticism ICE released new guidelines, mostly applicable to large raids. The guidelines instruct officers how to respond when they encounter single parents, pregnant women, nursing mothers and the like.

28. ICE claims that they intended to leave the two boys with their father before they learned that he had a criminal history. Alfonso Chardy, "US-born kids were in foster care as parents fought deportation," *The Miami Herald*, July 27, 2007.

29. Alfonso Chardy, "US-born kids were in foster care as parents fought deportation," *The Miami Herald*, July 27, 2007.

30. Declaration of Blanca Banegas-Benites to Florida Immigration Advocacy Center, March 23, 2007; Alfonso Chardy, "Sent Away," *The Miami Herald*, July 27, 2007.

31. See "Treatment of Immigration Detainees Housed at Immigration and Customs Enforcement Facilities," Department of Homeland Security Office of Inspector General, OIG-07-01, December 2006. The report notes that one detainee had to spend 16 days just trying to get permission to call his attorney. Half a dozen others had to file grievances in order to get permission to call their families and let them know they were in ICE detention.

32. See e.g., Spencer S. Hsu and Krissah Williams, "Illegal Workers Arrested in 6-State ID Theft Sweep," *The Washington Post*, December 13, 2006; Roxana Hegeman, "Immigration raids May Affect Meat Prices," The Associated Press; Ray Henry, "Children stranded After Immigration Raid," *The Washington Post*, March 7, 2007; N.C. Aizenman, "Pleading to Stay a Family; Raids on Illegal Immigrants Have Their U.S.-Born Children Fearing Separation—and Some Are Lobbying Capitol Hill," *The Washington Post*, April 2, 2007.

33. Randy Capps, Rosa Maria Castañeda, Ajay Chaudry, Robert Santos, "Paying the Price: The Impact of Immigration Raids on America's Children," The Urban Institute for the National Council of La Raza, 2007.

34. Randy Capps, Rosa Maria Castañeda, Ajay Chaudry, Robert Santos, "Paying the Price: The Impact of Immigration Raids on America's Children," The Urban Institute for the National Council of La Raza, 2007.

35. Randy Capps, Rosa Maria Castañeda, Ajay Chaudry, Robert Santos, "Paying the Price: The Impact of Immigration Raids on America's Children," The Urban Institute for the National Council of La Raza, 2007. Following their parents arrest, children felt abandoned and evidenced signs of "emotional trauma, psychological duress, and mental health problems." The Urban Institute has recommended that our government release parents to their children and that Congress hold hearings on the consequences of ICE raids on children. Randy Capps, Rosa Maria Castañeda, Ajay Chaudry, Robert Santos, "Paying the Price: The Impact of Immigration Raids on America's Children," The Urban Institute for the National Council of La Raza, 2007.

36. See e.g., Julia Preston, "Measures Would Offer Legal Status to Illegal Immigrant Student," *The New York Times*, September 20, 2007.

37. "I think in this case it's clear there should be an exception made because you have a situation where somebody has been 15, as much as 18 years who has been exemplary and through no fault of his or in other cases her responsibility. There's no question that there should be an exception made." Lou Dobbs, CNN July 31, 2007.

38. Kathy Kiely, "Children Caught in the Immigration Crossfire." *USA Today*, October 7, 2007.

39. The Development, Relief and Education for Alien Minors Act would permit students to gain conditional residency for six years, provided they have resided in the United States for at least 5 years prior to enactment, came to the U.S. before the age of 16, they graduated from high school or were admitted to an institution of higher learning, and they are of good moral character. After six years they could become permanent residents once they completed two years of college or served two years in the military. The Migration Policy Institute estimates that about 360,000 students could now be eligible for protection from deportation if the DREAM Act were to pass.

40. Last fall former Congressman Tom Tancredo (R-CO) asked federal authorities to arrest students who participated in a staff briefing in the DREAM Act because he suspected that some were illegal. Senator Dick Durbin (D-IL), who was sponsoring the DREAM Act, advised Tancredo that the legal status of the relevant students had been resolved. Tancredo responded that he did not expect Durbin to be able to "tell the difference between legal residents and illegal aliens." Klause Marre, "Durbin blasts Tancredo on immigration," October 25, 2007. http://thehill.com/leading-the-news/durbin-blasts-tancredo-on-immigration-2007-10-24.html.

41. A Broward County, Florida traffic court judge who was short listed for promotion routinely asked defendants about their legal status and, on at least one occasion, turned an immigrant over to ICE. Hispanic attorneys and judges protested. See e.g., Beth Reinhard," Judge on spot for way he treats illegals," *The Miami Herald*, March 14, 2004; Beth Reinhard, "Judges urged to act proper with minorities," *The Miami Herald*, March 14, 2006.

42. Deborah Baker, "Student's deportation sparks protest," *The Associated Press*, March 5, 2008.

43. This mother of three was arrested as she left her church in Greenacres in her car that had a broken taillight.

44. Dianna Smith, "Haitians shaken by arrest of churchgoer," *Palm Beach Post*, February 29, 2008. Some pastors are advising their parishioners to go to Canada, where Haitians are exempt from deportation.

45. S. Brady Calhoun, "Illegals gone from Bay County; Sheriff takes credit," *Florida Freedom Newspaper*, January 29, 2008.

46. Tal Abbady, "Letter sends a scare into immigrants at Deerfield complex," *The South Florida Sun-Sentinel*, October 20, 2007. The condo President resigned about a week after posting her notice, but some traumatized residents moved away nonetheless.

47. Tal Abbady, "Letter sends a scare into immigrants at Deerfield complex," *The South Florida Sun-Sentinel*, October 20, 2007.

48. Statement of Anne, June 30, 2006.

49. See e.g., Bill Kaczor, "Immigration bills get first heaving, but time running short," *The Associated Press*, April 8, 2008; "Plans for legislation cover wide spectrum," *The*

Miami Herald, March 31, 2008; Helena Poleo, "Bills Boost Power Over Immigration," *The Miami Herald*, February 17, 2008; Niala Boodhoo and Beth Reinhard, " State proposals target undocumented workers," *The Miami Herald*, February 7, 2007; Laura Wides-Munoz, "State Reps. Offer a Slew of Bills to Combat Illegal Immigration," *The Associated Press*, February 5, 2008.

50. "'Racist' Computer Game Targets Immigrants," Top News, *CBS 5*, April 13, 2006. By contrast, a video game, ICED!, was produced by the non-profit group Breakthrough. Its goal is to create empathy for immigrants.

51. Randal C. Archibold, "Illegal Immigrants Slain in an Attack in Arizona," *The New York Times*, February 9, 2007.

52. Andres Amerikaner, "Criminals targeting migrant fears," *The Miami Herald*, June 21, 2007.

53. See e.g., Casey Woods, "Opposing an 'Invasion,' *The Miami Herald*, March 31, 2008.

54. "When Hate Becomes Hurt," *Newsweek*, March 10, 2008.

55. Letter to Honorable John Conyers, Jr., Chairman, Committee on the Judiciary, U.S. House of Representative, from Peter R. Orszag, Director, Congressional Budget Office, April 4, 2008 http://www.cbo.gov/ftpdocs/91xx/doc9100/hr4088ltr.pdf

DISCUSSION QUESTIONS

1. Cheryl Little claims that America's war on terrorism has morphed into a war on immigrants. Is she right? If so, what's wrong with that? How might anti-immigration policies be hurting real people and families? How might such policies be making America less safe? How might our government be wasting precious resources targeting people who cause us no harm?

2. Little says that "a first step" toward solving America's immigrant crisis "must be to back away from the exclusive focus on law enforcement as a solution." What does she mean by this? How would backing away from an exclusive law enforcement focus help resolve this crisis?

3. Evaluate the role played by federal Immigration and Customs Enforcement (ICE) agents and local police and sheriff's departments in the current war on immigrants in the United States. How are immigrant children affected by the ICE and law enforcement dragnets, and by the ongoing war on immigrants?

THE NEW IMMIGRANTS

The Next America: Boomers, Millennials, and
the Looming Generational Showdown

BY **Paul Taylor; Pew Research Center**

ILLEGAL IMMIGRATION

Most of the political and media attention to immigrants in recent years has focused on those who have come illegally. Understandably so—the past few decades have seen the largest influx of such immigrants in the nation's history. The number living in the US more than tripled from 3.5 million in 1990 to a peak of 12.2 million in 2007 before declining somewhat during the 2007–2009 recession. The latest Pew Research Center estimate had 11.7 million here as of 2012, which means they accounted for slightly more than a quarter of the 41.7 million immigrants in the US that year.[1]

Unauthorized immigrants tend to live in the shadows and avoid contact with government agencies. How do we know how many there are? Mostly thanks to Jeffrey Passel, a brilliant former Census Bureau demographer who decades ago developed something called the "residual method" to estimate the number and characteristics of immigrants who are in the US illegally at any given time. Passel's methodology, which has since been adopted by the Department of Homeland Security and other researchers, involves totaling up the number of legal immigrants (computed from administrative data) and the number of all immigrants (computed from census data). The difference between those two numbers—the residual—is presumed to make up the universe of immigrants who are here illegally. It's a bit more complicated than that because various adjustments need to be made for undercounts. Once Passel has established the size of this universe, he can then make educated guesses about the characteristics of unauthorized immigrants. For example, if an immigrant is an accountant, a teacher, or a veteran, it's a pretty good bet he or she isn't here illegally. And so on.

Perhaps the most surprising finding from Passel's research is that a sizable share of unauthorized immigrants—nearly half—live in a household made up of an adult couple (married or not) and one or more children. This probably isn't the family constellation most people have in mind when they think about a migrant farm worker or a day laborer. However, unauthorized immigrants (46%) are much more likely to be parents of a minor child than are legal immigrants (38%) or native-born US adults (29%). The difference is driven both by the youth of unauthorized immigrant adults, who are typically in the child-rearing and -raising stage of life, and by their relatively high birthrates. It's also a clue to their motives for coming. Yes, they come for work. But they also come to put down roots, start a family, and create a future for their as-yet-unborn children. And it's those kids who are the greatest beneficiaries of their journey. Of the more than 5 million children of today's unauthorized immigrants, about 4 in 5 were born in this country and thus are automatic US citizens, despite the illegal status of their parents. The other 20 percent— the so-called Dreamers, who as young children were brought to this country illegally by their parents—have already been spared the threat of deportation by an Obama administration policy change in 2012 and are the leading candidates to be granted a pathway to citizenship in various immigration bills Congress was considering in 2013.

As for the roughly 10 million adult unauthorized immigrants, they broke the law, which means they live under the threat of employer exploitation, government deportation, or both. Most work long hours for low wages under lousy working conditions, often doing jobs their US-born counterparts consider beneath them. Tallying up their costs and benefits to society is

FIGURE 1 Estimates of the US Unauthorized Immigrant Population, 1990–2012

Note: Shading surrounding line indicates low and high points of the estimated 90% confidence interval. White data markers indicate the change from the previous year is statistically significant (for 1995, change is significant from 1990).

Source: Pew Research Center estimates based on residual methodology applied to March supplements to the Current Population Survey (1995–2004, 2012) or American Community Survey (2005–2011)

a complex and subjective exercise. Arguably the greatest harm they do is the illegal way they came to the country—which undermines the rule of law that helps makes the US a magnet for immigrants in the first place and is unfair to all who wait their turn to come legally. Once they get here, they tend to be more law-abiding than other Americans because they know any brush with the law could result in deportation. As for their economic impact, it's uneven. Most studies suggest that they depress wages (but only marginally) for the unskilled laborers with whom they directly compete, but raise wages for skilled laborers who

benefit from the increased economic activity and productivity associated with their presence in the labor force.[2] For consumers, they're a blessing, as they lower the cost of everything from food to housing to medical care to personal services. They're a net burden on state and local governments, which by law are obligated to educate their children and provide free health care to their indigent. But they're a net benefit to the federal government, mainly because many wind up paying into the Social Security system (up to $15 billion a year, by one estimate)[3] without ever receiving benefits from it.

ENDNOTES

1. Jeffrey Passel, D'Vera Cohn, and Ana Gonzalez-Barrera, "Population Decline of Unauthorized Immigrants Stalls, May Have Reversed," Pew Research Center, September 23, 2013.

2. See, for example, Giovanni Peri, "The Effect of Immigrants on U.S. Employment and Productivity," Federal Reserve Bank of San Francisco, August 30, 2010.

3. Adam Davidson, "Do Illegal Immigrants Actually Hurt the US Economy?" *New York Times*, February 12, 2013.

DISCUSSION QUESTIONS

1. What is the current state of undocumented immigration to the United States? How many undocumented immigrants are there in the United States? How do you know, and are these figures exact? Where do undocumented immigrants come from, and what kind of work do they do once they are in the United States?

2. Do you know anyone who is an undocumented immigrant? What is her or his life like?

3. Why are undocumented immigrants "invisible" to most of us? Typically, we don't see undocumented immigrants at the supermarket; we don't see them in hair salons; we don't see them in the doctor's or dentist's office, or in restaurants, or at the church or synagogue; and they don't mingle in society. Why is that?

4. What is the outlook for undocumented immigrants in the United States? Should a legal path to citizenship be made available to them? Or would that be "amnesty?" Should undocumented immigrants be rounded up, *en masse*, and deported? What would it cost to achieve this, and would such a nationwide program be tantamount to an act of "ethnic cleansing"?

READING 5.9

HELP NOT WANTED

BY **Paul Reyes**

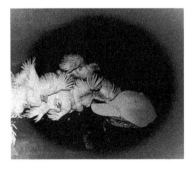

What happens when outside agitators work with state politicians to pass the nation's most draconian anti-immigration law yet? Alabama learned the hard way

By Paul Reyes

The last Saturday of September—game day in Alabama, the Crimson Tide and Tigers both at home—Birmingham seemed to have all but emptied out, fans having bolted west to the big one in Tuscaloosa, or south for the rout in Auburn. I was heading north to the farmland of Cullman County. The vista along I-65 still showed scars from tornadoes—some half a mile wide—that ripped through Alabama in April, part of a storm that carved a path all the way to the Carolinas. You could still see their mark in buzz-cut swaths of hillsides, in piles of pine and scrub oak smeared together on a bluff. Along the shoulder, a few of the slender, towering high-mast poles that light the interstate at night had been snapped in half. One even made for curious disaster art, bent and curved and twisted like a giant Calder sculpture.

Previous page: Sandra and David Bagwell's chicken-catching crew at their farm in Cullman, Alabama. This page: tornado damage in Tuscaloosa; the Bagwells. Opposite page: farmer Keith Smith.

Founded by a utopian German émigré who imagined it as "the garden spot of America," Cullman itself is a sundown town with storybook touches: early 20th-century storefronts, the yawp and clatter of a train and boxcars plodding through downtown. On the outskirts, I drove past piles of rock and rubble that flanked incomprehensibly lucky houses the storm had left untouched. Blue tarps covered the rooftops where branches had punched through and now flapped in the breeze like a school-play rendering of the sea.

Not too far outside Cullman, in an area known as Gold Ridge, I found Keith Smith's farm, a compound of chicken coops and warehouses at the end of a descending gravel drive, with fields rolling beyond. The chicken houses were open, empty and quiet. A tractor crept across one field, and I could see a row of baseball caps and pale straw hats bobbing above the frame of a seed setter being towed behind it.

Smith pulled up in a burly white pickup, trailed by a couple of collies, one with only one back leg, still hobbling at a pretty good clip. Smith's size befits his truck, and as he got out and led me to his office, he moved slowly, with great effort, heeding a pain in his ankles. In addition to sweet potatoes, Smith grows greens and raises pullets for Tyson. He was one of the first farmers in Alabama to complain publicly about the impact of the state's divisive anti-immigration bill, HB 56—a brave move, since doing so made him a potential target of the law, which criminalizes aiding or abetting undocumented immigrants in any way.

Signed by Gov. Robert Bentley in June, the law had been temporarily stayed after several groups—the ACLU, the Department of Justice, civil rights groups, and the leaders of four faiths—sued to stop it, forcing US District Judge Sharon Blackburn to consider its constitutionality. The dozen workers Smith had in the field that day were planting collard seeds and were about half the number he'd need to harvest the sweet-potato crop. He worried that most would be gone by the following week, when the law went into effect. "If I lose this crop," he said, "I'm out. I'll just have to do something else." Did he have a plan? "They ain't no plan," he said, tugging at his T-shirt. "If Blackburn rules in favor of the state and all the help leaves, then that's pretty much it. I'll try and find people. But I'm fighting a losing battle."

Less than a week later, Blackburn's ruling would allow many of the law's most extreme provisions to stand, triggering an exodus of Latinos that left fields abandoned just as the autumn harvest began. (Among those who fled: all the workers in Smith's field that game day.) Sitting in his John Deere-themed office—with hot sauce on his desk and a pocketknife sculpture as big as a hair dryer on the windowsill—Smith was blunt about the circumstances. "Majority of people that works for me," he said, "the kind of jobs I got, they're illegal. There ain't no use in beating around the bush saying they ain't or whatnot. That's just the way it is." Fake papers, no papers, tax-filing ambiguities, whatever. "I've worried about all this stuff for years," he said, "and I just got to where I threw my hands up and said, 'To hell with it. I'll just work 'em, pay 'em, and forget about it.'"

Smith's problem, which he spelled out in a deep, marbled drawl, is textbook by now: There simply aren't enough people in the United States legally who are willing or able or geographically situated to do the backbreaking work most farms have to offer, a truth that has become increasingly clear as farmers—first in Georgia, where legislation similar to HB 56 passed last year, and now in Alabama—have scrambled to fill the vacuum left by a labor force that evaporated overnight. Agriculture is a grueling, $5 billion industry in Alabama: $3.4 billion comes from poultry; the rest is from farms and nurseries that produce everything from cattle to cotton, peanuts to azaleas. One of every five jobs in Alabama is connected to agriculture. Most are paid as piecework—75 cents a bucket of potatoes, say, or a couple bucks per thousand chickens—and most of that piecework is mercilessly physical. Poultry catchers are expected to gather some 2,000 birds in an hour, while for pickers it's a matter of packing, say, 300 25-pound crates between sunrise and sunset. For the farmer, it's a necessity to keep skilled, reliable workers close at hand when profits are made or lost in the brief window of the harvest. This pressure bears down on the men and women willing to stoop and kneel and pick and haul and bleed in order to perform grueling tasks with awesome efficiency—and then, for many, to move on to where the seasons lead them next. And while anti-immigration arguments hang on the idea that if illegal workers were barred from these jobs Americans would eagerly fill them, Smith and other farmers say this doesn't square with reality. Cullman County is 93 percent white. Of the locals Smith has hired to replace the workers who fled, most lasted only a couple of hours he says, before they quit.

None of the farmers he knew were in favor of HB 56 as it stands, though "all of us would like to see an immigration law we can deal with." He mentioned guest-worker programs, background checks, tracking numbers—the same strategies that some state Republican legislators have recommended. But the argument over immigration has long been one of reform versus enforcement, and in the case of HB 56, enforcement is emphasized to the extreme. "The way this bill is now," Smith said, "if you have anything to do with them whatsoever, you're breaking the law. If you see 'em and they're hungry, or if they're out here run over by an automobile layin' in a ditch, and you help 'em, you're breakin' the

law." He swung to smash a fly on his desk and missed. "It's just not right."

IT COMES OFF as exaggeration, but the scenarios Smith described fall within the purview of HB 56. The

most draconian yet in a series of nativist laws taking root across the country, HB 56, like Arizona's SB 1070 before it, criminalizes being in the United States without proper documentation—which under federal law isn't a crime but a civil violation and cause for deportation. Both laws instruct law enforcement to act upon "reasonable suspicion" during routine traffic stops and arrests to determine whether to detain someone until his residency status can be confirmed through Immigration and Customs Enforcement (ICE). Both laws penalize anyone who knowingly employs, harbors, or transports (including giving a coworker a ride) undocumented immigrants, though Alabama's law goes further in that it penalizes anyone who rents to them. It prevents undocumented immigrants from receiving state or local public services (interpreted by some officials to include running water). It bans them from enrolling in public colleges, from seeking or soliciting work, and requires all businesses and agencies—from poultry plants to laundromats, from the governor's office to the sanitation department—to use the E-Verify system, a federal database used to determine the legal status of new hires.

One of the law's more incendiary measures requires the Alabama Department of Education to "accurately measure and assess the population of students who are aliens not lawfully present in the United States"—a provision that flirts with undermining the Supreme Court's 1982 ruling in *Plyler v. Doe*, which guarantees education to all students regardless of their immigration status. The measure was simply "part of the cost factor," state Sen. Scott Beason, cosponsor of HB 56, told the *Montgomery Advertiser*, stressing that public education for undocumented children "is one of our largest costs." Meanwhile, teachers and school administrators worried that as they became unwitting—and unwilling—enforcers of immigration law, undocumented students would be intimidated into dropping out.

Their fears were prescient. The Monday after Blackburn's ruling, which allowed the education provision to stand, more than 2,200 Latino students failed to show up for school statewide, double the average absentee rate. Sonia Smith, a school nurse at Tarrant Elementary, just north of Birmingham, fielded dozens of calls from parents offering excuses—panic attacks and fights over whether, and with whom, they should leave their American-born children should they be deported. Anne Pace, who teaches ESL at Tarrant, described some of her students arriving to class in tears; one started to hyperventilate, and the older kids seemed depressed and reticent, plagued by the idea that failure to produce the right paperwork would result in their parents' disappearance. "It's been very serious for them," Pace told me. "They're afraid for their parents. It's the unknown that scares them."

Alabama isn't exactly a logical front in the war on illegal immigration. It isn't a border state. Of the estimated 11 million undocumented immigrants in the United States, only 120,000 live in Alabama, and those people account for just 2.5 percent of Alabama's population. According to the Pew Hispanic Center, only a third of the state's 34,000 Latino children are undocumented—less than one-half of 1 percent of all of Alabama's students, according to the Census Bureau.

But the state's undocumented population is estimated to have doubled since 2005, prompting the law's proponents to use language that suggests an infestation.

The measure's sponsors, state Sen. Beason and state Rep. Micky Hammon, promoted the bill with campaign season hyperbole, calling out to the counties "most heavily hit" by illegal immigration, as if by some natural disaster. Hammon described it as being modeled after Arizona's notorious SB 1070, but stressed that it had an "Alabama flavor" in that it "attacks every aspect of an illegal immigrant's life." At a Republican Party breakfast prior to the bill's passage, Beason warned: "If you allow illegal immigration to continue in your area, you will destroy yourself eventually. If you don't believe illegal immigration will destroy a community, go and check out parts of Alabama around Arab and Albertville." (The mayors of both towns, both Republicans, bristled at the claim that their towns were going to hell.) Before returning to his seat, Beason called on his fellow Republicans to "empty the clip, and do what has to be done."

As HB 56 was moving through the Legislature, Hammon made remarkable claims, telling the *Anniston Star* that illegal immigrants cost Alabama between $600 and $800 million annually in "a lot of things," including unemployment benefits for pushed-aside legal residents, health care costs, education, and lost tax revenue. When the *Star* fact-checked his figures, it discovered that he'd simply extrapolated from a much-criticized Federation for American Immigration Reform (FAIR) study that claimed illegal immigration cost Arizona $2.6 billion. The study's own estimate of Alabama's burden was only $298 million. Beason, meanwhile, cast HB 56's purpose as "putting Alabamians back to work," promising it would be "the biggest jobs program for Alabamians that has ever been passed."

Yet for all the regional swagger, the Beason-Hammon Alabama Taxpayer and Citizen Protection Act (HB 56's official name) is part of a larger anti-immigration effort orchestrated by FAIR and its legal arm, the Immigration Reform Law Institute. The main architect is Kansas Secretary of State Kris Kobach, lawyer for IRLI, who crafted Arizona's SB 1070 and who, in town after town, state after state, has helped write and refine dozens of nativist laws and ordinances (see opposite page).

IRLI director Michael Hethmon calls these bills "field tests"—legal experiments launched wherever the political conditions are ripe, to see which will withstand court challenges in the hopes that one will eventually be upheld by the Supreme Court. Most of these field tests take the form of local ordinances or state laws with one or two provisions. What makes Alabama unique is that so many of the piecemeal experiments floated in other parts of the country were packed into one law.

ANALYZING THE ANTI-IMMIGRATION PUSH

Since 2010, state legislatures have churned out 164, often curiously similar, anti-immigration laws. We analyzed their roots, their architects (Kansas Secretary of State Kris Kobach and a gop legislators' group), and those who benefit from their passage (read: the private-prison industry). See more charts and data at motherjones.com/anti-immigration.

—Ian Gordon

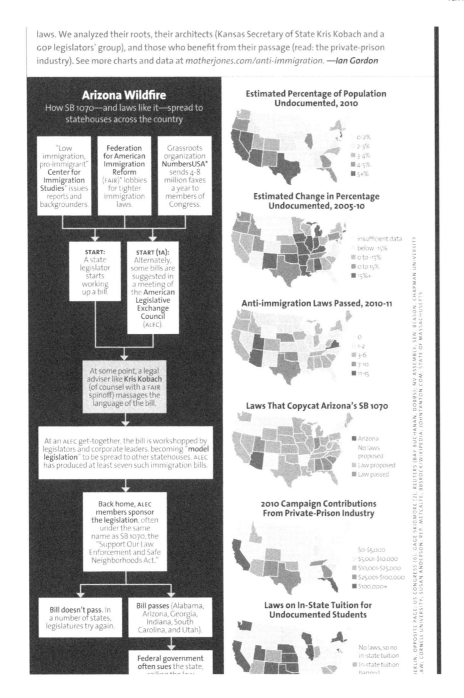

laws. We analyzed their roots, their architects (Kansas Secretary of State Kris Kobach and a GOP legislators' group), and those who benefit from their passage (read: the private-prison industry). See more charts and data at *motherjones.com/anti-immigration.* **—Ian Gordon**

Arizona Wildfire
How SB 1070—and laws like it—spread to statehouses across the country

"Low immigration, pro-immigrant" **Center for Immigration Studies** issues reports and backgrounders.

Federation for American Immigration Reform (FAIR)* lobbies for tighter immigration laws.

Grassroots organization **NumbersUSA*** sends 4-8 million faxes a year to members of Congress.

START: A state legislator starts working up a bill.

START (1A): Alternately, some bills are suggested in a meeting of the **American Legislative Exchange Council** (ALEC).

At some point, a legal adviser like **Kris Kobach** (of counsel with a FAIR spinoff) massages the language of the bill.

At an ALEC get-together, the bill is workshopped by legislators and corporate leaders, becoming "**model legislation**" to be spread to other statehouses. ALEC has produced at least seven such immigration bills.

Back home, ALEC members sponsor the legislation, often under the same name as SB 1070, the "Support Our Law Enforcement and Safe Neighborhoods Act."

Bill doesn't pass. In a number of states, legislatures try again.

Bill passes (Alabama, Arizona, Georgia, Indiana, South Carolina, and Utah).

Federal government often sues the state, calling the law

Estimated Percentage of Population Undocumented, 2010

0-2%
2-3%
3-4%
4-5%
5+%

Estimated Change in Percentage Undocumented, 2005-10

insufficient data
below -15%
0 to -15%
0 to 15%
15%+

Anti-immigration Laws Passed, 2010-11

0
1-2
3-6
7-10
11-15

Laws That Copycat Arizona's SB 1070

Arizona
No laws proposed
Law proposed
Law passed

2010 Campaign Contributions From Private-Prison Industry

$0-$5,000
$5,001-$10,000
$10,001-$25,000
$25,001-$100,000
$100,000+

Laws on In-State Tuition for Undocumented Students

No laws, so no in-state tuition
In-state tuition banned

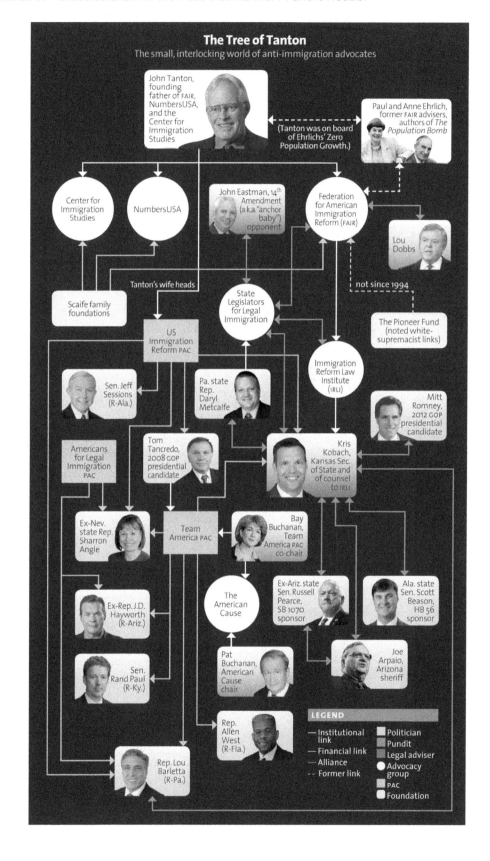

Tuscaloosa Police Chief Steven Anderson (bottom) says that Alabama's new law requires his officers (top) to check documentation during traffic stops and follow up on clearly frivolous tips—all with no extra training or funding.

It didn't start out that way. Back in 2007, Kobach had advised Beason on a series of anti-immigration bills, only to see them shot down by the Democratic majority. But fortunes changed in 2010, when the state GOP unveiled the "Republican Handshake With Alabama," an aggressive platform that pledged tax reductions, an end to wasteful spending and corruption in Montgomery, and a vow to protect Alabamians from federal "attack" in the form of "socialized health care." The most rousing rhetoric was reserved for illegal immigration, described as a force that "threatens our homeland security, reduces the quality of life for taxpaying citizens," and places Alabama's resources "under tremendous burden." The Handshake promised to give law enforcement the power to arrest an illegal immigrant "for simply setting foot in Alabama." In the end, the Handshake helped Alabama Republicans win a supermajority in the Legislature, their first since Reconstruction.

Once the GOP controlled the Statehouse, Kobach helped Beason and Hammon craft a more sweeping law than had ever been attempted anywhere. Kobach said the legislators "had already decided that this was going to cover the waterfront." His role was to take the blustering tone of the Handshake and transform it into "a state-of-the-art bill" that could withstand the lawsuits it would inevitably trigger—and serve as a template for similar efforts in other states.

"They were enthusiastic about trying virtually every area of law where immigration status could be a factor,"

IRLI's Hethmon said. "There was a sense that they wanted to be the toughest. They wanted bragging rights. But they were also sensitive to the fact that it would have to be scrubbed by the courts. Where Kobach was essential was the technical review. He had the background to convince them that it would be more productive to drop their cherished rhetorical expressions in their draft bills and use the denser, but more defensible, formulations that were coming out of our shop. So in our view, the stars lined up in Alabama."

However dense the language of HB 56 may be, its spirit is best understood as "attrition through enforcement." "If you ratchet up the level of enforcement," Kobach said, "people begin to comply with the law. That's a fundamental principle of deterrence. It's cheaper and it doesn't make that much of an imposition on the freedom of the illegal alien."

In other words, from the perspective of the immigration hardliners, the Alabama exodus since September isn't only the more cost-effective means of getting rid of undocumented aliens, but also the more humane way to do it—an exercise in free will.

"Illegal aliens are as logical as citizens," Hethmon added. "They make a rational calculation, both in coming to the country and deciding to stay. They say, Can I make money? Can I get my basic human needs—housing, medical care—taken care of? And most importantly, to what extent can I function below the radar? In other words, to what extent can I, in a practical sense, nullify the nation's legal distinctions between those who

> "Anybody promoting illegal-immigration enforcement as a job-creation bill has no clue of the real world," says a Georgia farm lobbyist. "Not only do we lack citizens *physically* capable of this work, we lack the *skill*."

are citizens and those who are not? Whether they're violating a federal criminal statute or federal civil statute or one at the state level is not that relevant. If they begin to believe that there are adverse consequences to their lawbreaking, they will self-deport."

Kobach—a charismatic 45-year-old former Eagle Scout (and former adviser to Attorney General John Ashcroft) whose bio stresses his missionary work as well as his Ivy League pedigree (see page 31)—insists that the laws he ghostwrites are saving taxpayers money by freeing jobs for Americans, driving up wages, and reducing the financial burden undocumented immigrants place on public resources, including the cost of deporting them. "There is absolutely no credible dispute to the fact that illegal immigration costs government a lot in terms of public benefits, in terms of incarceration costs, in terms of costs borne by government," he told me.

But Kobach omits the costs to defend the laws that Kobach crafts. Hazleton, Pennsylvania, a town of 25,000, racked up $2.8 million in legal fees; Farmers Branch, Texas, spent nearly $4.3 million. Kobach helped train the officers of Arizona's infamous Sheriff Joe Arpaio in immigration enforcement strategies; the DOJ recently ruled that Arpaio's department created "a pervasive culture of discriminatory bias against Latinos" and revoked its authority to conduct immigration screenings. The cost to the towns and states that have adopted his legislation, from Hazleton to Dallas, Missouri to Nebraska, is at least $6 million—money ill spent, some would argue, since many of the laws he's helped write have been blocked by the courts. For his efforts, Kobach says he's earned "less than a million dollars."

TUSCALOOSA WAS one of the towns hardest hit by April's tornadoes. Driving along University Avenue, Police Chief Steven Ander-son pointed toward empty lots: "There was a fire station back there," he said, motioning out the window. "There used to be an apartment complex behind it. There, that used to be Alberta Baptist Church." All told, more than 3,000 homes and businesses were damaged. It didn't bode well that construction lobbyists were complaining to the newspapers that a noticeable chunk of their workforce had fled the state following HB 56.

In the days after the storm, Anderson realized that very few Latinos had shown up at the FEMA aid stations set up around town, despite the damage done to their neighborhoods—in particular, to the Graceland Apartments complex, where the brick facades were shredded and the rubble of a roof piled up behind windows.

Following a hunch, Anderson sent officers into these buildings. They discovered Latino families hiding in the ruins, nursing cuts and broken bones. Many wouldn't ask for help from FEMA or the police or at hospitals for fear of being deported. Some had sought aid at Holy Spirit Catholic Church, which converted its parish hall into a makeshift shelter and even let some families sleep there, even though such sanctuary was criminalized by HB 56. (That provision was later enjoined by Judge Blackburn.)

As we toured the damage, Anderson said he supported the concept of immigration reform but then detailed a litany of complaints about HB 56. Could local law enforcement agencies—already gutted by layoffs and budget cuts—afford to train deputies to double as immigration officers? "We were told they were going to provide training for us," he said, "and that didn't happen. You just had a group of people who wanted a bill passed, and they did it. No guidance, no training, no funding." Then there is a county jail with capacity for 540 inmates that's already packed with more than 600. Not to mention the time suck: "We're not going to sit there for two hours with a traffic stop or with a suspect waiting for the federal government to get back to us on the paperwork," he told me as he turned down the crackled voices coming over his dispatch radio. "We have a job to do."

Worse, he said, was the damage the law has done to the social fabric. "The law actually tells citizens, if you see something, you call in and you report it. And if law enforcement doesn't do anything about it, you can file a civil suit against the heads of the departments for failing to enforce it." Essentially, officers are required to investigate even clearly frivolous tips—a scenario he fears will lead to profiling and harassment, and trigger a host of lawsuits down the line. "You'll have racist people that decide they're just going to pick up the phone and make a call," he said. "On other laws—murder, robbery, burglary—they don't have to put a statute in there that says, 'If you fail to enforce this law, chief of police, you could be held civilly responsible and can be fined X number of dollars per day that you fail to act.'" He shook his head. "They know how bad this law is, so they decided they needed to do something to give us extra incentive to enforce it."

As of this writing, under the new guidelines of the law, Tuscaloosa police have arrested 141 people for driving without proper identification: 97 blacks, 34 Latinos, and 10 whites. Twenty-eight people were handed over to ICE, though officials could not confirm how many, if any, have been deported.

QUANTIFYING THE impact of HB 56 on Alabama's economy has been a frustrating puzzle, especially with regard to its most visible and vulnerable component, agriculture. No entity has attempted to tabulate the size and cost of the labor exodus. The best effort comes from the University of Alabama Center for Business and Economic Research, which released a report estimating that the state could lose $40 million if even 10,000 undocumented workers stopped working—and that doesn't account for the $130 million in local, income, property, and consumption taxes that undocumented immigrants are estimated to pay. As for the claim that HB 56 would be "the biggest jobs program for Alabamians that has ever been passed," by January the governor's ballyhooed Work Alabama program, designed to fill the positions that opened following HB 56, had posted only 10 jobs, and officials had no idea if any had been filled.

Other states offer cautionary tales. In Georgia, a survey of just 233 farmers found that there was a shortage of 11,000 workers following passage of its new immigration law. Tomato growers who usually sent fleets of trucks into the fields found themselves with trucks sitting idle, fruit rotting on the ground. Georgia farmers lost about $300 million worth of crops, which in turn drained $1 billion from the state's economy, according to a study by the Center for American Progress.

"Anybody that's promoting illegal- immigration enforcement as a job-creation bill has no clue of the real world," says Charles Hall of the Georgia Fruit and Vegetable Grower's Association. "Talk to any employer needing workers for physically demanding jobs that have production standards, and those employers can't find dependable workers. And not only do we lack citizens who are *physically* capable of doing this work, we lack the *skill*. If you're trying to be a productive grower and you've got 200 acres of cucumbers that have to be harvested today, or they ruin, you need good, qualified, skilled workers out there."

Perhaps the most vivid example of the hurdles Alabama's farmers face comes from Jerry Spencer, who runs Grow Alabama, a CSA (community-supported agriculture) project that distributes for more than 100 farms statewide—and that uses Facebook to get the word out. On its page, most entries have to do with recipes or logistics or awareness of its mission. Then, on October 2, Spencer posted the following:

The immigration law has hit. From the big picture i agree with it...The cost of food is going beyond the moon and stars. Very sad day for our farmers and the people of Alabama...Anyone that wants a job please message me. Pay is based on production. There WERE Mexicans that earned $200/day—more than 90% are now gone. This is not play time. I'm only interested in people that want to work and make an honest living. We will form crews and go to the farms that need help for the day...

One farm belonged to Ellen Jenkins, who grows tomatoes on 50 acres an hour north of Birmingham. Jenkins had about 10 acres left to harvest when HB 56 went into effect, and with the strawberry season at hand in Florida, most of her workers decided to collect their checks and leave early. Jenkins is a recent widow, and she'd been having trouble running her farm alone. As an experiment to see whether Alabamians would indeed fill the void immigrants had left—and, more importantly, to help Jenkins—Spencer put the call out.

Every day for about a month, Spencer trucked unemployed Alabamians—out-of-work plumbers, electricians, dishwashers, construction workers—to Jenkins' farm. Each morning before leaving, Spencer would stand in front of the dozen or so who'd gathered at his office and give his "straight talk," describing the day ahead. "I tried to make it as unpleasant a talk as I could," he said, "so that people wouldn't arrive with expectations." Many would just walk out.

Over the course of the monthlong experiment, about 75 Alabamians worked on Jenkins' farm; 15 of them showed up more than once; only 3 lasted the entire month.

"A Mexican can honestly make $200 to $300 a day at the height of tomato season, but that's based on $3 per box," Spencer said. "The workers we took up there couldn't come close. I'm going to be generous and say $20 a day was average. I actually was proud to see how hard they did work, but they couldn't live up to the efficiency, and therefore the speed and production, that Mexicans could."

"I know what the governor wanted to have happen out of this," he said. "But it's going to take a *human* training—and I'm not talking about a worker-training program. People show up with expectations, hopes, assumptions that are unrealistic because they haven't done it before."

Victor and Jose, members of a Birmingham-based group advocating that undocumented college kids be granted permanent residency, worried that most of the families in their mobile-home community would flee following passage of HB 56. Bottom: Activist Helen Rivas calls the law "a man-made disaster; it's totally avoidable and preventable."

Spencer ended the program close to Halloween. "I couldn't afford to keep it going. I was handling all the transportation, the telephone communications, the scheduling, working with the farmer, training. I had my own business to run."

Jenkins won't know exactly what she lost until her distributors settle up. Normally, she said, picking a tomato field involves five passes; this time, with an inexperienced crew—not to mention reporters and photographers and television and radio crews looking on—she managed only one. How had the Alabamian crew done? She paused. "They tried," she said. "I'm not gonna put anybody down. Some done better than others; they just didn't know what they were doin'. Some never even probably seen a tomato plant. But they tried." Jenkins said she was considering greenhouse growing as an alternative to her 50 acres, to cut down on her need for labor. "It's like any other job," she said. "If you spend two or three days training 'em and they never show back up, that's a waste of time. They need to be trained before they come out here."

Spencer told me that many of the farmers he works with are reconsidering their futures—and not just how much seedling they should buy for a smaller planting if the labor doesn't arrive next spring, but also whether farming is even worth the trouble. "Farming is just so year to year, you really have to know your expenses," he

Casey Smith in the John Deere-themed office of his dad's farm

said. "You have to have a high degree of certainty about your labor."

LOSS OF A WORKFORCE is one thing, but it seemed that other, subtler losses were greater still. In September, I'd met with a Cullman couple named David and Sandra Bagwell, who ran a pair of chicken-catching crews, six men each, for the poultry giants. Sitting in their kitchen, Sandra played a home video to show me how the job was done. The video was shot from one end of a chicken house, with half the frame filled with the roiling, dusty white noise of 22,000 birds. A handful of workers are milling around and then begin stooping and swiping the birds up in handfuls, a half-dozen per hand, then tossing them into cages so swiftly, with such accuracy, that it seems as if the cage itself sucks them in.

Sandra stood near the TV and pointed out the workers—"my boys"—as each one snatched pom-poms of birds and dispatched them. With the relentless progression of a tide, the birds would disappear in two hours, including a short break for the men to wring out their clothes and change into something dry that they'd also sweat through by the end. As each figure moved across the screen, Sandra named him, told me of his quirks and talents. She was, she admitted, "a nervous wreck" about HB 56. She showed me the paperwork they'd provided her, but she wasn't certain whether it was fake or not. She worried that her crew might disappear after Blackburn's ruling, and that "if they don't leave, I'm going to have to tell them we can't work with them anymore. I'm going to be the one to tell them, 'I can't afford to be fined; I can't afford to go to jail. I gotta let y'all go.' That's me puttin' them out of work and hurtin' their families. And at the same time, it's gonna cost me and David everything if I can't find white boys to do this job."

Smith and his son Casey had even deeper bonds at risk. At their farm I met Shorty, a foreman who'd arrived from Durango, Mexico, in 1992 and had been working for Smith ever since. He looked tiny standing next to his boss, a seemingly incompatible pair, but between them I sensed a genuine friendship. We sat in a workshop: Keith leaning on a jerry-rigged recliner perched on a hubcap; Casey, 27, hunched on a bench; Shorty and I side by side on a discarded school bus seat. I asked Shorty what he knew of the workers who'd disappeared even before Blackburn's ruling. "Some left for Washington," he said, "some for Oklahoma. Supposedly they don't have laws like Alabama's, but I'm sure they'll pass it everywhere. Why just Alabama?"

Did he have plans?

"If I can't work, I'll go back to Mexico. I've got my money saved up. I'm ready."

"Just like that?"

"If there's no more work, I'm not going to sit here for a week or two just to spend everything I've saved up."

Both of Keith's sons grew up with Shorty—a fact that Casey made clear when he called me at my hotel later that night. He'd been quiet as we talked there in the shop, slapping at flies. But when he called he seemed compelled to speak, apologizing for the late interruption, tripping over what he needed to tell me. The circumstances had become depressingly clear to him—Shorty could be gone within days. "People like Shorty, who been working for us for all these years, they're not just people we employ," Casey said. "They're family members. A lot of people don't realize that. There's a tie there. Shorty's like an uncle. I'll flat out tell you, I got family members I think less of than I do him. For years I spent 8 to 10 hours of my day knowing Shorty was going to be *right there*. And I was going to see him *every day*. It's bigger than what people realize."

"Yeah, that's gonna be tough," Keith had said that afternoon, after a long pause, each of us staring at nothing in particular. "You know, somebody you've had a relationship with for 20 years and all of a sudden they gotta haul ass just for a stupid reason." But then he looked at Shorty, and as if on cue they both chuckled in a way that hinted at years of razzing. "Me and Shorty was planning on having our retirement party together. You know, we was gonna retire at the same day. We was hoping we could just ride around in the truck and tell everybody what to do. Chew everybody's ass out and go on about our business."

Retire when?

"Well, it ain't no time soon." Keith said and threw Shorty a sly grin—all it took to crack them both up.

IT DIDN'T TAKE LONG for the unintended consequences to seep into the lives of all Alabamians: epic lines at the DMV, exhausting delays at the courthouse, procedural pileups at the utility company—the result of the new onus on state and local agencies to verify citizenship for all transactions. In Tuscaloosa, Detlev Hager, a German Mercedes-Benz executive, was pulled over in a rental car without a license plate, then, in keeping with HB 56, arrested when he couldn't produce a license, passport, or any of the other documents he'd left back at his hotel. This episode made national headlines, much to the embarrassment of state officials who'd spent years and hundreds of millions in tax breaks courting Mercedes-Benz to build the SUV factory Hager

> In Tuscaloosa, a German Mercedes-Benz executive was pulled over in a rental car without a license plate, then, in keeping with HB 56, arrested when he couldn't produce any of the IDs he'd left back at his hotel.

was visiting. Before Hager's arrest, Gov. Bentley had brushed off the chaos the law was causing as kinks that would work themselves out. But the incidents kept piling up: the rotting crops; the citizens held hostage by technicalities because clerks, wanting to avoid any potential lawsuits, became sticklers; Homeland Security head Janet Napolitano—a former Arizona governor, no less—pointedly telling Congress that ICE agents wouldn't be helping Alabama enforce its new law.

And then there were the missteps of the bill's sponsors. Beason caught national flak when transcripts of an FBI bingo corruption sting emerged in which he quipped to fellow Republicans about the black clientele of the Greenetrack casino. "That's y'all's Indians," a colleague says. "They're aborigines," Beason says, "but they're not Indians." (It should be noted that Beason was the one wearing the wire.) In November, upon considering the "many realities" that made him politically radioactive, Republican Senate leaders removed Beason from his position as Senate Rules Committee chairman.

Hammon's missteps came during his hard sell of HB 56, when he'd repeatedly stressed that Alabama had "the second-fastest-growing population of illegal immigrants in the United States." When the *Anniston Star* again followed up, Hammon provided an article citing the Pew Hispanic Center, which listed Alabama as having the second-fastest-growing population of *Hispanics*.

Hammon's conflated research was noted by federal judge Myron Thompson in a December ruling that caused the attorney general to hold a provision forbidding state and local agencies from engaging in "business transactions" with undocumented immigrants. In the case before Thompson, the provision interfered with mobile-home registrations, which civil rights groups argued would leave numerous Latino families homeless. Thompson cited controversies surrounding the law, including Hammon's bad numbers, as proof that HB 56 is, at its core, "discriminatorily based." Thompson's ruling also took note of transcripts from legislative sessions, during which Democrats and Republicans continuously substituted "Hispanics" for "illegal immigrants" and bandied around stereotypes, like when Rep. John Rogers

(D-Birmingham) claimed that, as evidence of "illegals" in his district, he'd seen "about 30 of them get out of a car one day...I thought it was a circus." At the heart of Thompson's ruling, however, was the observation that "HB 56's treatment of children in mixed-status families, who are overwhelmingly Latino, is so markedly different from the State's historical treatment of children that it suggests strongly that the difference in treatment was driven by animus against Latinos in general..."

That generalized animus was costing the business community even its legal immigrant workforce, says Jay Reed, president of the Alabama chapter of Associated Builders and Contractors—and cofounder of Alabama Employers for Immigration Reform, a consortium of 18 industrial associations, including Alabama Poultry and Egg. "While the legislation wasn't meant to drive out those here legally working," he told me, "it has—especially in carpentry, masonry, landscaping." But "getting our members to talk about it publicly is tough," Reed admitted. "They worry about ICE raids and immigration compliance officers coming onto a job site, just because they said they lost their legals. You can't blame them."

More provisions of HB 56 were enjoined by the Circuit Court on October 14—including the one that forced the Education Department to tabulate its undocumented students. But until that court hears oral arguments on the entirety of the law on March 1, everybody—workers, employers, teachers, students—is in limbo.

Amid all this chaos, Republicans have offered mea culpas. Some claimed that they hadn't had time to fully consider the bill. "We've got just a couple of hours before adjourning the session," Gerald Dial, a senior Republican, recalled, "and I've got a bill that I haven't got time to read. But here's my predicament: I'm a state senator. I vote against this bill, it looks like I'm promoting illegal immigrants. So you've got me boxed in." Eventually party leaders admitted that the bill had been passed hastily, and even Gov. Bentley said that it needed to be "tweaked."

"We overreached," Dial insisted. "It's done some things we didn't want to do. We probably didn't have enough debate over it, because it was passed on the last day of a legislative session, at the last minute of the last hour. And hey, I made a mistake. But that's the great thing about being in the Legislature: You can come in the next year and make corrections if the bill is wrong." Dial hoped a bill that does just that would pass this spring.

I asked Dial whether, aside from the political fallout, he felt any personal regret in voting for HB 56. "I certainly do," he told me. "That's a big part of it. It opened up old wounds in this state that I and other legislators have worked for 40 years to overcome."

In december, when I caught up with Shorty again, he and a two-man crew were busy building pallets on which the sweet potatoes would be piled and cured. The exodus had pushed the harvest back three weeks, but even with an untrained, haphazard crew they were finally able to clear nearly all of their 120 acres. Smith thinks it was a fluke. "We got lucky 'cause of the weather," he told me. "You need to be done digging potatoes by Thanksgiving, and we dug on up into middle of December. If we hadn't had good weather, them last 40, 50 acres, we'd a lost 'em."

Lucky, too, in that being so outspoken against HB 56 had acted as an accidental recruiting tool. "As soon as all this stuff hit the news," Casey said, "we'd get people showing up wanting to work, and we didn't turn anybody away because we couldn't afford to." Out of the 50 or so workers who came through that fall, Casey said, "we probably ended up with about 7 that stayed with us till we got done." Many of the rest quit before lunch.

Shorty was also disillusioned with his experience running a crew of American workers. "They'd work an hour or two, then split," he told me. "Or they'd sit on a bucket and talk on the phone. How can you get any work done when you've got a cellphone in one hand and a cigarette in the other?"

Shorty still had his money saved, just in case, but in the meantime was going to "work until I'm not allowed to work. *Mi patrón* hasn't told me to go, so I'm still here." He spent more time at home, he said, and had cut back on driving—getting to and from the farm, and maybe sneaking to the bodega, but keeping his time on the road to a minimum. Otherwise, things were calm, relatively normal. I was surprised to hear his life hadn't changed much. "Not really," he said. "Those of us who've stuck it out, we've got work. And if we've got work, what else would we be looking to do?"

Things might very well change in April, when the law's E-Verify provision goes into effect, though Keith Smith seemed unfazed by the deadline. "It ain't gon' be worth shit for us," he said. "It's the same situation: There's not enough people that'll get out and do these jobs that you could run through E-Verify and get the results that you need." Was he just going to ignore the law? "I don't know," he sighed. "I ain't been complying with the law for years 'cause I haven't been able to. What other option do you have when you ain't got nobody else?"

And then, he clarified one of the most glaring but least considered faults of the unemployed citizen/undocumented immigrant conundrum: Smith has three year-round positions; the rest are seasonal, 8 to 10 weeks at most. "They help us when we're planting, leave, go do something else, and they come back when we get ready to harvest. The legislators talk about putting these people that are laid off to work. Well, a person would be stupid to quit unemployment and come work for me for four or five weeks. You can't blame 'em."

For now, the Smiths and Shorty and his two-man crew had their days full tending to chickens, repairing equipment, curing and shipping product, and trying to find 20 people just as good as the talent they've lost for the planting season in May. "I've talked with people I know in Florida and Mississippi," Shorty said, "but no one wants to come here to work."

If they do, chances are Smith will hire them, since he isn't inclined to turn away good help where he can find it, documents be damned. "I can't, unless they come and put me out of business."

I shared with him what Shorty had said about sticking it out until his boss told him it was time to go. "I ain't gonna kick him off," Smith said. "They'll have to come get him. I might go with him."

The Investigative Fund at The Nation Institute contributed additional support for this article.

Smith's foreman, Shorty, says he's going to "work until I'm not allowed to work."

DISCUSSION QUESTIONS

1. What happened on Keith Smith's farm, outside Cullman, Alabama, when HB 56 was passed by the Alabama Legislature? What was the intended outcome of HB 56–and why did the Alabama Legislature think that the new law was needed? What was the actual outcome of the new law?

2. What are the provisions of HB 56? How did the new law affect:
   —Undocumented immigrants in Alabama?
   —Alabama farmers and employers?
   —Alabama teachers and school administrators?
   —Alabama law enforcement officers?

3. Alabama does not share a border with Mexico; nor does it now or did it ever have many undocumented immigrants. Why then did the Alabama Legislature pass HB 56—encompassing some of the severest anti-undocumented-immigrant laws in the United States?

4. Discuss in detail the financial, administrative, and personal costs to Alabamans of the new law, as they are explained in the article.

5. If you were asked to "tweak" HB 56, how would you do it? Would you scrap it altogether? If so, why? Even if you think that many HB 56 provisions are excessive or counterproductive, what parts of HB 56 make sense? Is deterrence a good way to reduce undocumented immigrants? Why or why not? Should Alabama pass some kind of "guest worker" legislation that confers documented status to undocumented immigrants, and provides them with drivers' licenses and Medicare-style health insurance, and asks them to pay taxes on their wages? Why or why not?

¿VALE LA PENA?

The Women Who Pick Your Food

BY **Joseph Sorrentino**

Olga sings softly while working in the field, stooped over and stuffing onion plants into small holes that were made a few minutes earlier by a tractor. She places two or three plants in a hole, sweeps in a little dirt, takes a step, and does it again. It takes her about three hours to fill a row 1,400 feet long. For this, she earns $32. She usually plants two rows a day. Olga wears a red bandanna to protect herself from the dust and pesticides that are kicked up whenever a tractor or truck passes by. She is, it appears, the only one of about thirty workers who is worried about it.

Olga works on an onion farm in western New York, about an hour's drive from Rochester. The soil here—rich, dark, and moist—is called muck and is perfect for growing onions. It's late April, well past the normal time for planting onions, but an unusually wet spring has upset the schedule. Olga has been out in the cool damp weather for a couple of weeks, working eight to ten hours a day, six or seven days a week. When she's not in the fields, she's in a packing house sorting onions—a job she prefers. On a busy day, five thousand pounds of onions will roll down a conveyor belt every hour, as she and another woman try to find and toss out bad ones. She says working in the packing house is easier than working in the fields, but the work requires standing in one spot all day, leaving her with an aching back

Joseph Sorrentino is a freelance writer and photographer currently living in Rochester, New York. The names of some of the women profiled in this article have been changed to protect their identities.

and swollen legs. "Almost all the women have varicose veins," she told me. "I have them, too."

Like most farm workers in the United States, Olga is from Mexico. But unlike most farm workers, she didn't do farm work there; she worked in a stationery store. "I had never planted anything before [coming to the United States]," she said, "and the work was so difficult. I cried for months when I first came here.... I work in the heat, the sun, the dirt." Olga, who has three children, is older than most of the people she works with. She once saw another woman crying as she planted, just as Olga had done years earlier. Olga stopped working to talk with her. She asked the woman how long she'd been in the United States. The woman told her four months and asked Olga how long she'd been here. "Five years," Olga replied. "Don't worry, when you're here five years, you won't cry anymore."

Farm work is among the most difficult and dangerous jobs in the United States, consistently ranking as one of the three industries with the most accidents and injuries. It's also one of the lowest-paying jobs. Most workers earn about $10,000 a year. In New York State, farm workers are excluded from rights guaranteed to most other workers, including the rights to overtime pay, a weekly day of rest, and collective bargaining. In spite of all of this, several million Mexicans work on U.S. farms—60,000 to 80,000 in western New York alone. More than half of these workers are here illegally. Until recently, the majority were young men. Now more women are working in the fields.

The grinding poverty in rural Mexico is what's driving people north in search of work. Slightly over 80 percent of those who live in rural Mexico earn less than $2 a day, and their situation is worsening. The cost of staples like rice, beans, and eggs has almost doubled in the past few years. The price of seeds and fertilizers has also risen. These trends are partly a consequence of the North American Free Trade Act (NAFTA) and other neoliberal economic policies, which have benefited large corporations at the expense of rural workers, or *campesinos*. These policies and rising food costs have driven an already impoverished population further into poverty and forced millions of people off their land to seek work elsewhere.

Harvesting apples

Carina Diaz Garcia at home

Campesinos often supplemented their incomes at home by working a few months a year in Mexican cities or in the United States. Now, with little to return to in their villages, they're staying away longer, sometimes permanently. This is especially true for those fortunate enough to have made it into the United States. Border security, tightened right after 9/11, has become even tighter over the past few years. There are more fences, more border agents; unmanned aircraft now patrol the border. A decade ago, men could slip back and forth across the border fairly easily. Now they're afraid to return home because they know they may not get back in. This has left countless villages in rural Mexico with few able-bodied men. And now women are leaving their villages as well—married women who want to join their husbands in the United States and reunite their families, and single women who just want to escape poverty. In 2007, the U.S. Department of Labor reported that 22 percent of farm workers nationwide were women. One farmer in New York told me that during planting season upward of 40 percent of his workers are women.

In 2004, Carina Diaz Garcia was cooking and selling food on the streets of her hometown in the Mexican state of Morelos. She earned about $7 for thirty to thirty-five hours of work. She finally decided it was time to join her husband, who had been working on a farm in western New York for more than a year. Since she couldn't enter the United States. legally, she paid a "coyote" $2,000 to smuggle her across the border. A campesino family is lucky to earn $2,000 in a year, so people like Carina must borrow the money for the trip or go into debt to the coyote. It took Carina a week to cross the desert; she and her group spent much of that time dodging the Border Patrol. Her trip was made even more difficult because she had her one-year-old son with her. She ran out of food and water after a few days and twisted her ankle, but she pressed on. "We passed people who were dead," she told me.

Having arrived safely, Carina found her new life to be nearly as difficult as the one she had left behind in Mexico. She lives on the first floor of a small farmhouse just outside Albion, New York. The apartment is sparsely furnished with worn furniture bought at thrift stores or left behind by previous tenants. Carina keeps the apartment clean, but it's a bit chaotic, the result of having three young children and a brutal work schedule. During planting and harvesting seasons, her day begins around 5 a.m. "I get up, cook breakfast for my children and get them up at 6:10," she said. "Then I prepare lunch. At 6:50, the two older ones go to school. I leave the younger one with a woman who puts her on a bus later. I leave for work at seven." Depending on the time of year, Carina may work until six or seven at night, six or even seven days a week.

Every type of farm work has its challenges. Raspberries are easy to pick, but they're harvested during the hottest time of year. Still, the women with whom I spoke prefer picking raspberries to picking strawberries, which requires them to kneel all day,

Laura Gutierrez Lopez

leaving them with sore backs and aching knees. Even tying up tomatoes, though not very strenuous, leaves one's hands red, slightly swollen, and blistered. At the end of a workday, the women are exhausted and would like nothing more than to go straight to sleep. But they can't because there's more work for them to do at home.

Women in rural Mexico work alongside their husbands in the fields, but they're often viewed as "helping" rather than really working, and they're also expected to take care of the children and do all the domestic chores. The Mexican farm workers have brought these expectations with them to the United States. "Men think, 'I work outside of the home, that's enough,'" said Laura Gutierrez Lopez, a farm worker. "Many women work in the fields and they still have to clean, cook, and bathe their children." Some husbands do help out at home, but others can't because they're putting in even longer hours at the farm. So women farm workers end up doing almost all the household chores—the cooking and cleaning and childcare. This makes for very long days. Carina bristled slightly when I said she works twelve hours a day. "No," she replied. "I work from five in the morning until ten at night."

Life is hard for any farm worker, but it's especially hard for undocumented workers. It's a lot like house

arrest. Ana lives in a small, crowded one-bedroom apartment with her husband and their three daughters. She and her husband have the bedroom; the tiny living room doubles as a bedroom for the girls. When it's time to sleep, mattresses are dragged out and placed on the floor. Like most Mexican farm workers, Ana and her husband are here illegally and live in constant fear of being caught by the police or Immigration and Customs Enforcement (ICE) and deported. Not only would deportation end their chance of giving their daughters a better life here, it would hurt their extended families in Mexico, who depend on them for money. Ana estimates that she and her husband send their relatives in Mexico about a third of their income.

Before leaving for work in the morning, Ana checks the street from her second-floor apartment, looking for police or "*migración*" (ICE). Her husband calls a friend who's here legally and asks him to walk around the neighborhood, so that he can let them know if it's safe to leave. Ana and her husband rarely leave their apartment except to go to work; she figures they've been to a restaurant twice in five years. She won't even risk taking her younger daughters to a park. "It's not a life, really," she told me. "It makes us feel like criminals, like we're robbers or murderers...like a cockroach."

Just how restricted their lives are became evident one evening while Ana was preparing dinner. She opened the refrigerator. It was almost empty. "Look," she said. "No fresh fruits or vegetables." She said police and *migración* had been "everywhere" for the past couple of weeks and she had been afraid to go shopping. She lifted the lid off a large pot on the stove. It contained about a dozen ears of corn. "This is all we have for dinner," she said. "That—and maybe some bread."

Because of her immigration status, Ana won't go back to Mexico. She's afraid that if she did, she wouldn't be able to get back into the United States. She has two grandchildren in Mexico she's never seen and fears she won't see her parents again before they die. But she sounds more sad than bitter when she talks about her life here. "All we're doing is working. We're not hurting anyone. When people eat their delicious food, they need to think about who picks it: us. Mexicans. Come one day or even half a day and you'll quit because it's very difficult work."

Laura Gutierrez Lopez entered the country illegally in 2007. She wanted to earn enough money to build her parents a house in Mexico and then return home to open a store there. At first, she and her husband didn't go out of the house unless it was absolutely necessary. Finally, they decided they didn't want to live that way anymore and started to move around more freely. They paid for that freedom when Laura was stopped by police, who said her car registration had expired (she insists it hadn't). The police then called the ICE, which discovered she was here illegally. Laura, whose husband has already been deported, is still waiting to be deported herself. Until then, she's enjoying her freedom. "Before, I couldn't always shop when I wanted to, couldn't go out if there were police or *migración* around. Now, if I want to shop, I go. Now I'm freer, much calmer." She has even taken her children to amusement parks, something she never did before.

Women like Ana and Carina and Laura endure a great deal—difficult jobs that few others want, a restricted life in a foreign and often unwelcoming country, a workday that never seems to end. Yet they do it. I asked the women I interviewed, "Vale la pena?"—"Is it worth it?" They all answered, "Yes." And when I asked them why, they all had the same response: They wanted to give their children a chance at a better life. And so they go on working and saving and hiding from the ICE, whatever it takes to give their children something they themselves will never fully possess: a piece of the American Dream.

DISCUSSION QUESTIONS

1. What is daily life like, and what are the work conditions like, for undocumented immigrant farm workers in the United States?

2. Does it surprise you to learn that undocumented immigrants are so prevalent on many or even most U.S. farms, not just in border states such as Texas and Arizona, but even in northern states like New York? Why or why not?

3. In the final paragraphs of this article, the author asks the titular question: "Vale la pena?"—is it worth it? What's your answer? Given the extreme work conditions of agricultural work, why do so many undocumented immigrants seem to answer, "Yes!" when they are asked this question? Why do so many American farmers and employers of undocumented immigrants also answer, "Yes?"

AUTHOR AND TITLE INDEX

CPSIA information can be obtained
at www.ICGtesting.com
Printed in the USA
BVHW010235010222
627730BV00011B/298